MACROECONOMICS

Dean Karlan

Yale University and Innovations for Poverty Action

Jonathan Morduch

New York University

With special contribution by

Meredith L. Startz

Yale University and Innovations for Poverty Action

Rafat Alam

MacEwan University

Andrew Wong

University of Alberta

Mc
Graw
Hill
Education

MACROECONOMICS
First Canadian Edition

The Internet addresses listed in the text were accurate at the time of publication. The inclusion of a website does not indicate an endorsement by the authors or McGraw-Hill Education, and McGraw-Hill Education does not guarantee the accuracy of the information presented at these sites.

ISBN-13: 978-0-07-026094-8
ISBN-10: 0-07-026094-X

1 2 3 4 5 6 7 8 9 WEB 1 2 3 4 5 6 7

Care has been taken to trace ownership of copyright material contained in this text; however, the publisher will welcome any information that enables it to rectify any reference or credit for subsequent editions.

Portfolio and Program Manager: *Karen Fozard*

Product Manager: *Kevin O'Hearn*

Executive Marketing Manager: *Joy Armitage Taylor*

Product Developer: *Melissa Hudson*

Photo/Permissions Research: *Derek Capitaine*

Senior Product Team Associate: *Stephanie Giles*

Supervising Editor: *Jeanette McCurdy*

Copy Editor: *Judy Sturrup*

Plant Production Coordinator: *Sarah Strynatka*

Manufacturing Production Coordinator: *Sheryl MacAdam*

Cover Design: *Jodie Bernard*

Cover Image: *Wragg / Getty Images*

Interior Design: *Jodie Bernard*

Page Layout: *SPi Global*

Printer: *Webcom, Inc.*

All credits appearing on page or at the end of the book are considered to be an extension of the copyright page.

www.mhhe.com

ABOUT THE AUTHORS

Dean Karlan

Dean Karlan is Professor of Economics at Yale University and President and Founder of Innovations for Poverty Action (IPA). Dean started IPA in 2002, with two aims: to help learn what works and what does not in the fight against poverty and other social problems around the world, and then to implement successful ideas at scale. IPA now works in over 45 countries, with 800 employees around the world. Dean's personal research focuses on using field experiments to learn more about how microfinance works and how to make it work better. His research uses ideas from behavioural economics, and also covers fundraising, voting, health, and education. In recent work, for example, he has studied the impact of microcredit on the lives of the poor, and has worked to create better financial products in the United States to help people manage debt. Dean is also President and co-founder of stickK.com, a start-up that helps people use commitment contracts to achieve personal goals, such as losing weight or completing a problem set on time. Dean is a Sloan Foundation Research Fellow, and in 2007 was awarded a Presidential Early Career Award for Scientists and Engineers. He is co-editor of the *Journal of Development Economics* and on the editorial board of *American Economic Journal: Applied Economics*. He holds a BA from the University of Virginia, an MPP and MBA from the University of Chicago, and a PhD in Economics from MIT. In 2011, he coauthored *More Than Good Intentions: Improving the Ways the World's Poor Borrow, Save, Farm, Learn, and Stay Healthy.*

Jonathan Morduch

Jonathan Morduch is Professor of Public Policy and Economics at New York University's Wagner Graduate School of Public Service. Jonathan focuses on innovations that expand the frontiers of finance and how financial markets shape economic growth and inequality. Jonathan has lived and worked in Asia, but his newest study follows families in California, Mississippi, Ohio, Kentucky, and New York as they cope with economic ups and downs over a year. The new study jumps off from ideas in *Portfolios of the Poor: How the World's Poor Live on $2 a Day* (Princeton University Press, 2009), which he co-authored and which describes how families in Bangladesh, India, and South Africa devise ways to make it through a year living on $2 a day or less. Jonathan's research on financial markets is collected in *The Economics of Microfinance* and *Banking the World,* both published by MIT Press. At NYU, Jonathan is Executive Director of the Financial Access Initiative, a centre that supports research on extending access to finance in low-income communities. Jonathan's ideas have also shaped policy through work with the United Nations, World Bank, and other international organizations. In 2009, the Free University of Brussels awarded Jonathan an honorary doctorate to recognize his work on microfinance. He holds a BA from Brown and a PhD from Harvard, both in economics.

Karlan and Morduch first met in 2001 and have been friends and colleagues ever since. Before writing this text, they collaborated on research on financial institutions. Together, they've written about new directions in financial access for the middle class and poor, and in Peru they set up a laboratory to study incentives in financial contracts for loans to women to start small enterprises. In 2006, together with Sendhil Mullainathan, they started the Financial Access Initiative, a centre dedicated to expanding knowledge about financial solutions for the half of the world's adults who lack access to banks. This text reflects their shared passion for using economics to help solve problems, both in everyday life and in the broader world.

Rafat Alam

Dr. Rafat Alam is an assistant professor and discipline coordinator at the Department of Economics at MacEwan University in Edmonton, Alberta. He is engaged in undergraduate instruction in the areas of microeconomics, development economics, environmental economics, international trade, contemporary Canadian economic issues, and cost–benefit analysis. His research interests and current research are in the areas of economics of biodiversity conservation, environmental economics, development economics, and scholarship of teaching and learning in economics. Rafat has both a Bachelor and a Masters of Social Science in Economics from the University of Dhaka, Bangladesh, an MA in Economics from the University of British Columbia, and a PhD in Economics from the University of Ottawa.

Andrew Wong

Andrew Wong was born and grew up in Hong Kong before moving to Alberta as a teenager. After receiving his MA from the University of Alberta, he began teaching principles of micro- and macroeconomics at MacEwan University. During his time at MacEwan University, Andrew was connected with the University's distance learning program, eCampus Alberta, serving as a content expert and instructor for online course development in economics. In 2016, he was recognized for his twenty years of dedicated service to MacEwan University. He is also an instructor in the schools of economics and business at the University of Alberta. He successfully flipped his intermediate macroeconomics class, winning the Blended Learning Award in 2015.

BRIEF CONTENTS

CONTENTS

PREFACE

We offer this text, *Macroeconomics*, as a resource for professors who want to *keep their students engaged* and who have been seeking to *deliver core economic concepts* along with an introduction to *important new ideas* in economic thought. We designed the text to help students see economics as a common thread that enables us to understand, analyze, and solve problems in our local communities and around the world.

Why Do We Teach Economics?

Economics helps us solve problems.

Economic principles can help students understand and respond to everyday situations. Economic ideas are also helping us tackle big challenges, such as creating employment and keeping the government fiscally solvent. We show students how economic ideas are shaping their world, and we provide them with a wide-ranging set of practical insights to help develop their economic intuition.

Engagement with real-world problems is built into the fabric of our chapters, and throughout the text we present economic thinking as a common thread to help solve these. This compelling, problem-solving focus simplifies and streamlines the teaching of basic economic concepts by approaching topics intuitively and in a way that is useful to students. The text imparts to students the *immediacy* of how what they're learning *really matters*. As they read, faculty and students will find content that *breaks down barriers* between what goes on in the classroom and what is going on in our nation and around the world.

By providing a concrete, intuitive approach to introductory concepts, and by keeping the discussion always down-to-earth and lively, we make the learning materials easier to use in the classroom. The chapters are organized around a familiar curriculum while adding empirical context for ideas that students often find overly abstract or too simplified. The innovative, empirical orientation of the book enables us to incorporate intriguing findings from recent studies as well as to address material from such areas as game theory, finance, behavioural economics, and political economy. This approach connects concepts in introductory economics to important new developments in economic research, while placing a premium on *easy-to-understand explanations*.

In every chapter we fulfill three fundamental commitments:

- **To show how economics can solve real-life problems.** This text will engage students by approaching economics as a way of explaining real people and their decisions, and by providing a set of tools that serve to solve many different types of problems. *We show students that economics can make the world a better place*, while challenging them to reach their own conclusions about what "better" really means.

- **To teach principles as analytic tools for dealing with real situations.** The text is centred on examples and issues that resonate with students' experience. Applications come *first*, reinforcing the relevance of the tools that students acquire. Engaging empirical cases are interspersed throughout the content. The applications open up puzzles, anomalies, and possibilities that basic economic principles help explain. The aim is, first and foremost, to ensure that students gain an intuitive grasp of basic ideas.

- **To focus on what matters to students.** Students live in a digital, globalized world. We recognize that they are knowledgeable and care about both local and international issues. *Macroeconomics* takes a global perspective, with Canada as a leading example. We remain faithful to the core principles of economics, but we seek to share with students some of the ways that new ideas are expanding the "basics" of economic theory. We recognize and explain the rise of game theory, behavioural economics, and experimental and empirical approaches, in ways that matter to students.

We are excited to offer stand-alone chapters that dig into some of the new topics in economics, as part of our commitment to teaching economics as a way to help solve important problems. We've watched as topics like political economy, game theory, behavioural economics, and inequality figure more and more prominently in undergraduate curricula with each passing year, and we felt it was important to provide teachers with ways to share new ideas and evidence with their students—important concepts that most non-majors would usually miss. We know how selective teachers must be in choosing which material to cover during the limited time available. In light of this, we've been especially glad to have the guidance we've received from many teachers in finding ways to expose students to some of the newer, and most exciting, parts of economics today.

We promise you will find the discussion and writing style of *Macroeconomics* clear, concise, accessible, easy to teach from, and fun to read. We hope that this book will inspire students to continue their studies in economics, and we promise that *Macroeconomics* will give them something useful to take away even if they choose other areas of study.

Motivation

Who are we?

Macroeconomics draws on our own experiences as academic economists, teachers, and policy advisors. We are based at large research universities, offering advice to NGOs, governments, international agencies, donors, and private firms. Much of our research involves figuring out how to improve the way real markets function. Working with partners in Canada and on six continents, we are involved in testing new economic ideas. *Macroeconomics* draws on the spirit of that work, as well as similar research, taking students through the process of engaging with real problems, using analytical tools to devise solutions, and ultimately showing what works and why.

Why have we written this text?

One of the best parts of writing this text has been getting to spend time with instructors across the country. We've been inspired by their creativity and passion, and have learned from their pedagogical ideas. One of the questions we often ask is why the instructors originally became interested in economics. A common response, which we share, is an attraction to the logic and power of economics as a social science. We also often hear instructors describe something slightly different: the way that economics appealed to them as a tool for making sense of life's complexities, whether in business, politics, or daily life. We wrote this book to give instructors a way to share with their students both of those ways that economics matters.

Comprehensive and engaging, *Macroeconomics* will provide students a solid foundation for considering important issues that they will confront in life. We hope that, in ways small and large, the tools they learn in these pages will help them to think critically about their environment and to live better lives.

Dean Karlan
Yale University

Jonathan Morduch
New York University

Rafat Alam
MacEwan University

Andrew Wong
University of Alberta

ECONOMICS AS A COMMON THREAD

This text demonstrates how students can use basic economic principles to understand, analyze, and solve problems in their communities and around the world. Several basic pedagogical principles guide the organization of the content and support the implementation of the approach:

- **Uses the concrete to teach the abstract.** Interesting questions *motivate the learning of core principles* by showing how they are relevant to students. As often as possible, examples and cases lead into theory.
- **Explores current ideas and media.** The text provides students with a view of what is actually going on in the world and in economics *right now*. It is *current in its content, method, and media.*
- **Takes a problem-solving approach.** This text shows economics as a way to explain real people and their decisions, and provides tools that can be used to solve many different types of problems. To complement this problem-solving approach, the authors have taken special care to offer *high-quality end-of-chapter problem sets* that engage students with realistic questions. Smoothly integrated with the chapter text, there are at least two review questions and two problems for each learning objective. Four additional problems for each learning objective also are available in Connect.

Four Questions About How Economists Think

The text's discussion is framed by *four questions* that economists ask to break down a new challenge and analyze it methodically. These four questions are explored and then carried throughout *Macroeconomics* as a consistent problem-solving approach to a wide variety of examples and case studies so as to demonstrate how they can be used to address real issues. By teaching the *right questions to ask,* the text provides students with a method for working through decisions they'll face as consumers, employees, entrepreneurs, and voters.

Question 1: What are the wants and constraints of those involved? This question introduces the concept of *scarcity*. It asks students to think critically about the preferences and resources driving decision making in a given situation. It links into discussions of utility functions, budget constraints, strategic behaviour, and new ideas that expand our thinking about rationality and behavioural economics.

Question 2: What are the trade-offs? This question focuses on *opportunity cost*. It asks students to understand trade-offs when considering any decision, including factors that might go beyond the immediate financial costs and benefits. Consideration of trade-offs takes us to discussions of marginal decision making, sunk costs, non-monetary costs, and discounting.

Question 3: How will others respond? This question asks students to focus on *incentives,* both their incentives and the incentives of others. Students consider how individual choices aggregate in both expected and unexpected ways, and what happens when incentives change. The question links into understanding supply and demand, elasticity, competition, taxation, game theory, and monetary and fiscal policy.

Question 4: Why isn't everyone already doing it? This question relates to *efficiency*. It asks students to start from an assumption that markets work to provide desired goods and services, and then to think carefully about why something that seems like a good idea isn't already being put into practice. We encourage students to revisit their answers to the previous three questions and see if they missed something about the trade-offs, incentives, or other forces at work, or whether they are looking at a genuine market failure. This question ties in with a range of topics, including public goods, externalities, information gaps, monopoly, arbitrage, and how the economy operates in the long run versus the short run.

New for the First Canadian Edition

The first Canadian edition of *Macroeconomics* presents the core principles of economics, but also seeks to share with students some of the ways that new ideas are *expanding* the basics of economic theory. The sequence of chapters follows a fairly traditional route through the core principles. By thinking first about the choices faced by individuals, students can engage with ideas that more closely relate to their own experiences. In this way, the organization of the text makes core economic ideas more immediately intuitive and better prepares students to eventually understand the choices of firms, groups, and governments. The text proceeds step-by-step from the personal to the public, allowing students to build toward an understanding of aggregate decisions on a solid foundation of individual decision making.

The uniqueness of the first US edition was its application of global and international contexts in understanding macroeconomic concepts. The first Canadian edition of *Macroeconomics* emulates this design, but from a Canadian perspective. The first Canadian edition includes real-life examples and case studies from developing economies around the world, and reflects upon how they can be understood from within a Canadian, as well as a global, context. In addition to global examples, we have included Canadian examples and case studies that Canadian students will be able to relate to their everyday lives.

Beyond its basic coverage of macroeconomic principles, the first Canadian edition of *Macroeconomics* offers content that connects the core curriculum to today's macroeconomic concerns:

Chapter 1 aims to explain normative and positive economic analysis using the cost of Canadian education.

Chapter 2 explains absolute and comparative advantage using Canada–China trade scenarios. Canadian hockey players are used as an example to illustrate comparative advantage.

Chapter 3 explains the supply and demand and how markets work. It uses few Canadian examples, for example, the Canadian IT market, to explain market operations.

Chapter 4 provides the examples of Tim Horton's pricing decisions as well as Parks Canada entrance fees, to explain elasticity.

Chapter 5 uses the sale of Canadian airwaves to discuss efficiency.

Chapter 6 explores the impact of drug price control on R & D and the Canadian economy, Canadian supply management system in dairy industry and its impact, as well as the unintended consequences of biofuel subsidy.

Chapter 7 focuses on measuring economic performance. Tracing the production of a jar of jam helps us to understand how Canadian economic activity is measured and recorded. The chapter concludes with some of the drawbacks involved in using measurements.

Chapter 8 focuses on measuring economic performance. The Consumer Price Index is introduced to measure the cost of living and how changes in inflation affect our well-being in Canada.

Chapter 9 seeks to understand how economy grows and why growth rate varies among countries. The chapter concludes with some policy suggestions that helped Canada grow in the past.

Chapter 11 develops the aggregate demand/aggregate supply model to explain the business cycle. The purpose is to identify how the business cycle comes about and how to seek counter-cyclical solutions.

Chapter 12 starts off with the foundation of government fiscal policy via the theoretical framework. It then traces how Canada's Action Plan, following the Canadian recession in 2009, was used in putting the Canadian economy back on track.

Chapter 13 describes how financial markets fit into the overall economy, focusing on the market for loanable funds and how to connect borrowers and savers. The chapter concludes by locating saving and investment within the national accounts approach.

Chapter 14 starts with the role of money in the economy, and explores the role played by the Bank of Canada and how monetary policy can be used to influence economic variables.

Chapter 15 explains where inflation is coming from and how inflation varies around the world.

Chapter 16 begins with the economics of financial crises and explains why things sometimes go wrong in financial markets. The chapter focuses into how an event started in the US affected the Canadian economy, including the ways that governments responded through monetary and fiscal policy.

Chapter 17 uses the successful business of Lululemon to illustrate the importance of trade in our Canadian economy.

Chapter 18 starts with the basics of development economics and explores Canada's role in international aid program.

The text's most important commitment is to make sure that students understand the basic analytical tools of economics. Because students sometimes need reinforcement with the math requirements, *Macroeconomics* also contains four unique math appendixes that explain math topics important to understanding economics:

APPENDIX A	Math Essentials: Understanding Graphs and Slope
APPENDIX B	Math Essentials: Working with Linear Equations
APPENDIX C	Math Essentials: Calculating Percentage Change, Slope, and Elasticity
APPENDIX D	Math Essentials: The Area Under a Linear Curve

MODERN TEACHING APPROACH

In addition to the regular chapter features found in almost every textbook, this text includes several unique features that support a modern teaching approach.

Interesting Examples Open Each Chapter

Interesting examples open each chapter. These chapter-opening stories feature issues that consumers, voters, businesspeople, and family members face, and they are presented in an engaging, journalistic style. The examples then take students through relevant principles that can help frame and solve the economic problem at hand. Here is a sample of the chapter-opening features:

Making an Impact with Small Loans

The Origins of a T-Shirt

Mobiles Go Global

Canada's Everyday Drink

A Broken Laser Pointer Starts an Internet Revolution

Feeding the World, One Price Control at a Time

It's More than Counting Berries

Why Economic Growth Matters

Get Cracking

A Land of Opportunity...and Inflation

Special Features Build Interest

- **Real Life**—Describes a short case or policy question, findings from history or academic studies, and anecdotes from the field.

- **From Another Angle**—Shows a different way of looking at an economic concept. This feature can be a different way of thinking about a situation, a humorous story, or sometimes just an unusual application of a standard idea.

- **What Do You Think?**—Offers a longer case study, with implications for public policy and student-related issues. This feature offers relevant data or historical evidence and asks students to employ both economic analysis and normative arguments to defend a position. We leave the student with open-ended questions, which professors can assign as homework or use for classroom discussion.

- **Where Can It Take You?**—Directs students to classes, resources, or jobs related to the topic at hand. This feature shows students how they might apply what they learn in careers and as consumers.

- **Potentially Confusing** and **Hints**—Offer additional explanations of a concept or use of terminology that students may find confusing. Rather than smoothing over confusing ideas and language, the text calls attention to common misunderstandings and gives students the support they need to understand economic language and reasoning on a deeper level.

- **Concept Check**—Provides an opportunity at the end of each chapter section for students to quiz themselves on the preceding material before reading on. The Concept Check questions are keyed to related learning objectives, providing students with a built-in review tool and study device.

Sidebar features

REAL LIFE

Comparative Advantage: The Good, the Bad, and the Ugly

You may have noticed that when you call the customer service line for many large companies, you are likely to end up speaking with someone in India or the Philippines. Thirty years ago, that was not the case—call centres for Canadian customers were almost all located in Canada.

Canada has not become worse at running call centres. In fact, it may still have an absolute advantage at it.

FROM ANOTHER ANGLE

Story of Multi-Talented Athletes

Two of the most famous multi-talented athletes in Canadian sports history are Harvey Pulford and Lionel Conacher. They both won national championships in Canadian football, hockey, boxing, and lacrosse, and Conacher's name appears in the halls of fame of four different sports. Each could easily have become one of the best football players or boxers or lacrosse players of his generation, but both ended up as hockey players. From a practical point of view, they could not play multiple sports professionally for a long time, so they had to make a choice. Although both had an absolute advantage at

WHAT DO YOU THINK?

Is Self-Sufficiency a Virtue?

Why should Canada trade with other countries? If every other country in the world were to disappear tomorrow, Canada would probably manage to fend for itself. It has plenty of fertile land, natural resources, people, and manufacturing capacity.

Based on what you now know about specialization and the gains from trade, what do you think about the value of

POTENTIALLY CONFUSING

In Chapter 3 , "Markets," we distinguished between a curve *shifting* to the left or right and *movement along* the same curve. A shift represents a fundamental change in the quantity demanded or supplied at any given price; a movement along the same curve simply shows a switch to a different quantity and price point. Does a tax cause a *shift* of the demand or supply curve or a *movement along the curve*?

CONCEPT CHECK

☐ Could a person or country ever produce a combination of goods that lies outside the production possibilities frontier? Why or why not? [LO 2.1]

☐ Would an increase in productivity as a result of a new technology shift a production possibilities frontier inward or outward? [LO 2.1]

Strong Materials Support Learning

The chapters contain most of the standard end-of-chapter features to help students solidify and test their understanding of the concepts presented, as well as a few new ideas that expand on those concepts. The authors have taken particular care with student review and instructor materials to guide high-quality homework and test questions.

- **Summary**—Highlights and emphasizes the essential takeaways from the chapter.
- **Key Terms**—Lists the most important terms from the chapter.
- **Review Questions**—Guide students through review and application of the concepts covered in the chapter. The review questions range from straightforward questions about theories or formulas to more open-ended narrative questions.
- **Problems and Applications**—Can be assigned as homework, typically quantitative. All problems and applications are fully integrated with Connect, enabling online assignments and grading.

MARKET LEADING TECHNOLOGY

connect

Learn Without Limits

McGraw-Hill Connect® is an award-winning digital teaching and learning platform that gives students the means to better connect with their coursework, with their instructors, and with the important concepts that they will need to know for success now and in the future. With Connect, instructors can take advantage of McGraw-Hill's trusted content to seamlessly deliver assignments, quizzes, and tests online. McGraw-Hill Connect is a learning platform that continually adapts to each student, delivering precisely what they need, when they need it, so class time is more engaging and effective. Connect makes teaching and learning personal, easy, and proven.

Connect Key Features

SmartBook®

As the first and only adaptive reading experience, SmartBook is changing the way students read and learn. SmartBook creates a personalized reading experience by highlighting the most important concepts a student needs to learn at that moment in time. As a student engages with SmartBook, the reading experience continuously adapts by highlighting content based on what each student knows and doesn't know. This ensures that he or she is focused on the content needed to close specific knowledge gaps, while it simultaneously promotes long-term learning.

Connect Insight®

Connect Insight is Connect's new one-of-a-kind visual analytics dashboard—now available for instructors—that provides at-a-glance information regarding student performance, which is immediately actionable. By presenting assignment, assessment, and topical performance results together with a time metric that is easily visible for aggregate or individual results, Connect Insight gives instructors the ability to take a just-in-time approach to teaching and learning that was never before available. Connect Insight presents data that helps instructors improve class performance in a way that is efficient and effective.

Simple Assignment Management

With Connect, creating assignments is easier than ever, so instructors can spend more time teaching and less time managing.

- Assign SmartBook learning modules.
- Edit existing questions and create unique questions.
- Draw from a variety of text-specific questions, resources, and test bank material to assign online.
- Streamline lesson planning, student progress reporting, and assignment grading to make classroom management more efficient than ever.

Smart Grading

When it comes to studying, time is precious. Connect helps students learn more efficiently by providing feedback and practice material when they need it, where they need it.

- Automatically score assignments, giving students immediate feedback on their work and comparisons with correct answers.
- Access and review each response; manually change grades or leave comments for students to review.
- Track individual student performance—by question, assignment, or in relation to the class overall—with detailed grade reports.

- Reinforce classroom concepts with practice tests and instant quizzes.

- Integrate grade reports easily with Learning Management Systems including Blackboard, D2L, and Moodle.

Instructor Library

The Connect Instructor Library is a repository for additional resources to improve student engagement in and out of the class. It provides all the critical resources instructors need to build their course.

- Access instructor resources.

- View assignments and resources created for past sections.

- Post your own resources for students to use.

Instructor Resources

- Instructor's Manual
- Instructor's Solutions Manual
- Computerized Test Bank
- Microsoft® PowerPoint® Lecture Slides

Superior Learning Solutions and Support

The McGraw-Hill Education team is ready to help instructors assess and integrate any of our products, technology, and services into your course for optimal teaching and learning performance. Whether it's helping your students improve their grades or putting your entire course online, the McGraw-Hill Education team is here to help you do it. Contact your Learning Solutions Consultant today to learn how to maximize all of McGraw-Hill Education's resources.

For more information, please visit us online: http://www.mheducation.ca/he/solutions

ACKNOWLEDGMENTS

We could not have completed this text without the help of others. In particular, Andrew Wong would like to thank Sandi, Shannon, Katie, and Aidan for their support and patience, as well as their understanding and encouragement throughout the research and writing process.

Dr. Alam would like to thank his parents, Mr. Nurul Alam and Mrs. Nazmun Nahar; his wife, Nusrat Aireen; and his children, Nibras and Arisa.

A special thanks to the many talented staff and freelance members of the McGraw-Hill Education team—Kevin O'Hearn, Product Manager; Tammy Mavroudi and Melissa Hudson, Product Developers; Jeanette McCurdy, Supervising Editor; Judy Sturrup, Copy Editor; and Derek Capitaine, Permissions Editor—for their trust in us and helping to ensure the timely completion of our manuscript.

We gratefully acknowledge feedback and constructive criticism from colleagues across Canada.

Thank You!

This text has gone through a lengthy development process spanning several years, and it wouldn't be the same without the valuable feedback. The authors and McGraw-Hill thank you for sharing your insights and recommendations.

Hussein Alzoud
Athabasca University

Eric Moon
University of Toronto

Ron Bianchi
Vanier College

Fiona T. Rahman
University of Waterloo

Alan Chan
University of New Brunswick

Mark Raymond
Saint. Mary's University

xxii

Tak Yan Chan
Crandall University

Terri Rizzo
Lakehead University

Nafeez Fatima
University of Waterloo

Cheryl Roberts
University of British Columbia

David Gray
University of Ottawa

Bosu Seo
University of the Fraser Valley

Gordon Lee
University of Alberta

Claude Theoret
University of Ottawa

Michael Leonard
Kwantlen Polytechnic University

Angela Trimarchi
Wilfrid Laurier University

Junjie Liu
Simon Fraser University

Dr. Brian VanBlarcom
Acadia University

Michael Maschek
University of the Fraser Valley

Peter Wylie
UBC Okanagan

Leigh MacDonald
Western University

Sung Min Yoo
Trinity Western University

David Murrell
UNB at Fredericton

We are grateful to you all for helping shape our ideas about teaching economics today and for helping turn those ideas into the text you're reading.

Dean Karlan
Yale University

Jonathan Morduch
New York University

Rafat Alam
MacEwan University

Andrew Wong
University of Alberta

PART ONE

The Power of Economics

The two chapters in Part 1 will introduce you to ...

the tools and intuition essential to the study of economics.

Chapter 1 presents four questions that introduce the fundamental concepts of economic problem solving. We also describe how economists think about data and analyze policies, typically separating how people *want* the world to work (*normative* analysis) from how the world *actually* works (*positive* analysis).

Chapter 2 presents the ideas of absolute and comparative advantage to explain how people (and countries) can most effectively use their resources and talents. Should you hire a plumber or fix the pipes yourself? Should you become a pop star or an economist? We develop these ideas to show how trade can make everyone better off, on both a personal and a national level.

This is just a start. Throughout the book, we'll use these tools to gain a deeper understanding of how people interact and manage their resources, which in turn gives insight into tough problems of all sorts. Economic ideas weave a common thread through many subjects, from the purely economic to political, environmental, and cultural issues, as well as personal decisions encountered in everyday life. Economics is much more than just the study of money, and we hope you'll find that what you learn here sheds light far beyond your economics classes.

CHAPTER 1
Macroeconomics and Life

LEARNING OBJECTIVES

LO 1.1   Explain the historical thought behind macroeconomics.
LO 1.2   Explain the economic concept of scarcity.
LO 1.3   Explain the economic concepts of performance and decision making.
LO 1.4   Explain the economic concept of incentives.
LO 1.5   Explain the economic concept of efficiency.
LO 1.6   Distinguish between correlation and causation.
LO 1.7   List the characteristics of a good economic model.
LO 1.8   Distinguish between positive and normative analysis.

Making an Impact with Small Loans

On the morning of October 13, 2006, Bangladeshi economist Muhammad Yunus received an unexpected telephone call from Oslo, Norway. Later that day, the Nobel committee announced that Yunus and the Grameen Bank, which he founded in 1976, would share the 2006 Nobel Peace Prize. Past recipients of the Nobel Peace Prize include Mother Teresa, who spent over fifty years ministering to beggars and lepers; Martin Luther King, Jr., who used peaceful protest to oppose racial segregation; and the Dalai Lama, an exiled Tibetan Buddhist leader who symbolizes the struggle for religious and cultural tolerance. What were an economist and his bank doing in such company?

Grameen is not a typical bank. Yes, it makes loans and offers savings accounts, charging customers for its services, just like other banks. But it serves some of the poorest people in the poorest villages in one of the poorest countries in the world. It makes loans so small that it's hard for people in wealthy countries to imagine what good they can do: the first group of loans Yunus made totaled only $27. Before Grameen came along, other banks had been unwilling to work in these poor communities. They believed it wasn't worth bothering to lend such small amounts; many believed the poor could not be counted on to repay their loans.

Yunus disagreed. He was convinced that even very small loans would allow poor villagers to expand their small businesses—maybe buying a sewing machine, or a cow to produce milk for the local market—and earn more money. As a result, their lives would be more comfortable and secure, and their children would have a better future. Yunus claimed that they would be able to repay the loans and that his new bank would earn a profit.

Yunus proved the skeptics wrong, and today Grameen Bank serves more than 8 million customers. The bank reports that 98 percent of its loans are repaid—a better rate than some banks in rich countries can claim. Grameen also reports steady profits, which has inspired other banks to start serving poor communities on nearly every continent, including recent start-ups in New York City and Omaha, Nebraska.

© Karen Kasmauski/Corbis

Muhammad Yunus was trained as an economist. He earned a PhD at Vanderbilt University in Nashville and then taught in Tennessee before becoming a professor in Bangladesh. When a devastating famine struck Bangladesh, Yunus became disillusioned with teaching. What did abstract equations and stylized graphs have to do with the suffering he saw all around him?

Ultimately Yunus realized that economic thinking holds the key to solving hard problems that truly matter. The genius of Grameen Bank is that it is neither a traditional charity nor a traditional bank. Instead, it is a business that harnesses basic economic insights to make the world a better place.[1]

In this book, we'll introduce you to the tools economists use to tackle some of the world's biggest challenges, from health care reform, to climate change, to lifting people out of poverty. Of course, these tools are not just for taking on causes worthy of Nobel prizes. Economics can also help you become a savvier consumer, successfully launch a new cell phone app, or simply make smarter decisions about how to spend your time and money. Throughout this book, we promise to ask you not just to memorize theories, but also to apply the ideas you read about to the everyday decisions you face in your own life.

The Basic Insights of Macroeconomics

When people think of economics, they often think of the stock market, the unemployment rate, or media reports saying things like, "The Bank of Canada has raised its target for overnight rate." Although economics does include these topics, its reach is much broader.

Economics is the study of how people manage resources. Decisions about how to allocate resources can be made by individuals, but also by groups of people in families, firms, governments, and other organizations. In economics, *resources* are not just physical things like cash and gold mines. They are also intangible things, such as time, ideas, technology, job experience, and even personal relationships.

Traditionally, economics has been divided into two broad fields: microeconomics and macroeconomics. **Microeconomics** is the study of how individuals and firms manage resources. **Macroeconomics** is the study of the economy on a regional, national, or international scale. Microeconomics and macroeconomics are highly related and interdependent; we need both to fully understand how economies work.

LO 1.1 Explain the historical thought behind macroeconomics.

Economics prior to the Great Depression was mainly dominated by the Classical theory. Classical theory is what you may have learned in your introductory microeconomics class. It focuses on an equilibrium condition where supply and demand interact. It suggests that if demand and supply are not equal, the market will adjust in such a way that equilibrium ultimately will prevail. However, during the Great Depression, both the goods-and-services market and the labour market had a surplus and the markets were not in equilibrium. This contradicts the Classical theory that assumes demand will always equal supply.

Modern macroeconomics began with a book published by John Maynard Keynes titled *General Theory of Employment, Interest and Money* in 1936. Keynes introduced a new theory that explained why markets may not need to be in equilibrium for them to operate. This new theory became known as *Keynesian economics* and dominated policy making in the post-war 1940s and the 1950s, and more recently after the financial crisis that began in 2008.

People use economics every day, from Bay Street to neighbourhood stores, from government buildings to Bangladeshi villages. They apply economic ideas to everything from shoe shopping to hockey, from running a hospital to running for political office. What ties these topics together is a common approach to problem solving.

Economists tend to break down problems by asking a set of four questions:

1. What are the wants and constraints of those involved?
2. What are the trade-offs?
3. How will others respond?
4. Why isn't everyone already doing it?

Underlying these questions are some important economic concepts that we will begin to explore in later chapters. Although the questions, and the underlying concepts, are based on just a few common-sense assumptions about how people in society behave, they offer a surprising amount of insight into tough problems of all sorts. They are so important to economic problem solving that they will come up again and again in this book. In this chapter we'll take a bird's-eye view of economics, focusing on the fundamental concepts and skimming over the details. Later in the book, we'll return to each question in more depth.

Scarcity

Question 1: What are the wants and constraints of those involved?

LO 1.2 Explain the economic concept of scarcity.

For the most part, most people make decisions that are aimed at getting the things they want. Of course, you can't always get what you want. People want a lot of things, but they are *constrained* by limited resources. Economists define **scarcity** as the condition of wanting more than we can get with available resources. Scarcity is a fact of life. You have only so much time and only so much money. You can arrange your resources in a lot of different ways—studying or watching TV, buying a car or travelling to other parts of the country—but at any given time you have a fixed range of possibilities. Scarcity also describes the world on a collective level: as a society, we can produce only so many things, and we have to decide how those things are divided among many people.

The first question to ask in untangling a complex economic problem is: What are the wants and constraints of those involved? Given both rational behaviour and scarcity, we can expect people to work to get what they want, but to be constrained in their choices by the limited resources available to them. Suppose you *want* to spend as much time as possible this summer taking road trips around the country. You are *constrained* by the four months of summer vacation and by your lack of money to pay for gas, food, and places to stay. Behaving rationally, you might choose to work double shifts for two months to earn enough to spend two months on the road. Since you are now *constrained* by having only two months to travel, you'll have to prioritize your time, activities, and expenses.

Now put yourself in Muhammad Yunus's shoes, back in 1976. He saw extremely poor but entrepreneurial Bangladeshi villagers and thought that they could improve their lives with access to loans. Why weren't banks providing financial services for these people? In this case, those involved are traditional Bangladeshi banks and poor Bangladeshi villagers—what are the wants and constraints of both these groups?

*   The banks *want* to make profits by lending money to people who will pay them back with interest. They are *constrained* by having limited funds available to lend and to run branch banks. We can therefore expect banks to prioritize making loans to customers they believe are likely to pay them back. Before 1976, that meant wealthier, urban Bangladeshis, not the very poor in remote rural villages.

*   The villagers *want* the chance to increase their incomes. They have energy and business ideas but are *constrained* in their ability to borrow start-up money by the fact that most banks believe they are too poor to repay loans.

Analyzing the wants and constraints of those involved gives us some valuable information about why poor Bangladeshis didn't have access to loans. Banks *wanted* to earn profits and managed their *constrained* funds to prioritize those they thought would be profitable customers. Bangladeshi villagers *wanted* to increase their incomes but couldn't follow up on business opportunities due to *constrained* start-up money. That's good information, but we haven't yet come up with the solution that Dr. Yunus was looking for. To take the next step in solving the puzzle, we turn to another question economists often ask.

Performance and Decision Making

Question 2: What are the trade-offs?

LO 1.3 Explain the economic concepts of performance and decision making.

Measuring the macroeconomy requires us to develop ways to quantify our observations of the economy. When studying the economy on an international scale we always focus on its performance. We make comparisons among countries and determine rankings. On the regional and national scale we compare current performance with the past to determine whether the economy has improved or not. In macroeconomics, measurements are our performance indicators. They not only tell us where we are, they also help us to set goals.

Some of the most important performance measurements are Gross Domestic Product (GDP), unemployment rates, and the Consumer Price Index (CPI). These aggregate indicators help consumers, businesses, and governments to understand how the macroeconomy functions.

Gross Domestic Product (GDP) is usually a measurement of national income. It accounts for the dollar value of all the final goods and services a country has produced domestically for a specific period of time. Because income is generated when goods and services are produced, the measurement can also be viewed as a measurement of output. When an economy's output is rising over time, we have economic growth. But while an economy typically grows over a long period of time, there are periods when output decreases. These fluctuations in output in the short run are called *business cycles*.

Unemployment rates measure the number of unemployed workers in the labour force. This measurement tells us the labour utilization in the economy. Labour represents a significant input into an economy's production capacity, so when unemployment is high, the amount of output decreases. While some unemployment is inevitable in an economy, policy makers are more concerned with unemployment that comes from growth stagnation.

Inflation occurs when the overall price level is rising. While some rise in the overall price level is considered acceptable, a rapid rise in inflation may disrupt the saving–investment process. For example, during periods of high inflation, businesses may not want to borrow money to expand because the cost of borrowing typically rises. Households don't want to save money because the future value of their money may be lower. These disruptions will lead to lower economic output and affect long-run economic growth.

Armed with these performance indicators, policy makers look for policy decisions that lead to faster long-term growth and reduce the severity of recession. These policy decisions are usually concerned with two sets of tools: monetary policy and fiscal policy, which are used to keep economic output at a level that is consistent with full employment.

Monetary policy is conducted by the Bank of Canada. It involves controlling the money supply and the setting of interest rates. Low interest rates tend to stimulate output and employment but may create higher inflation. Higher interest rates tend to keep inflation low but may lower output and employment.

Fiscal policy is conducted by the federal government. It involves the use of government spending and taxation to influence the economy's output. Higher government spending and lower taxes will boost economic output but may bring a higher level of inflation and public debt. Lower government spending and higher taxes will keep inflation and public borrowing in check but may lead to lower output and employment.

Every decision in life involves weighing the trade-off between costs and benefits. We look at our options and decide whether it is worth giving up one in order to get the other. We choose to do things only when we think that the benefits will be greater than the costs. The potential *benefit* of taking an action is often easy to see: you can have higher economic growth; bank customers who take out a loan have the opportunity to expand their businesses. The *costs* of a decision, on the other hand, are not always clear.

You might think it *is* clear—that the cost of higher economic growth is simply the amount of money governments spend on infrastructure and education. But something is missing from that calculation. The true cost of something is not just the amount you have to pay for it, but also the opportunity you lose to do something else, instead. Suppose that a government chooses to spend money on infrastructure instead of spending the same money on a job-creation program. One of the true costs of government spending on infrastructure, then, is the number of jobs that were not generated by the job-creation program. Behaving rationally, governments should spend money on infrastructure only if it will be more valuable to the economy than the best alternative use for the money. Because governments and people have different priorities and place different values on things, they will make different decisions.

Economists call this true cost of your choice the **opportunity cost**, which is equal to the value of what you have to give up in order to get something. Put another way, opportunity cost is the value of your next-best alternative—the "opportunity" you must pass up in order to make a different choice.

Say you're planning a road trip with a friend, and she's taking the trip instead of using the money to buy a new computer, take a summer class, and visit her cousins. For her, the opportunity cost is the pleasure she would have had from a new computer, plus whatever benefits she might have gotten from the course, plus the fun she would have had with her cousins. If she's behaving rationally, she will go with you on the road trip only if she believes it will make her happier than what she's giving up.

Examining opportunity cost helps us think more clearly about trade-offs. If someone asked you how much your road trip cost and you responded by adding up the money you spent on gas, hotels, and food, you would be failing to capture some of the most important and interesting aspects of the trade-offs you made (such as how much fun you had). Opportunity cost helps us to see why, for example, a partner and a paralegal at a law firm face truly different trade-offs when they contemplate taking the same vacation for the same price. The partner makes a higher salary and therefore forgoes more money when taking unpaid time off from work. The opportunity cost of a vacation for the paralegal is therefore lower than it is for the lawyer, and the decision the paralegal faces is truly different.

Economists often express opportunity cost as a dollar value. Suppose you've been given a gift certificate worth $15 at a restaurant. The restaurant has a short menu: pizza and spaghetti, each of which costs $15. The gift certificate can be used only at this particular restaurant, so the only thing you give up for pizza is spaghetti, and vice versa. If you didn't have the certificate, you would be willing to pay as much as $15 for the pizza but no more than $10 for the spaghetti.

What is the opportunity cost of choosing the pizza? Even though the price on the menu is $15, the opportunity cost is only $10, because that is the value you place on your best (and only) alternative, the spaghetti. What is the opportunity cost of choosing the spaghetti? It's $15, the value you place on the pizza. Which do you choose? One choice has an opportunity cost of $10, the other $15. Behaving rationally, you should choose the pizza, because it has the lower opportunity cost.

A simpler way of describing this trade-off would be simply to say that you prefer pizza to spaghetti. The opportunity cost of spaghetti is higher because to get it, you have to give up something you like more. But putting it in terms of opportunity cost can be helpful when there are more choices, or more nuances to the choices.

For example, suppose the gift certificate could be used only to buy spaghetti. Now what is the opportunity cost of choosing the spaghetti? It is $0, because you can't do anything else with the gift certificate—your choice is spaghetti or nothing. The opportunity cost of pizza is now $15 because you're paying for it with money you could have spent on other purchases outside the restaurant. So, even though you like pizza better, you might now choose the spaghetti because it has a lower opportunity cost in this particular situation.

Once you start to think about opportunity costs, you see them everywhere. For an application of opportunity cost to a serious moral question, read the What Do You Think? box, The Opportunity Cost of a Life.

WHAT DO YOU THINK?

The Opportunity Cost of a Life

Throughout the book, What Do You Think? boxes ask for your opinion about an important policy or life decision. These boxes will present questions that require you to combine facts and economic analysis with values and moral reasoning. They are the sort of tough questions that people face in real life. There are many correct answers, depending on your values and goals.

The philosopher Peter Singer writes that opportunity costs can be a matter of life or death. Imagine you are a salesperson, and on your way to a meeting on a hot summer day, you drive by a lake. Suddenly, you notice that a child who has been swimming in the lake is drowning. No one else is in sight.

You have a choice. If you stop the car and dive into the lake to save the child, you will be late for your meeting, miss out on making a sale, and lose $250. The *opportunity cost* of saving the child's life is $250.

Alternatively, if you continue on to your meeting, you earn the $250 but you lose the opportunity to dive into the lake and save the child's life. The *opportunity cost* of going to the meeting is one child's life.

What would you do? Most people don't hesitate. They immediately say they would stop the car, dive into the lake, and save the drowning child. After all, a child's life is worth more than $250.

Now suppose you're thinking about spending $250 on a new iPod. That $250 could instead have been used for some charitable purpose, such as immunizing children in another country against yellow fever. Suppose that for every $250 donated, an average of one child's life ends up being saved. (In fact, $250 to save one child's life is not far from reality in many cases.) What is the opportunity cost of buying an iPod? According to Peter Singer, it is the same as the opportunity cost of going straight to the meeting: a child's life.

These two situations are not exactly the same, of course, but why does the first choice (jump in the lake) seem so obvious to most people, while the second seems much less obvious?

What do you think?

1. In what ways do the two situations presented by Singer—the sales meeting and the drowning child versus the iPod and the unvaccinated child—differ?

2. Singer argues that even something like buying an iPod is a surprisingly serious moral decision. Do you agree? What sort of opportunity costs do you typically consider when making such a decision?

3. What might be missing from Singer's analysis of the trade-offs people face when making a decision about how to spend money?

Another important principle for understanding trade-offs is the idea that rational people make decisions *at the margin*. **Marginal decision making** describes the idea that rational people compare the *additional* benefits of a choice against the *additional* costs, without considering related benefits and costs of past choices.

For example, suppose Canada's Wonderland has a $25 admission price and charges $5 per ride. If you are standing outside the park, the cost of the first ride is $30, because you will have to pay the admission price and buy a ticket to go on the ride. Once you are inside the park, the *marginal* cost of each additional ride is $5. When deciding whether to go on the roller coaster a second or third time, then, you should compare only the benefit or enjoyment you will get from one more ride with the opportunity cost of that additional ride.

This may sound obvious, but in practice many people don't make decisions on the margin. Suppose you get into Canada's Wonderland and start to feel sick shortly thereafter. If doing something else with your $5 for twenty minutes would bring you more enjoyment than another roller coaster ride while feeling sick, the rational thing to do would be to leave. The relevant trade-off is between the additional *benefits* that going on another ride would bring, versus the additional *costs*. You cannot get back the $25 admission fee or any of the other money you've already spent on rides. Economists call costs that have already been incurred and cannot be recovered **sunk costs**. Sunk costs should not have any bearing on your *marginal* decision about what to do next. But many people feel the need to go on a few more rides to psychologically justify the $25 admission.

Trade-offs play a crucial role in businesses' decisions about what goods and services to produce. Let's return to the example that started this chapter and apply the idea to a bank in Bangladesh: What are the trade-offs involved in making a small loan?

- For traditional banks, the opportunity cost of making small loans to the poor is the money that the bank could have earned by making loans to wealthier clients instead (clients who, in the traditional banking system, were believed to be more likely to pay back the loan plus interest).
- For poor borrowers, the opportunity cost of borrowing was whatever else they would have done with the time they spent travelling to the bank and with the money they would pay in fees and interest on the loan. The benefit, of course, was whatever the loan would enable them to do that they could not have done otherwise, such as starting a small business or buying food or livestock.

Based on this analysis of trade-offs, we can see why traditional banks made few loans to poor Bangladeshis. Because banks perceived the poor to be risky clients, the opportunity cost of making small loans to the poor seemed to outweigh the benefits—unless the banks charged very high fees. From the perspective of poor rural villagers, high fees meant that the opportunity cost of borrowing was higher than the benefits, so they chose not to borrow under the terms offered by banks.

Notice that the answer to this question built off the answer to the first: we had to know the wants and constraints of each party before we could assess the trade-offs they faced. Now that we understand the motivations and the trade-offs that led to the situation Dr. Yunus observed, we can turn to a third question he might have asked himself when considering what would happen when he founded the Grameen Bank.

Incentives

Question 3: How will others respond?

LO 1.4 Explain the economic concept of incentives.

You're in the mood for pizza, so you decide to go back to the restaurant with the short menu. When you get there, you discover that the prices have changed. Pizza now costs $50 instead of $15.

What will you do? Remember that your gift certificate is good for only $15. Unless you can easily afford to shell out $50 for a pizza or just really hate spaghetti, you probably won't be ordering the pizza. We're sure that you can think of ways to spend $35 that are worth more to you than your preference for pizza over spaghetti. But what if the prices had changed less drastically—say, $18 for pizza? That might be a tougher call.

As the trade-offs change, so will the choices people make. When the restaurant owner considers how much to charge for each dish, she must consider *how others will respond* to changing prices. If she knows the pizza is popular, she might be tempted to try charging more to boost her profits. But as she increases the price, fewer patrons will decide to order it.

If a trade-off faced by a lot of people changes, even by a small amount, the combined change in behaviour by everyone involved can add up to a big shift. The collective reaction to a changing trade-off is a central idea in economics and will come up in almost every chapter of this book. Asking "How will others respond?" to a trade-off that affects a lot of people gives us a complete picture of how a particular decision affects the world. What happens when prices change? What happens when the government implements a new policy? What happens when a company introduces a new product? Answering any of these questions requires us to consider a large-scale reaction, rather than the behaviour of just one person, company, or policy maker.

In answering this question about trade-offs, economists commonly make two assumptions. The first is that people respond to incentives. An **incentive** is something that causes people to behave in a certain way by changing the trade-offs they face. A positive incentive (sometimes just called an *incentive*) makes people *more likely* to do something. A negative incentive (sometimes called a *disincentive*) makes them *less likely* to do it. For example, lowering the price of spaghetti creates a positive incentive for people to order it because it lowers the opportunity cost—when you pay less for spaghetti, you give up fewer other things you could have spent the money on. Charging people more for pizza is a negative incentive to buy pizza, because they now have to give up more alternative purchases.

The second assumption economists make about trade-offs is that nothing happens in a vacuum. That is, you can't change just one thing in the world without eliciting a response from others. If you change your behaviour—even if only in a small way—that action will change the behaviour of the people around you in response. If you invent a new product, competitors will copy it. If you raise prices, consumers will buy less. If you tax a good or service, people will produce or consume less of it.

Asking *how others will respond* can help prevent bad decisions by predicting the undesirable side effects of a change in prices or policies. The question can also be used to design changes that elicit positive responses. When Muhammad Yunus was setting up Grameen Bank, he had to think carefully about the incentives that both rural villagers and traditional banks faced and to consider how those incentives could be changed without incurring negative side effects.

One reason that banks saw rural villagers as risky customers is that they were too poor to have anything to offer to the bank as collateral. *Collateral* is a possession, like a house or a car, pledged by a borrower to a lender. If the borrower cannot repay the loan, the lender keeps the collateral. The threat of losing the collateral increases the cost of choosing to not repay the loan, giving the borrower a positive incentive to repay. When traditional banks thought about lending to poor Bangladeshis, they concluded that without the threat of losing collateral, the villagers would be less likely to repay their loans.

Yunus needed to think up a different way of creating a positive incentive for poor customers to repay their loans. His best-known solution was to require borrowers to apply for loans in five-person groups. Every person in the group would have a stake in the success of the other members. If one person didn't repay a loan, no one else in the group could borrow from the bank again.

Yunus's idea, called *group responsibility,* was simple, but hugely significant. Yunus concluded that borrowers would have a strong incentive to repay their loans: they wouldn't want to ruin relationships with other members of the group—their fellow villagers, whom they live with every day and rely on for mutual support in hard times. This, in turn, changed the trade-off faced by banks, and they responded by being more willing to lend to the poor at lower rates. By asking himself how villagers would respond to the new kind of loan and how banks in turn would respond to the villagers' response, Yunus was able to predict that his idea could be the key to offering banking services to the poor.

Dr. Yunus's predictions proved to be correct. Seeing that poor villagers nearly always repaid their loans under Grameen's system gave other banks confidence that small borrowers could be reliable customers. Banks offering micro-loans, savings accounts, and other services to the very poor have spread around the world. As a result of Yunus's thoughtful creativity about incentives, the poor have better access to financial services, and banks earn money from providing them. Today, other ideas have proved even more effective in providing the right incentives for small borrowers, continuing in the tradition of experimentation and innovation pioneered by Yunus and Grameen Bank.

Throughout this book, you will see many examples of how the power of incentives can be harnessed to accomplish everything from increasing a company's profits to protecting the environment. But before we get carried away with brilliant economic innovations, we have to ask ourselves one more question, the final test of any solutions that come out of our problem-solving process.

Efficiency

Question 4: Why isn't everyone already doing it?

LO 1.5 Explain the economic concept of efficiency.

Economics tends to assume that people behave rationally. They clip coupons, compare car models before buying, and think hard about which major to choose at university. Although people are not calculating machines, they usually weigh trade-offs, respond to incentives, and are on the lookout for opportunities to get what they want in the most effective way possible.

The same goes for businesses. There are millions of businesses in the world, each trying to make a profit. When consumers want a good or service, some business will take the opportunity to earn money by providing it. That fact leads to our final assumption: *Under normal circumstances, individuals and firms will act to provide the things people want.* If a genuine profit-making opportunity exists, someone will take advantage of it, and usually sooner rather than later.

This final assumption comes from the idea of **efficiency**. Efficiency describes a situation in which resources are used in the most productive way possible to produce the goods and services that have the greatest total economic value to society. Increasing efficiency means finding a way to better use resources to produce the things that people want.

The definition of efficiency might raise some questions. How do we determine *value,* for example? What exactly do we mean by *resources?* Over the course of the book, we'll dive deeper into these issues. For now, we'll take a broad view: something is valuable if someone wants it, and a resource is anything that can be used to make something of value, from natural resources (such as water and trees) to human resources (such as talents and knowledge). This broad view leads to an important idea: when the economy is working efficiently, resources are *already* being allocated to valuable ends.

So when you think you see a big, unexploited opportunity—a new product, policy, technology, or business model that could change the world or earn you millions of dollars—ask yourself this: If it's such a great idea, *why isn't everyone* already *doing it?* One possible answer is simply that nobody has thought of it before. That's possible. But if *you* have seen the opportunity, doesn't it seem likely that at least one of the billions of other smart, rational people in the world will have seen it, too?

Don't get us wrong. We're not saying there is never an opportunity to do something new in the world. Great new ideas happen all the time—they drive progress. But there's a strong possibility that other people have already thought about the idea, and if they chose not to take advantage of it, that's a hint that you might be missing something. The first thing to do is backtrack to the first three economists' questions: Have you misjudged people's wants and constraints, miscalculated the trade-offs they face, or misunderstood how people will respond to incentives?

If you think back through those questions and still think you're on to something, here are some more possibilities to consider. We said that *under normal circumstances,* the economy is operating efficiently, and individuals or firms provide the things people want. What are some ways in which circumstances might not be normal?

- *Innovation:* Innovation is the explanation you're hoping is correct. Maybe your idea has not been used yet because it is too new. If you have come up with a truly new idea, whether it is new technology or a new business model, people cannot have taken advantage of it yet because it didn't exist before.

- *Market failure:* Market failures are an important cause of inefficiency. Sometimes people and firms fail to take advantage of opportunities because something prevents them from capturing the benefits of the opportunity or imposes additional costs on them. For instance, maybe your great new idea won't work because it would be impossible to prevent others from quickly copying it or because a few big companies have already got the market sewn up. Economists call such situations *market failure,* and we will discuss them in much greater depth later in the book.

- *Intervention:* If a powerful force—often the government—intervenes in the economy, transactions cannot take place the way they normally would. We'll see later in this book that many government economic policies intentionally or unintentionally interfere with people's ability to take advantage of profit-making opportunities.

- *Goals other than profit:* Maybe your idea won't produce a profit. Individuals and governments have goals other than profit, of course—for example, creating great art or promoting social justice. But if your idea doesn't also generate a profit, then it is less surprising that no one has taken advantage of it.

When Muhammad Yunus asked, "Why isn't everyone already lending to the poor?" he first identified a market failure involving lack of collateral and came up with the idea of group responsibility to fix it. But then he had to ask, "Why aren't all the banks already using the group responsibility idea?"

Maybe there was another market failure Yunus hadn't spotted. Maybe some government policy prevented it. Maybe traditional banks had considered it and decided it still wouldn't generate a profit. Yunus wasn't primarily interested in making profit, of course—he was interested in helping the poor. But if micro-loans weren't going to earn a profit for the banks even with group responsibility, then that would explain why no one was already doing it.

Fortunately, none of those answers were correct. This was a case in which the answer to *Why isn't everyone already doing it?* was that the idea was genuinely new. Grameen Bank was able to help very poor people in Bangladesh by lending them money, while making enough profit to expand and serve more customers. Today, over 20 million people in Bangladesh can get small loans from Grameen Bank and other organizations. Around the world, over 200 million low-income customers enjoy the same opportunity. Sometimes something that seems like a great new idea really is exactly that.

✓ CONCEPT CHECK

In every chapter of this book you will find a few Concept Checks. These questions test your understanding of the concepts presented in the preceding section. If you have trouble answering any of the questions, go back and review the section. Don't move forward until you understand these ideas.

- ☐ How do constraints affect decision making? [LO 1.2]
- ☐ What do opportunity costs represent? [LO 1.3]
- ☐ What is the name for something that changes the trade-offs that people face when making a decision? [LO 1.4]
- ☐ Give four reasons that might explain why a product isn't already in the market. [LO 1.5]

An Economist's Problem-Solving Toolbox

The concepts we've just discussed are some of the fundamental insights of macroeconomics. Using them to understand how the world *might* work is only half the battle. In the second part of this chapter we will describe some tools economists use to apply these insights to real situations.

Accurately spotting the fundamental economic concepts at work in the world is sometimes less obvious than you might think. Throughout history, people have observed the world around them and drawn conclusions that have proved hilariously—or sometimes tragically—wrong. We now know that the sun doesn't revolve around the Earth. Droughts are not caused by witches giving people the evil eye. Yet intelligent people once believed these things. It's human nature to draw meaning from the patterns we observe around us, but our conclusions are not always correct.

Economic analysis requires us to combine theory with observations and to subject both to scrutiny before drawing conclusions. In this section we will see how to put theories and facts together to determine what causes what. We will also distinguish between the way things *are* and the way we think they *should be.* You can apply these tools to various situations, from personal life choices to business decisions and policy analysis.

Correlation and Causation

LO 1.6 Distinguish between correlation and causation.

Many sports fans have a lucky jersey that they wear to help their team win a game. A die-hard fan might insist that his jersey is obviously lucky, because he was wearing it when his team won the Stanley Cup or the Grey Cup. This superstition is an exaggeration of a common human tendency: when we see that two events occur together, we tend to assume that one causes the other. Economists, however, try to be particularly careful about assuming what causes what.

To differentiate between events that simply occur at the same time and events that share a clear cause-and-effect relationship, we use two different terms. When we observe a consistent relationship between two events or variables, we say there is a **correlation** between them. If both tend to occur at the same time or move in the same direction, we say they are *positively correlated*. Wearing raincoats is positively correlated with rain. If one event or variable increases while a related event or variable decreases, we say they are *negatively correlated*. They move in opposite directions. High temperatures are negatively correlated with people wearing down jackets. If there is no consistent relationship between two variables, we say they are *uncorrelated*.

Correlation differs from causation. **Causation** means that one event brings about the other. As the preceding examples show, causation and correlation often go together. Weather and clothing are often correlated, because weather *causes* people to make certain choices about the clothing they wear.

Unfortunately, correlation and causation do not always go together in a straightforward way. Correlation and causation can be confused in three major ways: correlation without causation, omitted variables, and reverse causation.

Economists try to be particularly careful to differentiate between correlation and causation.

Correlation Without Causation

Does the strategy of *sell in May and go away* improve the return of a stock portfolio? A few decades ago, some people started to think it might. The idea is that the performance of the stock market grows stronger in the period from November to April than in any other part of the year. Bouman and Jacobsen in 2002 showed that this effect was supported in thirty-six out of thirty-seven countries (including Canada). In fact, a follow-up study by Andrade, Chhaochharia, and Fuerst in 2012 confirmed that the pattern persisted.

Would it have been a good idea to base your investment strategy on the above observation? We think not. There is no plausible cause-and-effect relationship here. Stock market outcomes happened to be *correlated with* the calendar for a number of years, but there is no logical way they could be *caused by* it. If you search long enough for odd coincidences, you will eventually find some.

Omitted Variables

Consider the following statement: there is a positive correlation between the presence of firefighters and people with serious burn injuries. Does this statement mean that firefighters cause burn injuries? Of course not. We know that firefighters are not burning people; they're trying to save them. Instead, there must be some common underlying factor, or *variable,* behind both observed outcomes—fires, in this case.

Sometimes two events that are correlated occur together because both are caused by the same underlying factor. Each has a causal relationship with a third factor rather than with each other. The underlying factor is called an *omitted variable,* because despite the fact that it is an important part of the cause-and-effect story, it has been left out of the analysis. The From Another Angle box, Does Ice Cream Cause Polio?" tells the story of an omitted variable that convinced some doctors to mistakenly campaign against a staple of summer fun: ice cream.

FROM ANOTHER ANGLE

Does Ice Cream Cause Polio?

From Another Angle boxes show you a different way of looking at an economic concept. Sometimes they will offer a humorous story, sometimes a different way of thinking about a situation, and sometimes just an unusual application of a standard idea. We find that a little bit of weirdness goes a long way in helping us to remember things, and we hope it will work for you, too.

A disease called polio once crippled or killed thousands of children in Canada every year. Before we knew what caused polio, doctors observed that polio infections seemed to be more common in children who had been eating lots of ice cream. Observing this *correlation* led some people to assume that there was a *causal* relationship between the two. Some doctors recommended an anti-polio diet that avoided ice cream. Many fearful parents understandably took their advice.

We now know that polio is caused by a virus that is transmitted from one person to another. The virus was spread through contaminated food and water—for example, dirty swimming pools or water fountains. It had nothing at all to do with how much ice cream a child ate. A polio vaccine was developed in 1955.

The ice cream confusion was caused by an *omitted variable:* warm weather. In warm weather, children are more likely to use swimming pools and water fountains. And in warm weather, children are also more likely to eat ice cream. Polio was therefore *correlated* with eating ice cream, but it certainly wasn't *caused* by it.

Sources: http://www.nytimes.com/2009/08/06/technology/06stats.html?_r=1. http://cpha.ca/en/programs/history/achievements/02-id/polio.aspx

Reverse Causation

A third common source of confusion between correlation and causation is called *reverse causation:* Did A cause B, or did B cause A? When two events always happen together, it can be hard to say which causes the other.

Let's return to the correlation between rain and raincoats. If we knew nothing about rain, we might observe that it often appears together with raincoats, and we might conclude that wearing a raincoat (A) causes rain (B). In this case, we all know that the causation goes the other way, but observation alone does not tell us that.

Looking at the timing of two correlated events can sometimes provide clues. Often, if A happens before B, it hints that A causes B rather than vice versa. But grabbing a raincoat as you leave home in the morning frequently happens *before* it rains in the afternoon. The timing notwithstanding, taking your raincoat with you in the morning clearly does not cause rain later in the day. In this case, your anticipation of B causes A to happen.

An important lesson for economists and non-economists alike is never to take observations at face value. Always make sure you can explain *why* two events are related. To do so, you need another tool in the economist's toolbox: a model.

Models

LO 1.7 List the characteristics of a good economic model.

A **model** is a simplified representation of a complicated situation. In economics, models show how people, firms, and governments make decisions about managing resources and how their decisions interact. An economic model can represent a situation as basic as how people decide what car to buy or as complex as what causes a global recession.

Because models simplify complex problems, they allow us to focus our attention on the most important parts. Models rarely include every detail of a given situation, but that is a good thing. If we had to describe the entire world with perfect accuracy before solving a problem, we'd be so overwhelmed with details that we'd never get the answer. By carefully simplifying the situation to its essentials, we can get useful answers that are *approximately* right.

One of the most basic models of the economy is the **circular flow model**. The economy involves billions of transactions every day, and the circular flow model helps show how all of those transactions work together. The model slashes through complexity to show important patterns. Figure 1-1 shows the circular flow of economic transactions in a graphic format called the *circular flow diagram.*

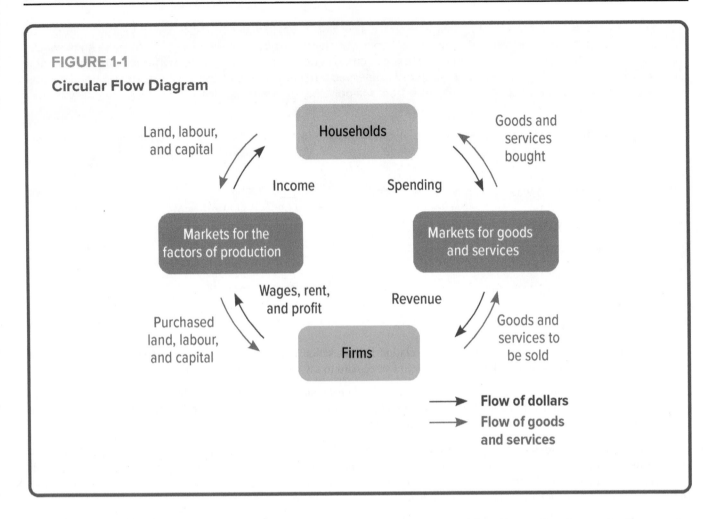

FIGURE 1-1

Circular Flow Diagram

The first simplification of the circular flow model narrows our focus to the two most important types of actors in the economy, households and firms:

- *Households* are vital in two ways. First, they supply land and labour to firms and invest capital in firms. (Land, labour, and capital are called the *factors of production*.) Second, they buy the goods and services that firms produce.

- *Firms,* too, are vital, but do the opposite of households. They buy or rent the land, labour, and capital supplied by households, and they produce and sell goods and services. The model shows that firms and households are tightly connected through both production and consumption.

In another helpful simplification, the circular flow model narrows the focus to two markets that connect households and firms:

- The *market for goods and services* is exactly what it sounds like. It reflects all of the activity involved in the buying and selling of goods and services. In this market, households spend their wages from labour and their income from land and capital, and firms earn revenue from selling their goods and services.

- The second market is the *market for the factors of production*. Here, households supply land, labour, and capital, and firms hire, purchase, or rent these inputs.

The model puts all of this together. The transactions we have described are part of two loops. One is a loop of inputs and outputs as they travel throughout the economy. The *inputs* are the land, labour, and capital firms use to produce goods. The *outputs* are the goods and services that firms produce using the factors of production.

Another loop represents the flow of dollars. Households buy goods and services using the money they get from firms for using their factors of production. Firms get revenues from selling these goods and services—and, in turn, firms can then use the money to buy or rent factors of production. This represents the flow of income. For a simple economy, expenditure must equal income. When applied to a nation, this model forms the basic foundation for calculating Gross Domestic Product (GDP), which we discuss in Chapter 7.

You might be a little dizzy at this point, with everything spinning in loops. To help straighten things out, let's follow $5 from your wallet as it flows through the economy. You could spend this $5 in any number of ways. As you're walking down the street, you see a box of doughnuts sitting in the window of your local bakery. You head in and give the baker your $5, a transaction in the market for goods. The money represents revenue for the baker and spending by you. The doughnuts are an output of the bakery.

The story of your $5 is not over, though. In order to make more doughnuts, the baker puts that $5 toward buying inputs in the market for the factors of production. This might include paying rent for the bakery or paying wages for an assistant. The baker's spending represents income for the households that provide the labour in the bakery or rent out the space. Once the baker pays wages or rent with that $5, it has made it through a cycle in the circular flow.

As the circular flow model shows, an economic model approximates what happens in the real economy. Later in the book we'll discuss other models that focus on specific questions—like how much gasoline prices will go up when the government raises taxes or how fast the economy is likely to grow in the next decade. The best models lead us to clearer answers about complicated questions and help us to devise policy to achieve desirable goals.

What makes a good economic model? We have already said that good models can leave out details that are not crucial and focus on the important aspects of a situation. To be useful, a model *should* do three additional things:

1. *A good model predicts cause and effect.* The circular flow model gives a useful description of the basics of the economy. Often, though, we want to go further. Many times we want a model not only to describe economic connections but also to predict how things will happen in the future. To do that, we have to get cause and effect right. If your model says that A causes B, you should be able to explain why. In Chapter 3 we'll learn about a central model in economics that shows that, for most goods and services, the quantity people want to buy goes down as the price goes up. Why? As the cost of an item rises but the benefit of owning it remains the same, more people will decide that the trade-off is not worth it.

2. *A good model makes clear assumptions.* Although models are usually too simple to fit the real world perfectly, it's important that they be clear about the simplifying assumptions. Doing so helps us to know when the model will predict real events accurately and when it will not. For example, we said earlier that economists often assume that people behave rationally. We know that isn't always true, but we accept it as an assumption because it is *approximately* accurate in many situations. As long as we are clear that we are making this assumption, we will know that the model will not be accurate when people fail to behave rationally.

3. *A good model describes the real world accurately.* If a model does not describe what actually happens in the real world, something about the model is wrong. We've admitted that models are not perfectly accurate, because they are intentionally simpler than the real world. But if a model predicts things that are not usually or approximately true, it is not useful. How do we tell if a model is realistic? Economists test their models by observing what happens in the real world and collecting data, which they use to verify or reject the model. In Chapter 7 and Chapter 8 we'll learn about the data in macroeconomics that helps us to understand the macroeconomy. In the Real Life box, Testing Models Against History, take a look at a model that has been tested over and over again in the last few hundred years.

REAL LIFE

Testing Models Against History

Real Life boxes show how the concept you're reading about relates to the real world. They are your chance to test models against the data. Often these boxes will describe a situation in which people used an economic idea to solve a business or policy question, or they present interesting research ideas or experiences.

Thomas Malthus, an early nineteenth-century economist, created a model that described the relationship between population growth and food production. The model predicted that mass starvation would occur as populations outgrew food supplies. In his famous work, *An Essay on the Principle of Population,* Malthus wrote:

> The power of population is so superior to the power in the earth to produce subsistence for man, that premature death must in some shape or other visit the human race...gigantic inevitable famine stalks...

Since Malthus wrote these words, famines have, in fact, killed millions of people. However, they have not been related to population growth in the way that Malthus predicted. Instead, the population of the world has increased from under a billion in 1800 to almost seven billion today. At the same time, nutrition standards have risen in almost every country.

Malthus's model left out a crucial part of the story: human ingenuity and technological progress. As the world's population has grown, people have found new ways to grow better food more efficiently, on more land. They have also found better ways to limit population growth.

Malthus's idea has not died out, though. Today, neo-Malthusian theory predicts that population will still outstrip the world's productive capacity. This theory updates Malthus's model to address more modern concerns, such as increasing environmental degradation that makes land unfit for farming. Others argue that non-renewable resources, such as oil, will be depleted. Still others warn that even if the world's farmers can produce enough food, unequal access to resources like fresh water will cause local famines and wars.

Critics of these arguments point out that human ingenuity has somehow averted catastrophe at every point in recent history when a Malthusian disaster seemed imminent. The population boom that followed World War II was supposed to lead to starvation, but it was counteracted by the Green Revolution, which increased food production manyfold.

Is the neo-Malthusian model accurate, then, or is it also missing some critical factor? Time will provide the data to answer this question.

Source: T. R. Malthus, *An Essay on the Principle of Population*, 1798.

Positive and Normative Analysis

LO 1.8 Distinguish between positive and normative analysis.

Economics is a field of study in which people frequently confuse facts with judgments that are based on beliefs. Think about the following example:

Statement #1: Income taxes reduce the number of hours that people want to work.

Statement #2: Income taxes should be reduced or abolished.

Many people have trouble separating these two statements. Some feel that the second statement flows logically from the first. Others disagree with the second statement, so they assume the first can't possibly be true.

If you read carefully, however, you'll see that the first sentence is a statement about cause and effect. Thus, it can be proved true or false by data and evidence. A statement that makes a factual declaration about how the world *actually* works is called a **positive statement**.

The second sentence, on the other hand, cannot be proved true or false. Instead, it indicates what *should be* done—but only if we share certain goals, understandings, and moral beliefs. A statement that makes a claim about how the world *should be* is called a **normative statement**.

To see how important the distinction between positive and normative statements can be, consider two claims that a physicist might make:

Positive statement: A nuclear weapon with the explosive power of 10 kilotons of TNT will have a fallout radius of up to 9.7 kilometres.

Normative statement: The United States was right to use nuclear weapons in World War II.

Although people could disagree about both of these statements, the first is a question of scientific fact, while the second depends heavily on a person's ethical and political beliefs. The first statement may inform your opinion of the second, but you can still agree with one and not the other.

Earlier in this chapter, we introduced a feature called What Do You Think? that asked for your opinion about an important policy or life decision. From this point forward, you can use your understanding of the differences between normative and positive analysis to untangle the questions asked in these boxes and combine the two kinds of analysis to arrive at a conclusion. Begin trying your hand at this with the What Do You Think? box, The Cost of University Cash.

WHAT DO YOU THINK?

The Cost of University Cash

In 2012–2013, the average yearly cost of university tuition and fees ranged from $6,348 at public universities to $50,000 at private universities. Students have a number of options for paying. They can take out student loans, private loans, or a combination of the two to defer payments until later, or they can use savings or earnings to foot the bill.

Students who qualify for student loans enjoy benefits such as limits on the interest rate they can be charged and the total payments they can be expected to make, and the possibility of loan forgiveness if they enter certain fields after graduation.

Lending to students is a controversial topic. Some people argue for more controls on private lending institutions, such as interest-rate caps and greater protection for students who default. They reason that lending programs should support students who would not otherwise be able to afford university. Furthermore, they argue, graduating with a lot of debt discourages students from going into lower-paid public service jobs.

Other people maintain that the existing lending system is fine. Getting a university degree, they argue, increases a person's future earning power so much that graduates should be able to handle the debt, even at high interest rates. They worry that over-regulation will discourage private lenders from offering student loans, defeating the purpose of giving students better access to financial assistance.

What do you think?

Use the four basic questions economists ask to break down the problem. Remember that your answer can draw on both positive analysis (what *will* happen if a certain policy is followed) and normative analysis (what *should* be done, given your values and goals). You should be able to say which parts of your answers fall into each category.

1. What motivations and constraints apply to students who are considering different schools and loan options? What motivations and constraints apply to private lenders?

2. What opportunity costs do students face when deciding how to pay for university? Should they avoid loans by skipping university altogether or by working their way through university?

3. How would prospective students respond to government limits on the interest rate on student loans? How would commercial banks that offer student loans respond?

4. Why do you think the government has not yet implemented interest-rate caps on private student loans? Do you anticipate any unintended side effects of that policy?

5. Consider your arguments in response to questions 1 through 4. Which parts are based on normative statements and which on positive statements?

Sources: "Trends in college pricing," http://nces.ed.gov/fastfacts/display.asp?id=76; "How much student debt is too much?" http://roomfordebate.blogs.nytimes.com/2009/06/14/how-much-student-debt-is-too-much/?scp=1&sq=student%20loans=cse. http://www.cbc.ca/news/canada/university-tuition-rising-to-record-levels-in-canada-1.1699103; http://news.nationalpost.com/2012/09/11/get-ready-for-10k-tuition-canadian-university-fees-rising-faster-than-incomes-and-inflation/

Throughout this book, remember that *you don't have to buy into a particular moral or political outlook in order for economics to be useful to you.* Our goal is to provide you with a toolbox of economic concepts that you can use to engage in positive analysis. We will also highlight important decisions you may face that will require you to engage in normative thinking, informed by economic analysis. Economics can help you to make better decisions and design more effective policies, regardless of your goals and beliefs.

✓ CONCEPT CHECK

☐   What does it mean when two variables are positively correlated? [LO 1.5]

☐   What are the characteristics of a good economic model? [LO 1.6]

☐   What is the difference between a positive statement and a normative statement? [LO 1.7]

Conclusion

Macroeconomists approach problems differently from many other people. Underlying economics is the basic principle of rational behaviour—that people make choices to achieve their goals in the most effective way possible.

In this chapter we have introduced the basic concepts economists use, as well as four questions they ask to break down problems. Throughout this book, you will see these concepts and questions over and over again:

1.   Scarcity: *What are the wants and constraints of those involved?*

2.   Opportunity cost: *What are the trade-offs?*

3.   Incentives: *How will others respond?*

4.   Efficiency: *Why isn't everyone already doing it?*

In later chapters, as we progress to more complicated problems, try using questions to break down problems into manageable pieces, ones you can understand using the fundamental concepts presented in this chapter.

Key Terms

economics	incentive
microeconomics	efficiency
macroeconomics	correlation
rational behaviour	causation
scarcity	model
opportunity cost	circular flow model
marginal decision making	positive statement
sunk cost	normative statement

Summary

LO 1.1 Explain the historical thought behind macroeconomics.

Classical thinking dominates economic thought until the Great Depression. Classical theory emphasizes the attainment of market equilibrium by the forces of demand and supply. While the theory was able to explain how markets perform most of the time, it failed to explain the existence of surplus in the labour market during the Great Depression. This led to the development of a new school of thought called Keynesian economics, and it forms the foundation for what is now called macroeconomics.

LO 1.2 Explain the economic concept of scarcity.

Economists usually assume that people behave rationally and live within a condition of scarcity. Answering the question, *What are the wants and constraints of those involved?* tells you what to expect from each player in the situation you are analysing. Given rational behaviour and scarcity, you can expect people to work to get what they want (their motivations) using the limited resources at their disposal (their constraints).

LO 1.3 Explain the economic concepts of performance and decision making.

Trade-offs arise when you must give up something to get something else. Answering *What are the trade-offs?* will tell you about the costs and benefits associated with a decision. The full cost of doing something is the opportunity cost. Economists assume that rational people make decisions at the margin, by comparing any additional benefits from a choice to the extra costs it brings. If people are behaving rationally when they face trade-offs, they will always choose to do something if the marginal benefit is greater than the opportunity cost. They will never do it if the opportunity cost is greater than the marginal benefit.

LO 1.4 Explain the economic concept of incentives.

The collective reaction to changing trade-offs is a central idea in economics. Asking *How will others respond?* will give you a complete picture of how a particular decision affects the world. You can assume that any action will bring a response, because people react to changes in their incentives.

LO 1.5 Explain the economic concept of efficiency.

Efficiency occurs when resources are used in the most productive way possible to produce the goods and services that have the greatest total economic value to society. In other words, efficiency means using resources to produce the things that people want. Under normal circumstances, markets are efficient.

So when you see what seems to be unexploited opportunity, you should ask, *If it's such a great idea, why isn't everyone already doing it?* Markets usually allocate resources efficiently. When they don't, a market failure may have occurred, government may have intervened in the economy, there may be goals other than profit involved, or there may be a genuine opportunity for innovation.

LO 1.6 Distinguish between correlation and causation.

When there is a consistently observed relationship between two events, we say they are correlated. This is different from a causal relationship, in which one event brings about the other. Three common ways in which correlation and causation are confused are correlation without causation, omitted variables, and reverse causation.

LO 1.7 List the characteristics of a good economic model.

A model is a simplified representation of the important parts of a complicated situation. In economics, models usually show how people, firms, and governments make decisions about managing resources and how their decisions interact. The circular flow model is a representation of how the transactions of households and firms flow through the economy. A good economic model should predict cause and effect, describe the world accurately, and state its assumptions clearly.

Economists test their models by observing what happens in the world and collecting data that can be used to support or reject their models.

LO 1.8 Distinguish between positive and normative analysis.

A statement that makes a factual claim about how the world actually works is called a positive statement. A statement that makes a claim about how the world should be is called a normative statement. Economics is a field in which people frequently confuse positive statements with normative statements. However, you do not have to adopt a particular moral or political point of view to use economic concepts and models.

Review Questions

1. Which economic theory dominates economic thinking prior to the Great Depression? [LO 1.1]

2. Suppose you are shopping for new clothes to wear to job interviews, but you're on a tight budget. In this situation, what are your wants and constraints? What does it mean to behave rationally in the face of scarcity? [LO 1.2]

3. You are a student with a demanding schedule of classes. You also work part time and your supervisor allows you to determine your schedule. In this situation, what is your scarce resource? How do you decide how many hours to work? [LO 1.2]

4. Think about the definition of scarcity that you learned in this chapter. Name three ways that you confront scarcity in your own life. [LO 1.2]

5. When shopping for your interview clothes, what are some trade-offs you face? What is the opportunity cost of buying new clothes? What are the benefits? How do you balance the two? [LO 1.3]

6. You have an 8:00 o'clock class this morning but you are feeling extremely tired. How do you decide whether to get some extra sleep or go to class? [LO 1.3]

7. It's Friday night. You already have a ticket to a concert, which cost you $30. A friend invites you to go out for a game of paintball instead. Admission would cost you $25, and you think you'd get $25 worth of enjoyment out of it. Your concert ticket is non-refundable. What is your opportunity cost (in dollars) of playing paintball? [LO 1.3]

8. Suppose you have two job offers and are considering the trade-offs between them. Job A pays $45,000 per year and includes health insurance and two weeks of paid vacation. Job B pays $30,000 per year and includes four weeks of paid vacation but no health insurance. [LO 1.3]

   a. List the benefits of Job A and the benefits of Job B.

   b. List the opportunity cost of Job A and the opportunity cost of Job B.

9. Your former neighbour gave you his lawnmower when he moved. You are thinking of using this gift to mow lawns in your neighbourhood this summer for extra cash. As you think about what to charge your neighbours and whether this idea is worth your effort, what opportunity costs do you need to consider? [LO 1.3]

10. Think of a few examples of incentives in your daily life. How do you respond to those incentives? [LO 1.4]

11. You supervise a team of salespeople. Your employees already receive a company discount. Suggest a positive incentive and a negative incentive you could use to improve their productivity. [LO 1.4]

12. Your boss decides to pair workers in teams and offer bonuses to the most productive team. Why might your boss offer team bonuses instead of individual bonuses? [LO 1.4]

13. Think of a public policy—a provincial or national law, tax, or public service—that offers an incentive for a particular behaviour. Explain what the incentive is, who is offering it, and what they are trying to encourage or discourage. Does the incentive work? [LO 1.4]

14. Why do individuals or firms usually provide the goods and services people want? [LO 1.5]

15. You may have seen TV advertisements for products or programs that claim to teach a surefire way to make millions on the stock market. Apply the *Why isn't everyone already doing it?* test to this situation. Do you believe the ads? Why or why not? [LO 1.5]

16. Describe an innovation in technology, business, or culture that had a major economic impact in your lifetime. [LO 1.5]

17. Why do people confuse correlation with causation? [LO 1.5]

18. Name two things that are positively correlated and two things that are negatively correlated. [LO 1.6]

19. Why is it important for a good economic model to predict cause and effect? [LO 1.7]

20. Why is it important for a good economic model to make clear assumptions? [LO 1.7]

21. Describe an economic model you know. What does the model predict about cause and effect? [LO 1.7]

22. Describe an economic model you know. What assumptions does the model make? Are the assumptions reasonable? [LO 1.7]

23. What is the difference between disagreeing with a positive statement and disagreeing with a normative statement? [LO 1.8]

24. Would a good economic model be more likely to address a positive statement or a normative statement? Why? [LO 1.8]

25. Write a positive statement and a normative statement about your favorite hobby. [LO 1.8]

Problems and Applications

1. Why you think a new theory was needed to explain the Great Depression? [LO 1.1]

2. Think about how and why goods and resources are scarce. Goods and resources can be scarce for reasons that are inherent to their nature at all times, temporary or seasonal, or that are artificially created. Separate the goods listed below into two groups; indicate which (if any) are artificially scarce (AS), and which (if any) are inherently scarce (IS). [LO 1.2]

    a. Air of any quality _____

    b. Land _____

    c. Patented goods _____

    d. Original Picasso paintings _____

3. You are looking for a new apartment in Toronto. Your income is $4,000 per month, and you know that you should not spend more than 25 percent of your income on rent. You have come across the following listing for one-bedroom apartments on Craigslist. You are indifferent about location, and transportation costs are the same to each neighbourhood. [LO 1.2]

Etobicoke	$1,200
Midtown	2,200
Scarborough	950
North York	1,500

    a. Which apartments fall within your budget? (Check all that apply.)

    b. Suppose that you adhere to the 25 percent guideline but also receive a $1,000 cost-of-living supplement every month, since you are living and working in Toronto. Which apartments fall within your budget now?

4. Suppose the price of a sweater is $15. Julia's benefit from purchasing each additional sweater is given in the table below. Julia gets the most benefit from the first sweater and less benefit from each additional sweater. If Julia is behaving rationally, how many sweaters will she purchase? [LO 1.3]

	Marginal benefit ($)
1st sweater	50
2nd sweater	35
3rd sweater	30

4th sweater	23
5th sweater	12
6th sweater	8

5. Sweaters sell for $15 at the crafts fair. Allie knits sweaters and her marginal costs are given in the table below. Allie's costs increase with each additional sweater. If Allie is behaving rationally, how many sweaters will she sell? [LO 1.3]

	Marginal cost ($)
1st sweater	5
2nd sweater	8
3rd sweater	12
4th sweater	18
5th sweater	25
6th sweater	32

6. Last year, you estimated you would earn $5 million in sales revenues from developing a new product. So far, you have spent $3 million developing the product, but it is not yet complete. Meanwhile, this year you have new sales projections that show expected revenues from the new product will actually be only $4 million. How much should you be willing to spend to complete the product development? [LO 1.3]
    a. $0
    b. Up to $1 million
    c. Up to $4 million
    d. Whatever it takes

7. Consider the following examples. For each one, say whether the incentive is positive or negative. [LO 1.4]
    a. Bosses who offer time-and-a-half for working on public holidays
    b. Mandatory minimum sentencing for drug offenses
    c. Fines for littering
    d. Parents who offer their children extra allowance money for good grades

8. Consider the following events that change prices. For each one, say whether the opportunity cost of consuming the affected good increases or decreases. [LO 1.4]

	Affected good
a. A local movie theater offers a student discount.	Movie tickets
b. A tax on soft drinks passes in your province.	Soft drinks
c. Subsidies on corn are cut in half.	Corn subsidies
d. Your student union begins offering bus passes for free.	Bus passes

9. Your best friend has an idea for a drive-through bar. Indicate the best explanation for why others have not taken advantage of her idea: true innovation, market failure, government intervention, unprofitableness. [LO 1.5]

10. Your best friend has an idea for a long-distance car service to drive people across the country. Indicate the best explanation for why others have not taken advantage of her idea: true innovation, market failure, government intervention, unprofitableness. [LO 1.5]

11. Determine whether each of the following questionable statements is best explained by correlation without causation, an omitted variable, or reverse causation. [LO 1.6]

    a. In cities that have more police, crime rates are higher.

    b. Many retired people live in provinces where everyone uses air conditioning during the summer.

    c. More people come down with the flu during the Winter Olympics than during the Summer Olympics.

    d. For the last five years, Wiarton Willie has seen his shadow on Groundhog Day and spring has come late.

12. For each of the pairs below, determine whether they are positively correlated, negatively correlated, or uncorrelated. [LO 1.6]

    a. Time spent studying and test scores

    b. Vaccination and illness

    c. Soft drink preference and music preference

    d. Income and education

13. Each statement below is part of an economic model. Indicate whether the statement is a prediction of cause and effect or an assumption. [LO 1.7]

    a. People behave rationally.

    b. If the price of a good falls, people will consume more of that good.

    c. Mass starvation will occur as population outgrows the food supply.

    d. Firms want to maximize profits.

14. From the list below, select the characteristics that describe a good economic model. [LO 1.7]

    a. Includes every detail of a given situation

    b. Predicts that A causes B

    c. Makes approximately accurate assumptions

    d. Fits the real world perfectly

    e. Predicts things that are usually true

15. Determine whether each of the following statements is positive or normative. (Remember that a positive statement isn't necessarily *correct;* it just makes a factual claim rather than a moral judgment.) [LO 1.8]

    a. People who pay their bills on time are less likely than others to get into debt.

    b. Hard work is a virtue.

    c. Everyone should pay his or her bills on time.

    d. China has a bigger population than any other country in the world.

    e. China's one-child policy (which limits families to one child each) helped to spur the country's rapid economic growth.

    f. Lower taxes are good for the country.

16. You just received your mid-term exam results and your professor wrote the following note: "You received a 70 on this exam, the average score. If you want to improve your grade, you should study more." Evaluate your professor's note. [LO 1.8]

    a. Is the first sentence positive or normative?

    b. Is the second sentence positive or normative?

CHAPTER 2

Specialization and Exchange

LEARNING OBJECTIVES

LO 2.1   Construct a production possibilities graph and describe what causes shifts in production possibilities curves.

LO 2.2   Define absolute and comparative advantage.

LO 2.3   Define specialization and explain why people specialize.

LO 2.4   Explain how the gains from trade follow from comparative advantage.

The Origins of a T-Shirt

How can we get the most out of available resources? It's one of the most basic economic questions. Factory managers ask it when looking for ways to increase production. National leaders ask it as they design economic policy. Activists ask it when they look for ways to reduce poverty or conserve the environment. And, in a different way, it's a question we all ask ourselves when thinking about what to do in life and how to make sure that we're taking full advantage of our talents.

To get a handle on this question, we start by thinking about resources at the highest level: the logic of international trade and the specialization of production between countries. By the end of the chapter, we hope that you'll see how the same ideas apply to decisions on any scale, right down to whether it makes more sense to fix your own computer or pay a specialist to do it for you.

We'll start with what seems to be a simple question: Where did your T-shirt come from? Look at the tag. We're betting it was made in a place you've never been to, and maybe never thought of visiting. China? Malaysia? Honduras? Sri Lanka? Bangladesh?

That "made in" label only tells part of the story. Chances are that your shirt's history spans other parts of the globe. Consider a standard T-shirt. The cotton might have been grown in Mali and then shipped to Pakistan, where it was spun into yarn. The yarn might have been sent to China, where it was woven into cloth, cut into pieces, and assembled into a shirt. That shirt might then have traveled all the way to the United States, where it was shipped to a store near you. A couple of years from now, when you are cleaning out your closet, you may donate the shirt to a charity, which may ship it to a secondhand clothing vendor in Mali—right back where your shirt's travels began.

Of course, this is not only the story of shirts. It is remarkably similar to the story of shoes, computers, and cars, among many other manufactured goods. Today, the products and services most of us take for granted come to us through an incredibly complex global network of farms, mines, factories, traders, and stores. Why is the production of even a simple T-shirt spread across the world? Why is the cotton grown in Mali and the sewing done in China, rather than vice versa? Why isn't the whole shirt made in Canada, so that it doesn't have to travel so far to reach you?

This chapter addresses fundamental economic questions about who produces which goods and why. The fact that millions of people and firms around the globe coordinate their activities to provide consumers with the right combination of goods and services seems like magic. This feat of coordination doesn't happen by chance, and no superplanner tells everyone where to go and what to do. Instead, the global production line is a natural outcome of people everywhere acting in their own self-interest to improve their own lives. Economists call this coordination mechanism the *invisible hand,* an idea that was first suggested by the eighteenth-century economic thinker Adam Smith.

David Malan/Photographer's Choice RF/Getty Images

To get some insight into the *who* and *why* of production, consider how the story of shirts has changed over the last few centuries. For most of the 1900s, North Americans wore shirts made in North America. Today, however, most shirts are made in China, Bangladesh, and other countries where factory wages are low. Have North American workers become worse at making shirts over the last two centuries? Definitely not. In fact, as we'll see in this chapter, it doesn't even mean that Chinese workers are better than North American workers at making shirts. Instead, each good tends to be produced by the country, company, or person with the lowest opportunity cost for producing that good.

Countries and firms *specialize* in making goods for which they have the lowest opportunity cost, and they trade with one another to get the combination of goods they want to consume. The resulting *gains from trade* can be split up so that everyone ends up better off. It's no surprise, then, that as transportation and communication between countries have improved, trade has taken off.

The concepts in this chapter apply not just to the wealth of nations and international trade. They also illuminate the daily choices most people face. Who should cook which dishes at Thanksgiving dinner? Should you hire a plumber or fix the pipes yourself? Should you become a rock star or an economist? The concepts these questions raise can be subtle and are sometimes misunderstood. We hope this chapter will provide insights that will help you become a better resource manager in all areas of your life.

Production Possibilities

In Chapter 1 we talked about models. Good models help us understand complex situations through simplifying assumptions that allow us to zero in on the important aspects. The story of why China now produces shirts for Canadians that Canadians themselves were producing a hundred years ago is a complex one, as you'd expect. But by simplifying it into a model we can reach useful insights.

Let's assume Canada and China produce only two things—shirts and bushels of wheat. (In reality, of course, they produce many things, but we're trying not to get bogged down in details right now.) The model uses wheat to stand in for "stuff other than shirts," allowing us to focus on what we're really interested in—shirts.

Using this model we'll perform a thought experiment about production using a tool called the *production possibilities frontier*. This tool is used in other contexts, as well, many of which have no connection to international trade. Here we use it to show what has changed over the last couple of centuries to explain why Canadians now buy shirts from China.

Drawing the Production Possibilities Frontier

LO 2.1 Construct a production possibilities graph and describe what causes shifts in production possibilities curves.

Let's step back in time to Canada in 1900. In our simple model, there are two million Canadian workers, and they have two choices of where to work: shirt factories or wheat farms. In shirt factories, each worker produces one shirt per day. On wheat farms, each worker produces two bushels of wheat per day.

What would happen if everyone worked on a wheat farm? Canada would produce 4 million bushels of wheat per day (2 bushels of wheat per worker × 2 million workers). This is one "production possibility." We represent it by point A in panel A of Figure 2-1. Alternatively, what would happen if everyone went to work in a shirt factory? Canada would produce 2 million shirts per day (1 shirt per worker × 2 million workers). This production possibility is represented by point E in Figure 2-1.

FIGURE 2-1

Possible Production Combinations

(A) Producing one good

Production possibilities	Bushels of wheat (millions)	Shirts (millions)
A	4	0
E	0	2

(B) Producing both goods

Production possibilities	Bushels of wheat (millions)	Shirts (millions)
B	3	0.5
C	2	1.0
D	1	1.5

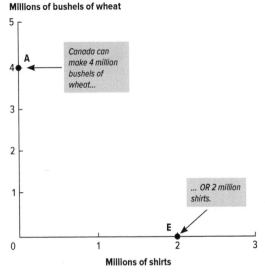

Canada can produce the maximum number of shirts or the maximum amount of wheat by devoting all its resources to one good or the other.

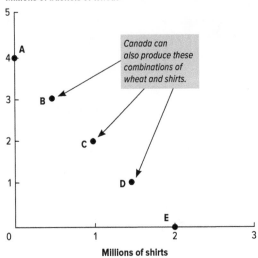

By allocating some resources to the production of each good, Canada can also produce many different combinations of wheat and shirts.

Of course, Canada wouldn't want just shirts or just wheat—and there is no reason that all workers have to produce the same thing. There are many different combinations of shirts and wheat that Canadian workers could produce, as panel B of Figure 2-1 shows. For example, if one quarter of the workers go to the shirt factory, they can make 500,000 shirts (1 shirt per worker × 500,000 workers) and the remaining workers can produce 3 million bushels of wheat (2 bushels per worker × 1.5 million workers). This production possibility is represented by point B in panel B. Or maybe 1 million workers make shirts (1 million shirts) and 1 million grow wheat (2 million bushels). That's point C.

We can continue splitting the workforce between shirts and wheat in different ways, each of which can be plotted as a point on the graph in Figure 2-1. If we fill in enough points, we create the solid green line shown in Figure 2-2. This is the **production possibilities frontier (PPF)**. It is a line or curve that shows all the possible combinations of outputs that can be produced using all available resources. In this case, the frontier plots all combinations of shirts and wheat that can be produced using all available workers in Canada. Points inside the frontier (such as point T) are achievable, but don't make full use of all available resources.

The production possibilities frontier helps us answer the first of the economists' questions that we discussed in Chapter 1: *What are the wants and constraints of those involved?* People in Canada want to consume shirts and wheat (and other things, of course; remember, we're simplifying). The production possibilities frontier gives us a way to represent the *constraints* on production. Canada cannot produce combinations of shirts and wheat that lie outside the frontier—such as point U in Figure 2-2. There just aren't enough workers or hours in the day to produce at point U, no matter how they are allocated between shirts and wheat.

FIGURE 2-2

Production Possibilities Frontier

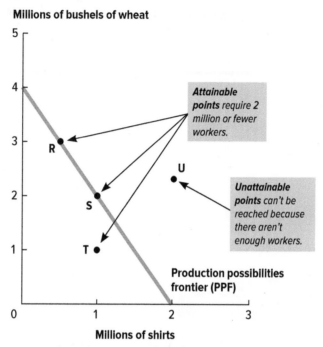

Millions of bushels of wheat

Attainable points require 2 million or fewer workers.

Unattainable points can't be reached because there aren't enough workers.

Production possibilities frontier (PPF)

Millions of shirts

Points on or below the production possibilities frontier, such as R, S, and T, represent combinations of goods that the Canada can produce with available resources. Points outside the frontier, such as U, are unattainable because there aren't enough resources.

The production possibilities frontier also addresses the second economists' question: *What are the trade-offs?* Each worker can make *either* one shirt *or* two bushels of wheat per day. In other words, there is a trade-off between the quantity of wheat produced and the quantity of shirts produced. If we want an extra shirt, one worker has to stop growing wheat for a day. Therefore, the opportunity cost of one shirt is two bushels of wheat. Growing another bushel of wheat takes one worker half a day, so the opportunity cost of a bushel of wheat is half a shirt. This opportunity cost is represented graphically by the slope of the production possibilities frontier. Moving up the frontier means getting more wheat at the cost of fewer shirts. Moving down the frontier means less wheat and more shirts. Looking at Figure 2-2, you'll notice that the slope of the line is −2. This is the same as saying that the opportunity cost of one shirt is always two bushels of wheat.

Let's start off with all workers growing wheat and nobody making shirts. If we reallocate the workers who are best at making shirts, we can get a lot of shirts without giving up too much wheat. In other words, the opportunity cost of making the first few shirts is very low. Now imagine almost all the workers are making shirts, so that only the very best farmers are left growing wheat. If we reallocate most of the remaining workers to shirt making, we give up a lot of wheat to get only a few extra shirts. The opportunity cost of getting those last few shirts is very high.

We can add a little more nuance to the model, to include land and machinery as resources also needed for production. We would find that the same pattern holds: the opportunity cost of producing an additional unit of a good typically increases

For a refresher on calculating and interpreting slopes, see Appendix A, Math Essentials: Understanding Graphs and Slope, which follows this chapter.

as more of each resource is allocated to it. For instance, growing more wheat probably requires reallocating not only workers but farmland. Making more shirts means setting up new factories and buying more sewing machines.

Once again, let's start with everyone growing wheat. With wheat production pushed to the maximum, some farmers probably have to work on land that isn't well suited to growing wheat. It could be that the land is swampy or the soil has been over-farmed and depleted of nutrients. When farmers who had been working on this poor land switch over to making shirts, the economy will lose only a little wheat and gain many shirts in return. In contrast, if only a small amount of wheat is being grown using only the best, most fertile land, reallocating the last few farmers will cause a relatively large decrease in wheat production for each additional shirt.

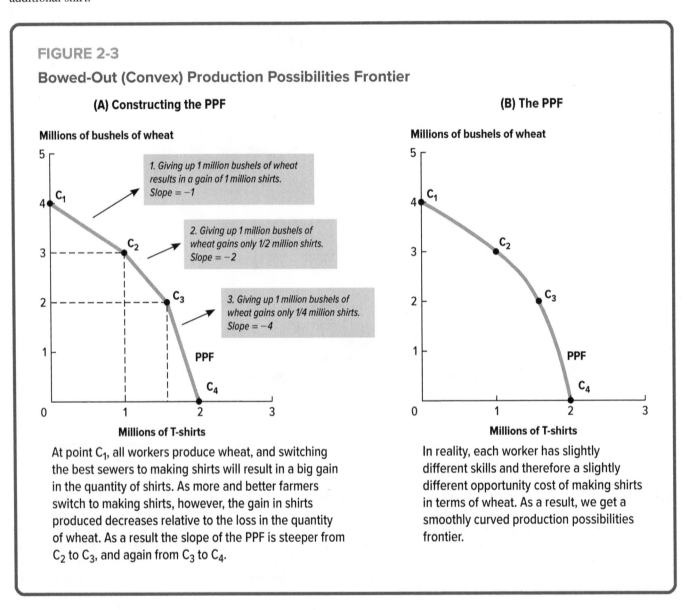

FIGURE 2-3

Bowed-Out (Convex) Production Possibilities Frontier

(A) Constructing the PPF

Millions of bushels of wheat

1. Giving up 1 million bushels of wheat results in a gain of 1 million shirts. Slope = -1

2. Giving up 1 million bushels of wheat gains only 1/2 million shirts. Slope = -2

3. Giving up 1 million bushels of wheat gains only 1/4 million shirts. Slope = -4

Millions of T-shirts

At point C_1, all workers produce wheat, and switching the best sewers to making shirts will result in a big gain in the quantity of shirts. As more and better farmers switch to making shirts, however, the gain in shirts produced decreases relative to the loss in the quantity of wheat. As a result the slope of the PPF is steeper from C_2 to C_3, and again from C_3 to C_4.

(B) The PPF

Millions of bushels of wheat

Millions of T-shirts

In reality, each worker has slightly different skills and therefore a slightly different opportunity cost of making shirts in terms of wheat. As a result, we get a smoothly curved production possibilities frontier.

Returning to the simplest model where workers are the only input to production, we can translate this increasing opportunity cost into the production possibilities frontier. Doing so, we get a curve that bows out (a convex curve) instead of a straight line, as shown in Figure 2-3. Panel A shows what happens if we have just three types of workers:

- For every bushel of wheat, some can make one shirt; they're the ones between points C_1 and C_2.
- For every bushel of wheat, some can make only 1/2 of a shirt (between points C_2 and C_3).
- For every bushel of wheat, some can make only 1/4 of a shirt (between points C_3 and C_4).

In other words, as we go down the curve, we move from those who are better at making shirts to those who are better at growing wheat. As we do so, the opportunity cost of making shirts versus growing wheat increases, and the slope of the curve gets steeper (-1 between C_1 and C_2, -2 between C_2 and C_3, and -4 between C_3 and C_4).

In reality there aren't just three types of workers—each worker will have slightly different skills. The many possibilities will result in a curve that looks smooth, as in panel B of Figure 2-3. At each point of the curved production possibilities frontier, the slope represents the opportunity cost of getting more wheat or more shirts, based on the skills of the next worker who could switch.

Choosing Among Production Possibilities

What can the production possibilities frontier tell us about what combination of goods an economy will choose to produce? Earlier, we noted that economies can produce at points inside the frontier as well as points on it. However, choosing a production point inside the frontier means a country could get more wheat, more shirts, or both, just by using all available workers. For instance, in Figure 2-4, Canada can get more wheat without giving up any shirts, by moving from point B_1 to point B_2. It can do the same by moving from point B_2 to B_3. But once at the frontier, it will have to give up some of one good to get more of the other. Points like B_3 that lie *on* the frontier are called **efficient**, because they squeeze the most output possible from all available resources. Points *within* (inside) the frontier are *inefficient* because they do not use all available resources.

FIGURE 2-4

Choosing an Efficient Production Combination

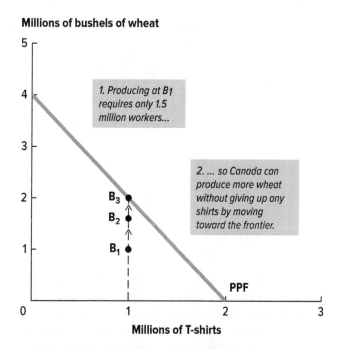

Millions of bushels of wheat

1. Producing at B_1 requires only 1.5 million workers...

2. ... so Canada can produce more wheat without giving up any shirts by moving toward the frontier.

PPF

Millions of T-shirts

Canada needs only 1.5 million workers to reach point B_1. If the country employs more workers, it can reach point B_2 and get more wheat without giving up any shirts. The country can keep employing more workers until it reaches point B_3 (or any other point on the frontier) and there are no more workers left. Once the frontier is reached, getting more of one good requires giving up some of the other.

In the real world, economies aren't always efficient. A variety of problems can cause some workers to be unemployed or other resources to be left idle. We'll return to these issues in detail in future chapters. For now, we'll assume that production is always efficient. People and firms usually try to squeeze as much value as they can out of the resources available to them, so efficiency is a reasonable starting assumption.

Based on the assumption of efficiency, we can predict that an economy will choose to produce at a point on the frontier rather than inside it. What the production possibilities frontier cannot tell us is *which* point on the frontier that will be. Will it be F_1 in Figure 2-5, for example? Or will Canada choose to move down the curve to F_2, producing more shirts at the expense of less wheat? We can't say whether point F_1 or F_2 is better without knowing more about the situation. If the Canadian economy is completely self-sufficient, the decision depends on what combination of shirts and wheat people in Canada want to consume. If trade with other countries is possible, it also depends on consumers and production possibilities in those countries, as we'll see later in the chapter.

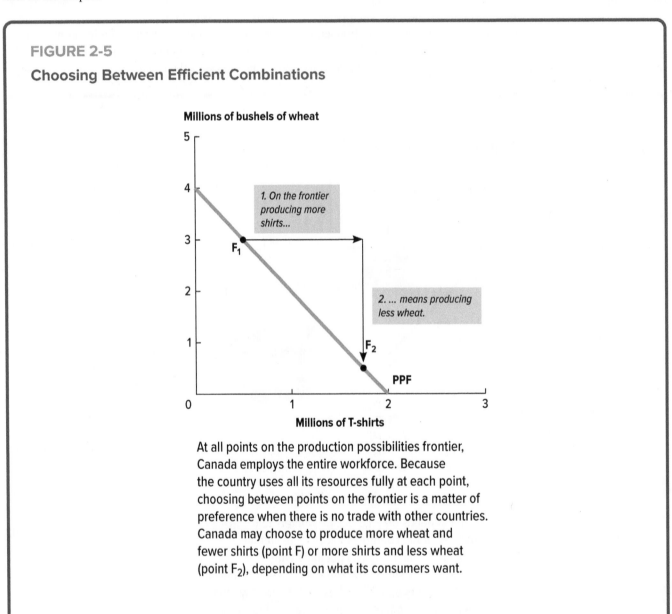

FIGURE 2-5

Choosing Between Efficient Combinations

At all points on the production possibilities frontier, Canada employs the entire workforce. Because the country uses all its resources fully at each point, choosing between points on the frontier is a matter of preference when there is no trade with other countries. Canada may choose to produce more wheat and fewer shirts (point F) or more shirts and less wheat (point F_2), depending on what its consumers want.

Shifting the Production Possibilities Frontier

Thus far, we've built a simple model that tells us what combinations of T-shirts and wheat Canada could produce in 1900. However, a lot of things have changed since 1900, including an incredible explosion in productive capacity. The production possibilities frontier is a useful tool for illustrating this change and understanding how it affects the constraints and trade-offs the country faces. Two main factors drive the change in Canadian production possibilities.

First, there are more workers. The Canadian population now is much larger than it was in 1900. Having more workers means more people available to produce shirts and wheat. Graphically, we can represent this change by shifting the entire frontier outward. Panel A of Figure 2-6 shows what happens to the frontier when the Canadian population doubles, with each worker still able to produce one shirt or two bushels of wheat per day.

However, the real magic of expanded productive capacity lies in the incredible technological advances that have taken place over the last couple of centuries. In 1810, a businessman from Boston named Francis Cabot Lowell traveled to England to learn about British textile factories and to copy their superior technology. He brought back the power loom, which enabled workers to weave much more cotton fabric every day than they could before.

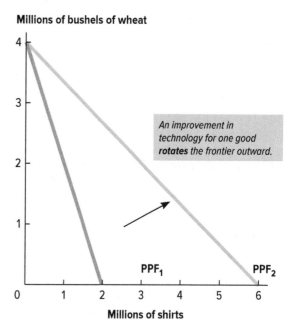

FIGURE 2-6

Shifting the Production Possibilities Frontier

(A) Change in resources: Population growth

Millions of bushels of wheat

*An increase in available resources **shifts** the entire frontier outward.*

PPF₁   PPF₂

Millions of shirts

Production possibilities expand when resources increase. If the working population grows, the country can make more of everything by producing at the same rate as before. This causes the frontier to shift outward. If the population doubled, so would the maximum possible quantities of shirts and wheat.

(B) Change in technology: Invention of the power loom

Millions of bushels of wheat

*An improvement in technology for one good **rotates** the frontier outward.*

PPF₁   PPF₂

Millions of shirts

Production possibilities expand when technology improves. If the textile industry adopts the power loom, workers can make more shirts in the same amount of time. This causes the frontier to rotate outward. The rate of wheat production remains constant while the rated of shirt production increases, so the slope of the frontier changes.

We can model this change in technology through the production possibilities frontier by changing the rate of shirt production from one to three shirts per day, as shown in panel B of Figure 2-6. As the rate of shirt production increases, while the rate of wheat production remains the same, the shape of the curve changes. In this case, it pivots outward along the x-axis, because for any given number of workers assigned to shirt-making, more shirts are produced than before. At every point except one (where all workers are growing wheat), the country can produce more with the same number of workers, thanks to improved technology.

For a refresher about shifts and pivots in graphs, see Appendix B, Math Essentials: Working with Linear Equations, which follows Chapter 3.

✓ CONCEPT CHECK

☐ Could a person or country ever produce a combination of goods that lies outside the production possibilities frontier? Why or why not? [LO 2.1]

☐ Would an increase in productivity as a result of a new technology shift a production possibilities frontier inward or outward? [LO 2.1]

Absolute and Comparative Advantage

In the mid-nineteenth century, armed with power looms, pre-Confederation Canada started mass producing clothing. Since then, the Canadian population has grown larger and manufacturing technology has improved even more. So, why are 30 percent of the world's clothing exports currently made in China while there are very few clothing factories in Canada?

Up to now, we have worked with a very simple model of production to highlight the key trade-offs faced by individual producers. If there is no trade between countries, Canada can consume only those goods that it produces on its own. In the real world, however, goods are made all over the world. If Canadians want to buy more shirts than are made in Canada, they can get them from somewhere else. Under these conditions, how can we predict which countries will produce which goods?

Understanding how resources are allocated among multiple producers is a step toward understanding why big firms work with specialized suppliers and why a wealthy, productive country like Canada trades with much poorer, less-productive countries. In this section we will see that trade actually increases total production, which can benefit everyone involved. To see why, let's turn to the question of why most T-shirts sold in Canada today are made in China.

Absolute and Comparative Advantage

> LO 2.2 Define absolute and comparative advantage.

Absolute Advantage

Suppose that taking into account all the improvements in shirt-making and wheat-growing technology over the last two centuries, a Canadian worker can now make 50 shirts or grow 200 bushels of wheat per day. A Chinese worker, on the other hand, can produce only 25 shirts (perhaps because Canadian workers use faster cloth-cutting technology) or 50 bushels of wheat (maybe because Canadian farmers use fertilizers and pesticides that farmers in China don't). In other words, given the same number of workers, Canada can produce twice as many shirts or four times as much wheat as China.

If a producer can generate more output than others with a given amount of resources, that producer has an **absolute advantage**. In our simplified model, Canada has an absolute advantage over China at producing both shirts and wheat because it can make more of both products than China can per worker.

Comparative Advantage

Absolute advantage is not the end of the story, though. If it were, Canada would still be producing lots of shirts. The problem is that for every T-shirt Canada produces, it uses resources that could otherwise be spent growing wheat. Of course, the same could be said of China. But in our model of T-shirt and wheat production, the opportunity cost of making one shirt in Canada is four bushels of wheat (200 bushels ÷ 50 shirts = 4 bushels per shirt); the opportunity cost of making one shirt in China is only two bushels of wheat (50 bushels ÷ 25 shirts = 2 bushels per shirt). Canada has to give up more to make a shirt than China does.

When a producer can make a good at a lower opportunity cost than other producers, we say it has a **comparative advantage** at producing that good. In our model, China has a comparative advantage over Canada at shirt-making, because its opportunity cost of producing a shirt is only two bushels of wheat compared to four bushels of wheat for Canada.

Canada, on the other hand, has a comparative advantage over China at growing wheat. Each time Canada produces a bushel of wheat, it gives up the opportunity to produce one-quarter of a shirt (50 shirts ÷ 200 bushels = 1/4 shirt per bushel). For China, however, the opportunity cost of growing a bushel of wheat is larger: it's one-half of a shirt (25 shirts ÷ 50 bushels = 1/2 shirt per bushel). Canada has a lower opportunity cost for producing wheat than China (1/4 shirt is less than 1/2 shirt), and therefore we say it has a comparative advantage at wheat production.

A country can have a comparative advantage without having an absolute advantage. In our scenario, Canada has an absolute advantage over China at producing both shirts and wheat. But it has a bigger advantage at producing wheat than at making shirts: it can make four times as much wheat per worker as China (200 versus 50 bushels) but only twice as many shirts per worker (50 versus 25). It's better at both—but it's "more better," so to speak, at producing wheat. (We know that "more better" is not good grammar, but it nicely expresses the idea.) China has a comparative advantage at the good it is "less worse" at producing shirts, even without an absolute advantage.

You may have noticed that for each country, the opportunity cost of growing wheat is the *inverse* of the opportunity cost of producing shirts. (For Canada, 1/4 is the inverse of 4; for China, 1/2 is the inverse of 2.) Mathematically, this means that it is impossible for one country to have a comparative advantage at producing both goods. Each producer's opportunity cost depends on its *relative* ability to produce different goods. Logic tells us that you can't be better at A than at B and also better at B than at A. (And mathematically, if X is bigger than Y, then 1/X will be smaller than 1/Y.) Canada can't be better at producing wheat than shirts relative to China and at the same time be better at producing shirts than wheat relative to China. As a result, no producer has a comparative advantage at everything, and each producer has a comparative advantage at something.

We can check this international trade scenario against an example closer to home. When your family makes Thanksgiving dinner, does the best cook make everything? If you have a small family, maybe one person can make the whole dinner. But if your family is anything like our families, you will need several cooks. Grandma is by far the most experienced cook, yet the potato peeling always gets outsourced to the kids. Is that because the grandchildren are better potato peelers than Grandma? We think that's probably not the case. Grandma has an absolute advantage at everything having to do with Thanksgiving dinner. Still, the kids may have a *comparative* advantage at potato peeling, which frees up Grandma to make those tricky pie crusts.

We can find applications of comparative advantage everywhere in life. Sports is no exception; look at the From Another Angle box, The Story of Lionel Conacher, for another example.

FROM ANOTHER ANGLE

Story of Multi-Talented Athletes

Two of the most famous multi-talented athletes in Canadian sports history are Harvey Pulford and Lionel Conacher. They both won national championships in Canadian football, hockey, boxing, and lacrosse, and Conacher's name appears in the halls of fame of four different sports. Each could easily have become one of the best football players or boxers or lacrosse players of his generation, but both ended up as hockey players. From a practical point of view, they could not play multiple sports professionally for a long time, so they had to make a choice. Although both had an *absolute* advantage at multiple sports, they had a *comparative* advantage as hockey players. So they took up hockey where they truly became stars. Pulford helped Ottawa to win four Stanley Cups and Conacher led more than one team to a Stanley Cup victory.

Two current examples would be Colorado Avalanche forward Jarome Ignila and Dallas Stars forward Jamie Benn. Both Benn and Ignila were also very talented baseball players. Ignila was a starting catcher on the Canadian National Junior Baseball Team and Benn was the MVP of the provincial AAA champion baseball team, the Victoria Capitals. But their comparative advantages as hockey players (and of course the income, too) made them to choose hockey over baseball.

Sources: http://definitivedose.com/sports/general/greatest-multi-sport-athletes; http://www.thesportster.com/entertainment/top-15-greatest-multi-sport-athletes-of-all-time-2/; http://www.thescore.com/news/815584; http://www.toptenz.net/top-10-multi-sport-athletes.php

✓ **CONCEPT CHECK**

☐ What does it mean to have an absolute advantage at producing a good? [LO 2.2]
☐ What does it mean to have a comparative advantage at producing a good? [LO 2.2]
☐ Can more than one producer have an absolute advantage at producing the same good? Why or why not? [LO 2.2]

Why Trade?

Canada is perfectly capable of producing its own shirts and its own wheat. In fact, in our simple model it has an absolute advantage at producing both goods. So, why buy shirts from China? We are about to see that both countries are actually able to consume more when they specialize in producing the good for which they have a comparative advantage and then trade with each other.

Specialization

LO 2.3 Define specialization and explain why people specialize.

If you lived 200 years ago, your everyday life would have been full of tasks that probably never even cross your mind today. You might have milked a cow, hauled water from a well, split wood, cured meat, mended a hole in a sock, and repaired a roof. Contrast that with life today. Almost everything we use comes from someone who specializes in providing a particular good or service. We bet you don't churn the butter you put on your toast and that you wouldn't even begin to know how to construct your computer. We are guessing you don't usually sew your own clothes or grow your own wheat. In today's world, all of us are dependent on one another for the things we need on a daily basis.

In our model, when Canada and China work in isolation, each produces some shirts and some wheat, each in the combinations that its consumers prefer. Suppose Canada has 20 million workers and China has 80 million. As before, each Canadian worker can make 50 shirts or 200 bushels of wheat, and each Chinese worker can make 25 shirts or 50 bushels of wheat. Suppose that, based on Canadian consumers' preferences, Canadian workers are split so that they produce 500 million shirts and 2 billion bushels of wheat. In China, workers are producing 1 billion shirts and 2 billion bushels of wheat. Even though China's productivity per worker is lower, it has more workers and so is able to produce a larger total quantity of goods. (The quantities of shirts and wheat are unrealistically large, because we are assuming they are the only goods being produced. In reality, of course, countries produce many different goods, but this simplifying assumption helps us to zero in on a real-world truth.)

If each country focuses on producing the good for which it has a comparative advantage, total production increases. Focusing in this way is called **specialization**, the practice of spending all of your resources producing a particular good. When each country specializes in making a particular good according to its comparative advantage, total production possibilities are greater than if each produced the exact combination of goods its own consumers want.

We have seen that if Canada and China are self-sufficient (each producing what its people want to consume), then together the two countries can make 1.5 billion T-shirts and 4 billion bushels of wheat, as shown at the top of Table 2-1 (Without specialization). What would happen if, instead, China put all its resources into making shirts, and Canaada put all its resources into growing wheat? The bottom section of Table 2-1 (With specialization) shows us:

Canada

200 bushels per worker × 20 million workers = 4 billion bushels

China

25 shirts per worker × 80 million workers = 2 billion shirts

TABLE 2-1 PRODUCTION WITH AND WITHOUT SPECIALIZATION

When China and Canada each specialize in the production of one good, the two countries can produce an extra 0.5 billion T-shirts using the same number of workers and the same technology.

	Country	Wheat (billions of bushels)	T-shirts (billions)
Without specialization	Canada	2	0.5
	China	2	1
	Total	**4**	**1.5**
With specialization	Canada	4	0
	China	0	2
	Total	**4**	**2**

By specializing, the two countries together can produce just as much wheat as before, *plus* 0.5 billion more shirts. Specialization increases total production, using the same number of workers and the same technology.

This rule applies to all sorts of goods and services. It explains why dentists hire roofers to fix a roof leak and why roofers hire dentists to fill a cavity. See the Real Life box, Specialization Sauce, for an example of the power of specialization in a setting you probably know well—McDonald's.

REAL LIFE

Specialization Sauce

Henry Ford pioneered the assembly-line method of automobile manufacturing, in which each worker does just one small task on each car before it moves down the line to the next worker, who does a different small task. Ford proved that he could build more cars in less time when each employee specialized in this way. Restaurants use the same principle: they can serve more customers faster if they split the work among managers, waitstaff, and chefs. Fast-food restaurants take specialization even further.

Fast food as we know it was born in 1948, when McDonald's founders Dick and Mac McDonald decided to implement a radically new method of preparing food. Inspired by factory assembly lines, they applied Ford's concept of specialization to the restaurant business. Instead of assigning several employees to general food preparation, they split each order into parts, parcelling out the steps required to prepare a meal. One employee became the grilling specialist; another added mustard and ketchup. A different employee operated the potato fryer, and yet another mixed the milkshakes.

Any single employee would almost certainly have been able to learn how to grill a hamburger, add condiments, make fries, *and* mix a milkshake. In each restaurant, one particularly skilled employee was probably faster than everyone else at all the steps in making a meal. Even so, specialization was more efficient. By assigning only one specific task to each employee, McDonald's founders revolutionized the speed and quantity of food preparation. Harnessing the power of specialization allowed them to grill more burgers, fry more potatoes, and feed more hungry customers.

Source: Eric Schlosser, *Fast Food Nation* (Boston: Houghton Mifflin, 2002), pp. 19–20.

Gains from Trade

> LO 2.4 Explain how the gains from trade follow from comparative advantage.

When countries specialize in producing the goods for which they have a comparative advantage, total production increases. The problem with specialization is that each producer ends up with only one good—in our model, wheat in Canada, shirts in China. If Canadians don't want to go naked and the Chinese don't want to starve, they must trade.

Suppose that China and Canada agree to trade 2 billion bushels of wheat for 0.75 billion T-shirts. As a result, each country ends up with just as much wheat as before, plus 0.5 billion more shirts. This improvement in outcomes that occurs when specialized producers exchange goods and services is called the **gains from trade**.

Figure 2-7 shows how the gains from trade affect a country's consumption. Before the trade, it was impossible for Canada and China to consume any combination of goods outside their production possibilities frontiers. After the trade between the two specialized producers, each country's consumption increases to a point that was previously unachievable. If Canada and China both consume the same amount of wheat as before, they are able to consume 0.5 million more T-shirts after opening up to trade.

In Figure 2.7, the gains from trade from the Canada–China trade are explained. Canada and China both consume same amount of wheat, but both consume 0.25 million extra shirts. In reality, the distribution can vary; there are other possible trading arrangements to benefit everyone.

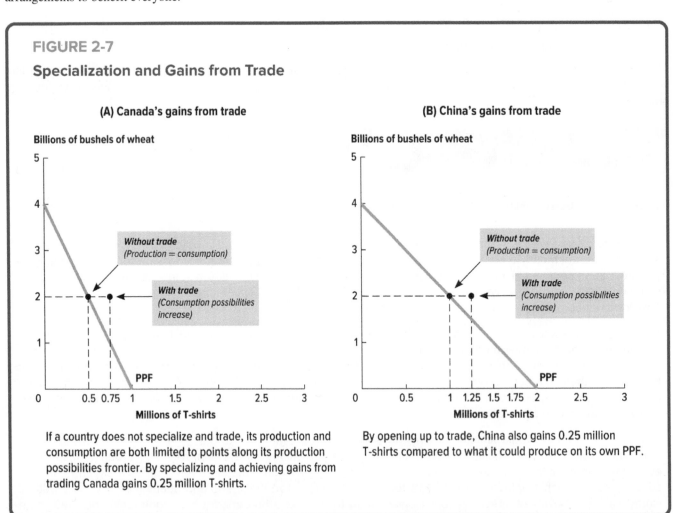

FIGURE 2-7

Specialization and Gains from Trade

(A) Canada's gains from trade

(B) China's gains from trade

If a country does not specialize and trade, its production and consumption are both limited to points along its production possibilities frontier. By specializing and achieving gains from trading Canada gains 0.25 million T-shirts.

By opening up to trade, China also gains 0.25 million T-shirts compared to what it could produce on its own PPF.

Overall, there is room for trade as long as the two countries differ in their opportunity costs to produce a good and they set a trading price that falls between those opportunity costs. In our example, the price at which China and Canada are willing to trade

T-shirts must fall between China's opportunity cost for producing T-shirts and Canada's opportunity cost for producing T-shirts. If China is the country that has specialized in T-shirts, it cannot charge a price greater than Canada's opportunity cost. If it does, Canada will simply make the T-shirts itself. Conversely, China must receive a price that covers its opportunity costs for making T-shirts or it will not be willing to trade.

Consider the *wants* that drive people to engage in exchanges. When people specialize and trade, everyone gets more of the things they want than they would if they were self-sufficient. Thus, trade can be driven entirely by self-interest. Just as Canada benefits from trading with China, an experienced worker or large firm benefits from trading with a less experienced employee or a small, specialized company.

For example, when Bill Gates was the CEO of Microsoft, he probably got IT assistants to fix bugs on his computer, even though he could have done it faster himself. Let's say Bill could fix the bug in an hour, but for every hour he was distracted from running Microsoft, the company's profits went down by $1,000. The IT assistant earns only $50 an hour, so even if he takes two to three times as long to do the work, it was still worth it for Bill to hire him and spend his own time keeping Microsoft's productivity up. Bill had an absolute advantage at fixing computer bugs, but the opportunity cost in lost profits means the IT assistant had a comparative advantage. (Bill's comparative advantage was at running Microsoft.) Everyone ends up better off if they specialize.

In spite of the gains from specializing and trading, not everyone considers this an obvious choice in every circumstance—which brings us to our fourth question from Chapter 1: *Why isn't everyone already doing it?* Some people argue that it's worth giving up the gains from trade for various reasons. For some examples, see the What Do You Think? box, Is Self-Sufficiency a Virtue?

WHAT DO YOU THINK?

Is Self-Sufficiency a Virtue?

Why should Canada trade with other countries? If every other country in the world were to disappear tomorrow, Canada would probably manage to fend for itself. It has plenty of fertile land, natural resources, people, and manufacturing capacity.

Based on what you now know about specialization and the gains from trade, what do you think about the value of exchange versus the value of self-sufficiency? Economists tend to line up in favour of free international trade; they argue that trade makes both countries economically better off. Serious and worthwhile arguments have also been made on the other side. The following are some reasons that have been proposed for developing national self-sufficiency.

- **National heritage.** Many people feel that a line has been crossed when a country loses its family farms or outsources a historically important industry—for example, automaking in the United States. Does a country lose its culture when it loses these industries?

- **Security.** Some people worry that trade weakens a country if it goes to war with a country that it depends on for essential goods. Is it safe to rely on other countries for your food supply, or does that kind of dependency pose a security risk? What about relying on another country for steel or uranium or oil?

- **Quality control and ethics.** When goods are made in other countries, production standards are harder to control than if the goods are made at home. Some people argue that international trade undermines consumer safety and environmental regulations, or that it fosters labour conditions that would be considered unethical or illegal in Canada.

What do you think?

1. Do you agree with any of these objections to free trade? Why? When is self-sufficiency more valuable than the gains from trade?

2. Is the choice between trade and self-sufficiency an either/or question? Is there a middle-of-the-road approach that would address concerns on both sides of this issue?

Comparative Advantage Over Time

Our simplified model of production possibilities and trade helps us to understand why Canadians now buy shirts from China. But we noted at the beginning of the chapter that this wasn't always the case—a hundred years ago, Canada was producing its own shirts. To understand why this changed, we can apply our model to shifts in comparative advantage over time. These shifts have caused significant changes in different countries' economies and trade patterns.

When the Industrial Revolution began, Great Britain led the world in clothing manufacturing. In the nineteenth century, the United States snatched the comparative advantage through a combination of new technology (which led to higher productivity) and cheap labour (which led to lower production costs). Gradually, the comparative advantage in making clothing shifted away from the United States to other countries. By the 1930s, 40 percent of the world's cotton goods were made in Japan, where workers from the countryside were willing to work long hours for low wages. In the mid-1970s, clothing manufacturing moved to Hong Kong, Taiwan, and Korea, where wages were even lower than in Japan. The textile industry then moved to China in the early 1990s, when millions of young women left their farms to work for wages as much as 90 percent lower than those in Hong Kong. There's an upside to the progressive relocation of this industry and its jobs: eventually high-wage jobs replaced low-wage jobs, and these countries experienced considerable economic growth.

Losing a comparative advantage in clothing production sounds like a bad thing at first. But as we know from our model, you can't lose comparative advantage in one thing without gaining it in another. Changes in clothing manufacturing were driven by by the fact that workers in each country were becoming more skilled in industries that paid better than making clothes—such as making cars, or programming computers, or providing financial services. This meant the opportunity cost of making clothes increased, and the comparative advantage in clothing production shifted to countries where the workers lacked skills in better-paying industries and so were willing to work in textile factories for lower wages.

Most historians would agree that it wasn't a sign of failure when countries lost their comparative advantage in clothing production—it was a sign of success. The same was true for the Canadian economy when the great Canadian fur trade started to decline in the 1920s. It was a sign of progress. This was also the time when the number of automobiles exported from Canada started to increase. Like former textile producers Great Britain, the United States, Japan, Korea, and Hong Kong, Canada is much wealthier now than when it was at the centre of the fur trade.

However, these changes probably didn't look or feel like success at the time, especially for workers in textile factories who saw their jobs disappearing overseas. This same controversy is unfolding today in other industries as companies outsource tasks that can be done more cheaply in other countries. The Real Life box, Comparative Advantage: The Good, the Bad, and the Ugly, considers whether a country's loss of comparative advantage at producing a particular good is something to worry about.

> Note that some boxed features appear in short, preview form within the chapter but are presented in greater detail online. Simply follow the directions at the end of the preview boxes to find the full story.

REAL LIFE

Comparative Advantage: The Good, the Bad, and the Ugly

You may have noticed that when you call the customer service line for many large companies, you are likely to end up speaking with someone in India or the Philippines. Thirty years ago, that was not the case—call centres for Canadian customers were almost all located in Canada.

Canada has not become worse at running call centres. In fact, it may still have an absolute advantage at it.

✓ CONCEPT CHECK

☐ Why do people or countries specialize? [LO 2.3]

☐ How do two countries benefit from trading with each other? [LO 2.4]

☐ Is it possible to not have a comparative advantage at anything? Why or why not? [LO 2.4]

Conclusion

Specialization and trade can make everyone better off. It is not surprising, then, that in an economy driven by individuals seeking to make a profit or to make the biggest difference in their communities, people specialize so as to exploit their comparative advantages. The principle is as true for countries such Canada and China as it is for individuals picking their careers.

No government intervention is required to coordinate production. The great economic thinker Adam Smith suggested the term *invisible hand* to describe this coordinating mechanism:

> It is not from the benevolence of the butcher, the brewer, or the baker that we expect our dinner, but from their regard to their [self-interest]. . . he intends only his own gain, and he is in this, as in many other cases, led by an invisible hand to promote an end which was no part of his intention. (A. Smith, *An Inquiry into the Nature and Causes of the Wealth of Nations*, 1776.)

The functioning of the invisible hand depends on a lot of other assumptions, such as free competition, full information, and many others that do not always hold true in the real world. Later in the book we will discuss these assumptions, and when they work and when they do not.

Most people take for granted the prevalence of specialization and trade in their everyday lives. Few stop to think about the benefits and where they come from. In this chapter we tried to dig down to the bottom of the assumptions people make and expose the logic behind the gains from trade. As we proceed—especially when we return to topics like international trade and government intervention in the markets—try to remember the underlying incentive that drives people to interact with one another in economic exchanges.

Key Terms

production possibilities frontier

efficient points

absolute advantage

comparative advantage

specialization

gains from trade

Summary

LO 2.1 Construct a production possibilities graph, and describe what causes shifts in production possibilities curves.

A production possibilities graph shows all the combinations of two goods that a person or an economy can produce with a given amount of time, resources, and technology. The production possibilities frontier is a line on that graph that shows all the maximum attainable combinations of goods. Producers of goods and services are not likely to choose a combination of goods inside the production possibilities frontier, because they could achieve a higher production level with the same amount of resources. And they cannot choose points outside the frontier, which would require more than the available resources. The choice between combinations on the production possibilities frontier is a matter of preference.

Shifts in the production possibilities frontier can be caused by changes in technology, as well as changes in population and other resources. Increases in technological capabilities and population will shift the PPF outward, while decreases in these factors will shift the PPF inward.

LO 2.2 Define absolute and comparative advantage.

Producers have an absolute advantage at making a good when they can produce more output than others with a given amount of resources. If you put two people or countries to work making the same good, the person or country that is more productive has an absolute advantage.

People or countries have a comparative advantage when they are better at producing one good than they are at producing other goods, relative to other producers. Everyone has a comparative advantage at something, whether or not they have an absolute advantage at anything.

LO 2.3 Define specialization and explain why people specialize.

Specialization means spending all or much of your time producing a particular good. Production is highest when people or countries specialize in producing the good for which they have a comparative advantage. Specialization increases total production but uses the same number of workers and the same technology.

LO 2.4 Explain how the gains from trade follow from comparative advantage.

The increase in total production that occurs from specialization and exchange is called the *gains from trade*. With specialization and trade, two parties can increase production and consumption, and each ends up better off. Shifts in comparative advantage over time have caused significant changes in different countries' economies and trade patterns. These changes generally signal economic success, although they can be painful for the individual workers and industries involved.

Review Questions

1. You've been put in charge of a bake sale for a local charity, at which you are planning to sell cookies and cupcakes. What would a production possibilities graph of this situation show? [LO 2.1]

2. You manage two employees at a pet salon. Your employees perform two tasks, giving flea baths and grooming animals. If you constructed a single production possibilities frontier for flea baths and grooming that combined both of your employees, would you expect the production possibilities frontier to be linear (a straight line)? Explain why or why not. [LO 2.1]

3. Back at the bake sale (see review question 1), suppose another volunteer is going to help you bake. What would it mean for one of you to have an absolute advantage at baking cookies or cupcakes? Could one of you have an absolute advantage at baking both items? [LO 2.2]

4. What would it mean for you or the other volunteer to have a comparative advantage at baking cookies or cupcakes? Could one of you have a comparative advantage at baking both items? [LO 2.2]

5. Suppose you have a comparative advantage at baking cookies, and the other volunteer has a comparative advantage at baking cupcakes. Make a proposal to the other volunteer about how to split up the baking. Explain how you can both gain from specializing, and why. [LO 2.3]

6. At the flower shop where you manage two employees, your employees perform two tasks, caring for the displays of cut flowers and making flower arrangements to fill customer orders. Explain how you would approach organizing your employees and assigning them tasks. [LO 2.3]

7. Suppose two countries produce the same two goods and have identical production possibilities frontiers. Do you expect these countries to trade? Explain why or why not. [LO 2.4]

8. Brazil is the largest coffee producer in the world, and coffee is one of Brazil's major export goods. Suppose that twenty years from now Brazil no longer produces much coffee and imports most of its coffee instead. Explain why Brazil might change its trade pattern over time. [LO 2.4]

Problems and Applications

1. Your friend Sam has been asked to prepare appetizers for a university reception. She has an unlimited amount of ingredients but only six hours to prepare them. Sam can make 300 mini-sandwiches or 150 servings of melon slices topped with smoked salmon and a dab of sauce per hour. [LO 2.1]

   a. Draw Sam's production possibilities frontier.

   b. Now suppose that the university decides to postpone the reception until after the big game, and Sam has an extra four hours to prepare. Redraw her production possibilities frontier to show the impact of this increase in resources.

   c. In addition to the extra time to prepare, suppose Sam's friend Chris helps by preparing the melon slices. Sam can now make 300 mini-sandwiches or 300 melon appetizers per hour. Redraw Sam's production possibilities frontier to show the impact of increased productivity in making melon appetizers.

2. Your friend Sam has been asked to prepare appetizers for the university reception. She has an unlimited amount of ingredients and six hours in which to prepare them. Sam can make 300 mini-sandwiches or 150 servings of melon slices topped with smoked salmon and a dab of sauce per hour. [LO 2.1]

   a. What is Sam's opportunity cost of making one mini-sandwich?

   b. What is Sam's opportunity cost of making one melon appetizer?

   c. Suppose the reception has been postponed, and Sam has an extra four hours to prepare. What is the opportunity cost of making one mini-sandwich now?

   d. Suppose the reception has been postponed, and Sam has an extra four hours to prepare. What is the opportunity cost of making one melon appetizer now?

   e. Suppose Sam's friend Chris helps by preparing the melon slices, increasing Sam's productivity to 300 mini-sandwiches or 300 melon appetizers per hour. What is the opportunity cost of making one mini-sandwich now?

   f. Suppose Sam's friend Chris helps by preparing the melon slices, increasing Sam's productivity to 300 mini-sandwiches or 300 melon appetizers per hour. What is the opportunity cost of making one melon appetizer now?

3. Suppose that Canada produces two goods: lumber and fish. It has 18 million workers, each of whom can cut 10 feet of lumber or catch 20 fish each day. [LO 2.1]

   a. What is the maximum amount of lumber Canada could produce in a day?

   b. What is the maximum amount of fish it could produce in a day?

   c. Write an equation describing the production possibilities frontier, in the form described in section 2.1 (Figure 2-1 and Figure 2-2).

   d. Use your equation to determine how many fish can be caught if 60 million feet of lumber are cut.

4. The graph in Figure 2P-1 shows Tanya's weekly production possibilities frontier for doing homework (writing papers and doing problem sets). [LO 2.1]

   a. What is the slope of the production possibilities frontier?

   b. What is the opportunity cost of doing one problem set?

   c. What is the opportunity cost of writing one paper?

FIGURE 2P-1

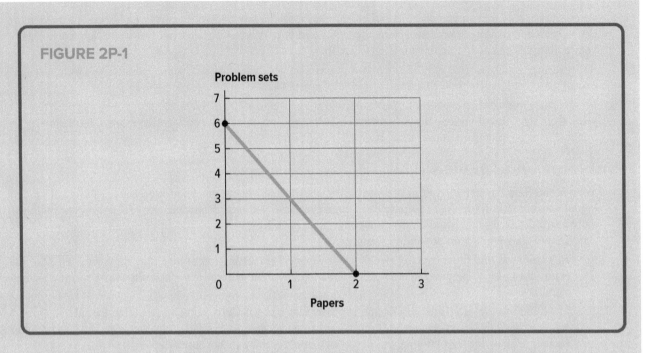

5. Use the production possibilities frontier in Figure 2P-2 to answer the following questions. [LO 2.1]

   a. What is the slope of the PPF between point A and point B?

   b. What is the slope of the PPF between point B and point C?

   c. Is the opportunity cost of producing hammers higher between points A and B or between points B and C?

   d. Is the opportunity cost of producing screwdrivers higher between points A and B or between points B and C?

FIGURE 2P-2

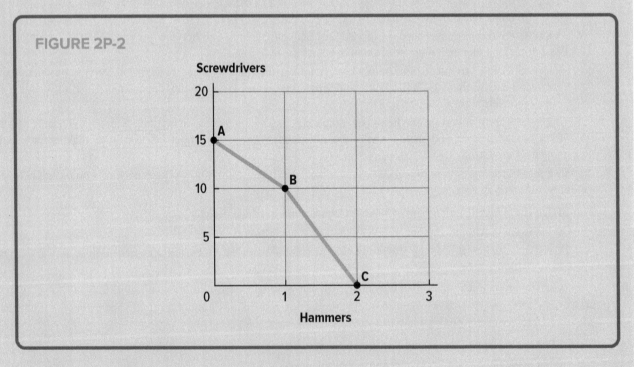

6. For each point on the PPF in Figure 2P-3, note whether the point is: [LO 2.1]

   • Attainable and efficient
   • Attainable and inefficient
   • Unattainable

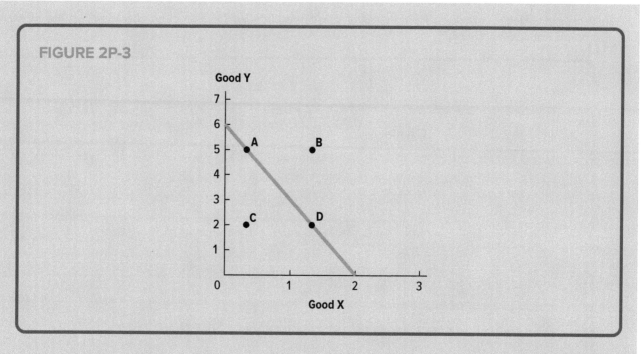

FIGURE 2P-3

7. For each point on the PPF in Figure 2P-4, note whether the point is: [LO 2.1]

   - Attainable and efficient
   - Attainable and inefficient
   - Unattainable

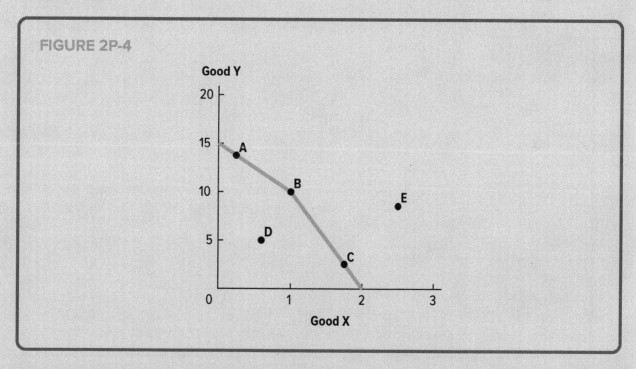

FIGURE 2P-4

8. Suppose that three volunteers are preparing cookies and cupcakes for a bake sale. Diana can make 27 cookies or 18 cupcakes per hour; Andy can make 25 cookies or 17 cupcakes; and Sam can make 10 cookies or 12 cupcakes. [LO 2.2]

   a. Who has the absolute advantage at making cookies?

   b. At making cupcakes?

9. Paula and Carlo are coworkers. Their production possibilities frontiers for counselling clients and writing memos are given in Figure 2P-5. [LO 2.2]

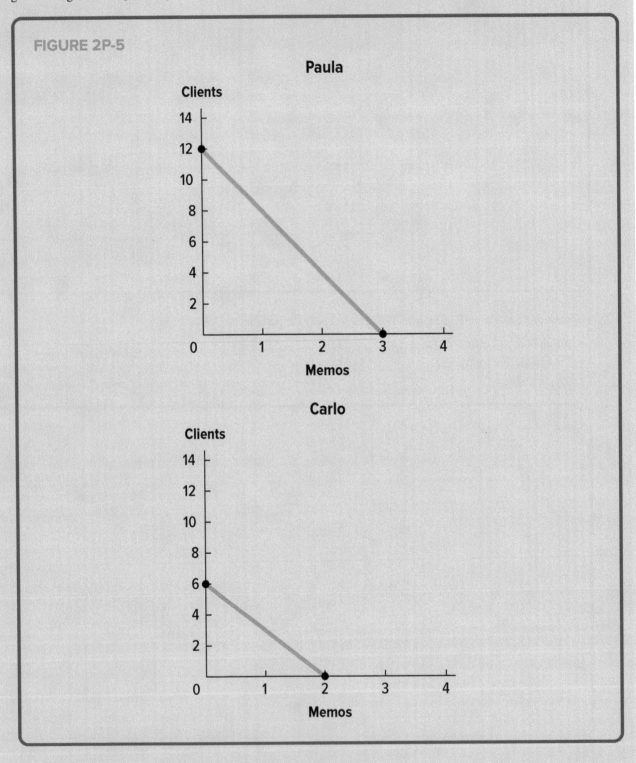

FIGURE 2P-5

a. Which worker has an absolute advantage in counselling clients?
b. Which worker has an absolute advantage in writing memos?
c. Which worker has a comparative advantage in counselling clients?
d. Which worker has a comparative advantage in writing memos?

10. Two students are assigned to work together on a project that requires both a written and an oral presentation. Steve can write 1 page or prepare 3 minutes of a presentation each day. Anna can write 2 pages or prepare 1 minute of a presentation each day. [LO 2.2]

   a. Who has a comparative advantage at writing?

   b. Suppose that Steve goes to a writing tutor and learns some tricks that enable him to write 3 pages each day. Now who has a comparative advantage at writing?

11. Suppose that the manager of a restaurant has two new employees, Rahul and Henriette, and is trying to decide which one to assign to which task. Rahul can chop 20 kilograms of vegetables or wash 100 dishes per hour. Henriette can chop 30 kilograms of vegetables or wash 120 dishes. [LO 2.3]

   a. Who should be assigned to chop vegetables?

   b. Who should be assigned to wash dishes?

12. The Dominican Republic and Nicaragua both produce coffee and rum. The Dominican Republic can produce 20 thousand tonnes of coffee per year or 10 thousand barrels of rum. Nicaragua can produce 30 thousand tonnes of coffee per year or 5 thousand barrels of rum. [LO 2.3]

   a. Suppose the Dominican Republic and Nicaragua sign a trade agreement in which each country would specialize in the production of either coffee or rum. Which country should specialize in coffee? Which country should specialize in producing rum?

   b. What are the minimum and maximum prices at which these countries will trade coffee?

13. Eleanor and her little sister Joanna are responsible for two chores on their family's farm, gathering eggs and collecting milk. Eleanor can gather 9 dozen eggs or collect 3 litres of milk per week. Joanna can gather 2 dozen eggs or collect 2 litres of milk per week. [LO 2.3]

   a. The family wants 2 litres of milk per week and as many eggs as the sisters can gather. Currently, Eleanor and Joanna collect one litre of milk each and as many eggs as they can. How many dozen eggs does the family have per week?

   b. If the sisters specialized, which sister should gather the milk?

   c. If the sisters specialized, how many dozen eggs would the family have per week?

14. Suppose Russia and Sweden each produce only paper and cars. Russia can produce 8 tonnes of paper or 4 million cars each year. Sweden can produce 25 tonnes of paper or 5 million cars each year. [LO 2.4]

   a. Draw the production possibilities frontier for each country.

   b. Both countries want 2 million cars each year and as much paper as they can produce along with 2 million cars. Find this point on each production possibilities frontier and label it A.

   c. Suppose the countries specialize. Which country will produce cars?

   d. Once they specialize, suppose they work out a trade of 2 million cars for 6 tonnes of paper. Find the new *consumption* point for each country and label it B.

15. Maya and Max are neighbours. Both grow lettuce and tomatoes in their gardens. Maya can grow 45 heads of lettuce or 9 kilograms of tomatoes this summer. Max can grow 42 heads of lettuce or 6 kilos of tomatoes this summer. If Maya and Max specialize and trade, the price of tomatoes (in terms of lettuce) would be as follows: 1 pound of tomatoes would cost between _____ and _____ kilos of lettuce. [LO 2.4]

APPENDIX A

Math Essentials: Understanding Graphs and Slope

LEARNING OBJECTIVES

LO A.1   Create four quadrants using *x*- and *y*-axes and plot points on a graph.
LO A.2   Use data to calculate slope.
LO A.3   Interpret the steepness and direction of slope, and explain what that says about a line.

Creating a Graph

LO A.1 Create four quadrants using *x*- and *y*-axes and plot points on a graph.

A graph is one way to visually represent data. In this book, we use graphs to describe and interpret economic relationships. For example, we use a graph called a production possibilities frontier to explore opportunity costs and trade-offs in production. We graph average, variable, and marginal costs to explore production decisions facing a firm. And—the favourite of economists everywhere—we use graphs to show supply and demand, and the resulting relationship between price and quantity.

Graphs of One Variable

Graphs of a single variable come in three main forms: the bar chart, the pie chart, and the line graph. In school you've probably made all three and plastered them on science-fair posters and presentations or used them in reports. These graphs are versatile; they can be used to present all sorts of information. Throughout economics, and in this book, you'll come across these graphs frequently.

Probably the most common single-variable graph is the *bar graph,* an example of which is shown in Figure A-1. The bar graph shows the size or frequency of a variable using bars—hence the name. The size of the bar on the *y*-axis shows the value of the variable, while the *x*-axis contains the categories of the variables. In Figure A-1, for example, the bar graph shows the number representing paid newspaper circulation each day. Since the bars stand next to each other, a bar graph makes it clear exactly where each news site stands in comparison with the others. As you can see, the larger bars for the *Globe and Mail* and *Toronto Star* mean that these sites get more visits than the *Toronto Sun.*

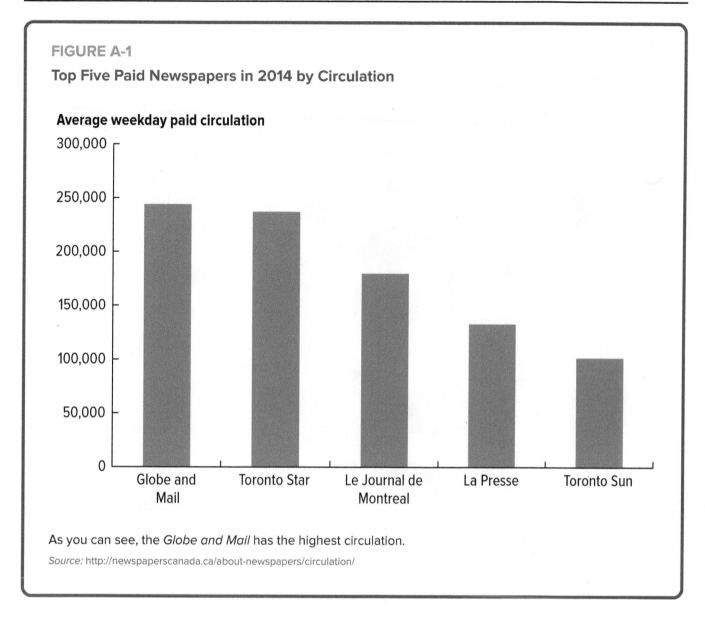

FIGURE A-1

Top Five Paid Newspapers in 2014 by Circulation

As you can see, the *Globe and Mail* has the highest circulation.

Source: http://newspaperscanada.ca/about-newspapers/circulation/

In general, bar graphs are versatile. You can show the distribution of letter grades in a class or the average monthly high and low temperatures in your city. Any time the size of a variable is important, you are generally going to want to use a bar graph.

Pie charts are often used to show how much of certain components make up a whole. Pie charts are usually a circle, cut into wedges that represent how much each makes up of the whole.

Figure A-2 shows the sales of the ten largest car manufacturers (Toyota, GM, Ford, etc.) as a percentage of overall new-car sales. The large wedges representing General Motors and Toyota show that these are large automakers compared to the small wedge representing Mercedes-Benz.

The most common use of pie charts is for budgeting. You'll often see government and business income and expenses broken down in a pie chart. Also, come election time, you'll see pie charts pop up all over the news media, representing the percentage of votes in an election that each candidate receives.

A final type of graph is called a *line* (or *time-series*) *graph*. This type of graph is helpful when you are trying to emphasize the trend of a single variable. In economics, the most common use for line graphs is to show the value of a variable over time. Inflation rates, GDP, and government debt over decades are all prime candidates for presentation on a line graph.

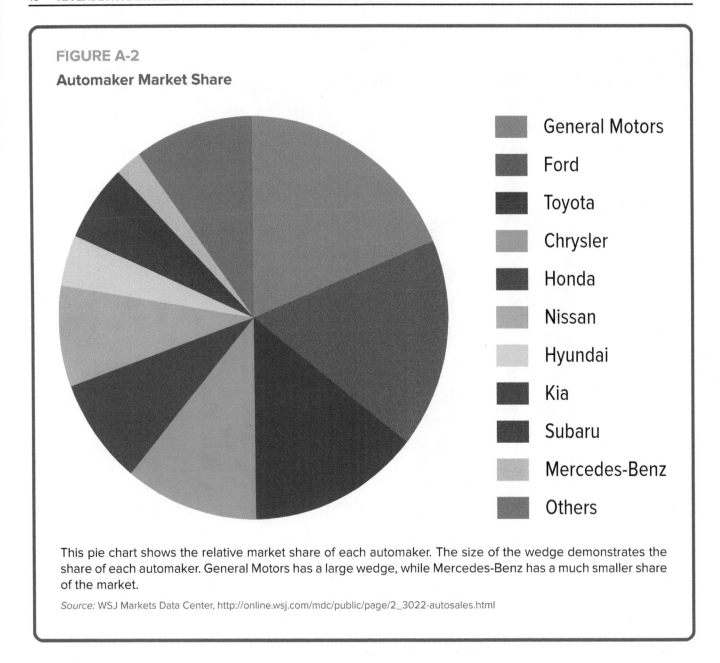

FIGURE A-2

Automaker Market Share

Legend:
- General Motors
- Ford
- Toyota
- Chrysler
- Honda
- Nissan
- Hyundai
- Kia
- Subaru
- Mercedes-Benz
- Others

This pie chart shows the relative market share of each automaker. The size of the wedge demonstrates the share of each automaker. General Motors has a large wedge, while Mercedes-Benz has a much smaller share of the market.

Source: WSJ Markets Data Center, http://online.wsj.com/mdc/public/page/2_3022-autosales.html

Figure A-3 shows the GDP growth rate in Mexico since 1960 on a time-series graph. Presenting the data this way makes it clear that Mexico had strong GDP growth (anything above 4 percent growth is very good) during the 1960s and 70s, but GDP growth was lower after that.

Ultimately, single-variable graphs can take us only so far. In order to get at some of the most fundamental issues of economics, we need to be able to plot the values of two variables (such as price and quantity) simultaneously.

Graphs of Two Variables

In order to present two or more variables on a graph, we are going to need something called the *Cartesian coordinate system*. With only two dimensions, this graphing system consists of two axes: the *x* (horizontal) axis and the *y* (vertical) axis. We can give these axes other names, depending on what economic variables we want to represent, such as price and quantity or inputs and outputs.

FIGURE A-3

GDP Growth in Mexico

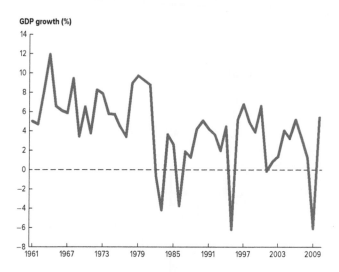

A line graph commonly shows a variable over a range of time. This allows the trend in the variable to be clear. In this case, you can see that GDP growth in Mexico has been highly variable, but overall, GDP growth was higher on average before 1980.

Source: World Bank World Development Indicators

In some cases it doesn't matter which variable we put on each axis. At other times, logic or convention will determine the axes. There are two common conventions in economics that it will be useful for you to remember:

1. **Price on the *y*-axis, quantity on the *x*-axis:** When we graph the relationship between price and quantity in economics, price is always on the *y*-axis and quantity is always on the *x*-axis.

2. **The *x*-axis "causes" the *y*-axis:** In general, when the values of one variable are dependent on the values of the other variable, we put the dependent variable on the *y*-axis and the independent variable on the *x*-axis. For example, if we were exploring the relationship between test scores and the number of hours a student spends studying, we would place hours on the *x*-axis and test scores on the *y*-axis, because hours spent studying generally affects scores rather than vice versa. Sometimes, though, the opposite is true. In economics, we often say that price (always the *y*-axis variable) causes the quantity demanded of a good (the *x*-axis variable).

The point where the two axes intersect is called the *origin.* Points to the right of the origin have *x*-coordinates with positive values, whereas points to the left of the origin have *x*-coordinates with negative values. Similarly, points above the origin have *y*-coordinates with positive values, and points below the origin have *y*-coordinates with negative values.

To specify a particular point, indicate the *x*- and *y*-coordinates in an ordered pair. Indicate the *x*-coordinate first and then the *y*-coordinate: (*x, y*). The intersection of the two axes creates four quadrants, as shown in Figure A-4.

Quadrant I: (*x,y*) The *x*- and *y*-coordinates are both positive.

Quadrant II: (−*x,y*) The *x*-coordinate is negative and the *y*-coordinate is positive.

Quadrant III: (−*x,*−*y*) The *x*- and *y*-coordinates are both negative.

Quadrant IV: (*x,*−*y*) The *x*-coordinate is positive and the *y*-coordinate is negative.

Origin: (**0,0**) The *x*- and *y*-coordinates are both zero at the origin.

FIGURE A-4

The Four Quadrants

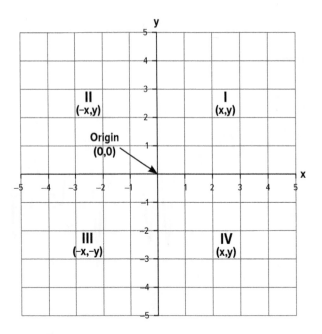

The Cartesian coordinate system is a way to plot values of two variables simultaneously. Different quadrants reflect whether the values of *x* and *y* are positive or negative.

Figure A-5 shows the following points plotted on a graph.

Quadrant I: (2,3)

Quadrant II: (−2,3)

Quadrant III: (−2,−3)

Quadrant IV: (2,−3)

In economics, we often isolate quadrant I when graphing. This is because there are many economic variables for which negative values do not make sense. For example, one important graph we use in economics shows the relationship between the price of a good and the quantity of that good demanded or supplied. Since it doesn't make sense to consider negative prices and quantities, we show only quadrant I when graphing supply and demand.

Figure A-6 shows a line in quadrant I that represents the relationship between the price of hot dogs at the ballpark and the quantity of hot dogs a family wants to buy. Price is on the *y*-axis, and the quantity of hot dogs the family demands is on the *x*-axis. For instance, one coordinate pair on this line is (3,2), meaning that if the price of hot dogs is $2, the family will want to buy three of them.

FIGURE A-5

Plotting Points on a Graph

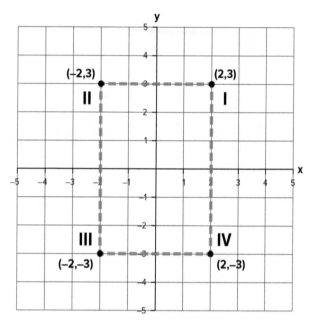

Each set of ordered pairs corresponds to a place on the Cartesian coordinate system.

FIGURE A-6

Thinking About the Logic Behind Graphs

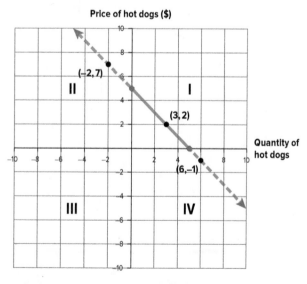

Plotting points in the four quadrants on a graph gives a line.

We could extend this demand curve in ways that make sense graphically but that don't represent logical price–quantity combinations in the real world. For instance, if we extend the demand curve into quadrant II, we have points such as (−2,7). If we extend the demand curve into quadrant IV, we have points such as (6,−1). However, it doesn't make sense to talk about someone demanding negative two hot dogs, nor does it make sense to think about a price of negative \$1.

Remember that we are not just graphing arbitrary points; we are illustrating a real relationship between variables that has meaning in the real world. Both (−2,7) and (6,−1) are points that are consistent with the equation for this demand curve, but neither point makes sense to include in our analysis. To graph this price–quantity relationship, we would limit our graph to quadrant I.

However, some variables you will study (such as revenue) may have negative values that make sense. When this is the case, graphs will show multiple quadrants.

Slope

Both the table and the graph in Figure A-7 represent a particular relationship between two variables, x and y. For every x there is a corresponding y. When we plot the points in the table we see that there is a consistent relationship between the value of x and the value of y. In this case, we can see at a glance that whenever the x value increases by 1, the y value increases by 0.5. We can describe this relationship as the *slope* of the line.

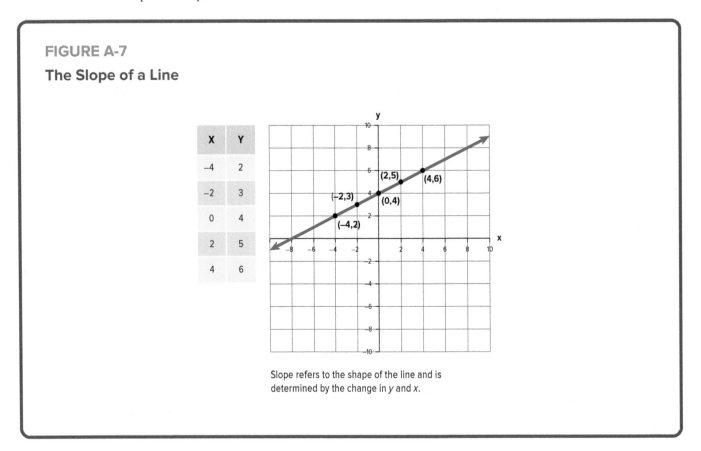

FIGURE A-7

The Slope of a Line

X	Y
−4	2
−2	3
0	4
2	5
4	6

Slope refers to the shape of the line and is determined by the change in *y* and *x*.

Slope is a ratio of vertical distance (change in y) to horizontal distance (change in x). We begin to calculate slope by labelling one point along the line point 1, which we denote (x_1, y_1), and another point along the line point 2, which we denote (x_2, y_2). We can then calculate the horizontal distance by subtracting x_1 from x_2. We calculate vertical distance by subtracting y_1 from y_2.

$$\text{Horizontal distance} \;=\; \Delta x \;=\; \left(x_2 - x_1\right)$$

$$\text{Vertical distance} \;=\; \Delta y \;=\; \left(y_2 - y_1\right)$$

The vertical distance is referred to as the **rise**, while the horizontal distance is known as the **run**. *Rise over run* is an easy way to remember how to calculate slope. (Note that the delta symbol, Δ, simply means *change in*.)

$$\text{Slope} = \frac{\text{rise}}{\text{run}} = \frac{\Delta y}{\Delta x} = \frac{(y_2 - y_1)}{(x_2 - x_1)}$$

When the relationship between x and y is linear (which means that it forms a straight line), the slope is constant. That is, for each one-unit change in the x-variable, the corresponding y-variable always changes by the same amount. Therefore, we can use any two points to calculate the slope of the line—it doesn't matter which ones we pick because the slope is the same everywhere on the line.

Slope gives us important information about the relationship between our two variables. As we are about to discuss, slope tells us something about both the direction of the relationship between two variables (whether they move in the same direction) and the magnitude of the relationship (how much y changes in response to a change in x).

Calculating Slope

LO A.2 Use data to calculate slope.

In Figure A-8, the run or horizontal distance between point (2,3) and point (4,5) is 4 minus 2, which equals 2. The rise or vertical distance is 5 minus 3, which equals 2. Therefore, the slope of the line in Figure A-8 is calculated as:

$$\text{Slope} = \frac{(y_2 - y_1)}{(x_2 - x_1)} = \frac{(5 - 3)}{(4 - 2)} = \frac{2}{2} = 1$$

Let's return to Figure A-7 and apply this same calculation. Because the relationship between x and y is linear, we can use any two points to calculate the slope. Let's designate point (2,5) as point 1, which we call (x_1, y_1), and point (4,6) as point 2, which we call (x_2, y_2).

$$\frac{(y_2 - y_1)}{(x_2 - x_1)} = \frac{(6 - 5)}{(4 - 2)} = \frac{1}{2} = 0.5$$

Note that it doesn't matter which point we pick as point 1 and which as point 2. We could have chosen 5 as y_2 and 6 as y_1 rather than vice versa. All that matters is that y_1 is from the same ordered pair as x_1 and y_2 is from the same pair as x_2. To prove that this is true, let's calculate slope again using (2,5) as point 2. The slope is still 0.5:

$$\frac{(y_2 - y_1)}{(x_2 - x_1)} = \frac{(5 - 6)}{(2 - 4)} = \frac{(-1)}{(-2)} = \frac{1}{2} = 0.5$$

FIGURE A-8

Calculating Slope

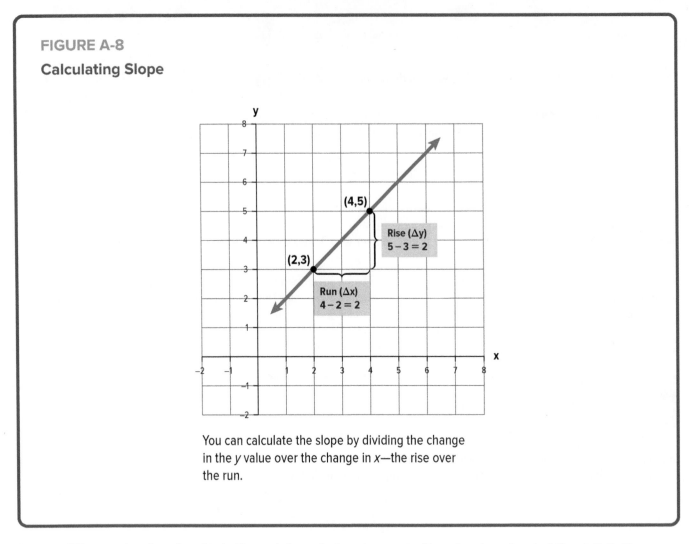

You can calculate the slope by dividing the change in the *y* value over the change in *x*—the rise over the run.

Use two different points from the table in Figure A-7 to calculate slope again. Try using the points (−4,2) and (0,4). Do you get 0.5 as your answer?

The Direction of a Slope

LO A.3 Interpret the steepness and direction of slope, and explain what that says about a line.

The direction of a slope tells us something meaningful about the relationship between the two variables we are representing. For instance, when children get older, they grow taller. If we represented this relationship in a graph, we would see an upward-sloping line, telling us that height increases as age increases, rather than decreasing. Of course, it is common knowledge that children get taller, not shorter, as they get older. But if we were looking at a graph of a relationship we did not already understand, the slope of the line would show us at a glance how the two variables relate to each other.

To see how we can learn from the direction of a slope and how to calculate it, look at the graphs in panels A and B of Figure A-9.

In panel A, we can see that when *x* increases from 1 to 2, *y* also increases, from 2 to 4. If we move the other direction down the line, we see that when *x* decreases from 2 to 1, *y* also decreases, from 4 to 2. In other words, *x* and *y* move in the same direction. Therefore, *x* and *y* are said to have a *positive relationship*. Not surprisingly, this means that the slope of the line is a positive number:

$$\text{Slope} = \frac{\Delta y}{\Delta x} = \frac{2}{1} = 2$$

When the slope of a line is positive, we know that y increases as x increases, and y decreases as x decreases. If a line slopes upward, then its slope is positive.

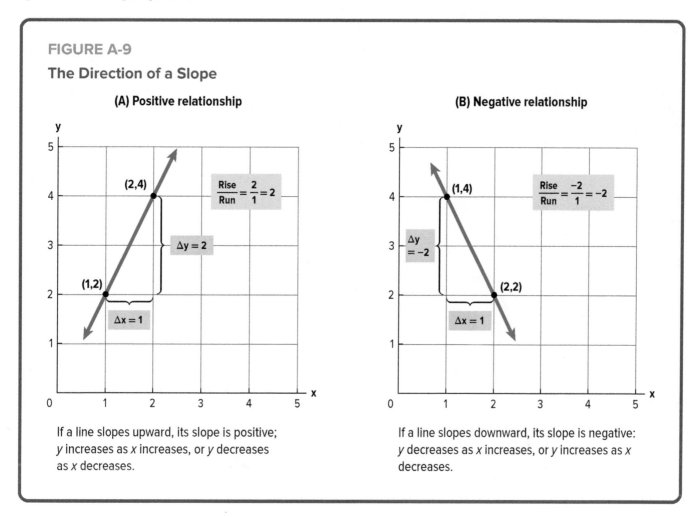

FIGURE A-9

The Direction of a Slope

(A) Positive relationship

If a line slopes upward, its slope is positive; y increases as x increases, or y decreases as x decreases.

(B) Negative relationship

If a line slopes downward, its slope is negative: y decreases as x increases, or y increases as x decreases.

Now turn to the graph in panel B. In this case, when x increases from 1 to 2, y decreases from 4 to 2. Reading from the other direction, when x decreases from 2 to 1, y increases from 2 to 4. Therefore, x and y move in opposite directions and are said to have a *negative relationship*. The slope of the line is a negative number:

$$\text{Slope} = \frac{\Delta y}{\Delta x} = \frac{-2}{1} = -2$$

When the slope of a line is negative, we know that y decreases as x increases, and y increases as x decreases. If a line slopes downward, its slope is negative.

In Chapter 3, you will see applications of these positive and negative relationships between the variables price and quantity. Here's a preview:

- You will see a positive relationship between price and quantity when you encounter a *supply curve*. You will learn the meaning of that positive relationship: as the price of a good increases, suppliers are willing to supply a larger quantity to markets. Supply curves, therefore, are upward sloping.

- You will see a negative relationship between price and quantity when you encounter a *demand curve*. You will learn the meaning of that negative relationship: as the price of a good increases, consumers are willing to purchase a smaller quantity. Demand curves are downward sloping.

From these examples, you can see that two variables (such as price and quantity) may have more than one relationship with each other, depending on whose choices they represent and under what circumstances.

The Steepness of a Slope

In addition to the *direction* of the relationship between variables, the *steepness* of the slope also gives us important information. It tells us how much y changes for a given change in x.

In both panels of Figure A-10 the relationship between x and y is positive (upward sloping), and the distance between the x values, Δx, is the same. However, the change in y that results from a one-unit change in x is greater in panel A than it is in panel B. In other words, the slope is *steeper* in panel A and *flatter* in panel B.

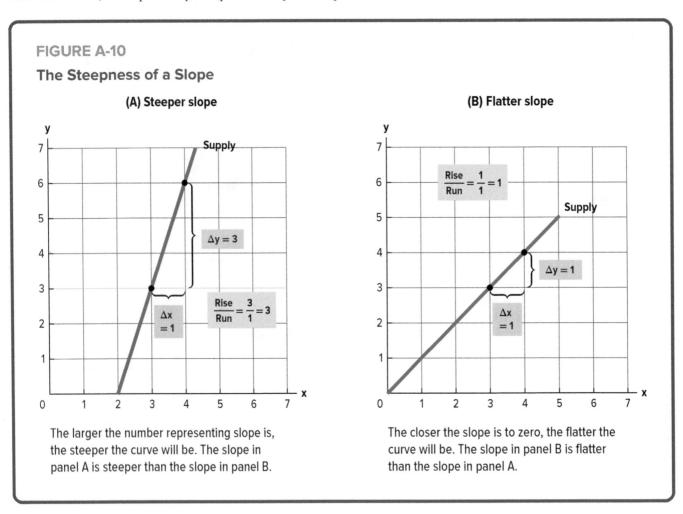

FIGURE A-10

The Steepness of a Slope

(A) Steeper slope

The larger the number representing slope is, the steeper the curve will be. The slope in panel A is steeper than the slope in panel B.

(B) Flatter slope

The closer the slope is to zero, the flatter the curve will be. The slope in panel B is flatter than the slope in panel A.

Numerically, the closer the number representing the slope is to zero, the flatter the curve will be. Remember that both positive and negative numbers can be close to zero. So a slope of −1 has the same steepness as a slope of 1, but one slopes downward and the other upward. Correspondingly, a line with a slope of −5 is steeper than a line with a slope of −1 or one with a slope of 1.

In general, slope is used to describe how much y changes in response to a one-unit change in x. In economics, we are sometimes interested in how much x changes in response to a one-unit change in y. In Chapter 4, for example, you will see how quantity (on the x-axis) responds to a change in price (on the y-axis).

Key Terms

slope
rise
run

Problems and Applications

1. Create four quadrants using *x*- and *y*-axes. Use your graph to plot the following points. **[LO A.1]**
   a. (1,4)
   b. (−2,1)
   c. (−3,−3)
   d. (3,−2)

2. Create four quadrants using *x*- and *y*-axes. Use your graph to plot the following points. **[LO A.1]**
   a. (0,4)
   b. (0,−2)
   c. (1,0)
   d. (−3,0)

3. Use the curve labeled Demand in Figure AP-1 to create a table (schedule) that shows Price in one column and Quantity in another. What is the slope of the curve labelled Demand? **[LO A.2]**

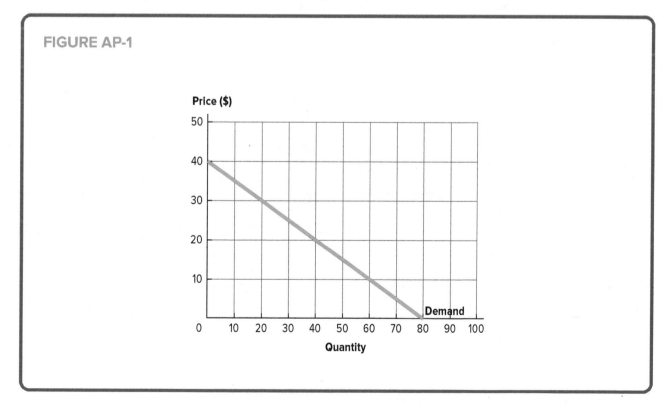

FIGURE AP-1

4. Use the curve labeled Demand in Figure AP-2 to create a table (schedule) that shows Price in one column and Quantity in another. What is the slope of the curve labelled Demand? [LO A.2]

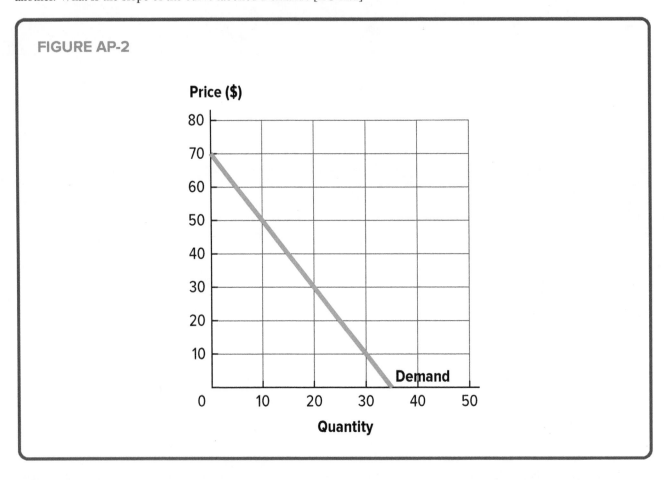

FIGURE AP-2

5. Use the information about price and quantity in Table AP-1 to create a graph, with Price on the y-axis and Quantity on the x-axis. Label the resulting curve Demand. What is the slope of that curve? [LO A.2]

TABLE AP-1

Price ($)	Quantity
0	120
2	100
4	80
6	60
8	40
10	20
12	0

6. Use the information about price and quantity in Table AP-2 to create a graph, with Price on the *y*-axis and Quantity on the *x*-axis. Label the resulting curve Demand. What is the slope of that curve? **[LO A.2]**

TABLE AP-2

Price ($)	Quantity
0	5
5	4
10	3
15	2
20	1
25	0

7. Use the curve labeled Supply in Figure AP-3 to create a table (schedule) that shows Price in one column and Quantity in another. What is the slope of the curve labelled Supply? **[LO A.2]**

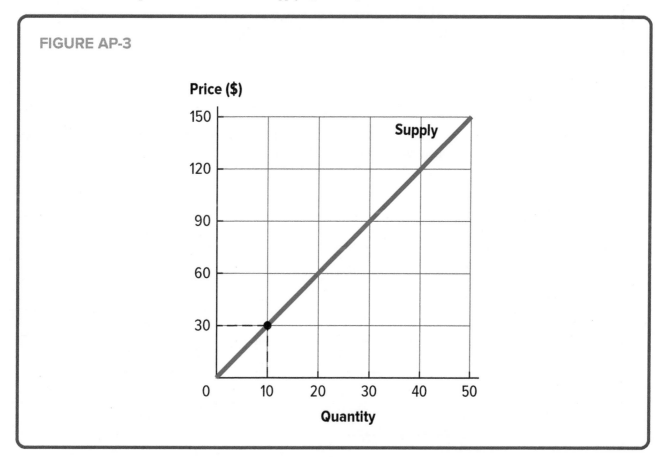

FIGURE AP-3

8. Use the curve labeled Supply in Figure AP-4 to create a table (schedule) that shows Price in one column and Quantity in another. What is the slope of the curve labelled Supply? [LO A.2]

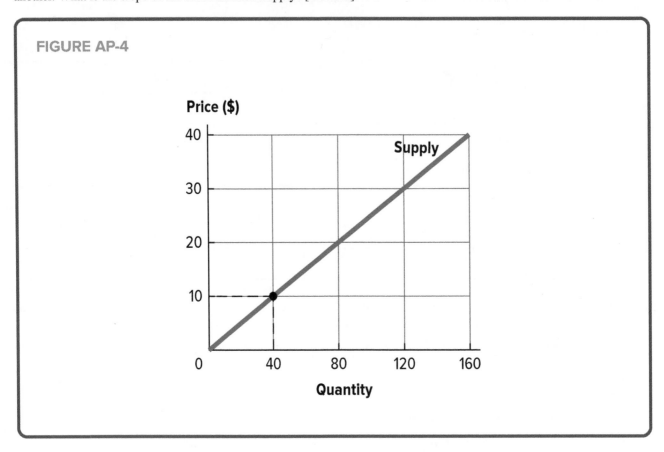

FIGURE AP-4

9. Use the information about price and quantity in Table AP-3 to create a graph, with Price on the y-axis and Quantity on the x-axis. Label the resulting curve Supply. What is the slope of that curve? [LO A.2]

TABLE AP-3

Price ($)	Quantity
0	0
25	5
50	10
75	15
100	20
125	25

10. Use the information about price and quantity in Table AP-4 to create a graph, with Price on the y-axis and Quantity on the x-axis. Label the resulting curve Supply. What is the slope of that curve? [LO A.2]

TABLE AP-4

Price ($)	Quantity
0	0
2	8
4	16
6	24
8	32
10	40
12	48

11. What is the direction of slope indicated by the following examples? [LO A.3]
    a. As the price of rice increases, consumers want less of it.
    b. As the temperature increases, the amount of people who use the town pool also increases.
    c. As farmers use more fertilizer, their output of tomatoes increases.

12. Rank the following equations by the steepness of their slope from lowest to highest. [LO A.3]
    a. $y = -3x + 9$
    b. $y = 4x + 2$
    c. $y = -0.5x + 4$

PART TWO

Supply and Demand

The four chapters in Part 2 will introduce you to ...

the basics of markets, which form the baseline for most economic analysis. Chapter 3 introduces supply and demand.

Anytime we go into a store and decide to buy something, we act on our demand for that good. The people who run the store figured out that it made sense for them to supply that good to us. The interaction between the forces of supply and demand determines the price we pay and how much is bought and sold.

The rest of the chapters in Part 2 will examine supply and demand to answer a variety of questions: Why do people rush to the store when Apple slashes the price of an iPhone? Why would the government ever want to set limits on prices in the market?

Together with Part 1, these chapters introduce the basic concepts of economic problem solving. To start, we've stripped the ideas down to their simplest form. These same concepts will return throughout the text, and we will build on them as we turn to different problems.

CHAPTER 3

Markets

LEARNING OBJECTIVES

LO 3.1   Identify the defining characteristics of a competitive market.
LO 3.2   Draw a demand curve and describe the external factors that determine demand.
LO 3.3   Distinguish between a shift in and a movement along the demand curve.
LO 3.4   Draw a supply curve and describe the external factors that determine supply.
LO 3.5   Distinguish between a shift in and a movement along the supply curve.
LO 3.6   Explain how supply and demand interact to drive markets to equilibrium.
LO 3.7   Evaluate the effect of changes in supply and demand on the equilibrium price and quantity.

Mobiles Go Global

For many people, a cell phone is on the list of things never to leave the house without, right up there with a wallet and keys. For better or worse, cell phones have become a fixture of everyday life.

It's hard to believe that as recently as the late 1990s, cell phones were a luxury. Before that, in the 1980s, they were big, heavy devices, seldom bought for personal use at all. In less than a quarter of a century, this expensive sci-fi technology became a relatively cheap, universal convenience. Today there are approximately 80 cell phones for every 100 people in Canada. There are almost as many cell-phone subscriptions (6.8 billion) as there are people on this Earth (seven billion)—and it took a little more than 20 years for that to happen. In 2013, there were some 96 cell-phone service subscriptions for every 100 people in the world.[1] The continent of Africa has 63.5 cell subscriptions per 100 people.[2] This phenomenal growth makes it easier to keep up with friends and family. It also connects small-town merchants to businesses in distant cities, opening up new economic possibilities.

How does a product move from expensive to cheap, from rare to commonplace, so quickly? The answer lies partly in the relationship between supply and demand. This chapter shows how the forces of supply and demand interact to determine the quantities and prices of goods that are bought and sold in competitive markets.

The basic story of how a new product takes hold is a familiar one. In the beginning, cell phones were expensive and rare. Over time, the

Tim Robberts/Getty Images

technology improved, the price dropped, the product caught on, and sales took off. Throughout this process of change, markets allow for ongoing communication between buyers and producers, using prices as a signal. Increases and decreases in price ensures that the quantity of a product that is available stays in balance with the quantity consumers want to buy.

To explain the leap in usage of cell phones over time, however, we need to go further than just price signals. Outside forces that influence supply and demand, such as changes in technology, fashion trends, and economic ups and downs, have driven that transformation. Markets have the remarkable ability to adjust to these changes without falling out of balance.

In this chapter, we'll step into the shoes of consumers and producers to examine the trade-offs they face. We'll see that the issues that drive supply and demand in the cell phone industry are not unique. In fact, the functioning of markets, as summarized in the theory of supply and demand, is the bedrock of almost everything in this book. Mastering this theory will help you to solve all kinds of problems, from how to price your product and find the cheapest gasoline to discovering the reasons for a shortage of hybrid cars.

Markets

In Chapter 2, we discussed the power of the *invisible hand* to coordinate complex economic interactions. The key feature of an economy organized by the invisible hand is that private individuals, rather than a centralized planning authority, make the decisions. Such an economy is often referred to as a **market economy**.

What Is a Market?

What do we mean by a *market*? The word might make you think of a physical location where buyers and sellers come together face-to-face—like a farmers' market or a mall. But people do not have to be physically near each other to make an exchange. For example, think of online retailers like Amazon.com or of fruit that is grown in South America but sold all over the world. The term **market** actually refers to the buyers and sellers who trade a particular good or service, not to a physical location.

Which buyers and sellers are included in the market depends on the context. The manager of a clothing store at your local mall might think about the market for T-shirts in terms of people who live locally and the other places they could buy T-shirts, like competing stores, garage sales, or online retailers. The CEO of a major clothing brand, on the other hand, might include garment factories in China and the fashion preferences of customers living all over the world in her idea of a market. Which boundaries are relevant depends on the scope of trades that are being made.

What Is a Competitive Market?

> LO 3.1 Identify the defining characteristics of a competitive market.

Making simplifying assumptions can help us zero in on important ideas. In this chapter, we will make a big simplifying assumption—that markets are *competitive*. A **competitive market** is one in which fully informed, price-taking buyers and sellers easily trade a standardized good or service.

Let's unpack this definition. Imagine you're driving up to an intersection where there is a gas station on each corner. This scenario will demonstrate the four important characteristics of a *perfectly* competitive market.

First, the gas sold by each station is the same—your car will run equally well regardless of where you fill your tank. This means that the gas being sold is a **standardized good.** In a competitive market, the good or service being bought and sold is standardized—any two units of it, no matter where they are purchased, have the same features and are interchangeable.

Second, the price at each gas station is prominently displayed on a big sign. As you drive by, you can immediately see how much a litre of each type of gas costs at each station. In a competitive market, you have *full information* about the price and features of the good being bought and sold.

Third, it's easy for you to choose any of the four gas stations at the intersection. The stations are very near each other and you don't have to have special equipment to fill up your tank or pay an entrance fee to get into the station. In competitive markets, there are no **transaction costs**—the costs incurred by buyer and seller in agreeing to and executing a sale of goods or services. Thus, in competitive markets, you don't have to pay anything for the privilege of buying or selling in the market. You can easily do business in this four-station market for gasoline.

Finally, we bet you'd find that a litre of gas costs the same at each station at the intersection. Why? Recall the third economists' question from Chapter 1: *How will others respond?* Assuming the stations are offering standardized gas, customers should be indifferent to buying from one station or another at a given price. If one raises its price, all the drivers will simply go to a station where the gas is cheaper. The gas station that raised prices will lose customers. For this reason, no individual seller has the power to change the market price. In economic terminology, a buyer or seller who cannot affect the market price is called a **price taker**.

The drivers going by are also price takers. If you try to negotiate a discount at one of the gas stations before filling your tank, you won't get far—the owner would rather wait and sell to other customers who will pay more. The price is the price; your choice is to take it or leave it. In competitive markets, both buyers and sellers are price takers.

By thinking about the gas stations at a single intersection, you have learned the four characteristics of perfectly competitive markets. Table 3-1 summarizes the four characteristics of a perfectly competitive market: a standardized good, full information, no transaction costs, and price-taking participants.

TABLE 3-1 FOUR CHARACTERISTICS OF PERFECTLY COMPETITIVE MARKETS

Standardized good	Any two units of the good have the same features and are interchangeable.
Full information	Market participants know everything about the price and features of the good.
No transaction costs	There is no cost to participating in exchanges in the market.
Participants are price takers	Neither buyers nor sellers have the power to affect the market price.

In reality, very few markets are *perfectly* competitive. Even gas stations at the same intersection might not be: maybe one can charge a few cents more per gallon because it uses gas with less ethanol or offers regular customers an attractive loyalty scheme or has a Tim Hortons to entice drivers. In future chapters, we'll spend a lot of time thinking about the different ways that markets in the real world are structured and why it matters when they fall short of perfect competition.

The market for cell phones is not perfectly competitive, either. Cell phones are not standardized goods—some models look cooler, have better cameras, or have access to different apps or calling plans. You may have been indifferent about which station to buy gas from, but you're unlikely to be completely indifferent when choosing between two different cell phones at the same price. Furthermore, the fact that there are a limited number of service providers means that sellers aren't always price takers. If only one network has good coverage in your area or offers an exclusive deal on a popular type of phone, it can get away with charging a premium.

So why assume perfect competition if markets in the real world are rarely perfectly competitive? The answer is that the simple model of competitive markets we will develop in this chapter leads us to useful insights, even in markets that aren't perfectly competitive. And taking the time now to make sure you understand perfect competition will better prepare you to understand why it matters when markets aren't perfectly competitive. As we go through this chapter we'll note some ways in which the real cell phone market departs from perfect competition. By the end of the chapter, we hope you'll agree that the simple model of perfect competition tells us a lot, if not everything, about how a real market works.

✓ CONCEPT CHECK

☐ What is a market? What are the characteristics of a competitive market? [LO 3.1]

☐ Why are participants in competitive markets called *price takers?* [LO 3.1]

Demand

Demand describes how much of something people are willing and able to buy under certain circumstances. Suppose someone approached you and asked if you would like a new cell phone. What would you answer? You might think, "Sure," but as a savvy person, you would probably first ask, "For how much?" Whether you want something (or how much of it you want) depends on how much you have to pay for it.

These days most people in the Canada have cell phones, but that hasn't been the case for very long. Let's assume for the sake of our model that cell phones are standardized—one model, with the same features and calling plans. Now, put yourself in the position of a consumer in the mid-1990s. Maybe you've seen cell phones advertised at $499 and think it's not worth it to you. As the price goes down over time to $399, and $299, you're still not tempted to buy it. At $199, you start to consider it. Then, the first time you see a cell phone advertised for less than $125, you decide to buy.

Different people bought their first cell phone at different prices: at any given time, at any given price, some people are willing to buy a phone and others aren't. If we add up all of these individual choices, we get overall *market demand.* The amount of a particular good that buyers in a market will purchase at a given price during a specified period is called the **quantity demanded**. For almost all goods, the lower the price, the higher the quantity demanded.

This inverse relationship between price and quantity demanded is so important that economists refer to it as the **law of demand**. The first requirement for the law of demand is the idea sometimes known as *ceteris paribus,* the Latin term for "all other things being the same." In other words, the law of demand says that when all else is held equal, quantity demanded rises as price falls. Economists frequently rely on the idea of *ceteris paribus* to isolate the effect of a single change in the economy. If all else is not held equal, it is very difficult to see the true effect of something like a price change, because it may be accompanied by other changes that also affect quantity demanded. For instance, studies show that the demand for cell phones increases with people's incomes. So when we see both incomes *and* prices rising at the same time, we cannot immediately predict what will happen to cell phone sales. When we talk about the law of demand, therefore, it is important to remember that we are assuming that nothing other than price changes.

The law of demand isn't a made-up law that economists have imposed on markets. Rather, it holds true because it describes the underlying reality of individual people's decisions. The key is to think about the *trade-offs* that people face when making the decision to buy.

What happens when the price of something falls? First, the benefit that you get from purchasing it remains the same, because the item itself is unchanged. But the opportunity cost has fallen, because when the price goes down you don't have to give up as many other purchases in order to get the item. When benefits stay the same and opportunity cost goes down, this trade-off suddenly starts to look a lot better. When the trade-off between costs and benefits tips toward benefits, more people will want to buy the good.

Of course, falling prices were not the only consideration in people's decisions to buy their first cell phone. Some might have decided to buy one when they got a pay raise at work. Others might have bought one at the point when most of their friends owned one. Incomes, expectations, and tastes all play a role; economists call these factors *non-price determinants* of demand. We'll discuss their potential effects later in this chapter. First, let's focus on the relationship between price and quantity demanded.

The Demand Curve

LO 3.2 Draw a demand curve and describe the external factors that determine demand.

The law of demand says that the quantity of cell phones demanded will be different at every price level. For this reason, it is often useful to represent demand as a table, called a **demand schedule**, which shows the quantities of a particular good or service that consumers are willing to purchase (demand) at various prices. Panel A of Figure 3-1 shows a hypothetical annual demand schedule for cell phones in Canada. (Remember, we're assuming that cell phones are a standardized good. This isn't quite right, but the basic principle holds true: when cell phone prices are lower, you're more likely to buy a new one.) The demand schedule assumes that factors other than price remain the same.

Panel B of Figure 3-1 shows another way to represent demand, by drawing each price–quantity combination from the demand schedule as a point on a graph. That graph, called a **demand curve**, visually displays the demand schedule. That is, it is a graph that shows the quantities of a particular good or service that consumers will demand at various prices. The demand curve also represents consumers' *willingness to buy:* it shows the highest amount consumers will pay for any given quantity.

On the demand curve, quantity goes on the *x*-axis (the horizontal axis) and price on the *y*-axis (the vertical axis). The result is a downward-sloping line that reflects the inverse relationship between price and quantity. The demand curve in Figure 3-1 represents exactly the same information as the demand schedule.

Since demand curves and other material in this chapter make extensive use of lines and linear equations, you may want to review those concepts in Appendix B, Math Essentials: Working with Linear Equations, which follows this chapter.

FIGURE 3-1

Demand Schedule and Demand Curve

(A) Demand schedule

Cell phones (millions)	Price ($)
5	180
10	160
15	140
20	120
25	100
30	80
35	60
40	40
45	20

This demand schedule shows the quantity of cell phones demanded each year at various prices. As prices decrease, consumers want to purchase more cell phones.

(B) Demand curve

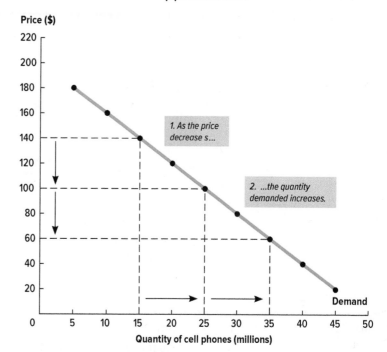

This demand curve is a graphic representation of the demand schedule for cell phones in Canada. Each entry in the demand schedule is plotted on this curve.

Determinants of Demand

The demand curve represents the relationship between price and quantity demanded *with everything else held constant.* If everything else is *not* held constant—that is, if one of the non-price factors that determines demand changes—the curve will shift.

The downward-sloping demand curve reflects the trade-offs that people face between (1) the benefit they expect to receive from a good and (2) the opportunity cost they face for buying it. Therefore, any factor that changes this balance at a given price will change people's willingness to buy and thus their purchasing decisions.

The non-price determinants of demand can be divided into five major categories: consumer preferences, the prices of related goods, incomes, expectations of future prices, and the number of buyers in the market. Table 3-2 summarizes the impact of each factor on demand. Each of these non-price determinants affects either the benefits or the opportunity cost of buying a good, even if the price of the good itself remains the same.

POTENTIALLY CONFUSING

Although the five determinants of demand include price-related issues such as the price of related goods and expectations about future prices, we refer to them as *non-price determinants* to differentiate them from the effect of the current price of the good on demand for that good.

TABLE 3-2 DETERMINANTS OF DEMAND

Determinant	Examples of an increase in demand	Examples of a decrease in demand
Consumer preferences	A Buy Canadian ad campaign appeals to national pride, increasing the demand for Canadian-made sneakers.	An outbreak of *E. coli* decreases the demand for spinach.
Prices of related goods	A decrease in the price of hot dogs increases the demand for relish, a complementary good.	A decrease in taxi fares decreases the demand for subway rides, a substitute good.
Incomes	An economic downturn lowers incomes, increasing the demand for ground beef, an inferior good.	An economic downturn lowers incomes, decreasing the demand for steak, a normal good.
Expectations	A hurricane destroys part of the world papaya crop, causing expectations that prices will rise and increasing the current demand for papayas.	An announcement that a new smartphone soon will be released decreases the demand for the current model.
Number of buyers	An increase in life expectancy increases the demand for nursing homes and medical care.	A falling birthrate decreases the demand for diapers.

Consumer preferences are the personal likes and dislikes that make buyers more or less inclined to purchase a good. We don't need to know *why* people like what they like or to agree with their preferences; we just need to know that these likes and dislikes influence their purchases. At any given price, some consumers will get more enjoyment (i.e., benefit) out of a cell phone than others, simply based on how much they like talking to friends, or whether they use their phones for work, or any number of other personal preferences.

Some consumer preferences are fairly constant across time, such as those that arise from personality traits or cultural attitudes and beliefs. For example, a recluse may have little desire for a cell phone, while an on-the-go executive may find a cell phone (or two) to be essential. Other preferences will change over time, in response to external events or fads. For instance, it's more useful to own a cell phone when all your friends already have one.

Prices of Related Goods

Another factor that affects the demand for a particular good is the prices of related goods. There are two kinds of related goods—substitutes and complements.

We say that goods are **substitutes** when they serve similar-enough purposes that a consumer might purchase one in place of the other—for example, rice and pasta. If the price of rice doubles while the price of pasta stays the same, demand for pasta will increase. That's because the opportunity cost of pasta has decreased: you can buy less rice for the same amount of money, so you give up less potential rice when you buy pasta. If the two goods are quite similar, we call them *close substitutes*. Similar fishes, such as salmon and trout, might be considered close substitutes.

For many Canadians deciding whether to buy their first cell phone, the nearest substitute would be a landline phone. Cell phones and landlines are not very close substitutes. You can use them for the same purposes at home or the office, but only one of them can go for a walk with you. Still, if the price of landline phone service suddenly skyrocketed, we can be sure that change would increase the demand for cell phones.

In fact, the very high cost of landline phone services in many developing countries is one reason cell phones spread very quickly. In Canada, almost every household had a landline phone before it had a cell phone. In many poor countries landlines are so expensive that very few people can afford one. That's why cell phones are often called a *leapfrog technology*: people go straight from no phone to a cell phone, hopping over an entire stage of older technology.

Goods that are consumed together—so that purchasing one will make a consumer more likely to purchase the other—are called **complements**. Peanut butter and jelly, cereal and milk, cars and gasoline are all complements. If the price of one of the two goods increases, demand for the other will likely decrease. Why? As consumers purchase less of the first good, they will want less of the other to go with it. Conversely, if the price of one of the two goods declines, demand for the other will likely increase. For example, when the prices of new cell phones fall, consumers will be more likely to buy new accessories to go with them.

Incomes

Not surprisingly, the amount of income people earn affects their demand for goods and services: The bigger your paycheque, the more money you can afford to spend on the things you want. The smaller your paycheque, the more you have to cut back. Many goods are **normal goods**, meaning that an increase in income causes an increase in demand and a decrease in income causes a decrease in demand. For most people, cell phones are a normal good. If someone cannot afford a cell phone, she's more likely to buy one when her income rises. If someone already has a cell phone, she's more likely to upgrade to a newer, fancier cell phone when her income rises.

For some goods, called **inferior goods**, the opposite relationship holds: as income increases, demand decreases. Typically, people replace inferior goods with more expensive and appealing substitutes when their incomes rise. For many people, inexpensive grocery items like instant noodles, some canned foods, and generic store brands might be inferior goods. When their incomes rise, people replace these goods with fresher, more expensive ingredients. Decreases in income occur for many people during economic downturns; thus, the demand for inferior goods reflects the overall health of the economy. For an example, see the Real Life box, Can Instant-Noodle Sales Predict a Recession?

REAL LIFE

Can Instant-Noodle Sales Predict a Recession?

If you were to open a typical university student's kitchen cupboard, what would you find? Many students rely on a decidedly unglamorous food item: ramen instant noodles. Packed with cheap calories, this tasty snack is famously inexpensive.

Ramen noodles are an example of an inferior good. When people's budgets are tight (as are those of most students), these noodles sell well. When incomes rise, ramen sales drop and more expensive foods replace them.

In Thailand, ramen noodles have even been used as an indicator of overall economic health. The Mama Noodles Index tracks sales of a popular brand of instant ramen noodles. Because the demand for inferior goods increases when incomes go down, an increase in ramen sales could signal a downturn in incomes and an oncoming recession. In fact, observers of the Thai economy say that the Mama Noodles Index does a pretty good job of reflecting changing economic conditions.

Even the demand for inferior goods may decrease during severe economic downturns, however. Although the Mama Noodles Index has risen as expected when the Thai economy falters, the index unexpectedly dropped 15 percent during the deep recession of early 2009.

So are instant noodles an inferior good or a normal good? In Thailand, the answer may depend on who you are or how severely your income has dropped. For the middle class, who choose between ramen and more expensive foods, ramen may indeed be an inferior good. For the poor, whose choice more likely is whether or not they will get enough to eat, ramen may be a normal good. When their incomes rise they may buy more ramen; when their incomes fall, even noodles may be a luxury.

Sources: "Using their noodles," Associated Press, September 5, 2005, http://www.theage.com.au/news/world/using-their-noodles/2005/09/04/1125772407287.html; "Downturn bites into instant-noodle market as customers tighten belts," *The Nation*, March 20, 2009, http://www.nationmultimedia.com/business/Downturn-bites-into-instant-noodle-market-as-custo-30098402.html.

Expectations

Changes in consumers' expectations about the future—especially future prices—can also affect demand. If consumers expect prices to fall in the future, they may postpone a purchase until a later date, causing current demand to decrease. Think about waiting to buy a new cell phone until it goes on sale, or holding off on purchasing a smartphone in the hope that the next model will be cheaper and faster than the prior one. When prices are expected to drop in the future, demand decreases.

Conversely, if consumers expect prices to rise in the future, they may wish to purchase a good immediately, to avoid a higher price. This reasoning often occurs in speculative markets, like the stock market or sometimes the housing market. Buyers purchase stock or a house expecting prices to rise, so they can sell at a profit. In these markets, then, demand increases when prices are low and are expected to rise.

Number of Buyers

The demand curve represents the demand of a particular number of potential buyers. In general, an increase in the number of potential buyers in a market will increase demand; a decrease in the number of buyers will decrease it. Major population shifts, like an increase in immigration or a drop in the birthrate, can create nationwide changes in demand. As the number of teenagers and college students increases, the demand for cell phones increases, too.

Shifts in the Demand Curve

LO 3.3 Distinguish between a shift in and a movement along the demand curve.

What happens to the demand curve when one of the five non-price determinants of demand changes? The entire demand curve shifts, either to the right or to the left. The shift is horizontal rather than vertical, because non-price determinants affect the quantity demanded at *each* price. The quantity demanded at a given price is now higher (or lower), so the point on the curve corresponding to that price is now further right (or left).

Consider what happens, for example, when the economy is growing and people's incomes are rising. The price of cell phones does not necessarily change, but more people will choose to buy a new one at any given price, causing quantity demanded to be higher at every possible price. Panel A of Figure 3-2 shows the resulting shift of the demand curve to the right, from D_A to D_B. In contrast, if the economy falls into a recession and people begin pinching pennies, quantity demanded will decrease at every price, and the curve will shift to the left, from D_A to D_C.

It is important to distinguish between these *shifts* in demand, which move the entire curve, and *movements along* a given demand curve. Remember this key point: s*hifts in the demand curve are caused by changes in the non-price determinants of demand*. A recession, for example, would lower incomes and move the whole demand curve left. When we say "demand decreases," this is what we are talking about.

In contrast, suppose that the price of phones increases but everything else stays the same—that is, there are no changes in the non-price determinants of demand. Because the demand curve describes the quantity consumers will demand at any possible price, not just the current market price, we don't have to shift the curve to figure out what happens when the price goes up. Instead, we simply look at a different point on the curve that describes what is actually happening in the market right now.

To find the quantity that consumers will want to purchase at this new price, we move along the existing demand curve from the old price to the new one. If, for instance, the price of cell phones increases, we find the new quantity demanded by moving up along the demand curve to the new price point, as shown in panel B of Figure 3-2. The price change does not shift the curve itself, because the curve already describes what consumers will do at any price.

To summarize, panel A of Figure 3-2 shows a *shift in demand* as the result of a change in the non-price determinants; panel B shows a *movement along the demand curve* as the result of a change in price.

Economists use very specific terminology to distinguish between a shift in the demand curve and movement along the demand curve. We say that a change in one of the non-price determinants of demand causes an *increase in demand* or *decrease in demand*—that is, a shift of the entire demand curve. To distinguish this from movement along the demand curve, we say that a change in price causes an *increase in quantity demanded* or *decrease in the quantity demanded*. Just keep in mind that a "change in demand" is different from a "change in the quantity demanded." Observing this seemingly small difference in terminology prevents a great deal of confusion.

Understanding the effects of changes in both price and the non-price determinants of demand is a key tool for businesspeople and policymakers. Suppose you are in charge of the Cell Phone Manufacturers' Association, an industry lobby group, and your members want to spur demand for phones. One idea might be to start an advertising campaign. If you understand the determinants of demand, you know that an advertising campaign aims to change consumer preferences, increasing the real or perceived benefits of owning a cell phone. In other words, a successful advertising campaign would shift the demand curve for cell phones to the right. Similarly, if the government is considering a tax cut to stimulate the economy, you know that a tax cut increases consumers' disposable incomes, increasing the demand for all normal goods. In other words, you are hoping that the resulting increase in incomes will shift the demand curve for cell phones to the right.

FIGURE 3-2

Movement Along the Demand Curve versus Shifts in the Demand Curve

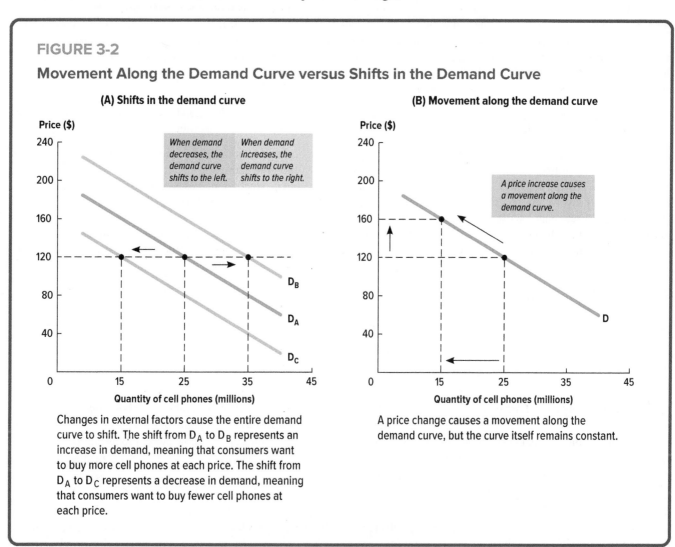

Changes in external factors cause the entire demand curve to shift. The shift from D_A to D_B represents an increase in demand, meaning that consumers want to buy more cell phones at each price. The shift from D_A to D_C represents a decrease in demand, meaning that consumers want to buy fewer cell phones at each price.

A price change causes a movement along the demand curve, but the curve itself remains constant.

✓ CONCEPT CHECK

☐ What are the five determinants of demand? [LO 3.2]
☐ What is the difference between a change in quantity and a change in quantity demanded? [LO 3.3]

Supply

We've discussed the factors that determine how many phones consumers want to buy at a given price. But are cell phone producers necessarily willing to sell that many? The concept of *supply* describes how much of a good or service producers will offer for sale under given circumstances. The **quantity supplied** is the amount of a particular good or service that producers will offer for sale at a given price during a specified period.

As with demand, we can find overall market supply by adding up the individual decisions of each producer. Imagine you own a factory that can produce cell phones or other consumer electronics. If the price of cell phones is $110, you might decide there's good money to be made and use your entire factory space to produce cell phones. If the price is only $80, you might produce some cell phones but decide it will be more profitable to devote part of your factory to producing laptop computers. If the cell phone price drops to $55, you might decide you'd make more money by producing only laptops. Each producer will have a different price point at which it decides it's worthwhile to supply cell phones. This rule—all else held equal, quantity supplied increases as price increases, and vice versa—is called the **law of supply**.

(In reality, it's costly to switch a factory from making cell phones to laptops or other goods. However, the simple version illustrates a basic truth: the higher the price of a good, the more of that good producers will want to sell.)

As with demand, supply varies with price because the decision to produce a good is about the *trade-off* between the benefit the producer will receive from selling the good and the opportunity cost of the time and resources that go into producing it. When the market price goes up and all other factors remain constant, the benefit of production increases relative to the opportunity cost, and the trade-off involved in production makes it more favourable to produce more. For instance, if the price of phones goes up and the prices of raw materials stay the same, existing phone producers may open new factories and new companies may start looking to enter the cell phone market. The same holds true across other industries. If air travellers seem willing to pay higher prices, airlines will increase the frequency of flights, add new routes, and buy new planes so they can carry more passengers. When prices drop, they cut back their flight schedules and cancel their orders for new planes.

The Supply Curve

LO 3.4 Draw a supply curve and describe the external factors that determine supply.

Like demand, supply can be represented as either a table or a graph. A **supply schedule** is a table that shows the quantities of a particular good or service that producers will supply at various prices. A **supply curve** is a graph of the information in the supply schedule. Just as the demand curve showed consumers' willingness to buy, so the supply curve shows producers' *willingness to sell:* it shows the minimum price producers must receive to supply any given quantity. Figure 3-3 shows Canadian cell phone providers' supply schedule and their supply curve for cell phones.

Determinants of Supply

The law of supply describes how the quantity that producers are willing to supply changes as price changes. But what determines the quantity supplied at any given price? As with demand, a number of non-price factors determine the opportunity cost of production and therefore producers' willingness to supply a good or service. *When a non-price determinant of supply changes, the entire supply curve will shift.* Such shifts reflect a change in the quantity of goods supplied at *every* price.

The non-price determinants of supply can be divided into five major categories: prices of related goods, technology, prices of inputs, expectations, and the number of sellers. Each of these factors determines the opportunity cost of production relative to a given benefit (i.e., the price) and therefore the trade-off that producers face. Table 3-3 shows how the supply of various products responds to changes in each determinant.

FIGURE 3-3

Supply Schedule and the Supply Curve

(A) Supply schedule

Cell phones (millions)	Price ($)
45	180
40	160
35	140
30	120
25	100
20	80
15	60
10	40
5	20

This supply schedule shows the quantity of cell phones supplied each year at various prices. As prices decrease, suppliers want to produce fewer cell phones.

(B) Supply curve

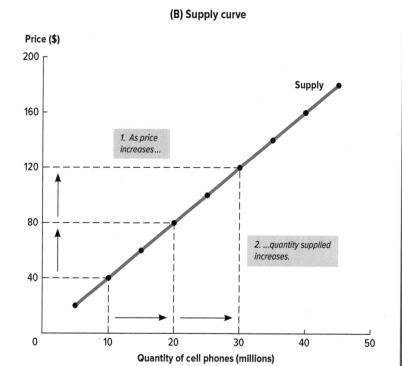

This supply curve is a graphic representation of the supply schedule for cell phones in Canada. It shows the quantity of cell phones that suppliers will produce at various prices.

TABLE 3-3   DETERMINANTS OF SUPPLY

Determinant	Examples of an increase in supply	Examples of a decrease in supply
Price of related goods	The price of gas rises, so an automaker increases its production of smaller, more fuel-efficient cars.	The price of clean energy production falls, so the power company reduces the amount of power it supplies using coal-power plants.
Technology	The installation of robots increases productivity and lowers costs; the supply of goods increases.	New technology allows corn to be made into ethanol, so farmers plant more corn and fewer soybeans; the supply of soybeans decreases.
Prices of inputs	A drop in the price of tomatoes decreases the production cost of salsa; the supply of salsa increases.	An increase in the minimum wage increases labour costs at food factories; the supply of processed food decreases.
Expectations	Housing prices are expected to rise, so builders increase production; the supply of houses increases.	New research points to the health benefits of eating papayas, leading to expectations that the demand for papayas will rise. More farmers plant papayas, increasing the supply.

Determinant	Examples of an increase in supply	Examples of a decrease in supply
Number of sellers	Subsidies make the production of corn more profitable, so more farmers plant corn; the supply of corn increases.	New licensing fees make operating a restaurant more expensive; some small restaurants close, decreasing the supply of restaurants.

Prices of Related Goods

Return to your factory, where you can produce either cell phones or laptops. Just as you chose to produce more laptops and fewer cell phones when the price of cell phones dropped, you would do the same if the price of laptops increased while the price of cell phones stayed constant.

The price of related goods determines supply because it affects the opportunity cost of production. When you choose to produce cell phones, you forgo the profits you would have earned from producing something else. If the price of that something else increases, the amount you forgo in profits also increases. For instance, imagine a farmer who can grow wheat or corn (or other crops, for that matter) on his land. If the price of corn increases, the quantity of wheat (the substitute crop) he is willing to grow falls, because each acre he devotes to wheat is one fewer acre he can use to grow corn.

Technology

Improved technology enables firms to produce more efficiently, using fewer resources to make a given product. Doing so lowers production costs, increasing the quantity producers are willing to supply at each price.

Improved technology has played a huge role in the changing popularity of cell phones. As technological innovation in the construction of screens, batteries, and mobile networks, and in the processing of electronic data has leapt forward, the cost of producing a useful, consumer-friendly cell phone has plummeted. As a result, producers are now willing to supply more cell phones at lower prices.

Prices of Inputs

The prices of the inputs used to produce a good are an important part of its cost. When the prices of inputs increase, production costs rise and the quantity of the product that producers are willing to supply at any given price decreases.

For example, small amounts of silver and gold are used inside cell phones. When the prices of these precious metals rise, the cost of manufacturing each cell phone increases, and the total number of units that producers collectively are willing to make at any given price goes down. Conversely, when input prices fall, supply increases.

Expectations

Suppliers' expectations about prices in the future also affect quantity supplied. For example, when the price of real estate is expected to rise in the future, more real estate developers will wait to embark on construction projects, decreasing the supply of houses in the near future. When expectations change and real estate prices are projected to fall in the future, many of those projects will be rushed to completion, causing the supply of houses to rise.

Number of Sellers

The market supply curve represents the quantities of a product that a particular number of producers will supply at various prices in a given market. This means that the number of sellers in the market is considered to be one of the fixed parts of the supply curve. We've already seen that the sellers in the market will decide to supply more if the price of a good is higher. This does not mean that the number of sellers will change based on price in the short run.

There are, however, non-price factors that cause the number of sellers to change in a market and move the supply curve. For example, suppose cell phone producers must meet strict licensing requirements. If those licensing requirements are dropped, more companies may enter the market, willing to supply a certain number of cell phones at each price. These additional phones must be added to the number of cell phones that existing producers are already willing to supply at each price point.

In 1980, this cutting-edge technology cost $4,000.

C. Borland/Photolink/Getty Images

Shifts in the Supply Curve

LO 3.5 Distinguish between a shift in and a movement along the supply curve.

Just as with demand, changes in price cause suppliers to move to a different point on the same supply curve, while changes in the non-price determinants of supply shift the supply curve itself. A change in a non-price determinant increases or decreases *supply,* while a change in price increases or decreases the *quantity supplied.*

A change in one of the non-price determinants increases or decreases the supply at any given price. These shifts are shown in panel A of Figure 3-4. An increase in supply shifts the curve to the right. A decrease in supply shifts the curve to the left. For instance, an improvement in battery technology that decreases the cost of producing cell phones will shift the entire supply curve to the right, from S_A to S_B, so that the quantity of phones supplied at every price is higher than before. Conversely, an increase in the price of the gold needed for cell phones raises production costs, shifting the supply curve to the left, from S_A to S_C.

As with demand, we differentiate these shifts in the supply curve from a movement along the supply curve, which is shown in panel B of Figure 3-4. If the price of cell phones changes, but the non-price determinants of supply stay the same, we find the new quantity supplied by moving along the supply curve to the new price point.

FIGURE 3-4

Movement Along the Supply Curve versus Shifts in the Supply Curve

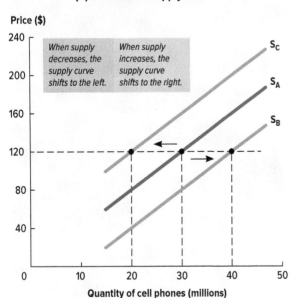

(A) Shifts in the supply curve

When supply decreases, the supply curve shifts to the left. When supply increases, the supply curve shifts to the right.

Changes in external factors cause the entire supply curve to shift. The shift from S_A to S_B represents an increase in supply, meaning that producers are willing to supply more cell phones at each price. The shift from S_A to S_C represents a decrease in supply, meaning that producers are willing to supply fewer cell phones at each price.

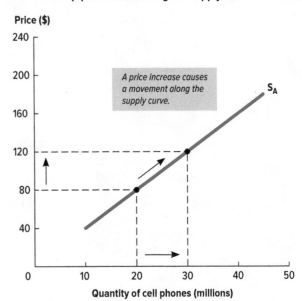

(B) Movement along the supply curve

A price increase causes a movement along the supply curve.

A price change causes a movement along the supply curve, but the curve itself remains constant.

✓ CONCEPT CHECK

☐ What does the law of supply say about the relationship between price and quantity supplied? [LO 3.4]

☐ In which direction does the supply curve shift when the price of inputs increases? [LO 3.5]

Market Equilibrium

We've discussed the factors that influence the quantities supplied and demanded by producers and consumers. To find out what actually happens in the market, however, we need to combine these concepts. The prices and quantities of the goods that are exchanged in the real world depend on the *interaction* of supply with demand.

Bear with us for a moment as we point out the obvious: there is no sale without a purchase. You can't sell something unless someone buys it. Although this point may be obvious, the implication for markets is profound. When markets work well, the quantity supplied exactly equals the quantity demanded.

Graphically, this convergence of supply with demand happens at the point where the demand curve intersects the supply curve, a point called the market **equilibrium**. The price at this point is called the **equilibrium price**, and the quantity at this point is called the **equilibrium quantity**. We can think of this intersection, where quantity supplied equals quantity demanded, as the point at which buyers and sellers agree on the quantity of a good they are willing to exchange at a given price. At higher prices, sellers want to sell more than buyers want to buy. At lower prices, buyers want to buy more than sellers are willing to sell. Because every seller finds a buyer at the equilibrium price and quantity, and no one is left standing around with extra goods or an empty shopping cart, the equilibrium price is sometimes called the *market-clearing price*.

In reality, things don't always work so smoothly: short-run *friction* sometimes slows the process of reaching equilibrium, even in well-functioning markets. As a result, smart businesspeople may hold some inventory for future sale, and consumers may need to shop around for specific items. On the whole, though, the concept of equilibrium is very accurate (and important) in describing how markets function.

Figure 3-5 shows the market equilibrium for cell phones in Canada. It was constructed by combining the market supply and demand curves shown in Figures 3-1 and 3-3. In this market, the equilibrium price is $100, and the equilibrium quantity supplied and demanded is 30 million phones.

FIGURE 3-5

Market Equilibrium in the Canadian Market for Cell Phones

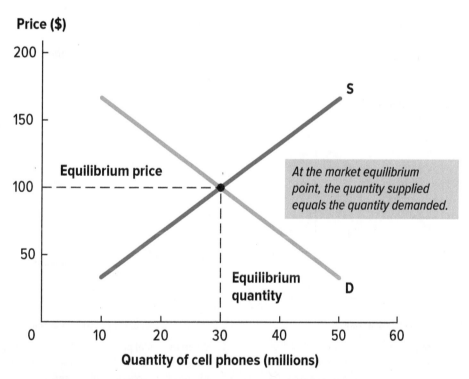

The point where the supply curve intersects the demand curve is called the equilibrium point. In this example, the equilibrium price is $100, and the equilibrium quantity is 30 million cell phones.
At this point, consumers are willing to buy exactly as many cell phones as producers are willing to sell.

Reaching Equilibrium

LO 3.6 Explain how supply and demand interact to drive markets to equilibrium.

How does a market reach equilibrium? Do sellers know intuitively what price to charge? No. Instead, they tend to set prices by trial and error, or by past experience with customers. The incentives buyers and sellers face will naturally drive the market toward equilibrium, as sellers raise or lower their prices in response to customers' behaviour.

Figure 3-6 shows two graphs, one in which the starting price is above the equilibrium price and the other in which it is below the equilibrium price. In panel A, we imagine that cell phone suppliers think they'll be able to charge $160 for a cell phone, so they produce 40 million phones, but they find that consumers will buy only 10 million. (We can read the quantities demanded and supplied at a price of $160 from the demand and supply curves.) When the quantity supplied is higher than the quantity demanded, we say that there is a **surplus** of phones, or an **excess quantity supplied**. Manufacturers are stuck holding extra phones in their warehouses; they want to sell that stock and must reduce the price to attract more customers. They have an incentive to keep lowering the price until quantity demanded increases to reach quantity supplied.

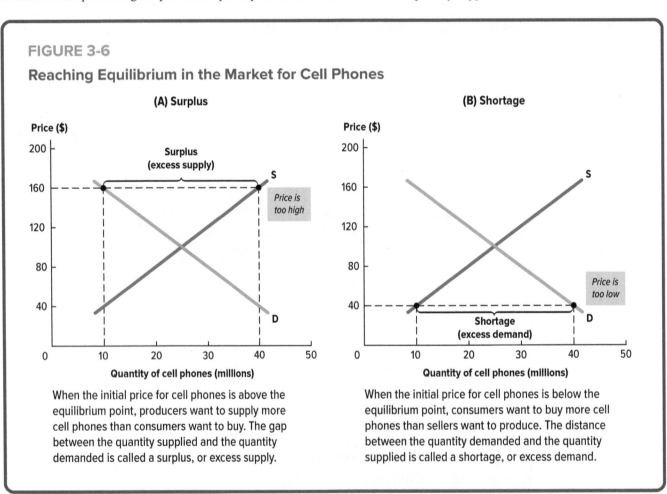

FIGURE 3-6

Reaching Equilibrium in the Market for Cell Phones

(A) Surplus

When the initial price for cell phones is above the equilibrium point, producers want to supply more cell phones than consumers want to buy. The gap between the quantity supplied and the quantity demanded is called a surplus, or excess supply.

(B) Shortage

When the initial price for cell phones is below the equilibrium point, consumers want to buy more cell phones than sellers want to produce. The distance between the quantity demanded and the quantity supplied is called a shortage, or excess demand.

In panel B of Figure 3-6, we imagine that cell phone producers make the opposite mistake—they think they'll be able to charge only $40 per phone. They make only 10 million cell phones, but discover that consumers actually are willing to buy 40 million cell phones at that price. When the quantity demanded is higher than the quantity supplied, we say there is a **shortage**, or **excess quantity demanded**. Producers will see long lines of people waiting to buy the few available cell phones and will quickly realize that they could make more money by charging a higher price. They have an incentive to increase the price until quantity demanded decreases to equal quantity supplied and no one is left standing in line.

Thus, at any price above or below the equilibrium price, sellers face an incentive to raise or lower prices. No one needs to engineer the market equilibrium or share secret information about what price to charge. Instead, money-making incentives drive the market toward the equilibrium price, at which there is neither a surplus nor a shortage. The Real Life box, Labour Shortage in the Canadian IT Industry, describes a case in which an increase in the market wage rate (which is the price for labour) solved the problem of shortage.

REAL LIFE

Labour Shortage in Canadian IT industry

In 2015, 811,200 ICT professionals were employed in Canada. But Canada is heading for a looming shortage of about 182,000 IT professionals over the next five years. Several factors are creating this shortage. There are not enough IT graduates coming out of the postsecondary sector to meet the market demand. Fast pace of the technological changes in the IT sector is also creating skill mismatches. Increased international competition for IT graduates and an aging workforce are two other factors. Currently there are not enough youth attracted to IT professions. Only 5 percent of IT jobs are held by youth. But market will eventually take care of the problem. Some IT jobs will be supplied by outsourcing, the immigration system will fill in some of the shortages by attracting internationally trained IT professionals, and domestic market wages will increase. These three events together will clear the market. The higher wage will eventually attract more Canadian youth to take up IT as a profession and will also help Canada to attract IT professionals from international market.

Sources: http://www.itworldcanada.com/article/canada-needs-182000-people-to-fill-these-it-positions-by-2019/287535; http://www.parl.gc.ca/content/hoc/committee/411/huma/reports/rp5937523/humarp09/humarp09-e.pdf; http://www.itbusiness.ca/blog/canadas-it-labour-shortage-challenges-and-opportunities/50250

Changes in Equilibrium

> **LO 3.7** Evaluate the effect of changes in supply and demand on the equilibrium price and quantity.

We've seen what happens to the supply and demand curves when a non-price factor changes. Because the equilibrium price and quantity are determined by the interaction of supply and demand, a shift in either curve will also change the market equilibrium. Some changes will cause only the demand curve to shift; some, only the supply curve. Some changes will affect both the supply and demand curves.

To determine the effect on market equilibrium of a change in a non-price factor, ask yourself a few questions:

1. Does the change affect demand? If so, does demand increase or decrease?
2. Does the change affect supply? If so, does supply increase or decrease?
3. How does the combination of changes in supply and demand affect the equilibrium price and quantity?

HINT

Remember, when we say that supply or demand increases or decreases we're referring to a *shift in the entire curve,* not a movement along it, which is a change in quantity demanded.

Shifts in Demand

We suggested earlier that landline service is a *substitute* for cell phones and that if the price of landline phone service suddenly skyrocketed, demand for cell phones would increase. In other words, the demand curve shifts to the right. The price of landline service probably doesn't affect the supply of cell phones, because it doesn't change the costs or expectations that cell phone manufacturers face. So the supply curve stays put. Figure 3-7 shows the effect of the increase in landline price on the market equilibrium for cell phones. Because the new demand curve intersects the supply curve at a different point, the equilibrium price and quantity change. The new equilibrium price is $120, and the new equilibrium quantity is 35 million.

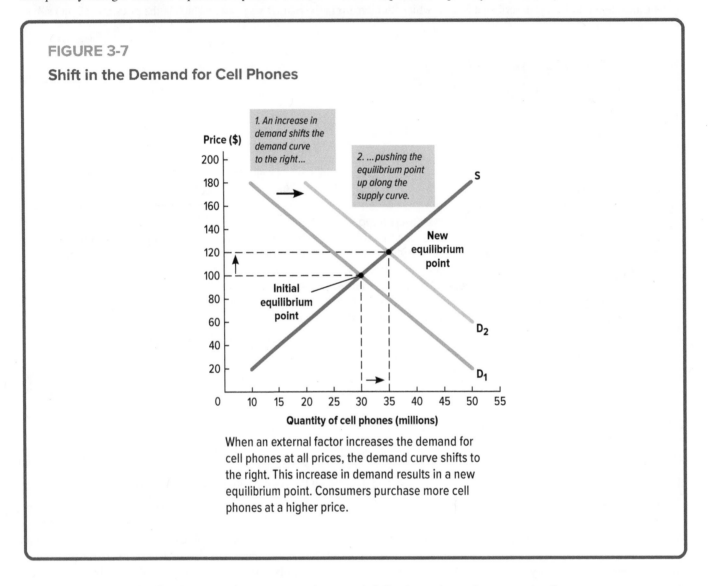

FIGURE 3-7

Shift in the Demand for Cell Phones

When an external factor increases the demand for cell phones at all prices, the demand curve shifts to the right. This increase in demand results in a new equilibrium point. Consumers purchase more cell phones at a higher price.

We can summarize this effect in terms of the three questions to ask following a change in a non-price factor:

1. *Does demand increase/decrease?* Yes, the change in the price of landline phone service increases demand for cell phones at every price.

2. *Does supply increase/decrease?* No, the change in the price of landline phone service does not affect any of the non-price determinants of supply. The supply curve stays where it is.

3. *How does the combination of changes in supply and demand affect equilibrium price and quantity?* The increase in demand shifts the demand curve to the right, pushing the equilibrium to a higher point on the stationary supply curve. The new point at which supply and demand meet represents a price of $120 and a quantity of 35 million phones.

> To improve your understanding of shifts in demand, try the online interactive graphing tutorial.

Shifts in Supply

What would happen if a breakthrough in battery technology enabled cell phone manufacturers to construct phones with the same battery life for less money? Once again, asking *How will others respond?* helps us predict the market response. We can see that the new technology does not have much impact on demand: customers probably have no idea how much the batteries in their phones cost to make, nor do they care as long as battery life stays the same. However, cheaper batteries definitely decrease production costs, increasing the number of phones manufacturers are willing to supply at any given price. So the demand curve stays where it is, and the supply curve shifts to the right. Figure 3-8 shows the shift in supply and the new equilibrium point. The new supply curve intersects the demand curve at a new equilibrium point, representing a price of $80 and a quantity of 35 million phones.

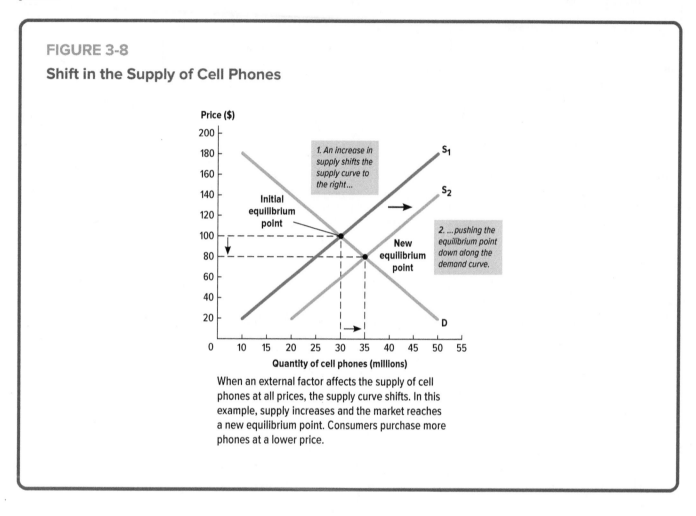

FIGURE 3-8

Shift in the Supply of Cell Phones

When an external factor affects the supply of cell phones at all prices, the supply curve shifts. In this example, supply increases and the market reaches a new equilibrium point. Consumers purchase more phones at a lower price.

Once again, we can analyze the effect of the change in battery technology on the market for cell phones in three steps:

1. *Does demand increase/decrease?* No, the non-price determinants of demand are not affected by battery technology.

2. *Does supply increase/decrease?* Yes, supply increases because the new battery technology lowers production costs.

3. *How does the combination of changes in supply and demand affect equilibrium price and quantity?* The increase in supply shifts the supply curve to the right, pushing the equilibrium to a lower point on the stationary demand curve. The new equilibrium price and quantity are $80 and 35 million phones.

> To improve your understanding of shifts in supply, try the online interactive graphing tutorial.

Table 3-4 summarizes the effect of some other changes in demand or supply on the equilibrium price and quantity.

Shifts in Both Demand and Supply

In our discussion so far, we've covered examples in which only demand or supply shifted. However, it's possible that factors that shift demand (such as a hike in landline cost) and supply (such as an improvement in battery technology) in the market for cell phones could happen at the same time. It's also possible that a single change could affect both supply and demand.

TABLE 3-4   EFFECT OF CHANGES IN DEMAND OR SUPPLY ON THE EQUILIBRIUM PRICE AND QUANTITY

Example of change in demand or supply	Effect on equilibrium price and quantity	Shift in curve
A successful Buy Canadian advertising campaign increases the demand for Tim Hortons coffee.	The demand curve shifts to the right. The equilibrium price and quantity increase.	
An outbreak of *E. coli* reduces the demand for spinach.	The demand curve shifts to the left. The equilibrium price and quantity decrease.	
The use of robots decreases production costs.	The supply curve shifts to the right. The equilibrium price decreases, and the equilibrium quantity increases.	
An increase in the minimum wage increases labour costs.	The supply curve shifts to the left. The equilibrium price increases, and the equilibrium quantity decreases.	

For instance, suppose that in addition to reducing the cost of production, the new battery technology makes cell phone batteries last longer. We already know that cheaper batteries will increase supply. As we saw before with increases in supply, price decreases while the quantity increases. Asking *How will consumers respond?* allows us to see that the improvement in battery life will also increase demand, because longer-lasting batteries will make a cell phone more valuable to consumers at any price. As a result, both the demand curve and the supply curve shift to the right. Panels A and B of Figure 3-9 both show that the effect of a double change is a new equilibrium point at a higher price and a higher quantity.

Even without looking at a graph, we could have predicted that in this case the equilibrium *quantity* would rise. Increases in demand and increases in supply both independently lead to a higher equilibrium quantity—and the combination will certainly do so as well. Without more information, however, we cannot predict the change in equilibrium *price*. Holding all else equal, an increase in demand leads to an increase in price, but an increase in supply leads to a decrease in price. To find the net effect on equilibrium price, we would have to know whether the shift in demand outweighs the shift in supply shown in panel A of Figure 3-9, or the opposite, which is shown in panel B.

FIGURE 3-9

Shifts in Both Demand and Supply

An increase in supply and demand shifts both curves to the right, resulting in a higher quantity traded. However, the direction of the price shift depends on whether supply or demand increases more.

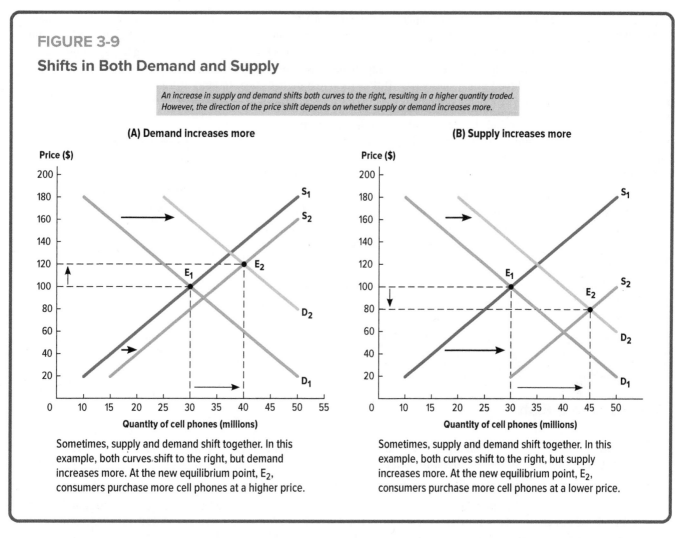

(A) Demand increases more

Sometimes, supply and demand shift together. In this example, both curves shift to the right, but demand increases more. At the new equilibrium point, E_2, consumers purchase more cell phones at a higher price.

(B) Supply increases more

Sometimes, supply and demand shift together. In this example, both curves shift to the right, but supply increases more. At the new equilibrium point, E_2, consumers purchase more cell phones at a lower price.

We can state this idea more generally: when supply and demand shift together, it is possible to predict *either* the direction of the change in quantity *or* the direction of the change in price without knowing how much the curves shift. Table 3-5 shows some rules you can use to predict the outcome of these shifts in supply and demand. When supply and demand move in the *same* direction, we can predict the direction of the change in quantity but not the direction of the change in price. When supply and demand move in *opposite* directions, the change in price is predictable but the change in quantity is not.

TABLE 3-5   PREDICTING CHANGES IN PRICE AND QUANTITY WHEN SUPPLY AND DEMAND CHANGE SIMULTANEOUSLY

Supply change	Demand change	Price change	Quantity change
Decrease	Decrease	?	↓
Decrease	Increase	↑	?
Increase	Increase	?	↑
Increase	Decrease	↓	?

Thinking about the intuition behind these rules may help you to remember them. Any time you are considering a situation in which supply and demand shift at the same time, ask yourself, *What do buyers and sellers agree on?* For instance, when both supply and demand increase, buyers and sellers agree that at any given price, the quantity they are willing to exchange is higher. The reverse is true when both supply and demand decrease: buyers and sellers agree that at a given price, the quantity they are willing to exchange is lower.

Applying this reasoning to opposite shifts in supply and demand—when one increases but the other decreases—is trickier. To find out what buyers and sellers agree on, try rephrasing what it means for demand to increase. One way to say it is that consumers are willing to buy a *higher* quantity at the *same* price. Another way to say it is that consumers are willing to pay a *higher* price to buy the *same* quantity. So, when demand increases and supply decreases, buyers are willing to pay more for the same quantity; also, sellers are willing to sell the same quantity only if they receive a higher price. In other words, they can agree on a higher price at any given quantity. We can therefore predict that the equilibrium price will increase.

The opposite is true when demand decreases and supply increases. Buyers are willing to buy the same quantity as before only if the price is lower, and sellers are willing to supply the same quantity at a lower price. Because the two groups can agree on a lower price at any given quantity, we can predict that the price will decrease.

Of course, you can always work out the effect of simultaneous shifts in demand and supply by working through the three questions described in the previous section. Draw the shifts in each curve on a graph, as is done in two cases in panels A and B in Figure 3-9, and find the new equilibrium.

To improve your understanding of simultaneous shifts in demand and supply, try the online interactive graphing tutorial.

Before you finish this chapter, read the Real Life box, Give a Man a Fish, for some information about how cell phones affected supply and demand in one developing country.

REAL LIFE

Give a Man a Fish

Are cell phones a technological luxury or a practical necessity? Maybe you can't imagine life without the ability to call or text your friends anywhere, anytime. But are cell phones as important as shelter, food, or water? A recent study in India showed that being able to communicate may help people to meet their basic needs.

In a competitive market, the price of a particular good is found at the point where the quantity supplied equals the quantity demanded. This model assumes that everywhere in the market, buyers and sellers are fully informed about prices and can adjust their behaviour accordingly. If buyers and sellers do not have good information about prices, shortages can develop in some locations and surpluses in others.

When economist Robert Jensen studied the market for fish in Kerala, a state in southwestern India, he found that it did not reach one equilibrium price. Instead, each local fish market had its own equilibrium. In this area, many people rely on fishing for their daily income. Fishers tend to sell their fish at a single local market; they take the price that prevails at that market on a particular day. If that market has only a few buyers that day, the fishers end up with too much fish. At the same time, if the fishers in a neighbouring village have a poor catch that day, some buyers will go home empty-handed—even if they are willing to pay a high price. Without a way to know if there is a shortage or surplus in a nearby market, the fishers can't adjust their prices to reach equilibrium with customers.

Jensen found that the fishers could solve this problem using cell phones. By communicating with one another and with people on land while out fishing, they were able to find out where it would be most profitable to sell their catches. They used that information to travel to the right village to sell their fish. Supply began to better match the demand in each village and prices became more uniform across villages. Access to the right information allowed the market for fish to reach an efficient equilibrium. Sellers earned an average of 8 percent more in profits, and buyers paid an average of 4 percent less for their fish. Fishers increased their incomes and consumers stretched their incomes further.

As the saying goes, "Give a man a fish and he will eat for a day. Teach a man to fish and he will eat for a lifetime." To this wisdom, we might add, "Give a man a cell phone. . ."

Source: R. Jensen, "The digital provide: Information (technology), market performance, and welfare in the South Indian fisheries sector," *The Quarterly Journal of Economics,* vol. CXXII (2007), issue 3.

✓ CONCEPT CHECK

☐ What is the market equilibrium? [LO 3.6]

☐ What happens to the equilibrium price and quantity if the supply curve shifts right but the demand curve stays put? [LO 3.7]

Conclusion

By the time you reach the end of this course, you'll be quite familiar with the words *supply* and *demand*. We take our time on this subject for good reason. An understanding of supply and demand is the foundation of economic problem solving. You'll be hard-pressed to make wise economic choices without it.

Although markets are not always perfectly competitive, you may be surprised at how accurately many real-world phenomena can be described using the simple rules of supply and demand. In the next chapters we'll use these rules to explain how consumers and producers respond to price changes and government policies.

Key Terms

market economy

market

competitive market

standardized good

transaction costs

price taker

quantity demanded

law of demand

demand schedule

demand curve

substitutes

complements

normal goods

inferior goods

quantity supplied

law of supply

supply schedule

supply curve

equilibrium

equilibrium price

equilibrium quantity

surplus (excess quantity supplied)

shortage (excess quantity demanded)

Summary

LO 3.1 Identify the defining characteristics of a competitive market.

A market is the group of buyers and sellers who trade a particular good or service. In competitive markets, a large number of buyers and sellers trade standardized goods and services. They have full information about the goods, and there is no cost to participating in exchanges in the market. Participants in competitive markets are called price takers because they can't affect the prevailing price for a good.

LO 3.2 Draw a demand curve and describe the external factors that determine demand.

A demand curve is a graph that shows the quantities of a particular good or service that consumers will demand at various prices. It also shows consumers' highest willingness to pay for a given quantity. The law of demand states that for almost all goods, the quantity demanded increases as the price decreases. This relationship results in a downward-sloping demand curve.

Several non-price factors contribute to consumers' demand for a good at a given price: consumer preferences, the prices of related goods, incomes, and expectations about the future. On a market-wide level, the number of buyers can also increase or decrease total demand. When one of these underlying factors changes, the demand curve will shift to the left or the right.

LO 3.3 Distinguish between a shift in and a movement along the demand curve.

When one of the non-price factors that drives demand changes, the entire curve shifts to the left or the right. With this shift, the quantity demanded at any given price changes. When demand increases, the curve shifts to the right; when demand decreases, it shifts to the left.

When the underlying demand relationship stays the same, a change in the price of a good leads to a movement along the curve, rather than a shift in the curve.

LO 3.4 Draw a supply curve and describe the external factors that determine supply.

A supply curve is a graph that shows the quantities of a particular good or service that producers will supply at various prices. It shows the minimum price producers must receive to supply any given quantity. The law of supply states that the quantity supplied increases as the price increases, resulting in an upward-sloping supply curve.

Several non-price factors determine the supply of a good at any given price: they include the prices of related goods, technology, prices of inputs, expectations about the future, and the number of sellers in the market. If one of these underlying factors changes, the supply curve will shift to the left or the right.

LO 3.5 Distinguish between a shift in and a movement along the supply curve.

Just as with demand, a change in the non-price determinants of supply will cause the entire supply curve to shift to the left or the right. As a result, the quantity supplied is higher or lower at any given price than it was before. When supply increases, the curve shifts to the right; when supply decreases, it shifts to the left.

A shift in the supply curve differs from movement along the supply curve. A movement along the curve happens when the price of a good increases but the non-price determinants of supply stay the same.

LO 3.6 Explain how supply and demand interact to drive markets to equilibrium.

When a market is in equilibrium, the quantity supplied equals the quantity demanded. The incentives that individual buyers and sellers face drive a competitive market toward equilibrium. If the prevailing price is too high, a surplus will result and sellers will lower their prices to get rid of the excess quantity supplied. If the prevailing price is too low, a shortage will result and buyers will bid up the price until the excess quantity demanded disappears.

LO 3.7 Evaluate the effect of changes in supply and demand on the equilibrium price and quantity.

When one or more of the underlying factors that determine supply or demand changes, one or both curves will shift, leading to a new market equilibrium price and quantity.

To calculate the change in the equilibrium price and quantity, you must first determine whether a change affects demand and, if so, in which direction the curve will shift. Then you must determine whether the change also affects supply and, if so, in which direction that curve will shift. Finally, you must determine the new equilibrium point where the two curves intersect.

Review Questions

1. Think about a competitive market in which you participate regularly. For each of the characteristics of a competitive market, explain how your market meets these requirements. [LO 3.1]

2. Think about a noncompetitive market in which you participate regularly. Explain which characteristic(s) of competitive markets your market does not meet. [LO 3.1]

3. Explain why a demand curve slopes downward. [LO 3.2]

4. In each of the following examples, name the factor that affects demand and describe its impact on your demand for a new cell phone. [LO 3.2]
   a. You hear a rumour that a new and improved model of the phone you want is coming out next year.
   b. Your grandparents give you $500.
   c. A cellular network announces a holiday sale on a text-messaging package that includes the purchase of a new phone.
   d. A friend tells you how great his new cell phone is and suggests that you get one, too.

5. Consider the following events:
   a. The price of cell phones goes down by 25 percent during a sale.
   b. You get a 25 percent raise at your job.

   Which event represents a shift in the demand curve for cell phones? Which represents a movement along the curve? What is the difference? [LO 3.3]

6. What is the difference between a change in demand and a change in quantity demanded? [LO 3.3]

7. Explain why a supply curve slopes upward. [LO 3.4]

8. In each of the following examples, name the factor that affects supply and describe its impact on the supply of cell phones. [LO 3.4]
   a. Economic forecasts suggest that the demand for cell phones will increase in the future.
   b. The price of plastic goes up.
   c. A new screen technology reduces the cost of making cell phones.

9. Consider the following events:
   a. A maggot infestation ruins a large number of apple orchards in British Columbia.
   b. Demand for apples goes down, causing the price to fall.

   Which event represents a shift in the supply curve for apples? Which represents a movement along the curve? What is the difference? [LO 3.5]

10. What is the difference between a change in supply and a change in quantity supplied? [LO 3.5]

11. What is the relationship between supply and demand when a market is in equilibrium? Explain how the incentives facing cell phone companies and consumers cause the market for cell phones to reach equilibrium. [LO 3.6]

12. Explain why the equilibrium price is often called the market-clearing price. [LO 3.6]

13. Suppose an economic boom causes incomes to increase. Explain what will happen to the demand and supply of phones, and predict the direction of the change in the equilibrium price and quantity. [LO 3.7]

14. Suppose an economic boom drives up wages for the sales representatives who work for cell phone companies. Explain what will happen to the demand and supply of phones, and predict the direction of the change in the equilibrium price and quantity. [LO 3.7]

15. Suppose an economic boom causes incomes to increase and at the same time drives up wages for the sales representatives who work for cell phone companies. Explain what will happen to the demand for and supply of phones and predict the direction of the change in the equilibrium price and quantity. [LO 3.7]

Problems and Applications

1. Consider shopping for cucumbers in a farmers' market. For each statement below, note which characteristic of competitive markets the statement describes. *Choose from: standardized good, full information, no transaction costs, and participants are price takers.* [LO 3.1]

   a. All of the farmers have their prices posted prominently in front of their stalls.

   b. Cucumbers are the same price at each stall.

   c. There is no difficulty moving around between stalls as you shop and choosing between farmers.

   d. You and the other customers all seem indifferent about which cucumbers to buy.

2. Suppose two artists are selling paintings for the same price in adjacent booths at an art fair. By the end of the day, one artist has nearly sold out of her paintings while the other artist has sold nothing. Which characteristic of competitive markets has not been met and best explains this outcome? [LO 3.1]

   a. Standardized good

   b. Full information

   c. No transaction costs

   d. Participants are price takers

3. Using the demand schedule in Table 3P-1, draw the daily demand curve for slices of pizza in a university town. [LO 3.2]

TABLE 3P-1

Price ($)	Quantity demanded (slices)
0.00	350
0.50	300
1.00	250
1.50	200
2.00	150
2.50	100
3.00	50
3.50	0

4. Consider the market for cars. Which determinant of demand is affected by each of the following events? *Choose from: consumer preferences, prices of related goods, incomes, expectations, and the number of buyers.* [LO 3.2]

   a. Environmentalists launch a successful One Family, One Car campaign.

   b. A baby boom occurred sixteen years ago.

   c. Layoffs increase as the economy sheds millions of jobs.

   d. An oil shortage causes the price of gasoline to soar.

   e. The government offers tax rebates in return for the purchase of commuter rail tickets.

   f. The government announces a massive plan to bail out the auto industry and subsidize production costs.

5. If a decrease in the price of laptops causes the demand for cell phones to increase, are laptops and cell phones substitutes or complements? [LO 3.2]

6. If rising incomes cause the demand for beer to decrease, is beer a normal or inferior good? [LO 3.2]

7. Consider the market for corn. Say whether each of the following events will cause a shift in the demand curve or a movement along the curve. If it will cause a shift, specify the direction. [LO 3.3]

   a. A drought hits corn-growing regions, cutting the supply of corn.

   b. The government announces a new subsidy for biofuels made from corn.

   c. A global recession reduces the incomes of consumers in poor countries, who rely on corn as a staple food.

   d. A new hybrid variety of corn seed causes a 15 percent increase in the yield of corn per acre.

   e. An advertising campaign by the beef producers' association highlights the health benefits of corn-fed beef.

8. The demand curve in Figure 3P-1 shows the monthly market for sweaters at a local clothing store. For each of the following events, draw the new outcome. [LO 3.3]

   a. Sweaters fall out of fashion.

   b. There is a shortage of wool.

   c. The winter is particularly long and cold this year.

   d. Sweater vendors offer a sale.

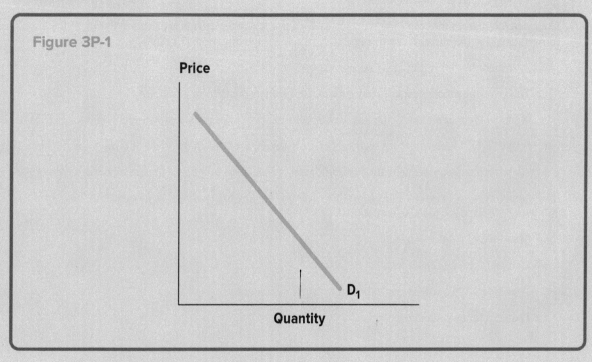

Figure 3P-1

9. Using the supply schedule found in Table 3P-2, draw the daily supply curve for slices of pizza in a university town. [LO 3.4]

TABLE 3P-2

Price ($)	Quantity supplied (slices)
0.00	0
0.50	50
1.00	100
1.50	150
2.00	200
2.50	250
3.00	300
3.50	350

10. Consider the market for cars. Which determinant of supply is affected by each of the following events? *Choose from: prices of related goods, technology, prices of inputs, expectations, and the number of sellers in the market.* [LO 3.4]

   a. A steel tariff increases the price of steel.

   b. Improvements in robotics increase efficiency and reduce costs.

   c. Factories close because of an economic downturn.

   d. The government announces a plan to offer tax rebates for the purchase of commuter rail tickets.

   e. The price of trucks falls, so factories produce more cars.

   f. The government announces that it will dramatically rewrite efficiency standards, making it much harder for automakers to produce their cars.

11. Consider the market for corn. Say whether each of the following events will cause a shift in the supply curve or a movement along the curve. If it will cause a shift, specify the direction. [LO 3.5]

   a. A drought hits corn-growing regions.

   b. The government announces a new subsidy for biofuels made from corn.

   c. A global recession reduces the incomes of consumers in poor countries, who rely on corn as a staple food.

   d. A new hybrid variety of corn seed causes a 15 percent increase in the yield of corn per acre.

   e. An advertising campaign by the beef producers' association highlights the health benefits of corn-fed beef.

12. The supply curve in Figure 3P-2 shows the monthly market for sweaters at a local craft market. For each of the following events, draw the new outcome. [LO 3.5]

   a. The price of wool increases

   b. Demand for sweaters decreases

   c. A particularly cold winter is expected to begin next month

   d. Demand for sweaters increases

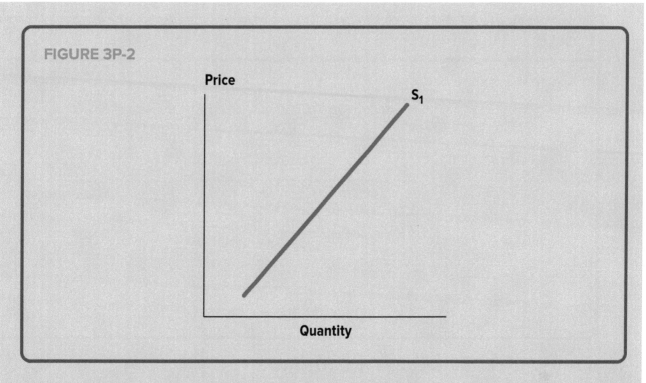

FIGURE 3P-2

13. Refer to the demand and supply schedule shown in Table 3P-3. [LO 3.6]

   a. If pizza parlors charge $3.50 per slice, will there be excess quantity supplied or excess quantity demanded? What is the amount of excess quantity supplied or excess quantity demanded at that price?

   b. If pizza parlors charge $1.00 per slice, will there be excess quantity supplied or excess quantity demanded? What is the amount of excess quantity supplied or excess quantity demanded at that price?

   c. What are the equilibrium price and quantity in this market?

TABLE 3P-3

Price ($)	Quantity demanded (slices)	Quantity supplied (slices)
0.00	350	0
0.50	300	100
1.00	250	150
1.50	200	200
2.00	150	250
2.50	100	300
3.00	50	350
3.50	0	400

The graph in Figure 3P-3 shows the weekly market for compact discs in a small town. Use this graph to answer problems 14–16.

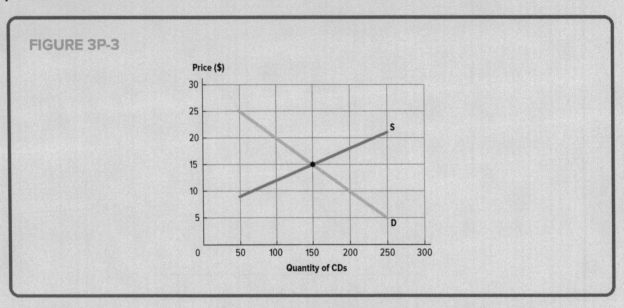

FIGURE 3P-3

14. Which of the following events will occur at a price of $20? [LO 3.6]

    a. Equilibrium

    b. Excess quantity demanded

    c. Excess quantity supplied

    d. No CDs supplied

    e. No CDs demanded

15. Which of the following events will occur at a price of $10? [LO 3.6]

    a. Equilibrium

    b. Excess quantity demanded

    c. Excess quantity supplied

    d. No CDs supplied

    e. No CDs demanded

16. What are the equilibrium price and quantity of CDs? [LO 3.6]

17. The graph in Figure 3P-4 shows supply and demand in the market for automobiles. For each of the following events, draw the new market outcome and say whether the equilibrium price and quantity will increase or decrease. [LO 3.7]

    a. Environmentalists launch a successful One Family, One Car campaign.

    b. A steel tariff increases the price of steel.

    c. A baby boom occurred sixteen years ago.

    d. An oil shortage causes the price of gasoline to soar.

    e. Improvements in robotics increase efficiency and reduce costs.

    f. The government offers a tax rebate for the purchase of commuter rail tickets.

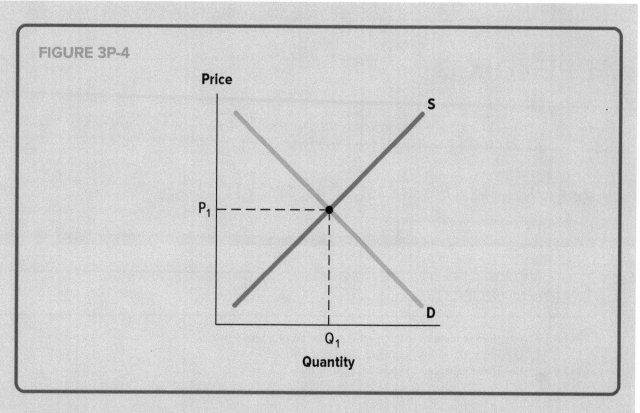

FIGURE 3P-4

18. Say whether each of the following changes will increase or decrease the equilibrium price and quantity, or whether the effect cannot be predicted. [LO 3.7]

   a. Demand increases; supply remains constant

   b. Supply increases; demand remains constant

   c. Demand decreases; supply remains constant

   d. Supply decreases; demand remains constant

   e. Demand increases; supply increases

   f. Demand decreases; supply decreases

   g. Demand increases; supply decreases

   h. Demand decreases; supply increases

Math Essentials: Working with Linear Equations

LEARNING OBJECTIVES

LO B.1   Use linear equations to interpret the equation of a line.
LO B.2   Use linear equations to explain shifts and pivots.
LO B.3   Use linear equations to solve for equilibrium.

Relationships between variables can be represented with algebraic equations as well as with graphs and tables. You should be comfortable moving among all three representations. We addressed graphs in Appendix A (following Chapter 2); if you didn't read it then, you might want to do so now.

Interpreting the Equation of a Line

LO B.1 Use linear equations to interpret the equation of a line.

If the relationship between two variables is linear, it can be represented by the equation for a line, commonly written as:

Equation B-1

$$y = mx + b$$

In this form, called the *slope intercept form*, m is the slope of the line, and b is the y-intercept.

All linear equations provide information about the slope and y-intercept of the line. From our discussion in Appendix A, we already know that slope is the ratio of vertical distance (change in y) to horizontal distance (change in x). So what does the y-intercept tell us? It is the point at which the line crosses the y-axis. Put another way, it is the value of y when x is zero. Knowing these values is useful in turning an equation into a graph. Also, as we'll see, they can allow us to get information about the real economic relationship being represented without even having to graph it.

Although you might see the equation for a line rearranged in several different forms, just remember that if y is on the left side of the equation, whatever number is multiplying x (known as the *coefficient of x*) is your slope. If you don't see a number in front of x, the slope is 1. The number being added to or subtracted from a multiple of x is a constant that represents the y-intercept. If you don't see this number, you know that the y-intercept is zero. Take a look at a few examples in Table B-1.

TABLE B-1 EXAMPLES OF LINEAR EQUATIONS

Equation	Slope	y-intercept
$y = 6x + 4$	6	4
$y = x - 2$	−1	−2
$y = 10 - 2x$	−2	10
$y = -4x$	−4	0

Turning a Graph into an Equation

To see how to translate a graph into an algebraic equation, look at Figure B-1. What equation represents this relationship?

FIGURE B-1

Translating a Graph into an Algebraic Equation

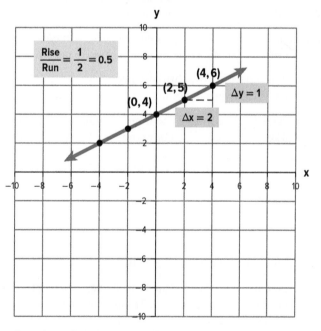

By using information provided on a graph, you can easily construct an equation of the line in the form $y = mx + b$. The slope, m, is calculated by taking the rise of a line over its run. The value of the y-intercept provides the b part of the equation.

To derive this equation, we need to find the values of the slope and the *y*-intercept. We can calculate the slope at any point along the line:

$$\text{Slope} \quad = \quad \frac{\Delta y}{\Delta x} = \frac{(y_2 - y_1)}{(x_2 - x_1)}$$

$$= \quad \frac{(6 - 5)}{(4 - 2)} = \frac{1}{2} = 0.5$$

By looking at the graph to see where the line intersects the *y*-axis, we can tell that the *y*-intercept is 4. Therefore, if we write the equation in the form $y = mx + b$, we get $y = 0.5x + 4$. Our table, graph, and equation all give us the same information about the relationship between *x* and *y*.

Turning an Equation into a Graph

Let's work in the opposite direction now, starting with an equation and seeing what information it gives us.

The following equation takes the form $y = mx + b$, with P (price) and Q (quantity) substituted for *y* and *x*, respectively.

$$P = -5Q + 25$$

We know from looking at this equation that it represents a line with a slope of −5 and a *y*-intercept of 25. Suppose that we know this equation represents supply or demand, but we're not sure which. How can we tell whether this is a demand equation or a supply equation? Easy. The slope is negative. We don't need a graph to tell us that the relationship between P and Q is negative and the line will be downward-sloping. Therefore, the equation must represent demand rather than supply.

Because the *y*-intercept in our equation is 25, we know that the demand curve will cross the *y*-axis at 25. This tells us that when price is 25, quantity demanded is 0. In order for consumers to demand a positive quantity, price must be lower than 25.

If we need to know more about the relationship represented by the equation, we can graph the demand curve. Since we know that 25 is the *y*-intercept, we can use the point (0,25) to begin plotting our graph as shown in Figure B-2.

It takes only two points to define a line, and we already have one from the *y*-intercept. To find a second point, we can plug in any value of Q and solve for the corresponding P (or vice versa). For example, if we let Q = 2 and solve for P we get:

$$P \quad = \quad -5\,(2) + 25$$

$$P \quad = \quad -10 + 25$$

$$P \quad = \quad 15$$

We can now plot the point (2,15) and connect it to the *y*-intercept at (0,25).

Rather than plugging in random points, though, it is often useful to know the *x*-intercept as well as the *y*-intercept. On a demand curve, this will tell us what quantity is demanded when price is 0. To find this intercept, we can let P = 0 and solve for Q:

$$0 \quad = \quad -5Q + 25$$

$$-25 \quad = \quad -5Q$$

$$5 \quad = \quad Q$$

FIGURE B-2

Translating an Algebraic Equation into a Graph

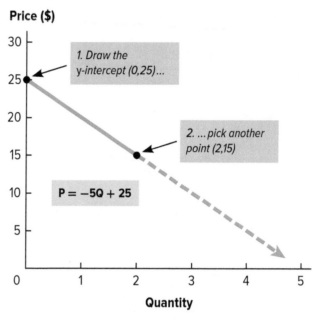

Price ($)

1. Draw the y-intercept (0,25)...

2. ...pick another point (2,15)

$P = -5Q + 25$

Quantity

The first step in graphing the equation of a line in the form $y = mx + b$ is to plot the y intercept, given by b. Then pick another point by choosing any value of x or y, and solving the equation for the other variable to get an ordered pair that represents another point on the line. Connecting these two points gives the line.

We can now plot the point (5,0) and connect it to (0,25) to graph the demand curve.

Finding intercepts is useful for interpreting other types of graphs, as well. In a production possibilities frontier, the intercepts tell you how much of one good will be produced if all resources are used to produce that good and none are used to produce the other good. In the production possibilities frontier shown in Figure B-3, for example, we can find the y-intercept to see that by devoting all workers to making shirts and none to producing wheat, 2 million T-shirts can be produced. Alternatively, we can find the x-intercept to see that if all workers grow wheat and none make shirts, 4 million bushels of wheat can be produced.

We saw in Chapter 2 that the slope of the frontier represents the trade-off between producing two goods. We can use our intercepts as the two points we need to calculate the slope.

$$\text{Slope} = \frac{\Delta y}{\Delta x} = \frac{(4 \text{ million} - 0)}{(0 - 2 \text{ million})} = \frac{4}{-2} = -2$$

You know from Chapter 2 that the slope of the frontier will be negative because it represents a trade-off: you can't make more wheat without giving up some shirts. Because an increase in wheat means a decrease in shirts, the two variables move in opposite directions and have a negative relationship. This frontier has a constant slope, which means that the trade-off between the two goods—which we can also think of as the opportunity cost of producing shirts in terms of wheat—is also constant.

FIGURE B-3

Using Intercepts to interpret a Production Possibilities Frontier

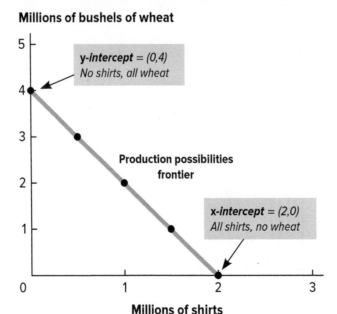

Millions of bushels of wheat

y-intercept = (0,4)
No shirts, all wheat

Production possibilities frontier

x-intercept = (2,0)
All shirts, no wheat

Millions of shirts

The intercepts of a production possibilities frontier give the maximum amount of a good a country can produce by dedicating all resources in the economy to the production of that good. In this case, with all workers dedicated to the production of one good or the other, the economy can make either 4 million bushels of wheat or 2 million shirts.

Equations with *x* and *y* Reversed

Thus far, we have represented demand and supply equations with P (or *y*) isolated on the left side of the equation. For example, our demand equation was given as P = −5Q + 25. You may find, however, that in some places, demand and supply equations are given with Q (or *x*) isolated on the left side of the equation.

When you see this, you cannot read the equation as giving you the slope and the *y*-intercept. Instead, when an equation is in this form, you have the inverse of slope and the *x*-intercept.

Look at our demand equation again. If we rearrange the equation to solve for Q, we have an equation of the form $x = ny + a$:

$$P = -5Q + 25$$

$$P - 25 = -5Q$$

$$-\frac{1}{5}P + 5 = Q \text{ or } Q = -\frac{1}{5}P + 5$$

We know that the starting equation represents the same underlying relationship as the final equation. For instance, we know that our slope is -5, but in the rearranged form where we have solved for Q, the coefficient multiplying P is the inverse of slope, or $-1/5$. We can generalize this observation to say that when we have an equation of the form $x = ny + a$, $n = 1/m$ where m is the slope of the line from the same equation expressed in the form $y + mx + b$. We also know that 25 is the y-intercept. But in our rearranged form, a represents the x-intercept, which is 5. The graph in Figure B-4 shows that these two equations represent different aspects of the same line.

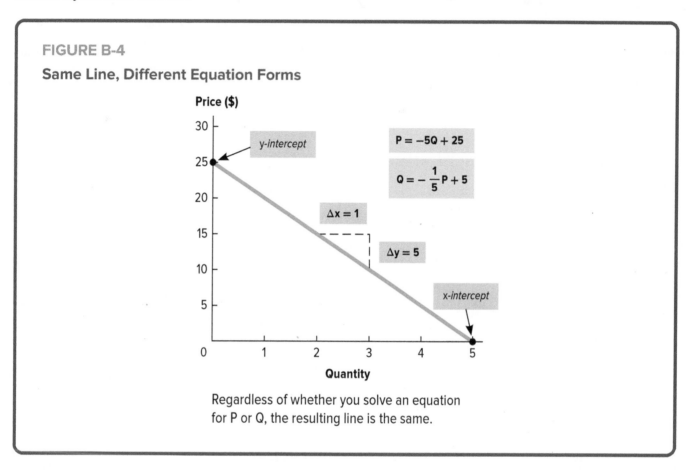

FIGURE B-4

Same Line, Different Equation Forms

Regardless of whether you solve an equation for P or Q, the resulting line is the same.

Keep in mind that $P = -5Q + 25$ is the same equation as $Q = -1/5\ P + 5$; we have simply rearranged it to solve for Q instead of P.

Shifts and Pivots

LO B.2 Use linear equations to explain shifts and pivots.

Imagine that your campus cafeteria has a deli with a salad bar and that the price of a salad depends on the number of ingredients you add to it. This relationship is represented by the following equation:

$$y = 0.5x + 4$$

where

y = total price of the salad
x = number of added ingredients

Because our variables are the price of a salad and the number of ingredients, negative quantities do not make sense: you can't have negative carrots in your salad, and we doubt that the cafeteria is paying you to buy salads. Therefore, we can isolate the graph of this equation to the first quadrant, as shown in panel A of Figure B-5.

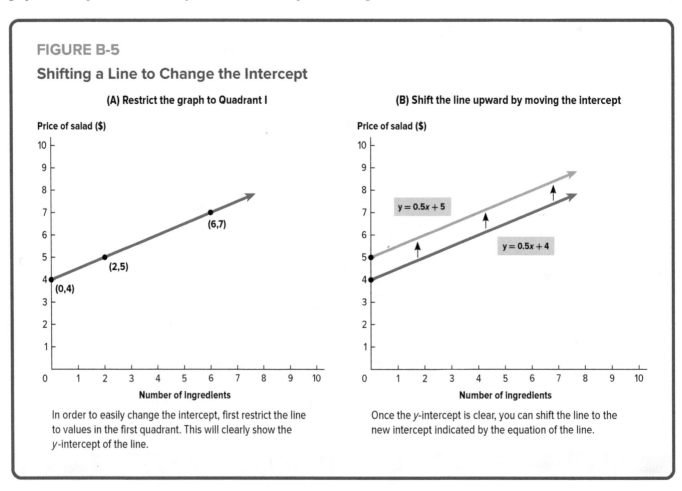

FIGURE B-5

Shifting a Line to Change the Intercept

(A) Restrict the graph to Quadrant I

In order to easily change the intercept, first restrict the line to values in the first quadrant. This will clearly show the y-intercept of the line.

(B) Shift the line upward by moving the intercept

Once the y-intercept is clear, you can shift the line to the new intercept indicated by the equation of the line.

Our y-intercept of 4 represents the price of a salad if you add zero ingredients. In other words, a plain bowl of lettuce costs $4. The slope of 0.5 represents the cost of adding ingredients to the salad. Each additional ingredient costs 50 cents. The fact that (2,5) is a point along the line shows that the price of a salad with two added ingredients is $5.

How much is a salad with six added ingredients?

$$
\begin{aligned}
y &= 0.5(6) + 4 \\
y &= 3 + 4 \\
y &= 7
\end{aligned}
$$

A salad with six added ingredients is $7, and (6,7) is another point on the graph.

Now let's see what happens to our graph when the baseline price of a bowl of lettuce without additional ingredients increases to $5. This baseline price is represented by the y-intercept, which changes from 4 to 5. The slope of the graph does not change, because each additional ingredient still costs 50 cents.

Thus, our equation changes to $y + 0.5x + 5$. Rather than re-graphing this new question from scratch, we can simply *shift* the original line to account for the change in the y-intercept, as shown in panel B of Figure B-5.

Suppose, instead, that the price of lettuce remains at $4, but the price of additional ingredients increases to $1 each. How will this change the graph and equation?

If the price of lettuce with zero additional ingredients remains at $4, the y-intercept will also stay the same. However, the slope will change, increasing from 50 cents to $1. Figure B-6 shows that this change of slope will *pivot* the line in our graph.

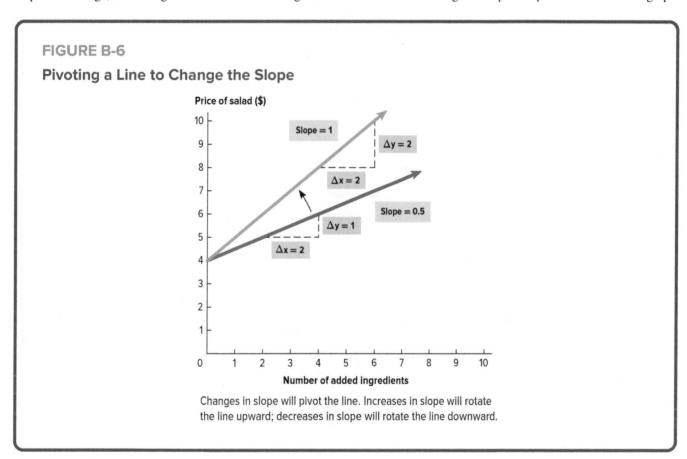

FIGURE B-6

Pivoting a Line to Change the Slope

Changes in slope will pivot the line. Increases in slope will rotate the line upward; decreases in slope will rotate the line downward.

Our equation changes, as well. This time, we substitute 1 in place of 0.5 for the slope. Thus, $y = x + 4$. (Remember that no coefficient on x indicates that the slope is 1.)

What happens if the baseline price of lettuce goes up to $5 *and* the price of toppings goes up to $1? We have to both shift *and* pivot the line to represent the change in the intercept and the slope. (Sounds like a fitness routine, doesn't it?) Figure B-7 shows both changes.

You will need to shift and pivot lines in many places throughout this book to represent changes in the relationship between two variables. For instance, we saw in Chapter 3 that when a non-price determinant of demand changes, you need to *shift* the demand curve to show that people demand a higher or lower quantity of a good at any given price. When consumers become more or less sensitive to changes in price, you need to *pivot* the demand curve to represent a change in slope.

FIGURE B-7

Shift and Pivot

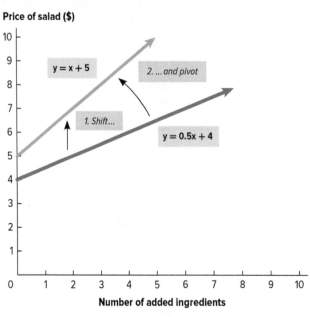

In order to handle a change in slope and intercept, you first shift the line to the new intercept and then pivot the line to reflect the new slope.

Solving for Equilibrium

> **LO B.3** Use linear equations to solve for equilibrium.

One graph can show multiple relationships between the same two variables. The most frequent case we encounter in this book is graphs showing both the demand relationship and the supply relationship between price and quantity.

Panel A of Figure B-8 shows data from supply and demand schedules. Remember from Chapter 3 that as P increases, the quantity demanded decreases. Since P and Q are moving in opposite directions, the relationship is negative. When these values are plotted in panel B, we have a downward-sloping line for the demand curve. Conversely, as P increases, the quantity supplied increases. Plotting these points yields an upward-sloping supply curve.

When we use one graph to show multiple equations of the same variables, we do so in order to show something meaningful about the relationship between them. For instance, when we show supply and demand on the same graph, we usually want to find the equilibrium point—the point at which the quantity supplied and the quantity demanded are equal to each other at the same price.

FIGURE B-8

Supply and Demand

(A) Supply and demand schedules

Price ($)	Q$_{demand}$	Q$_{supply}$
20	180	0
30	160	10
40	140	20
50	120	30
80	60	60
90	40	70
100	20	80
110	0	90

The supply and demand schedules show the quantities demanded and supplied for a given price.

(B) Graphing the schedules

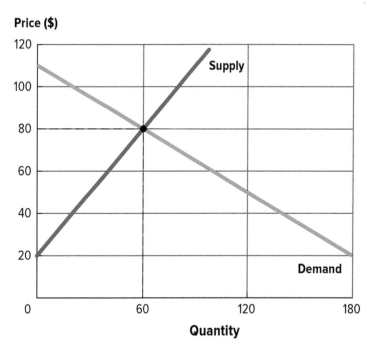

Graphing the values from the schedules gives a downward-sloping demand curve and an upward-sloping supply curve.

We can find the equilibrium point in several ways. If we have schedules showing both demand and supply data, the easiest way to find equilibrium is to locate the price that corresponds to *equal supply and demand quantities*. What is that price in panel A of Figure B-8? At a price of 80, Q is 60 in the demand schedule as well as in the supply schedule.

We can also find the equilibrium point easily by looking at a graph showing both supply and demand. The single point where the two lines intersect is the equilibrium.

Sometimes, however, it is useful to find equilibrium from equations alone, without having to graph them or to calculate a whole schedule of points by plugging in different prices. Usually you'll want to use this method when you are given equations but no graph or schedule. However, just for practice, let's first derive the supply and demand equations from Figure B-8 and then figure out the equilibrium point.

We want to start by representing supply and demand as equations of the form $y = mx + b$. Let y = price and x = quantity. We need to determine the slope (m) and the y-intercept (b) for each equation.

First, the demand equation: What is the y-intercept? It is the value of y when x is zero. Looking at panel A in Figure B-8, we can see that when Q is zero, P is 110. The y-intercept of the demand equation is 110. Now we need the slope. Because this is a linear relationship and the slope is constant, we can determine the slope using any two points. Let's use the points (180,20) and (160,30).

$$\frac{\Delta y}{\Delta x} = \frac{(P_2 - P_1)}{(Q_2 - Q_1)} = \frac{(20 - 30)}{(180 - 160)} = \frac{-10}{20} = -0.5$$

Thus, our demand equation is P = −0.5Q + 110.

We'll use the same procedure to derive the supply equation. Looking at the supply schedule, we can see that when Q is zero, P is 20. The y-intercept is 20. To determine slope, let's use the points (0,20) and (10,30).

$$\frac{\Delta y}{\Delta x} = \frac{(P_2 - P_1)}{(Q_2 - Q_1)} = \frac{(20 - 30)}{(0 - 10)} = \frac{-10}{-10} = -1$$

Thus, our supply equation is P = Q + 20.

Now that we have our equations, we can use them to solve for equilibrium. Equilibrium represents a point that is on both the demand and supply curves; graphically, it is where the two curves intersect. This means that P on the demand curve must equal P on the supply curve, and the same for Q. Therefore, it makes sense that we find this point by setting the two equations equal to each other.

$$P_D = -0.5Q + 110$$

$$P_S = Q + 20$$

$$P_D = P_S,$$

Therefore,

$$-0.5Q + 110 = Q + 20$$

This allows us to solve for a numeric value for Q.

$$1.5Q + 20 = 110$$

$$1.5Q = 90$$

$$Q = 60$$

Now that we have a value for Q, we can plug it into either the supply or demand equation to get the value for P. Let's use our supply equation.

$$P = 20 + Q$$

$$P = 20 + 60$$

$$P = 80$$

Solving for equilibrium using the equations gives us the same point we found using the demand and supply schedules: P = 80 and Q = 60 ($80,60).

Problems and Applications

1. Use the demand curve in Figure BP-1 to derive a demand equation. [LO B.1]

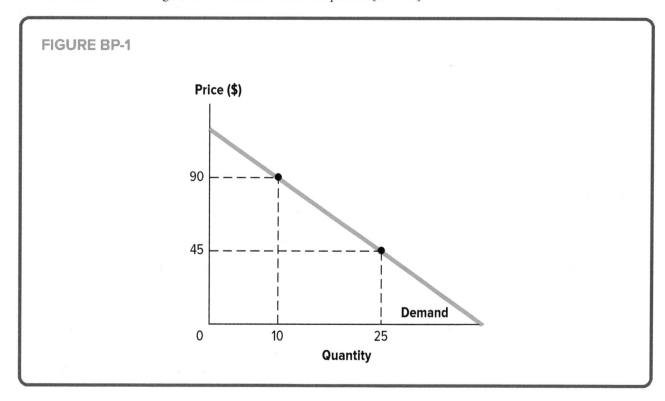

FIGURE BP-1

2. Use the demand schedule in Table BP-1 to derive a demand equation. [LO B.1]

TABLE BP-1

Price ($)	Quantity
0	320
10	280
20	240
30	200
40	160
50	120
60	80
70	40
80	0

3. Use the supply curve in Figure BP-2 to derive a supply equation. [LO B.1]

FIGURE BP-2

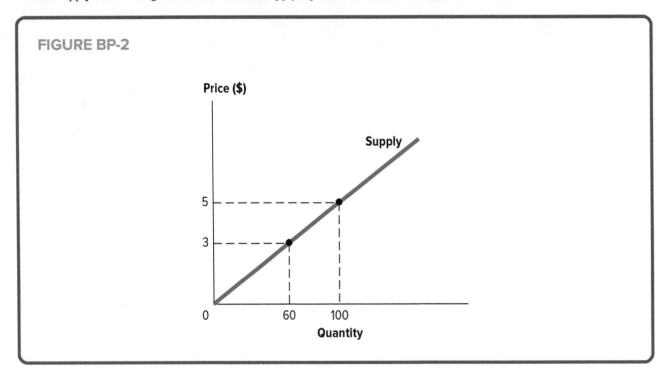

4. Use the supply schedule in Table BP-2 to derive a supply equation. [LO B.1]

TABLE BP-2

Price ($)	Quantity
100	0
200	25
300	50
400	75
500	100
600	125

5. Graph the equation P = 2Q + 3. Is this a supply curve or a demand curve? [LO B.1]
6. Graph the equation P= −8Q + 10. Is this a supply curve or a demand curve? [LO B.1]
7. Rearrange the equation Q = 5 − 0.25P and sketch the graph. Is this a supply curve or a demand curve? [LO B.1]
8. Rearrange the equation Q = 0.2P and sketch the graph. Is this a supply curve or a demand curve? [LO B.1]
9. The entrance fee at your local amusement park is $20 for the day. The entrance fee includes all rides except roller coasters. Roller coasters cost an extra $2 per ride. [LO B.2]
    a. Write an equation that represents how much money you will spend on rides as a function of the number of rides you go on: S = total spending on rides; Q = the quantity of roller coaster rides.
    b. What is your total spending on rides if you ride four roller coasters?
    c. Draw a graph of the relationship between total spending on rides and the number of roller coaster rides.
    d. Redraw the graph from part (c) to show what will change if the entrance fee increases to $25.

e. Rewrite the equation from part (a) to incorporate the increased entrance fee of $25.

f. After the entrance fee increases to $25, what is your total spending on rides if you ride four roller coasters?

10. Use the following two equations: [LO B.3]

    (1) $P = 12 - 2Q$

    (2) $P = 3 + Q$

a. Find the equilibrium price and quantity.

b. Graph the demand and supply equations. Illustrate the equilibrium point.

11. With reference to Table BP-3: [LO B.3]

a. Use the information from the table to create the demand and supply equations.

b. Use your demand and supply equations to solve for equilibrium.

c. Graph supply and demand curves. Illustrate the equilibrium point.

TABLE BP-3

Price ($)	Quantity demanded	Quantity supplied
0	12	0
20	10	4
40	8	8
60	6	12
80	4	16
100	2	20
120	0	24

CHAPTER 4

Elasticity

LEARNING OBJECTIVES

LO 4.1	Calculate price elasticity of demand using the mid-point method.
LO 4.2	Explain how the determinants of price elasticity of demand affect the degree of elasticity.
LO 4.3	Calculate price elasticity of supply using the mid-point method.
LO 4.4	Explain how the determinants of price elasticity of supply affect the degree of elasticity.
LO 4.5	Calculate cross-price elasticity of demand, and interpret the sign of the elasticity.
LO 4.6	Calculate income elasticity of demand, and interpret the sign of the elasticity.

Canada's Everyday Drink

Canadians are addicted to Tim Hortons coffee. Over the course of fifty-one years, Tim Hortons coffee has become Canada's everyday drink. Though Tim Hortons is now American owned, it is still an integral part of Canadian lifestyle.

The Tim Hortons chain was first opened in 1964 in Hamilton, Ontario. Since then it has grown into Canada's largest national chain in the coffee and fresh baked-goods segment, with more than 2,200 stores right across the country and approximately 160 locations in key markets in the United States. The first Tim Hortons stores offered only two products—coffee and doughnuts. But as consumer tastes grew, so did the choices at Tim Hortons. And in addition to standard stores, Tim Hortons locations can also be found in shopping malls, highway outlets, universities, and hospitals, providing prominent visibility of the chain. Most standard Tim Hortons locations offer 24-hour drive-through service, catering to consumers on the go.[1]

Keeping the coffee price affordable is key to Tim Hortons' success, and the chain recently increased the sizes of their coffee cups while keeping the prices the same.

So, how do businesses like Tim Hortons make pricing decisions? How do they anticipate and react to changing circumstances? If Tim Hortons raised the price of its coffee—perhaps due to a supply shortage caused by poor weather in Ethiopia—this would reduce the quantity demanded by consumers.

This chapter introduces the idea of elasticity, which describes how much a change in price will affect consumers.

Like the market for cell phones, the market for coffee is not perfectly competitive. Managers of a big company like Tim Hortons have some ability to set prices, and they try to choose prices that will earn the largest profits. They also try to respond to changing market conditions: How much will sales fall if the price of coffee beans drives up the cost of a double-double coffee? How much will people decrease their coffee consumption during a recession? How many customers will be lost if competitors like McDonald's offer less-expensive coffee? Even in perfectly competitive markets, producers want to predict how their earnings will change in response to economic conditions and changes in the market price.

Non-profit service providers also often need to think about price elasticity. For instance, a non-profit organization wants to set the price of its services so so as to cover costs without driving away too many people. Similarly, non-profit Sunday schools or summer schools want to cover costs and keep education affordable for students. The ability to address issues like these is crucial for any public or private organization. Understanding how to price a Tim Hortons coffee requires the same kind of thinking as figuring out whether to raise entrance fees to national parks to cover the costs of maintaining the wilderness. Solving these challenges relies on understanding *elasticity,* a measure of how much supply and demand will respond to changes in price and income.

Benoit Daoust/Shutterstock.com

In this chapter you will learn how to calculate the effect of a price change on the quantity supplied or demanded. You will become familiar with some rules that businesses and policy makers follow when they cannot measure elasticity exactly. Using what you know about supply and demand, you will be able to categorize different types of goods by noting whether their elasticities are positive or negative. You will also learn how to use a rough approximation of price elasticity to tell whether raising prices will raise or lower an organization's total revenue.

What Is Elasticity?

If Tim Hortons raises the price of a coffee, we can expect the quantity of coffees demanded to fall. But by how much? Although we saw in Chapter 3 that price increases cause the quantity demanded to fall in a competitive market, we have not yet been able to say *how big* that movement will be. That question is the subject of this chapter.

Elasticity is a measure of how much consumers and producers will respond to a change in market conditions. The concept can be applied to supply or demand, and it can be used to measure responses to a change in the price of a good, a change in the price of a related good, or a change in income.

The concept of elasticity allows economic decision makers to anticipate *how others will respond* to changes in market conditions. Whether you are a business owner trying to sell cars or a public official trying to set sales taxes, you need to know how much a change in prices will affect consumers' willingness to buy.

The most commonly used measures of elasticity are *price elasticity of demand* and *price elasticity of supply.* These two concepts describe how much the quantity demanded and the quantity supplied change when the price of a good changes. The *cross-price elasticity of demand* describes what happens to the quantity demanded of one good when the price of another good changes. Another helpful measure, *income elasticity of demand,* measures how much the quantity demanded reacts to changes in consumers' incomes. Let's begin with price elasticity of demand.

Price Elasticity of Demand

Price elasticity of demand describes the size of the change in the quantity demanded of a good or service when its price changes. We showed in Chapter 3 that quantity demanded generally decreases when the price increases, but so far we have not been able to say *how much* it decreases. Price elasticity of demand fills this gap in our understanding of supply and demand.

Another way to think about price elasticity of demand is as a measure of consumers' sensitivity to price changes. When consumers' buying decisions are highly influenced by price, we say that their demand curve is *more elastic,* meaning that a small change in price causes a large change in the quantity demanded. When consumers are not very sensitive to price changes—that is, when they will buy approximately the same quantity regardless of the price—we say that their demand curve is *less elastic.*

Calculating Price Elasticity of Demand

LO 4.1 Calculate price elasticity of demand using the mid-point method.

Consider the challenge Hortons faced in shoring up falling sales during the recession. In this situation, a business might lower its prices by offering a sale. But would a sale work? How much could Hortons' managers expect purchases to increase as a result of the sale? In other words, *How will customers respond* to a sale? The ability to answer this question is an essential tool for businesses. To do so, we need to know the price elasticity of demand for Tim Hortons coffee.

Let's say that Hortons usually charges $2 for a cup of coffee. What might happen if it offered a special sale price of $1.50? Suppose that, before the sale, Hortons sold 10 million cups of coffee each day. Now suppose that consumers react to the sale by increasing the quantity demanded to 15 million cups per day. Figure 4-1 shows the quantity demanded before and after the sale as two points on the demand curve for coffee. Based on the results of this sale, what can we say about consumers' sensitivity to the price of coffee at Tim Hortons?

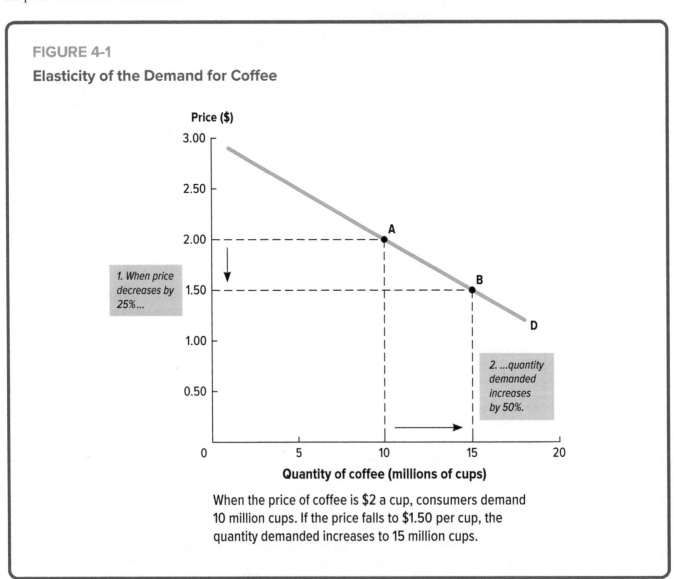

FIGURE 4-1

Elasticity of the Demand for Coffee

When the price of coffee is $2 a cup, consumers demand 10 million cups. If the price falls to $1.50 per cup, the quantity demanded increases to 15 million cups.

Mathematically, price elasticity is the percentage change in the quantity of a good that is demanded in response to a given percentage change in price. The formula looks like this:

Equation 4-1

$$\text{Price elasticity of demand} = \frac{\% \text{ change in Q demanded}}{\% \text{ change in P}}$$

HINT

A *percentage change* is the difference between the starting and ending levels divided by the starting level, expressed as a percentage. So a percentage change in quantity would be expressed as:

$$\text{Percentage change in quantity} = \left[\frac{(Q_2 - Q_1)}{Q_1}\right] \times 100$$

Similarly, a percentage change in price would be expressed as:

$$\text{Percentage change in price} = \left[\frac{(P_2 - P_1)}{P_1}\right] \times 100$$

If we plug the original and sale quantities and prices into Equation 4-1, what do we find? The price was cut by 25 percent and the quantity demanded rose by 50 percent. That tells us that the price elasticity of demand is −2.0.

$$\text{Price elasticity of demand} = \frac{(15 \text{ million} - 10 \text{ million})/10 \text{ million}}{(1.50 - 2.00)/2.00} = \frac{50\%}{-25\%} = -2.0$$

Note that the *price elasticity of demand will always be a negative number.* Why? Because price and quantity demanded move in opposite directions. That is, a positive change in price will cause a negative change in the quantity demanded and vice versa. However, be aware that economists often drop the negative sign and express the price elasticity of demand as a positive number, just for the sake of convenience. Don't be fooled! Under normal circumstances, price elasticity of demand is always negative, whether or not the negative sign is printed.

POTENTIALLY CONFUSING

Some books print the negative sign of elasticity estimates; others do not. Another way to think of an elasticity measure is as an absolute value. The *absolute value* of a number is its distance from zero, or its numerical value without regard to its sign. For example, the absolute values of 4 and −4 are both 4. The absolute value of elasticity measures the *size* of the response, while the sign measures its direction. Sometimes only the absolute value will be printed, when it is assumed that you know the direction of the change.

You might be wondering why we work with percentages in calculating elasticity. Why not just compare the change in the quantity demanded to the change in price? The answer is that percentages allow us to avoid some practical problems. Think about what would happen if one person measured coffee in 350-millilitre cups, while another measured it by the pot or the litre. Without percentages, we would have several different measures of price elasticity, depending on which unit of measurement we used. To avoid this problem, economists use the *percentage change* in quantity rather than the *absolute change* in quantity. That way, the elasticity of demand for coffee is the same whether we measure the quantity in cups, pots, or litres.

Using the Mid-Point Method

Unfortunately, even when using percentages, we still have a measurement problem: the answer changes depending on which direction we move along the demand curve. We saw that when the price dropped from $2 to $1.50, the elasticity of demand was −2.0:

$$\text{Price elasticity of demand} = \frac{(15 \text{ million} - 10 \text{ million})/10 \text{ million}}{(1.50 - 2.00)/2.00} = \frac{50\%}{-25\%} = -2.0$$

What happens if we calculate the price elasticity from the other direction? Suppose that Hortons ends the sale and puts the price of coffee back up from $1.50 to $2. This action causes the quantity demanded to fall from 15 million cups back down to 10 million. Note that while dropping from $2 to $1.50 was a 25 percent reduction in price ($0.50/$2.00 = 25 percent), increasing from $1.50 to $2 is a 33 percent increase ($0.50/$1.50 = 33 percent). Similarly, going from a quantity of 15 million to 10 million is a 33 percent decrease, whereas going from 10 million to 15 million is a 50 percent increase. Plugging these figures into our equation, we find that the elasticity of demand now seems to be −1.0:

$$\text{Price elasticity of demand} = \frac{(10 \text{ million} - 15 \text{ million})/15 \text{ million}}{(2.00 - 1.50)/1.50} = -\frac{33\%}{33\%} = -1.0$$

This is a headache. We're moving between the same two points on the demand curve, with the same change in price and quantity ($0.50 and 5 million cups), but in one direction we find an elasticity of demand of −2.0 and in the other direction it's −1.0. We'd like to have a consistent way to estimate the elasticity of demand between two points on the demand curve, regardless of the direction of the movement.

The **mid-point method** solves our problem: it measures the percentage change relative to a point *midway between the two points*. Using the mid-point method, we find the percentage change in quantity by dividing the change in quantity by the average of (that is, the mid-point between) the old and new quantities:

Equation 4-2

$$\% \text{ change in Q} = \frac{\text{change in Q}}{\text{average of Q}}$$

In the denominator of this expression, the mid-point (average) quantity is equal to the sum of the two quantities divided by 2. We can find the mid-point price in the same way:

$$\text{Mid-point of Q} = \frac{(Q_1 + Q_2)}{2}$$

$$\text{Mid-point of P} = \frac{(P_1 + P_2)}{2}$$

In our example, the demand for coffee went from 10 million cups at $2 to 15 million cups at $1.50. So the average (mid-point) quantity was 12.5 million, and the average (mid-point) price was $1.75.

The formula for the price elasticity of demand using the mid-point method is shown in Equation 4-3.

Equation 4-3

$$\text{Price elasticity of demand} = \frac{(Q_2 - Q_1)/[(Q_1 + Q_2)/2]}{(P_2 - P_1)/[(P_1 + P_2)/2]}$$

Using Equation 4-3, we find that the price elasticity of demand is the same whether we move from a lower price to a higher one or vice versa. For a price decrease, the elasticity is:

$$\text{Price elasticity of demand} = \frac{(15 \text{ million} - 10 \text{ million})/12.5 \text{ million}}{(1.50 - 2.00)/1.75} = \frac{40\%}{-29\%} = -1.38$$

For a price increase, the elasticity is:

$$\text{Price elasticity of demand} = \frac{(10 \text{ million} - 15 \text{ million})/12.5 \text{ million}}{(2.00 - 1.50)/1.75} = \frac{-40\%}{29\%} = -1.38$$

Our measure for the price elasticity of demand is now consistent.

Determinants of Price Elasticity of Demand

> **LO 4.2** Explain how the determinants of price elasticity of demand affect the degree of elasticity.

How would the quantity of coffees demanded change if the price fell from $3 to $1.50? Now, how much would the quantity demanded of cotton socks change if the price fell from $10 per pack to $5? Although both represent a 50 percent price reduction, we suspect that the former might change your buying habits more than the latter. Socks are socks, and a $5 saving probably won't make you rush out and buy twice as many.

The underlying idea here is that consumers are more sensitive to price changes for some goods and services than for others. Why isn't price elasticity of demand the same for all goods and services? Many factors determine consumers' responsiveness to price changes. The availability of substitutes, relative need and relative cost, and the time needed to adjust to price changes all affect price elasticity of demand.

Availability of Substitutes

Recall from Chapter 3 that substitutes are goods that are distinguishable from one another but have similar uses. When the price of a good with a close substitute increases, consumers will buy the substitute instead. If close substitutes are available for a particular good, then the demand for that good will be *more elastic* than it would be if only distant substitutes are available. For example, the price elasticity of demand for cranberry juice is likely to be relatively elastic; if the price gets too high, many consumers may switch to grape juice.

"Great idea, Pete!"

Would you expect this price change to reduce the quantity demanded of lobsters?

www.CartoonStock.com. Used with permission.

Degree of Necessity

When a good is a basic necessity, people will buy it even if prices rise. The demand for socks probably is not very elastic, nor is the demand for home heating during the winter. Although people may not like it when the prices of these goods rise, they will buy them to maintain a basic level of comfort. And when prices fall, they probably won't buy vastly more socks or make their homes a lot hotter.

In comparison, the demand for luxuries like vacations, expensive cars, and jewellery is likely to be much more elastic. Most people can easily do without these goods when their prices rise. Note, however, that the definition of a necessity depends on your standards and circumstances. In Florida air conditioning may be a necessity and heating a luxury; the opposite is likely to be true in Yukon.

Cost Relative to Income

All else held equal, if consumers spend a very small share of their incomes on a good, their demand for the good will be less elastic. For instance, most people can get a year's supply of salt for just a few dollars. Even if the price doubled, a year's supply would still cost less than $10, so consumers probably would not bother to adjust their salt consumption.

The opposite is also true: if a good costs a very large proportion of a person's income, like going on a luxury three-week vacation to the beach, the demand for the good will be more elastic. If the price of rooms at high-end beach-front hotels doubles, then a lot of people will decide to do something else with their vacations.

Adjustment Time

Goods often have much more elastic demand in the long run than in the short run. Often adjusting to price changes takes some time. Consider how you might react to an increase in the price of gasoline. In the short run you might cancel a weekend road trip, but you would still have to do the same amount of driving as usual to school, work, or the grocery store. Over a year, however, you could consider other choices that would further reduce your consumption of gas, such as buying a bus pass or a bicycle, getting a more fuel-efficient car, or moving closer to work or school.

Scope of the Market

A major caveat with regard to the determinants just described is that each depends on how you define the market for a good or service. The price elasticity of demand for bananas might be high, but the price elasticity of demand for *fruit* could still be low, because there are more substitutes for bananas than for the broader category of fruit. Similarly, although water might have a very low price elasticity of demand as a basic necessity, the demand for *bottled* water could be extremely elastic.

Using Price Elasticity of Demand

When we make decisions in the real world, we often don't know the exact price elasticity of demand. But we don't always need to estimate elasticity precisely to know that consumers will react differently to price changes for cups of coffee than for socks. Instead, businesses and other decision makers often know something general about the shape of the demand curve they are facing. Being able to place goods in several broad categories of elasticity can facilitate real pricing decisions in situations without full information.

At the extremes, demand can be perfectly elastic or perfectly inelastic. When demand is **perfectly elastic**, the demand curve is horizontal, as shown in panel A of Figure 4-2. This graph indicates that consumers are very sensitive to price, because demand drops to zero when the price increases even a minuscule amount. When demand is **perfectly inelastic**, the demand curve is vertical, as shown in panel B of Figure 4-2. In this case, the quantity demanded is the same no matter what the price. These two extremes rarely occur in real life.

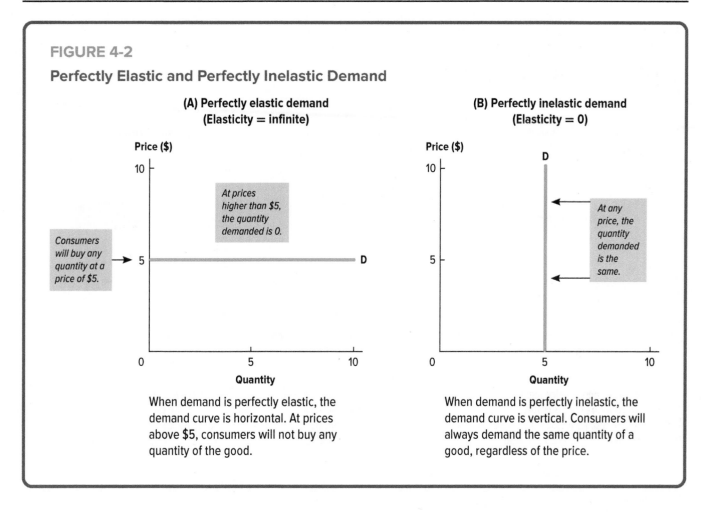

FIGURE 4-2

Perfectly Elastic and Perfectly Inelastic Demand

(A) Perfectly elastic demand (Elasticity = infinite)

Price ($)

At prices higher than $5, the quantity demanded is 0.

Consumers will buy any quantity at a price of $5.

When demand is perfectly elastic, the demand curve is horizontal. At prices above $5, consumers will not buy any quantity of the good.

(B) Perfectly inelastic demand (Elasticity = 0)

Price ($)

At any price, the quantity demanded is the same.

When demand is perfectly inelastic, the demand curve is vertical. Consumers will always demand the same quantity of a good, regardless of the price.

Between these two extremes, elasticity is commonly divided into three quantifiable categories: elastic, inelastic, and unit-elastic. When the absolute value of the price elasticity of demand is greater than 1, we call the associated demand **elastic**. With elastic demand, a given percentage change in the price of a good will cause an even larger percentage change in the quantity demanded. For example, a 40 percent change in price might lead to a 60 percent change in the quantity demanded. Panel A of Figure 4-3 illustrates elastic demand.

When the absolute value of the price elasticity of demand is less than 1, we say that demand is **inelastic**. With inelastic demand, a given percentage change in price will cause a smaller percentage change in the quantity demanded. For example, a 40 percent change in price might lead to a 20 percent change in the quantity demanded. Panel B of Figure 4-3 illustrates inelastic demand.

FIGURE 4-3

Elastic, Inelastic, and Unit-Elastic Demand

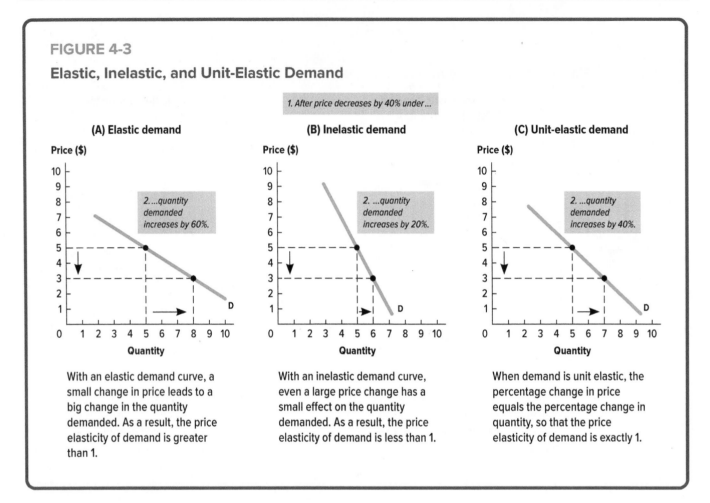

1. After price decreases by 40% under...

(A) Elastic demand

Price ($)

2. ...quantity demanded increases by 60%.

With an elastic demand curve, a small change in price leads to a big change in the quantity demanded. As a result, the price elasticity of demand is greater than 1.

(B) Inelastic demand

Price ($)

2. ...quantity demanded increases by 20%.

With an inelastic demand curve, even a large price change has a small effect on the quantity demanded. As a result, the price elasticity of demand is less than 1.

(C) Unit-elastic demand

Price ($)

2. ...quantity demanded increases by 40%.

When demand is unit elastic, the percentage change in price equals the percentage change in quantity, so that the price elasticity of demand is exactly 1.

If the absolute value of elasticity is exactly 1—that is, if a percentage change in price causes the same percentage change in the quantity demanded—then we say that demand is **unit-elastic**. In this case, a 40 percent change in price leads to a 40 percent change in the quantity demanded. Panel C of Figure 4-3 illustrates unit-elastic demand.

As we'll see later in this chapter, these terms—elastic, inelastic, and unit-elastic—can be used to describe any sort of elasticity, not just the price elasticity of demand. Although these categories may sound academic, they can have serious implications for real-world business and policy decisions. The Real Life box, Does Charging for Bednets Decrease Malaria? describes a case in which knowing whether the price elasticity of demand is elastic or inelastic is a matter of life and death.

To improve your understanding of elastic, inelastic, and unit-elastic demand, try the online interactive graphing tutorial.

REAL LIFE

Does Charging for Bednets Decrease Malaria?

Around the world, malaria kills millions of people every year. There is no vaccine to protect people from malaria. There is a way to escape the disease, though: sleep under a bednet that has been treated with insecticide. Bednets prevent malaria by shielding sleepers from disease-carrying mosquitoes.

Organizations that want to promote the use of bednets to fight malaria face a practical question: Would charging a fee for bednets be more effective in reducing the illness than handing out the nets for free?

Those who advocate charging a fee argue that people who pay for the nets will value them more, and will probably use them more, than those who receive the nets for free. These advocates expect that fewer nets will be wasted on people who don't really want them and that people who do buy them will be more likely to use them. Moreover, if people pay for their bednets, provider organizations will be able to afford to distribute more of them. On the other hand, the law of demand states that the higher the price, the lower the quantity demanded is likely to be. Even if charging a fee would make some people more likely to use the nets, it might dissuade others from getting them, thus undermining the aim of the anti-malaria campaign.

To settle this question, health organizations needed to know the price elasticity of the demand for bednets. Working in Kenya, economists Jessica Cohen of the Harvard School of Public Health and Pascaline Dupas of Stanford set up an experiment to try both methods and to measure the price elasticity of demand for bednets. As it turned out, charging a fee greatly reduced the quantity of the nets demanded. In the experiment, the number of people who took bednets dropped by 75 percent when the price increased from zero to $0.75. Nor did people who bought bednets at that price use them more effectively than those who received them for free.

If profit were the goal in this campaign, a few bednets sold at $0.75 would generate more revenue than a lot of bednets given away for free. But the goal was to protect people from malaria, not to make a profit. For organizations with a social mission, free distribution of bednets seems more effective than charging a fee.

Source: J. Cohen and P. Dupas, "Free distribution or cost sharing? Evidence from a randomized malaria prevention experiment," *Quarterly Journal of Economics* 125, no. 1 (February 2010): 1–45.

Knowing whether the demand for a good is elastic or inelastic is extremely useful in business, because it allows a manager to determine whether a price increase will cause total revenue to rise or fall. **Total revenue** is the amount that a firm receives from the sale of goods and services, calculated as the quantity sold multiplied by the price paid for each unit. This number is important for an obvious reason: it tells us how much money sellers receive when they sell something.

An increase in price affects total revenue in two ways:

- It causes a *quantity effect,* or a decrease in revenue that results from selling fewer units of the good.

- It causes a *price effect,* or an increase in revenue that results from receiving a higher price for each unit sold.

> To improve your understanding of the quantity and price effects of a price change, try the online interactive graphing tutorial.

Figure 4-4 shows both the quantity effect and the price effect. When the quantity effect outweighs the price effect, a price increase will cause a drop in revenue, as it does in Figure 4-4. When the price effect outweighs the quantity effect, a price increase will raise total revenue.

When demand is elastic, a price increase causes total revenue to fall. We already know that when demand is elastic, a change in price will cause a larger percentage change in quantity demanded. Another way of saying this is that the quantity effect outweighs the price effect. So when demand is elastic, a price increase causes a proportionally larger decrease in the quantity demanded, and total revenue falls.

Conversely, when demand is inelastic, the percentage change in price is larger than the percentage change in quantity demanded. The price effect outweighs the quantity effect, and total revenue increases. With inelastic demand, then, consumers will purchase less of a good when prices rise, but the change in the quantity demanded will be proportionally less than the change in price. Figure 4-5 shows this trade-off between the price and quantity effects. As you can see, panel A shows an elastic demand in which a $1 change in price causes the quantity demanded to increase by 4,000. With the inelastic demand curve in panel B, a $2 decrease in price increases quantity demanded by only 1,000.

There is one final point to make. So far, everything we've said has described elasticity *at a particular spot on the demand curve.* For most goods, however, elasticity varies along the curve. So when (using Equation 4-3) we determined that the price elasticity of demand for coffee was 1.38, we meant that it was 1.38 for a price change from $1.50 to $2 a cup. If the price changes from $2 to $2.50, the elasticity will be different.

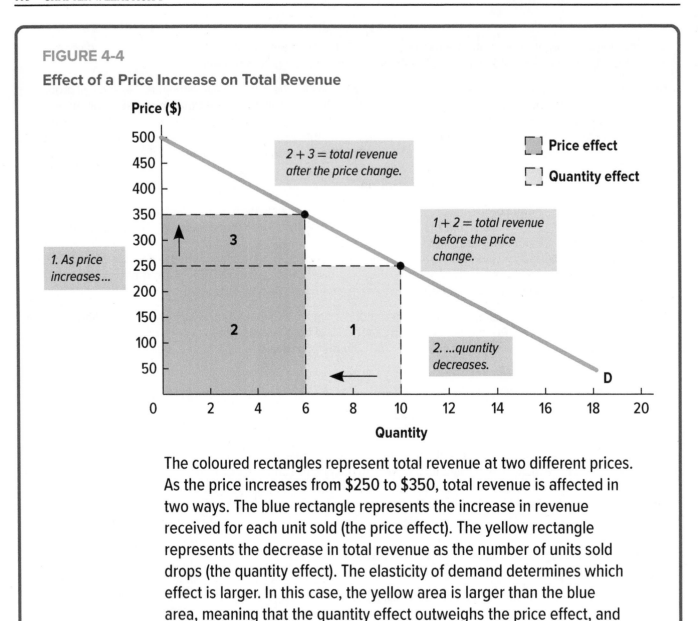

FIGURE 4-4

Effect of a Price Increase on Total Revenue

The coloured rectangles represent total revenue at two different prices. As the price increases from $250 to $350, total revenue is affected in two ways. The blue rectangle represents the increase in revenue received for each unit sold (the price effect). The yellow rectangle represents the decrease in total revenue as the number of units sold drops (the quantity effect). The elasticity of demand determines which effect is larger. In this case, the yellow area is larger than the blue area, meaning that the quantity effect outweighs the price effect, and total revenue decreases.

The reasoning behind this fact is common sense. Imagine that the price of a cup of coffee plummets to 10 cents, and you get into the habit of buying one every morning. What would you do if you showed up one morning and found that the price had doubled overnight, to 20 cents? We bet you'd shrug and buy one anyway.

Now, imagine the price of coffee is $10 a cup, and you buy it only as an occasional treat. If you arrive at the coffee shop and find the price has doubled to $20, what will you do? You'd probably consider very carefully whether you really need that latte. In both cases, you would be responding to a 100 percent increase in price for the same product, but you would react very differently. This makes perfect sense: in one case, the latte costs you only 10 more cents, but in the other, it costs an additional $10.

Your reactions to the latte illustrate a general rule: demand tends to be more elastic when price is high and more inelastic when price is low. This brings us to an important caveat about the three graphs shown in Figure 4-3. Although the example of an elastic demand curve in panel A has a steeper *slope* than the inelastic demand curve in panel B, we now know that slope is not the same as elasticity.

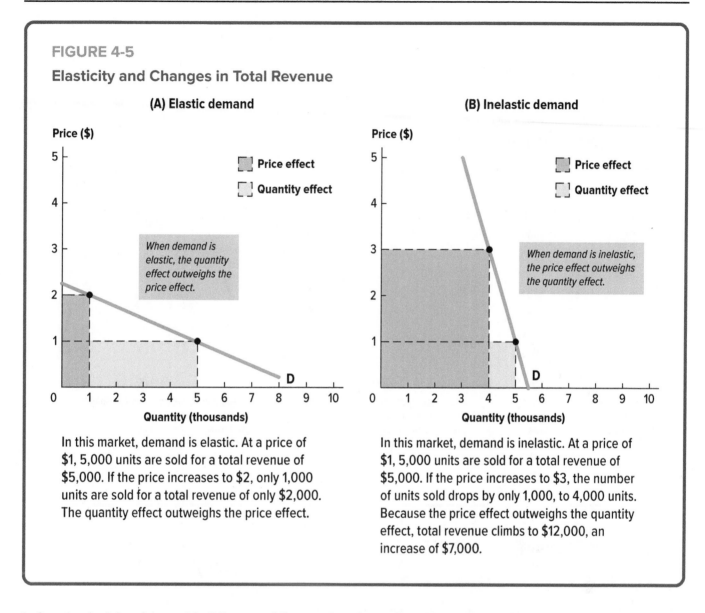

FIGURE 4-5

Elasticity and Changes in Total Revenue

(A) Elastic demand

(B) Inelastic demand

In this market, demand is elastic. At a price of $1, 5,000 units are sold for a total revenue of $5,000. If the price increases to $2, only 1,000 units are sold for a total revenue of only $2,000. The quantity effect outweighs the price effect.

In this market, demand is inelastic. At a price of $1, 5,000 units are sold for a total revenue of $5,000. If the price increases to $3, the number of units sold drops by only 1,000, to 4,000 units. Because the price effect outweighs the quantity effect, total revenue climbs to $12,000, an increase of $7,000.

In fact, the elasticity of demand is different at different points along a linear demand curve. The reasoning is not intuitive, but becomes straightforward when you think about it graphically. Look at Figure 4-6. The line in panel B has a constant slope, but the percentage changes in price and quantity are very different at each end of the curve. For instance, going from $45 to $40 is a much smaller difference (in percentage terms) than from $10 to $5, but the slope of the curve is the same between both sets of points.

It becomes apparent that as we move along a linear demand curve, revenue first increases and then decreases with higher prices. Panel C shows graphically the total revenue curve associated with the demand curve in panel B, using calculations from the schedule in panel A. Note that when the price is high, lowering the price will increase revenue. For example, when the price decreases from $45 to $40 (see the schedule), total revenue almost doubles, from $45 to $80. When the price is low, however, lowering it further decreases total revenue. Moving from $10 to $5, for example, decreases total revenue from $80 to $45.

> For a refresher on slope versus elasticity, see Appendix C, Math Essentials: Calculating Percentage Change, Slope, and Elasticity, which follows this chapter.

An understanding of price elasticity of demand has all sorts of real-world applications. See, for example, the issue discussed in the What Do You Think? box, Should Entrance Fees at National Parks Be Raised?

FIGURE 4-6

Changes in Elasticity Along the Demand Curve

(A) Demand and revenue schedule

Price ($)	Quantity	Total revenue ($)
50	0	0
45	1	45
40	2	80
35	3	105
30	4	120
25	5	125
20	6	120
15	7	105
10	8	80
5	9	45
0	10	0

(B) Price elasticity

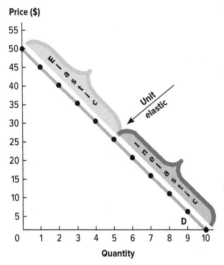

(C) Total revenue

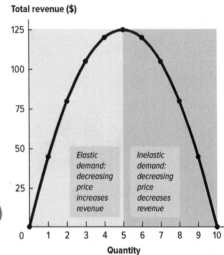

This table lists the data shown in the graphs in panels B and C. Quantity demanded always increases as price falls. Total revenue rises until the price falls to $25, then falls at lower prices.

Price elasticity of demand varies along the demand curve. Above a certain price, demand is elastic; below it, demand is inelastic.

This graph shows total revenue along the demand curve shown above. Total revenue first rises, but then begins to fall as demand moves from elastic to inelastic.

WHAT DO YOU THINK?

Should Entrance Fees at National Parks Be Raised?

Parks Canada is the steward of forty-four national parks including Banff National Park, Thousand Islands National Park, and Cape Breton Highlands National Park. According to its 2014 report, nearly $670 million of Parks Canada's operating budget comes from the federal government. Entrance fees contribute approximately $59 million in non-government revenue to the federal agency.[2] Since 2013, cash-strapped Parks Canada started consulting the public about fee hikes. But there is significant opposition to any discussion of higher fees.

A day at Canada's Wonderland costs a family of four at least $188, not counting food, drinks, and souvenirs. A three-day pass to enter Jasper National Park costs $59 per car, which means that the same family spending three days among elk, mountains, glaciers, and lakes would pay the equivalent of $5 per person per day.

Which is why it's perplexing to see opposition to any fee hikes. Their principal objections are economic: tourism-dependent communities fret that higher fees will reduce visitation and cut into profits, while others argue that the increases will keep out those of limited financial means. It's true, in theory at least, that raising the price of something should decrease demand for it.

On the other hand, it's absurd to expect a finite amount of parkland to accommodate a continually increasing number of people. Anyone who has visited Lake Louise in Banff National Park on a holiday weekend is unlikely to regard a drop in park visitation as entirely a bad thing.

Slightly higher user fees are unlikely to have much effect on park use, but they could have a significant effect on the quality of the park experience. Most of that money will stay at individual parks, where it can be spent on upkeep and repairs—the sort of unglamorous expenditures that typically get shortchanged in the politically driven federal budget process. Smaller crowds and plumbing that works—what's not to like?

What do you think?

1. Do you agree with the argument that the demand for national park visits is inelastic at current price levels, so that higher fees are "unlikely to have much effect on park use"? Think about the factors that affect price elasticity, such as the availability and price of substitutes.

2. How would you weigh the following trade-offs?

   a. Should Parks Canada intentionally try to shrink the demand for visits in order to reduce crowding? In order to protect parks from environmental damage?

   b. Does Parks Canada has a responsibility to keep national parks accessible to families who cannot afford to pay higher fees?

   c. Should Parks Canada be concerned about the economic impact of a reduced demand for visits on surrounding communities?

✓ CONCEPT CHECK

☐ What is the formula for calculating the price elasticity of demand? [LO 4.1]

☐ Why should you use the mid-point method to calculate the price elasticity of demand? [LO 4.1]

☐ If demand is inelastic, will an increase in price increase or decrease revenue? [LO 4.2]

Price Elasticity of Supply

What happens when an increase in coffee consumption drives up the price of coffee beans? *How will the coffee market respond* to the price change? We can predict, based on the law of supply, that coffee growers will respond to an increase in price by increasing their production—but by how much?

Price elasticity of supply is the size of the change in the quantity supplied of a good or service when its price changes. Price elasticity of supply measures producers' responsiveness to a change in price, just as price elasticity of demand measures consumers' responsiveness to a change in price.

Chapter 3 showed that when prices rise, producers supply larger quantities of a good; when prices fall, they supply smaller quantities. Just as the price elasticity of demand for a good tells us how much the quantity *demanded* changes as we move along the demand curve, the price elasticity of supply tells us how much the quantity *supplied* changes as we move along the supply curve.

Calculating Price Elasticity of Supply

> **LO 4.3** Calculate price elasticity of supply using the mid-point method.

Price elasticity of supply is measured in the same way as price elasticity of demand: as the percentage change in quantity divided by the percentage change in price (see Equation 4-4).

Equation 4-4

$$\text{Price elasticity of supply} = \frac{\% \text{ change in quantity supplied}}{\% \text{ change in price}}$$

To ensure that elasticity will be the same whether you move up or down the supply curve, you should use the mid-point method, as in Equation 4-5.

Equation 4-5

$$\text{Price elasticity of supply} = \frac{(Q_2 - Q_1)/\left[(Q_1 + Q_2)/2\right]}{(P_2 - P_1)/\left[(P_1 + P_2)/2\right]}$$

Suppose that when the price of coffee beans goes from $1 to $1.20 per pound, production increases from 90 million pounds of coffee beans per year to 100 million pounds. Using the mid-point method, the percentage change in quantity supplied would be:

$$\% \text{ change in quantity supplied} = \frac{(100 \text{ million} - 90 \text{ million})}{95 \text{ million}} = 11\%$$

The percentage change in price would be:

$$\% \text{ change in price} = \frac{(1.2 - 1)}{1.1} = 18\%$$

So the price elasticity of supply at this point on the supply curve is:

$$\text{Price elasticity of supply} = \frac{11\%}{18\%} = 0.6$$

An elasticity of 0.6 tells us that the supply of coffee beans is relatively inelastic, at least in the short run. Does this result make sense? As it turns out, coffee takes a long time to grow. Coffee plants don't produce a full yield for four to six years after they are planted. Because coffee growers can't increase production quickly, it makes sense that the supply of coffee would be inelastic. (Remember that if prices had fallen from $1.20 to $1, instead of rising from $1 to $1.20, the elasticity would be the same using the mid-point method.)

HINT

- The elasticity of demand is calculated by dividing a positive number by a negative number, or by dividing a negative number by a positive number, so the answer is always negative.

- The elasticity of supply, on the other hand, is calculated by dividing either a positive number by another positive number, or a negative number by another negative number. In either case, the answer is always positive.

Remembering the above rules can help you to check your numerical calculations.

As with the price elasticity of demand, we can describe the price elasticity of supply using three categories:

- *Elastic,* if it has an absolute value greater than 1.

- *Inelastic,* if it has an absolute value less than 1.

- *Unit-elastic,* if it has an absolute value of exactly 1.

In extreme cases, we can also describe supply as being *perfectly elastic* (if the quantity supplied could be anything at a given price and is zero at any other price), or *perfectly inelastic* (if the quantity supplied is the same regardless of the price).

> To improve your understanding of price elasticity, try the online interactive graphing tutorial.

Determinants of Price Elasticity of Supply

> **LO 4.4** Explain how the determinants of price elasticity of supply affect the degree of elasticity.

Whether supply is elastic or inelastic depends on the supplier's ability to change the quantity produced in response to price changes. Three factors affect a supplier's ability to expand production: the availability of inputs, the flexibility of the production process, and the time needed to adjust to changes in price. Recall that this last factor—time—is also a determinant of the elasticity of demand. Just as consumers take time to change their habits, suppliers need time to ramp up production.

Availability of Inputs

The production of some goods can be expanded easily, just by adding extra inputs. For example, a bakery can easily buy extra flour and yeast to produce more bread, probably at the same cost per loaf. Increasing the supply of other goods is more difficult, however, and sometimes is impossible. If the price of Picasso paintings goes up, there isn't much anyone can do to produce more of them, since we cannot bring the artist back to life.

In other words, the elasticity of supply depends on the elasticity of the supply of inputs. If producing more of a good will cost a lot more than the initial quantity did, because the extra inputs will be harder to find, then the producer will be reluctant to increase the quantity supplied. Higher and higher prices will be needed to convince the producer to go to the extra trouble.

Flexibility of the Production Process

The easiest way for producers to adjust the quantity supplied of a particular good is to draw production capacity away from other goods when prices rise, or to reassign capacity to other goods when prices fall. Farmers may find this sort of substitution relatively simple: when corn prices are high they will plant more acres with corn; when corn prices are low they will reassign acres to more profitable crops. Other producers have much less flexibility. If you own a company that manufactures specialized parts for Toyota, you might need to buy new machinery to begin making parts for Ford, let alone switch to another type of product entirely.

Adjustment Time

As with demand, supply is more elastic over long periods than over short periods. That is, producers can make more adjustments in the long run than in the short run. In the short run, the number of hotel rooms at Disneyland is fixed; in the medium and long run, old rooms can be renovated and new hotels can be built. Production capacity can also increase or decrease over time as new firms start up or old ones shut down.

✓ CONCEPT CHECK

☐ How would you calculate the price elasticity of supply? [LO 4.3]
☐ What are the three determinants of the price elasticity of supply? [LO 4.4]

Other Elasticities

The quantity of a good that is demanded is sensitive to more than just the price of the good. Because people are clever, flexible, and always on the lookout for ways to make the most of opportunities, the quantity demanded also responds to changing circumstances, such as the prices of other goods and the incomes consumers earn. Let's consider two other demand elasticities, the *cross-price elasticity of demand* and the *income elasticity of demand*.

Cross-Price Elasticity of Demand

LO 4.5 Calculate cross-price elasticity of demand, and interpret the sign of the elasticity.

We have noted that the substitutability of goods affects price elasticity. That is, consumers' willingness to start or stop buying a good depends on the availability of other goods that serve the same purpose. For example, we might expect a Starbucks coffee to have relatively price-elastic demand, because some people will buy regular coffee from Tim Hortons when the price of a Starbucks coffee rises. Once again, recalling the four economists' questions we presented in Chapter 1, asking *How will others respond?* is the key to understanding the situation.

What happens if the price of Tim Hortons coffee falls but the price of a Starbucks coffee stays the same? **Cross-price elasticity of demand** describes how the quantity demanded of one good changes when the price of a *different* good changes. Because Starbucks coffee and Tim Horton's coffee are substitutes, we expect the quantity of Starbucks coffees demanded to go down when the price of Tim Horton's coffee falls, as some people switch from Starbucks coffees to Tim Horton's coffee. The reverse also holds: if the price of a cup of Tim Hortons coffee rises, while the price of a Starbucks coffee doesn't, we expect the quantity of Starbucks coffee demanded to rise as some people switch from Tim Hortons coffee to the relatively cheaper Starbucks coffee. Equation 4-6 gives the formula for the cross-price elasticity of demand.

Equation 4-6

$$\text{Cross-price elasticity of demand between A and B} = \frac{\%\text{ change in quantity of A demanded}}{\%\text{ change in price of B}}$$

When two goods are substitutes, we expect their cross-price elasticity of demand to be positive. That is, an increase in the price of one will cause an increase in the quantity demanded of the other. On the other hand, a decrease in the price of one substitute good will cause a decrease in the quantity demanded of the other. Just how elastic demand is depends on how close the two substitutes are. If they are very close substitutes, a change in the price of one will cause a large change in the quantity demanded of the other, so that cross-price elasticity will be high. If they are not close substitutes, cross-price elasticity will be low.

Cross-price elasticity can also be negative. Unlike the price elasticity of demand, which can be expressed as an absolute value because it is always negative, the sign of a cross-price elasticity tells us about the relationship between two goods. We have seen that when two goods are substitutes, their cross-price elasticity will be positive. However, when two goods are complements (that is, when they are consumed together), cross-price elasticity will be negative.

For example, when people drink more coffee, they want more cream to go with it. Coffee and cream are complements, not substitutes. So when the demand for coffee increases, the demand for cream will increase, all else held equal. When two goods are linked in this way, their cross-price elasticity will be negative, because an increase in the price of one good will decrease the quantity demanded of both goods. Again, the relative size of the elasticity tells us how strongly the two goods are linked. If the two goods are strong complements, their cross-price elasticity will be a large negative number. If the two goods are loosely linked, their cross-price elasticity will be negative but not far below zero.

Income Elasticity of Demand

> **LO 4.6** Calculate income elasticity of demand, and interpret the sign of the elasticity.

There are some goods that people buy in roughly the same amounts, no matter how wealthy they are. Salt, toothpaste, and toilet paper are three examples. These are not the sort of products people rush out to buy when they get a raise at work. Other goods, though, are very sensitive to changes in income. If you get a raise, you might splurge on new clothes or a meal at a fancy restaurant.

The **income elasticity of demand** for a good describes how much the quantity demanded changes in response to a change in consumers' incomes. As Equation 4-7 shows, it is expressed as the ratio of the percentage change in the quantity demanded to the percentage change in income:

Equation 4-7

$$\text{Income elasticity of demand} = \frac{\% \text{ change in quantity demanded}}{\% \text{ change in income}}$$

Recall from Chapter 3 that increases in income raise the demand for normal goods and lower the demand for inferior goods. Income elasticity tells us how much the demand for these goods changes.

For example, a Starbucks Frappuccino is a normal good that might be fairly responsive to changes in income. When people become wealthier, they will buy more of a small luxury item like this. Therefore, we would guess that the income elasticity of demand for fancy iced coffee drinks is positive (because the drink is a normal good) and relatively large (because the drink is a non-necessity that has many cheaper substitutes).

Regular coffee is also generally a normal good, so its income elasticity should be positive. However, we might guess that it will be less elastic than a Frappuccino's. Many people consider their standard cup of coffee every day before work to be more of a necessity than a luxury and will buy it regardless of their incomes. Another way to put it is that the demand for Frappuccinos is income-elastic, while the demand for plain coffee is relatively income-inelastic. For normal goods like these, income elasticity is positive, because the quantity that is demanded increases as incomes rise. Both necessities and luxuries are normal goods. If the good is a necessity, income elasticity of demand will be positive but less than 1. If the good is a luxury, income elasticity will be positive but more than 1.

As with the cross-price elasticity of demand, the income elasticity of demand can be negative as well as positive. The income elasticity of demand is negative for inferior goods because quantity demanded decreases as incomes increase.

In 2009 Starbucks introduced a new retail product, VIA instant coffee. Although some coffee enthusiasts sneered, others thought it was a shrewd move at a time of economic hardship. Instant coffee mix may be an inferior good in some places: as incomes increase, people will drink more expensive beverages and *decrease* their consumption of instant coffee. During a recession, however, budgets tighten, and people may increase their consumption of instant coffee as they cut back on more expensive drinks. At least, that is what Starbucks was hoping. In this scenario, the income elasticity of instant coffee would be small and negative. A less-appealing inferior good that people quickly abandon as they grow richer would have a large, negative income elasticity.

Once again, the sign and size of a good's elasticity tell us a lot about the good. Table 4-1 summarizes what we have learned about the four types of elasticity.

TABLE 4-1   FOUR MEASURES OF ELASTICITY

Measure	Equation	Negative	Positive	More elastic	Less elastic
Price Elasticity of Demand	$\dfrac{\text{\% change in quantity demanded}}{\text{\% change in price}}$	Always	Never	Over time, for substitutable goods and luxury items	In the short run, for unique and necessary items
Price Elasticity of Supply	$\dfrac{\text{\% change in quantity supplied}}{\text{\% change in price}}$	Never	Always	Over time, with flexible production	In the short run, with production constraints
Cross-Price Elasticity	$\dfrac{\text{\% change in quantity demanded of A}}{\text{\% change in price of B}}$	For complements	For substitutes	For near-perfect substitutes and strong complements	For loosely related goods
Income Elasticity	$\dfrac{\text{\% change in quantity demanded}}{\text{\% change in income}}$	For inferior goods	For normal goods	For luxury items with close substitutes	For unique and necessary items

If you find this discussion particularly interesting, you might want to consider work as a pricing analyst. You can read more about this in the Where Can It Take You? box, Pricing Analyst.

WHERE CAN IT TAKE YOU?

Pricing Analyst

In most industries, keeping an eye on competitors' prices and responding accordingly is a major task. Large businesses hire *pricing analysts* to perform this crucial function. Pricing analysts use their knowledge of elasticity and markets to help businesses determine the right price to charge for their products.

✓ CONCEPT CHECK

☐ Why is the cross-price elasticity of demand positive for substitutes? [LO 4.5]

☐ Why does the income-elasticity of demand depend on whether a good is normal or inferior? [LO 4.6]

Conclusion

Supply and *demand* may be the most common words in economics, but applying these concepts to the real world requires a bit of elaboration. Elasticity is the first of several concepts we will study that will help you to apply the concepts of supply and demand to business and policy questions. In this chapter we saw how elasticity can be used to set prices so as to maximize revenue. In the coming chapters we will use elasticity to predict the effects of government intervention in the market, and we will dig deeper into the consumer and producer choices that drive elasticity.

Key Terms

elasticity	inelastic
price elasticity of demand	unit-elastic
mid-point method	total revenue
perfectly elastic demand	price elasticity of supply
perfectly inelastic demand	cross-price elasticity of demand
elastic	income elasticity of demand

Summary

LO 4.1 Calculate price elasticity of demand using the mid-point method.

Elasticity is a measure of consumers' and producers' responsiveness to a change in market conditions. Understanding the elasticity for a good or service allows economic decision makers to anticipate the outcome of changes in market conditions and to calibrate prices so as to maximize revenues.

Price elasticity of demand is the size of the change in the quantity demanded of a good or service when its price changes. Elasticity should be calculated as a percentage using the mid-point method to avoid problems with conflicting units of measurement and with the direction of a change. Price elasticity of demand is almost always negative, because the quantity demanded falls as the price rises. It is usually represented as an absolute value, without the negative sign.

LO 4.2 Explain how the determinants of price elasticity of demand affect the degree of elasticity.

In general, demand is inelastic for goods that have no close substitutes, are basic necessities, or cost a relatively small proportion of consumers' incomes. Demand is also inelastic over short periods and for broadly defined markets. When demand is elastic, a percentage change in the price of a good will cause a larger percentage change in the quantity demanded; the absolute value of the elasticity will be greater than 1. When demand is inelastic, a percentage change in price will cause a smaller percentage change in the quantity demanded; the absolute value of the elasticity will be less than 1. When demand is unit-elastic, the percentage changes in price and quantity will be equal, and the elasticity will be exactly 1.

LO 4.3 Calculate price elasticity of supply using the mid-point method.

Price elasticity of supply is the size of the change in the quantity supplied of a good or service when its price changes. Price elasticity of supply is almost always positive, because the quantity supplied increases as the price increases.

LO 4.4 Explain how the determinants of price elasticity of supply affect the degree of elasticity.

Supply is generally inelastic when additional inputs to the production process are difficult to get and the production process is inflexible. Supply is also inelastic over short periods. Supply is considered elastic when the absolute value of its price elasticity is greater than 1, inelastic when the absolute value is less than 1, and unit-elastic when it is exactly 1.

LO 4.5 Calculate cross-price elasticity of demand, and interpret the sign of the elasticity.

Cross-price elasticity of demand is the percentage change in the quantity demanded in response to a given percentage change in the price of a *different* good. The cross-price elasticity of demand between two goods will be positive if they are substitutes and negative if they are complements.

LO 4.6 Calculate income elasticity of demand, and interpret the sign of the elasticity.

Income elasticity of demand is the percentage change in the quantity of a good demanded in response to a given percentage change in income. Income elasticity of demand will be positive for normal goods and negative for inferior goods.

Review Questions

1. You are advising a coffee shop manager who wants to estimate how much sales will change if the price of a coffee rises. Explain why he should measure elasticity in percentage terms rather than in terms of dollars and cups. [LO 4.1]

2. Explain why the coffee shop manager should measure elasticity using the mid-point method in his calculations. [LO 4.1]

3. You are working as a private math tutor to raise money for a trip during spring break. First explain why the price elasticity of demand for math tutoring might be elastic. Then explain why the price elasticity of demand for math tutoring might be inelastic. [LO 4.2]

4. You are working as a private math tutor to raise money for a trip during spring break. You want to raise as much money as possible. Should you should increase or decrease the price you charge? Explain. [LO 4.2]

5. You have been hired by the government of Kenya, which produces a lot of coffee, to examine the supply of gourmet coffee beans. Suppose you discover that the price elasticity of supply is 0.85. Explain this figure to the Kenyan government. [LO 4.3]

6. You have noticed that the price of tickets to your university's basketball games keeps increasing but the supply of tickets remains the same. Why might supply be unresponsive to changes in price? [LO 4.3]

7. Which will have a more price-elastic supply over six months, real estate in downtown Toronto or real estate in rural Winnipeg? Explain your reasoning. [LO 4.4]

8. Certain skilled labour, such as hair cutting, requires licensing or certification, which is costly and takes a long time to acquire. Explain what would happen to the price elasticity of supply for haircuts if this licensing requirement were removed. [LO 4.4]

9. Although we could describe both the cross-price elasticity of demand between paper coffee cups and plastic coffee lids, and the cross-price elasticity of demand between sugar and artificial sweeteners as highly elastic, the first cross-price elasticity is negative and the second is positive. What is the reason for this? [LO 4.5]

10. Name two related goods you consume that have a positive cross-price elasticity. What happens to your consumption of the second good if the price of the first good increases? [LO 4.5]

11. Name two related goods you consume that have a negative cross-price elasticity. What happens to your consumption of the second good if the price of the first good increases? [LO 4.5]

12. In France, where cheese is an important and traditional part of people's meals, people eat over twice as much cheese per person as in Canada. In which country do you think the demand for cheese will be more income-elastic? Why? [LO 4.6]

13. Name a good you consume for which your income elasticity of demand is positive. What happens when your income increases? [LO 4.6]

14. Name a good you consume for which your income elasticity of demand is negative. What happens when your income increases? [LO 4.6]

Problems and Applications

1. When the price of a bar of chocolate is $1, demand is 100,000 bars. When the price rises to $1.50, demand falls to 60,000 bars. Calculate the price elasticity of demand according to the instructions below and express your answer in absolute value. [LO 4.1]
   a. Suppose price increases from $1 to $1.50. Calculate the price elasticity of demand in terms of percent change.
   b. Suppose price decreases from $1.50 to $1. Calculate the price elasticity of demand in terms of percent change.
   c. Suppose the price increases from $1 to $1.50. Calculate the price elasticity of demand using the mid-point method.
   d. Suppose the price decreases from $1.50 to $1. Calculate the price elasticity of demand using the mid-point formula.

2. If the price elasticity of demand for used cars priced between $3,000 and $5,000 is −1.2 (using the mid-point method), what will be the percent change in quantity demanded when the price of a used car falls from $5,000 to $3,000? [LO 4.1]

3. Three points are identified on the graph in Figure 4P-1. [LO 4.2]

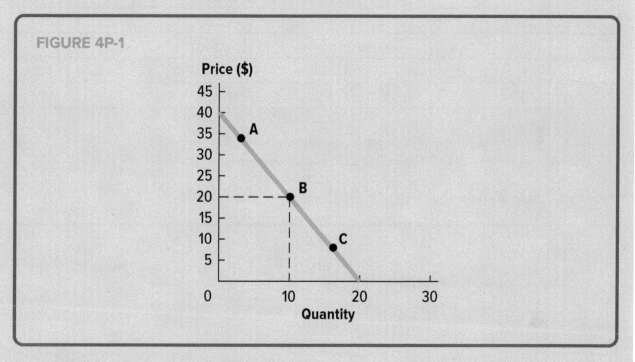

FIGURE 4P-1

   a. At point A, demand is _____.
   b. At point B, demand is _____.
   c. At point C, demand is _____.

4. Which of the following has a more elastic demand in the short run? [LO 4.2]
   a. Pomegranate juice or drinking water?
   b. Cereal or Rice Krispies?
   c. Speedboats or gourmet chocolate?

5. In each of the following instances, determine whether demand is elastic, inelastic, or unit-elastic. [LO 4.2]
   a. If price increases by 10 percent and quantity demand decreases by 15 percent, demand is _____.
   b. If price decreases by 10 percent and quantity demanded increases by 5 percent, demand is _____.

6. In each of the following instances, determine whether quantity demanded will increase or decrease, and by how much. [LO 4.2]
   a. If price elasticity of demand is −1.3 and price increases by 2 percent, quantity demanded will _____ by _____ percent.
   b. If price elasticity of demand is −0.3 and price decreases by 2 percent, quantity demanded will _____ by _____ percent.

Problems 7 and 8 refer to the demand schedule shown in Table 4P-1. For each price change, say whether demand is **elastic, unit-elastic,** *or* **inelastic,** *and say whether total revenue* **increases, decreases,** *or* **stays the same.**

TABLE 4P-1

Price ($)	Quantity demanded
80	0
70	50
60	100
50	150
40	200
30	250
20	300
10	350
0	400

7. Price increases from $10 to $20. Demand is _____ and total revenue _____ . **[LO 4.2]**
8. Price decreases from $70 to $60. Demand is _____ and total revenue _____ . **[LO 4.2]**

Problems 9–12 refer to Figure 4P-2.

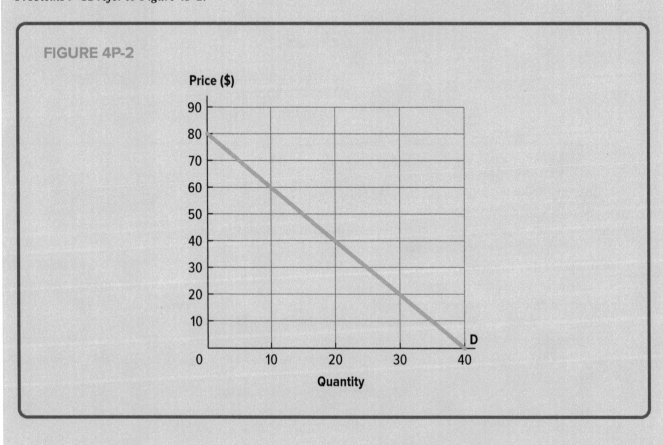

FIGURE 4P-2

9. Draw the price effect and the quantity effect for a price change from $60 to $50. Which effect is larger? Does total revenue increase or decrease? No calculation is necessary. [LO 4.2]

10. Draw the price effect and the quantity effect for a price change from $30 to $20. Which effect is larger? Does total revenue increase or decrease? No calculation is necessary. [LO 4.2]

11. Draw the price effect and the quantity effect for a price change from $60 to $70. Which effect is larger? Does total revenue increase or decrease? No calculation is necessary. [LO 4.2]

12. Draw the price effect and the quantity effect for a price change from $10 to $20. Which effect is larger? Does total revenue increase or decrease? No calculation is necessary. [LO 4.2]

13. Use the graph in Figure 4P-3 to calculate the price elasticity of supply between points A and B using the mid-point method. [LO 4.3]

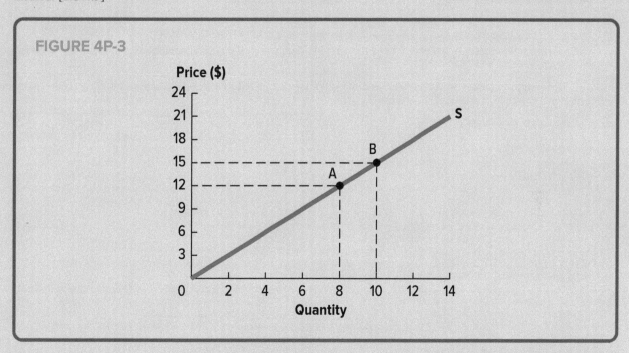

FIGURE 4P-3

14. If the price of a haircut is $15, the number of haircuts provided is 100. If the price rises to $30 per haircut, barbers will work much longer hours, and the supply of haircuts will increase to 300. What is the price elasticity of supply for haircuts between $15 and $30? [LO 4.3]

15. Which of the following has a more elastic supply in the short run? [LO 4.4]
    a. Hospitals or mobile clinics?
    b. Purebred dogs or pet rabbits?
    c. On-campus courses or online courses?

16. In each of the following instances, determine whether supply is elastic, inelastic, or unit-elastic. [LO 4.4]
    a. If price increases by 10 percent and quantity supplied increases by 15 percent, supply is _____.
    b. If price decreases by 10 percent and quantity supplied decreases by 5 percent, supply is _____.

17. In each of the following instances, determine whether quantity supplied will increase or decrease, and by how much. [LO 4.4]
    a. If price elasticity of supply is 1.3 and price increases by 2 percent, quantity supplied will _____ by _____ percent.
    b. If price elasticity of supply is 0.3 and price decreases by 2 percent, quantity supplied will _____ by _____ percent.

18. Suppose that the price of peanut butter rises from $2 to $3 per jar. [LO 4.5]
    a. The quantity of jelly purchased falls from 20 million jars to 15 million jars. Use the mid-point formula to find the cross-price elasticity of demand between peanut butter and jelly. Are they complements or substitutes?
    b. The quantity of jelly purchased rises from 15 million jars to 20 million jars. What is the cross-price elasticity of demand between peanut butter and jelly? Are they complements or substitutes?

19. For each of the following pairs, predict whether the cross-price elasticity of demand will be positive or negative: [LO 4.5]
    a. Soap and hand sanitizer
    b. CD players and MP3s
    c. Sheets and pillowcases

20. Suppose that when the average family income rises from $30,000 per year to $40,000 per year, and the average family's purchases of toilet paper rise from 100 rolls to 105 rolls per year. [LO 4.6]
    a. Use the mid-point formula to calculate the income-elasticity of demand for toilet paper.
    b. Is toilet paper a normal or an inferior good?
    c. Is the demand for toilet paper income-elastic or income-inelastic?

21. In each of the following instances, determine whether the good is normal or inferior, and whether it is income-elastic or income-inelastic. [LO 4.6]
    a. If income increases by 10 percent and the quantity demanded of a good increases by 5 percent, the good is _____ and _____.
    b. If income increases by 10 percent and the quantity demanded of a good decreases by 20 percent, the good is _____ and _____.

APPENDIX C

Math Essentials: Calculating Percentage Change, Slope, and Elasticity

LEARNING OBJECTIVES

LO C.1   Understand how to calculate percentage changes.
LO C.2   Use slope to calculate elasticity.

The math associated with the concept of elasticity covers a wide variety of topics. In order to be able to calculate elasticity, you need to be able to calculate percentage changes. In order to talk about shape of a line and its elasticity, you need to understand slope and the relationship between variables, particularly price and quantity.

Percentage Change

LO C.1 Understand how to calculate percentage changes.

In Chapter 4, we calculated elasticity in all its forms. If you're not entirely comfortable calculating percentage change, though, elasticity can be a daunting idea. Percentage changes represent the relative change in a variable from an old value to a new one. In general, the formula can be reduced in plain English to saying, "New minus old, divided by old, times 100."

The mathematical equivalent is shown as Equation C-1. There, X_1 represents the original value of any variable X, and X_2 is the new value of this variable.

Equation C-1

$$\text{Percentage change} = \left[\frac{(X_2 - X_1)}{X_1} \right] \times 100$$

Overall, you can use this method to calculate the percentage change in variables of various kinds. A percentage change in quantity, for example, would be expressed as:

$$\text{Percentage change in quantity} = \left[\frac{(Q_2 - Q_1)}{Q_1}\right] \times 100$$

where Q_2 represents the new value of quantity demanded and Q_1 the original quantity demanded.

Similarly, a percentage change in price would be expressed as:

$$\text{Percentage change in price} = \left[\frac{(P_2 - P_1)}{P_1}\right] \times 100$$

Let's try an example for practice. For weeks, you have been watching the price of a new pair of shoes. They normally cost $80, but you see that the store has a sale and now offers them for $60. You find the percentage change in the price of the shoes by first subtracting the old price ($80) from the new one ($60) to find the change in price, which is $20. To find how much of a change this is, you take this $20 price change and divide it by the original cost of the shoes ($80). This gives you the decimal that you multiply by 100 to get the percentage change:

$$\frac{\$60 - \$80}{\$80} = -0.25$$

$$-0.25 \times 100 = -0.25\%$$

In this case, the $20 price reduction was a 25 percent decrease in price. Not a bad sale!

Notice that in this case, the percentage change is negative, which indicates that the new value is less than the original. If the prices of shoes had increased instead, the associated percentage change would be a positive value.

The best way to do get comfortable with calculating percentage changes is through lots of practice. You can find a few extra problems to try on your own at the end of this appendix, and you also could challenge yourself to calculate price changes you see in your everyday life.

Slope and Elasticity

LO C.2 Use slope to calculate elasticity.

In Appendix A, Math Essentials: Understanding Graphs and Slope, we showed that the direction of a slope tells us something meaningful about the relationship between the two variables we are representing: when x and y move in the same direction, they are said to have a *positive* relationship. Not surprisingly, this means that the slope of the line is a positive number. When the slope of a line is positive, we know that y increases as x increases, and y decreases as x decreases. Similarly, when x and y move in opposite directions, they are said to have a *negative* relationship. The slope of the line is a negative number. When the slope of a line is negative, we know that y decreases as x increases, and y increases as x decreases.

In Chapter 3, we saw a positive relationship between price and quantity in the supply curve. We saw a negative relationship between price and quantity in the demand curve. Two variables (such as price and quantity) may have more than one relationship to each other, depending on whose choices they represent and under what circumstances.

The steepness of a slope is also important. Numerically, the closer the number representing the slope is to zero, the flatter the curve will be. Remember that both positive and negative numbers can be close to zero. So, a slope of −1 is the same as a slope of 1, although one slopes downward and the other upward. Correspondingly, a line with a slope of −5 is steeper than a line with a slope of −1 or one with a slope of 1. You can tell just from looking at an equation how steep the line will be. If this idea is still a little hazy, you might want to review Appendix A to refresh your memory, as the steepness of slope is important to understanding the concept of elasticity.

Although the ideas of slope and elasticity are related, there are two basic mathematical distinctions between them:

1. Slope describes the change in y per the change in x, whereas elasticity measures are based on the change in x per the change in y.

2. We usually measure elasticity in terms of *percentage changes,* rather than absolute (unit-based) changes.

Why would we be interested in how much x changes in response to a one-unit change in y? To get at this difference, let's look at Figure C-1. It is similar to Figure A-10 (in Appendix A), but replaces the variables x and y with the quantity of a good (Q) and its price (P).

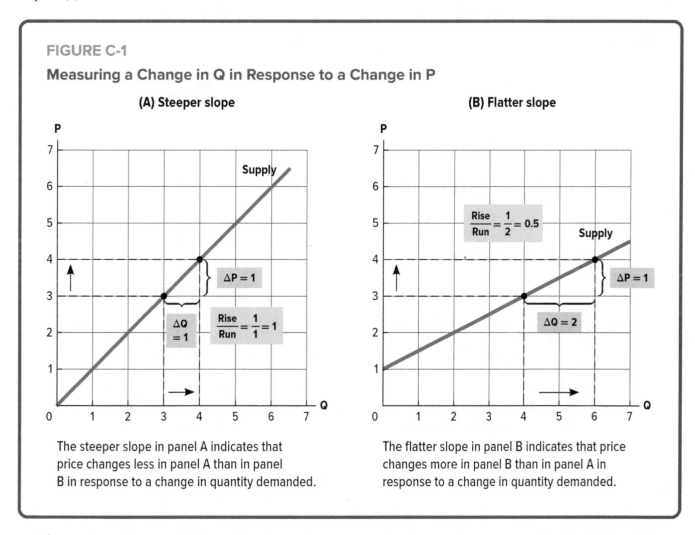

FIGURE C-1

Measuring a Change in Q in Response to a Change in P

(A) Steeper slope

The steeper slope in panel A indicates that price changes less in panel A than in panel B in response to a change in quantity demanded.

(B) Flatter slope

The flatter slope in panel B indicates that price changes more in panel B than in panel A in response to a change in quantity demanded.

In Chapter 4 you learned that *price elasticity* is a measure of the responsiveness of supply (or demand) to changes in price. In other words, it is a measure of how quantity (on the x-axis) responds to a change in price (on the y-axis). So this time, let's make the change in price (vertical distance) the same and look at how much quantity changes (horizontal distance).

Looking at Figure C-1, we can see that when price moves from 3 to 4, quantity supplied changes by less in panel A than it does in panel B. When price increases from 3 to 4 in panel A, quantity increases by one unit, from 3 to 4. In contrast, panel B shows an increase of two units from 4 to 6 for the same change in P. This means supply is less responsive to a price change in panel A compared to panel B.

X over Y, or Y over X?

We have noted that slope is indicated by $\Delta y/\Delta x$. In contrast, elasticity is commonly indicated by $\%\Delta Q/\%\Delta P$, which corresponds to $\Delta y/\Delta x$. In some sense, then, elasticity is computed as the mirror image of slope. The easiest way to picture this is to see the difference between slope and elasticity for vertical and horizontal lines.

In Figure C-2, the horizontal line pictured in panel A has a slope of zero. This is because a one-unit change in x results in zero change in y. Therefore, slope is calculated as $0/\Delta x$. Zero divided by any number is zero. If we think of the horizontal line as a demand curve mapping price to quantity demanded, however, the price elasticity is infinity.

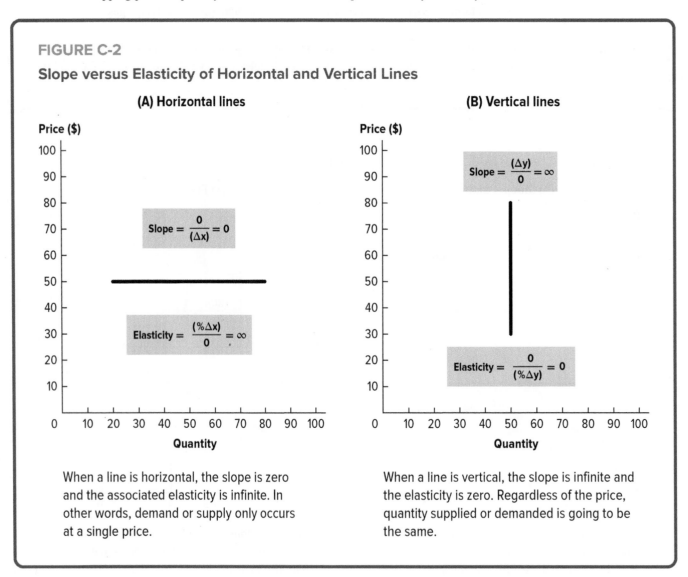

FIGURE C-2

Slope versus Elasticity of Horizontal and Vertical Lines

(A) Horizontal lines

$$\text{Slope} = \frac{0}{(\Delta x)} = 0$$

$$\text{Elasticity} = \frac{(\%\Delta x)}{0} = \infty$$

(B) Vertical lines

$$\text{Slope} = \frac{(\Delta y)}{0} = \infty$$

$$\text{Elasticity} = \frac{0}{(\%\Delta y)} = 0$$

When a line is horizontal, the slope is zero and the associated elasticity is infinite. In other words, demand or supply only occurs at a single price.

When a line is vertical, the slope is infinite and the elasticity is zero. Regardless of the price, quantity supplied or demanded is going to be the same.

How can slope be zero and elasticity infinity? Remember that slope measures how much y changes in response to a change in x. Elasticity, however, measures the sensitivity of P (on the y-axis) to a change in Q (on the x-axis). Whereas x is in the denominator when calculating slope, it is in the numerator when calculating elasticity. For a horizontal line, then, elasticity will be $\%\Delta Q/0$, since there is no change in P. Division by zero is mathematically undefined, or known as infinity.

The reverse is true when we look at a vertical line. When a graph is vertical, there is zero change in x for any change in y. Therefore, slope is calculated as $\Delta y/0$. In this case, slope is undefined (infinity). But elasticity will be $0/\%\Delta P$. Again, zero divided by any number is zero.

Elasticity Changes Along Lines with Constant Slope

The second important mathematical difference between slope and elasticity is that we usually measure slope in terms of absolute changes, but we measure elasticity in terms of percent changes. This means that at different points along a straight line slope is constant, but elasticity varies.

As an example, take a look at the demand schedule in Table C-1. First, calculate the slope between two different sets of points. Using the first two prices and quantities at the top of the demand schedule, we see that the slope between these points is -1.

TABLE C-1   DEMAND SCHEDULE

Price ($)	Quantity
80	0
70	10
60	20
50	30
40	40
30	50
20	60
10	70
0	80

$$\text{Slope \#1} = \frac{\Delta P_1}{\Delta Q_1} = \frac{(0-10)}{(80-70)} = \frac{-10}{10} = -1$$

Now pick another two points. Using the quantities 30 and 20 and their respective prices, we can calculate that the slope is still -1.

$$\text{Slope \#2} = \frac{\Delta P_2}{\Delta Q_2} = \frac{(30-20)}{(50-60)} = \frac{10}{-10} = -1$$

No matter what two points along the demand curve we choose, the slope is the same. *Slope is constant because the demand curve is linear.*

Now let's calculate elasticity between these same two sets of points. We will use the mid-point method described in Chapter 3 to calculate elasticity:

$$\text{Elasticity} = \frac{\%\Delta Q}{\%\Delta P} = \frac{\Delta Q/Q_{\text{midpoint}}}{\Delta P/P_{\text{midpoint}}}$$

Let's start with the top of the demand curve and calculate the price elasticity of demand for a price change from 80 to 70. Using the midpoint method, we have:

$$\frac{\Delta Q/Q_{midpoint}}{\Delta P/P_{midpoint}} = \frac{(0 - 10)/5}{(80 - 70)/60} = \frac{-10/5}{10/60} = \frac{-2}{0.17} = -11.8$$

Now let's calculate the price elasticity of demand at the bottom of the demand curve for a price change of 30 to 20.

$$\frac{\Delta Q/Q_{midpoint}}{\Delta P/P_{midpoint}} = \frac{(50 - 60)/55}{(30 - 20)/25} = \frac{-10/55}{10/25} = \frac{-0.18}{0.4} = -0.45$$

Even though both of these calculations represented a 10-unit change in quantity in response to a $10 change in price, elasticity changes along a linear demand curve. Moving down along the demand curve means less elasticity. This is because the same change in Q or P is a different *percentage* of the mid-point at different points on the line.

Problems and Applications

1. Calculate the percentage change in each of the following examples: [LO C.1]
    a. 8 to 12
    b. 16 to 14
    c. 125 to 120
    d. 80 to 90
2. Find the percentage change in price in these examples: [LO C.1]
    a. The price of a $4 sandwich increases to $5.
    b. A sale discounts the price of a sofa from $750 to $500.
3. Use the demand curve in Figure CP-1 to answer the questions. Use the mid-point method in your calculations. [LO C.2]

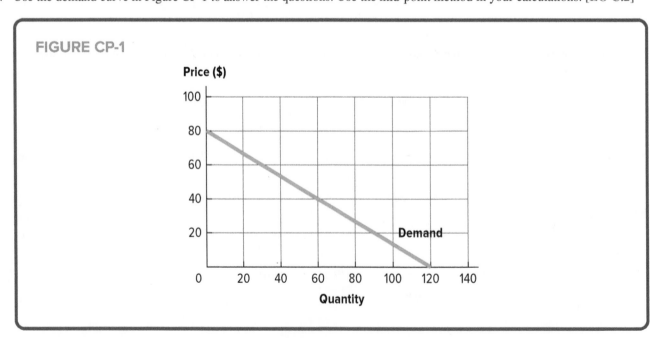

FIGURE CP-1

a. What is the price elasticity of demand for a price change from $0 to $20?

b. What is the price elasticity of demand for a price change from $20 to $40?

c. What is the price elasticity of demand for a price change from $40 to $60?

4. Use the demand schedule in Table CP-1 to answer the following questions. Use the mid-point method in your calculations. [LO C.2]

TABLE CP-1

Price ($)	Quantity
0	60
4	50
8	40
12	30
16	20
20	10
24	0

a. What is the price elasticity of demand for a price change from $4 to $8?

b. What is the price elasticity of demand for a price change from $8 to $16?

c. What is the price elasticity of demand for a price change from $20 to $24?

5. Use the demand schedule in Table CP-2 to answer the questions. Use the mid-point method when calculating elasticity. [LO C.2]

TABLE CP-2

Price ($)	Quantity
0	56
1	48
2	42
3	35
4	28
5	21
6	14
7	7
8	0

a. What is the price elasticity of demand for a price change from $2 to $3? What is the slope of the demand curve for a price change from $2 to $3?

b. What is the price elasticity of demand for a price change from $3 to $5? What is the slope of the demand curve for a price change from $3 to $5?

c. What is the price elasticity of demand for a price change from $6 to $7? What is the slope of the demand curve for a price change from $6 to $7?

CHAPTER 5

Efficiency

A Broken Laser Pointer Starts an Internet Revolution

In 1995, a young software developer named Pierre Omidyar spent his Labour Day weekend building a website he called AuctionWeb. His idea was to create a site where people could post their old stuff for sale online and auction it off to the highest bidder. Soon after, he sold the first item on AuctionWeb for $14.83. It was a broken laser pointer that he had posted on the site as a test, never expecting anyone to bid on it. When Pierre pointed out that the pointer was broken, the bidder explained that he was "a collector of broken laser pointers."

As you might have guessed, AuctionWeb became the wildly successful company we now know as eBay. In 2011, the total value of items sold on eBay was nearly $68.6 billion, and 100 million people around the world were active users.

Like many creation stories, the tale of eBay's first sale gives us insight into what makes it tick. People are interested in some pretty odd things (like broken laser pointers), but given a big enough audience, someone who wants to sell can usually find someone who wants to buy. When buyers and sellers are matched up and they trade, each is made better off. The buyers get items they want, and the sellers get money. Because both parties benefit from engaging in such transactions, they are willing to pay eBay to provide the marketplace where they can find each other.

eBay's success is based on one of the most fundamental ideas in economics, and its importance stretches far beyond the company itself: *voluntary exchanges create value and can make everyone involved better off.* This principle drives a range of businesses that do not manufacture or grow anything themselves, but instead facilitate transactions between producers and consumers—from grocery stores, to investment banks, to online retailers.

But this principle raises a question: How do we know that people are better off when they buy and sell things? Can we say anything about *how much* better off they are?

To answer these questions, we need a way to describe the size of the benefits that result from transactions and who receives them. In this chapter we will introduce the concept of *surplus,* which measures the benefit that people receive when they buy something for less than they would have been willing to pay or sell something for more than they would have been willing to accept. *Surplus* is the best way to look at the benefits people receive from successful transactions.

Bloomberg via Getty Images

Surplus also shows us why the equilibrium price and quantity in a competitive market are so special: they maximize the total well-being of those involved. Even when we care about outcomes other than total well-being (like inequality in the distribution of benefits), surplus gives us a yardstick for comparing different ideas and policies. For instance, calculations of surplus can clearly show who benefits and who loses from policies such as taxes and minimum wages. As we'll see, *efficiency,* in the sense of maximizing total surplus, is one of the most powerful features of a market system. Even more remarkable is that it is achieved without centralized coordination.

Surplus also shows us how simply enabling people to trade with one another can make them better off. Often, creating a new market for goods and services (as the Grameen Bank did in Bangladesh, in the example in Chapter 1) or improving an existing market (as eBay did on the Internet) can be a good way to help people. Knowing how and when to harness the power of economic exchanges to improve well-being is an important tool for businesspeople and public-minded problem solvers alike.

Willingness to Pay and Sell

> **LO 5.1** Use *willingness to pay* and *willingness to sell* to determine supply and demand at a given price.

eBay is an online auction platform that allows people to create a web page advertising an item for sale. People who want to buy the item make bids offering to pay a particular price. This decentralized marketplace supports all sorts of transactions, from real estate to used cars to rare books, and even (in one extraordinary case) a half-eaten cheese sandwich said to look like the Virgin Mary (which sold for $28,000).

Who uses eBay? What do they want? At the most basic level, they are people who want to buy or sell a particular good. We're not sure what's going on with people who want broken laser pointers or old cheese sandwiches, so let's stick with something a little more typical. How about digital cameras? (Just as we did in Chapter 3, we'll make the simplifying assumption that there is just one kind of digital camera rather than thousands of slightly different models.)

Imagine you see a digital camera posted for sale on eBay. Who might bid on it? What are their *wants and constraints?* Most obviously, people who bid will be those who *want* a camera. But they will also care about the price they pay. Why spend $200 for a camera if you can get it for $100 and spend the other $100 on something else? Potential buyers *want* to pay as little as possible, but on top of this general preference, all buyers have a maximum price they are willing to pay.

Economists call this maximum price the buyer's **willingness to pay** or **reservation price**. Economists use these two terms interchangeably; in this book, we'll stick with *willingness to pay.* This price is the point above which the buyer says, "Never mind. I'd rather spend my money on something else." Potential buyers want to purchase a camera for a price that is as low as possible and no higher than their maximum *willingness to pay.* On eBay, we can see willingness to pay in action. When the price of a product remains below any bidders' willingness to pay, they'll continue to bid on it. Individuals will drop out as the going price passes their willingness to pay.

Of course, buyers are only half the story. Who posted the camera for sale on eBay in the first place? To create a functioning market for digital cameras, someone has to want to sell them. Whereas buyers want to buy a camera for as low a price as possible, sellers want to sell for as high a price as possible. Why take less money if you could get more? Just as each potential buyer has a willingness to pay, each potential seller has a *willingness to sell*. **Willingness to sell** is the minimum price that a seller is willing to accept in exchange for a good or service. A seller always wants to sell for a price that is as high as possible above a certain minimum. We can see willingness to sell in action on eBay through the "reserve price" that sellers can set when they post an item. This reserve price sets a bar below which the seller will not accept any bids. If there are no higher bids, the seller simply keeps the item.

So far, so good: buyers want to buy low, sellers want to sell high. What does this have to do with markets? We're about to see that willingness to pay and willingness to sell are actually the forces that drive the shape of demand and supply curves.

Willingness to Pay and the Demand Curve

Let's return to potential camera buyers and take a closer look at how they choose to bid on the camera posted on eBay. To keep things simple, let's imagine that there are five buyers who are considering bidding on this particular camera.

- The first potential buyer is a bird watcher, who cares passionately about having a good camera to document the rare birds she finds. She is willing to pay up to $500 for the camera.
- The next bidder is an amateur photographer; he has an outdated camera and is willing to pay $250 for this newer model.
- The third bidder is a real estate agent, who will be willing to pay $200 or less to be able to take better pictures of her properties.
- Next is a journalist, who wouldn't mind having a newer camera than the one her newspaper provided, but would pay no more than $150 for it.
- Finally there is a teacher, who will spend no more than $100—the amount of the eBay gift certificate given to him by appreciative parents for his birthday.

We can plot each potential buyer's willingness to pay on a graph. In panel A of Figure 5-1, we've graphed possible prices for the camera against the number of buyers who would be willing to bid that price for it. Remember that each person's willingness to pay is a *maximum*—he or she would also be willing to buy the camera at any lower price. Therefore, at a price of $100, all five buyers are willing to bid; at $350, only one will bid.

If you squint a bit, you might notice that the graph in panel A looks a lot like a demand curve—price on the *y*-axis, quantity on the *x*-axis, and a line showing that quantity demanded increases as price decreases. In fact this *is* a demand curve, albeit one representing only five potential buyers. If we conducted the same exercise in a bigger market and plotted out the willingness to pay of millions of people, rather than just five, we'd get a smooth demand curve, as shown in panel B of Figure 5-1.

Notice that although each buyer's willingness to pay is driven by different factors, we can explain the motivations behind all of their decisions by asking, *What are the trade-offs?* Money that is spent to buy a camera on eBay cannot be spent on other things. Willingness to pay is the point at which the benefit that a person will get from the camera is equal to the benefit of spending the money on another alternative—in other words, the opportunity cost.

At prices above the maximum willingness to pay, the opportunity cost is greater than the benefits; at lower prices, the benefits outweigh the opportunity cost. For instance, $250 is the point at which the enjoyment that the amateur photographer gets from a camera is the same as the enjoyment he would get from, say, buying $250 worth of stamps for his stamp collection instead. Since everyone has things they want other than cameras, this same logic applies to each of the potential buyers represented in the demand curve.

To figure out which of our five individual buyers will actually purchase a camera, we have to know the market price. To find the market price, we have to know something about the supply of digital cameras. Therefore, we turn next to investigating the supply curve.

FIGURE 5-1

Willingness to Pay and the Demand Curve

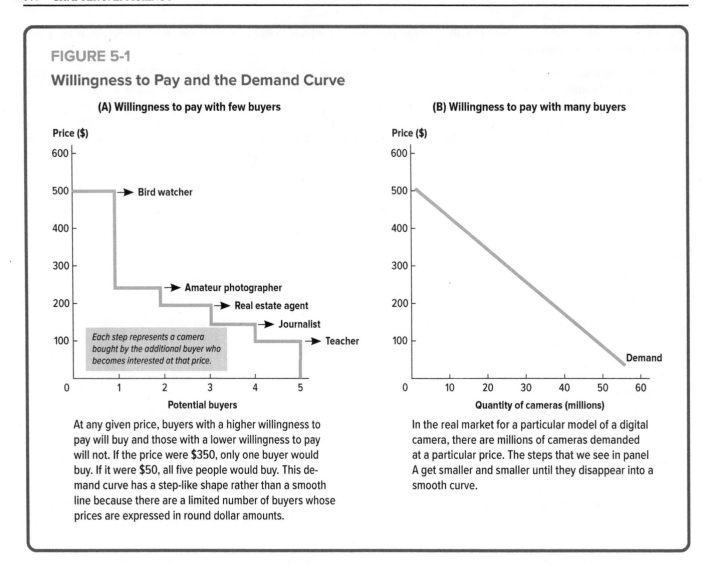

(A) Willingness to pay with few buyers

Price ($)

- Bird watcher
- Amateur photographer
- Real estate agent
- Journalist
- Teacher

Each step represents a camera bought by the additional buyer who becomes interested at that price.

Potential buyers

At any given price, buyers with a higher willingness to pay will buy and those with a lower willingness to pay will not. If the price were $350, only one buyer would buy. If it were $50, all five people would buy. This demand curve has a step-like shape rather than a smooth line because there are a limited number of buyers whose prices are expressed in round dollar amounts.

(B) Willingness to pay with many buyers

Price ($)

Demand

Quantity of cameras (millions)

In the real market for a particular model of a digital camera, there are millions of cameras demanded at a particular price. The steps that we see in panel A get smaller and smaller until they disappear into a smooth curve.

Willingness to Sell and the Supply Curve

As you may have guessed, just as the shape of the demand curve was driven by potential buyers' willingness to pay, the shape of the supply curve for digital cameras is driven by potential sellers' willingness to sell. To simplify things, let's imagine five particular sellers who have posted their cameras for sale on eBay.

- The first prospective seller is a comic book collector. He was given a camera as a birthday present, but all he really cares about is having money to spend on comic books. He's willing to part with his camera for as little as $50.
- Then there's a sales representative from a big company that makes digital cameras. She's authorized to sell for $100 or higher.
- Next is a professional nature photographer who owns several cameras but won't sell for anything less than $200; at a lower price he'd rather give it as a gift to his nephew.
- Another seller is a sales representative at a smaller company that is just setting up in the camera business and has much higher costs of production than the larger company; it can make money only by selling its cameras for $300 or more.
- The fifth seller is an art teacher who is sentimentally attached to her camera, given to her by a friend. She won't give it up unless she can get at least $400.

We can represent these five individuals by plotting their willingness to sell on a graph. Panel A of Figure 5-2 shows a graph of potential prices and the number of cameras that will be up for bid at each price. This graph is a supply curve representing only five potential sellers. As with the demand curve, if we added all of the millions of digital cameras that are actually for sale in the real world, we see the smooth supply curve we're accustomed to, as in panel B.

Sellers' willingness to sell is determined by the *trade-offs* they face, and in particular, the opportunity cost of the sale. The opportunity cost of selling a camera is the use or enjoyment that the seller could get from keeping the camera—or, in the case of the two camera manufacturers, from doing something else with the money that would be required to manufacture it. Each seller's opportunity cost will be determined by different factors—not all of them strictly monetary, as in the case of the teacher who is sentimentally attached to her camera.

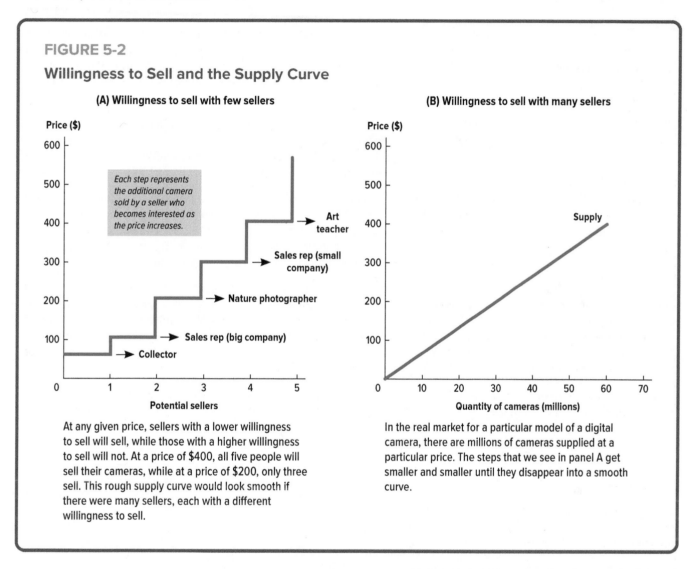

FIGURE 5-2

Willingness to Sell and the Supply Curve

(A) Willingness to sell with few sellers

Each step represents the additional camera sold by a seller who becomes interested as the price increases.

At any given price, sellers with a lower willingness to sell will sell, while those with a higher willingness to sell will not. At a price of $400, all five people will sell their cameras, while at a price of $200, only three sell. This rough supply curve would look smooth if there were many sellers, each with a different willingness to sell.

(B) Willingness to sell with many sellers

In the real market for a particular model of a digital camera, there are millions of cameras supplied at a particular price. The steps that we see in panel A get smaller and smaller until they disappear into a smooth curve.

For items that the seller just wants to get rid of, the starting price might be one cent. If opportunity cost is zero, anything is better than nothing! On the other hand, in a market where manufacturers are producing and selling new products, the minimum price will have to be high enough to make it worth their while to continue making new products. If the sale price didn't cover their costs of production, the manufacturers would simply stop making the item—otherwise, they would actually lose money every time they made a sale. (Occasionally, we do see manufacturers selling below the cost of production, but only when they've made a mistake and have to get rid of already-produced goods.)

Having met five potential buyers and five potential sellers, we're now in a position to understand what happens when the two groups come together in the market to make trades. But first, take a look at the Real Life box, Haggling and Bluffing, to consider how buyers' willingness to pay interacts with sellers' willingness to sell in the real world.

REAL LIFE

Haggling and Bluffing

If you've ever visited a flea market or bought a used car, you have probably haggled over price. In much of the world haggling for goods is an integral part of daily life. Even in wealthy countries, bargaining over salaries and promotions is commonplace—employees offer to sell their time and skills, and employers offer to buy them. In any bargaining situation, the seller wants to sell for as high a price as possible, and the buyer wants to buy for as low a price as possible. How do they reach an agreement?

The idea of willingness to pay explains a lot of bargaining strategies. Usually, the seller will start with a price much higher than the minimum she is actually willing to accept. Likewise, the buyer starts with an offer much lower than what he is actually willing to pay. Neither will reveal the price he or she thinks is reasonable. Isn't this a waste of time? They both know that they'll end up somewhere in the middle. Why not just start there?

Put yourself in the shoes of a flea-market vendor. If you knew for certain how much a potential customer was willing to pay, would you accept anything short of that amount? Probably not. As the would-be buyer, then, you have a strong incentive to make sure that the vendor doesn't know your true willingness to pay. The same is true for the vendor, who wants to hide from the potential buyer the minimum price he'll accept. Both parties start bidding far from their actual reservation price, hoping to end up with the most favourable price possible.

The same principle also explains a trick that is sometimes used by hagglers: bluffing about your willingness to pay. What would you do if the cost of an item were above your maximum willingness to pay? On eBay, you'd stop bidding; in the flea market, you'd walk away. Walking away from the bargaining table signals that the current price is higher than your willingness to pay—whether or not that is truly the case. If the seller realizes he won't get a higher price, he will sometimes settle rather than lose the sale entirely. On the other hand, if you're a bad bluffer or if your offered price is below the seller's willingness to sell, you lose the deal.

The next time you hear that "labour has walked out on talks" in a union wage negotiation or that a party to a civil lawsuit has "withdrawn from mediation," you will know that they're signalling their minimum or maximum price. The question is, are they bluffing?

✓ CONCEPT CHECK

☐ How is willingness to pay determined by opportunity cost? [LO 5.1]
☐ What is the relationship between willingness to pay and the demand curve? [LO 5.1]

Measuring Surplus

Surplus is a way of measuring who benefits from transactions and by how much. Economists use this word to describe a fairly simple concept: if you get something for less than you would have been willing to pay, or sell it for more than the minimum you would have accepted, that's a good thing. Think about how nice it feels to buy something on sale that you would have been willing to pay full price for. That "bonus" value that you would have paid if necessary, but didn't have to, is *surplus*. We can talk about surplus for both buyers and sellers, individually and collectively.

Surplus is the difference between the price at which a buyer or seller would be *willing* to trade and the actual price. Think about willingness to pay as the price at which someone is completely indifferent between buying an item and keeping her money. At a higher price, she would prefer to keep the money; at a lower price, she would prefer to buy. By looking at the distance between this *indifference point* and the actual price, we can describe the extra value the buyer (or the seller) gets from the transaction.

Surplus is a simple idea, but a surprisingly powerful one. It turns out that this is a better measure of the value that buyers and sellers get from participating in a market than price itself. To see why this is true, read the From Another Angle box, How Much Would You Pay to Keep the Internet from Disappearing?

FROM ANOTHER ANGLE

How Much Would You Pay to Keep the Internet from Disappearing?

Why is surplus a better measure of value than how much we pay for something? Consider the difference between what we pay for the Internet versus a particular model of computer.

Most people can access the Internet for very little, or even for free. You might pay a monthly fee for high-speed access at home, but almost anyone can use the Internet for free at schools, libraries, or coffee shops. Once you're online there are millions of websites that will provide information, entertainment, and services at no charge. Computer owners, on the other hand, pay a lot for particular types of computers. For instance, consumers might pay $999 for a MacBook laptop. Does this mean that we value access to the Internet less than a MacBook? Probably not.

To see why simply measuring price falls short of capturing true value, think about how much you would pay to prevent the particular type of computer you own from disappearing from the market. You might pay something. After all, there's a reason you chose it in the first place, and you might be willing to cough up a bit extra to get your preferred combination of technical specifications, appearance, and so on. But if the price got very steep, you'd probably rather switch to another, similar type of computer instead of paying more money. That difference—the maximum extra amount you would pay over the current price to maintain the ability to buy something—is your consumer surplus. It is the difference between your willingness to pay and the actual price.

Now consider the same question for the Internet. Imagine that the Internet is going to disappear tomorrow (or, at least, that you will be unable to access it in any way). How much would you pay to keep that from happening? Remember, no Internet means no email, no Google search or maps, no Facebook, no Twitter, no YouTube, no video streaming, and no online shopping. We suspect that you might be willing to pay a lot. The amount that you're willing to pay represents the true value that you place on the Internet, even though the amount that you currently spend on it might be very little. That's the magic of surplus.

Consumer Surplus

> **LO 5.2** Calculate consumer surplus based on a graph or table.

Let's go back to our five eBay buyers and calculate the surplus they would receive from buying a camera at a given price. Suppose it turns out that the going rate for cameras on eBay is $160. The bird watcher was willing to bid up to $500. Therefore, her **consumer surplus** from buying the camera is $340—the difference between her willingness to pay and the $160 she actually pays. Two other potential buyers will also buy a camera if the price is $160: the real estate agent (willing to pay up to $200) and the amateur photographer (willing to pay $250). The consumer surplus they receive is $40 and $90, respectively. The other two potential buyers will have dropped out of bidding when the price rose above $100 and then above $150, so they buy nothing and pay nothing. Their consumer surplus is zero.

We can add up each individual's consumer surplus to describe the overall benefits that buyers receive in a market. (Confusingly, economists use the same term for individual and collective surplus, but you should be able to tell from the context whether we mean one person's consumer surplus or total consumer surplus for all buyers in the market.) If the market for digital cameras consisted only of our five individuals, then the total consumer surplus would be:

$$\$340 + \$90 + \$40 + \$0 + \$0 = \$470$$

Panel A in Figure 5-3 shows consumer surplus for these five individuals when the price is $160. Consumer surplus is represented graphically by the area underneath the demand curve and above the horizontal line of the equilibrium price.

How does a change in the market price affect buyers? Since buyers would always prefer prices to be lower, a decrease in price makes them better off and an increase in price makes them worse off. Some people will choose not to buy at all when prices rise—which means that their surplus becomes zero. Those who do buy will have a smaller individual surplus than they had at the lower price. The opposite is true when prices fall. Measuring consumer surplus tells us *how much* better or worse off buyers are when the price changes.

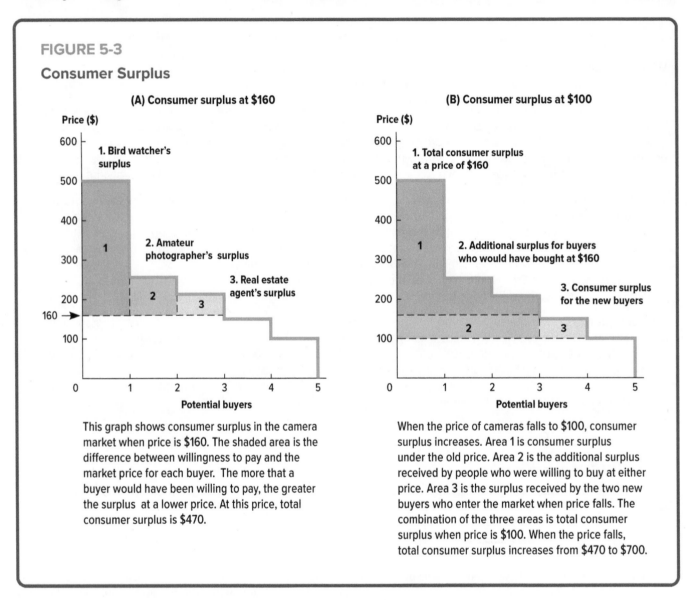

FIGURE 5-3

Consumer Surplus

(A) Consumer surplus at $160

1. Bird watcher's surplus
2. Amateur photographer's surplus
3. Real estate agent's surplus

This graph shows consumer surplus in the camera market when price is $160. The shaded area is the difference between willingness to pay and the market price for each buyer. The more that a buyer would have been willing to pay, the greater the surplus at a lower price. At this price, total consumer surplus is $470.

(B) Consumer surplus at $100

1. Total consumer surplus at a price of $160
2. Additional surplus for buyers who would have bought at $160
3. Consumer surplus for the new buyers

When the price of cameras falls to $100, consumer surplus increases. Area 1 is consumer surplus under the old price. Area 2 is the additional surplus received by people who were willing to buy at either price. Area 3 is the surplus received by the two new buyers who enter the market when price falls. The combination of the three areas is total consumer surplus when price is $100. When the price falls, total consumer surplus increases from $470 to $700.

Panel B of Figure 5-3 shows what happens to total consumer surplus if the going price of cameras on eBay falls to $100. You can see by comparing panel A and panel B that when the price level falls, the area representing consumer surplus gets bigger. The consumer surplus of each of the three buyers who were already willing to buy increases by $60 each, and an additional two buyers join the market. The journalist gains a consumer surplus of $50, because her willingness to pay is $150. The teacher buys a camera but gains no consumer surplus, because the price is exactly equal to his willingness to pay. When the camera's price was $160, consumer surplus was $470. When the camera's price drops to $100, total consumer surplus among our five individuals increases by $230, equaling $700:

$$\$470 + \$60 + \$60 + \$60 + \$50 + \$0 = \$700$$

> For a refresher on the area under a linear curve, see Appendix D, Math Essentials: The Area under a Linear Curve, which follows this chapter

Producer Surplus

> **LO 5.3** Calculate producer surplus based on a graph or table.

Like buyers, sellers want to increase the distance between the price at which they are willing to trade and the actual price. Sellers are better off when the market price is higher than their minimum willingness to sell. **Producer surplus** is the net benefit that a producer receives from the sale of a good or service, measured by the difference between willingness to sell and the actual price. It's called *producer* surplus regardless of whether the sellers actually produced the good themselves or—as often happens on eBay—are selling it secondhand.

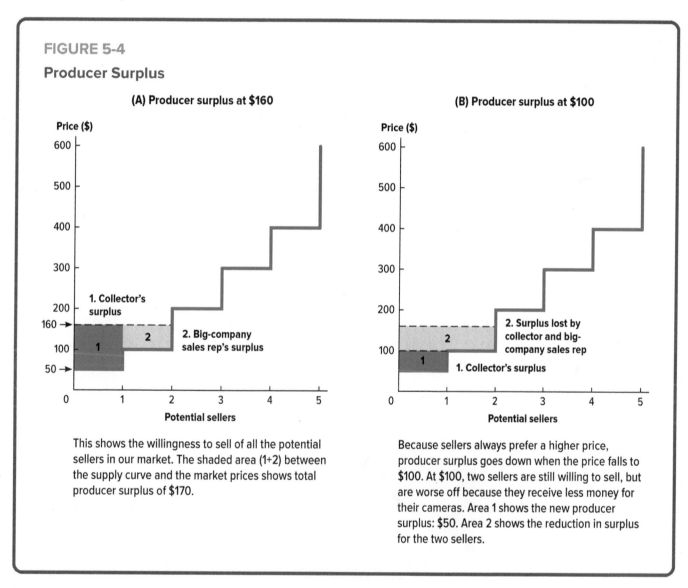

FIGURE 5-4

Producer Surplus

(A) Producer surplus at $160

This shows the willingness to sell of all the potential sellers in our market. The shaded area (1+2) between the supply curve and the market prices shows total producer surplus of $170.

(B) Producer surplus at $100

Because sellers always prefer a higher price, producer surplus goes down when the price falls to $100. At $100, two sellers are still willing to sell, but are worse off because they receive less money for their cameras. Area 1 shows the new producer surplus: $50. Area 2 shows the reduction in surplus for the two sellers.

If our five potential sellers find that the going price of cameras on eBay is $160, two of them will sell—and will be happy because they will get more for their cameras than the minimum they were willing to accept. The comic book collector, whose willingness to sell is $50, has a producer surplus of $110. The sales rep for the bigger camera company with willingness to sell of $100 has a surplus of $60. The three potential sellers who won't trade at this price have a surplus of zero. If our five sellers are the only ones in the market, then total producer surplus at this price level is:

$$\$110 + \$60 + \$0 + \$0 + \$0 = \$170$$

A change in the market price affects sellers in the opposite way it affects buyers. Sellers would always prefer prices to be higher, so a decrease in price makes them worse off. Some will choose not to sell at all when prices fall; their surplus becomes zero. Those who do sell will have a smaller individual surplus than at the higher price. The opposite is true when the market price rises, which makes sellers better off. Measuring producer surplus tells us *how much* better or worse off sellers are when the price changes.

Panel B in Figure 5-4 shows what happens to producer surplus if the price drops from $160 to $100. The two sellers still sell, but their surplus is reduced. Total producer surplus falls to $50. Notice that producer surplus is represented graphically by the area underneath the horizontal line of equilibrium price and above the supply curve. The higher the price, the bigger the area and the greater the producer surplus.

Total Surplus

LO 5.4 Calculate total surplus based on a graph or table.

We now understand how to calculate consumer surplus and producer surplus at any given price. But what will the actual market price be? To find out, we have to put the demand and supply curves together and locate the point where they intersect. Let's broaden our focus beyond just five buyers and sellers to the entire market for digital cameras on eBay. To represent this big market, we can bring back the smooth demand and supply curves from Figures 5-1 and 5-2. When we put the two together in Figure 5-5, we find that the equilibrium price is $200, and the equilibrium quantity of cameras traded is 30 million. (We're assuming a standardized model of digital camera and all the other features of a competitive market outlined in Chapter 3.)

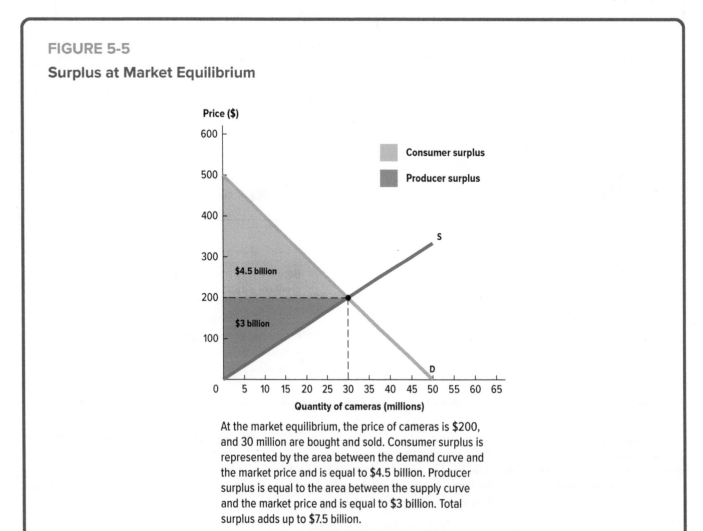

FIGURE 5-5

Surplus at Market Equilibrium

At the market equilibrium, the price of cameras is $200, and 30 million are bought and sold. Consumer surplus is represented by the area between the demand curve and the market price and is equal to $4.5 billion. Producer surplus is equal to the area between the supply curve and the market price and is equal to $3 billion. Total surplus adds up to $7.5 billion.

Total consumer surplus is represented graphically by the area underneath the demand curve and above the equilibrium price. That's the area shaded gold in Figure 5-5. Total producer surplus is represented by the area of the graph above the supply curve and below the equilibrium price—the area shaded blue.

Added together, those two areas—consumer surplus and producer surplus—make up the total surplus created by those 30 million sales of digital cameras on eBay. **Total surplus** is a measure of the combined benefits that everyone receives from participating in an exchange of goods or services.

We can also think of total surplus as value created by the existence of the market. Total surplus is calculated by adding up the benefits that every individual participant receives ($300 consumer surplus for the bird watcher, plus $150 producer surplus for the comic book collector, and so on). But these benefits exist only as a result of their participation in exchanges in the market.

To improve your understanding of consumer, producer, and total surplus, try the online interactive graphing tutorial.

This is an important point, because sometimes people mistakenly think of the economy as a fixed quantity of money, goods, and well-being, in which the only question is how to divide it up among people. That idea is referred to as a **zero-sum game**. A zero-sum game is a situation in which whenever one person gains, another loses an equal amount, such that the net value of a transaction is zero. Playing poker is an example of a zero-sum game: whatever one player wins, another player, logically, has to lose.

The concept of surplus shows us that the economy generally does not work like a poker game. Voluntary transactions, like selling cameras on eBay, do not have a winner or loser. Rather, both the buyer and seller are winners, since they both gain surplus. Everyone ends up better off than they were before. Total surplus cannot be *less* than zero—if it were, people would simply stop buying and selling.

As a rule, markets generate value, but the distribution of that value is a more complicated issue. In the following sections, we will look at what surplus can tell us about the well-being generated by market transactions and by deviations from the market equilibrium. Then, in the next chapter, we'll use these tools to evaluate the effects of some common government policies when they are implemented in a competitive market. Later in the book, we will revisit some of the assumptions about how competitive markets operate, and we will discuss what happens to surplus when those assumptions don't hold true in the real world. First, for a real-world recap of some of the ideas we've encountered so far in this chapter, read the Real Life box, Airwaves that Cost $2.1 Billion.

REAL LIFE

Airwaves that Cost $2.1 Billion

We've seen the auction process in action with private buyers and sellers on eBay. But auctions can be an important public policy tool, too. Take, for instance, an auction in the spring of 2014, in which the Canadian government raised almost $2.1 billion by selling the airwaves to mobile phone service companies. *To learn more about this auction, continue reading by going online at http://www.ic.gc.ca/eic/site/ic-gc.nsf/eng/07389.html.*

✓ CONCEPT CHECK

☐ What consumer surplus is received by someone whose willingness to pay is $20 below the market price of a good? [LO 5.2]

☐ What is the producer surplus earned by a seller whose willingness to sell is $40 below the market price of a good? [LO 5.3]

☐ Why can total surplus never fall below zero in a market for goods and services? [LO 5.4]

Using Surplus to Compare Alternatives

In a competitive market, buyers and sellers will naturally find their way to the equilibrium price. In our eBay example, we expect that buyers and sellers of digital cameras will bargain freely, offering different prices until the number of people who want to buy is matched with the number of people who want to sell. This is the invisible hand of market forces at work, and it doesn't require any eBay manager to coordinate or set prices. But, as we're about to see, the magic of the invisible hand doesn't stop there.

Market Equilibrium and Efficiency

LO 5.5 Define efficiency in terms of surplus, and identify efficient and inefficient situations.

The concept of surplus lets us appreciate something very important about market equilibrium: it is not only the point at which buyers are perfectly matched to sellers; it is also the point at which total surplus is maximized. In other words, equilibrium makes the total well-being of all participants in the market as high as possible.

FIGURE 5-6

Changing the Distribution of Surplus

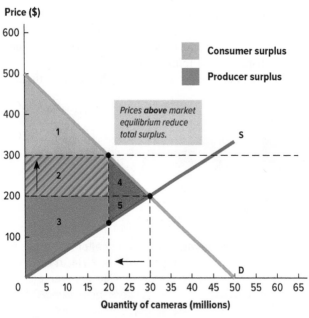

When the price rises above the market equilibrium, fewer transactions take place. The surplus shown in area 2 is transferred from consumers to producers as a result of the higher price paid for transactions that do still take place. The surplus in areas 4 and 5 is lost to both consumers and producers as a result of the reduced number of transactions.

To see why this is so, let's look at what would happen to surplus if, for some reason, the market moved away from equilibrium. Suppose an eBay manager decides to set the price of cameras so that people don't have to go to the trouble of bidding. He decides that $300 seems like a reasonable price. How will potential buyers and sellers *respond* to this situation? Figure 5-6 shows us. Buyers who wanted 10 million cameras at the equilibrium price of $200 are no longer willing to buy at $300, reducing their consumer surplus to zero. That means that sellers who would have sold those 10 million cameras to buyers also miss out and get producer surplus of zero. For the 20 million cameras that still are sold, buyers pay a higher price and lose surplus. The sellers of those 20 million cameras benefit from the higher price and gain the surplus lost by consumers. Overall, total surplus in the market is lower than it was at the equilibrium price, because there are now 10 million fewer cameras sold.

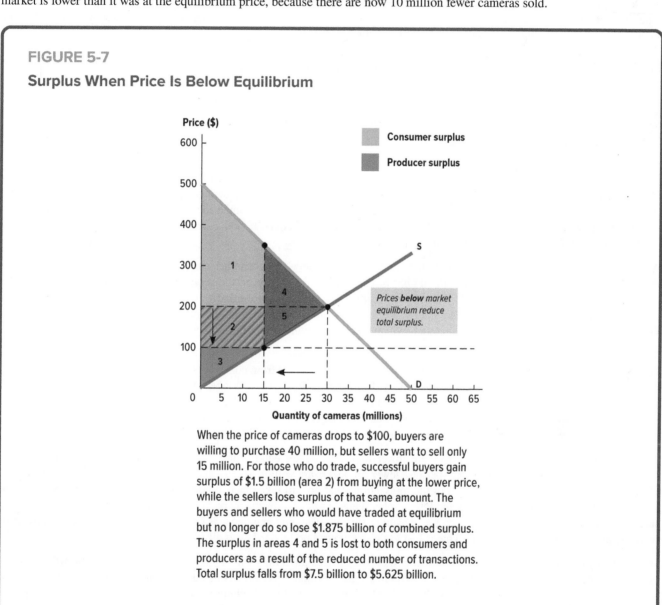

FIGURE 5-7

Surplus When Price Is Below Equilibrium

When the price of cameras drops to $100, buyers are willing to purchase 40 million, but sellers want to sell only 15 million. For those who do trade, successful buyers gain surplus of $1.5 billion (area 2) from buying at the lower price, while the sellers lose surplus of that same amount. The buyers and sellers who would have traded at equilibrium but no longer do so lose $1.875 billion of combined surplus. The surplus in areas 4 and 5 is lost to both consumers and producers as a result of the reduced number of transactions. Total surplus falls from $7.5 billion to $5.625 billion.

What happens if the interfering eBay manager instead decides to sell digital cameras for $100? As Figure 5-7 shows, buyers are willing to purchase 40 million cameras but sellers are willing to sell only 15 million at prices between $100 and $200. Since 15 million fewer cameras sell (compared to equilibrium), buyers and sellers lose the surplus that would have been gained through their sale. For the 15 million transactions that still take place, consumers gain surplus of $1.5 billion ($100 × 15 million) from buying at a lower price (area 2), which is exactly equal to the surplus the remaining sellers lose from selling at a lower price. The buyers and sellers who would have traded at equilibrium but no longer do so lose $1.875 billion of combined surplus. Breaking this down, we find that the 15 million buyers no longer in the market lose $1.125 billion (area 4) and sellers lose $0.75 billion (area 5) in surplus. This $1.875 billion total (areas 4 + 5) in lost surplus is subtracted from the amount of total surplus before the price ceiling. Overall, total surplus falls from $7.5 billion to $5.625 billion.

In both cases—when the price is $300 (above the equilibrium price) or when it is $100 (below the equilibrium price)—total surplus decreases relative to the market equilibrium. In fact, we find this same result at *any price* other than the equilibrium price. The key is that a higher or lower price causes fewer trades to take place, because some people are no longer willing to buy or sell. The value that would have been gained from these voluntary trades no longer exists. As a result, *the equilibrium in a perfectly competitive, well-functioning market maximizes total surplus.*

Another way to say this is that the market is **efficient** when it is at equilibrium: there is no exchange that can make anyone better off without someone becoming worse off. Efficiency is one of the most powerful features of a market system. Even more remarkable is that it is achieved without centralized coordination.

Changing the Distribution of Total Surplus

LO 5.6 Describe the distribution of benefits that results from a policy decision.

A reduction in total surplus was not the only interesting thing that happened when the meddling eBay manager moved the price of digital cameras away from equilibrium. Another outcome was reassignment of surplus from customers to producers, or vice versa, for the transactions that did take place. When the price was raised, sellers gained some well-being at the expense of buyers. When it was lowered, buyers gained some well-being at the expense of sellers. In both cases, achieving this transfer of well-being from one group to the other came at the expense of reduced total surplus.

When an artificially high price is imposed on a market, it's bad news for consumer surplus. Consumers lose surplus due to the reduced number of transactions and the higher price buyers have to pay on the remaining transactions. The situation for producers, though, is more complex. They lose some surplus from the transactions that would have taken place under equilibrium and no longer do. On the other hand, they gain more surplus from the higher price on the transactions that do still take place. These two effects will compete with one another. Whichever effect "wins" will determine whether the producer surplus increases or decreases overall.

To see why, let's go back to Figure 5-6. Area 2 is surplus that is transferred from consumers to producers. Areas 4 and 5 represent surplus lost to consumers and producers, respectively, from transactions that no longer take place. Whether area 2 is bigger or smaller than area 5 will decide whether producer surplus increases or decreases. That depends on the shape of the demand curve and the supply curve. In this case, we can see that area 2 is bigger than area 5. The effect of the artificially high price was to make sellers better off (while making buyers even more worse off).

The opposite situation occurs when prices are lower than the market equilibrium, which you can see by looking again at Figure 5-7. Fewer transactions take place (because fewer producers are willing to sell), and so both producers and consumers lose some surplus from missed transactions. For the transactions that do still take place, consumers pay less and gain surplus at the expense of producers, who get paid less and lose surplus. Thus, a price below the market equilibrium will always reduce producer surplus. That price might increase or decrease consumer surplus. The outcome depends on how much surplus is gained by those who buy at a lower price compared to what is lost to those who can no longer buy at all.

We don't expect eBay managers to start imposing their own prices anytime soon—that would be contrary to the whole idea of eBay as a decentralized virtual marketplace. But there are times when governments or other organizations do decide to impose minimum or maximum prices on markets. After all, efficiency is not the only thing we care about; many fundamental public policy questions revolve around possible trade-offs between economic efficiency and other concerns such as fairness and equity. We'll look in much more detail at this in the next chapter.

Deadweight Loss

LO 5.7 Define and calculate deadweight loss.

An intervention that moves a market away from equilibrium might benefit either producers or consumers, but it always comes with a decrease in total surplus. Where does that surplus go? It disappears and becomes what is known as a **deadweight loss**. Deadweight loss is the loss of total surplus that results when the quantity of a good that is bought and sold is below the market equilibrium quantity. Figure 5-8 shows deadweight loss for sales of the cameras on eBay. Any intervention that moves a market away from the equilibrium price and quantity creates deadweight loss. Fewer exchanges take place, so there are fewer opportunities for the generation of surplus.

FIGURE 5-8

Deadweight Loss

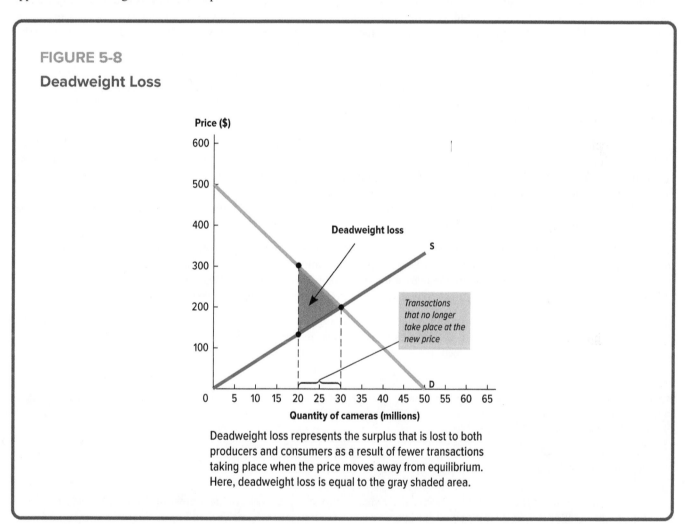

Deadweight loss represents the surplus that is lost to both producers and consumers as a result of fewer transactions taking place when the price moves away from equilibrium. Here, deadweight loss is equal to the gray shaded area.

We can calculate deadweight loss by subtracting total surplus *after* a market intervention from total surplus at the market equilibrium *before* the intervention. Or we can calculate deadweight loss directly by determining the area of the triangle on a graph. We'll see in the next chapter that deadweight loss is an important concept for understanding the costs of government intervention in markets, through mechanisms such as taxes and controls on the prices of goods.

To improve your understanding of deadweight loss on a supply and demand graph, try the online interactive graphing tutorial.

Missing Markets

LO 5.8 Explain why correcting a missing market can make everyone better off.

A price change is the indirect cause of deadweight loss in the examples we've just seen. But the direct cause is actually the reduction in the quantity of cameras traded. The non-equilibrium price causes fewer transactions to take place, and the surplus that would have been generated by those transactions at equilibrium is lost. Now look at the flip side: more voluntary transactions mean more surplus. The deeper lesson of the story is that by enabling transactions to take place, the invention of eBay has created surplus where none existed before.

When there are people who would like to make exchanges but cannot, for one reason or another, we are missing opportunities for mutual benefit. In this situation, we say that a market is *missing*: there is no place for potential buyers and sellers to exchange a particular good or service. We can think of a missing market as a special case of a market in which quantity is below the equilibrium—in this case, at or close to zero. This means that total surplus is lower than it could be if a well-functioning market existed.

Markets can be missing for a variety of reasons. Sometimes public policy prevents the market from existing—for instance, when the production or sale of a particular good or service is banned. But markets can also be missing or shrunk due to other types of hold-ups: a lack of accurate information or communication between potential buyers and sellers, or a lack of technology that would make the exchanges possible.

eBay is an example of how new technology can generate new value by creating or expanding a market. Prior to the existence of the Internet and companies like eBay that enable potential buyers and sellers to find one another online, people's scope for transactions was much more limited. You could hold a garage sale to get rid of your extra stuff; you could go to your local stores or post an ad in a newspaper if you were looking to buy an unusual item. But it was very difficult to find out if someone on the other side of the country was offering a rare product or a better price. eBay allows more buyers to find sellers and vice versa, encouraging more mutually beneficial trades.

The idea that we can increase total surplus by creating new markets and improving existing ones has important implications for public policy. Policies and technologies that help people share information and do business more effectively can increase well-being. For instance, ideas like serving the market for small loans by the Grameen Bank or expanding access to cell phones in Indian fishing villages don't just redistribute pieces of the pie to help the poor. Instead, they make the whole pie bigger.

Think about the many situations in the world in which new technology, new strategies, and outreach to new clients have enabled the market to bring value to the people who participate in it. Think also about some controversial situations in which markets don't exist, but could be created, as described in the What Do You Think? box, Kidneys for Sale.

WHAT DO YOU THINK?

Kidneys for Sale

Markets create value that would not otherwise exist, when buyers and sellers come together to participate in voluntary transactions. The idea that well-functioning markets maximize surplus is an important descriptive fact. But people may have moral and political priorities that go beyond maximizing surplus. In fact, many important public policy questions revolve around trade-offs between economic efficiency and other goals.

For instance, the law in Canada (and many other countries) prohibits certain types of market transactions. Consider the following cases:

- It's illegal to buy or sell organs for medical transplants.

- It's illegal to buy or sell certain drugs, such as cocaine and heroin.

- It's illegal to buy or sell children for adoption.

- It's illegal to buy or sell certain types of weapons, such as nuclear devices.

Looking at it from one angle, these are all examples of missing markets. You now know that when markets are missing, we are missing opportunities to create surplus by enabling voluntary transactions to take place. For instance, a market for organs could make a lot of people better off. Some healthy people would gain surplus by selling their kidneys: they would rather have money and one remaining kidney than two kidneys and no money. Meanwhile, some people with kidney disease would happily pay for the donation of a healthy kidney. Because the law prevents this transaction from happening, both miss out on surplus.

If maximizing surplus is our highest goal, it's plausible that we should allow organs and other such goods to be traded on the market. But allowing markets for organs goes against many people's morality—perhaps because they hold other goals higher than maximizing surplus.

What do you think?

1. Do you agree that the law should prevent trade in organs?

2. How about drugs, children, and nuclear weapons?

3. Are there any reasons that markets for these goods might not end up maximizing surplus?

4. What values and assumptions are driving your answers?

✓ CONCEPT CHECK

☐ What can we say about the size and distribution of total surplus in an efficient market? [LO 5.5]

☐ Why does an intervention that moves a market away from the equilibrium price and quantity create a deadweight loss? [LO 5.7]

☐ What does it mean to say that a market is "missing"? [LO 5.8]

Conclusion

In this chapter we've introduced the concepts of willingness to pay and willingness to sell, which help explain when individual buyers and sellers will choose to make a trade. We've also discussed what it means to measure consumer and producer surplus and shown that the market equilibrium is efficient because it maximizes total surplus.

As we'll see in the next chapter, surplus and deadweight loss are powerful tools for understanding the implications of business ideas and public policies. Who will benefit from the policy? Who will be harmed by it? What effect will it have on the economy overall? The language of surplus, efficiency, and distribution of benefits is particularly helpful for getting to the bottom of controversial decisions. Later in the book, we will describe important cases where the efficiency rule about market equilibrium does not always hold true, and we'll see how surplus can also help us understand these cases.

Key Terms

willingness to pay (reservation price)

willingness to sell

surplus

consumer surplus

producer surplus

total surplus

zero-sum game

efficient market

deadweight loss

Summary

LO 5.1 Use willingness to pay and willingness to sell to determine supply and demand at a given price.

Willingness to pay (also sometimes known as the reservation price) and willingness to sell describe the value that individuals place on a particular good or service. Willingness to pay is the maximum price that a buyer would be willing to pay for a particular good or service. Willingness to sell is the lowest price a seller is willing to accept in exchange for a particular good or service. Consumers will buy only if the price is lower than their willingness to pay, and producers will sell only if the price is higher than their willingness to sell.

LO 5.2 Calculate consumer surplus based on a graph or table.

Surplus is a way of measuring who benefits from transactions and by how much. Consumer surplus is the net benefit that consumers receive from purchasing a good or service, measured by the difference between each consumer's willingness to pay and the actual price. Graphically, it is equal to the area below the demand curve and above the market price.

LO 5.3 Calculate producer surplus based on a graph or table.

Producer surplus is a measure of the net benefits that a producer receives from the sale of a good or service, measured by the difference between the producer's willingness to sell and the actual price. Graphically, it is equal to the area above the supply curve and below the market price.

LO 5.4 Calculate total surplus based on a graph or table.

Total surplus is a measure of the combined benefits that everyone receives from participating in an exchange of goods or services. It is calculated by adding consumer surplus and producer surplus. Graphically, it is equal to the total area between the supply and demand curves, to the left of the equilibrium quantity.

LO 5.5 Define efficiency in terms of surplus, and identify efficient and inefficient situations.

A market is *efficient* if there is no exchange that can make anyone better off without someone becoming worse off. An efficient market maximizes total surplus, but doesn't tell us how the surplus is distributed between consumers and producers. In a competitive market, efficiency is achieved only at the market equilibrium price and quantity; higher prices and lower prices will both decrease the quantity bought and sold and reduce total surplus.

LO 5.6 Describe the distribution of benefits that results from a policy decision.

Prices above or below the market equilibrium reduce total surplus but also redistribute surplus between producers and consumers differently. A price above the equilibrium always decreases consumer surplus; some producers win and others lose, and the overall effect on producer surplus depends on the shape of the supply and demand curves. A price below the equilibrium always decreases producer surplus; some consumers win and others lose.

LO 5.7 Define and calculate deadweight loss.

Deadweight loss is the loss of total surplus that occurs when the quantity of a good that is bought and sold is below the market equilibrium quantity. Any intervention that moves a market away from the equilibrium price and quantity causes deadweight loss. Fewer exchanges take place, so there are fewer opportunities for the generation of surplus.

LO 5.8 Explain why correcting a missing market can make everyone better off.

A market is *missing* when there is a situation in which people would like to engage in mutually beneficial trades of goods and services but can't because no market for them exists. We can think of a missing market as a special case of a market where quantity is held below the equilibrium—in this case, at zero. Missing markets can occur for many reasons, including government intervention or a lack of information or technology. When missing markets are filled, people are able to trade, which generates surplus.

Review Questions

1. Bill is a professional photographer. His camera is broken, and he needs a new one within the next hour or he will miss an important deadline. Lisa is a high-school student who doesn't have a camera but wants to get one to take pictures at her prom next month. Who do you think would have a higher willingness to pay for a particular camera today? Why? [LO 5.1]

2. You are in the market for a new couch and have found two advertisements for the kind of couch you want to buy. One seller notes in her ad that she is selling because she is moving to a smaller apartment and the couch won't fit in the new space. The other seller says he is selling because the couch doesn't match his other furniture. Which seller do you expect to buy from? Why? (*Hint:* Who would be the more motivated seller.) [LO 5.1]

3. Suppose you are at a flea market and are considering buying a box of vintage records. You are trying to bargain down the price, but the seller overhears you telling a friend that you are willing to pay up to $50. Why is your consumer surplus now likely to be lower than it would have been if the seller hadn't overheard you? [LO 5.2]

4. Consider a market in equilibrium. Suppose supply in this market increases. How will this affect consumer surplus? Explain. [LO 5.2]

5. You currently have a television that you want to sell. You can either pick a price and try to sell it at a yard sale or auction it off on eBay. Which method do you think will yield a higher producer surplus? Why? [LO 5.3]

6. Consider a market in equilibrium. Suppose demand in this market decreases. How will this affect producer surplus? Explain. [LO 5.3]

7. Consider the market for plane tickets to the Caribbean. A bad winter in Eastern and Central Canada increases demand for tropical Caribbean vacations, shifting the demand curve to the right. The supply curve stays constant. Does total surplus increase or decrease? (*Hint:* Sketch a generic supply and demand curve and look at what happens to the size of the triangle that represents total surplus when the demand curve shifts right.) [LO 5.4]

8. You need to paint your fence but you really hate this task. You decide to hire the kid next door to do it for you. You would be willing to pay him up to $100, but you start by offering $50, expecting to negotiate. To your great surprise, he accepts your $50 offer. When you tell your friend about the great deal you got, she is shocked that you would take advantage of someone. What can you tell your friend to assure her that you did not cheat the kid next door? [LO 5.4]

9. Ontario has rent control for any rental unit built before 1991. Rent control, in essence, is a price ceiling on rent. Is the market for apartments built before 1991 likely to be efficient or inefficient? What does this imply for the size of total surplus? [LO 5.5]

10. Total surplus is maximized at the equilibrium price and quantity. When demand increases, price increases. Explain how total surplus is still maximized if price increases due to an increase in demand. [LO 5.5]

11. The Atlantic provinces of Canada have a price ceiling on gasoline to keep it affordable. How does this policy affect producer and consumer surplus? How does this policy affect total surplus? [LO 5.6]

12. Consider a policy to help struggling farmers by setting a minimum trade price for wheat. Will this be an effective way to increase their surplus? Explain. [LO 5.6]

13. If rent control creates deadweight loss for both consumers and suppliers of housing, why are consumers often in favor of this policy? [LO 5.7]

14. Suppose price is 5 percent above equilibrium in two markets: a market for a necessity and a market for a luxury good. All else equal (including supply conditions), in which market do you expect deadweight loss to be greater? Explain. [LO 5.7]

15. Your grandmother likes old-fashioned yard sales and doesn't understand why everyone is so excited about eBay. Explain to her why the creation of a market that enables people who don't live in the same town to buy and sell used goods increases total surplus over the yard-sale market. [LO 5.8]

16. At Zooey's elementary school, children are not allowed to trade lunches or components of their lunches with other students. Lunchroom monitors watch closely and strictly enforce this policy. Help Zooey make an argument about the inefficiency of this policy to her principal. [LO 5.8]

Problems and Applications

1. Answer the following questions based on Table 5P-1 and Table 5P-2. [LO 5.1]
   a. What is the quantity demanded at $10? What is the quantity supplied at $10?
   b. What is the quantity demanded at $25? What is the quantity supplied at $25?

TABLE 5P-1

Buyer	A	B	C	D	E	F	G	H	I
Willingness to pay for one unit	$6	$27	$13	$21	$33	$35	$12	$13	$22

TABLE 5P-2

Seller	A	B	C	D	E	F	G	H	I
Willingness to sell for one unit	$21	$4	$30	$14	$12	$15	$51	$9	$23

2. Use the information below to construct a step graph of the six consumers' willingness to pay. [LO 5.1]

	Willingness to pay for one unit ($)
Fred	8
Ann	2
Morgan	16
Andre	12
Carla	2
Hanson	4

3. Use the information below to construct a step graph of the six sellers' willingness to sell. [LO 5.1]

	Willingness to sell one unit ($)
Joseph	25
Juan	20
Kristin	60
Peter	10
Candice	25
Solomon	50

4. Based on Table 5P-1, calculate consumer surplus for each consumer when the price is $17. What is the total consumer surplus at this price? [LO 5.2]

5. Use the market represented in Figure 5P-1 to draw the consumer surplus when the market is in equilibrium. What is the value of consumer surplus at the equilibrium price? [LO 5.2]

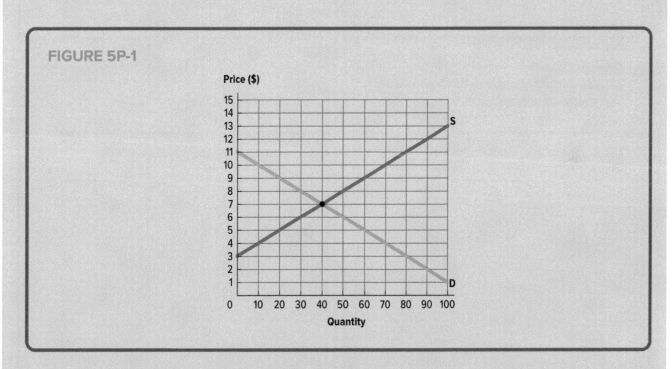

FIGURE 5P-1

6. Use the market represented in Figure 5P-1 to draw the consumer surplus when the market price is $8. What is the value of consumer surplus at this price? [LO 5.2]

7. Based on Figure 5P-1, consumer surplus is $0 when price is greater than or equal to what price? [LO 5.2]

8. Based on Table 5P-2, calculate producer surplus for each producer when the price is $12. What is total producer surplus at this price? [LO 5.3]

9. Use the market represented in Figure 5P-1 to draw the producer surplus when the market is in equilibrium. What is the value of producer surplus at the equilibrium price? [LO 5.3]

10. Use the market represented in Figure 5P-1 to draw the producer surplus when the market price is $5. What is the value of producer surplus at this price? [LO 5.3]

11. Based on Figure 5P-1, producer surplus is $0 when price is less than or equal to what price? [LO 5.3]

12. What is the value of the existence of the market represented in Figure 5P-2? [LO 5.4]

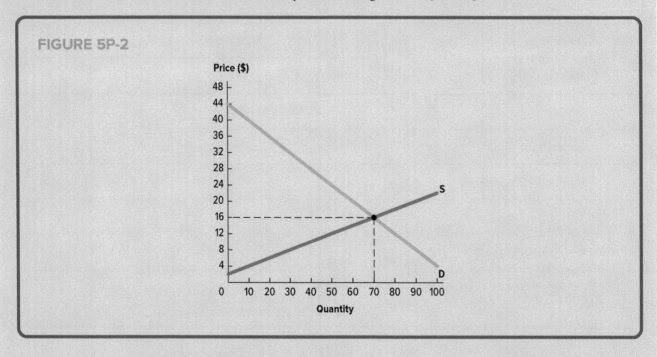

FIGURE 5P-2

13. Consider the market represented in Figure 5P-3. [LO 5.4]
    a. Calculate total surplus when demand is D_1.
    b. Calculate total surplus when demand decreases to D_2.

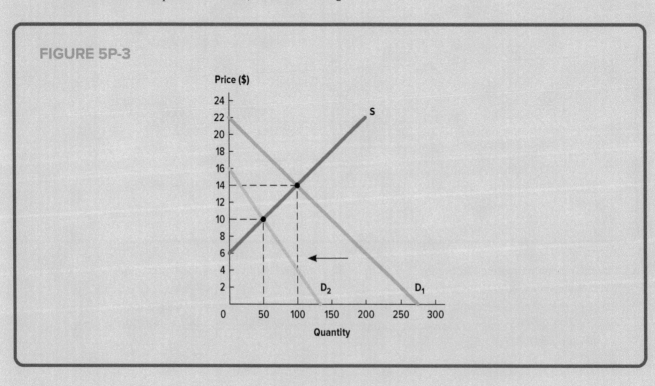

FIGURE 5P-3

14. Consider the market represented in Figure 5P-4. [LO 5.4]
    a. Calculate total surplus when supply is S_1.
    b. Calculate total surplus when supply increases to S_2.

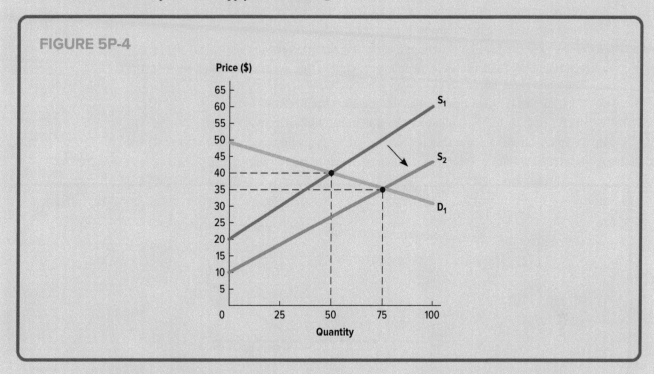

FIGURE 5P-4

15. Consider the market represented in Figure 5P-5. [LO 5.5]
    a. Draw the consumer surplus and producer surplus if the market is functioning at the equilibrium price and quantity. Compute the total surplus if the market is functioning at the equilibrium price and quantity.
    b. Compute the consumer surplus and producer surplus if the price is $30.
    c. Compute the consumer surplus and producer surplus if the price is $10.

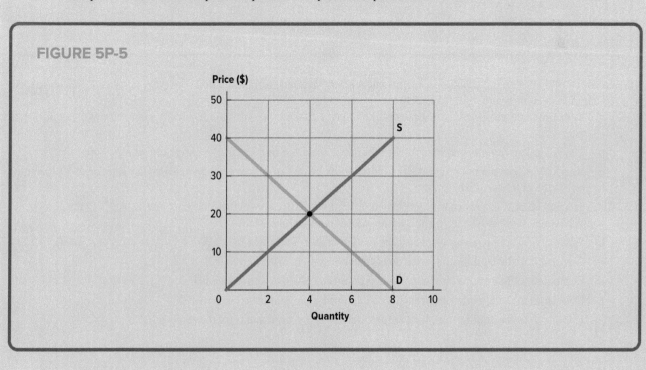

FIGURE 5P-5

16. Assume the market for wine is functioning at its equilibrium. For each of the following situations, say whether the new market outcome will be *efficient* or *inefficient*. [LO 5.5]
    a. A new report shows that wine is good for heart health.
    b. The government sets a minimum price for wine, which increases the current price.
    c. An unexpected late frost ruins large crops of grapes.
    d. Grape pickers demand higher wages, increasing the price of wine.

17. Based on Figure 5P-6, choose all of the following options that are true. [LO 5.5], [LO 5.6]
    a. The market is efficient.
    b. Total surplus is higher than it would be at market equilibrium.
    c. Total surplus is lower than it would be at market equilibrium.
    d. Producer surplus is lower than it would be at market equilibrium.
    e. Consumer surplus is lower than it would be at market equilibrium.

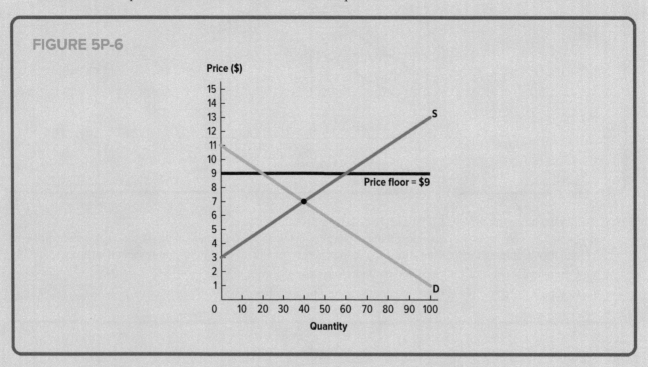

FIGURE 5P-6

18. In which of the following situations can you say, without further information, that consumer surplus decreases relative to the market equilibrium level? [LO 5.6]
    a. Your province passes a law that pushes the interest rate (i.e., the price) for payday loans below the equilibrium rate.
    b. The federal government enforces a law that raises the price of dairy goods above the equilibrium.
    c. Your city passes a local property tax, under which buyers of new houses have to pay an additional 5 percent on top of the purchase price.

19. Use the areas labeled in the market represented in Figure 5P-7 to answer the following questions. [LO 5.6]
    a. What area(s) are consumer surplus at the market equilibrium price?
    b. What area(s) are producer surplus at the market equilibrium price?
    c. Compared to the equilibrium, what area(s) do consumers lose if price is P_2?
    d. Compared to the equilibrium, what area(s) do producers lose if the price is P_2?
    e. Compared to the equilibrium, what area(s) do producers gain if the price is P_2?
    f. Compared to the equilibrium, total surplus decreases by what area(s) if the price is P_2?

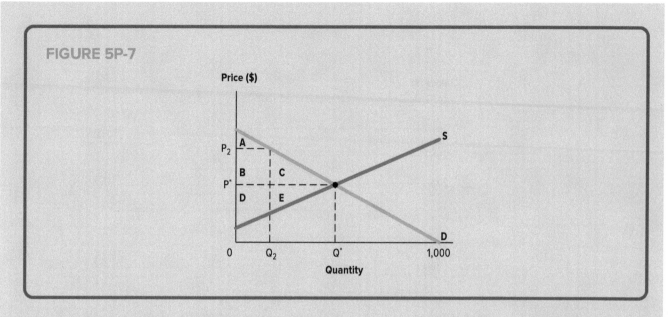

FIGURE 5P-7

20. Figure 5P-8 shows a market for cotton, with the price held at $0.80 per kilogram. Calculate the deadweight loss caused by this policy. [LO 5.7]

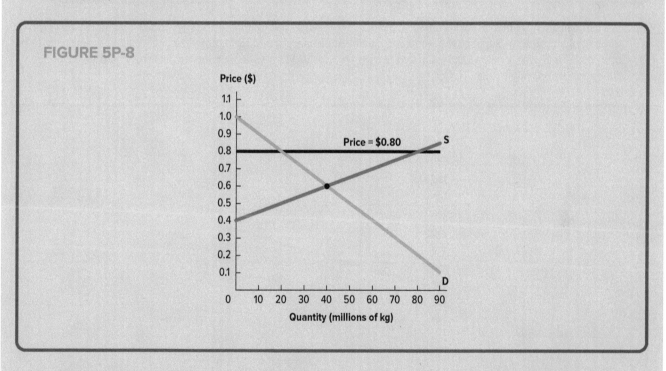

FIGURE 5P-8

21. Consider the market represented in Figure 5P-9. [LO 5.7]
   a. Suppose the government sets a minimum price of $25 in the market. Calculate the deadweight loss.
   b. Suppose the government sets a maximum price of $25 in the market. Calculate the deadweight loss.

FIGURE 5P-9

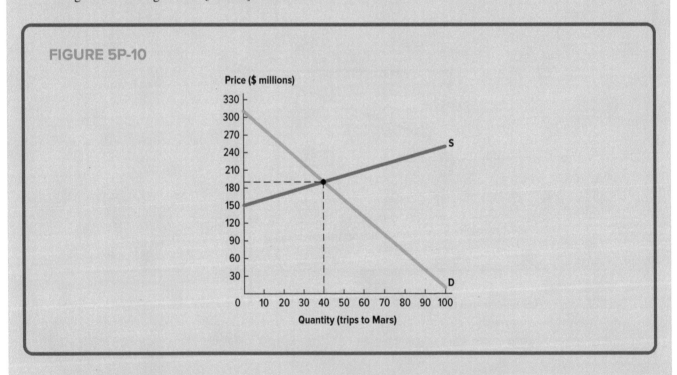

22. We can consider the market for traveling to Mars to be missing, because no technology exists that allows this service to be bought and sold. Suppose that someone has invented space-travel technology that will enable this service to be provided. Figure 5P-10 shows the estimated market for trips to Mars. Calculate the surplus that could be generated by filling in this missing market. [LO 5.8]

FIGURE 5P-10

23. Consider the market for travelling to Mars represented in Figure 5P-10. Assuming consumers knew they would each eventually pay $190,000 for the trip itself, how much would they collectively be willing to invest to support the space program that would make this trip possible? [LO 5.8]

APPENDIX D

Math Essentials: The Area Under a Linear Curve

LEARNING OBJECTIVE

LO D.1   Calculate surplus by finding the area under a linear curve.

The Area Under a Linear Curve

LO D.1 Calculate surplus by finding the area under a linear curve.

Chapter 5 introduced you to the concept of surplus. Surplus measures the gains or losses in well-being resulting from transactions in a market. You will often need to calculate a numerical value for surplus. To do that, you need to know how to find the area under a linear curve, so we will review a little geometry.

Graphically, surplus is represented as the area between a supply or demand curve and the market price. The area between these curves and the market price will take the form of a triangle. In order to find surplus, you are going to need to be able to calculate the area of a triangle:

Equation D-1

$$\text{Area of triangle} = \frac{1}{2} \times \text{base of triangle} \times \text{height of triangle} = \frac{1}{2}\,bh$$

The key, then, is to figure out which length to use as the base and which as the height.

In panel A of Figure D-1, consumer surplus is the shaded triangle below the demand curve and above the market price.

The base of this triangle is the *horizontal distance* from the equilibrium point to the y-axis, $(12 - 0) = 12$. The height is the *vertical distance* from the equilibrium price to the y-intercept of the demand curve, $(50 - 20) = 30$. Therefore the area of the triangle—and the consumer surplus—is:

$$\frac{1}{2} \times \left(12 \times 30 \right) = \$180$$

FIGURE D-1

Measuring the Area Under a Curve

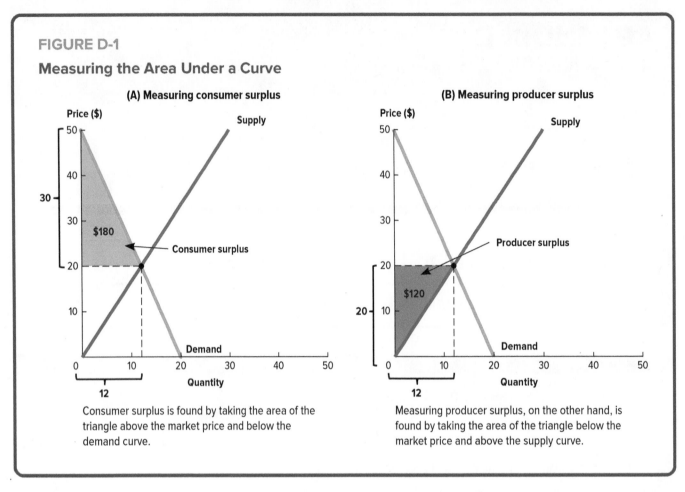

(A) Measuring consumer surplus

Consumer surplus is found by taking the area of the triangle above the market price and below the demand curve.

(B) Measuring producer surplus

Measuring producer surplus, on the other hand, is found by taking the area of the triangle below the market price and above the supply curve.

Producer surplus is the shaded area below the market price and above the supply curve in panel B of Figure D-1. The base of the triangle is again the *horizontal distance* from the equilibrium point to the y-axis, $(12 - 0) = 12$. The height is the vertical distance from the equilibrium price to the y-intercept of the supply curve, $(20 - 0) = 20$. Therefore the area of the triangle—and the producer surplus—is:

$$\frac{1}{2} \times \left(12 \times 20\right) = \$120$$

You learned in the chapter that total surplus is consumer surplus plus producer surplus:

$$\text{Total surplus} = \$180 + \$120 = \$300$$

We can also calculate total surplus directly by calculating the area of the larger triangle that encompasses both. This time, the calculation of this triangle is slightly different. The base is the amount of space in between the y-intercept of the supply and demand curves. This gives a base of 50. The height of the triangle, on the other hand, is the distance from the y-axis to the equilibrium point. The area is thus $1/2 \times 50 \times 12 = \$300$, the same result as before.

Occasionally, you will see oddly shaped surplus areas. You can always calculate these by breaking them down into familiar rectangles and triangles. Then calculate the area of each using length times width (for a rectangle) and $1/2$ bh (for a triangle), and add the results to find the total area.

Problems and Applications

1. Use the graph in Figure DP-1 to answer the following questions. [LO D.1]
    a. What is the amount of consumer surplus?
    b. What is the amount of producer surplus?
    c. What is the amount of total surplus?

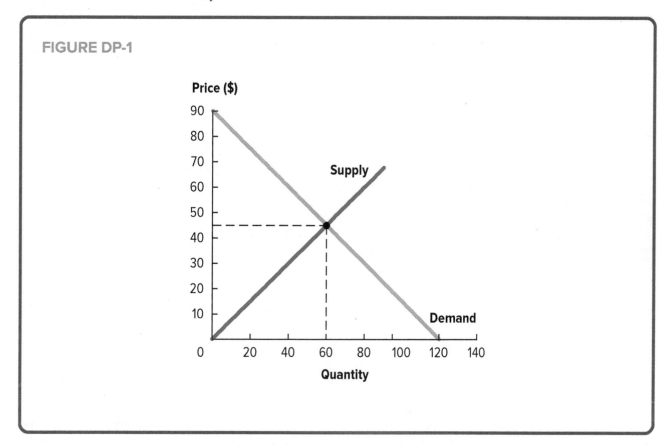

FIGURE DP-1

2. Use these two supply and demand equations to answer the following questions. [LO D.1]

    Equation D-1

    $$P = 50 - 4Q$$

    Equation D-2

    $$P = 2 + 2Q$$

    a. What is the equilibrium price? What is the equilibrium quantity?
    b. Draw a graph of supply and demand and illustrate the equilibrium.
    c. What is the amount of consumer surplus?
    d. What is the amount of producer surplus?
    e. What is the amount of total surplus?

Government Intervention

Feeding the World, One Price Control at a Time

In the spring of 2008, a worldwide food shortage caused food prices to skyrocket. In just a few months, the prices of wheat, rice, and corn shot up as much as 140 percent. But Canada was less affected than many countries. Overall, consumer prices for food consumed at home in Canada had risen only 1.2 percent in the 12 months ending in April 2008. This stability was unique compared with most nations. Food prices jumped 7.1 percent in the EU and 5.9 percent in the US over the same period. Increases in China were larger at 22 percent for food.[1] In the United States, the number of people living on food stamps rose to the highest level since the 1960s. By June, low-income Americans were facing tough choices, as the prices of basics like eggs and dairy products rose. Many reported giving up meat and fresh fruit; others said they began to buy cheap food past its expiration date.[2]

Rising food prices caused trouble all over the world. The *Economist* magazine reported on the political fallout:

> [In Côte d'Ivoire,] two days of violence persuaded the government to postpone planned elections...In Haiti, protesters chanting "We're hungry" forced the prime minister to resign; 24 people were killed in riots in Cameroon; Egypt's president ordered the army to start baking bread; [and] the Philippines made hoarding rice punishable by life imprisonment.[3]

Faced with hunger, hardship, and angry outbursts, many governments felt obliged to respond to the crisis. But what to do? Responses varied widely across countries. Many countries made it illegal to charge high prices for food. Others subsidized the price of basic necessities. In the United States and Europe, policy makers tried to alleviate the shortage by paying farmers to grow more food. Were these responses appropriate? What, if anything, should governments do in such a situation?

Food is a tricky issue for policy makers because it's a basic necessity. If prices rise too high, people go hungry. If prices fall too low, farmers go out of business, which raises the risk of food shortages in the future. So, while policy makers aren't too concerned if the prices of many goods—like digital cameras or lattes—jump up and down, they often do care about food prices. But attempts to lower, raise, or simply stabilize prices can backfire or create unintended side effects. Sometimes the cure ends up being worse than the problem itself.

Abdurashid Abdulle/AFP/Getty Images

In this chapter, we'll look at the logic behind policies that governments commonly use to intervene in markets and their consequences—both intended and unintended. We will start with *price controls,* which make it illegal to sell a good for more or less than a certain price. Then we will look at *taxes* and *subsidies,* which discourage or encourage the production of particular goods. These tools are regularly applied to a broad range of issues, from unemployment to home ownership, air pollution to education. For better or worse, they have a huge effect on our lives as workers, consumers, businesspeople, and voters.

Why Intervene?

In Chapter 3, we saw that markets gravitate toward equilibrium. When markets work well, prices adjust until the quantity of a good that consumers demand equals the quantity that suppliers want to produce. At equilibrium, everyone gets what they are willing to pay for. In Chapter 5, we saw that equilibrium price and quantity also maximize total surplus. Thus, at equilibrium, there is no way to make some people better off without harming others.

So, why intervene? Why not let the invisible hand of the market determine prices and allocate resources? Some would argue that's exactly what should be done. Others believe the government has to intervene sometimes—and the fact is that every single government in the world intervenes in markets in some fashion.

Three Reasons to Intervene

The arguments for intervention fall into three categories: correcting market failures, changing the distribution of surplus, and encouraging or discouraging consumption of certain goods. As we discuss different policy tools throughout the chapter, ask yourself which of these motivations is driving the intervention.

Correcting Market Failures

Our model of demand and supply has so far assumed that markets work efficiently—but, in the real world, that's not always true. For example, sometimes there is only one producer of a good who faces no competition and can charge an inefficiently high price. In other cases, one person's use of a product or service imposes costs on other people that are not captured in prices paid by the first person, such as the pollution caused by burning the gas in your car. Situations in which the assumption of efficient, competitive markets fails to hold are called **market failures**. When there is a market failure, intervening can actually increase total surplus. We'll have much more to say about market failures in future chapters. In this chapter, we will stick to analyzing the effect of government interventions in efficient, competitive markets.

Changing the Distribution of Surplus

Efficient markets maximize total surplus, but an efficient outcome may still be seen as unfair. (Of course, the definition of fairness is up for debate.) Another reason to intervene in the market, therefore, is to change the distribution of surplus.

For example, even if the job market is efficient, wages can still drop so low that some workers fall below the poverty line while their employers make healthy profits. The government might respond by intervening in the labour market to impose a minimum wage. This policy will change the distribution of surplus, reducing employers' profits and lifting workers' incomes. Reasonable people can—and often do—argue about whether a policy that benefits a certain group (such as minimum-wage workers) is justified or not. Our focus will be on accurately describing the benefits and costs of such policies. Economics can help us predict whose well-being will increase, whose well-being will decrease, and who may be affected in unpredictable ways.

Encouraging or Discouraging Consumption

Around the world, many people judge certain products to be good or bad based on culture, health, religion, or other values. At the extreme, certain "bad" products are banned altogether, such as hard drugs. More often, governments use taxes to discourage people from consuming bad products, without banning them altogether. Common examples are cigarettes and alcohol; many governments tax them heavily, with the aim of reducing smoking and drinking. In some cases, minimizing costs imposed on others (such as from pollution or second-hand smoke) is also part of the motivation for discouraging consumption.

On the other hand, governments use *subsidies* to encourage people to consume "good" products or services. For instance, many governments provide public funding for schools to encourage education and for vaccinations to encourage parents to protect their children against disease.

Four Real-World Interventions

In this chapter we'll look at four real-world examples of how governments have intervened or could intervene in the market for food. For each, we'll consider the motives for the intervention and what its direct and indirect consequences were or could be:

1. For many Mexican families, tortillas are an important food. What happened when the Mexican government set a maximum price for tortillas, in an effort to keep them affordable?
2. Farming is a risky business that is subject to bad weather and other uncertainties. In order to support the income of farmers, governments typically set a minimum legal price at which agricultural goods can be sold. What happens when the Canadian Dairy Commission sets a minimum price for milk?
3. Many Europeans struggle with health problems caused by overeating and poor nutrition. Several countries have responded by taxing certain food products. What happens if governments taxes high-fat or high-calorie foods?
4. What would happen if, instead of setting a maximum price for tortillas, the Mexican government *subsidized* tortillas?

As we walk through these examples of real policies, we want you to apply both positive and normative analysis. Remember the difference:

*   *Positive* analysis is about facts: Does the policy actually accomplish the original goal?
*   *Normative* analysis is a matter of values and opinions: Do you think the policy is a good idea?

Few policies are all good or all bad. The key question is, *What are the trade-offs* involved in the intervention? Do the benefits outweigh the costs?

✓ CONCEPT CHECK

☐   What are three reasons that a government might want to intervene in markets?

Price Controls

Suppose you are an economic policy advisor and food prices are rising. What should you do? If you were living in a region with many low-income consumers, you might want to take action to ensure that everyone gets enough to eat. One policy tool you might consider using is a **price control**—a regulation that sets a maximum or minimum legal price for a particular good. The direct effect of a price control is to hold the price of a good up or down when the market shifts, thus preventing the market from reaching a new equilibrium.

Price controls can be divided into two opposing categories: *price ceilings* and *price floors.* We encountered this idea already in the chapter on surplus, when we imagined an interfering eBay manager setting prices for digital cameras. In reality, eBay would never do such a thing, but governments often do, particularly when it comes to markets for food items. What are the effects of using price controls to intervene in a well-functioning, competitive market?

Price Ceilings

LO 6.1 Calculate the effect of a price ceiling on the equilibrium price and quantity.

A **price ceiling** is a maximum legal price at which a good can be sold. Many countries have price ceilings on staple foods, gasoline, and electricity, as policy makers try to ensure everyone can afford the basic necessities.

Historically, the government of Mexico has set a price ceiling for tortillas, with the intent of guaranteeing that this staple food will remain affordable. Panel A of Figure 6-1 illustrates a hypothetical market for tortillas without a price ceiling. The equilibrium price is $0.50 per kilogram, and the equilibrium quantity is 50 million kilograms.

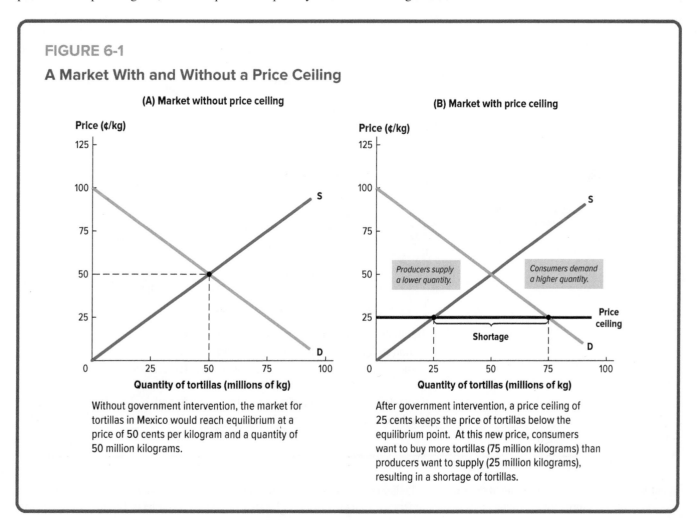

FIGURE 6-1

A Market With and Without a Price Ceiling

Without government intervention, the market for tortillas in Mexico would reach equilibrium at a price of 50 cents per kilogram and a quantity of 50 million kilograms.

After government intervention, a price ceiling of 25 cents keeps the price of tortillas below the equilibrium point. At this new price, consumers want to buy more tortillas (75 million kilograms) than producers want to supply (25 million kilograms), resulting in a shortage of tortillas.

Let's say that the government of Mexico responded to rising tortilla prices by setting a price ceiling of approximately $0.25 per kilo, as shown in panel B of Figure 6-1. How should we expect producers and consumers to respond to this intervention? When price falls, consumers will want to buy more tortillas. In this example, the price fell from $0.50 to $0.25, and as a result, quantity demanded increased from 50 million to 75 million kilos.

Predictably, however, a lower price means fewer producers will be willing to sell tortillas. When the price fell to $0.25, the quantity supplied dropped from 50 million to 25 million kilos. A lower price means higher quantity demanded but lower quantity supplied. Supply and demand were no longer in equilibrium. The price ceiling created a *shortage* of tortillas, equal to the 50 million kilo difference between the quantities supplied and demanded.

Did the price ceiling meet the goal of providing low-priced tortillas to consumers? Yes and no. Consumers were able to buy *some* tortillas at the low price of $0.25 a kilogram—but they wanted to buy three times as many tortillas as producers were willing to supply. We can assess the full effect of the price ceiling by looking at what happened to consumer and producer surplus. Without looking at the graph, we already know that a price ceiling will cause producer surplus to fall: sellers are selling fewer tortillas at a lower price. We also know that total surplus—that is, producer and consumer surplus combined—will fall, because the market has moved away from equilibrium. Some trades that would have happened at the equilibrium price do not happen, and the surplus that would have been generated by those mutually beneficial trades is lost entirely. This is known as *deadweight loss* and is represented by area 1 in Figure 6-2. As we discussed in Chapter 5, **deadweight loss** represents the loss of total surplus that occurs because the quantity of a good that is bought and sold is below the market equilibrium quantity.

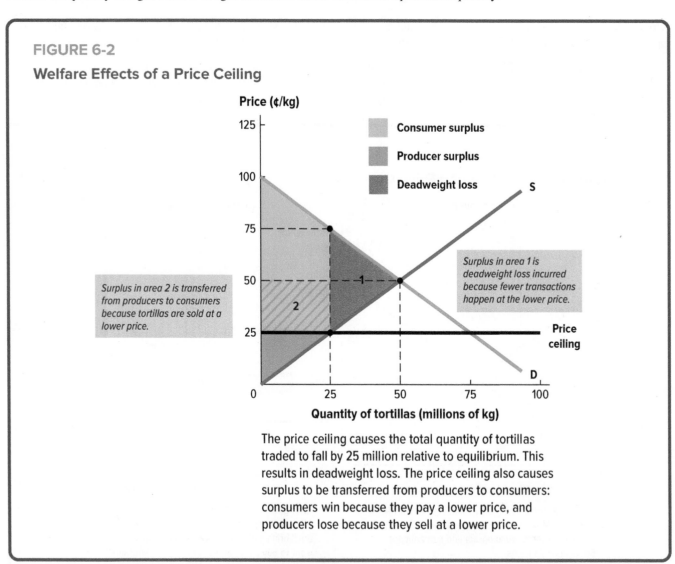

FIGURE 6-2

Welfare Effects of a Price Ceiling

The price ceiling causes the total quantity of tortillas traded to fall by 25 million relative to equilibrium. This results in deadweight loss. The price ceiling also causes surplus to be transferred from producers to consumers: consumers win because they pay a lower price, and producers lose because they sell at a lower price.

What we can't tell without looking at the graph is whether consumer surplus will increase or decrease—that response depends on the shape of the supply and demand curves. Consumers lose surplus from trades that no longer take place. But for the trades that still do take place, consumers gain surplus from paying $0.25 instead of $0.50 (while producers lose the same amount of surplus from receiving the lower price).

This direct transfer of surplus from producers to consumers is represented by area 2 in Figure 6-2. The fact that area 2 is larger than half of area 1 (the portion of deadweight loss that would have gone to consumers at equilibrium) represents the goal the price ceiling was intended to achieve: a net increase in the well-being of consumers. Was the policy worthwhile? On the one hand, consumers gained surplus. On the other hand, the surplus lost by producers was greater than that gained by consumers, meaning that total surplus decreased. Is it a price worth paying? That is a normative question about which reasonable people can disagree.

Another factor we may want to consider in our overall analysis of the price ceiling is the way in which the scarce tortillas are allocated. Because a price ceiling causes a shortage, goods must be rationed. This could be done in a number of ways. One possibility is for goods to be rationed by using coupons, with each family entitled to buy a certain amount of tortillas per week using government sanctioned coupons. This is what happened when food was rationed in Canada during the Second World War.

Another possibility is to allocate goods on a first-come, first-served basis. This forces people to waste time standing in lines. In still other cases, rationed goods might go to those who are given preference by the government, or to the friends and families of sellers. Finally, shortages open the door for people to bribe whoever is in charge of allocating scarce supplies, which would mean even more deadweight loss than in the example shown in Figure 6-2. Economists call this *rent-seeking behaviour,* and it is often cited as an argument against imposing price ceilings.

Price ceilings are sometimes used with noble intentions. The What Do You Think? box, How Beneficial is Drug Price Control for Canada? asks you to weigh the costs and benefits of a controversial price ceiling on the control of drug prices in Canada.

WHAT DO YOU THINK?

How Beneficial Is Drug Price Control for Canada?

To moderate the prices of pharmaceutical drugs, over the last thirty years federal and provincial governments in Canada have used a variety of policy tools. The federal government established the Patented Medicine Prices Review Board (PMPRB) to control factory gate prices. Different provinces have instituted formulary management, use of generics, reference-based pricing, price freezes, and limits on markups. If inflation is taken into account, these policy tools have been effective in keeping drug prices relatively low in Canada. But some argue that these price control policies adversely affect innovation and may reduce economic growth and the quality of Canadian health care.

The extremely high cost of research and development in the pharmaceutical sector may create these adverse impacts. "The costs—and risks—of discovering and launching a new drug have been rising sharply. After adjusting for inflation, the average R&D cost of a new drug went from $318 million US in 1991 to $802 million US in 2001 (in 2000 dollars). The entire R&D process can last 10 to 15 years" (Petkantchin, 2004).

It is also becoming increasingly difficult to find an effective new molecule that can be used to produce a commercial drug. "For each 10,000 molecules at the pre-clinical testing stage, only one will obtain approval and go on commercial sale" (Petkantchin, 2004). Price controls may further inhibit these discoveries by increasing the already-significant costs and risks inherent in the development of new drugs. If that is the case, then only a high price charged to consumers can provide the profit that will incentivize a company to launch a new drug in Canada. "It has been reported that because of some PMPRB rulings, certain drugs have not been launched in Canada, although they have undergone regulatory review and received a Notice of Compliance" (Menon, 2001).

Pharmaceuticals is also a high-growth sector, so price controls or any policy with a negative impact on R&D may discourage multinational pharmaceutical companies from conducting pharmaceutical research in Canada, which would mean losing well-paid jobs and private research centers. Petkantchin (2004) cites a study showing that in Germany the result of drug price controls was an overall loss to their economy of US$3 billion. Recently, Alexion Pharmaceuticals, a US company, filed a lawsuit challenging the validity and authority of price control by PMPRB.

Drug price controls are used to make drugs affordable and reduce inequality in the health care sector. But while controls cut the cost of drugs to all Canadians, the lack of availability of a medication could adversely affect Canadians' health, and a reduction of R&D in this sector may negatively affect economic growth.

Sources: Valentin Petkantchin; 2004. "The dark side of drug price controls," *Medical Post*, Vol. 40, no 17 (http://www.iedm.org/fr/2421-the-dark-side-of-drug-price-controls);

Devidas Menon; 2001. "Pharmaceutical Cost Control In Canada: Does It Work?," *Health Affairs* 20, no.3, 92-103;(http://content.healthaffairs.org/content/20/3/92)

http://www.theglobeandmail.com/report-on-business/industry-news/the-law-page/company-behind-500000-drugchallenges-ottawas-ability-to-control-drug-prices/article26549512/.

What do you think?

1. What effect do you think price control can have on R&D activities for new drugs?

2. Price ceilings hold down prices, but may also cause shortages and transfer surplus from drug companies to drug users. Would you support a cap on drug prices?

3. What would you expect the outcome of such a policy to be for buyers (patients) and sellers (pharmaceutical companies)?

FIGURE 6-3

Non-binding Price Ceiling

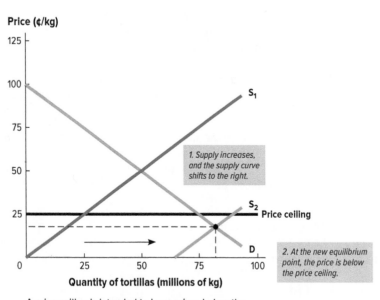

A price ceiling is intended to keep prices below the equilibrium level. However, changes in the market can reduce the equilibrium price to a level below the price ceiling. When that happens, the price ceiling no longer creates a shortage, because the quantity supplied equals the quantity demanded.

A price ceiling does not always affect the market outcome. If the ceiling is set above the equilibrium price in a market, it is said to be *non-binding.* That is, the ceiling doesn't "bind" or restrict buyers' and sellers' behaviour because the current equilibrium is within the range allowed by the ceiling. In such cases, the equilibrium price and quantity will prevail.

Although price ceilings are usually binding when they are first implemented (otherwise, why bother to create them?), shifts in the market over time can render the ceilings non-binding. Suppose the price of corn decreases, reducing the cost of making tortillas. Figure 6-3 shows how the supply curve for tortillas would shift to the right in response to this change in the market, causing the equilibrium price to fall below the price ceiling. The new equilibrium is 80 million kilograms of tortillas at $0.20 a kilo, and the price ceiling becomes non-binding.

Price Floors

LO 6.2 Calculate the effect of a price floor on the equilibrium price and quantity.

A **price floor** is a minimum legal price at which a good can be sold. Canada has a long history of establishing price floors for certain agricultural goods. The rationale is that farming is a risky business—subject to bad weather, crop failure, and unreliable prices—but also an essential one, if people are to have enough to eat. A price floor is seen as a way to guarantee farmers a minimum income in the face of these difficulties, keeping them in business and ensuring a reliable supply of food.

FIGURE 6-4

A Market With and Without a Price Floor

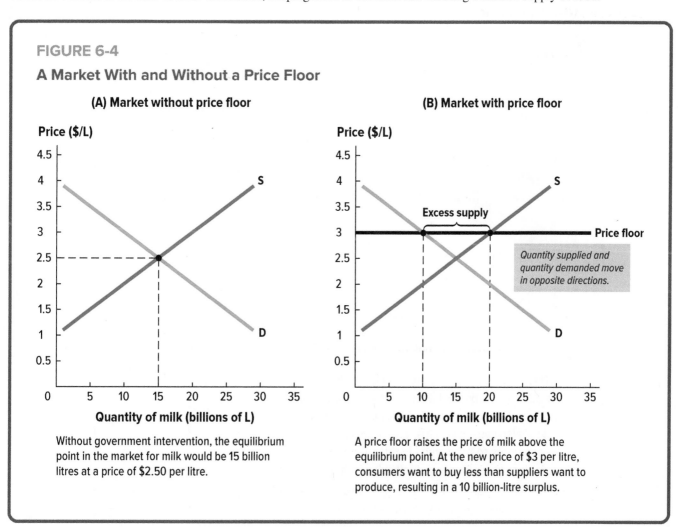

(A) Market without price floor

Price ($/L)

Without government intervention, the equilibrium point in the market for milk would be 15 billion litres at a price of $2.50 per litre.

(B) Market with price floor

Price ($/L)

A price floor raises the price of milk above the equilibrium point. At the new price of $3 per litre, consumers want to buy less than suppliers want to produce, resulting in a 10 billion-litre surplus.

Canada has maintained price floors for dairy products for fifty years; the supply management system in the dairy industry began in 1970. Under the supply management system, price is regulated at the retail and wholesale stages. The Canadian Dairy Commission sets the price that serves as a benchmark for each provincial agency across Canada.

What effect has this system had on the market for milk? In panel A of Figure 6-4, we show a hypothetical unregulated market for milk in Canada, with an annual equilibrium quantity of 15 billion litres and an equilibrium price of $2.50 per litre.

Now suppose the Canadian Dairy Commission implements a price floor, so that the price of milk cannot fall below $3 per litre, as shown in panel B of Figure 6-4. *How will producers and consumers respond?* At $3 per litre, dairy farmers will want to increase milk production from 15 to 20 billion litres, moving up along the supply curve. At that price, however, consumers will want to *decrease* their milk consumption from 15 to 10 billion litres, moving up along the demand curve. As a result, the price floor creates an excess quantity supplied of milk that is equal to the difference between the quantity supplied and the quantity demanded—in this case, 10 billion litres.

Has the government accomplished its aim of supporting dairy farmers and providing them with a reliable income? As with price ceilings, the answer is yes and no. Producers who can sell all their milk will be happy, because they are selling more milk at a higher price. However, producers who cannot sell all their milk because demand no longer meets supply will be unhappy. Consumers will be unhappy because they are getting less milk at a higher price.

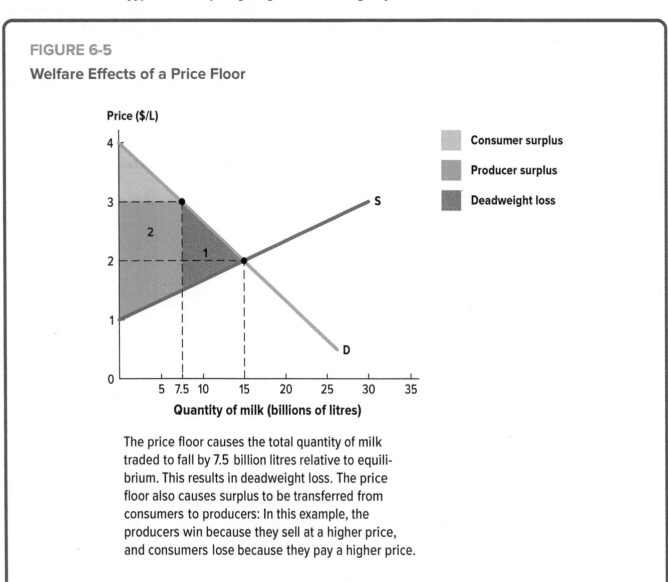

FIGURE 6-5

Welfare Effects of a Price Floor

The price floor causes the total quantity of milk traded to fall by 7.5 billion litres relative to equilibrium. This results in deadweight loss. The price floor also causes surplus to be transferred from consumers to producers: In this example, the producers win because they sell at a higher price, and consumers lose because they pay a higher price.

Again, we can apply the concept of surplus to formally analyze how this change in total surplus is distributed between consumers and producers. According to Figure 6-5, before the price floor, 60 billion litres of milk were sold and bought; afterward, only 30 billion. Five billion litres of milk that could have been traded were not, reducing total surplus. This deadweight loss is represented by area 1 in Figure 6-5.

Like price ceilings, price floors change the distribution of surplus, but in this case producers win at the expense of consumers. When the price floor is in effect, the only consumers who buy are those whose willingness to pay is above $3 a litre. Their consumer surplus falls, because they are buying the same milk at a higher price, and their lost surplus is transferred directly to the producers who sell milk to them. This transfer of surplus is represented by area 2 in Figure 6-5. Whether producers gain or lose overall will depend on whether this area is bigger or smaller than their share of the deadweight loss. The fact that area 2 is larger than the section of area 1 lost to producers shows that in this case the price floor policy increased well-being for producers.

Is the price of reduced total and consumer surplus worth paying to achieve increased producer surplus? One factor to consider is how the extra surplus is distributed among producers. Producers who are able to sell all their milk at the higher price will be happy. But producers who do not manage to sell all of their goods will be left holding an excess quantity supplied. They may be worse off than before the imposition of the price floor. With excess quantity supplied, customers may choose to buy from firms they like based on familiarity, political preference, or any other decision-making process they choose.

FIGURE 6-6

Non-binding Price Floor

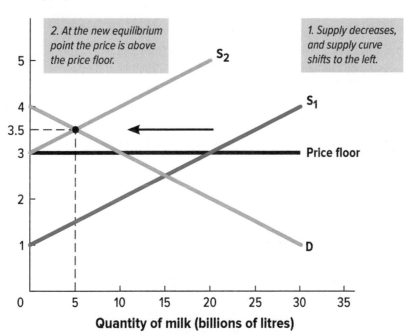

Although a price floor is usually set so as to raise prices above the equilibrium level, changes in the supply can raise the equilibrium price above the price floor. When that happens, the surplus that was created by the price floor disappears, and the quantity supplied equals the quantity demanded.

To prevent some producers from being left in the lurch, the government may decide to buy up all the excess quantity supplied of milk, ensuring that *all* producers benefit. Of course, paying for the milk imposes a cost on taxpayers and is often cited as an argument against price floors. How much milk will the government have to buy? The answer is the entire amount of the excess quantity supplied created by the price floor. According to Figure 6-4, in the case of the hypothetical milk price floor, the government will have to buy 10 billion litres at a price of $3 per litre. The cost to taxpayers of maintaining the price floor in this example would be $30 billion each year.

Price floors are not always binding. The price floor may become binding, however, in response to changes in the market. Consider the effect of the increased demand for ethanol on the market for milk. Ethanol is a fuel additive made from corn. The sudden rise in demand for ethanol pushes up the price of corn, which pushes up the cost of livestock feed for dairy farmers. As a result, the supply curve for milk shifts to the left, pushing the equilibrium price for milk above the $3 price floor to $3.50. Figure 6-6 shows how such a decrease in supply could render a price floor non-binding.

✓ CONCEPT CHECK

☐ Why does a price ceiling cause a shortage? [LO 6.1]

☐ What can cause a price ceiling to become non-binding? [LO 6.1]

☐ Explain how a government can support a price floor through purchases. [LO 6.2]

Taxes and Subsidies

Taxes are the main way that governments raise revenue to pay for public programs. Taxes and subsidies can also be used to correct market failures and encourage or discourage production and consumption of particular goods. As we will see, like price floors and price ceilings, they can have unintended consequences.

Taxes

LO 6.3 Calculate the effect of a tax on the equilibrium price and quantity.

We began this chapter by discussing hunger, which is (relatively speaking) a minor problem in wealthy countries. Indeed, Canada, US and European countries have the opposite problem: diseases associated with overeating and poor nutrition, such as obesity, heart disease, and diabetes.

How can policy makers respond to this new type of food crisis? In 2011, Hungary imposed taxes on foods with high fat, sugar, and salt content, as well as increased tariffs on soft drinks and alcohol. When a good is taxed, either the buyer or seller must pay some extra amount to the government on top of the sale price. How should we expect people to *respond* to a tax on fatty foods? Taxes have two primary effects. First, they discourage production and consumption of the good that is taxed. Second, they raise government revenue through the fees paid by those who continue buying and selling the good. Therefore, we would expect a tax to both reduce consumption of fatty foods and to provide a new source of public revenue.

Figure 6-7 illustrates this scenario by showing the impact of a trans fat tax on the market for Chocolate Whizbangs. A delicious imaginary candy, Chocolate Whizbangs are unfortunately rather high in trans fats. Suppose that, currently, 30 million Whizbangs are sold every year, at $0.50 each.

FIGURE 6-7

Effect of a Tax Paid by the Seller

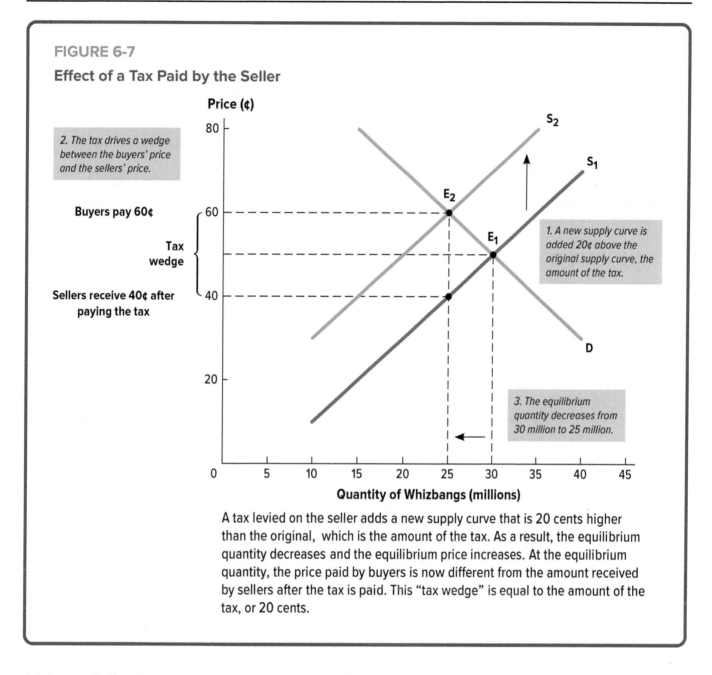

2. The tax drives a wedge between the buyers' price and the sellers' price.

Buyers pay 60¢

Tax wedge

Sellers receive 40¢ after paying the tax

1. A new supply curve is added 20¢ above the original supply curve, the amount of the tax.

3. The equilibrium quantity decreases from 30 million to 25 million.

A tax levied on the seller adds a new supply curve that is 20 cents higher than the original, which is the amount of the tax. As a result, the equilibrium quantity decreases and the equilibrium price increases. At the equilibrium quantity, the price paid by buyers is now different from the amount received by sellers after the tax is paid. This "tax wedge" is equal to the amount of the tax, or 20 cents.

A Tax on Sellers

Let's say that the government of British Columbia enacts a tax of $0.20, which the seller must pay for every Whizbang sold. *How will buyers and sellers respond?* The impact of a tax is more complicated than the impact of a price control, so let's take it one step at a time.

1. **Does a tax on sellers affect supply?** *Yes, supply decreases.*

   When a tax is imposed on sellers, they must pay the government $0.20 for each Whizbang sold. At any market price, sellers will behave as if the price they are receiving is actually $0.20 lower. Put another way, for sellers to be willing to supply any given quantity, the market price must be $0.20 higher than it was before the tax.

   Figure 6-7 shows this change in supply graphically, by adding a new supply curve (S_2). (Technically, this "shift" isn't really a shift of the curve, but a way of showing the new equilibrium price; see the following Potentially Confusing box.) Note that the new supply curve is $0.20 higher, the exact amount of the tax. At any given market price, sellers will now produce the same quantity as they would have at a price $0.20 lower before the tax. At $0.60 on curve S_2, the quantity supplied will be the same as at a price of $0.40 on curve S_1. At a price of $0.50 on curve S_2, the quantity supplied will be the same as at a price of $0.30 on curve S_1, and so on.

2. Does a tax on sellers affect demand? *No, demand stays the same.*

Demand remains the same because the tax does not change any of the non-price determinants of demand. At any given price, buyers' desire to purchase Whizbangs is unchanged. Remember, however, that the *quantity demanded* may still change—does change, in fact—although the curve itself doesn't change.

3. How does a tax on sellers affect the market equilibrium? *The equilibrium price rises and quantity demanded falls.*

The new supply curve causes the equilibrium point to move up along the demand curve. At the new equilibrium point, the price paid by the buyer is $0.60. Because buyers now face a higher price, they demand fewer Whizbangs, so the quantity demanded falls from 30 million to 25 million. Notice that at the new equilibrium point, the quantity demanded is lower and the price is higher. Taxes usually reduce the quantity of a good or service that is sold, shrinking the market.

POTENTIALLY CONFUSING

In Chapter 3, "Markets," we distinguished between a curve *shifting* to the left or right and *movement along* the same curve. A shift represents a fundamental change in the quantity demanded or supplied at any given price; a movement along the same curve simply shows a switch to a different quantity and price point. Does a tax cause a *shift* of the demand or supply curve or a *movement along* the curve?

The answer is neither, really. When we add a tax, we're not actually shifting the curve; rather, we are adding a second curve. The original curve is still needed to understand what is happening. This is because the price that sellers receive is actually $0.20 lower than the price at which they sell Whizbangs, due to the tax. So we need one curve to represent what sellers receive and another curve to represent what buyers pay. Notice in Figure 6-7 that the price suppliers receive is on the original supply curve, S_1, but the price buyers pay is on the new supply curve, S_2. The original curve *does not move,* but we add the second curve to indicate that, because of the tax, buyers face a different price than the sellers will get. In order for the market to be in equilibrium, the quantity that buyers demand at $0.60 must now equal the quantity that sellers supply at $0.40.

Look at the new equilibrium price in Figure 6-7. The price paid by buyers to sellers is the new market price, $0.60. However, sellers do not get to keep all the money they receive. Instead, they have to pay the tax to the government. Since the tax is $0.20, the price that sellers receive once they have paid the tax is only $0.40. Ultimately, sellers do not receive the full price that consumers pay, because the tax creates what is known as a *tax wedge* between buyers and sellers. A **tax wedge** is the difference between the price paid by buyers and the price received by sellers, which equals the amount of the tax. In Figure 6-7, the tax wedge is calculated as shown in Equation 6-1.

Equation 6-1

$$\text{Tax wedge} = P_{buyers} - P_{sellers} = \text{tax}$$

For each Whizbang sold at the new equilibrium point, the government collects tax revenue, as calculated in Equation 6-2. Specifically, the government receives $0.20 for each of the 25 million Whizbangs sold, or $5 million total. Graphically, the government revenue equals the green-shaded area in Figure 6-8.

FIGURE 6-8

Government Revenue and Deadweight Loss from a Tax

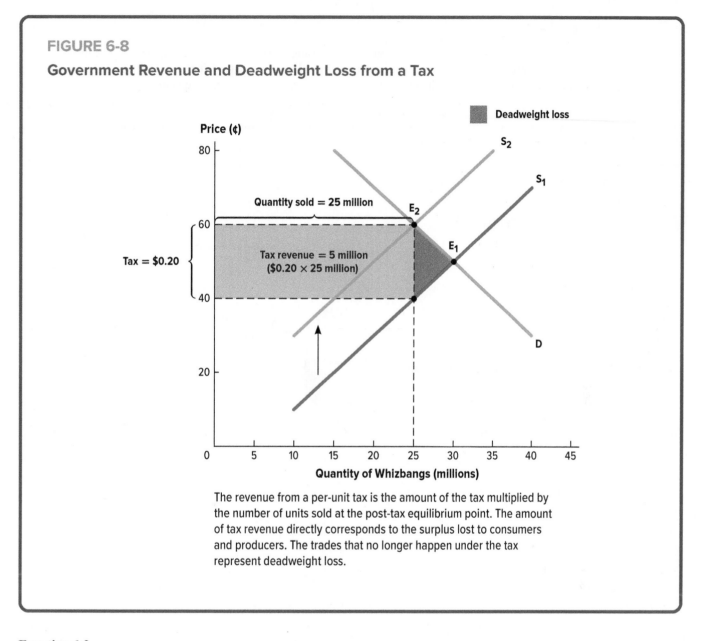

The revenue from a per-unit tax is the amount of the tax multiplied by the number of units sold at the post-tax equilibrium point. The amount of tax revenue directly corresponds to the surplus lost to consumers and producers. The trades that no longer happen under the tax represent deadweight loss.

Equation 6-2

$$\text{Government tax revenue} = \text{Tax} \times Q_{\text{post-tax}}$$

Just like a price control, a tax causes deadweight loss and redistributes surplus. We can see the deadweight loss caused by the reduced number of trades in Figure 6-8. It is surplus lost to buyers and sellers who would have been willing to make trades at the pre-tax equilibrium price.

The redistribution of surplus, however, is a little trickier to follow. Under a tax, *both* producers and consumers lose surplus. Consumers who still buy pay more for the same candy than they would have under equilibrium, and producers who still sell receive less for the same candy. The difference between this lost surplus and deadweight loss, however, is that it doesn't disappear. Instead, it becomes government revenue. In fact, the area representing government revenue in Figure 6-8 is exactly the same as the surplus lost to buyers and sellers still trading in the market after the tax has been imposed. This revenue can pay for services that might transfer surplus back to producers or consumers, or both, or to people outside of the market.

A Tax on Buyers

What happens if the tax is imposed on buyers instead of sellers? Surprisingly, the outcome is exactly the same. Suppose British Columbia enacts a sales tax of $0.20, which the buyer must pay for every Whizbang bought. In this case the demand curve, rather than the supply curve, moves by the amount of the tax, but the resulting equilibrium price and quantity are the same (see Figure 6-9).

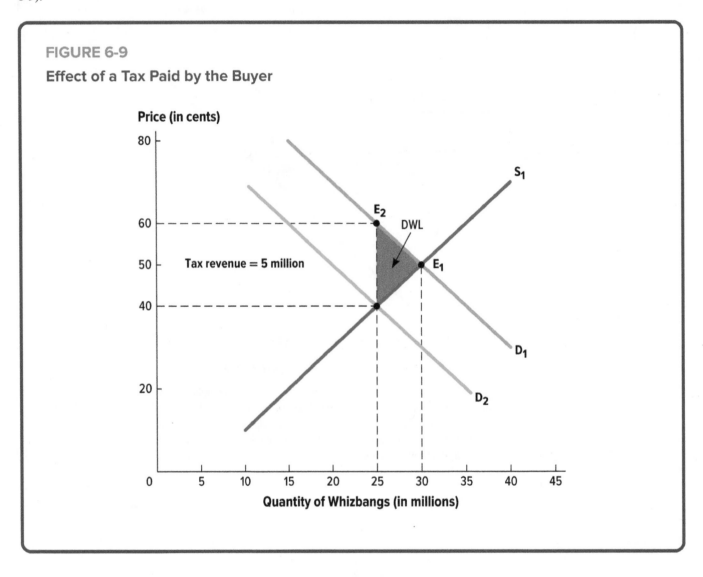

FIGURE 6-9

Effect of a Tax Paid by the Buyer

To double-check this result, let's walk step by step through the effect of a tax levied on buyers.

1. **Does a tax on buyers affect the supply curve?** *No, supply stays the same.*

    The supply curve stays the same because the tax does not change the incentives producers face. None of the non-price determinants of supply are affected.

2. **Does a tax on buyers affect the demand curve?** *Yes, demand decreases.*

    Demand decreases because the price buyers must pay per unit, including the tax, is now $0.20 higher than the original price. As Figure 6-9 shows, we take the original demand curve D_1 and factor in the amount of the tax to get a second demand curve D_2, which represents the price buyers pay under the tax. At any given price, buyers will now behave as if the price were actually $0.20 higher. For example, at $0.40 on curve D_2, the quantity demanded is as if the price were $0.60 on curve D_1. At $0.30 on curve D_2, the quantity demanded is as if the price were $0.50.

3. **How does a tax on buyers affect the market equilibrium?** *The equilibrium price and quantity both fall.*

As a result, the equilibrium point with the new demand curve is further down the supply curve. The equilibrium price falls from $0.50 to $0.40, and the quantity demanded and supplied falls from 30 million to 25 million. Although the market equilibrium price goes down instead of up, as it does with a tax on sellers, the actual amount that buyers and sellers pay is the same no matter who pays the tax. When buyers pay the tax, they pay $0.40 to the seller and $0.20 to the government, or a total of $0.60. When sellers pay the tax, buyers pay $0.60 to the seller, who then pays $0.20 to the government. Either way, buyers pay $0.60 and sellers receive $0.40.

As Figure 6-9 shows, a tax on buyers creates a tax wedge just as a tax on sellers does. At the new equilibrium point, the price sellers receive is $0.40. The buyer pays $0.40 to the seller and then the $0.20 tax to the government, so that the total effective price is $0.60. Once again, the tax wedge is $0.20, exactly equal to the amount of the tax.

Equation 6-3

$$\text{Tax wedge} = \$0.60 - \$0.40 = \$0.20$$

Furthermore, the government still collects $0.20 for every Whizbang sold, just as under a tax on sellers. Again, the post-tax equilibrium quantity is 25 million, and the government collects $5 million in tax revenue.

Equation 6-4

$$\text{Tax revenue} = \$0.20 \times 25 \text{ million} = \$5 \text{ million}$$

What is the overall impact of the tax on Whizbangs? Regardless of whether a tax is imposed on buyers or sellers, there are four effects that result from all taxes:

1. Equilibrium quantity falls. The goal of the tax has been achieved—consumption of Whizbangs has been discouraged.
2. Buyers pay more for each Whizbang and sellers receive less. This creates a tax wedge, equal to the difference between the price paid by buyers and the price received by sellers.
3. The government receives revenue equal to the amount of the tax multiplied by the new equilibrium quantity. In this case, the BC provincial government receives an additional $5 million in revenue from the tax on Whizbangs—which could be used to offset the public health expenses caused by obesity-related diseases.
4. The tax causes deadweight loss. This means that the value of the revenue the government collects is always less than the reduction in total surplus caused by the tax.

In evaluating a tax, then, we must weigh its goal—in this case, reducing the consumption of trans fats—against the loss of surplus in the market.

Who Bears the Burden of a Tax?

We've seen that the outcome of a tax does not depend on who pays it. Whether a tax is levied on buyers or on sellers, the cost is shared. But which group bears more of the burden?

In our example, the burden was shared equally. Buyers paid $0.50 for a Whizbang before the tax; after the tax, they pay $0.60. Therefore, buyers bear $0.10 of the $0.20 tax burden. Sellers received $0.50 for each Whizbang before the tax; after the tax, they receive $0.40. Therefore, sellers also bear $0.10 of the $0.20 tax burden. The shaded rectangles in panel A of Figure 6-10 represent graphically this 50/50 split.

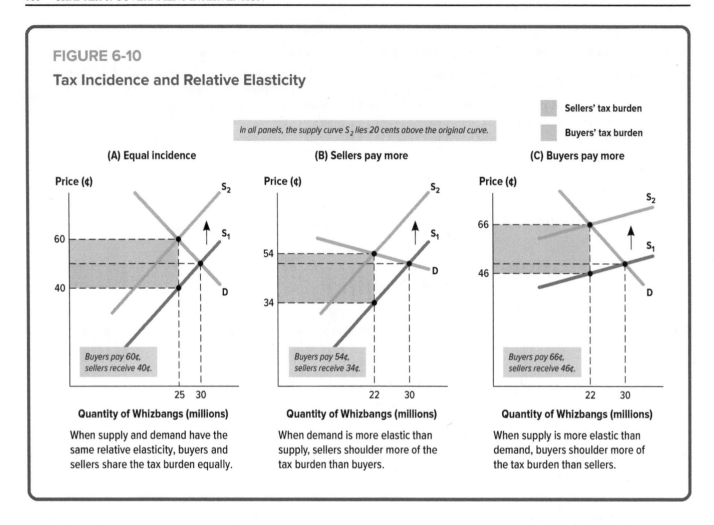

FIGURE 6-10

Tax Incidence and Relative Elasticity

Sellers' tax burden

Buyers' tax burden

In all panels, the supply curve S₂ lies 20 cents above the original curve.

(A) Equal incidence

Price (¢)

S₂
S₁

60

40

D

Buyers pay 60¢, sellers receive 40¢.

25 30

Quantity of Whizbangs (millions)

When supply and demand have the same relative elasticity, buyers and sellers share the tax burden equally.

(B) Sellers pay more

Price (¢)

S₂
S₁

54

34

D

Buyers pay 54¢, sellers receive 34¢.

22 30

Quantity of Whizbangs (millions)

When demand is more elastic than supply, sellers shoulder more of the tax burden than buyers.

(C) Buyers pay more

Price (¢)

S₂
S₁

66

46

D

Buyers pay 66¢, sellers receive 46¢.

22 30

Quantity of Whizbangs (millions)

When supply is more elastic than demand, buyers shoulder more of the tax burden than sellers.

Often, however, the tax burden is not split equally. Sometimes one group carries much more of it than the other. Compare the example just given to another possible market for Whizbangs, represented in panel B of Figure 6-10. In this case, buyers paid $0.50 before the tax. After the tax, they pay $0.54, so their tax burden is $0.04 per Whizbang. Sellers, on the other hand, receive only $0.34 after the tax, so their tax burden, at $0.16 per Whizbang, is four times as large as that of buyers. Panel C shows the opposite case, in which buyers bear more of the burden than sellers. There, buyers pay $0.66 and sellers receive $0.48. The relative tax burden borne by buyers and sellers is called the **tax incidence**.

What determines the incidence of a tax? The answer has to do with the relative elasticity of the supply and demand curves. Recall from Chapter 4 that price elasticity describes how much the quantity supplied or demanded changes in response to a change in price. Since a tax effectively changes the price of a good to both buyers and sellers, the relative responsiveness of supply and demand will determine the tax burden. Essentially, the side of the market that is more price elastic will be more able to adjust to price changes and will shoulder less of the tax burden.

Panel B of Figure 6-10 imagines a market in which demand is more elastic: many consumers easily give up their Whizbang habit and buy healthier snacks, instead. In that case, Whizbang producers pay a higher share of the tax. Panel C imagines a market in which demand is less elastic: consumers are so obsessed with Whizbangs that they will buy even at the higher price. In that case, buyers pay a higher share of the tax.

Recall that the market outcome of a tax—the new equilibrium quantity and price—is the same regardless of whether a tax is imposed on buyers or on sellers. Thus, the tax burden will be the same no matter which side of the market is taxed. Note in panel C of Figure 6-10 that buyers bear the greater part of that burden, even though the tax is imposed on sellers. The actual economic incidence of a tax is unrelated to the *statutory incidence*—that is, the person who is legally responsible for paying the tax.

This is an important point to remember during public debates about taxes. A politician may say that companies that pollute should be held accountable for the environmental damage they cause, through a tax on pollution. Regardless of how you may feel about the idea of taxing pollution, remember that levying the tax on companies that pollute does not mean that they will end up bearing the whole tax burden. Consumers who buy from those producers will also bear part of the burden of the tax, through higher prices. Policy makers have little control over how the tax burden is shared between buyers and sellers.

Subsidies

A **subsidy** is the reverse of a tax: it's a requirement that the government pay an extra amount to producers or consumers of a good. Governments use subsidies to encourage the production and consumption of a particular good or service. They can also use subsidies as an alternative to price controls to benefit certain groups without generating a shortage or an excess quantity supplied.

Let's return to the Mexican dilemma—what to do when hungry people cannot afford to buy enough tortillas. What would happen if the government subsidized tortillas rather than imposed a price ceiling on them?

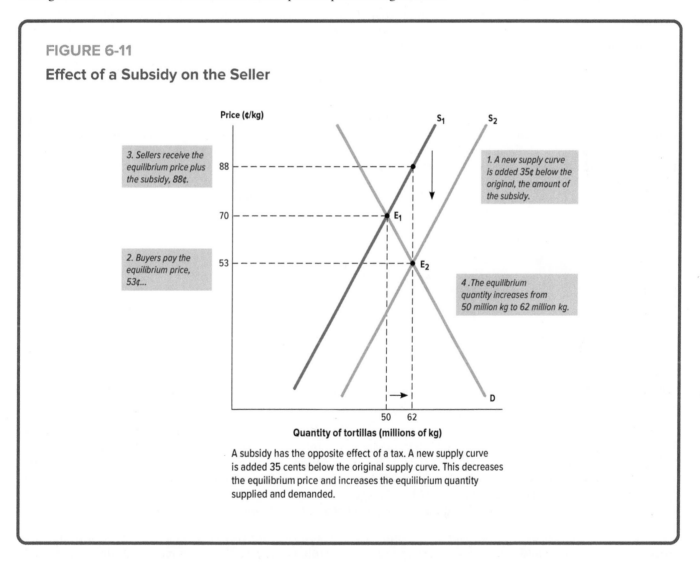

FIGURE 6-11

Effect of a Subsidy on the Seller

3. Sellers receive the equilibrium price plus the subsidy, 88¢.

1. A new supply curve is added 35¢ below the original, the amount of the subsidy.

2. Buyers pay the equilibrium price, 53¢...

4. The equilibrium quantity increases from 50 million kg to 62 million kg.

A subsidy has the opposite effect of a tax. A new supply curve is added 35 cents below the original supply curve. This decreases the equilibrium price and increases the equilibrium quantity supplied and demanded.

Figure 6-11 shows the tortilla market we discussed earlier in the chapter. The figure shows that before the subsidy, the market is in equilibrium at a price of $0.70 per kilogram and a quantity of 50 million kilos. Now suppose the government offers tortilla makers a subsidy of $0.35 per kilo. *How will buyers and sellers respond to the subsidy?* They will respond in the opposite way that they respond to a tax: With a tax, the quantity supplied and demanded decreases, and the government collects revenue. With a subsidy, the quantity supplied and demanded increases, and the government spends money.

We can calculate the effect of a $0.35 tortilla subsidy by walking through the same three steps we used to examine the effect of a tax.

1. **Does a subsidy to sellers affect the supply curve?** *Yes, supply increases.*

   When producers receive a subsidy, the real price they receive for each unit sold is higher than the market price. At any market price, therefore, they will behave as if the price were $0.35 higher. Put another way, for sellers to supply a given quantity, the market price can be $0.35 lower than it would have to be without the subsidy. As a result, the new supply curve is drawn $0.35 below the original. In Figure 6-11, S_2 shows the new supply curve that is the result of the subsidy.

2. **Does a subsidy to sellers affect the demand curve?** *No, demand stays the same.*

   The demand curve stays where it is, because consumers are not directly affected by the subsidy.

3. **How does a subsidy to sellers affect the market equilibrium?** *The equilibrium price decreases and the equilibrium quantity increases.*

   The equilibrium quantity with the new supply curve increases as consumers move down along the demand curve to the new equilibrium point. At the new, post-subsidy equilibrium, the quantity supplied increases from 50 million pounds of tortillas to 62 million pounds. As with a tax, the price buyers pay for tortillas differs from the price sellers receive after the subsidy, because the subsidy creates a wedge between the two prices. This time, however, sellers receive a *higher* price than the pre-subsidy equilibrium of $0.70, and buyers pay a *lower* one. Buyers pay $0.53 per pound and sellers receive $0.88 per pound. The government pays the $0.35 difference.

A subsidy benefits both buyers and sellers, increasing total surplus *within* the market. However, the subsidy imposes a cost on the government and ultimately on taxpayers. In this example, the government must pay $0.35 for each of the 62 million pounds of tortillas produced, for a total expenditure of $21.7 million. Is the subsidy worth the cost? That depends on how much we value the increased production of tortillas and the reduced cost to consumers versus the opportunity cost of the subsidy—that is, whatever other use the government or taxpayers might have made of that $21.7 million. And as the Real Life box, The Unintended Consequences of Biofuel Subsidies, shows, the obvious benefits of a subsidy can sometimes be swamped by unexpected costs.

REAL LIFE

The Unintended Consequences of Biofuel Subsidies

The Brazilian government has been providing subsidies to expand the production and use of biofuels. Biofuels are a potential low-carbon energy source, but whether biofuels offer carbon savings depends on how they are produced.

The planned expansion of biofuel plantations in Brazil could potentially cause both direct and indirect land-use changes (e.g., biofuel plantations replace rangelands, which replace forests). In one research paper, simulations show that indirect land-use changes, especially those pushing the rangeland frontier into the Amazonian forests, could offset the carbon savings from biofuels. Sugarcane ethanol and soybean biodiesel each contribute to nearly half of the projected indirect deforestation of 121,970 square kilometres by 2020, creating a carbon debt that would take about 250 years to be repaid using these biofuels instead of fossil fuels.

Converting rainforests, peatlands, savannas, or grasslands to produce food-crop-based biofuels in Brazil, Southeast Asia, and the United States creates a biofuel carbon debt by releasing 17 to 420 times more CO_2 than the annual greenhouse gas (GHG) reductions that these biofuels would provide by displacing fossil fuels.

The United States subsidizes the production of biofuels such as ethanol, a cleaner fuel than gasoline. The professed goal of the subsidy is to reduce pollution; unfortunately, it has also had some unintended effects. In *Time* magazine, Michael Grunwald argues that, indirectly, biofuels can actually increase pollution:

> [T]he basic problem with most biofuels is amazingly simple, given that researchers have ignored it until now: using land to grow fuel leads to the destruction of forests, wetlands and grasslands that store enormous amounts of carbon... More deforestation results from a chain reaction so vast it's subtle: U.S. farmers are selling one-fifth of their corn to ethanol production, so U.S. soybean farmers are switching to corn, so Brazilian soybean farmers are expanding into cattle pastures, so Brazilian cattlemen are displaced to the Amazon.

Through a complex chain of market reactions that policy makers probably didn't anticipate, Grunwald argues, ethanol subsidies are having the opposite of the hoped-for reduction in air pollution. Unfortunately, unintended consequences aren't always just a postscript to market interventions. Sometimes they can change the whole story.

Sources: https://www.researchgate.net/profile/Joerg_Priess/publication/41416829_Indirect_land-use_changes_can_overcome_carbon_savings_from_biofuels_in_Brazil/links/00b49518632e47a0e9000000.pdf http://citeseerx.ist.psu.edu/viewdoc/download?doi=10.1.1.333.8744&rep=rep1&type=pdf M. Grunwald, "The clean energy scam," *Time,* March 27, 2008, http://www.time.com/time/magazine/article/0,9171,1725975,00.html. The *New York Times* had a follow-up in its environmental blog: http://green.blogs.nytimes.com/2008/11/03/the-biofuel-debate-good-bad-or-too-soon-to-tell/. The *New York Times* had a follow-up in its environmental blog: http://green.blogs.nytimes.com/2008/11/03/the-biofuel-debate-good-bad-or-too-soon-to-tell/.

As with a tax, the effect of a subsidy is the same regardless of whether it is paid to producers or consumers. If consumers received a $0.35 subsidy for every pound of tortillas they bought, their demand curve would be $0.35 above the original, the supply curve would remain unchanged, and the equilibrium outcome would be the same as if producers received the subsidy: quantity increases from 50 million pounds to 62 million pounds, buyers pay $0.53 per pound, and sellers receive $0.88.

Also as with a tax, the way in which the benefits of a subsidy are split between buyers and sellers depends on the relative elasticity of the demand and supply curves. The side of the market that is more price elastic receives more of the benefit. In our example, both have almost the same benefit: buyers are better off by $0.17 per pound of tortillas, and producers by $0.18. As with taxes, it is important to note that who gets what share of benefit from the subsidy does not depend on who receives the subsidy. Sometimes in debates about subsidies you will hear someone argue that a subsidy should be given either to buyers or sellers because they deserve it more. This argument doesn't make much sense in a competitive market (although it might in a non-competitive market).

In sum, a subsidy has the following effects, regardless of whether it is paid to buyers or sellers:

1. Equilibrium quantity increases, accomplishing the goal of encouraging production and consumption of the subsidized good.
2. Buyers pay less and sellers receive more for each unit sold. The amount of the subsidy forms a wedge between buyers' and sellers' prices.
3. The government has to pay for the subsidy, the cost of which equals the amount of the subsidy multiplied by the new equilibrium quantity.

✓ CONCEPT CHECK

☐ What is a tax wedge? [LO 6.3]

☐ How does a subsidy affect the equilibrium quantity? How does it affect the price that sellers receive and the price that buyers pay? [LO 6.4]

☐ Does it matter whether a subsidy is paid to buyers or sellers? Why or why not? [LO 6.4]

Evaluating Government Interventions

LO 6.5 Explain how elasticity and time period influence the impact of a market intervention.

We began this chapter with a discussion of three reasons policy makers might decide to intervene in a market. To decide whether policy makers have achieved their goals by implementing a price control, tax, or subsidy, we need to assess the effects of each intervention, including its unintended consequences.

We've established a few rules about the expected outcomes of market interventions. Table 6-1 summarizes the key effects of price controls, taxes, and subsidies. In general, we can say the following:

- Price controls have opposing impacts on the quantities supplied and demanded, causing a shortage or excess quantity supplied. In contrast, taxes and subsidies move the quantities supplied and demanded in the same direction, allowing the market to reach equilibrium at the point where the quantity supplied equals the quantity demanded.
- Taxes discourage people from buying and selling a particular good, raise government revenue, and impose a cost on both buyers and sellers.
- Subsidies encourage people to buy and sell a particular good, cost the government money, and provide a benefit to both buyers and sellers.

In the following sections we will consider some of the more complicated details of market interventions. These details matter. Often the details of an intervention make the difference between a successful policy and a failed one.

How Big is the Effect of a Tax or Subsidy?

Regardless of the reason for a market intervention, it's important to know exactly *how much* it will change the equilibrium quantity and price. Can the effect of a tax or subsidy on the equilibrium quantity be predicted ahead of time? The answer is yes, if we know the price elasticity of supply and demand. The more elastic supply or demand is, the greater the change in quantity. This rule follows directly from the definition of price elasticity, which measures buyers' and sellers' responsiveness to a change in price—and a tax or subsidy is effectively a change in price.

TABLE 6.1 GOVERNMENT INTERVENTIONS: A SUMMARY

Intervention	Reason for using	Effect on price	Effect on quantity	Who gains and who loses?
Price floor	To protect producers' income	Price cannot go below the set minimum	Quantity demanded decreases and quantity supplied increases, creating excess quantity supplied.	Producers who can sell all their goods earn more revenue per item; other producers are stuck with an unwanted excess quantity supplied.
Price ceiling	To keep consumer costs low	Price cannot go above the set maximum	Quantity demanded increases and quantity supplied decreases, creating a shortage.	Consumers who can buy all the goods they want benefit; other consumers suffer from shortages.

Intervention	Reason for using	Effect on price	Effect on quantity	Who gains and who loses?
Tax	To discourage an activity or collect money to pay for its consequences; to increase government revenue	Price increases	Equilibrium quantity decreases	Government receives increased revenue; society may gain if the tax decreases socially harmful behaviour. Buyers and sellers of the good that is taxed share the cost. Which group bears more of the burden depends on the price elasticity of supply and demand.
Subsidy	To encourage an activity; to provide benefits to a certain group	Price decreases	Equilibrium quantity increases	Buyers purchase more goods at a lower price. Society may benefit if the subsidy encourages socially beneficial behaviour. The government and ultimately the taxpayers bear the cost.

Figure 6-12 shows the effect of a $0.20 tax on the quantity demanded under four different combinations of price elasticity of supply and demand—again, for Whizbangs.

- In panel A, both supply and demand are relatively inelastic. In this case the tax causes the equilibrium quantity to decrease, but not by much. Both buyers and sellers are willing to continue trading, even though they now must pay the tax.
- In panel B, demand is more elastic than supply, so when the supply curve is $0.20 higher, the change in quantity is much larger than in panel A.
- In panel C, supply is elastic but demand is relatively inelastic. Again, because suppliers are highly responsive to the cost of the tax, the quantity changes more than in panel A.
- Finally, panel D shows what happens if supply and demand are both elastic. In this case, the quantity goes down even more than in the second and third examples.

To predict the size of the effect of a tax or subsidy, then, policy makers need to know the price elasticity of both supply and demand. As we have seen, they can also use that information to determine who will bear more of the burden or receive more of the benefit.

If you are interested in the role of government in the economy, read the Where Can It Take You? box, Public Economics, to learn more about the field.

WHERE CAN IT TAKE YOU?

Public Economics

Are you more interested in elections and legislation than in how to run a business? If so, we hope you are beginning to realize that understanding the economics behind public policy is incredibly important. Although well-designed policies can accomplish great things, well-intentioned but poorly designed policies can backfire badly.

To learn more about the economics of public policy, consider taking a *public economics* course. We will discuss policy issues throughout this book, but there is a lot more to learn, whether you want to be a politician, an analyst at a think tank, or just an informed voter.

FIGURE 6-12

Price Elasticity and the Effect of a $0.20 Tax

(A) Inelastic supply and demand

The equilibrium quantity decreases by 3 million.

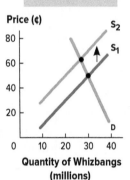

Quantity of Whizbangs (millions)

When both supply and demand are relatively price-inelastic, the equilibrium quantity does not decrease significantly because of a tax.

(B) Inelastic supply and elastic demand

The equilibrium quantity decreases by 7 million.

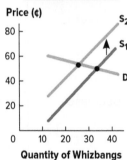

Quantity of Whizbangs (millions)

When supply is inelastic but demand is relatively elastic, the equilibrium quantity decreases more than it does in panel A in response to a tax.

(C) Elastic supply and inelastic demand

The equilibrium quantity decreases by 4 million.

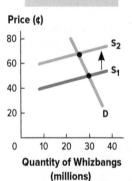

Quantity of Whizbangs (millions)

When supply is relatively elastic compared to inelastic demand, the equilibrium quantity decreases more than it does in panel A in response to a tax.

(D) Elastic supply and demand

The equilibrium quantity decreases by 20 million.

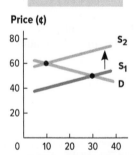

Quantity of Whizbangs (millions)

The greatest decrease in the equilibrium quantity occurs when both demand and supply are relatively elastic; both buyers and sellers react strongly to the change in price that is caused by a tax.

Long-Run versus Short-Run Impact

We have seen that in addition to changing the price of a good or service, price controls cause shortages or excess quantity supplied. Because buyers and sellers take time to respond to a change in price, sometimes the full effect of price controls becomes clear only in the long run.

Suppose the Canadian government imposed a price floor on gasoline in an attempt to reduce air pollution by discouraging people from driving. Panel A of Figure 6-13 shows the short-run impact of a price floor in the market for gasoline. Note that in the short run, the quantity of gas demanded might not change very much. Although people would cut down on unnecessary driving, the greater part of demand would still be based on driving habits that are difficult to change, such as commuting to work or going to the grocery store. And unless gasoline producers have a lot of unused oil wells sitting around, sellers might have trouble ramping up production quickly. In the short run, demand and supply are not very elastic, and the price floor results in only a small excess quantity supplied.

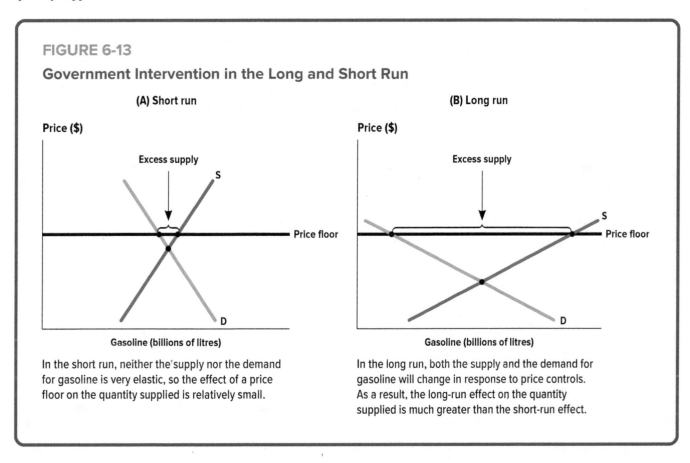

FIGURE 6-13

Government Intervention in the Long and Short Run

(A) Short run

Price ($)

Excess supply

S

Price floor

D

Gasoline (billions of litres)

In the short run, neither the supply nor the demand for gasoline is very elastic, so the effect of a price floor on the quantity supplied is relatively small.

(B) Long run

Price ($)

Excess supply

S

Price floor

D

Gasoline (billions of litres)

In the long run, both the supply and the demand for gasoline will change in response to price controls. As a result, the long-run effect on the quantity supplied is much greater than the short-run effect.

Recall that for both supply and demand, one of the determinants of price elasticity is the period over which it is measured. On both sides of the market, elasticity is often greater over a long time period than over a short one. On the demand side, consumers might make small lifestyle changes over the medium term, such as buying a bus pass or shopping closer to home. Over a longer time period (long run), they might make even bigger changes. When they need to buy a new car, for example, they will be inclined to buy a model that offers high gas mileage. If they move to a new job or home, they may place more weight than in the past on commuting distance.

Supply will also be more elastic over the long run. Because a higher price gives suppliers an incentive to produce more, they may invest in oil exploration, dig new wells, or take steps to increase the pumping capacity of existing wells. Panel B of Figure 6-13 shows the long-run impact of a price floor in the market for gasoline. Because both supply and demand are more elastic in the long run than in the short run, the excess quantity supplied of gasoline is much larger in the long run than in the short run.

If the goal of the price floor was to reduce air pollution by giving consumers an incentive to cut down on driving, the impact might look disappointing in the short run: the quantity of gas burned will decrease very little. Over the long run, however, the quantity of gas burned will decrease further, and the policy will look more successful. If, on the other hand, the reason for the price floor was to support gasoline suppliers, the short-run response would look deceptively rosy, because suppliers will sell almost the same quantity of gas at a higher price. As the quantity falls over the long run, however, more producers will be stuck with an excess quantity supplied and the policy will start to look less successful.

In the European Union and the United States, farmers are given very generous subsidies. Without these subsidies, many farmers would be forced to quit farming. Critics argue that subsides distort the market by keeping prices of certain foods much higher than they would be without subsidies. Read the full debate in the What Do You Think? box, Farm Subsidies.

WHAT DO YOU THINK?

Farm Subsidies

Many wealthy countries spend a lot of money on price floors and subsidies that encourage domestic agricultural production. For instance, the costs associated with Europe's Common Agricultural Policy (CAP) currently account for almost half the European Union's budget, or approximately $50 billion per year.

CAP was established in 1957 with the following objectives:

1. To increase agricultural productivity by encouraging technical progress and by ensuring the rational development of agricultural production and the optimum utilization of the factors of production, particularly labour.

2. To thereby ensure a fair standard of living for the agricultural population, particularly by increasing of the individual earnings of persons engaged in agriculture.

3. To stabilize markets.

4. To guarantee regular supplies.

5. To ensure reasonable prices in supplies to consumers.

Supporters believe that these are important and worthwhile policy goals. However, CAP has come under heavy criticism for many reasons. Critics say that CAP imposes a huge cost on taxpayers; creates excess supplies of crops by distorting farmers' incentives; hurts farmers in poor countries, whose produce must compete with Europe's subsidized crops; and channels public funds to big agribusinesses.

The European Union is not alone in its policies. Every year the *United States Farm Bill* allocates many billions of dollars to crop price supports. Japan also intervenes heavily in agricultural markets. Canada provides some direct subsidy and indirect support by allowing supply management.

What do you think?

1. Do you approve of the stated objectives of Europe's Common Agricultural Policy? Which, if any, do you think merit the market distortions they may create?

2. Do wealthy nations have a responsibility to consider the impact of their agricultural policies on poorer countries, or are domestic farming interests more important?

Source: "Cap explained," European Commission website, 2009, http://ec.europa.eu/agriculture/publi/capexplained/cap_en.pdf.

✓ CONCEPT CHECK

☐ If the demand for a good is inelastic, will a tax have a large or small effect on the quantity sold? Will buyers or sellers bear more of the burden of the tax? [LO 6.5]

☐ Would you expect a tax on cigarettes to be more effective over the long run or the short run? Explain your reasoning. [LO 6.5]

Conclusion

If you listen to the news, it might seem as if economics is all about business and the stock market. Business matters, but many of the most important, challenging, and useful applications of economic principles involve public policy.

This chapter gives you the basic tools you need to understand government interventions and some of the ways they can affect your everyday life. Of course, the real world is complicated, so this isn't our last word on the topic. Later we discuss how to evaluate the benefits of both markets and government policies. We'll also discuss market failures and whether and when governments can fix them.

Key Terms

market failures

price control

price ceiling

deadweight loss

price floor

tax wedge

tax incidence

subsidy

Summary

LO 6.1 Calculate the effect of a price ceiling on the equilibrium price and quantity.

Government usually intervenes in a market for one or more of the following reasons: to correct a market failure, to change the distribution of a market's benefits, or to encourage or discourage the consumption of particular goods and services. Governments may also tax goods and services in order to raise public revenues.

A price ceiling is a maximum legal price at which a good can be sold. A binding price ceiling causes a shortage, because at the legally mandated price, consumers will demand more than producers supply. This policy benefits some consumers, because they are able to buy what they want at a lower price, but other consumers are unable to find the goods they want. Producers lose out because they sell less at a lower price than they would without the price ceiling.

LO 6.2 Calculate the effect of a price floor on the equilibrium price and quantity.

A price floor is a minimum legal price at which a good can be sold. A price floor causes an excess quantity supplied, because at the minimum price, sellers will supply more than consumers demand. This policy benefits some producers, who are able to sell their goods at a higher price, but leaves other producers with goods they can't sell. Consumers lose because they buy less at a higher price. Maintaining a price floor often requires the government to buy up the excess quantity supplied, costing taxpayers money.

LO 6.3 Calculate the effect of a tax on the equilibrium price and quantity.

A tax requires either buyers or sellers to pay some extra price to the government when a good is bought and sold. A tax shrinks the size of a market, discouraging the consumption and production of the good being taxed. The effect is the same regardless of whether the tax is levied on buyers or sellers. The tax burden is split between consumers and producers, and the government collects revenues equal to the amount of the tax times the quantity sold.

LO 6.4 Calculate the effect of a subsidy on the equilibrium price and quantity.

A subsidy is a payment that the government makes to buyers or sellers of a good for each unit that is sold. Subsidies increase the size of a market, encouraging the consumption and production of the good being subsidized. The effect is the same regardless of whether the subsidy is paid to buyers or sellers. Both consumers and producers benefit from a subsidy, but taxpayers must cover the cost.

LO 6.5 Explain how elasticity and time period influence the impact of a market intervention.

In evaluating the effects of a government intervention in the market, it is important to consider both the intended and unintended consequences of the policy. The size of the impact of a tax or subsidy and the distribution of the burden or benefit will depend on the price elasticities of supply and demand. Furthermore, the impact of a government intervention is likely to change over time, as consumers and producers adjust their behavior in response to the new incentives.

Review Questions

1. You are an advisor to the Egyptian government, which has placed a price ceiling on bread. Unfortunately, many families still cannot buy the bread they need. Explain to government officials why the price ceiling has not increased consumption of bread. [LO 6.1]

2. Suppose there has been a long-standing price ceiling on housing in your city. Recently, population has declined, and demand for housing has decreased. What will the decrease in demand do to the efficiency of the price ceiling? [LO 6.1]

3. Suppose Canada maintains a price floor for spinach. Why might this policy decrease revenues for spinach farmers? [LO 6.2]

4. Suppose Colombia maintains a price floor for coffee beans. What will happen to the size of the deadweight loss if the price floor encourages new growers to enter the market and produce coffee? [LO 6.2]

5. Many provinces tax cigarette purchases. Suppose that smokers are unhappy about paying the extra charge for their cigarettes. Will it help smokers if the province imposes the tax on the stores that sell the cigarettes rather than on smokers? Why or why not? [LO 6.3]

6. Consider a tax on cigarettes. Do you expect the tax incidence to fall more heavily on buyers or sellers of cigarettes? Why? [LO 6.3]

7. In the Philippines, rice production is lower than rice consumption, resulting in a need to import rice from other countries. In this situation, the Philippine government might consider subsidizing rice farmers. What are the potential benefits of such a policy? What are the costs? [LO 6.4]

8. A subsidy will increase consumer and producer surplus in a market and will increase the quantity of trades. Why, then, might a subsidy (such as a subsidy for poultry farms in Canada) be considered inefficient? [LO 6.4]

9. Suppose the government imposes a price ceiling on gasoline. One month after the price ceiling, there is a shortage of gasoline, but it is much smaller than critics of the policy had warned. Explain why the critics' estimates might still be correct. [LO 6.5]

10. A province facing a budget shortfall decides to tax soft drinks. You are a budget analyst for the province. Do you expect to collect more revenue in the first year of the tax or in the second year? Why? [LO 6.5]

Problems and Applications

1. Many people are concerned about the rising price of gasoline. Suppose that government officials are thinking of capping the price of gasoline below its current price. Which of the following outcomes do you predict will result from this policy? Check all that apply. [LO 6.1]
   a. Drivers will purchase more gasoline.
   b. Quantity demanded for gasoline will increase.
   c. Long lines will develop at gas stations.
   d. Oil companies will work to increase their pumping capacity.

2. Figure 6P-1 shows a market in equilibrium.

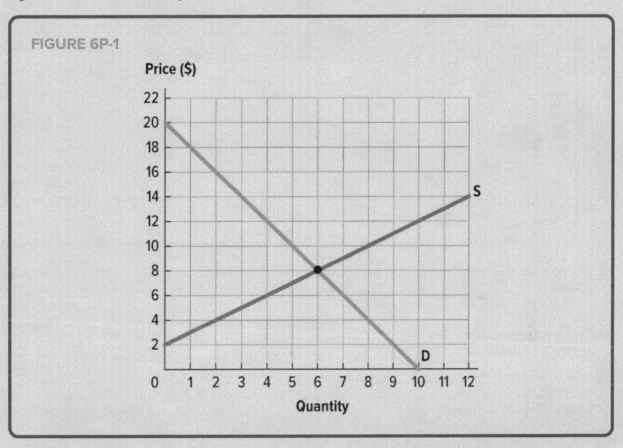

FIGURE 6P-1

   a. Draw a price ceiling at $12. What is the amount of shortage at this price? Draw and calculate the deadweight loss. [LO 6.1]
   b. Draw a price ceiling at $4. What is the amount of shortage at this price? Draw and calculate the deadweight loss. [LO 6.1]

3. Decades of overfishing have dramatically reduced the world supply of cod (a type of whitefish). Farm-raised halibut is considered a close substitute for ocean-fished cod. [LO 6.1]
   a. On the graph in Figure 6P-2, show the effect of overfishing cod on the market for farmed halibut.

   A fast-food chain purchases whitefish for use in its Fish 'n' Chips meals. Already hurt by the reduced supply of cod, the fast-food chain has lobbied aggressively for price controls on farmed halibut. As a result, Parliament has considered imposing a price ceiling on halibut at the former equilibrium price—the price that prevailed before overfishing reduced the supply of cod.

b. On your graph, show what will happen in the market for farmed halibut if Parliament adopts the price control policy. Draw and label the price ceiling, quantity demanded, quantity supplied, and deadweight loss.

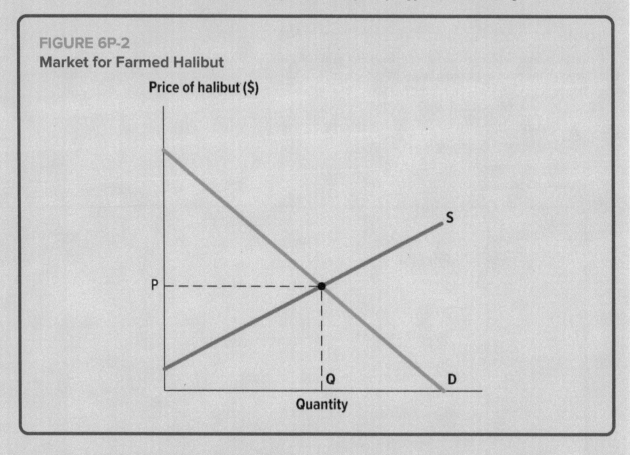

FIGURE 6P-2
Market for Farmed Halibut

4. The Organization for the Promotion of Brussels Sprouts has convinced the government of Ironia to institute a price floor on the sale of brussels sprouts, at $8 per bushel. Demand is given by $P = 9 - Q$ and supply by $P = 2Q$, where Q is measured in thousands of bushels. [LO 6.2]
    a. What will be the price and quantity of brussels sprouts sold at market equilibrium?
    b. What will be the price and quantity sold with the price floor?
    c. How big will be the excess quantity supplied of brussels sprouts produced with the price floor?
5. The traditional diet of the citizens of the nation of Ironia includes a lot of red meat, and ranchers make up a vital part of Ironia's economy. The government of Ironia decides to support its ranchers through a price floor, which it will maintain by buying up excess meat supplies. Table 6P-1 shows the supply and demand schedule for red meat; quantities are given in thousands of pounds. [LO 6.2]

TABLE 6P-1

Price ($)	Quantity demanded (thousands of kg)	Quantity supplied (thousands of kg)
6	5	80
5	20	70
4	35	60
3	50	50

Price ($)	Quantity demanded (thousands of kg)	Quantity supplied (thousands of kg)
2	65	40
1	80	30

    a. How many thousands of kilos of meat would you recommend that the government purchase to keep the price at $4 per kilo?

    b. How much money should the government budget for this program?

6. Suppose you have the information shown in Table 6P-2 about the quantity of a good that is supplied and demanded at various prices. [LO 6.3]

TABLE 6P-2

Price ($)	Quantity demanded	Quantity supplied
45	10	160
40	20	140
35	30	120
30	40	100
25	50	80
20	60	60
15	70	40
10	80	20
5	90	0

    a. Plot the demand and supply curves on a graph, with price on the y-axis and quantity on the x-axis.

    b. What are the equilibrium price and quantity?

    c. Suppose the government imposes a $15 per unit tax on sellers of this good. Draw the new supply curve on your graph.

    d. What is the new equilibrium quantity? How much will consumers pay? How much will sellers receive after the tax?

    e. Calculate the price elasticity of demand over this price change.

    f. If demand were less elastic (holding supply constant), would the deadweight loss be smaller or larger? [LO 6.5]

7. The weekly supply and demand for fast-food cheeseburgers in your city is shown in Figure 6P-3. In an effort to curb a looming budget deficit, the mayor recently proposed a tax that would be levied on sales at fast-food restaurants. [LO 6.3]

    a. The mayor's proposal includes a sales tax of 60 cents on cheeseburgers, to be paid by consumers. What is the new outcome in this market (how many cheeseburgers are sold and at what price)? Illustrate this outcome on your graph.

b. How much of the tax burden is borne by consumers? How much by suppliers?

c. What is the deadweight loss associated with the proposed tax?

d. How much revenue will the government collect?

e. What is the loss of consumer surplus from this tax?

FIGURE 6P-3

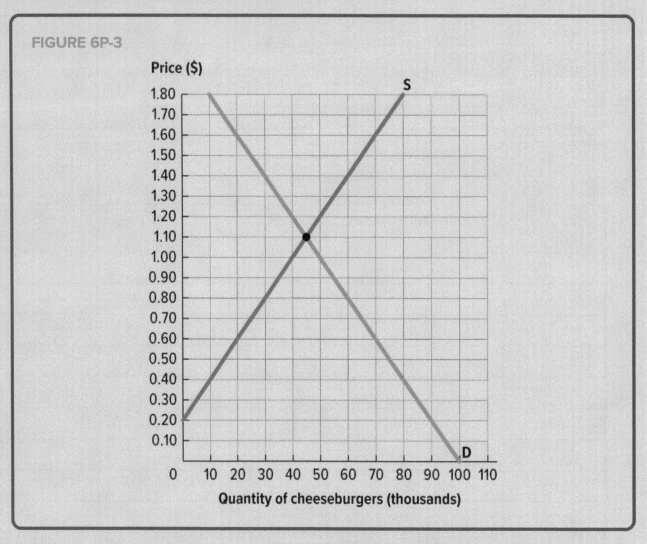

8. Demand and supply of laptop computers are given in Figure 6P-4. The quantity of laptops is given in thousands. Suppose the government provides a $300 subsidy for every laptop computer that consumers purchase. [LO 6.4]

a. What will be the quantity of laptops bought and sold at the new equilibrium?

b. What will be the price consumers pay for laptops under the subsidy?

c. What will be the price that sellers receive for laptops under the subsidy?

d. How much money should the government budget for the subsidy?

FIGURE 6P-4

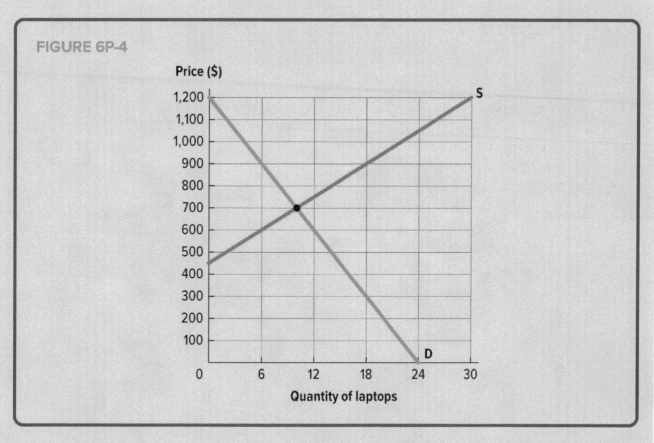

9. Suppose government offers a subsidy to laptop sellers. Say whether each group of people gains or loses from this policy. [LO 6.4]
    a. Laptop buyers
    b. Laptop sellers
    c. Desktop computer sellers (assuming that they are different from laptop sellers)
    d. Desktop computer buyers

10. Suppose that for health reasons, the government of the nation of Ironia wants to increase the amount of broccoli citizens consume. Which of the following policies could be used to achieve the goal? [LO 6.1], [LO 6.4]
    a. A price floor to support broccoli growers
    b. A price ceiling to ensure that broccoli remains affordable to consumers
    c. A subsidy paid to shoppers who buy broccoli
    d. A subsidy paid to farmers who grow broccoli

11. The following scenarios describe the price elasticity of supply and demand for a particular good. In which scenario will a subsidy increase consumption the most? Choose only one. [LO 6.5]
    a. Elastic demand, inelastic supply
    b. Inelastic demand, inelastic supply
    c. Elastic demand, elastic supply
    d. Inelastic demand, elastic supply

12. The following scenarios describe the price elasticity of supply and demand for a particular good. All else equal (equilibrium price, equilibrium quantity, and size of the tax), in which scenario will government revenues be the highest? Choose only one. [LO 6.5]
    a. Elastic demand, inelastic supply
    b. Inelastic demand, inelastic supply
    c. Elastic demand, elastic supply
    d. Inelastic demand, elastic supply

PART THREE

The Data of Macroeconomics
The two chapters in Part 3 will introduce you to ...

the topic of macroeconomics and two important macroeconomic concepts, gross domestic product (GDP) and consumer prices.

How well off do you think you will be in ten years? In twenty years? Your answers probably depend in part on choices that you may already be considering—especially choices about where to live, family plans, and your career.

Of course, your future financial position will also depend on forces outside of your control. Some of those forces will be economic, like how many jobs are available, how housing prices change, and how fast prices rise over time. These forces are the focus of macroeconomics, the study of how billions of daily decisions made by individuals add up to shape the overall economy. It's the study of economic growth, inflation, booms and busts, and unemployment.

Chapter 7 covers the calculation of gross domestic product (GDP), the most useful metric of macroeconomics, which sums up the amount of economic activity in a country. It's the first number economists look at when tracking overall economic growth as well as the ups and downs of the economy.

Chapter 8 covers another important part of macroeconomic record keeping: consumer prices. Decades ago, a soft drink cost a dime and a brand-new car could be purchased for hundreds of dollars. Both items cost a lot more today, but that doesn't mean that we're worse off—our incomes have risen along with prices. As you'll see, accounting for consumer prices gives an important part of the macro picture.

As we progress through the study of macroeconomics, the concepts of GDP and changing price levels will come up over and over again; they are useful tools for answering questions about the health and direction of the economy. These two chapters offer insight into forces that will affect your job and income, as well as the wealth and well-being of the whole country.

CHAPTER 7

Measuring the Wealth of Nations

LEARNING OBJECTIVES

LO 7.1   Justify the importance of using the market value of final goods and services to calculate GDP, and explain why each component of GDP is important.

LO 7.2   Explain the equivalence of the expenditure and income approaches to valuing an economy.

LO 7.3   Explain the three approaches that are used to calculate GDP, and list the categories of spending that are included in the expenditure approach.

LO 7.4   Explain the difference between real and nominal GDP, and calculate the GDP deflator.

LO 7.5   Calculate and explain the meanings of GDP per capita and the real GDP annual growth rate.

LO 7.6   Discuss some limitations to GDP, including its measurement of home production, the underground economy, environmental degradation, and well-being.

It's More than Counting Berries

If we made a list of the economic changes that are most dramatically reshaping the world, the rapid growth of China's economy would likely be at the top. In 1978, when China's leaders moved to open up its economic system, it was the world's fifteenth-largest economy. The size of China's economy doubled. Then it doubled, and doubled, and doubled again. By 2014, China's economy clocked in at more than $10 trillion. It passed Japan's in 2011 to become the second-largest economy in the world. Rapid economic growth can create jobs, reduce poverty, and improve standards of living. In China, the fraction of the population living below the international poverty line ($1.25 per person per day) fell from over 80 percent in 1978 to under 20 percent today.

Economic growth has increased living standards all over the world in recent decades, although typically in less dramatic fashion than in China. The health of the national economy has a powerful effect on everyday life in any country. When the economy is doing well, jobs are plentiful and most people can live well and securely. When the economy does poorly, jobs are scarce, businesses close down, and people struggle. It's no wonder that politicians spend a lot of energy debating the best plan to expand the economy. Over the next few chapters, we'll discuss many of the ideas and terms used in those debates.

But first we need to answer a basic question: How do we measure the size of the economy? If we can answer that, we can compare China's economy to economies of other nations, and we can determine whether an economy is growing or not over time. What does it really *mean* to say that China has a $10 trillion economy?

The answers to these questions require some careful accounting. As a start, think about just one of the many transactions that take place in the Canadian economy. Say you bought a jar of jam when you went to the grocery store. Although you may not have thought beyond your next peanut butter and jam sandwich, your purchase contributed to the size of the economy.

Consider some of the things that happened before that jar of jam made it into your shopping cart: A farmer grew the berries. The farmer sold his berries to a wholesaler. The wholesaler then sold the berries to a jam factory, which combined the berries with other ingredients to produce a jar of jam. The factory then sold that jar to a grocery store chain, which delivered it to your neighbourhood store.

Many people were employed to produce that jar of jam: farmers, accountants, truck drivers, custodians, and cashiers at the grocery store. Many firms earned profits from the jar of jam, too: the berry farm, the wholesaler, the factory, the shipping company, and your local store. Clearly, the activities that went into making and buying the jar of jam added value to the economy. Can we measure how much?

The berries passed through many stages, from seed, to harvest, to being combined with other ingredients, to a jar on the grocery store shelf. At each stage, the berries were sold as an output of one firm and purchased as an input by another firm. Should we add up all of these sales individually to calculate the value the jar of jam added to the economy? No—if we did that, we'd be overcounting the value of the berries. All of the sales were just steps toward one end product: your jar of jam. How then *do* we calculate the total value of your jar of jam to the economy?

This is the problem that economists faced in the 1930s when they first attempted to calculate the value of the Canadian economy. How can you add up all economic activity to arrive at an overall value for the economy, *without* double-counting items that are resold more than once before they reach the consumer?

Photo: Stephanie Seaton/Unlimited Vision. Summerland Sweets.

The solution is a system called *national income accounting,* created by Nobel Prize winners Simon Kuznets and Richard Stone. In Canada, the 1945 White Paper on Employment and Income by W. A. Mackintosh set the foundation necessary for the development of the National Income and Expenditure Accounts. In this chapter, we'll see how to use this system to calculate the value of a national economy. We'll see why it's so useful to measure a country's total output and also why the most commonly used measure has some limitations. In later chapters, we'll put these ideas to work to explain economic growth, unemployment, and economic booms and slowdowns.

Valuing an Economy

Economics has traditionally been divided into two broad fields, microeconomics and macroeconomics. *Microeconomics* is the study of how individuals and firms manage resources. In microeconomics, we zero in on a single person's budget, or one firm's cost of production, or the price of a particular good. **Macroeconomics**, on the other hand, is the study of the economy on a broad scale, focusing on issues such as economic growth, unemployment, and inflation. In macroeconomics, we talk about consumption, production, and prices in the *aggregate,* on a national level, and we look at the effects of those aggregate forces on the whole economy.

Compared to microeconomics, the concepts may often seem distant from decisions we make and challenges we face, but macroeconomic issues can have profound impacts on our daily lives. Everyone tends to do better in times of steady economic growth, stable prices, and low unemployment. On the flip side, long periods of stagnation, inflation, and high unemployment can do great damage to families and communities.

At the start of the chapter, we introduced one of the most important macroeconomic issues of our time: the incredible growth of the Chinese economy. But how do we know how big the Chinese economy is? How do we know that it is larger than Japan's but smaller than that of the United States? What does it mean to say that the size of China's economy doubled? To talk about these crucial issues, we need a tool for measuring the size or value of a national economy. Based on the kind of questions it lets us answer, you can see why this metric is one of the most important and commonly used data points in macroeconomics. It gives us a sense of the well-being of the average person in a country. It also allows us to gauge the direction in which an economy is headed by looking at changes over time.

We'll see later in the chapter that we have to think carefully about what we mean by the *size* or *value* of an economy, because there are various ways to measure it. Just as you might measure the economic status of a family by looking at what it can afford to spend or by looking at what its members earn, we can measure the status of a national economy by looking at expenditures or at income. In the end, we'll see that these add up to the same thing: giving a single measure of the total value of everything produced in the economy.

The most commonly used metric for measuring the value of a national economy is **gross domestic product**, or **GDP**. Gross domestic product is the sum of the market values of all final goods and services produced within a country in a given period of time. That's a mouthful of a definition. Before we look at how economists calculate GDP, let's briefly unpack its component parts.

Unpacking the Definition of GDP

LO 7.1 Justify the importance of using the market value of final goods and services to calculate GDP, and explain why each component of GDP is important.

The definition of GDP has four important pieces:

1. *Market value*
2. Of *final goods and services*
3. Produced *within a country*
4. In a *given period of time*

Let's take each piece one at a time, and explain its importance.

Market Value

If we measured the output of economies by listing every single good and service, we wouldn't learn much—100.5 million kilograms of blueberries, 78.1 million pounds of honey, 8.6 million gallons of maple syrup, and so on. The list would go on for thousands of pages. It wouldn't be very interesting. Nor would it be useful for comparing the overall size of national economies, which tend to make different things. Say we want to compare the Canadian economy, which produces lots of maple syrup, with the Mexican economy, which produces lots of tortillas. How do we do it?

Clearly, we need to translate the production of jam, tortillas, honey, maple syrup, and all the other goods and services into a common unit so we can add them up. That common unit is their *market value*—in Canada, measured in dollars.

Final Goods and Services

Consider the berries that end up in your jar of jam. Suppose our blueberry farmer sells enough berries to make one jar of jam to a wholesaler for 12 cents. The wholesaler sells them to the jam factory for 24 cents. The jam factory sells the jar of jam to the grocery store for $1.85. Finally, the grocery store sells it to you for $3.40 per 500-gram jar. How much does this process contribute to GDP?

If we simply add up all the transactions, we might think that the jar of jam contributed $5.61 to GDP ($0.12 + $0.24 + $1.85 + $3.40). But, if that were true, producing the jar of jam would contribute more to GDP than its final selling price. That can't be right. If it were, we could grow the economy just by trading the same jar of jam for the same dollar, over and over again, and adding up each transaction.

PhotoStock-Israel/Science Photo Library

To avoid double-counting, we should ignore the price of *intermediate* goods and services—that is, goods and services used only to produce something else, like the fresh berries that were sold to the jam factory. Instead, we want to count only expenditures on *final goods and services*—those that get sold to the consumer. In this case, the only final good was the jar of jam you bought at the store. Its price was $3.40, so that is how much your purchase contributed to GDP.

Produced Within a Country

The goods and services that count toward GDP are defined in terms of the *location of production,* not the citizenship of the producer. So if a Canadian company owns a factory in Mexico, the value of the goods produced in that factory will count toward Mexican GDP, not Canadian GDP. A Canadian citizen working in France will contribute to French GDP. Likewise, a French or Mexican citizen working in Canada will contribute to Canadian GDP.

What if we want to measure the value of what is produced by all Canadian companies regardless of their location? In this case, we use a metric called **gross national product (GNP)**. GNP is the sum of the market values of all final goods and services produced and capital owned by the *permanent residents* of a country in a given period of time, no matter where in the world the production occurs. It is similar to GDP except that it (1) includes *worldwide* income earned by a country's enterprises and permanent residents and (2) excludes production by foreign nationals working domestically.

Given Period of Time

In theory, we could calculate the output of the economy over any time period—a day, a month, a year. When you hear people talking about GDP, they're usually referring to an annual figure. However, a year is a long time to wait for an update on how the economy is doing, so GDP is usually calculated on a *quarterly* basis—that is, four times a year.

Typically what we really want is an estimate of annual GDP, using the most recent quarterly information. We can't just multiply this quarter's GDP by four, however, because the economy seldom rolls along at the same pace all year. For instance, December usually has more economic activity than other months because people are buying presents and travelling. Therefore, we need to adjust quarterly GDP estimates to account for these seasonal patterns. That's why quarterly GDP is typically shown as an estimate that has been *seasonally adjusted at an annual rate.* By taking account of predictable seasonal patterns, we can make a good guess at what annual GDP will be if the economy continues at its current pace.

Production Equals Expenditure Equals Income

> **LO 7.2** Explain the equivalence of the expenditure and income approaches to valuing an economy.

Now that we have defined gross domestic product, how do we go about measuring it? First of all, let's zero in on what we really mean when we talk about the size of an economy: it's the amount of "stuff" people in the economy are making. Economists refer to this "stuff" as either *output* or *production,* and it includes both goods and services. Indeed, about one-third of Canadian output is services, not goods. As we've seen, though, there's not much point in simply listing thousands of pages of goods and services. So how do we put a dollar value on it? There are two ways of approaching this problem.

The market value of a good or service is the price at which it is bought and sold. If we add up all the money people spend buying final goods and services—being careful to omit spending on intermediate goods so as not to double-count—the sum will be the market value of all output sold in the economy. In other words, we can measure total output by measuring total *expenditure.*

Of course, every transaction has both a buyer who spends on a good or service and a seller who earns income from the sale. Thus, expenditures by one person translate directly into *income* for someone else. So we can also measure production by adding up everyone's income. This may sound familiar if you remember the *circular flow model* of the economy that was presented in Chapter 1 and is repeated here in Figure 7-1.

Households buy things from firms in the market for goods and services. Firms then use some of the money they earn in revenue to pay wages to workers and rent to landowners in the market for the factors of production. In each of these transactions, expenditures by one party are income for another.

The circular flow model is a major simplification of the economy. (What about the money paid in taxes, or the money that is saved instead of spent, for example?) Yet it shows that we should get to the same figure for GDP regardless of whether we measure expenditure or income in an economy:

$$\text{National production} = \text{national expenditure} = \text{national income}$$

This equality is a crucial idea in the study of macroeconomics.

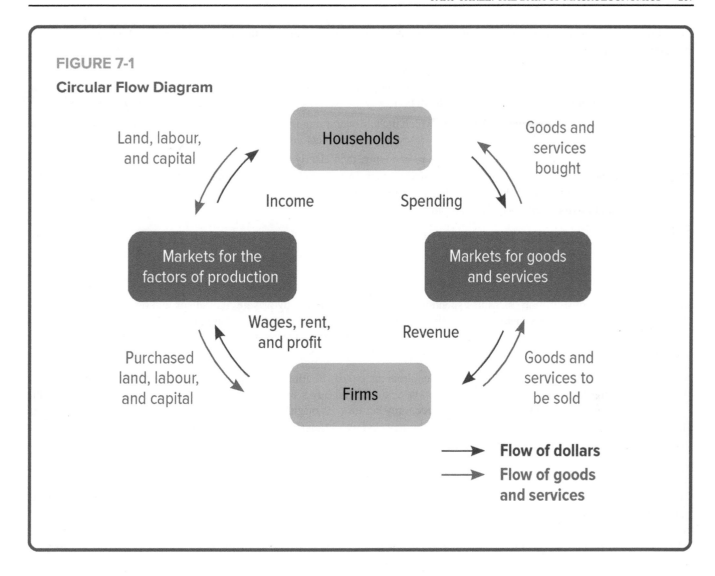

FIGURE 7-1

Circular Flow Diagram

Approaches to Measuring GDP

LO 7.3 Explain the three approaches that are used to calculate GDP, and list the categories of spending that are included in the expenditure approach.

The equality of production, expenditure, and income would hold true in a literal, straightforward way if we lived in *closed economy*—an economy in which all goods were produced and sold domestically, and everything was consumed as soon as it was made. The actual economy is more complicated, but the basic equality still holds—as long as we're a little more careful about how we define each part.

One complication is international trade. Once we start to consider imports and exports, we see that expenditure in one country can translate into income in *another* country. Also, what happens when goods are produced but not sold? In this section, we will consider the various approaches to measuring GDP and see how economists deal with these complications.

The Expenditure Approach

To measure output using the *expenditure method,* we start by breaking *expenditure* down into categories. We don't want to double-count, so we don't include intermediate products, like fresh berries and the labour of jam factory workers, which firms buy only to transform into final goods and services. But we *do* include the following:

- Most final goods and services are bought by people who intend to *consume* them, such as a family buying groceries or clothes or haircuts.

- Firms buy some goods as an *investment* in future production, such as a farmer buying a new tractor to use in growing berries or a jam factory buying new machinery. The reason we count these is that the tractor and the machinery are not used up in producing a jar of jam in the same way that fresh berries are.

- We also want to count *government* purchases, which include everything from fighter planes to asphalt for road repair to those plastic bins that go through the scanner at airport security checkpoints.

- If we're interested in the output of the Canadian economy, then clearly we want to count goods and services produced in Canada and bought by foreigners, which are called *exports*. But we *don't* want to count expenditures by Canadians on items produced outside of Canada, which are called *imports*. For that reason, we subtract the amount of imports from the amount of exports and use the result—*net exports*—to calculate expenditures.

To find total expenditure we add together these four categories: consumption, investment, government purchases, and net exports. Let's look at each in more detail.

Consumption

The first category, **consumption**, measures spending on goods and services by private individuals and households. It includes almost anything you'd buy for yourself, from basic, non-durable goods (like food and clothing), to durable goods (like computers and cars), to services (like tutoring and plumbing). If you pay rent or university tuition, those expenses are also included in consumption.

Note that what is consumed has to be *new*. This requirement avoids the illogical conclusion that we could grow the economy simply by reselling the same jar of jam over and over again. If you buy a used camera from a classified ad, for example, the camera itself is not counted toward the size of the economy because the original purchase of the camera was already recorded in GDP when it was sold new. However, the fee the seller pays to buy a classified ad *is* counted as consumption, and so is the price the seller pays Purolator to deliver the camera to you.

Investment

The second category, **investment**, includes spending on productive inputs, such as factories, machinery, and inventories—goods bought by people or firms who plan to use those purchases to produce other goods and services in the future rather than consuming them. It includes *capital goods,* which are items like machines or tools that will be used for production of other goods or services. It also includes buildings and structures, like warehouses, that will be involved in providing goods and services.

It's worth noting that newly built houses are also counted as investment. In contrast, if you rent a house, the expenditure falls under consumption. Why the difference? A newly built house will provide a place for you to live (or to rent out) now and for years to come, just as a newly built factory will generate output now and in future years. But when you *rent* a house, you are paying its owner for the service of letting you live there. You are consuming place-to-live services, but you're not making an investment because the house belongs to someone else and won't generate future revenues for you.

Again, note that investment goods are counted only if they are *new*. We don't count buying an existing factory or secondhand tools as investment. Nor do we count an individual's purchase of an existing house. (The services of the realtor selling you the house, though, would be counted toward consumption.)

POTENTIALLY CONFUSING

You may have heard people talk about their investments—stocks, bonds, mutual funds, and other products bought and sold in the financial markets. While it may seem as if these financial products should be counted under the "I" (investment) term in GDP, *they are not counted as a part of GDP* for two reasons. First, if you buy a share of Bombardier stock through the Toronto Stock Exchange, your money does not go to Bombardier. Instead, you are buying stock from some other investor who has decided to sell stock in Bombardier. (We'll cover how economists think about buying stocks and making other financial investments in a chapter called "The Basics of Finance.")

A second problem is that including stock purchases in GDP calculations would be another type of double-counting. If we added to GDP every time someone bought shares, we could make the economy seem to be growing simply by having people resell the same shares over and over again—just like passing the same jar of jam back and forth.

Finally, our definition of investment also includes a less-obvious type of purchase: spending on inventories. When we equated production, income, and expenditure, we raised the question of how to deal with goods that are produced but not sold. **Inventory** is the answer: it's the stock of goods that a company produces now, but keeps to sell at a future time. If Ford manufactures a car this year in Ontario, but the car sits on the lot until next year, the car becomes part of Ford's inventory. If Blackberry makes a batch of smartphones, but keeps them in a warehouse until it's time to release the new model for public sale, they become part of Blackberry's inventory.

When a good is added to a company's inventory, we treat it as if the producing company has bought it, to keep in stock for the future. The value of that sale is included in our calculation of investment for the year. What happens next year when a consumer buys the Blackberry phones? We don't want to count the same phone toward GDP in two different years. So its value will be subtracted from Blackberry's inventory at the same time as it is counted as consumption. These two transactions cancel out, meaning the purchase results in no net increase in GDP.

Government Purchases

The next category of spending, **government purchases**, represents goods and services bought by all levels of government. This includes *consumption*-type purchases on goods (for instance, buying new bulbs to go in streetlights) and services (buying the labour of government workers who repair streetlights). It also includes *investment*-type purchases (for instance, buying a truck that government workers will use to repair streetlights in the future). In fact, the technical name for this category of spending is *general government final consumption expenditures and gross fixed capital formation*. We'll stick with the term *government purchases* because it's less of a mouthful.

However, one important category of government spending does *not* count as a government purchase: spending that simply *transfers* resources to individuals through the Canada Pension Plan or similar programs. When an elderly person spends money from her Canada Pension Plan cheque to buy groceries, the spending will then be counted as private consumption, and the payment to the elderly person from the government does not count toward government purchases.

Net Exports

The three categories of spending we've considered—consumption, investment, and government purchases—include spending on goods and services produced abroad as well as those produced domestically. Let's think about the GDP of Canada. Our calculation of consumption will include instances when people in Canada buy goods made abroad—say, a sweater imported from Scotland. If we're trying to measure the value of the goods produced *within Canada,* we don't want to count this spending. On the flip side, we don't want to miss spending by people in other countries on goods or services made in Canada and exported for sale abroad.

These two forces work in opposite directions: domestic spending on imports should be subtracted from our GDP calculations, while international spending on exports should be added. We can simplify these international transactions by combining exports and imports into one term, called **net exports** or NX. Net exports represents the value of goods and services produced domestically and consumed abroad minus the value of goods and services produced abroad and consumed domestically. If exports are higher than imports, NX will be positive. If imports are higher than exports, NX will be negative.

When we add together spending in all four categories—consumption, investment, government purchases, and net exports—the total will be equal to expenditures on all goods and services produced in a country, which in turn is equal to the value of that production. This equation is represented as follows.

Equation 7-1

$$\text{Expenditure} = C + I + G + NX = \text{production}$$

As you can see in Figure 7-2, consumption is by far the largest single category of expenditure in Canada, but investment and government purchases are also significant. We can also see that Canadian residents *buy* more goods from abroad than they *sell* to people abroad. That's why net exports is a negative number, 0.9 percent of total 2014 GDP. In other words, in 2014 Canadian consumers spent more abroad than Canadian producers earned from foreigners buying Canadian-made goods, and the size of that difference was equal to 0.9 percent of GDP. If exports had been higher than imports, this number would have been positive.

FIGURE 7-2

Canadian GDP Breakdown

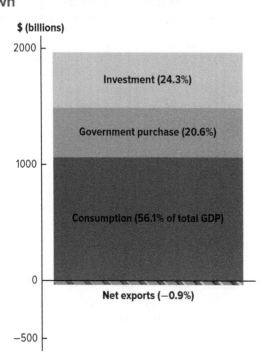

This figure shows the *expenditure method* of calculating GDP, which adds consumption, investment, government purchases, and net exports (exports minus imports). In Canada, imports are currently higher than exports, so the value of net exports is negative and is subtracted from the total.

Source: Statistics Canada, CANSIM, Table 380-0064, "Gross domestic product, expenditure-based."

Figuring out what goes into GDP and what isn't counted in the expenditure method takes a little practice. To help you keep track, Table 7-1 summarizes some of the examples presented in this chapter.

TABLE 7-1 IS IT GDP?

Situation	GDP Category	Why?
Buying a new digital camera	Consumption	Purchasing a *new* good or service always counts toward GDP.
Buying a used camera on a classified site	Not counted	As a used good, the camera does not count toward GDP, as it was already counted when new. The fees paid to list the camera for sale count as consumption, though.
Buying a new house	Investment	Since the house can increase or fall in value, it makes sense to think of it as an investment.
Renting an apartment	Consumption	You are paying the owner of the house for a service, so it is counted as consumption.

Situation	GDP Category	Why?
Blackberry making a new batch of phones but not selling them until next year	Investment	Counted as a part of investment, as Blackberry is holding these phones as a part of its inventory.
Buying shares of Bombardier stock	Not counted	Shares of stock are a transfer of money from one owner of the stock to another. Including stocks would cause a double-counting problem.
CATSA buying plastic bins for airport security	Government spending	Any consumption or investment purchases made by the government are counted in GDP as government spending.
Babysitting for your neighbour	Not counted	In principle, it should be included in GDP, but such income is often not reported to Revenue Canada and thus it can't be included in official statistics.

The Income Approach

A different way to think about the value of a national economy is to add up the income earned by everyone in the country. To value an economy this way, we add up wages earned by workers, interest earned on capital investments, rents earned on land and property, and profits earned by firms (plus a couple of additional technical adjustments). These cover all the types of income earned by people in a country, which can be shown in an equation as:

Equation 7-2

$$\text{Income} = \text{wages} + \text{interest} + \text{rental income} + \text{profits}$$

This *income method* will give us the same result as the expenditure method in an economy without any imports and exports. In every transaction, there is not only a buyer who spends but also a seller who earns the same amount in income. If you spend $20 on gasoline, that same $20 is both expenditure to you and income to the owner of the gas station. The expenditure approach added up everything on one side of this transaction. Now the income approach adds up everything on the *other side* of the transaction, which comes out to the same amount.

What happens, though, when you want to add to the equation any trades that occur *outside* of the country? The term *net exports* is what allows us to equate expenditure and income in an economy that trades internationally. Figure 7-3 shows how we can think about the income and expenditure approaches using the visual tool of a two-by-two matrix: When goods produced in Canada are exported, that's expenditure by other countries and income for Canada. When people in Canada spend money on goods made in another country, that's expenditure in Canada and income for the other country.

FIGURE 7-3

Expenditure Approach: Adding up Expenditures and Income

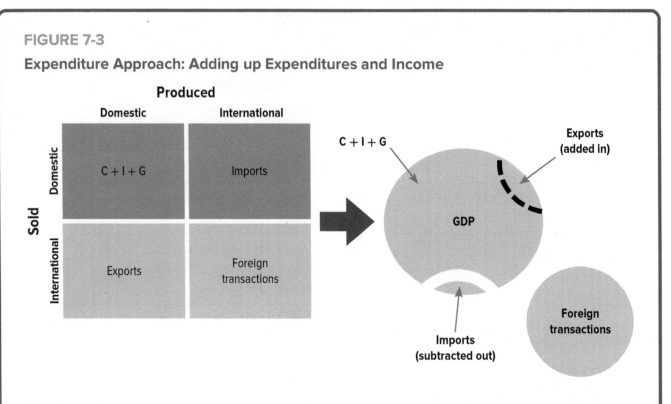

Everything that is produced domestically is added to GDP, whether it is purchased for consumption, investment, by the government, or by people abroad (exports). Goods that are produced internationally but bought domestically, otherwise known as imports, are subtracted from GDP because they represent expenditures leaving the country. Transactions between foreign producers and foreign buyers do not involve domestic production or expenditure and therefore do not figure into GDP calculations.

The Value-Added Approach

Before we move on, we should mention a third approach that economists sometimes use to measure economic output: the *value-added approach*. We have seen that the expenditure approach solves the double-counting problem by considering only transactions that represent final, and not intermediate, goods and services. For example, we count a consumer's purchase of a jar of jam from a store, but not a jam factory's purchase of berries from a berry wholesaler. What if, instead, we looked at *all* transactions, but counted only the *value they add* to the economy?

To see the reasoning behind this approach, let's stick with a jar of jam. At each stage of the jam production process, we're going to look at the difference between the sale value of the product and the value of the inputs that went into it. This difference represents the value added at that stage of production. For instance:

- The farmer *adds value* to the economy by taking seeds, land, and water, and growing berries. Just for simplicity, imagine the farmer didn't pay anything for his inputs. The value added to the economy is the $0.12 the farmer gets from selling enough berries for a jar of jam to the wholesaler, minus the value of the inputs, which we are imagining to be zero.
- If the wholesaler buys that $0.12 in berries and sells them to a jam factory for $0.24, then the wholesaler has added $0.12 ($0.24 − $0.12) in value to the economy by helping to link up farmers and factories.
- The jam factory adds value by pressing the berries into jam and putting it into jars. If the factory is able to get $1.85 per jar, it has added $1.61 ($1.85 − $0.24) in value to the economy.
- The grocery store adds value by transporting jars to a convenient location in your neighbourhood, where clerks are on hand to help you to purchase it for the final price of $3.40 per jar, a value added of $1.55 ($3.40 − $1.85).

To see the final value added, simply sum up the value added at each stage of the process: $0.12 + $0.12 + $1.61 + $1.55 = $3.40. You'll notice that this is the same as the final price for the jar of jam in the store, which is what is counted in the expenditure method. The value-added approach is an alternative, and equally valid, way of avoiding the problem of double-counting the berries. The value-added approach lets us break down the total value paid and see how much of it was created at each step of the production process.

The value-added approach is especially useful when thinking about services involved in the resale of existing goods. We've already seen, for example, that resale of used cameras, existing houses, and shares of company stock do not count toward GDP—but the related services provided by classified sites, realtors, and stockbrokers do. Added value helps us to think about why this is so. A stockbroker adds value by handling the paperwork associated with purchasing shares of stock. A realtor adds value by publicizing the fact that a house is for sale, showing potential purchasers around, and helping negotiate a sale. Classified sites add value by connecting buyers with sellers. In general, any intermediary involved in the sale of used goods adds value by sourcing those goods and making them available for sale in a convenient way.

Why are there three approaches to calculating GDP, and how do you know when to use one instead of another? All three approaches end up with the same number, but each provides a slightly different picture of how the different pieces make up the big picture. Do you want to know about consumer activity versus government purchases? The expenditure approach highlights that data. The income approach emphasizes information about the relative importance of different factors of production. Calculating the value added at each stage of production avoids the problem of double-counting and is especially useful in clarifying the resale of existing goods. Many countries use all three approaches to calculate GDP so that policy makers and researchers can get a full picture of economic activity.

✓ CONCEPT CHECK

- ☐ Why are only final goods and services counted under GDP? Why are sales of used goods not counted? [LO 7.1]
- ☐ Why is total income in a country equal to total expenditures on goods produced in that country? [LO 7.2]
- ☐ What is the difference between consumption spending and investment spending? [LO 7.3]
- ☐ Under which category of expenditure do inventories fall? [LO 7.3]
- ☐ Does the sale of intermediate goods count toward GDP in the expenditure approach? [LO 7.3]
- ☐ How do GDP calculations account for the value added in the sale of an existing house by a realtor? [LO 7.3]

Using GDP to Compare Economies

Canadian GDP increased from $1.57 trillion in 2009 to $1.97 trillion in 2014. Does this mean that people in Canada produced more goods and services in 2014 than in 2009? Or does it mean that we just paid more for the same things because prices were higher? GDP is a function of both the quantity of goods and services produced (output) and their market value (prices).

Often, an increase in GDP is the result of growth in both components—an increase in output *and* an increase in prices. If we want to use GDP to compare the health of a national economy over time, or to compare economies of different countries, we need to know how much of the growth to attribute to each factor.

Real versus Nominal GDP

LO 7.4 Explain the difference between real and nominal GDP, and calculate the GDP deflator.

GDP enables us to track changes in the value of output over time. But if you compare levels of just GDP in different years, you can't be sure whether differences are due to changes in production, or prices, or both. To zero in on changes in production, we need a new measure. We use the term *real GDP* to refer to GDP measurement that focuses solely on output, controlling for price changes. Formally, **real GDP** is calculated based on goods and services valued at *constant prices*. Those constant prices are given for a specific year. We might, for example, measure real GDP by valuing output in 2014 at the prices that prevailed in 2010.

If we report GDP *without* controlling for price changes, we are talking about *nominal GDP*. **Nominal GDP** is calculated based on goods and services valued at *current prices* (current at the time of production). Thus, in nominal GDP measurement, output for 2014 would be valued in 2014 prices.

Calculating Nominal and Real GDP

To see the difference between real and nominal GDP measures in practice, let's imagine an economy with only two goods: pizza and spaghetti. For ease of discussion, let's call this fictional economy Pizzetta. Suppose that in 2010, Pizzetta produced 5 million pizzas at a price of $10 each and 20 million plates of spaghetti at a price of $8. Table 7-2 shows this output. In 2011, the number of pizzas and plates of spaghetti increased to 6 million and 22 million, respectively, and prices stayed the same. In 2012, Pizzetta produced the same number of pizzas and plates of spaghetti, but prices increased. In 2013, both quantity and prices increased.

TABLE 7-2   CALCULATING REAL VERSUS NOMINAL GDP GROWTH

Nominal GDP is the sum of the market values of all final goods and services, which we calculate by multiplying the quantity of each output by its market price in the current year. To calculate *real GDP,* we want to value those goods and services at their prices in the base year. When prices stay the same, nominal GDP and real GDP increase at the same rate. If prices rise, nominal GDP will be higher than real GDP.

(1) Year	(2) Pizzas (millions)	(3) Price of pizza ($)	(4) Spaghetti (millions)	(5) Price of spaghetti ($)	(6) Nominal GDP (millions of $)	(7) Real GDP in 2010 prices (millions of $)	(8) What's happening
2010 (base year)	5	10	20	8	(5 × $10) + (20 × $8) = **$210**	(5 × $10) + (20 × $8) = **$210**	In the base year, nominal GDP and real GDP are equal by definition.
2011	6	10	22	8	(6 × $10) + (22 × $8) = **$236**	(6 × $10) + (22 × $8) = **$236**	When output rises and prices stay constant, nominal and real GDP rise at the same rate.
2012	6	12	22	10	(6 × $12) + (22 × $10) = **$292**	(6 × $10) + (22 × $8) = **$236**	When prices rise and output stays constant, nominal GDP rises but real GDP does not.
2013	7	13	25	11	(7 × $13) + (25 × $11) = **$366**	(7 × $10) + (25 × $8) = **$270**	When both output and prices rise, nominal and real GDP rise at different rates.

In order to calculate nominal GDP, we simply multiply the quantity of each good produced in a given year by its price in that year, as shown in column 6 of Table 7-2. We can see that Pizzetta's nominal GDP increased between 2010 and 2011, and again in 2012 and 2013. What doesn't nominal GDP tell us? If we looked just at nominal GDP, we wouldn't be able to tell that in one year (2011) the increase was due to larger output, while in another year (2012) the increase was due only to an increase in prices with no increase in output.

To calculate real GDP (GDP valued at constant prices), we have to choose a *base year.* In the base year, nominal GDP and real GDP are equal. In every other year, we multiply the quantity of a good produced in that year by its price in the base year. In essence, we are holding prices constant while allowing quantities to rise and fall. This method isolates increases in output from increases in prices. Suppose we pick 2010 as our base year. We can see in Table 7-2 that in 2011, the increase in real GDP is actually the same as the increase in nominal GDP ($236 million). That makes sense. Prices didn't change between the two years, so base-year prices are the same as current-year prices.

Between 2011 and 2012, however, we see the difference between nominal and real GDP show up. Nominal GDP increases because prices increased. (Prices of pizza and spaghetti increased by $2 each.) But real GDP stays constant because output stayed constant.

Between 2012 and 2013 both nominal *and* real GDP increase, because both prices *and* output increased. However, the increase in real GDP ($34 million) is smaller than the increase in nominal GDP ($74 million). What does that tell us? It indicates that only $34 million of the $74 million growth in nominal GDP was due to rising output; the rest was due to rising prices.

In summary, real GDP isolates changes in an economy's output, while nominal GDP encompasses changes in both output and prices. As a result, economists and policy makers typically use real GDP numbers as a reference point.

The GDP Deflator

Calculating real GDP allows us to isolate output growth from price increases. But what if it's price increases that we're interested in? The **GDP deflator** is a measure of the overall change in prices in an economy, using the ratio between real and nominal GDP. We calculate the GDP deflator as follows:

Equation 7-3

$$\text{GDP deflator} = \frac{\text{nominal GDP}}{\text{real GDP}} \times 100$$

We saw in the previous section that the difference between nominal and real GDP is the difference between current prices and base-year prices. If we want to know about how prices have changed, we could always directly compare the price of each good in the current and base years. But that would be much like listing every good and service instead of reporting total GDP: it's not incorrect, but it's long, boring, and doesn't do much to summarize what's going on in the economy as a whole. The GDP deflator is one way of summarizing how prices have changed across the entire economy. It takes changes in the price of each individual good and service, and sums them up according to how much of that good or service was produced. In other words, the GDP deflator is a weighted average of all of the individual price changes in the economy.

The GDP deflator equation gives us the ratio between the base-year value of current output and the current-year value of current output. In the base year, the GDP deflator is always equal to 100, because current prices *are* base-year prices. Thus, in the base year, nominal GDP equals real GDP. If prices rise, nominal GDP will be higher than real GDP, and the deflator will be greater than 100. So if the GDP deflator is 115 in a given year, we infer that the overall price level is 15 percent higher than it was in the base year. If prices fall, the deflator will be less than 100. Similarly, if we are looking at a year before the base year, when prices were lower, the deflator will be less than 100. Table 7-3 shows the GDP deflator for the imaginary Pizzetta in 2010–2013.

TABLE 7-3   CALCULATING THE GDP DEFLATOR AND INFLATION RATES

Using the values of nominal and real GDP, we can calculate the GDP deflator, a measure of price changes over time. It is set to 100 for a base year; as prices increase, the value of the deflator increases, as well. With the GDP deflator we can calculate inflation, the percentage change of prices.

Year	Nominal GDP (millions of $)	Real GDP (millions of $)	Deflator	Inflation
2010	210	210	$\frac{\$210}{\$210} \times 100 = 100$	—
2011	236	236	$\frac{\$236}{\$236} \times 100 = 100$	(100 − 100)/100 = **0%**
2012	292	236	$\frac{\$292}{\$236} \times 100 = 124$	(124 − 100)/100 = **24%**
2013	366	270	$\frac{\$366}{\$270} \times 100 = 136$	(136 − 124)/124 = **9.7%**

The GDP deflator gets its name from its relationship to inflation. *Inflation* is an idea we'll discuss at length in future chapters; in fact, we have an entire chapter devoted to the topic. For now, it's enough to note that inflation describes how fast the overall level of prices is changing. Inflation is defined in terms of a year-to-year increase in prices, rather than an increase over a base year. So, we can calculate inflation by looking at the increase in the GDP deflator between any two years. For instance, as shown in Table 7-3, the inflation rate in Pizzetta between 2012 and 2013 is:

$$\text{Inflation rate} = \left[\frac{(\text{deflator}_{2013} - \text{deflator}_{2012})}{\text{deflator}_{2012}} \right] \times 100$$
$$= \frac{(136 - 124)}{124} \times 100$$
$$= 9.7\%$$

The GDP deflator is one simple way of measuring changes in the price level. It allows us to "deflate" nominal GDP by controlling for price changes. In official government statistics, the GDP deflator is actually calculated using a somewhat more elaborate method called a *chain-weighted index*. The basic intuition is the same as the simpler approach we've described here.[1] We'll return to the idea of changes in the overall price level in the chapter titled "Cost of Living."

Using GDP to Assess Economic Health

LO 7.5 Calculate and explain the meanings of GDP per capita and the real GDP annual growth rate.

How do we use GDP to compare economies? We could, of course, simply look at the GDPs of two countries side by side to see their relative sizes. High GDP means a big economy. Figure 7-4 shows the GDPs of a number of countries around the world. As you can see, the United States has the largest economy, by far, followed by China.

FIGURE 7-4

GDP Around the World (2014)

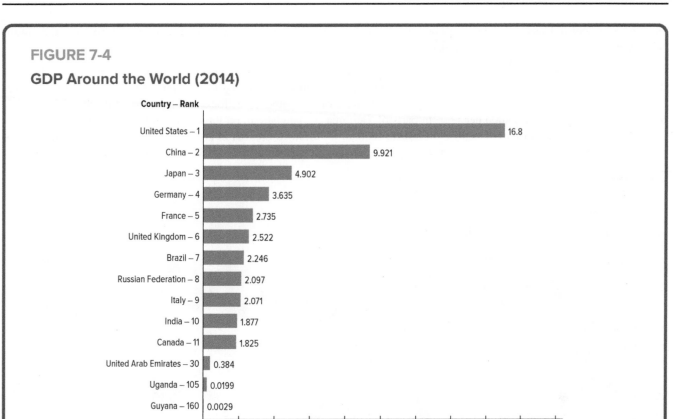

The top eleven countries in terms of overall nominal GDP include rich countries—with both large populations (the United States) and small (Denmark)—as well as some poorer countries with large populations (China and India).

Source: World Bank World Development Indicators 2014, World Bank

However, if we really want to know the income of an average individual in these countries, GDP will paint a misleading picture because the populations of the countries are of quite different sizes. China's GDP is just over half as high as that of the United States, but its population is more than four times as large. India has just under four times as many people as the United States but only one-tenth the GDP. The total income earned in China and India is spread across far more people, so the average person has lower income. Meanwhile, Norway has a much smaller economy than Canada, but because its population is also much smaller, the average Norwegian is actually richer than the average Canadian.

GDP per Capita

If we want get an idea of how much is produced *per person* in a country, we need to divide GDP by population size. This measure is called **GDP per capita**. (*Per capita* simply means per person.) Figure 7-5 shows GDP per capita in each country in the world. When we compare this map to Figure 7-4, the most noticeable pattern is that the wealthy but small countries of Europe and the Middle East rise to the top, while populous countries like China, Brazil, and India move down.

GDP per capita is a useful measure. Knowing, for example, that GDP per capita in Switzerland is $67,246, while in Haiti it is only $673, suggests a lot about differences in life in these two countries. However, GDP per capita doesn't tell us everything. First, it is a measure of *average* income; it doesn't tell us anything about how that income is distributed. A country with deep poverty and a rich elite could have higher GDP per capita than a country where everyone has a moderate standard of living.

Second, it doesn't tell us what you can buy with a given amount of money in that country. The same goods might be more expensive in some countries than in others. For instance, GDP per capita in Canada and the Netherlands are both about $50,000. But many goods and services are more expensive in the Netherlands than in Canada. A dollar in the Netherlands won't buy you as much as it does in Canada. When we account for this difference in the cost of living, the real value of GDP per capita in the Netherlands falls to about $41,700, which is *lower* than in Canada.

Conversely, many poor countries are cheaper to live in than rich ones. This doesn't mean that every single thing costs less, but that overall the cost of living is lower. Looking at GDP per capita without accounting for differences in the cost of living makes poor countries look even poorer than they really are. In Canada or the Netherlands, for example, it would be almost impossible to survive on an income of $3,000 per year. In parts of Tanzania or Bangladesh, on the other hand, it would buy you a decent basic lifestyle. We will return to the subject of how to account for these differences in price levels in the next chapter. For now, just remember that GDP per capita is only a start in understanding people's real ability to consume goods and services.

FIGURE 7-5

Global GDP per Capita (in 2014 US dollars)

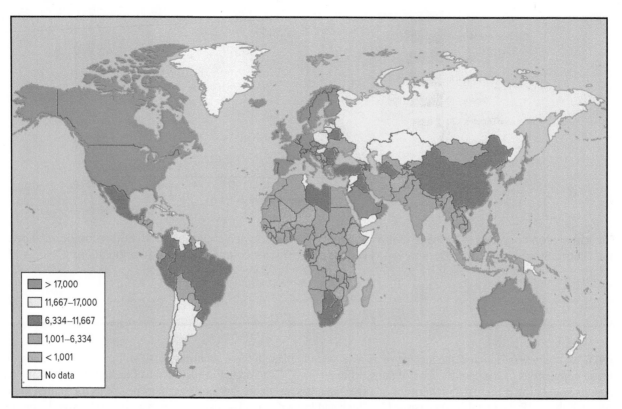

Sources: The World Bank, *World Development Indicators 2014* Data Set, data.worldbank.org. Map made by StatWorld: http://www.statsilk.com/maps/world-stats-open-data.

GDP Growth Rates

One of the most common uses of GDP is to track changes in an economy over time. We usually talk about changes in GDP in terms of the *growth rate.* This is often measured as the percent change in real GDP from one time period to the next, typically annually or quarterly at an annual rate. For instance, if Canadian real GDP grew from $1.8 trillion in one year to $1.85 trillion (in constant dollars) the next, the annual growth rate would be:

$$\text{GDP growth rate} = \left[\frac{(\$1.85 \text{ trillion} - \$1.8 \text{ trillion})}{\$1.8 \text{ trillion}}\right] \times 100 = 2.8\%$$

If the economy shrinks, the growth rate will be negative. For instance, the Canadian economy shrank between 2008 and 2009, with a negative annual real GDP growth rate of −4.2 percent (third quarter of 2008 to second quarter 2009).

We can think about GDP growth rates in several ways. Let's think first about how economic growth changes year to year for the same country. A shrinking economy is a big deal. It means that people are actually producing less than they did the year before.

We have special terms for a period in which the economy contracts. A **recession** is a period of significant decline in economic activity. There is no hard-and-fast rule about what constitutes a "significant decline," but a recession is usually marked by falling GDP, rising unemployment, and an increased number of bankruptcies. A **depression** is a severe or extended recession. Again, there is no hard-and-fast rule about when a recession becomes a depression.

In Canada, there is no official agency that announces business cycles. Generally, a recession or depression is considered official when Statistics Canada reports two consecutive quarters with a decline in real GDP. The country often feels the effects of a recession long before they register in government statistics: people start losing their jobs and businesses experience falling sales.

Another way we can look at economic growth is to compare how fast different countries are growing. High growth rates are not necessarily associated with high total GDP or high GDP per capita, as Figure 7-6 shows. We can see that real GDP growth in the world's rich places, such as the United States, Canada, and Europe, has been relatively slow in recent years (albeit from a much higher starting level). Much more rapid growth has occurred in middle-income and poorer places, led by China and followed by South Asia and East Africa.

FIGURE 7-6

GDP Growth Around the World (2013)

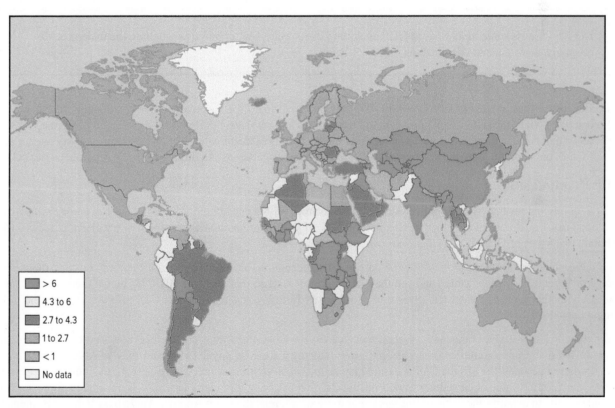

■	> 6
□	4.3 to 6
■	2.7 to 4.3
■	1 to 2.7
■	< 1
□	No data

In contrast with the map of overall income, on average poorer countries grew faster than more developed countries.

Source: The World Bank, *World Development Indicators 2014 Data Set*, data.worldbank.org. StatWorld, http://www.statsilk.com/maps/world-stats-open-data.

✓ CONCEPT CHECK

☐ What is the difference between real and nominal GDP? [LO 7.4]

☐ What does it mean if country A has higher GDP than country B, but country B has higher GDP per capita? [LO 7.5]

Limitations of GDP Measures

GDP is a powerful and versatile way of measuring the size of an economy. How much do people produce in different countries? What is the average income per person? Is the economy growing? How quickly? The uses of GDP in answering these questions make it one of the most important measures in a macroeconomist's toolbox.

However, we can't expect *everything* important to be measured by just one number. In this section, we'll talk about some types of economic activity that are excluded from GDP by design. We'll also look at which aspects of economic well-being are and are not captured by GDP. GDP is a powerful start when describing the health and direction of an economy, but we can get an even richer picture by supplementing it with other metrics.

Data Challenges

LO 7.6 Discuss some limitations to GDP, including its measurement of home production, the underground economy, environmental degradation, and well-being.

When critics argue that we should look beyond GDP, they point out that GDP calculations leave out some important types of economic activity. GDP measures the market value of final goods and services, but it doesn't include anything that is not traded in a market or that isn't reported to the government. That means that three major categories of economic activity are not counted as part of GDP: home production, the underground economy, and non-market externalities such as environmental degradation.

Home Production

In general, goods and services that are both produced and consumed within one household—which we call *home production*—are not included in GDP. If you eat out, your meal is part of GDP; if you eat at home, it's not. If you hire a cleaning service to clean your home, that's part of GDP; if you clean your own home, it's not.

Similarly, the same goods might or might not be part of GDP, depending on whether you sell them or consume them yourself. If you grow vegetables in your garden and sell them at a farmers' market, that's part of GDP; if you eat them yourself, it's not. If your grandmother knits a sweater and gives it to you for your birthday, that's not part of GDP; if your grandmother sells her knitting on a website, it is.

Home production is a major component of economic activity in most places and can change how one country compares to another. In relatively poor countries, many people grow their own food on small farms and may make their own tools and clothes. In these instances, the official GDP measure may be missing a significant percentage of real production. Even in wealthy countries, much of the value of caretaking work—raising children or caring for elderly parents—is uncounted. Some economists have made efforts to quantify the value of this work. For more detail, read the From Another Angle box, Valuing Homemakers.

Valuing Homemakers

If you were to compare the GDP growth of the United States and Germany between the 1970s and the 1990s, you'd find that the US economy grew more than Germany's. Does this mean that life got better in the US during that period relative to life in Germany? Estimates of home production cast an interesting light on this question.

One major difference between the United States and Germany over those three decades is the change in the number of people in the workforce. In the 1970s, comparable proportions of Germans and Americans were in paid employment; by the 1990s, a higher proportion of Americans had jobs. This difference can be largely explained by the rising rate of female participation in the US labour force. A larger workforce makes for a larger GDP.

But the larger GDP does not necessarily mean that the United States is better off. The women who stayed at home in the 1970s weren't sitting around doing nothing. They were running households and raising families, growing and making goods for home consumption, doing volunteer work in their communities, and so on. Although these are valuable activities, a mother or father who stays home to look after children and bake cookies contributes nothing to GDP. But when she or he goes out to work, hires someone to look after the children, and buys cookies at the store, that adds to GDP. Therefore, we can't automatically conclude from the rise in US GDP relative to that of Germany that more goods and services were being produced in the US in the 1990s. Could it be that some goods and services simply moved from the uncounted area of home production to the documented area of GDP?

Studies suggest this may, in fact, be the case. When you add up paid work, home production, and volunteer work, Americans and Germans put in about the same number of hours per week. But workers in Germany spent 5.3 hours less on paid work and 6 hours more on household production than did Americans. Estimating home production suggests that a lower German employment rate does not necessarily imply lower overall production or a lower standard of living.

Consideration of home production can also change the way we view recessions. US GDP dropped in 2008, but home production went up. Feeling a financial squeeze, people substituted home-cooked meals for restaurant meals, planted gardens, and did their own repairs rather than hire someone. When the economy was doing well, people's choices suggest that they preferred to hire others to do these tasks, so the recession clearly reduced people's well-being. But economist Nancy Folbre, who has led efforts to quantify the value of home production, argues that it might not have reduced well-being by nearly as much as official GDP statistics suggest.

Sources: http://economix.blogs.nytimes.com/2009/05/04/including-home-production-gdp-might-not-look-so-bad; http://www.nber.org/papers/w8797.pdf; http://scholar.harvard.edu/alesina/publications/work-and-leisure-us-and-europe-why-so-different-0

The Underground Economy

Many goods and services are sold below the radar, outside of official records. These transactions make up the *underground economy*.

On the extreme end, there is trade in goods and services that are themselves illegal—banned drugs, restricted weapons, endangered animals and plants, and so on. Sales of illegal goods and services are part of what is called the *black market*. Because black-market transactions are illegal, they are, of course, not reported to the government or tax authorities. As a result, they don't show up in government statistics, and they aren't counted as part of the official GDP. In principle, though, black market activities belong in the GDP calculation.

At the less extreme end are economic transactions that are otherwise legal but are sometimes not reported to the government. Failure to report can be either accidental or deliberate (to avoid paying taxes). For instance, were you ever hired to mow a neighbour's lawn, or babysit, or run errands for a few bucks when you were in high school? If you didn't report those amounts to Revenue Canada,[2] you were participating in what's known as the *gray market*—so called because it sits somewhere between the black market and the documented economy.

Gray-market transactions aren't counted in GDP for the same reason that black-market transactions aren't counted: if it's not reported, it doesn't show up in government statistics. And if it doesn't show up in government statistics, it can't be counted in GDP.

Even though black- and gray-market transactions aren't reported, researchers try to quantify them to get a sense for what's missing in our GDP calculations. It turns out that the underground economy accounts for a significant portion of the total economy in many countries. On average across the world, the underground economy is worth about one-third of GDP. This average hides wide variations, though. In Canada, for example, the underground economy has been valued at only around 2.2 percent of GDP. It is estimated at more than half of GDP in Nigeria, and more than two-thirds in some Latin American countries.[3]

The typical explanation for this pattern reflects the cost of doing business legally. In some countries you have to pay extremely high taxes or pay bribes to officials to cut through bureaucratic red tape. When the cost of doing business legally is high, people are much more likely to conduct their business through other channels. In such countries, GDP may significantly underestimate the true size of the economy. In the case of Nigeria, it would mean increasing the official GDP figure by 50 percent.[4]

Environmental Externalities

Suppose an electricity company causes air pollution by burning coal. The electricity generated ends up being counted in GDP. It may appear in the price paid by households for their electricity. Or it may be wrapped up in the price of goods and services that other firms make using the electricity as an input.

Some economists feel that GDP, as a metric, is missing the costs associated with pollution. They argue that we need to account for the *negative externalities* of economic activities. In a sense, we can think of the value of negative externalities as *negative output*. They are final "goods" that do harm to people, and therefore have negative value, but that negative value is not counted in production or expenditure measures.

Increasingly, those who deal with economic statistics are trying to incorporate the value of negative externalities into GDP. Some countries have tried to calculate **green GDP**. This alternative measure of GDP subtracts the environmental costs of production from the positive outputs normally counted in GDP.

In some countries that are growing rapidly, such as China and India, there are few regulations to guard against environmental degradation. When the Chinese government attempted to calculate green GDP in 2007, it came up with some shocking results. Once adjusted for pollution, the soaring GDP growth rates in many provinces in China dropped to almost zero. This was such an inconvenient finding that the government abandoned the green-GDP project. The Chinese government is not alone in its concerns about the political implications of GDP measures. For more about the intersection of politics and national accounting, read the From Another Angle box, The Politics of Green GDP.

FROM ANOTHER ANGLE

The Politics of Green GDP

Since GDP is widely viewed as the measure of the overall health of the economy, politicians have an incentive to make GDP numbers look as strong as possible, to help their re-election chances. As a result, deciding the best way to measure the economy isn't left to number-crunching economists—it can also be deeply political.

A perfect example of this is green GDP. Recognizing that GDP may not capture the negative externalities of environmental production, statistics officials around the world started to work on how to measure a more complete measure of economic activity. This idea started off with the typical GDP equation: C + I + G + NX. What made the new GDP calculation "green" was that it would weigh the value of this production against its overall environmental costs. Included in those costs would be the consumption of non-renewable resources—such as oil and coal—and some of the costs from pollution.

You may have noticed that we don't see this figure reported in the news. Why not? Statistics Canada does not supplement existing national account aggregates with the "green aggregates." It seems they were worried that measuring green GDP might be too complex and uncertain in practice to be able to guide policy making.

By contrast, a similar French effort had top-level support. Former President Nicolas Sarkozy recruited several prominent economists—including two Nobel laureates, Amartya Sen and Joseph Stiglitz—to serve on the grandly named Commission on the Measurement of Economic and Social Progress.

The commission published a 300-page report in September 2009, outlining twelve recommendations. These included measures of the state of health, education, the environment, and income inequality that could be used to build a more inclusive measure of overall well-being. This measure was never officially calculated. But we can guess roughly what it might show by seeing how France scores in other, already-crafted measures such as the Better Life Index from the OECD (Organisation for Economic Co-operation and Development): France ranked 18th among 34 OECD member countries. That ranking is seven positions *lower* than France's position when the same countries are ranked by the size of their GDP per capita.

If President Sarkozy had been hoping for a new metric that would make the French feel good about their country on the world stage, then this type of calculation would have fallen far short. As we have seen, the traditional measurement of GDP is more than just a metric favored by economists—it can be quite useful for politicians, as well.

Sources: http://www.oecd.org/statistics/datalab/bli.htm; http://www.nytimes.com/2010/05/16/magazine/16GDP-t.html?pagewantedmall=all; http://www.stiglitz-sen-fitoussi.fr/en/index.htm.

GDP versus Well-Being

GDP tells us a lot about the living standards in a country, but it can't tell us everything. Suppose you are offered the chance to live in a country that you know nothing about. You could quickly learn more by finding out the country's average income as measured by its GDP per capita. Which data would you turn to next to find out about the quality of life there? *Quality of life* is a nuanced idea, and it's hard to capture perfectly with any number. However, metrics like infant or child mortality (how many babies and children die), literacy rates (how many people can read), and life expectancy (how long people live) can give us a fuller picture of the well-being of a country's inhabitants.

You might assume that countries with high GDP per capita are likely to do well on these other metrics. The wealthier a country is, the more easily it can afford good health care and education for its people. Broadly speaking, you would be right. As Table 7-4 shows, GDP per capita is highly correlated with these quality of life measures. However, the correlation is not perfect: look at Equatorial Guinea in Africa. Countries that are much poorer than Equatorial Guinea—such as Brazil, Bulgaria, and China—nonetheless seem to do a much better job of caring for the health of their children and elderly.

TABLE 7-4   GDP COMPARED WITH OTHER MEASURES OF WELL-BEING

While GDP is commonly used to measure average income in a country, it can't capture all aspects of quality of life. Overall, metrics of well-being and quality of life—like infant mortality, literacy, and life expectancy—are correlated with GDP per capita, but in extreme cases, like that of Equatorial Guinea, they can diverge dramatically.

Country	GDP per capita (current US $)	Literacy rate (% of population over 15)	Life expectancy at birth (years)	Child mortality (deaths per 1,000 under age 5)	Life satisfaction index (0 to 10)
Norway	100,819 (2)	—	81.5 (13)	3 (8)	8.1 (4)
United States	53,143 (10)	—	78.94 (36)	7 (37)	7.8 (10)

Country	GDP per capita (current US $)	Literacy rate (% of population over 15)	Life expectancy at birth (years)	Child mortality (deaths per 1,000 under age 5)	Life satisfaction index (0 to 10)
Canada	51,911 (11)	—	81.48	5	7.9 (6)
Brazil	11,208 (55)	90.4 (63)	73.94 (102)	14 (109)	7.6 (22)
Bulgaria	7,296 (74)	98.4 (28)	73.55 (94)	12 (61)	4.4 (108)
China	6,807 (77)	95.1 (43)	75.33 (95)	14 (102)	5.2 (92)
Mali	715 (164)	33.4 (176)	55.03 (176)	128 (195)	3.7 (117)

Note: Numbers in brackets denote country rank.

Sources: 2014 World Bank HDI, https://data.undp.org/dataset/HDI-Indicators-By-Country-2014/5tuc-d2a9? (Life Expectancy, Child Mortality); https://data.undp.org/dataset/Table-9-Education/xn26-t7qa? (Literacy rate) http://data.worldbank.org/data-catalog/world-development-indicators (GDP per capita); http://www.earth.columbia.edu/sitefiles/file/Sachs%20Writing/2012/World%20Happiness%20Report.pdf (Life Satisfaction Index), 2012.

There are good reasons to expect that GDP per capita might not perfectly correlate with people's well-being. Let's take an obvious example. When people take more vacation or leisure time, they aren't working to manufacture goods or provide services. More time off from work may reduce GDP, but vacations generally make people happier. In this sense, pursuing GDP growth as the highest priority can be in opposition to improving quality of life in other ways, at least in the short term.

If what we care about is not so much the output of an economy but the happiness of the people who comprise it, can we measure happiness directly? Economists and others are trying to do this systematically. These efforts are just underway, though, and nobody is suggesting that such measures replace GDP. One of the measures they've developed is the Life Satisfaction Index. (See the final column in Table 7-4.) It suggests that the correlation between GDP per capita and happiness is, indeed, far from perfect. For example, people in Bulgaria seem to be less happy than we might expect from their average income; people in Mali seem to be happier. For more on measuring happiness, read the Real Life box, Can Money Buy You Happiness?

REAL LIFE

Can Money Buy You Happiness?

Everyone has heard the saying, "Money can't buy you happiness." But is it actually true? The answer turns out to depend on how much money, and how you define happiness.

First, how can we tell whether someone is happy? Researchers have generally relied on just asking people how they feel. Studies show consistently that people who are married tend to be happier, as do people who are religious, and people who are in good health. Income seems to matter a lot, too.

However, we need to remember the difference between *causation* and *correlation*. The fact that wealth and life satisfaction are correlated doesn't mean that having more money *causes* happiness. In fact, when you look at the same country over time, people don't necessarily get happier as the country they live in gets richer. For instance, the United States has much higher GDP per capita now than it did fifty years ago. But researchers have found that Americans are not noticeably happier than they were fifty years ago. One possible explanation for this puzzle is that people naturally tend to compare their lifestyles and material wealth to those of their peers rather than to their parents or grandparents.

How about the relationship between money and happiness for individuals within a country? Research in the United States has found that there *is* a correlation between happiness and money—up to a point. That point happens to be an income level of about $75,000 per year. Below that income level, more money appears to be related to higher levels of happiness on average. Above that income level, it's much less clear—whether money buys happiness seems to depend on the way in which you ask people if they're happy.

Typically, researchers use two distinct methods. One is to ask something like, "How satisfied are you with your life as a whole these days?" This measure, usually called *life satisfaction,* continues to rise with income. In other words, someone earning $750,000 is likely to tell a researcher that she is more satisfied than someone earning $75,000.

The other method is to ask people about the emotions they felt *on the previous day.* For example, did you feel happiness yesterday? Enjoyment? Anger? Stress? Worry? Here, we find that overall someone earning $75,000 is more likely to have experienced positive emotions than someone earning $25,000. But despite what you would think, someone earning $750,000 did not report more positive emotions and less negativity than someone earning $75,000. Although money doesn't always buy happiness, it seems to help up to a certain point.

Sources: Angus Deaton, "Income, health, and well-being around the world: Evidence from the Gallup World Poll," *Journal of Economic Perspectives,* 2008; http://economix.blogs.nytimes.com/2009/03/10/the-happiest-states-of-america/; http://www.princeton.edu/~deaton/downloads/deaton_kahneman_high_income_improves_evaluation_August2010.pdf.

✓ CONCEPT CHECK

☐ What is home production? [LO 7.6]
☐ Why might GDP fall if environmental damages caused by production were taken into account? [LO 7.6]
☐ What supplemental metrics are commonly used to measure quality of life alongside GDP per capita? [LO 7.6]

Conclusion

GDP is a powerful and versatile metric. There are good reasons that it is one of the most commonly used tools in macroeconomics. It gives a simple measure of the size of an economy and the average income of its participants. It also allows us to make comparisons over time or across countries. The system of national income accounts gives us a picture of how output, expenditure, and income are linked, and a framework for adding up the billions of daily transactions that occur in an economy.

Comparing nominal and real GDP allows us to examine the role of increasing prices versus increasing output in a growing economy. The GDP deflator and the inflation rate track changes in overall price levels over time—which, as we'll see in the next chapter, is a major task in macroeconomics. GDP per capita gives us a sense of the average income within a country, although it doesn't tell us about the distribution of income or quality of life. Finally, calculating real GDP growth rates shows us which direction the economy is moving in, and is an important indicator of recession or depression.

In the next chapter, we'll dig deeper into the tools that economists use to measure price changes and the cost of living. When we combine these tools with GDP, we have a menu of macroeconomic metrics that will allow us to describe and analyze national and international economies.

Key Terms

macroeconomics	real GDP
gross domestic product (GDP)	nominal GDP
gross national product (GNP)	GDP deflator
consumption	GDP per capita
investment	recession
inventory	depression
government purchases	green GDP
net exports	

Summary

LO 7.1 Justify the importance of using the market value of final goods and services to calculate GDP, and explain why each component of GDP is important.

Most goods and services go through several production steps and may pass through multiple firms before ending up in the hands of the consumer. However, when calculating GDP, we should consider only the value of the final good or service in order to avoid double-counting. The value added by each step of the production process will be included in the price of the final product.

The most commonly used variable for measuring the value of a national economy is gross domestic product, or GDP. GDP is the sum of the market values of all final goods and services produced within a country in a given period of time. The goods and services that count toward GDP are defined in terms of the location of production, not the citizenship of the producer. GDP is usually calculated on an annual and quarterly (three-month) basis; only new goods and services being produced within that time period are counted. Quarterly GDP estimates are typically given as a seasonally adjusted annual rate, which projects what annual GDP will be based on the current quarter's output if the economy continues to follow expected seasonal patterns.

LO 7.2 Explain the equivalence of the expenditure and income approaches to valuing an economy.

Economists can think about the size of a national economy in three different ways: how much is produced (output), how much is spent (expenditure), and how much income is earned (income). All three of these methods add up to the same thing. Total output is the *value* of the things produced in an economy in dollar terms, which is the same as the price for which those outputs sell, which is the same as what people spent to buy those outputs. Therefore, the value of output is equal to expenditures. Every transaction has both a buyer and a seller, so expenditures by one person translate directly into income for someone else; therefore, income equals expenditure.

LO 7.3 Explain the three approaches that are used to calculate GDP, and list the categories of spending that are included in the expenditure approach.

The *expenditure* approach to calculating the size of an economy involves adding up all spending on goods and services produced in an economy and subtracting spending on imports. We can break expenditures into four categories: *Consumption* (C) measures spending on goods and services to be consumed by private individuals and families. *Investment* (I) includes any goods that are bought in order to produce other goods and services in the future. *Government purchases* (G) are goods and services bought by all levels of government, for either consumption or investment. Finally, *net exports* (NX) is foreign spending on domestically produced goods and services minus domestic spending on foreign-produced goods and services. The sum of these categories and the equivalence of income (Y) and expenditure gives us the equation $Y = C + I + G + NX$.

The income approach adds up the income earned by everyone in a country—including wages (earned by workers), interest (earned on capital investments), rental income (earned on land and property), and profits (earned by firms).

The *value-added* approach accounts for the value that is added at each stage of production in the economy. This approach allows economists to investigate the contribution of each transaction in the economy to overall GDP. It also solves the double-counting problem because only part of the value of each transaction is registered, and it does not register the total price of intermediate goods and services.

Many countries use all three approaches to calculate GDP so that policy makers and researchers can get a full picture of economic activity.

LO 7.4 Explain the difference between real and nominal GDP, and calculate the GDP deflator.

GDP is a function of both the quantity of goods and services produced (output) and their market value (prices); an increase in GDP can result from growth in either or both components. To isolate the role of growing output, we can control for price changes. *Real GDP* is calculated based on goods and services valued at constant prices. *Nominal GDP* is calculated based on goods and services valued at current prices. If we want to measure price changes, we can calculate the GDP deflator, a measure that summarizes the overall increase in prices in an economy using the ratio between real and nominal GDP.

LO 7.5 Calculate and explain the meanings of GDP per capita and the real GDP annual growth rate.

GDP per capita is total GDP divided by the population of a country. It tells us the average income or productivity per person in the economy. To track changes in an economy over time, we can calculate the real GDP growth rate, measured as the percentage change in real GDP from one time period to the next, typically annually or quarterly at an annual rate. When the economy shrinks the growth rate is negative, and this is one of the major indicators used to determine whether the economy is in a recession or depression.

LO 7.6 Discuss some limitations to GDP, including its measurement of home production, the underground economy, environmental degradation, and well-being.

GDP is a rough measure of the average standard of living in a country, but does not tell us about the distribution of wealth. Furthermore, three important segments of the economy are not included in GDP by design: home production (goods and services that are produced and consumed within a household); the underground economy (illegal transactions, or legal transactions that simply aren't reported to the government); and externalities (such as pollution) that are not fully accounted for in regular production or consumption measures. Higher GDP is often associated with other indicators of higher well-being, such as health, education, and life satisfaction, but does not guarantee those things.

Review Questions

1. Canadian car dealers sell both used cars and new cars each year. However, only the sales of the new cars count toward GDP. Why does the sale of used cars not count? [LO 7.1]
2. There is an old saying, "You can't compare apples and oranges." When economists calculate GDP, are they able to compare apples and oranges? Explain. [LO 7.1]

3. When Canadians buy goods produced in the US, Americans earn income from Canadian expenditures. Is the value of this American output and Canadian expenditure counted in the GDP of Canada or the United States? Why? [LO 7.2]

4. Economists sometimes describe the economy as having a *circular flow*. In the most basic form of the circular flow model, companies hire workers and pay them wages. Workers then use these wages to buy goods and services from companies. How does the circular flow model explain the equivalence of the expenditure and income methods of valuing an economy? [LO 7.2]

5. In 2013, the average baseball player earned $3.4 million per year. Suppose that these baseball players spend all of their income on goods and services each year and save nothing. Argue why the sum of the incomes of all baseball players must equal the sum of expenditures made by the baseball players. [LO 7.2]

6. Determine whether each of the following counts as consumption, investment, government purchases, net exports, or none of these, under the expenditure approach to calculating GDP. Explain your answer. [LO 7.3]
    a. The construction of a court house
    b. A taxicab ride
    c. The purchase of a taxicab by a taxicab company
    d. A student buying a textbook
    e. The trading of municipal bonds (a type of financial investment offered by city government)
    f. A company's purchase of foreign minerals

7. If car companies produce a lot of cars this year but hold the new models back in warehouses until they release them in the new model year, will this year's GDP be higher, lower, or the same as it would have been if the cars had been sold right away? Why? Does the choice to reserve the cars for a year change which category of expenditures they fall under? [LO 7.3]

8. The value-added method involves taking the price of intermediate outputs (i.e., outputs that will in turn be used in the production of another good) and subtracting the cost of producing each one. In this way, only the value that is added at each step (the sale value minus the value that went into producing it) is summed up. Explain why this method gives us the same result as the standard method, which counts only the value of final goods and services. [LO 7.3]

9. Imagine a painter is trying to determine the value she adds when she paints a picture. Assume that after spending $200 on materials, she sells one copy of her painting for $500. She then spends $50 to make 10 copies of her painting, each of which sells for $100. What is the value added of her painting? What if a company then spends $10 per copy to sell 100 more copies, each for $50? What is the value the painter adds then? If it's unknown how many copies the painting will sell in the future, can we today determine the value added? Why or why not? [LO 7.3]

10. At a press conference, the president of a small country displays a chart showing that GDP has risen by 10 percent every year for five years. He argues that this growth shows the brilliance of his economic policy. However, his chart uses nominal GDP numbers. What might be wrong with this chart? If you were a reporter at the press conference, what questions could you ask to get a more accurate picture of the country's economic growth? [LO 7.4]

11. Suppose that the GDP deflator grew by 10 percent from last year to this year. That is, the inflation rate this year was 10 percent. In words, what does this mean happened in the economy? What does this inflation rate imply about the growth rate in real GDP? [LO 7.4]

12. An inexperienced researcher wants to examine the average standard of living in two countries. In order to do so, she compares the nominal GDPs in those two countries. What are two reasons why this comparison does not lead to an accurate measure of the countries' average standards of living? [LO 7.4, LO 7.5]

13. In 2013, according to the International Monetary Fund, India had the world's 10th-highest nominal GDP, the 140th-highest nominal GDP per capita, and the 43rd-highest real GDP growth rate. What does each of these indicators tell us about the Indian economy and how life in India compares to life in other countries? [LO 7.5]

14. China is a rapidly growing country. It has high levels of bureaucracy and business regulation, low levels of environmental regulation, and a strong tradition of entrepreneurship. Discuss several reasons why official GDP estimates in China might miss significant portions of the country's economic activity. [LO 7.6]

15. Suppose a college student is texting while driving and gets into a car accident causing $2,000 worth of damage to his car. Assuming the student repairs the car, does GDP rise, fall, or stay constant with this accident? What does your answer suggest about using GDP as a measure of well-being? [LO 7.6]

Problems and Applications

1. Suppose a gold miner finds a gold nugget and sells the nugget to a mining company for $500. The mining company melts down the gold, purifies it, and sells it to a jewellery maker for $1,000. The jewellery maker fashions the gold into a necklace, which it sells to a department store for $1,500. Finally, the department store sells the necklace to a customer for $2,000. How much has GDP increased as a result of these transactions? [LO 7.1], [LO 7.3]

2. Table 7P-1 shows the price of inputs and the price of outputs at each step in the production process of making a shirt. Assume that each of these steps takes place within the country. [LO 7.1], [LO 7.3]
   a. What is the total contribution of this shirt to GDP, using the standard expenditure method?
   b. If we use the value-added method (i.e., summing the value added by producers at each step of the production process, equal to the price of inputs minus the price of outputs), what is the contribution of this shirt to GDP?
   c. If we mistakenly added the price of both intermediate and final outputs without adjusting for value added, what would we find that this shirt contributes to GDP? By how much does this overestimate the true contribution?

TABLE 7P-1

	Cotton farmer ($)	Fabric maker ($)	Sewing and printing ($)
Inputs	0	1.10	3.50
Value of output	1.10	3.50	18.00

3. The Canadian government gives income support to many families living in poverty. How does each of the following aspects of this policy contribute to GDP? [LO 7.2]
   a. Does this government's expenditure on income support count as part of GDP? If so, into which category of expenditure does it fall?
   b. When the families buy groceries with the money they've received, does this expenditure count as part of GDP? If so, into which category does it fall?
   c. If the families buy new houses with the money they've received, does this count as part of GDP? If so, into which category does it fall?

4. Given the following information about each economy, either calculate the missing variable or determine that it cannot be calculated. [LO 7.2], [LO 7.3]
   a. If C = $20.1 billion, I = $3.5 billion, G = $5.2 billion, and NX = −$1 billion, what is total income?
   b. If total income = $1 trillion, G = $0.3 trillion, and C = $0.5 trillion, what is I?
   c. If total expenditure = $675 billion, C = $433 billion, I = 105 billion, and G = $75 billion, what is NX? How much are exports? How much are imports?

5. Using Table 7P-2, calculate the following. [LO 7.2], [LO 7.3]
   a. Total gross domestic product and GDP per person.
   b. Consumption, investment, government purchases, and net exports, each as a percentage of total GDP.
   c. Consumption, investment, government purchases, and net exports per person.

TABLE 7P-2

Sector	Value (millions)
Consumption	$ 770,000
Investment	$ 165,000
Government spending	$ 220,000
Net exports	–$ 55,000
Population	50

6. Determine which category each of the following economic activities falls under: consumption (C), investment (I), government purchases (G), net exports (NX), or not included in GDP. [LO 7.3]
    a. The mayor of Edmonton authorizes the construction of a new arena using public funds.
    b. A student pays rent on her apartment.
    c. Parents pay university tuition for their son.
    d. Someone buys a new Toyota car produced in Japan.
    e. Someone buys a used Toyota car.
    f. Someone buys a new General Motors car produced in Canada.
    g. A family buys a house in a newly constructed housing development.
    h. The Canadian Armed Forces pays its soldiers.
    i. A Brazilian driver buys a Ford car produced in Canada.
    j. The Department of Transportation buys a new machine for printing driver's licenses.
    k. An apple picked in British Columbia in October is bought at a grocery store in Ontario in December.
    l. Hewlett-Packard produces a computer and sends it to a warehouse in another province for sale next year.
7. Table 7P-3 shows economic activity for a very tiny country. Using the expenditure approach determine the following: [LO 7.3]
    a. Consumption
    b. Investment
    c. Government purchases
    d. Net exports
    e. GDP

TABLE 7P-3

Activity	Total value (thousands of $)
Families buy groceries	600
Electronics company sells HD projectors to households	100

Activity	Total value (thousands of $)
Personal trainer gives Zumba class	5
Custard stand sells pistachio ice cream	2
Police department buys new cars	500
Mayor leads creation of new education budget	300
Elevator construction company builds new factory	600
Local businessperson purchases corn from Mexico	400
Sports-gear company sells hockey gloves to Canadian team	200
Bike store sells used carbon-fibre bikes	200
Value of stock local stockbroker executes for clients	2,000

8. During the recent recession sparked by financial crisis, the US economy suffered tremendously. Suppose that, due to the recession, the US GDP dropped from $14 trillion to $12.5 trillion. This decline in GDP was due to a drop in consumption of $1 trillion and a drop in investment of $500 billion. The US government responded to this recession by increasing government purchases. [LO 7.3]
    a. Suppose that government spending had no impact on consumption, investment, or net exports. If the administration wanted to bring GDP back up to $14 trillion, how much would government spending have to rise?
    b. Many economists believe that an increase in government spending doesn't just directly increase GDP, but that it also leads to an increase in consumption. If government spending rises by $1 trillion, how much would consumption have to rise in order to bring GDP back to $14 trillion?
9. Assume Table 7P-4 summarizes the income of Paraguay. [LO 7.3]
    a. Calculate profits.
    b. Calculate the GDP of Paraguay using the income approach.
    c. What would GDP be if you were to use the value-added approach?
    d. What would GDP be if you were to use the expenditure approach?

TABLE 7P-4

Category	Value (billions of $)
Wages	8.3
Interest	0.7
Total business expenditures	21.0
Total business revenues	30.0

10. Table 7P-5 shows the prices of the inputs and outputs for the production of a road bike. [LO 7.3]
    a. What value is added by the supplier of the raw materials?
    b. What value is added by the tire maker?
    c. What value is added by the maker of the frame and components?
    d. What value is added by the bike mechanic?
    e. What value is added by the bike store?
    f. What is the total contribution of the bike to GDP?

TABLE 7P-5

Raw materials	Manufacturing	Construction	Sale by the retailer
• Rubber for one tire ($20) • Aluminum for the frame ($80) • Other component materials ($70)	• Tire maker sells tires for $30 each • Bike frame and components maker sell their products for a total of $250	• Bike mechanic puts everything together and sells the bike for $350	• Retailer sells the bike for $500

11. Imagine that Canada produces only three goods: apples, bananas, and carrots. The quantities produced and the prices of the three goods are listed in Table 7P-6. [LO 7.4]
    a. Calculate the GDP of Canada in this three-good version of its economy.
    b. Suppose that a drought hits the province of British Columbia. This drought causes the quantity of apples produced to fall to 2. Assuming that all prices remain constant, calculate the new Canadian GDP.
    c. Assume, once again, that the quantities produced and the prices of the three goods are as listed in Table 7P-6. Now, carrot sellers decide that the price of carrots is too low, so they agree to raise the price. What would the price of carrots have to be in order for the Canadian GDP to be $60?

TABLE 7P-6

Good	Quantity produced	Price ($)
Apples	5	2.00
Bananas	10	1.00
Carrots	20	1.50

12. Based on Table 7P-7, calculate nominal GDP, real GDP, the GDP deflator, and the inflation rate in each year, and fill in the missing parts of the table. Use 2010 as the base year. [LO 7.4]

TABLE 7P-7

Year	Quantity of oranges	Price of orange ($)	Quantity of beach balls	Price of beach ball ($)	Nominal GDP ($)	Real GDP ($)	GDP deflator	Inflation rate (%)
2010	500	1.00	850	5.00				
2011	600	1.50	900	7.50				
2012	750	1.65	1,000	8.25				

13. Suppose that the British economy produces two goods: laptops and books. The quantity produced and the prices of these items for 2010 and 2011 are shown in Table 7P-8. **[LO 7.4]**
    a. Let's assume that the base year was 2010, so that real GDP in 2010 equals nominal GDP in 2010. If the real GDP in Britain was $15,000 in 2010, what was the price of books?
    b. Using your answer from (a), if the growth rate in nominal GDP was 10 percent, how many books must have been produced in 2011?
    c. Using your answers from (a) and (b), what is the real GDP in 2011? What was the growth rate in real GDP between 2010 and 2011?

TABLE 7P-8

Year	Quantities produced	Price ($)
2010	Laptops = 50 Books = 1,000	Laptops = 200 Books = ?
2011	Laptops = 100 Books = ?	Laptops = $150 Books = 10

14. Based on Table 7P-9, calculate nominal GDP per capita in 2008 and 2009, and the real GDP growth rate between the two years. Which countries look like they experienced recession in 2008–2009? **[LO 7.5]**

TABLE 7P-9

	2008			2009		
	Nominal GDP (billions of $)	Real GDP (billions of $)	Population	Nominal GDP (billions of $)	Real GDP (billions of $)	Population
Argentina	328.03	383.48	39,746,000	310.17	386.68	40,134,000
Egypt	162.44	123.21	75,200,000	188.61	128.97	76,800,000

	2008			2009		
	Nominal GDP (billions of $)	Real GDP (billions of $)	Population	Nominal GDP (billions of $)	Real GDP (billions of $)	Population
Germany	3,651.62	2,100.54	82,013,000	3,338.68	2,002.46	81,767,000
Ghana	28.53	11.27	22,532,000	26	11.8	23,108,000
United States	14,319	13,228.65	304,718,000	14,119	12,880.53	307,374,000

15. Table 7P-10 describes the real GDP and population of a fictional country in 2009 and 2010. [LO 7.5]
    a. What is the real GDP per capita in 2009 and 2010?
    b. What is the growth rate in real GDP?
    c. What is the growth rate in population?
    d. What is the growth rate in real GDP per capita?

TABLE 7P-10

Year	Real GDP (billions of $)	Population (millions)
2009	10	1.0
2010	12	1.1

16. Table 7P-11 shows data on population and expenditures in five countries, as well as the value of home production, the underground economy, and environmental externalities in each. [LO 7.5], [LO 7.6]
    a. Calculate GDP and GDP per capita in each country.
    b. Calculate the size of home production, the underground economy, and environmental externalities in each country as a percentage of GDP.
    c. Calculate total and per capita "GDP-plus" in each country by including the value of home production, the underground economy, and environmental externalities.
    d. Rank countries by total and per capita GDP, and again by total and per capita "GDP-plus." Compare the two lists. Are the biggest and the smallest economies the same or different?

TABLE 7P-11

Country	C ($)	I ($)	G ($)	Net exports ($)
Bohemia	9,800,000,000	230,000,000	950,000,000	−120,000,000
Silesia	450,000,000	78,000,000	100,000,000	13,000,000

Country	C ($)	I ($)	G ($)	Net exports ($)
Bavaria	2,125,000,000	319,000,000	597,000,000	134,000,000
Saxony	2,750,000,000	75,000,000	1,320,000,000	−45,000,000
Ottoman Empire	6,225,000,000	567,000,000	1,435,000,000	1,000,000

Country	Population	Home production ($)	Underground economy ($)	Environmental externalities ($)
Bohemia	1,200,000	1,250,000,000	5,770,000,000	−1,560,000,000
Silesia	160,000	75,000,000	128,000,000	−45,000,000
Bavaria	425,000	386,000,000	1,450,000,000	.−523,000,000
Saxony	760,000	146,000,000	250,000,000	−820,000,000
Ottoman Empire	800,000	432,000,000	654,000,000	−396,300,000

17. Suppose a parent was earning $20,000 per year working at a local firm. The parent then decides to quit his job in order to care for his child who was being watched by a babysitter for $10,000 per year. Does GDP rise, fall, or stay constant with this action, and how much does GDP change (if at all)? [LO 7.6]

Chapter Sources

http://www.nytimes.com/2010/08/16/business/global/16yuan.html

http://data.worldbank.org/indicator/NY.GDP.MKTP.KD?page=5 [China GDP stats]

http://data.worldbank.org/indicator/SI.POV.DDAY [China poverty stats]

http://www23.statcan.gc.ca/imdb/p2SV.pl?Function=getSurvey&SDDS=1901

http://www.statcan.gc.ca/daily-quotidien/160531/dq160531a-eng.htm

http://nordhaus.econ.yale.edu/documents/Env_Accounts_052609.pdf

http://link.springer.com/article/10.1007/s10797-011-9187-7

http://www.nytimes.com/2007/08/26/world/asia/26china.html?pagewanted=2

CHAPTER 8

The Cost of Living

Get Cracking

In 1995, a dozen Grade A large eggs cost about $1.60. In the same year, the average minimum wage in Canada was about $5.78. By 2014, the price of eggs had risen to $3.29 and the average minimum wage was $10.40. Did wages keep up with the price of eggs? Clearly, prices and wages are much higher today than they were in 1995. As prices increased over time, a dollar bought less and less.

The price of eggs draws our attention to an important idea: a dollar now is very different from a dollar in the past. More generally, it reminds us that a *dollar* is just a word or a piece of paper; what really matters is what we can buy with the dollar. And what we can buy with a dollar changes over time. When we talk about what a dollar actually buys, we are talking about the *cost of living*. When we say the cost of living has gone up, we mean that, looking broadly over a range of goods and services, a dollar buys less today than it used to buy.

In this chapter we'll describe the most important measures of changing prices and discuss how to measure changes of prices over time. Along the way, you'll get a sense of how the cost of living factors into everything from how far your paycheque will stretch, to debates over the size of pension payments.

© McGraw-Hill Education

The Cost of Living

In the previous chapter we discussed how to measure output on a national level. Now we turn our attention to the second pillar of macroeconomic data: prices. In the previous chapter we calculated real GDP to see how output increases over time, independent of price changes. Now we want to focus on the price changes themselves.

Measuring prices in a national economy helps us answer the question, "What's a dollar (or euro or yen or peso) worth?" This question is trickier than it might sound. What a dollar will buy you changes from year to year as the prices of goods rise or fall (but usually rise) over time. It also changes as you go from place to place; in general, a dollar will get you a lot more in Thunder Bay, Ontario, than in Calgary, Alberta.

Of course, people earn more money now than they used to. And, on average, people earn more in Calgary than they do in Thunder Bay. If higher income goes with higher prices, people's actual ability to consume the things they want may remain the same. The key to understanding the cost of living is to look at the full picture.

If all prices and incomes rose at the same rate everywhere in the world, tracking the cost of living would be a simple accounting question. What makes it an interesting and important macroeconomic topic is the fact that, in the real world, prices change at different speeds across time and place. This means that at any given time wages might be rising more slowly than the price of consumer goods. That difference effectively shrinks people's ability to buy things. Or, if you have $5,000 in student debt, rising price levels mean that the real value of that debt (in terms of the quantity of goods and services you have to give up in order to pay back the loan) is getting smaller over time. Or suppose you have competing job offers in Calgary and Thunder Bay. You will want to consider not only the salaries offered but also the costs of living in both places. These can differ greatly, even for two cities in the same country, as shown in the Real Life box, The Cost of Living in Calgary versus Thunder Bay in the next section.

As these examples show, changing price levels can have real effects on people's incentives and choices. They determine the relative value of your salary, of saving or borrowing, of living in one city or another, and a multitude of other decisions. When you add up all of these microeconomic choices, you can get big macroeconomic effects.

Measuring Price Changes Over Time

What does it mean to track how prices change? After all, people buy many different goods and services, each with its own price. Some prices go up and some go down. Some prices move a lot, some don't budge. Perhaps your rent held steady, but gasoline became more expensive. Maybe it became cheaper to buy an older iPhone once the new iPhone came out. Maybe the price of clothing rose only slightly in the last year, but cable bills went through the roof. To understand how the overall cost of living has increased, we want a single number that summarizes changes in the prices of many goods rather than single items.

If we want to talk about prices in general, then, how do we know how much weight to give to the price of each good and service? And how do we know which goods and services to look at in the first place? The idea of a *market basket* gives us a method for comparing prices over time and locations.

REAL LIFE

The Cost of Living in Calgary versus Thunder Bay

Today, Calgary is one of the most expensive cities in Canada. A simple one-bedroom apartment can cost $1,400 a month in rent. In fact, the average home price in Calgary is $545,000, while the Canadian average is about $398,000. Other things are quite expensive, as well. "Cheap" eats in the city will cost you about $15. A three-course dinner, according to the online price-tracker Numbeo, is going to set you back at least $70 per couple.

As you would expect, though, people also get paid more in Calgary. The latest data from Statistics Canada (2013) show the median Calgary household income as $101,260. Thunder Bay had a median income of $82,690. That's a difference in incomes of 22 percent.

TABLE 8-1   MEDIAN HOUSEHOLD INCOME, BY CENSUS METROPOLITAN AREA (2013)

Abbotsford-Mission (BC)	$ 68,310
Vancouver (BC)	$ 73,390
Toronto (Ontario)	$ 72,830
Montreal (Quebec)	$ 73,250
Thunder Bay (Ontario)	$ 82,690
Calgary (Alberta)	$ 101,260

Source: Statistics Canada, CANSIM Table 111-0009, "Family characteristics, summary."

The income difference is pretty substantial, but it's less than half of the difference in prices. In other words, the median household in Thunder Bay is substantially better off than the median household in Calgary, at least in terms of the quantity of goods and services they can afford to buy.

Why, then, do people choose to live in Calgary? Why doesn't everyone prefer to move to places like Thunder Bay? We can deduce that people who choose to live in Calgary get some kind of additional utility from their choice, worth many thousands of dollars a year to them. If that's not true for you, you're likely to find greater happiness—and cheaper meals—in another part of the country.

Sources: http://www.creb.com/public/seller-resources/housing-statistics.php; http://crea.ca/content/national-average-price-map; http://www.numbeo.com/cost-of-living/city_result.jsp?country=Canada&city=Calgary

The Market Basket

> **LO 8.1** Define a market basket and explain its importance in tracking price changes.

When comparing the cost of living across time and places, we have to consider the prices of many different goods and services—housing, food, clothing, transportation, entertainment, and so on. To accomplish this, we construct something that looks like a really long shopping list, called a **market basket.** The list includes specific goods and services, in fixed quantities that roughly correspond to a typical consumer's spending. (Who's a typical consumer? Good question. We'll come back to that later.) The goal is to see how the cost of buying the goods and services on the list changes over time. By keeping goods and quantities constant, we can be sure that any change in the total cost of the basket is caused by a change in prices, rather than the type or amount of things being consumed.

To see how this method works, imagine that you noticed changes from last year to this year in the prices of four items you typically buy at the grocery store:

	Price last year ($)	Price this year ($)
Bread (per loaf)	3.00	3.15
Milk (per litre)	2.50	2.55
Beef (per kilogram)	3.50	3.64
Carrots (per kilogram)	1.00	1.25

How much did the price of groceries increase since last year? It depends on which type of food we look at. The price of bread rose by 5 percent, milk by 2 percent, beef by 4 percent, and carrots by a whopping 25 percent.

Suppose we want to know, overall, how much the cost of *your* groceries rose—a very reasonable and practical question. To answer it, we have to know how much of each food you typically buy. For instance, if you typically buy a loaf of bread, a litre of milk, three kilograms of beef, and a kilogram of carrots, then:

Cost in 2012 = ($3.00 × 1) + ($2.50 × 1) + ($3.50 × 3) + ($1.00 × 1) = $17.00

Cost in 2013 = ($3.15 × 1) + ($2.55 × 1) + ($3.64 × 3) + ($1.25 × 1) = $17.87

Price increase from 2012 to 2013 = $\left[\dfrac{(\$17.87 - \$17)}{\$17}\right] \times 100 = 5.1\%$

> *Reminder:* The formula for calculating a percentage change is $\left[\dfrac{(X_2 - X_1)}{X_1}\right] \times 100$
>
> So the change in the price of bread is $\dfrac{(\$3.15 - \$3)}{\$3} \times 100 = 5\%$

This is the *basket approach.* It measures changes in the cost of your shopping basket, assuming that you buy the same items in the same quantities. This approach gives us a single number to measure how much your total costs rise over time.

The basket approach makes a lot more sense than simply averaging the increase in the price of each grocery item (bread, 5 percent; milk, 2 percent; beef, 4 percent; carrots, 25 percent). If we did that, we would find a completely different answer:

Incorrect calculation of price increase

$$= \frac{(5\% + 2\% + 4\% + 25\%)}{4}$$

$$= 9\% \text{ (Remember, \textit{this answer is wrong!})}$$

You don't spend nearly as much on carrots as you do on beef or milk or bread. Therefore the relatively big increase in the price of carrots doesn't affect you as much as simply averaging the percentage increases would suggest. After all, we want a meaningful answer to the original question, "How much have groceries gone up in price?" To get that, what we really want to know is how much extra you can expect to be charged when you take your usual basket of groceries to the store checkout.

Of course, most people don't buy exactly the same thing all the time, especially when they see that prices are changing. In fact, we know that when prices rise, quantity demanded usually falls. In reality, you might decide to buy less beef and switch from carrots to potatoes. If we allowed your basket to change, though, we'd be capturing both the change in prices and the change in your behaviour. To focus on the price change alone, we have to keep the basket fixed, even though we know that is not entirely realistic. We'll come back to ways of dealing with this challenge later in the chapter. For now, the basket approach gives us a way to capture lots of different prices changes in a single number that (approximately) represents the purchases of a typical consumer.

Consumer Price Index

> **LO 8.2** Calculate and use a price index to measure changes in the cost of living over time.

The basket approach allows us to track changes in the cost of living. To summarize these changes, we construct a **price index**, which measures how much the cost of a market basket has risen or fallen relative to the cost in a base time period or location.

The most commonly used index tool for tracking changes in the cost of living in Canada is the **Consumer Price Index**, or **CPI**. The CPI tracks changes in the cost of a basket of goods and services purchased by a typical Canadian household. It is calculated by Statistics Canada, a statistical agency in the Canadian federal government, and the data is released monthly.

The method for calculating the CPI is relatively simple. First, Statistics Canada comes up with a basket of goods and services purchased by a typical household. Then, every month it collects data on the prices of those goods and services in a variety of places around the country. Using these data, Statistics Canada calculates the cost of buying that market basket.

The CPI measures the increase in the cost of the market basket relative to the cost in a given base year. For instance, suppose that the annual cost of the market basket was $40,000 in 2012 (the base year) and $40,400 in 2013. To find the index for 2013 relative to 2012, we use the following formula:

Equation 8-1

$$\text{CPI} = \frac{\text{cost of desired-year basket in base-year prices}}{\text{cost of base-year basket in base-year prices}} \times 100$$

$$= \left(\frac{\text{basket}_{\text{desired-year}}}{\text{basket}_{\text{base-year}}}\right) \times 100$$

$$= \left(\frac{\text{basket}_{2013}}{\text{basket}_{2012}}\right) \times 100$$

$$= \left(\frac{\$40,400}{\$40,000}\right) \times 100 = 101$$

In the base year, by definition, the index will always be 100. In future years, if the cost of the basket rises higher than that of the base year, the index will be more than 100. If the cost of the basket falls below the base-year cost, the index will be less than 100. In our example, with 2012 as the base year, the CPI increases from 100 to 101. This change indicates a 1 percent increase in the basket of consumer goods, which also means a 1 percent increase in the cost of living for a typical household.

Statistics Canada's stated goal for the CPI is to answer this question: What is the cost, at this month's market prices, of achieving the standard of living attained in the base period? In other words, the CPI helps us understand how the cost of living today compares with the cost of living at some time in the past. As Figure 8-1 shows, the CPI has risen consistently over the last hundred years.

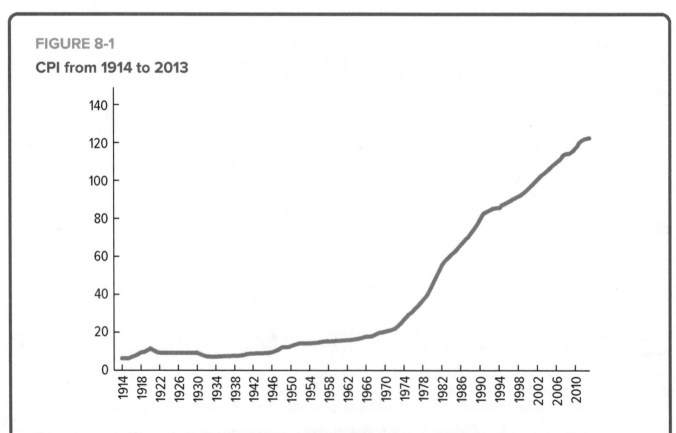

FIGURE 8-1

CPI from 1914 to 2013

Prices increased more dramatically in the second half of the last century than they did in the first half. Over the first fifty years, prices tripled. In 2013, prices were seven times greater than they were in 1966.

Source: Statistics Canada, CANSIM Table 326-0021, "Consumer Price Index, annual (2002=100)"

The Challenges in Measuring Price Changes

LO 8.3 Name the two main challenges Statistics Canada faces when measuring price changes and outline how it responds to these challenges.

The idea behind the CPI is straightforward, but turning that idea into reality requires addressing two big challenges. The first is to figure out which goods should go into the market basket so that the CPI reflects the average purchases of the widest group of people. The second challenge is how to measure changes over time. Take this simple question as an example: Is it a price increase if a computer costs 10 percent more but is also 10 percent faster? In this section, we'll address both of these challenges in turn.

FIGURE 8-2

Spending by Urban Consumers Represented in the CPI

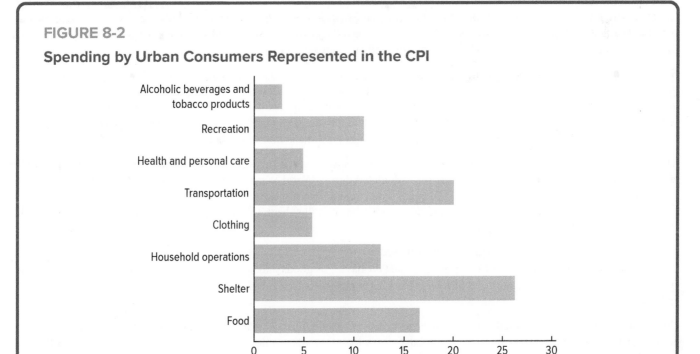

This bar chart shows how much prices in certain sectors are weighted in the calculation of the Consumer Price Index. By far, the largest component of the Consumer Price Index is shelter costs, at over 25 percent. The next two largest components are food and transportation, which together make up over a third of the CPI. The rest of the categories together comprise the final quarter.

Source: Statistics Canada, Table 1, "Consumer Price Index and major components, Canada--not seasonally adjusted"
http://www.statcan.gc.ca/daily-quotidien/140919/t140919a001-eng.htm.

Which Goods?

The first question is, *which goods* should go into the market basket to measure price changes? Your next-door neighbour may love carrots and you may love beef. As a result, your grocery bills will probably look very different and will increase at different rates as the prices of carrots and beef change. There is no way to have a single number that perfectly describes changes in the cost of living for everyone because people buy different things. The best we can do is to come up with a basket that tries to represent a *typical* household.

Who is typical? The CPI is based on an average of the goods and services purchased by *urban consumers*—anyone living in a city of 100,000 or more. This accounts for 69 percent of the Canadian population and includes people in all sorts of jobs as well as unemployed and retired people. It doesn't, however, include people living in rural areas, members of the military, or the institutionalized population (mostly people living in prisons or mental hospitals).

The CPI tries to balance out the consumption of different types of people in different life stages and situations. Rather than representing the exact consumption of any particular household, it is an average across a very large group of Canadian consumers. A particular family's cost of living might increase more or less than the CPI, depending on exactly how much of which things the family buys. Figure 8-2 shows the breakdown of spending in 2011 in the average urban-consumer household across eight major categories.

Changes Over Time: Substitution and Innovation

Earlier, we noted that a price index like the CPI measures pure price changes only if the types and quantities of goods in the market basket remain constant. However, there is an accuracy trade-off involved. Keeping the basket fixed accurately isolates price changes from behaviour changes. However, when real people's behaviour has changed enough, keeping the basket fixed also means that it will no longer accurately represent the consumption of a typical household. Price indexes also have to deal with the fact that, as tastes and prices change, households tend to buy different goods and services. There are two main reasons for changes in consumption patterns over time—substitution and innovation.

Substitution is the idea that people switch between similar goods and services when relative prices shift. If the price of carrots goes up by 25 percent while the prices of other vegetables increase by a smaller amount, people will tend to buy fewer carrots and more other vegetables. If the price of going out to the movies goes up and the price of streaming video goes down, people will tend to watch more videos at home and fewer at the movie theatre. If the market basket doesn't reflect the fact that people buy less of particular goods as they get more expensive, it will overstate actual changes in the cost of living.

The second reason the market basket has to change over time is *innovation:* as new goods and services become available, people change what they consume. When the CPI was first calculated during World War I, for example, it did not include refrigerators, washing machines, telephones, computers, and many other goods that almost all households today purchase at one time or another. Some of these things couldn't be bought at any price because they hadn't been invented. Others existed but hadn't made it into the general consumer market yet.

Statistics Canada does occasionally update the basket used to calculate the CPI, to account both for substitution and new products. These updates undermine the idea of comparing a *constant* basket of goods and services. But the underlying aim is to capture the cost of achieving a certain *standard of living.* Creating a basket that balances these competing goals requires some tricky judgment calls.

Similar judgment calls are required when products get better. For example, cars today are far safer, more reliable, and offer more features than in the 1950s. So if cars are more expensive now than they were in the 1950s, how do we tease apart the fact that the price of the basic product has increased from the fact that car quality is now higher?

If a higher price represents higher quality, the true cost of living may not actually have increased. Think about the reverse situation. Suppose that the price of a car stayed the same, but its features improved. We would say that the cost of living has fallen, because you are able to achieve higher well-being for the same price. In the same sense, if the price of the car increases as its features improve, the cost of living may actually be constant, as you pay more but also achieve greater well-being. The question is how we weigh the quality change against the price change. In trying to make these judgment calls, Statistics Canada has to attempt something called *hedonic quality adjustment.* It tries to estimate what the price of the item would be *without* the improved features.

As you might guess, the nitty-gritty of coming up with a CPI figure every month involves detailed calculations, performed by an army of data collectors visiting or calling tens of thousands of stores in thirty-three cities. Google has recently come up with a less precise but much simpler approach using Internet searches to find prices. Read about it in the Real Life box, The Google Price Index.

REAL LIFE

The Google Price Index

One day, Hal Varian's favorite pepper grinder broke. He headed to Google Shopping, a search function that allows shoppers to browse the web for the best deals, to look for a new grinder. But Varian was quickly distracted from his quest by the realization that Google could be used to collect an immense amount of data on prices.

Varian had stumbled into a gold mine of economic data. Suddenly he lost interest in his pepper grinder. In his words, "The first thing I wanted to do was create a price index." Conveniently, as Google's chief economist, he was uniquely well situated to turn his vision into reality. In October 2010, he announced that Google was working on a Google Price Index (GPI) that would measure changes in the cost of living using pricing data found on the Internet.

✓ CONCEPT CHECK

- ☐ What is the purpose of a market basket? [LO 8.1]
- ☐ What is a price index? [LO 8.2]
- ☐ Does the CPI show price changes for people living in rural areas? [LO 8.3]
- ☐ Name the two challenges that complicate the calculation of inflation? [LO 8.3]

Using Price Indexes

Now that we know how to measure price changes over time, what do we *do* with that knowledge? As we saw with GDP in the last chapter, many economic variables give an incomplete picture when expressed in nominal terms—that is, without accounting for price differences. To solve this problem, we can use price indexes to turn nominal variables into real ones. With price indexes, we can isolate changes in prices from changes in fundamentals like income and output and express those changes in constant dollars relative to a base year. The **inflation rate**, the size of the change in the overall price level, is one of the central concepts in macroeconomics. In this section we'll discuss how to calculate the inflation rate and how to use it.

The Inflation Rate

LO 8.4 Calculate the inflation rate by three methods and adjust nominal variables into real variables using a price index.

The inflation rate is the percent change in the CPI from year to year. Using the CPI method, the inflation rate is calculated as follows:

Equation 8-2

$$\text{Inflation rate} = \left[\frac{(\text{CPI}_{year2} - \text{CPI}_{year1})}{\text{CPI}_{year1}} \right] \times 100$$

Table 8-2 shows increases in the CPI from 2005 to 2011, using 2002 as the base year. If we want to know how much prices have increased since the base year, the change in the CPI provides a direct answer. For instance, the 2005 CPI of 107 means that price levels in 2005 were 7 percent higher than they were in the base year, 2002.

TABLE 8-2   CALCULATING THE INFLATION RATE

To calculate the inflation rate, subtract the CPI of the previous year from the current year, divided by the CPI of the previous year. In most years, prices have increased, but in 2009, inflation was close to zero.

Year	CPI	Calculation	Inflation rate (%)
2005	107	—	
2006	109.1	$\dfrac{109.1 - 107}{107} \times 100$	1.96
2007	111.5	$\dfrac{111.5 - 109.1}{109.1} \times 100$	2.2
2008	114.1	$\dfrac{114.1 - 111.5}{111.5} \times 100$	2.33
2009	114.4	$\dfrac{114.4 - 114.1}{114.1} \times 100$	0.26
2010	116.5	$\dfrac{116.5 - 114.4}{114.4} \times 100$	1.84
2011	119.9	$\dfrac{119.9 - 116.5}{116.5} \times 100$	2.92

Source: Statistics Canada, CANSIM Table 326-0020 "Consumer Price Index monthly (2002=100)".

But what if we want to compare 2006 to 2005, rather than to 2002? When you read about inflation in the news, it is typically expressed as an increase over the previous year. We can calculate the percent increase in prices from year to year as follows:

$$\text{Inflation rate}_{2006} = \left[\frac{(CPI_{2006} - CPI_{2005})}{CPI_{2005}} \right] \times 100$$

$$= \left[\frac{(109.1 - 107)}{107} \right] \times 100 = 1.96\%$$

An inflation rate of 1.96 percent means that the overall price level increased at that rate between 2005 and 2006.

If you follow news reports about the economy, you may hear discussion of two different inflation measures—all-items inflation and core inflation:

- *All-items inflation* measures the changes in prices for the entire market basket of the average urban consumer. It's just another term for inflation measured using the CPI.

- *Core inflation* measures price changes using eight of the CPI's most volatile components (mostly related to energy and food) taken out of the basket.

Why use both the all-items and core measures? Compared to many goods, energy and food prices go up and down a lot. Because they might be very high or very low at the time the CPI is calculated, including them might over- or understate the real change in overall prices. On the other hand, most Canadians spend a large part of their income on food and gas. Any basket that does not include these goods is missing a large part of the cost-of-living picture. Looking at both all-items and core inflation can give us a more accurate sense of what's really happening in the economy.

The difference between the all-items and core measurements suggests a more general idea: we can measure inflation using any basket of goods or price index we want. The resulting measures of inflation will reflect changes in the prices of different sets of goods. The CPI focuses on prices paid by consumers.

An alternative price index, the *Producer Price Index (PPI),* measures the prices of goods and services purchased by firms. The PPI includes things that are not part of the typical person's consumption basket, such as industrial machinery. Because increases in input prices eventually make it to consumers when they buy the final product, the PPI is considered a good predictor of future consumer prices. Regardless of the index we use, inflation is measured as a *percent increase in the index from one year to the next.*

A third option is to calculate the inflation rate using the *GDP deflator,* as we did in the previous chapter. The GDP deflator measures price changes for *everything produced in the country.* It doesn't, however, include goods produced abroad that might have a real effect on the typical household's cost of living, such as imported food items. Another key difference is that the GDP deflator is computed using the actual quantities that are produced in the economy each year, rather than using a fixed basket of goods.

All three measures of inflation—CPI, PPI, and GDP deflator—are useful; they simply measure different things. In practice, inflation rates calculated using the three methods track each other quite closely.

Deflating Nominal Variables

Often, we want to study how the real value of a variable, such as income, has changed over time. To do this, we can use the CPI (or another price index) to *deflate* the nominal variable and state it in constant, real terms.

You might be shocked if your grandparents told you how much money they made in their younger days. For instance, in 1976, a salary of $28,454 would have allowed your grandparents to live a comfortable life, send their kids to university, and put away a little for retirement. In 2013, that income would be very little for a family of four.

Suppose we want to know how much money your grandparents would have to earn now to have purchasing power equivalent to their income in 1976. We can translate nominal income in any past year into constant, real dollars to allow us to compare changes in purchasing power over time. Equation 8-3 shows how any dollar amount from the past can be translated into its current value (i.e., the value of year X income in year Y dollars).

Equation 8-3

$$\text{Real value}_{\text{year Y}} = \text{nominal value}_{\text{year X}} \times \left(\frac{\text{CPI}_{\text{year Y}}}{\text{CPI}_{\text{year X}}}\right)$$

Let's apply this equation to find the purchasing power of $28,454 in 2011 dollars. We multiply $28,454 by the ratio of the CPI in 2011 and 1976 to find the value of 1976 income in 2011 dollars, as shown in Equation 8-3a:

Equation 8-3a

$$\text{Real value}_{2011} = \text{nominal value}_{1976} \times \left(\frac{\text{CPI}_{2011}}{\text{CPI}_{1976}}\right)$$

$$= \$28,454 \times \left(\frac{119.9}{31.1}\right)$$

$$= \$109,700$$

What does this result mean? It means that the goods and services your grandparents were able to buy with $28,454 in 1976 cost $109,700 in 2011. It turns out that they were doing pretty well, after all.

We can make this same calculation using any base year and any nominal variable. For instance, suppose we want to know how much of the increase in the income of the wealthy is attributable to inflation and how much it represents an increase in real wealth. The first two columns of Table 8-3 show average income for the top 20 percent of the population in nominal terms. The third column shows the CPI for each decade. The fourth column uses the CPI to translate income into a direct comparison of purchasing power in 2011 dollars. This shows that although the cost of living has increased, the income of the wealthiest 20 percent of Canadians has increased faster. In other words, increased nominal incomes are partly due to inflation and partly due to a real increase in purchasing power.

TABLE 8-3   CALCULATING THE DEFLATION OF NOMINAL VARIABLES

The average income of those living in 1976 looks much lower than in 2011. When 1976 incomes are inflated so that the value of these dollars is the same between the two decades, the gap decreases dramatically.

Year	Average income of top 20 percent ($)	CPI (2002 = 100)	Value in 2011 dollars
1976	28,454	31.1	$28,454 \times \left(\frac{119.9}{31.1}\right) = \$109,700$
1981	43,926	49.5	$43,926 \times \left(\frac{119.9}{49.5}\right) = \$106,400$
1991	71,198	82.8	$71,198 \times \left(\frac{119.9}{82.8}\right) = \$103,100$
2001	101,715	97.8	$101,715 \times \left(\frac{119.9}{97.8}\right) = \$124,700$
2011	139,400	119.9	$139,400

Inflation adjustment can make a huge difference in how we perceive things that happen *now* relative to things that happened *in the past*.

Adjusting for Inflation: Indexing

How can we be sure that wages will keep up with inflation? One fundamental theory in macroeconomics says that, with enough time, wages should naturally rise to offset the effects of inflation, so in the end inflation should not matter to people's well-being and their choices.

However, most economists agree that there are times when some prices are changing so fast that the rest of the economy struggles to keep up. If prices increase faster than wages, for instance, people will experience a drop in their standard of living. Everyone will face a very strong incentive to buy things *now* if they are afraid prices will be higher next week or next month. Inflation can then distort economic choices. We'll talk a lot more about problems like these later in the book, particularly in the chapter about inflation. For now, let's look at how *measuring* inflation can be an important step toward solving problems that inflation causes.

One very practical application of the CPI is to index payments to inflation. In Canada, the first pension benefit came in 1927 for British subjects aged seventy years and older who had lived in Canada for at least twenty years and in their current province of residence for five years. These citizens were entitled to a maximum of $20 a month ($20 in 1927 dollars is about $270 today). A "means test" was also in place to determine eligibility, and the benefits stayed constant. In 1951 the Liberals passed the Old Age Security Act. It replaced the old age pension system by establishing a universal pension plan that paid a monthly benefit of $40.

In the early years of social insurance, no accommodation was made for inflation. Retirees expected to receive the same nominal dollar amount monthly for the rest of their lives. It assumed most elderly Canadians had other sources of savings, since the monthly benefits fell well below the amount needed for basic necessities.

From 1951 to 1966, government adjusted the benefits every few years. Each time, it increased the level of benefits in accord with the cost of living. However, these increases were sporadic and required a concerted effort on the part of lawmakers. Then, in 1966, government implemented a different solution: indexing. **Indexing** automatically increases payments in proportion to the cost of living (to a maximum of 2 percent per year). Such payments are said to be *indexed to inflation.* Government indexes all Social Security benefits directly to the CPI. If the CPI increases 2 percent, so does the nominal value of monthly benefits. As a result, the dollar amount of benefits has increased most years since 1966, keeping pace with changes in the cost of living.

Indexed payments are usually referred to as *cost-of-living adjustments,* or COLAs. In Canada, few salaries or income payments are indexed to inflation (except for those with union contracts, where they are more common), but Social Security does have a COLA and affects millions of retirees. Indexing is much more common in other countries. In much of Europe, government employees' salaries receive automatic COLAs, as do retirees' pensions.

The reasoning behind indexing is straightforward: if you want the real value of a payment to stay constant over time, make the adjustment for inflation automatic. The alternative is to rewrite a law or a contract every year—a process that involves more work and less certainty. However, indexing is not uncontroversial. To consider some reasons why COLAs can be a mixed blessing, read the What Do You Think? box, COLAs for Better or Worse.

WHAT DO YOU THINK?

COLAs for Better or Worse

Cost-of-living adjustments (COLAs) provide increases in payments to offset inflation that occurred in the past year. Without an adjustment for the cost of living, what you could buy with a given wage or social security cheque would shrink steadily. Inflation would eat away at the value of these payments.

Traditionally, COLAs for the people who receive social security have been pegged to the CPI All-Items Index. This is the most widely used indicator of price changes in Canada. Some argue that the government should shift to a method more sensitive to the actual spending patterns of the elderly, who buy different things than average households. One proposed alternative is a measure that uses a price basket geared to elderly consumers. In this alternative, for example, health and personal care would represent more of the total, compared with their current lower weight in CPI.

There often are calls for COLAs to be applied to the minimum wage. Although the cost of living goes up every year, the 2013 average minimum wage in Canada of $10.14 per hour was almost identical to the average minimum wage of $10.13 (2013 dollars) in 1975. In other words, increases in the minimum wage have not kept up with prices. The result is that the real value of the minimum wage has remained the same since the 1970s.

✓ CONCEPT CHECK

☐ What are the three main measures of inflation? [LO 8.4]

☐ How does Social Security adjust payments based on changes to the cost of living? [LO 8.4]

Accounting for Price Differences Across Places

So far, we've seen how to capture the fact that our grandparents paid less for a loaf of bread than we do today. Now, how do we capture the fact that a loaf of bread today costs less in Mexico than in the United States? Or, indeed, that a loaf of bread costs less in Iowa City than in New York City? Just as we need to adjust economic variables for price changes over time, we sometimes need a tool that allows us to adjust for differences in prices across locations.

An idea called *purchasing power parity* enables us to compare the true cost of living in various locations. Here is how it works.

Purchasing Power Parity

> **LO 8.5** Explain purchasing power parity.

In theory, goods ought to cost the same everywhere, once they have been translated into a common currency using foreign exchange rates. To see why, imagine a pair of jeans that costs less in Mexico than in the United States. Wouldn't entrepreneurs travel from the US to Mexico, convert their dollars into pesos, buy the jeans, take them back to the US, and sell them for a profit?

In principle, yes. These entrepreneurs will continue until the increased quantity of jeans supplied in the US and the increased quantity demand in Mexico causes the prices in the two countries to equalize. At that point, no one has an incentive to buy jeans abroad. The result is that purchasing power should theoretically be the same everywhere, when stated in a common currency. This idea is called **purchasing power parity (PPP)**.

In reality, PPP almost never holds exactly. Overall price levels are lower in Mexico. For most goods, $100 exchanged into pesos buys you more in Mexico than $100 would buy you in the US. Why? There are three main factors: transaction costs, non-tradable goods and services, and trade restrictions. Let's briefly consider them.

- **Transaction costs:** One reason that PPP doesn't hold is transportation costs. It costs money to move goods from place to place. However, the difference in PPP is usually larger than what would be explained by transport costs alone. There are other transaction costs; for example, it costs time and money to find sellers in another country. If the price difference is small and the costs of making transactions in another country are high, the *trade-off* involved may not be worth it, and those entrepreneurs will decide not to bring cheap jeans in from Mexico.
- **Non-tradables:** Some goods and services just can't be taken from place to place very easily, or at all. For instance, you can't buy an apartment in Iowa City and transport it to Manhattan. You can't buy a pizza in Italy and transport it to North Dakota. (Well, you could, but it wouldn't be worth eating when you got it there.) You can't buy a haircut in India if you live in New Orleans. (Of course, you could fly to India to get your hair cut, but the transaction costs would be extremely high relative to the few bucks you'd save.) These types of goods and services are called *non-tradables*.
- **Trade restrictions:** Finally, international trade isn't free. There are often tariffs and trade restrictions that increase the cost or difficulty of making exchanges across national borders. Such restrictions discourage people from fully taking advantage of lower prices in other countries.

For these three reasons, we frequently see substantially different prices for individual goods and services, and different overall price levels, across countries or locations within a country. For example, the purchasing power of a dollar is higher in Mexico than in the US and lower in Switzerland. If we want to compare incomes or costs across different countries, we're going to need to adjust nominal prices; this is similar to what we do when comparing standards of living in different time periods. To compare prices in different places, economists have developed the idea of purchasing power indexes.

Purchasing Power Indexes

> **LO 8.6** Use a price index to calculate PPP-adjusted variables and compare the cost of living across different places.

Just as we can use a price index to account for changes in prices over time, we can also construct a price index that describes differences in prices across locations. The methodology is quite similar. First, we need to find a market basket of goods and services that we can compare across countries. Next, we measure the price of the goods in the basket in each country, and calculate the overall cost of purchasing it in each country. Then, we build an index showing how much the basket costs in each country relative to some base.

FIGURE 8-3

The Big Mac Index

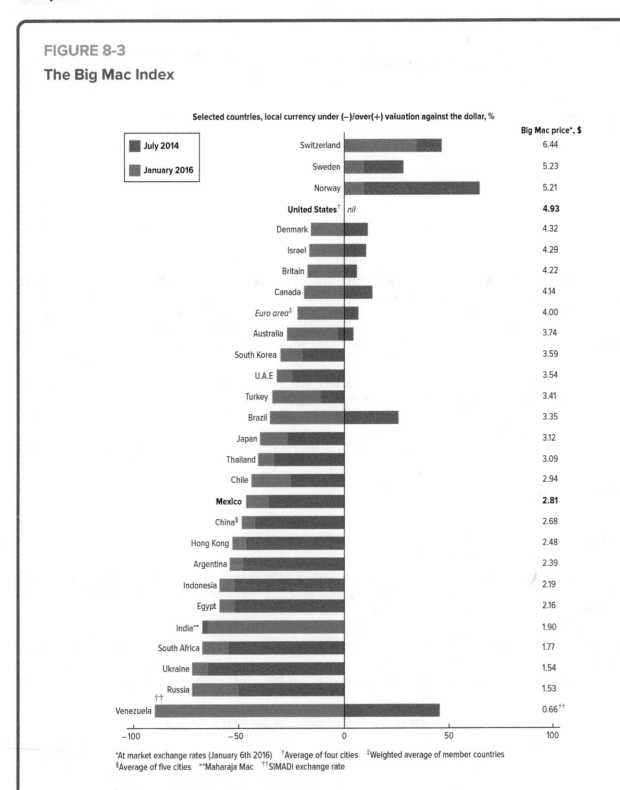

Selected countries, local currency under (−)/over(+) valuation against the dollar, %

	Big Mac price*, $
Switzerland	6.44
Sweden	5.23
Norway	5.21
United States[†] *nil*	**4.93**
Denmark	4.32
Israel	4.29
Britain	4.22
Canada	4.14
Euro area[‡]	4.00
Australia	3.74
South Korea	3.59
U.A.E	3.54
Turkey	3.41
Brazil	3.35
Japan	3.12
Thailand	3.09
Chile	2.94
Mexico	**2.81**
China[§]	2.68
Hong Kong	2.48
Argentina	2.39
Indonesia	2.19
Egypt	2.16
India**	1.90
South Africa	1.77
Ukraine	1.54
Russia	1.53
Venezuela[††]	0.66[††]

Legend: July 2014, January 2016

Axis: −100   −50   0   50   100

*At market exchange rates (January 6th 2016)   [†]Average of four cities   [‡]Weighted average of member countries
[§]Average of five cities   **Maharaja Mac   [††]SIMADI exchange rate

The Big Mac Index is one way to measure differences in purchasing power across countries. According to the index, China and other countries in Asia, including Malaysia and Thailand, have a low cost of living. Rich countries generally have costs of living that are similar to the US or even higher.

Source: The Big Mac Index © The Economist Newspaper Limited, London (January 9, 2016). Used with permission.

For a simple example, let's think about the price of Big Macs around the world. The *Economist* magazine measures these prices in 120 countries in what it calls the Big Mac Index. The Big Mac isn't a basket that represents the full cost of living, of course. But it has the advantage of being similar in each country, due to McDonald's international production and sourcing policies. It also requires a variety of inputs, such as beef, bread, lettuce, labour, advertising, and real estate.

The Big Mac Index takes the United States as the base country and compares the cost of a Big Mac there to the cost in another country. In the US, the price of a Big Mac in 2012 was $4.20; in Mexico it was 37 pesos. If the theory of purchasing power parity held true, Big Macs would have the same real price in the US and Mexico. In that case, the exchange rate between dollars and pesos should be 8.81 pesos per dollar (37 pesos = $4.20). In reality, the official exchange rate between pesos and dollars was 13.68 pesos per dollar. We can calculate the Big Mac Index by comparing the official exchange rate (13.68) to the exchange rate predicted by PPP (8.81):

$$\text{Big Mac Index for Mexico} = \frac{(8.81 - 13.68) \times 100}{13.68}$$

$$= \frac{-4.87 \times 100}{13.68} = -36\%$$

What does a negative Big Mac Index for Mexico tell us? It means that price levels in Mexico are lower than we'd expect if PPP held true. As a result, real purchasing power is higher in Mexico than it is in the US. If you exchange your dollars for pesos, they'll go further at a McDonald's in Mexico than at one in the US. A positive Big Mac Index (as in expensive countries, like Norway and Australia) would imply that price levels are higher than predicted by PPP. Therefore, real purchasing power is lower in such places than in the U.S. Figure 8-3 shows how price levels differ across a number of countries, using the United States as the base level.

The Big Mac Index is a simple way of looking at price differences. The main measure actually used for international price comparisons is the World Bank's International Comparison Program (ICP) index. It uses a broad market basket that tries to represent the full cost of living across countries. The question is how to construct that market basket. People in different places consume different things depending on their culture, climate, religion, and so on. As a result, it's impossible to create a market basket that is "typical" everywhere. The methods behind the PPP are still being improved, but for now, even imperfect PPP data is better than no data at all.

PPP-Adjustment

Suppose that we are comparing GDP per capita around the world. What we want from this statistic is some sense of the differences in the average standard of living across countries. If the cost of living varies, the nominal level of GDP per capita will actually mean very different things in different countries.

PPP-adjustment involves recalculating economic statistics to account for differences in price levels across countries. When we do this, we say that we are calculating *PPP-adjusted* variables. PPP-adjustment using a price index is quite similar to adjusting for cost of living increases using a price index like the CPI.

For example, let's calculate PPP-adjusted GDP per capita in the United States and Mexico. In 2011, nominal GDP per capita in the US was $48,442; in Mexico it was $10,064. According to the World Bank's PPP index, the purchasing power of a given amount of dollars was about 34.4 percent lower in the United States. In other words, on average, in Mexico goods and services cost about 34.4 percent less than they do in the US. (Notice that this number is similar to what we found using the Big Max Index.)

To find PPP-adjusted GDP per capita of any country relative to the US, we can use Equation 8-4.

Equation 8-4

$$\text{PPP-adjusted GDP} = \text{nominal dollars}_{\text{country A}} \times \left[\frac{1}{\left(1 - \text{price-level adjustment}_{\text{country A}}\right)}\right]$$

We can plug the numbers for Mexico into this equation:

Equation 8-4a

$$\text{PPP-adjusted GDP} = \$10{,}064 \times \left[\frac{1}{1 - 0.344}\right]$$

$$= \$10{,}064 \times 1.5244 = \$15{,}341.56$$

If we looked only at the nominal figure, we might think that the average person in Mexico has a standard of living comparable to someone earning $10,064 in the US. In reality, as the PPP-adjusted figure shows us, the average Mexican lives about as well as someone who earns $15,340 in the US. PPP-adjustment gives us a more realistic sense of differences in living standards around the world. In general, price levels are lower in poorer countries, so PPP-adjustment lets us see that poorer countries are not quite so poor as suggested by their nominal GDP per capita.

Making international comparisons of purchasing power is not straightforward. This is especially true when trying to get a realistic sense of how the living standards of the world's poorest citizens translate into dollar terms. The much-quoted "dollar-a-day" figure for international poverty comes from the World Bank's attempts to figure out the true purchasing power of the poor. For insight into some of the challenges with this measure, and how economists are tackling them, read the Real Life box, Counting the Poor, Give or Take 400 Million.

REAL LIFE

Counting the Poor, Give or Take 400 million

What can you buy for $1.25 in your town? Maybe some gum, or a chocolate bar, or a few vegetables at the grocery store. Could you live on US$1.25 a day? It's probably pretty difficult to imagine. Yet an estimated 1.3 billion people around the world do live on this amount, or less. It is the current level of the World Bank's *absolute poverty measure,* the most common measure of international poverty. As shorthand, it's usually referred to as the *dollar-a-day poverty measure.*

If you've travelled to low-income countries you'll know that prices are very different than in the United States. Some-times, $1.25 (converted into local currency) can buy you lunch in a nice café, or even some clothes. But that $1.25 poverty measure is actually already adjusted for PPP. In other words, it measures the equivalent of what $1.25 *would buy in the United States* (that chocolate bar or a few vegetables).

It's hard to believe that over a billion people in the world are trying to survive on the equivalent of what $1.25 would buy in the US. Could there be something wrong with how we adjust the incomes of the poor in local currencies to get to that figure in US dollars?

Economists Angus Deaton and Olivier Dupriez think so. They argue that rather than calculating the cost of living for typical households in a country, we need to determine what the typical *poor* household buys and use this basket of goods to get a meaningful estimate of the cost of living for the poor. They call this the *poverty-weighted purchasing power parity index*—also known as PPPP, or simply P4.

By grounding poverty estimates in more realistic data, Deaton and Dupriez say, we can better understand the poor's cost of living. Due to spotty information about housing costs, for example, the World Bank underestimated global poverty figures by about 400 million people in 2005. When figuring out who lives on less than a dollar per day, it turns out that the cost of living is an important part of the calculation.

✓ CONCEPT CHECK

☐ How can transaction costs partially explain differences in purchasing power parity? [LO 8.5]

☐ What does the Big Mac Index show? [LO 8.5]

☐ Why do economists adjust international statistics based on purchasing power? [LO 8.6]

Conclusion

What can a dollar buy? The answer today is not the same as it will be next year, and it's not the same in Calgary as it is in Thunder Bay. The result is that a nominal dollar amount in a particular time or place is just part of the answer. What we really care about is the *purchasing power* of that dollar amount. That's what determines how much you can buy at the store.

In this chapter, we've developed tools that allow us to track changes in the overall price level. These tools help us understand how the purchasing power of a dollar changes over time and across locations. Using the cost of a constant market basket allows us to construct a price index that shows relative price levels over time, such as the CPI.

Using price indexes, we can adjust economic variables such as wages, income, GDP, and interest rates to see the difference between their nominal and real values. This lets us answer questions like, "What would today's salaries have bought in our grandparents' time?" It can also help us make better choices when deciding how to invest money, write contracts, or set up policies that account for the effects of inflation.

This chapter and the previous one have introduced the basic language and metrics of macroeconomics. We've discussed output and prices, and how to measure the both the size of an economy and the cost of living there. In the next chapter, we'll move on to one of the most central questions in macroeconomics: Why are some countries richer than others, and how does a country grow richer?

Key Terms

market basket

price index

Consumer Price Index (CPI)

inflation rate

indexing

purchasing power parity

PPP-adjustment

Summary

LO 8.1 Define a market basket, and explain its importance in tracking price changes.

To understand how the overall cost of living has increased, we need a way to measure the combined change in the prices of multiple goods, whose individual prices may be changing at different rates. To accomplish this, we can construct a market basket that includes specific goods and services in fixed quantities. By keeping goods and quantities constant, we can be sure that any change in the total cost of the basket is caused by a change in prices, rather than the type or amount of things being consumed.

LO 8.2 Calculate and use a price index to measure changes in the cost of living over time.

To summarize changes in price levels, we can construct a price index, which measures how much the cost of a market basket has risen or fallen relative to the cost in the base year or location. The most commonly used tool for measuring the cost of living in Canada is the Consumer Price Index, or CPI. It tracks the cost of a basket of goods and services that is representative of the purchases of Canadian households. The price index in a given year is equal to the ratio of the cost of the market basket in that year to the cost in the base year, multiplied by 100. In the base year, the index will always be 100. In future years, if the price of the basket rises, the index will be more than 100. If the price of the basket falls below that in the base year, the index will be less than 100. An index of 120 implies a 20 percent increase in price levels over the base year.

LO 8.3 Name the two main challenges Statistics Canada faces when measuring price changes and outline how Statistics Canada responds to these challenges.

Statistics Canada faces two major challenges in constructing a basket: how to decide which consumption should be measured and how to account for changes in consumption over time. To deal with the first challenge, the CPI is based on an average of the goods and services purchased by urban consumers. It also presents two broad measures of this basket: all-items inflation (another term for the CPI) and core inflation. Core inflation measures price changes for the CPI market basket, but with food and energy costs taken out. Removing those costs may miss a large part of the inflation picture.

The second challenge comes from changes to consumption and products over time. If the market basket doesn't change to reflect the substitutions consumers make as prices change, it will overstate the effect due to the rising prices. Finally, in trying to measure changes in the standard of living, economists need to tease out differences between mere changes in prices of products versus changes in quality as a result of innovation and technological advances.

LO 8.4 Calculate the inflation rate by three methods and adjust nominal variables into real variables using a price index.

The inflation rate describes the size of changes in the overall price level year to year, calculated by measuring the percent change in a price index from one year to the next. Inflation estimates based on the CPI include price changes in imported consumer goods. Estimates based on the PPI measure the prices of goods and services purchased by firms and may predict future increases in consumer prices. Estimates based on the GDP deflator exclude imports but include domestically produced items that are not part of the typical person's consumption basket. In practice, inflation rates based on the CPI, PPI, and GDP deflator track each other quite closely.

One of the most important applications of price indexes is the ability to be able to determine the purchasing power of money from a different time period. This enables us to see the value of what a certain amount of dollars from the past could buy today, or how much a certain amount of dollars today would have been be worth in the past. Indexing is an important application of the need to adjust nominal values into their real purchasing power. Recognizing that the purchasing power of money changes over time, payments and paycheques can be indexed to inflation, so that their purchasing power stays equal even as prices change.

LO 8.5   Explain purchasing power parity.

Purchasing power parity (PPP) is the idea that price levels in different countries should be the same, once they have been stated in a common currency. For a number of reasons—including transaction costs, non-tradable goods and services, and trade restrictions—PPP doesn't typically hold true; the real purchasing power of a dollar differs from place to place.

LO 8.6   Use a price index to calculate PPP-adjusted variables and compare the cost of living across different places.

When we recalculate economic variables to account for differences in purchasing power across countries, we say that we are calculating PPP-adjusted variables. To measure this difference in purchasing power, we can calculate a price index by comparing the cost of purchasing a market basket in each country. If the cost of living is lower than the base country, then PPP-adjusted GDP will be higher than nominal GDP. If the cost of living is higher than the base country, then PPP-adjusted GDP will be lower than nominal GDP.

Review Questions

1. If we want to look at changes in the cost of living, why don't we track differences in each household's *actual* expenditures from one year to the next, rather than a market basket? Offer several reasons why this method would fail to capture changes in the overall price level accurately. [LO 8.1]

2. There are many different types of market baskets that economists measure. For example, the market basket for consumers—called the Consumer Price Index—tracks the prices associated with the typical consumer's purchases of goods and services. The Producer Price Index tracks the prices that firms receive when selling their goods and services. A third type of market basket is the Home Price Index, which tracks the value of residential housing. In what scenarios would each of these market baskets be useful? [LO 8.1]

3. Why is the top of the list of the highest-grossing films of all times dominated by movies made within the last ten years? (*Hint:* Did *The Dark Knight,* made in 2008, really sell considerably more movie tickets than the classic *Gone with the Wind,* or is something else going on?) [LO 8.2]

4. How would you use the idea of the Consumer Price Index to compare prices across distances? [LO 8.2]

5. What type of price index would a basket measuring the inflation rate for farmers include? Why doesn't Statistics Canada calculate the price levels for a market basket approximating the purchases of farmers? [LO 8.3]

6. Does the CPI represent the actual change in the cost of living for any given household? Explain why or why not. [LO 8.3]

7. Suppose wages rise in China, leading to an increase in the price of toys imported from China. How would this change affect CPI, PPI, and the GDP deflator in Canada differently? [LO 8.4]

8. If the growth rate in income was larger than the inflation rate (as measured by the change in CPI or GDP deflator), has the real value of income grown? [LO 8.4]

9. What is the better measure of inflation to determine how much should be paid to employees for cost-of-living adjustments, the Producer Price Index (PPI) or the CPI? Why? [LO 8.4]

10. Why are people unlikely to buy Big Macs in the places where they are relatively cheap, according to purchasing power parity, and sell them where they are relatively more expensive, in order to make a profit? [LO 8.5]

11. In many poor countries even middle-class families may have full-time servants, a luxury reserved for only the very wealthiest households in rich countries like Canada. How does the existence of low-cost domestic help affect PPP-adjusted GDP statistics in poor countries? [LO 8.5], [LO 8.6]

12. Would a province with a very low cost of living, have a PPP-adjusted GDP higher or lower than its GDP calculated without PPP-adjustment? Why? [LO 8.6]

Problems and Applications

1. Subscribing to the theory that life is, indeed, a beach, the residents of La Playa spend all of their money on three things: every year, they collectively buy 250 bathing suits, 600 tubes of sunscreen, and 400 beach towels. Using the data in Table 8P-1, calculate: [LO 8.1]
    a. The total cost of this basket each year from 2006 through 2009
    b. How much the price of this basket has changed from year to year in percentage terms

TABLE 8P-1

Item (amount purchased)	Price 2006 ($)	Price 2007 ($)	Price 2008 ($)	Price 2009 ($)
Bathing suits (250)	10.00	12.00	15.00	18.00
Sunscreen (600)	4.00	5.00	5.00	6.00
Beach towels (400)	5.00	5.50	7.00	9.00
Total cost of basket				
Price increase from year before	—			

2. Suppose a typical Canadian consumer purchases three goods, creatively named Good A, Good B, and Good C. The prices of these goods are listed in Table 8P-2. [LO 8.1]
   a. If the typical consumer purchases two units of each good, what was the percentage increase in the price paid by the consumer for this basket between 2011 and 2012?
   b. If the typical consumer purchases 10 units of Good B and 2 units of both Good A and Good C, what was the percentage increase in the price paid by the consumer for this basket?
   c. Given your answers to (a) and (b), what is the relationship between the market basket and the percentage price change?

TABLE 8P-2

Good	Price in 2011 ($)	Price in 2012 ($)
A	10	15
B	5	4
C	1	2

3. Using the data in Table 8P-3, calculate the CPI in each year, using 2005 as the base year. [LO 8.2]

TABLE 8P-3

Year	Cost of basket ($)	CPI	Percent change in CPI
2005	20,000	100	—
2006	21,500		
2007	22,800		

Year	Cost of basket ($)	CPI	Percent change in CPI
2008	26,150		
2009	28,825		
2010	32,700		

4. Table 8P-4 lists the prices and quantities consumed of three different goods from 2010 to 2012. [LO 8.2]
   a. Calculate how much money the typical consumer pays each year to purchase the quantities listed in the table.
   b. Using the amounts you found in part (a), calculate the percentage change in how much the consumer paid from 2010 to 2011, and from 2011 to 2012.
   c. Why is it problematic to use your answers to part (b) as a measure of inflation?
   d. Suppose we take 2010 as the base year, which implies that the market basket is fixed at the consumption levels of 2010. Now find the rate of inflation from 2010 to 2011 and from 2011 to 2012.
   e. Repeat the exercise from part (d), now assuming that the base year is 2011.
   f. Why were your answers from parts (d) and (e) different?

TABLE 8P-4

	2010		2011		2012	
Good	Price ($)	Quantity	Price ($)	Quantity	Price ($)	Quantity
A	10	10	15	8	20	5
B	5	18	3	30	4	25
C	1	10	2	5	5	10

5. Which of the following goods have likely required hedonic price adjustment over time if they were included in the Consumer Price Index (CPI)? [LO 8.3]
   a. Word-processing equipment
   b. Cell phones
   c. Salt
   d. Televisions
   e. Housing
   f. Tennis rackets
6. Use Table 8P-5 to calculate core and all-items inflation relative to the base year in each time frame, assuming that each category is weighted equally in the calculation of all-items inflation. [LO 8.2], [LO 8.3]
   a. 2008 to the base year
   b. 2012 to the base year
   c. 2008 to 2012

TABLE 8P-5

	Food and energy	Other goods and services
2008	120	102
2012	105	107

7. The median North American household earned \$9,387 in 1973 and \$49,445 in 2010. During that time, though, the CPI rose from 44.4 to 218.1. **[LO 8.4]**
   a. Calculate the total growth rate in nominal median household income from 1973 to 2010.
   b. Calculate the total growth rate in real median household income from 1973 to 2010.

8. Table 8P-6 shows the GDP deflator and CPI for five recent years. How much did prices change between years in each measure? **[LO 8.4]**

TABLE 8P-6

Year	GDP deflator	Change in GDP deflator	CPI	Change in CPI
2005	100		100	
2006	105		104	
2007	112		110	
2008	123		113	
2009	127		120	
2005–2009				

9. Using Table 8P-7, find the real value of a \$1,000 payment and find the amount that this \$1,000 should be adjusted to in subsequent years, in order to keep its real value at \$1,000. **[LO 8.4]**

TABLE 8P-7

Year	CPI	Real value of \$1,000	Cost-of-living adjusted payment
2005	100	1,000	0
2006	103		
2007	105		
2008	110		

10. Tim Hortons paid its line workers $10 per hour last year when the Consumer Price Index was 100. Suppose that over the past year deflation occurred and the aggregate price level fell to 80. **[LO 8.4]**
    a. What must Tim Hortons pay its workers this year in order to keep the real wage fixed?
    b. What must Tim Hortons pay its workers this year if it wants to increase the real wage by 10 percent?
    c. If Tim Hortons keeps its workers' wages fixed at $10 per hour, how big a raise do its workers get in real terms?

11. Table 8P-8 shows the prices of a tall Starbucks latte in countries around the world. Using the data, and the fact that a latte costs $3 in Canada, calculate how much a country's currency is under- or overvalued according to purchasing power. **[LO 8.5]**

TABLE 8P-8

Country	Price	Official exchange rate
Thailand	60 baht	30 baht/dollar
Argentine	15 pesos	6 pesos/dollar
United Kingdom	2 pounds sterling	0.5 pound/dollar
Japan	450 yen	80 yen/dollar

12. An employee asks her boss whether she can transfer offices, so that she can work in a different part of the country. The boss responds positively and says that the employee can choose to work in Victoria, Toronto, or Calgary. The boss then hands the employee a list, as shown in Table 8P-9, of the salaries that she would earn in the different cities and the average price levels in those same cities. **[LO 8.5]**, **[LO 8.6]**
    a. From a standpoint of maximizing the employee's consumption possibilities, which office should she choose?
    b. What would be the minimum salary in Toronto the boss could offer the employee to make the employee indifferent between moving to Calgary and to Toronto?

TABLE 8P-9

Office location	Salary ($)	CPI
Calgary	80,000	100
Victoria	120,000	155
Toronto	150,000	210

13. Calculate the PPP-adjusted GDP for each of four countries, using the information found in Table 8P-10. **[LO 8.6]**

TABLE 8P-10

Country	GPD ($)	Price level (%)	PPP-adjusted GDP
Ona	10,000	6	
Rye	12,700	-27	
Zolfo	14,100	-10	
Avon	23,400	20	

Chapter Sources

http://research.stlouisfed.org/publications/review/03/11/pakko.pdf

http://www.servicecanada.gc.ca/eng/subjects/benefits/index.shtml

http://www.census.gc.ca/ccr16_r000-eng.html

http://www.statcan.gc.ca/daily-quotidien/160122/dq160122c-eng.htm

PART FOUR

Economic Growth and Unemployment

The two chapters in Part 4 will introduce you to …

economic growth and unemployment. As we explore economic growth, we turn to the forces that determine why some countries are richer and others are poorer. Moving on to unemployment, we ask why everyone who wants to work can't always find a job.

Chapter 9 focuses on one of the great challenges in economics: How can policy and resources be combined to create healthy economic growth? Growth increases economic opportunities, creates a dynamic business environment, and generates new wealth that allows people to lead more comfortable, secure lives. In recent years, economic growth has lifted hundreds of millions of people around the world out of poverty. In the search for the combination of policies that will lead to economic growth, we look to success stories like the astounding advances in China in the last few decades, and we take cautionary lessons from countries that still search for ways to lift living standards.

Chapter 10 covers unemployment. The unemployment rate reflects the struggles of individuals looking for work, but it is also considered to be an important barometer of the overall health of the economy. A strong economy has many benefits: factories and businesses create new jobs, people find it relatively easy to get work, and unemployment is usually low. But when the economy falters, firms lay off workers to cut production and unemployment is high. Because it acts as a signal of the state of the economy, the unemployment rate is tracked closely from month to month and is influential in debates about government policy and politics.

CHAPTER 9

Economic Growth

LEARNING OBJECTIVES

LO 9.1	Calculate the growth rate of real GDP per capita, accounting for changes in price levels and population.
LO 9.2	Describe the relationship between productivity and growth, and list the factors that determine productivity.
LO 9.3	Explain the difference between a country's level of income and its rate of growth.
LO 9.4	Assess the empirical evidence for and against convergence theory.
LO 9.5	Discuss policies that could promote growth, and relate them to productivity.
LO 9.6	Explain how good governance and economic openness lay the foundation for growth.

Why Economic Growth Matters

Between 2005 and 2010, a miracle occurred: more than half a billion people around the world rose out of poverty. These people moved from worrying about where their next meal was coming from to being able to worry instead about finding a better place to live or a more satisfying job.

What triggered this miracle? It wasn't a humanitarian intervention or massive government program. It was two little numbers: average annual GDP growth rates of 11 percent for China and 8 percent for India.

If you had traveled through those countries in recent years, you'd have found them buzzing with entrepreneurial spirit. Buildings and infrastructure sprouted like mushrooms and highways roared with people and goods rushing between enormous cities. The bridge of new wealth connected millions of people to the Internet and a global consumer culture.

High rates of economic growth have produced more than just tall buildings and smoother roads. The newly minted middle classes in China and India have cash to spend, buying the latest cell phones and flooding the roads with new cars. The middle class in China alone is bigger than the entire population of many nations. The bright lights of Shanghai and Mumbai also offer promise to millions of people who have migrated from poorer rural areas hoping to land jobs in factories or hotels, trading rural lifestyles for urban ones. Wages are rising and poverty rates are plummeting.

It is easy to get excited by these transformations and to proclaim that we've found the solution to global poverty. But saying that economic growth is the solution to poverty is a bit like saying that brilliant medical research is the solution

Leung Cho Pan/Flickr/Getty Images

to curing diseases or that scoring lots of touchdowns is a good way to win a football game. Of course it's important, but how do you make it happen? That's the hard part.

Leaders all over the world seek economic growth. It means wealthier, healthier, and better-educated citizens enjoying more comfortable lives, higher tax revenues for governments, and enticing opportunities for investors. Sadly, we have no magic formula for economic growth. Decades of research have helped us see why some countries are rich and others poor. But history has also shown that it's not easy for policy makers to translate this understanding into action.

The search for a recipe for economic growth captivates economists. It is simultaneously one of the most important and fascinating questions in economics, and one about which we're still learning. In this chapter we will describe three aspects of the study of growth. First, we'll discuss how growth is measured and show the patterns that have emerged around the world in the last century. Second, we'll create a basic framework for understanding why growth happens, and how savings, capital, labour, and technology contribute to it. Finally, we'll dig into details on how public policy choices can affect growth.

Economic Growth Through the Ages

Over the last hundred years, real GDP per capita in Canada has grown at an average rate of about 2 percent per year. That might not sound so impressive compared to the growth experienced by China and India. In the context of history, however, it's revolutionary. In this section, we'll explore two reasons why this is so.

History of World Growth

> **LO 9.1** Calculate the growth rate of real GDP per capita, accounting for changes in price levels and population.

Imagine you were alive in 1800. Almost anywhere in the world at that time, income per person was almost the same as it had been a millennium earlier. The possibility of growth has always been around, of course, but rapid economic growth is a modern phenomenon.

Take a look at Figure 9-1, which shows world population and income per person over the last 3,000 years. Historical records and archaeological evidence allow us to get a general sense of prices and standards of living in ancient days. Notice that for the first 2,800 of the last 3,000 years, *very little was happening economically.* The population was growing slowly, and the economy was growing just fast enough to keep up with the snail's pace of the population. The result was that real income per person barely changed at all.

Suddenly, in the 1800s, the global economy underwent a radical transformation. After staying about the same size for thousands of years, it started to grow. This growth was even more striking given that the world's population exploded at roughly the same time. The red line in Figure 9-1 shows real GDP (the level of GDP adjusted for changes in prices, but not for the size of the population). The blue line shows world population growth. When we put the two together, we get *real GDP per capita.*

The growth rate of real GDP per capita is typically the number we care about; it describes the change in actual purchasing power for each person. In order to get an accurate picture of the real GDP per capita growth rate, we need to subtract both changes in prices and population from the nominal GDP growth rate, as follows:

Equation 9-1

$$\text{Real GDP per capita growth rate} = \text{nominal GDP growth rate} - \text{inflation rate} - \text{population growth rate}$$

Just from glancing at Figure 9-1, you can see that real GDP growth in the last few centuries not only kept pace with population growth, but surpassed it. (In other words, nominal GDP grew faster than inflation and population combined.) As a result, the purchasing power of the average person in the world today is more than thirty times as high as it was 200 years ago. This represents a transformative change in the way people live. A growth rate like 2 percent may not sound revolutionary, but it is a big jump from what had been essentially zero growth in the centuries before.

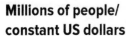

History of World Economic Growth: GDP per Capita, 1000 BC to 2000 AD

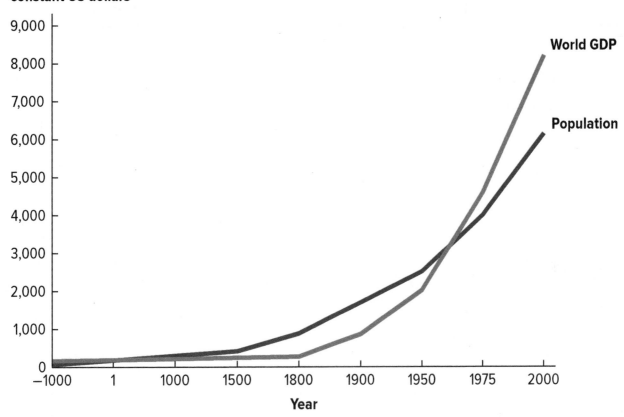

For the first 2,800 years of this graph, world GDP per capita was essentially constant. Then, in 1800, with the Industrial Revolution, incomes in Europe began to increase rapidly. In the last 50 years, global GDP per capita quadrupled.

Source: http://www.j-bradford-delong.net/macro_online/ms/ch5/chapter_5.pdf.

HINT

Growth rates usually compare the level of a variable in one year to its level the previous year (though growth rates can be calculated for other time frames, too). To get a concrete sense of a growth rate, here's how to calculate the Canadian nominal GDP growth rate in 2013. First, find the level of Canadian nominal GDP in 2013 ($1.9 trillion) and the level in 2012 ($1.8 trillion). Then subtract to find the absolute change, an increase of $100 billion. The growth rate is then calculated as the absolute change between 2012 and 2013 expressed as a percentage of the level of nominal GDP in 2012:

$$\left(\frac{\$0.1 \text{ trillion}}{\$1.8 \text{ trillion}}\right) \times 100 = 5.6 \text{ percent}$$

Compounding and the Rule of 70

The second reason that the historical Canadian growth rate of 2 percent per year is more impressive than it sounds is that economic growth builds on itself over time. This process is the same as the compounding of interest in a savings account, with earlier interest payments getting added to the account and earning interest in turn. The result is that a relatively modest annual growth rate can add up to a large change in the economy over time. In fact, real per capita GDP in Canada is *much higher* now than what it was 80 years ago. Figure 9-2 shows this growth in real purchasing power.

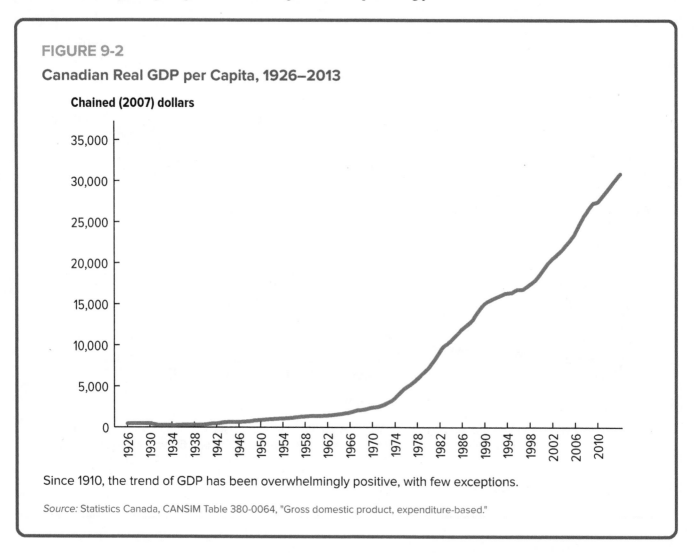

FIGURE 9-2

Canadian Real GDP per Capita, 1926–2013

Chained (2007) dollars

Since 1910, the trend of GDP has been overwhelmingly positive, with few exceptions.

Source: Statistics Canada, CANSIM Table 380-0064, "Gross domestic product, expenditure-based."

Total changes in GDP over time that are bigger than the annual growth rate would at first suggest are the result of compounding. The key insight is that the base from which growth is measured gets bigger every year. To see how this works, let's refer to Canadian GDP in 1910 as Y. If the economy is growing at 2 percent per year, then in 1911, GDP will be:

$$GDP_{1911} = Y + (0.02 \times Y) = 1.02Y$$

To simplify the math, notice that a 2 percent growth rate means that every year GDP is 1.02 times GDP in the previous year. In 1912, the base is now larger—1.02Y rather than just Y:

$$GDP_{1912} = 1.02 \times GDP_{1911} = 1.02 \times 1.02Y = (1.02)^2 Y$$

And in 1913:

$$GDP_{1913} = 1.02 \times GDP_{1912} = 1.02 \times (1.02)^2 Y = (1.02)^3 Y$$

Are you seeing the pattern? Because 1913 is three years after 1910, we find GDP in 1913 by multiplying the base 1910 GDP by one plus the growth rate three times—that is, by 1.02 to the power of three. If we generalize this formula, we can predict GDP per capita in any year A. We start from year B and multiply by 1 plus the growth rate, as many times as there are years are between B and A:

Equation 9-2

$$\text{GDP}_{\text{yearA}} = \text{GDP}_{\text{yearB}} \times \left(1 + \text{growth rate}\right)^{(A-B)}$$

Let's apply this equation to Canadian growth over the last century. In 1910, per capita real GDP was roughly \$5,800. Plugging that amount for $\text{GDP}_{\text{yearB}}$ into Equation 9-2, we forecast that real GDP per capita in 2010 would be roughly \$42,000:

$$\text{GDP per capita}_{2010} = \$5,800 \times \left(1 + 0.02\right)^{100} = \$42,000$$

A simple shortcut for approximating this calculation is the *rule of 70*. The rule states that the number of years it will take for income to double at the current real growth rate is approximately equal to 70 divided by the growth rate:

Equation 9-3

$$\text{Years until income doubles} = \frac{70}{\text{real growth rate}}$$

How well does the rule of 70 do at approximating the Canadian experience? Dividing 70 by 2 percent, we find that real GDP per capita should double every 35 years. This means income should have doubled just under three times in the last 100 years. Real GDP per capita in 1910 doubled three times is \$46,800 (\$5,800 × 2 × 2 × 2). Not too far off, for a shortcut.

Thinking of growth in terms of *years to double* makes it easier to appreciate how small differences in growth rates can add up to huge differences in income over time. What if the growth rate in Canada had been a bit higher, say, 3.5 percent? That might not sound very different from 2 percent, but it would mean incomes doubled every 20 years instead of every 35. Over 100 years, income would have doubled five times instead of three. And, instead of earning an average \$42,000, Canadians would be earning an average of \$168,000—approximately four times greater than with a 2 percent growth rate.

To see the effect that differences in growth rates can make, consider the incredible economic story of East Asia. Starting in 1960, four countries in Asia (Hong Kong, Singapore, Taiwan, and South Korea) managed growth rates of over 8 percent per year. That implies that real incomes doubled more than once every ten years! In just fifty years, this impressive economic growth managed to vault many people in these countries out of poverty. For insight into the debate about why this "Asian miracle" hasn't happened elsewhere, see the Real Life box, What a Difference 50 Years Makes.

REAL LIFE

What a Difference 50 Years Makes: The Story of Korea and Ghana

In 1960, Ghana and South Korea had similar levels of development. Both were quite poor, and most of the population eked out a living on small farms. Ghana, however, had good prospects—most economists thought it was poised to grow by at least 7 percent per year.

The consensus prediction for South Korea, on the other hand, was far less rosy. The first World Bank mission to the country called South Korea's growth plan "ridiculously optimistic"; it predicted sluggish growth. Fast-forwarding fifty years, South Korea is now a major manufacturing force, making sophisticated, high-end electronics and cars. Its brands include Samsung, LG, Hyundai, and Kia. It is now a wealthy country, with a GDP per capita over \$22,000.

Ghana's economy also grew, though much more slowly. But its population grew faster than South Korea's, so its average income per capita was actually *higher* in 1960 than in 2000. Today, Ghana is one of the richer countries in Africa, but it is much less well-off than South Korea. Ghana's GDP per capita in 2011 was a little over $1,500 per person, and over half of the workforce is still employed in the agricultural sector, either growing export crops such as cocoa, or subsistence crops such as cassava and maize.

Why did South Korea take off while Ghana failed to meet its early promise? The story is complicated, but an important part of it is that Ghana suffered years of political instability after 1960. Government intervention in the economy was heavy-handed and discouraged foreign trade.

South Korea, on the other hand, focused relentlessly on educating its citizens and encouraging people to save. The government gave firms generous incentives to export, including tax benefits and low-interest loans. South Korea's expanding manufacturing sector led it to an average growth rate of real GDP per capita of 5.4 percent in the half century between 1961 and 2011. The rule of 70 estimates that Korea doubled in size about every thirteen years. Put another way, between 1961 and 2011 Korea doubled its income nearly four times, leaving the current generation of young adults in South Korea with incomes that are about thirteen times that of their grandparents after adjusting for inflation.

Economists don't have a foolproof formula for creating growth miracles. But by studying how South Korea grew and why Ghana didn't, we can get closer to a real understanding of economic growth.

Sources: http://siteresources.worldbank.org/DEC/Resources/84797-1275071905763/Lessons_from_Korea_Lim.pdf; http://countrystudies.us/south-korea/; http://www.nber.org/chapters/c8548.pdf; http://apps.cimmyt.org/english/docs/special_publ/del/3rd_EcoLec99.pdf; http://economistsview.typepad.com/economistsview/2006/03/amartya_sen_dem.html; http://databank.worldbank.org.

✓ CONCEPT CHECK

☐   What was the overall trend of economic growth in the world before 1800? [LO 9.1]

☐   What is the rule of 70? [LO 9.1]

Determinants of Productivity

Growth may seem like an abstract concept, but it has a huge impact on people's standard of living. If you happen to have been born in Canada or South Korea, for instance, you likely enjoy a standard of living much higher than that of your grandparents and great-grandparents. You are probably taller, healthier, better educated, more widely travelled, and have more luxury and comfort in your life. Other regions of the world have grown much more slowly or not at all, and as a result, people live in ways relatively similar to earlier generations.

What determines the dramatic differences between countries and their growth paths over time? In this section, we will build a framework to understand factors that determine the level of income in a country and the rate at which it grows over time. With this framework, we will have a basis for discussing the historical circumstances and policy choices that cause some economies to grow and others to stagnate.

Productivity Drives Growth

Imagine a single household—say, a family that lives away from others on a farm in a remote place. The only goods available to this family are things its members can produce. If the family wants food or clothes or toys or a house, it will have to grow or make them. Suppose some family members learn to sew more quickly; they will make clothes more quickly and have more time left over to make toys for their children. Or suppose they make a plow that allows them to plant vegetables more easily, freeing up time and energy to build an extra room onto their house. The total amount of goods they produce will increase, and so will their standard of living.

In fact, the *only* way that the family can consume more and enjoy a higher standard of living is to increase the amount each person produces. We call that output **productivity**. Productivity can be measured in various ways, but it's typically measured as output per worker.

From Chapter 7 we know that *output per person on a country level* is the same thing as GDP per capita. Just like the farm family, we can think of a country as a self-contained economic unit that can earn and consume only as much as it produces. Thus, a country's income—like that of the farm family—depends on how productive its workers are.

Of course, hardly any family or country today consumes exactly what it produces itself. Typically, both sell some of the goods and services they produce, and they then use the money they earn to buy goods and services that others produce. Still, the underlying relationship holds: the more a country produces, the more it can consume. In the short term, it can temporarily push consumption higher than production by borrowing money. But in the long run, debts have to be paid, and the only way to be able to consume more is to produce more.

As a result, the standard of living in a country is driven by the average productivity of its people. Increases in productivity per person lead to increases in per capita income, which we call *economic growth*. So now the question is: What makes a country's people more productive?

Components of Productivity

> **LO 9.2** Describe the relationship between productivity and growth, and list the factors that determine productivity.

To find out what makes people more productive, we'll go back to the enterprising farm family. What determines how many vegetables they can grow in a year? The answer depends on several other questions: How skilled and experienced are they at farming? How fertile is their land, and what is the climate like? Do they have plows and fertilizer? Do they have state-of-the-art computerized irrigation systems, or do they depend on rainfall? Do they use the latest high-yield seed varieties?

Most of us are not farmers. But the factors that determine our productivity as workers fall into the same categories: physical capital (like plows and tractors), human capital (farming experience), technology (high-tech tools and crop varieties), and natural resources (land quality and rainfall). Let's walk through each determinant to see how it affects productivity.

Physical Capital

Most types of production require tools, and better tools allow workers to be more productive. A farmer with a sturdy horse-drawn plow will outperform a farmer with a hoe, but won't do as well as his neighbour with a tractor. These are examples of **physical capital**, the stock of equipment and structures that allows for the production of goods and services. Elsewhere in the economy, examples of physical capital include a manufacturer's factory and machines, a cellular network's towers and cables, and so on.

We calculate the amount of physical capital in an economy by adding up the value of all tools, equipment, and structures. Every year, some new physical capital is added through investment (farmers buy new tractors), and some old physical capital wears out or becomes obsolete (old tractors stop working). Taking into account both new investment and the retirement of older capital, we can tell the net amount of physical capital that has been added to the economy.

Where does the money for investment in physical capital come from? It largely comes from the savings of ordinary households. You put away money in the bank, and the bank loans funds to farmers and factories and cellular networks so that they can purchase new equipment. Thus, the level of savings in an economy can be an important determinant of investment in capital, and through that mechanism, a determinant of future productivity. In countries with low levels of savings, firms have trouble finding the money they need to invest in their factories and businesses. We will look in more detail at the relationship between savings and investment in later chapters.

Human Capital

Having new machines is usually a plus for productivity, but only if workers know how to use them. **Human capital** refers to the set of skills, knowledge, experience, and talent that determines the productivity of workers. Education is one of the main ways that we think about people building human capital. By taking an economics course, you are learning things that will make you more productive in the workplace. Human capital can also be acquired through training or job experience.

Note that the human capital of an individual or a nation is not always improving—it can also become outdated or deteriorate. People who are unemployed for long periods of time can forget some of the skills that were valuable in the workplace, for instance.

Human capital contributes to growth because it helps workers in the economy produce more with the same amount of physical capital. In other words, people can work smarter. A large increase in human capital is one explanation for the growth in the Canadian economy over the last hundred years. A century ago, the average person in Canada completed only around eight years of school; today, the average is more than twelve years of school. The average worker today knows more than the average worker at the start of the century and so will be more productive.

Countries with low levels of GDP per capita usually also have low levels of schooling. For example, the average person in Malawi or India has approximately five years of schooling. Helping people to invest in their human capital through better access to schools and job training is a priority for many developing countries.

Technology

The word *technology* may conjure up the image of a sleek new consumer gadget. When we think of how technology contributes to productivity, though, we need to understand the term more broadly. Technology comes in all forms and sizes. It can be big developments, such as the invention of the Internet or cell phones. It can also be seemingly small advances, like a more efficient water pump for irrigating crops or an engine design that allows cars to travel farther on the same amount of fuel. Big or small, technology means that the same inputs will produce more outputs. In 1956, Robert Solow and Trevor Swan independently developed the

Schools around the world aim to build human capital. Here, a school in Kenya shows attentive students in a jam-packed classroom.

Courtesy of Aude Guerrucci

neoclassical growth model. The model explains how technological progress induces saving and investment that encourage the capital per unit of labour to increase. In other words, countries with better technology will be able to produce more with the same amount of physical and human capital.

One of the most striking examples of the power of technology is the transformation of agriculture in Asia starting in the 1960s. Scientists developed new varieties of seeds for crops like rice and wheat, and these new varieties produced much higher yields than traditional seeds. These high-yielding seed varieties doubled the amount of food that could be produced on a plot of land. This "green revolution" not only erased the prospect of famine but also set the stage for the incredible overall growth that occurred in Asia over the past five decades. We'll come back to this story later in the chapter.

Natural Resources

Natural resources are production inputs that come from the Earth—lakes, mineral deposits, forests, and so on. Natural resources can be split into two categories: renewable and non-renewable.

- *Renewable resources* can be replenished naturally over time. For instance, after cutting down a tree for lumber, you can plant another one to grow in its place. Likewise, when a hydroelectric plant harnesses the power of a river to generate electricity, it doesn't "use up" the river, which continues to flow. Of course some things take longer to renew than others. The river renews immediately, but the trees take many years to replenish.

- Mineral deposits such as coal, oil, and gold, on the other hand, are *non-renewable*. When you take them out of the ground and use them, they are not replenished.

The availability of natural resources can account for some of the differences in economic development around the world. Canada has been blessed with a lot of fertile land, for example. Britain got a big boost from having easily accessible coal with which to power its manufacturing. But natural resources aren't everything. Japan and Switzerland are wealthy countries without an abundance of natural resources; Guinea and Kazakhstan are poor countries, despite having many natural resources. Economists have sometimes overestimated the importance of natural resources in productivity, as discussed in the From Another Angle box, Does the Planet Have a Maximum Capacity?

FROM ANOTHER ANGLE

Does the Planet Have a Maximum Capacity?

By all accounts, the eighteenth-century scholar and early economist Reverend Thomas Robert Malthus had a rather pessimistic view of the future. He argued that sooner or later the world's population would grow so big that it would not be able to produce enough food to feed itself.

Fortunately, Malthus has been wrong so far. Will we continue to beat Malthus's dire predictions?

Rates versus Levels

LO 9.3 Explain the difference between a country's level of income and its rate of growth.

Imagine that you're driving a car and merging onto the highway, pressing the accelerator pedal to the floor. Your speedometer says you are doing 50 kmph, then a second later 60 kmph, then second later 70 kmph. Your *level* of speed is fairly low, but your *rate of change* is high. Now imagine you are on the highway and cruising at 100 kmph. You are at a high *level* of speed, but the speed is constant—your *rate of change* is zero.

This analogy is useful for thinking about the differences between wealthy countries and fast-growing countries. Switzerland, for example, has high levels of physical and human capital, and access to sophisticated technology; consequently, it has high productivity and a high standard of living. Its current rate of growth is low, but it's starting from a high level. It's like the driver cruising along on the highway.

By contrast, China has lower levels of physical and human capital, and less widespread access to the latest technologies. As a result, Chinese workers have lower productivity than Swiss workers, and GDP per capita in China is lower than in Switzerland. However, incomes are increasing very rapidly in China. They have not yet achieved the same level as Switzerland, but they are moving quickly in that direction. China is like the car merging onto the highway, not yet going as fast as the cars already on the highway, but with a high *rate of change*. Its level of speed is increasing all the time.

As we discuss policies that can influence future growth, the distinction between the *level of income* and the *rate of increase in income* is crucial. The factors that took a country to its current economic level may or may not be related to those that can lead to future growth. For instance, Kuwait has grown rapidly in the last few decades and enjoys high productivity and incomes. This growth was almost entirely due to its incredible natural endowment of oil. But Kuwait would be foolish to base its future economic growth strategy only on exploiting its oil reserves. The people of Kuwait might hope that there are untapped oil reservoirs hiding somewhere in the desert, but there's nothing they can do to make more oil than already exists.

Similarly, we saw in Chapter 7 that increasing participation of women in the labour market partially explained Canadian growth rates from the 1970s to the 1990s. But clearly, as with Kuwait's oil, it would not be sensible to think you can grow an economy forever by encouraging more and more stay-at-home parents to get jobs or current workers to work

The spread of technology is a key driver of economic growth and can speed up rates of convergence. This Bedouin youth talks on a mobile phone as he leads a camel in southern Iraq.
AFP/Getty Images

longer hours. Sooner or later there will be no stay-at-home parents left, and no more hours in the day for people to work overtime.

Such one-time changes in the economy can cause growth spurts that lead to higher income *levels,* but they cannot sustain a higher *rate of change* over time.

In contrast, improvements in technology *can* sustain high rates of change. Sure, when an inventor creates a new gizmo, that invention is a one-time change. If technology stops improving, the economy won't continue to grow. But often improvements in technology lead to *more* improvements in technology. For example, computing capacity has approximately doubled every two years since the invention of computers, a phenomenon called Moore's law. People are constantly finding better and more effective ways to do things, and as a result, their productivity is continuously increasing.

Convergence

> **LO 9.4** Assess the empirical evidence for and against convergence theory.

Are poor countries doomed to stay poor, like cars poking along forever at 20 or 30 kmph? Or does the fact that a country is poor right now just mean that we are seeing it early in the development process, like a car moving slowly but accelerating toward highway speed? Will China and other countries with low incomes but fast growth eventually reach a level of wealth similar to those of Canada and Switzerland? If they do, will they keep accelerating forever, or will they eventually see their rates of growth slow and settle in on the highway alongside the world's rich countries?

One classic model of economic growth suggests the "settling in" story is the correct one. This model relates to the idea of *decreasing marginal returns* to factors of production: countries that start with very little physical capital will get a higher return from adding a unit of capital than will a country that starts at a higher initial level. This leads to the general hypothesis that countries starting at low levels of income (which correspond to low levels of capital) will tend to grow at much faster rates than those starting with high levels of income. Each additional unit of capital provides larger gains when you're coming from behind.

This idea is called **convergence theory** (or the *catch-up effect*). It says that poor countries will grow faster than rich ones, until they catch up and all countries "converge" at the same growth rate. The theory predicts that even if countries differ in their rates of savings, population growth, and other features, they will still converge at the same *growth rate,* although not the same *level of income.* In other words, countries that start out poor should initially grow faster than ones that start out rich, but will eventually slow to the same growth rate.

In some ways, convergence theory fits the evidence from the real world. Figure 9-3 shows the differences between growth rates in countries around the world over the past 20 years. Looking at the map, you'll see that richer countries have mostly been growing slowly and that most of the fastest growth rates are occurring in some of the poorest countries. However, you can also see plenty of poor countries on the map that have not been growing quickly, especially in Africa.

Further, many economists think convergence theory explains the incredible growth of the East Asian countries: those countries experienced very high marginal returns as they began to accumulate physical and human capital. They also were well positioned to take advantage of technologies and capital flows from wealthier countries.

In other places, however, convergence is clearly not happening. Most African countries started at levels of physical and human capital as low as East Asia's half a century ago, but they have not experienced the same growth spurt. In fact, many actually got poorer during the 1980s and early 1990s. Clearly, simply starting out poor is not a guarantee of achieving impressive growth rates.

To try to understand what allows some low income countries to take off while others stagnate, we need to consider how public policy affects economic growth.

FIGURE 9-3

FIGURE 9-3

World GDP per Capita Rates, 1990–2010*

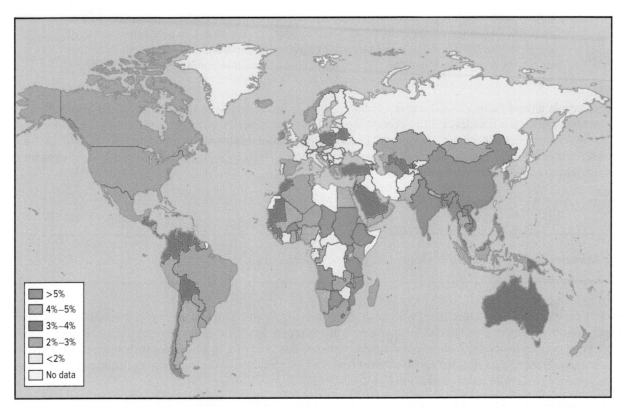

Legend:
- >5%
- 4%–5%
- 3%–4%
- 2%–3%
- <2%
- No data

Over the past twenty years, there has been a wide disparity in the rate of economic growth. This growth has been strongest in Southeast Asia, while the rate of economic growth in most of Western Europe has been sluggish.

*In most of the former Soviet bloc, data start in 1991 after the fall of the USSR.

Source: World Bank, *World Development Indicators,* http://databank.worldbank.org/ddp/home.do.

✓ CONCEPT CHECK

☐ What are the main determinants of productivity? [**LO 9.2**]

☐ How are rates different from levels when talking about economic growth? [**LO 9.3**]

☐ What does convergence theory predict about growth rates? About income levels? [**LO 9.4**]

Growth and Public Policy

Nobel Prize winner Robert Lucas captured the fascination and sense of possibility that come with thinking about economic growth in this way:

> Is there some action a government of India could take that would lead the Indian economy to grow like Indonesia's or Egypt's? If so, what, exactly? If not, what is it about the "nature of India" that makes it so? The consequences for human welfare involved in questions like these are simply staggering: Once one starts to think about them, it is hard to think about anything else.[1]

Billions of people around the world still live in conditions that are unimaginable to those living in wealthy countries. Recent history has shown that a few decades of strong economic growth like that experienced by South Korea could transform their lives. What can be done to spark and sustain that growth? Unfortunately, no one has a simple answer to this question. In this section, we discuss some of the factors that are generally believed to promote or hold back growth. We also look at policy solutions that some countries have implemented successfully.

Investment and Savings

> **LO 9.5** Discuss policies that could promote growth, and relate them to productivity.

If physical capital increases productivity, why don't countries simply put as much money as possible into infrastructure, machinery, and other capital investments? In some cases, this is precisely what they do. However, there is an opportunity cost involved. For a country to acquire more physical capital, someone has to pay for it, which means that money can't also be spent on consumption. This problem is called the **investment trade-off**—a reduction in current consumption to pay for the investment in capital intended to increase future production.

Savings that pay for capital investment can come either from within a country or from outside it. The former is called **domestic savings**, and is equal to domestic income minus consumption spending. It can come from two sources: private households spending less than they earn, or government revenues exceeding non-capital expenditures.

Household savings rates vary enormously across countries, as Figure 9-4 shows. On one end of the spectrum, we have China, where households typically put away a whopping 40 percent of their earnings. In contrast, households in Canada save very little: in 2005 the household savings rate was 3.6 percent; the rate rebounded to a more healthy rate of about 5 percent in 2011.

REAL LIFE

Planning for Growth

"We are fifty or a hundred years behind the advanced countries. We must make good this distance in ten years. Either we do it, or they will crush us." These words were delivered by Joseph Stalin, leader of the Soviet Union, in 1931. Rather than relying on the invisible hand of the market to guide the economy, Russia called for a central planning agency to set targets for production.

Although the lofty goals were not met, production of many industrial goods doubled.

Market-oriented economies have also created plans, investing public funds in industries the government considered strategically important.

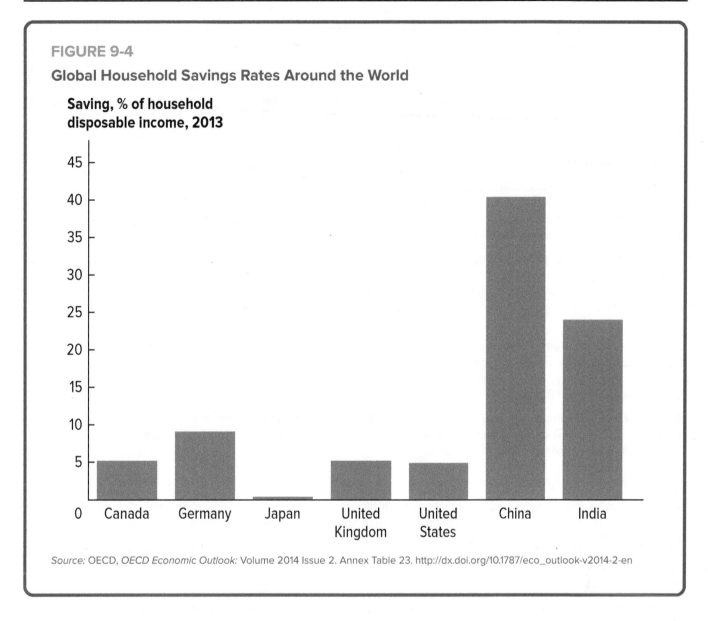

FIGURE 9-4

Global Household Savings Rates Around the World

Saving, % of household disposable income, 2013

Source: OECD, OECD Economic Outlook: Volume 2014 Issue 2. Annex Table 23. http://dx.doi.org/10.1787/eco_outlook-v2014-2-en

Governments also can use tax revenues (or borrow money) to invest in physical capital. Governments often fund the underlying infrastructure that private companies rely on for their operations, such as roads, bridges, ports, and sewer systems. This infrastructure can have a major effect on growth. In many developing countries, for example, even if farmers could grow more, it would be hard to get their goods to market because of poor roads. Many governments are currently investing heavily in communications infrastructure such as high-speed Internet, in the expectation that this will improve private companies' productivity.

Governments can also focus resources on industries they believe can contribute the most to national growth. Some people attribute the rapid growth of the East Asian economies in the 1980s and 1990s to the success of their industrial policies. Through these policies, governments picked industries to support with investments and favorable tax and trade policies. The idea that governments can effectively plan growth by "picking winners" is controversial, though. Consider the arguments on either side in the Real Life box, Planning for Growth.

Funds for capital investment can also come from outside a country. **Foreign direct investment (FDI)** is investment that occurs when a firm runs part of its operation abroad or invests in another company abroad. For example, when Toyota operates a plant in Ontario, the Japanese firm owns the machinery and buildings, even though the production takes place in Canada. Similarly, factories owned by Canadian firms in Europe are an important source of FDI for the EU.

Many governments actively work to attract FDI, hoping it will build up their capital stock when domestic savings aren't sufficient. Another benefit of FDI is that when foreign companies invest in local firms, they can transfer human capital to local managers and workers. Perhaps managers from the foreign country travel to oversee the investment. In doing so, they can train local staff or set up more efficient procedures.

However, FDI has its critics. Foreign firms with money to invest often have numerous governments competing to attract the investment. The firm can drive a hard bargain, demanding special tax breaks or legal exemptions that governments cannot easily afford. The transfer of knowledge or technology may also not happen to the extent some would wish, if foreign managers oversee operations without training local talent. As a result, some argue that a policy of attracting FDI might not ultimately be as beneficial as it first appears.

Education and Health

In rich countries, we take free basic education for granted. In many countries, however, schools may be few and far between, charge unaffordable fees to students, or simply provide very low-quality education. One of the major efforts of the Millennium Development Goals—a collection of targets set by the United Nations to tackle aspects of poverty in developing countries by 2015—has been to push countries to provide free elementary school education.

Ensuring that high-quality public education is freely available to all children is one of the most important ways that a country can increase its stock of human capital. Education teaches skills such as literacy, basic math, and communication—all essential to perform more than the most elementary jobs. High-quality education also builds the pool of scientists, thinkers, and entrepreneurs who develop new technologies and business models.

Using public policy to promote health can also contribute to growth. Workers who are in good health will be more productive and less likely to miss work days. Some economic benefits of improved health are less visible, especially in low-income countries. For instance, health economists have found that reducing vitamin and mineral deficiencies, such as anemia (the result of a diet with not enough iron in it), and parasites, such as worms, can improve people's mental and physical energy. Treatment increases the ability to focus, making it easier for children to learn in school and for adults to do their best at work.

The combination of health problems and lack of educational opportunities often combine in poor countries to make it hard to accumulate greater levels of human capital. Public policy can help to push a country out of this negative cycle by improving public health services and the quality of education.

Technological Development

A lot of research and development takes place at private institutions—in firms, private laboratories, and so on. However, public policy can also encourage technological development through the educational system, funding for research and study, and tax structures that encourage firms to develop and adopt new technologies. In Canada, about \$30.6 billion a year goes into research and development. About \$12.4 billion of the investment takes place at universities and research institutes, but most spending is done by business.[2]

Advancements in technology can be fantastic, but they can also be fickle. The green revolution, which introduced new agricultural technologies, was a rousing success in Asia, but has been more complicated in Africa. The Real Life box, Green Revolutions in Asia and Africa, provides details of this story.

REAL LIFE

Green Revolutions in Asia and Africa

In 1961, India was at risk of famine. The population was booming, and no more farmland was available. How would everyone be fed? Incredibly, by 1985, the spectre of famine had all but disappeared, not only in India but across Asia. In just twenty-five years, crop yields doubled, easily outpacing the growth of the population.

This transformation in agriculture, called the green revolution, was the result of painstaking research and development funded by private charities such as the Rockefeller Foundation. It resulted in new crop varieties, such as strain IR8, or "miracle rice," developed in 1968 by the International Rice Research Institute in the Philippines. "Miracle rice" required more intensive fertilizer and irrigation treatments than traditional varieties but produced about double the amount of rice per plant.

Unfortunately, the green revolution did not reach Africa. While climate, soil, and growing conditions are fairly similar across much of Asia, they vary widely in Africa. The high-yield varieties of rice and wheat simply didn't grow as well there. A variety of rice that doubles yields in most Asian countries may wilt in the drier climate of Ethiopia or be swamped in the equatorial rains of the Congo.

African farmers today mostly still farm as their grandparents did, and as farmers in Asia did fifty years ago, with little fertilizer and limited tools. Growing enough food in Africa requires the agricultural sector to employ a large percentage of the labour force. Many economists believe that this difference partly explains why Asia's economies have grown more quickly than Africa's in the last half century: when you don't need as many workers to grow food, they can do something else instead, such as working in factories in the city.

The search is now on for ways to make the green revolution work in Africa. The Bill and Melinda Gates Foundation and the Rockefeller Foundation are funding a regional approach that tries to tailor plant varieties and practices to local conditions. This new work may not be as immediate or dramatic as the Asian green revolution, but may lead to innovations that put ample food in every bowl—and help Africa along the path to greater prosperity.

Laying the Groundwork: Good Government, Property Rights, and Economic Openness

> **LO 9.6** Explain how good governance and economic openness lay the foundation for growth.

Imagine that you live in a country where, if someone stole your truck, there was nothing you could do about it. The police wouldn't help you unless you bribed them. Even if you could get police help, it might take five years and a lot of money to prosecute someone in court. Would you still buy a truck? You might, if you thought that the potential benefits were high enough to outweigh the risk of losing your investment. But you'd certainly be less inclined to invest in trucks and other expensive capital goods than you would if you thought that your property would be protected.

This is just one example of the ways in which enforceable laws and effective, trustworthy government services are essential to a well-functioning economy. Most countries have mechanisms to punish those who violate the property rights of others and to enforce contracts between buyers and sellers. Institutions like police forces, courts of law, and government bureaucracies are meant to protect property, settle disputes, and provide a predictable legal framework in which people can make plans and agreements. However, these institutions are more effective and reliable in some countries than in others.

Stability in leadership and institutions is important, as is effectiveness. Would you want to build an expensive new factory if you thought there was a good chance of new leaders coming to power who might seize it? Would you risk investing in a business if the tax policies or laws that determined its profitability changed from month to month?

Many economists believe that good government has a major impact on economic growth and can help us understand why some economies have grown rapidly while others have stagnated. How to improve government is a tricky question, though. It is challenging to design effective policies to tackle corruption, make courts more efficient, limit the powers of politicians, and so on.

Government policy also determines how open a country will be to trade. Firms often argue that governments need to protect them from competition by placing tariffs on foreign goods. However, the "Asian miracle" countries succeeded by combining industrial policy with outward-oriented policies to gear their economies toward exporting goods. Later in the book we'll discuss free trade and why most economists believe that there are important gains to keeping economies open.

The Juggling Act

As with many things in life, there are *trade-offs* between different ways of promoting growth through public policy. Most governments—especially those in poor countries—can't pay for education *and* health *and* highways *and* better police all at the same time. Unfortunately, this is a vicious cycle: the richer you are, the better able you are to pay for things that will help you be even richer in the future. The poorer you are, the less able you are to pay for the things that can make you richer.

Earlier in the chapter, we noted the trade-off between current consumption and investment in physical capital, human capital, and research that will contribute to growth and to higher future income. The poorer the country, the tougher this trade-off becomes. It's harder for people who live close to the edge on a dollar or two a day to save a given amount of money or pay more taxes than it would be for wealthier people. This logic leads to the vicious cycle described above. If you can't afford to pay for a good court system or to invest in a tractor or a computer, you will find it harder to climb out of poverty. This *poverty trap* is one of the main justifications for foreign aid that provides loans or funding for infrastructure and human capital development.

Why don't countries take one element at a time—for example, focusing limited resources first on infrastructure, and then on education or health, and so on? Unfortunately, it's not usually that simple. Growth often requires concurrent improvements in many aspects of the economy. For instance, translating new technology into growth often requires a population with sufficient human capital to take advantage of it, and sometimes specific infrastructure. Imagine a country trying to build an Internet-based economy. This would be difficult, if not impossible, if much of the population can't read, or if the electrical grid experiences regular blackouts due to insufficient power generation. Harnessing the power of the Internet to promote commerce, and thus growth, would require simultaneous improvements in literacy, computer skills, the power grid, a trustworthy postal service, and payment mechanisms.

Another trade-off that governments face is how much to sacrifice the natural environment in pursuit of economic growth. The What Do You Think? box, Should Poor Countries Be as Earth-Friendly as Rich Ones? explores this particular trade-off.

WHAT DO YOU THINK?

Should Poor Countries Be as Earth-Friendly as Rich Ones?

During the Industrial Revolution, European factories spewed pollution into the atmosphere as they rolled out a steady stream of textiles, steel, and other goods. Power plants fueled by dirty coal dotted cities throughout Western Europe and eventually the United States. Miners and factory workers often died of lung diseases and other health problems associated with dirty air and unsafe working conditions.

After many years of unchecked pollution, conditions got so bad that London suffered from chronic smog that would settle over the city for days, blotting out the sun. In 1952, one particularly severe smog episode killed over 4,000 people. In retrospect, the environmental and health consequences of Europe's industrialization seem awful. At the time, though, they were simply part and parcel of a massive increase in wealth and economic power.

In the past fifty years, technologies have been developed that allow firms to produce goods and energy with far less pollution. Developing countries today don't necessarily have to go through the same painful arc that marked earlier industrial transformations. Despite this, China's economic explosion has been accompanied by smog, toxic rivers, and a few actual explosions at factories that have killed thousands of people and filled the atmosphere with pollutants. Why haven't firms in China chosen to use the new, cleaner technology now available?

There are two reasons. First, acquiring clean technologies is not always straightforward, due to stringent trade policies and intellectual property laws. Second, even when these technologies are accessible, they may be very expensive. Factories and power plants in Europe and Canada are now relatively clean, not because the new technologies are always cheaper than the older, dirtier methods, but because governments in those countries have introduced strict regulations requiring firms to mitigate their impact on the environment and protect the health and safety of their workers and neighbours.

China and other developing countries are forced to ask themselves some difficult questions. Do they want to introduce strict environmental laws, forcing companies to use expensive clean technology? Or do they want to grow their economies as quickly as possible by using cheaper ways of doing things, even if they are environmentally damaging?

Many in richer countries feel that fast-growing countries such as India and China should have to protect the environment by using the cleaner technologies now available. They point out that production in developing countries is releasing vast amounts of greenhouse gases that affect other countries, too. For example, China is already the largest producer of carbon dioxide in the world. The effects, through climate change, could be disastrous all over the world.

Developing countries, on the other hand, counter that being forced to use the cleaner technologies would make their goods more expensive and less competitive in the world market. They argue that developed countries created the problem of climate change by releasing greenhouse gases during their own industrial revolutions, and it's not fair to expect poorer countries to pay the penalty. It's also not clear what the more humane policy is; we've seen that economic growth can decrease poverty and alleviate suffering, and stricter regulations likely mean slower growth and slower poverty reduction.

To help solve this impasse, the United Nations has launched a Green Climate Fund. Starting in 2020, the fund will distribute $100 billion per year to developing countries, partly to help them acquire and pay for cleaner technologies. The fund may help countries avoid some of the pollution associated with economic growth, but probably won't solve the whole problem.

What do you think?

1. Should all countries be held to the same environmental standards?

2. Do rich countries have a responsibility to help poorer countries acquire cleaner technologies?

3. Is it worth implementing cleaner technologies if it means slower growth?

Sources: http://www.reuters.com/article/2011/04/15/us-climate-fund-idUSTRE73E3WG20110415; http://www.cnbc.com/id/43139649; http://news.bbc.co.uk/2/hi/uk_news/england/2545759.stm; http://www.nytimes.com/2010/07/29/world/asia/29china.html; http://www.law.duke.edu/journals/dltr/articles/2009dltr001.html.

✓ CONCEPT CHECK

☐ What determinant of economic growth is influenced by domestic saving? [LO 9.5]

☐ Why do police protection and efficient courts matter for economic growth? [LO 9.6]

Conclusion

Economic growth can make the rich richer; it has emerged as a powerful way to make the poor richer, too. In this chapter we looked at how we define and measure economic growth and why growth is so important. Because of compounding, even a small increase in the growth rate will have a large impact on the level of income in the long run. A country that is growing at 3.5 percent, instead of 2 percent, will end up approximately four times richer after 100 years.

In order to grow, a country needs to be able to put together the ingredients: savings that can be invested in physical capital, healthy and skilled workers, appropriate technology, and supportive public policies and institutions. All governments face tough trade-offs: How much should the country invest in health, education, and infrastructure? How can the government create a secure legal environment for people to invest? The goal is a positive cycle in which people gain human capital, invent better technology, become more productive at their jobs, get richer and able to afford more physical capital, and so on.

This process is not easy, but it is important. If policy makers, businesses, and workers come together effectively to build the right environment for investment, their contributions can deliver a foundation for the prosperity of future generations.

Key Terms

productivity	investment trade-off
physical capital	domestic savings
human capital	foreign direct investment (FDI)
convergence theory	

Summary

LO 9.1 Calculate the growth rate of real GDP per capita, accounting for changes in price levels and population.

The fact that growth compounds over time makes it hard to tell what the total effect on incomes will be just by looking at the annual growth rate. GDP growth rates are often stated without taking population growth into account and sometimes without taking inflation into account. To find the rate of real GDP growth, take the nominal growth rate and subtract both population growth and inflation growth rates.

National economic growth builds on itself over time. The result is that a relatively modest annual growth rate, like 2 percent, actually adds up to quite a large total growth rate over time. The rate at which GDP increases incomes can be found through the *rule of 70*: to find how long it takes incomes to double within a country, divide 70 by the rate of real GDP growth.

LO 9.2 Describe the relationship between productivity and growth, and list the factors that determine productivity.

The only way that a country can consume more and enjoy a higher standard of living is to increase its *productivity*—the amount it produces per worker. Productivity can be measured for any unit of labour, whether that unit is an hour of time worked or how much one worker produces; it is typically measured as output per person. The factors that influence labour productivity are physical capital, human capital, technology, and natural resources.

LO 9.3 Explain the difference between a country's level of income and its rate of growth.

There are two important distinctions to make in terms of economic development. One is about the *level* of well-being. Countries like Canada or Switzerland that have very high amounts of physical and human capital are said to be at a high level of development. The other distinction is about the *rate* of economic growth. While Canada may have a high level of development, the rate of growth in Canadian GDP is not nearly as fast as China's. Level matters because it tells how wealthy a country currently is. Rates matter because they tell how quickly a country is increasing its wealth.

LO 9.4 Assess the empirical evidence for and against convergence theory.

Convergence theory predicts that countries that are starting at lower levels of income will grow at a faster rate than those starting at higher levels, until they catch up and converge to the same growth rate.

In some ways, convergence theory fits evidence from the real world. The four East Asian countries that experienced incredible growth since the 1960s started from low levels of physical and human capital, but were well positioned to take advantage of technologies and capital flows from wealthier countries. However, even though half a century ago most African countries had similar or even lower levels of physical and human capital than East Asia, they have not experienced high growth rates.

LO 9.5 Discuss policies that could promote growth, and relate them to productivity.

Countries face an investment trade-off, in which they must reduce current consumption to pay for the capital investment needed to increase future production. Funds to pay for capital investment can come either from domestic savings or from foreign direct investment (FDI) from outside the country.

A variety of policies can promote economic growth. Education teaches skills such as literacy, basic math, and communication, which are essential to perform more than the most elementary jobs. Education is also a way to develop the training and skills that countries need in order to undertake technological research and development. Public health systems can also contribute to growth by increasing the portion of the population that is fit, healthy, and able to work. Public policy can also encourage technological development through the education system, funding for research and study, and tax structures that encourage firms to develop and adopt new technologies.

LO 9.6 Explain how good governance and economic openness lay the foundation for growth.

Enforceable laws and effective, trustworthy government services are critical to a well-functioning economy. The most important is the provision of property rights, giving people the ability to have control over the resources they own. Most countries have institutions and infrastructure that are at least partially designed to protect these property rights. Courts enforce the contracts between buyers and sellers. They also are responsible, through the criminal justice system, for punishing people who are accused of violating the property rights of others.

Review Questions

1. Explain why inflation reduces the real value of nominal GDP per capita. [LO 9.1]

2. When policy makers discuss policies that encourage long-run growth in per capita real GDP, they often mention policies aimed at reducing the growth rate in the population. If effective, why might these policies improve long-run growth? Also, what are the potential costs associated with these policies? [LO 9.1]

3. Does the rule of 70 predict greater increases in the amount of income for richer or poorer countries when both have the same growth rate? Why? [LO 9.1], [LO 9.3]

4. Explain why many rich countries are able to continuously grow, even though they already have very high levels of physical and human capital. [LO 9.2]

5. At a young age, would you rather have a large level of savings or a pool of savings that was increasing at a faster rate? [LO 9.3]

6. Using the growth rates for countries over the past twenty years (found in Figure 9-3), is there evidence that poorer countries in Africa and Asia are converging to the level of income found in Western Europe? Why or why not? [LO 9.4]

7. Southern states in the US are, on average, poorer than northern states. Southern states also have higher growth rates in real GDP per capita, on average, than northern states. Use these facts to draw a conclusion about whether the theory of convergence is correct. What other factors should be considered? [LO 9.4]

8. Many believe that technology is very costly to create, but cheap to transfer. For example, think of the personal computer. The technology underpinning the personal computer took a generation of time and a ton of money to create. However, now that the personal computer has been created, it is easy for others to purchase and reap the benefits. Given this insight, what do you believe will be the growth implications for Canada (traditionally more apt to create new technology) and China (traditionally more apt to adopt technologies created elsewhere)? [LO 9.4], [LO 9.5]

9. How might low rates of saving in Canada limit the accumulation of physical capital? [LO 9.5]

10. Realizing that poor countries must solve many problems at once has shifted benefactors away from the idea of giving multiple small payments to the idea of a Big Push. This Big Push entails giving a very large sum of money that could be used to fix multiple problems at once. In fact, the amount of money required might be so large that other countries might be the only ones who could afford the donation. What are the trade-offs associated with this idea? [LO 9.5]

11. How is it possible that Switzerland, a landlocked country with almost no natural resources, is one of the richest countries in the world, while the Democratic Republic of the Congo, a huge country with vast deposits of many strategically important minerals, is one of the poorest? [LO 9.2], [LO 9.5], [LO 9.6]

12. Why could a free press be important for economic growth? (*Hint:* Think about the connection between the press and government.) [LO 9.6]

Problems and Applications

1. Fill in the blanks in Table 9P-1. [LO 9.1]

TABLE 9P-1

Country	Nominal GDP growth (%)	Population growth (%)	Inflation (%)	Real GDP growth per capita (%)
Svea	5	3		−1
Bonifay	2	1	0	
Chaires		2	7	4
Drifton	5	0	−1	
Estiffanulga	7		3	3

2. Equation 9-1 states that Real GDP per capita growth rate = nominal GDP per capita growth rate − inflation rate − population growth rate.

   This equation is an approximation of the exact rate of growth of GDP per capita, and so it results in some errors when calculating this rate. However, the simplified equation is both easy to use and results in small error terms when inflation, nominal GDP growth, and population growth are low, and so it is a useful approximation. Table 9P-2 lists a fictional country's nominal GDP, real GDP, GDP deflator, and population over two years. [LO 9.1]
   a. Use your knowledge from Chapter 7, "The Cost of Living," to verify that the real GDP figures in Table 9P-2 are accurate.
   b. Calculate this country's real GDP per capita for both 2012 and 2013.
   c. Calculate the growth rate in this country's real GDP per capita between 2012 and 2013.
   d. Calculate the growth rates in the nominal GDP, GDP deflator, and the population.

TABLE 9P-2

Year	Nominal GDP ($)	GDP deflator	Real GDP ($)	Population
2012	1,000,000	1.00	1,000,000	1,000
2013	1,050,000	1.02	1,029,412	1,005

3. For each growth rate below, use the rule of 70 to calculate (1) how long it will take incomes to double, and (2) what the income will be in 30 years if each country starts with an income of $1,000 per capita. [LO 9.2]
   a. 4 percent
   b. 7 percent
   c. 2.5 percent
   d. 10 percent
   e. 3 percent

4. For each part below, determine whether the following actions will increase or decrease productivity, and name the component of productivity that each affects. [LO 9.2]

   a. The local government builds a new school.

   b. Teachers in the new school hold classes for young students.

   c. A manufacturer installs robots on its assembly line.

   d. A research team designs a more efficient system of irrigation.

   e. A soft drink company discovers a new source of underground water that can be used to make its products.

   f. A professor writes a new and improved economics textbook.

   g. A large number of people have less access to health care.

   h. A worker receives on-the-job training to be a mechanic.

5. Which of the countries shown in Table 9P-3 had the highest level of income in 2010? Which had the highest rate of income growth from 2005 to 2010? Do incomes in these countries appear to be converging? [LO 9.3], [LO 9.4]

TABLE 9P-3

Country	GDP per capita 2005 ($)	GDP per capita 2010 ($)
Bolivia	3,664	4,592
China	4,102	7,519
Ghana	2,007	2,615
Argentina	10,860	15,854
Brazil	8,603	11,239

6. The median household income in New Brunswick is approximately $65,910 per year, while the income per household in Alberta is about $94,460. However, suppose the growth rate of per capita real GDP in New Brunswick is higher than in Alberta (3 percent versus 2 percent). [LO 9.3], [LO 9.4]

   a. In which province would you rather live over the next few years if you are trying to maximize your income per capita?

   b. In which province would you rather live in the long run if you are trying to maximize your income per capita?

7. Will the three countries in Table 9P-4 converge at the same level of economic development given enough time? [LO 9.3], [LO 9.4]

TABLE 9P-4

Country	Income per capita ($)	Real per capita GDP growth rate (%)
Ansonia	5,000	7.0
Trumbull	7,500	4.5
Shelton	10,000	2.0

8. For each of the following examples, state whether this activity would likely hinder or promote economic growth and name a component of productivity each produces or reduces. [LO 9.2], [LO 9.5]
   a. Not requiring students to attend school
   b. Granting patents on new inventions
   c. Building a solid infrastructure system
   d. Allowing local rivers and streams to become polluted

9. Policy makers in Canadian government have long tried to write laws that encourage growth in per capita real GDP. These laws typically do one of three things, as listed below. For each of the three points, name a law or government program with that intention. [LO 9.5]
   a. They encourage firms to invest more in research and development in order to boost technology.
   b. They encourage individuals to save more in order to boost the physical capital stock.
   c. They encourage individuals to invest more in education in order to boost the stock of human capital.

10. Name the type of institution that is responsible for promoting a stable environment for the economy regarding each of the following situations. [LO 9.6]
   a. Someone steals your car, but is caught.
   b. You claim that your employer violated the terms of your employment contract.

Chapter Sources

J. Bradford DeLong and Martha Olney, *Macroeconomics,* 2nd edition (New York: McGraw-Hill/Irwin, 2005).

Ralph Landau, Timothy Taylor, and Gavin Wright, eds., *The Mosaic of Economic Growth* (Palo Alto, CA: Stanford University Press, 1996).

CHAPTER 10

Unemployment and the Demand for Labour

LEARNING OBJECTIVES

LO 10.1   Explain how economists measure employment and unemployment.
LO 10.2   Explain how wage rates above equilibrium cause unemployment.
LO 10.3   Explain why there is a natural rate of unemployment in an economy.
LO 10.4   Explain why unemployment has a cyclical component.
LO 10.5   Identify factors that may stop wages from falling to the equilibrium level.
LO 10.6   Describe the challenges policy makers face when designing employment insurance.

What Does It Mean to Be Unemployed?

Unemployment is frustratingly common, especially during a recession. In tough times jobs are hard to find. In June 2009, the unemployment rate in Canada rose to 8.7 percent. Unemployment was even higher for certain groups of the population. For young adults without a high-school degree, the unemployment rate was over 18 percent.[1] Even many university graduates struggled to find work and ended up living back at home with their parents.

Of course, unemployment exists even when the economy is not in a recession. The natural churn of the labour market, which causes people to be unemployed for short periods as they move between jobs, is a normal part of economic life. Even when there's no recession, regional unemployment occurs as factories close and when the needs of local employers shift. Such unemployment is made worse when laid-off workers find that their skills no longer match the jobs that are available. Ironically, policies designed to protect workers—like minimum wage laws and unionization—also can lead to unemployment; while they help existing workers, they often make it harder for those out of work to find jobs.

Sean De Burca/Getty Images

Some unemployment may be unavoidable, but too much of it can have serious consequences, both for the economy as a whole and on an individual level. One consequence of unemployment is that some of the productive potential of the economy—the time and skills of the unemployed—is not being put to use. Another consequence is much more personal. Many unemployment stories show that prolonged unemployment can be one of the most difficult experiences a person suffers. It creates uncertainty about the future and can bring on feelings of hopelessness, especially for someone who is trying to support a family. Studies show that being unemployed is correlated with higher rates of depression and lower assessments of self-worth. Unemployment is an economic problem with potentially serious social and psychological consequences.

Unfortunately the difficulties of finding a job are in large part shaped by macroeconomic forces outside of an individual's control. What are these forces? Why does unemployment exist in the first place? These questions pose a puzzle for economists.

We start by assuming that a market reaches an equilibrium where quantity demanded is equal to quantity supplied at the prevailing price. The fact that unemployment exists suggests that people want to supply more labour at the prevailing wage than firms are demanding. Why don't wages drop until unemployment is eliminated? In this chapter, we'll investigate the reasons why wages might not drop to an equilibrium level. We'll also see why some unemployment will exist even when the labour market is in equilibrium. As we distinguish between different sources of unemployment, we'll see the logic of different strategies that attempt to address the underlying problems.

Defining and Measuring Unemployment

Measuring unemployment turns out to be more complicated than simply counting the number of people who aren't working. We want to count individuals as unemployed when they're *actively searching* for a job. For example, retired people don't have jobs, but they also don't *want* jobs. How do we differentiate those two forms of being unemployed? And how do we represent the situation when people get so discouraged they stop looking for work? Defining unemployment in a clear and consistent way is an important step toward getting a handle on the underlying issues.

Unemployment occurs when someone wants to work but cannot find a job. People are unemployed for many reasons: job-seekers may lack relevant skills, for example, or they may be holding out for high salaries; sometimes they have the right skills and appropriate ambitions but still can't land a job in the current market. The government's definition of unemployment attempts to capture all of these situations. Statistics Canada, the government agency in charge of collecting employment statistics via the Labour Force Survey, defines unemployment in this way:

> Persons aged 15 years and older who had no employment during the reference week, were available for work, except for temporary illness, and had made specific efforts to find employment sometime during the 4-week period ending with the reference week.[2]

This definition means that Canada counts people as being unemployed only if they meet three criteria:

1. They didn't work at all in the prior week.
2. They were available to work if they had been offered a job.
3. They were making efforts to look for a job.

Measuring Unemployment

> **LO 10.1** Explain how economists measure employment and unemployment.

In this section we will put together all the pieces you need to understand the sort of unemployment figures you might see in the newspaper or a Statistics Canada official report. These reports are extremely influential in the worlds of business and politics; everyone wants to know what the latest information about unemployment says about the health of the economy.

First, we need to define some key groups of people. The *working-age population* is the civilian, non-institutionalized population aged fifteen and over. That means all adults except those who are in the armed forces (such as soldiers) or who are inmates in an institution (such as a prison or mental-health facility).

However, not everyone who is over fifteen wants to work. In the official definition of unemployment, we want to count only those people who are "available for work" and "making specific efforts to find employment." That means we don't count full-time students as unemployed, or parents who are staying home to look after their children. Nor do we count people who cannot work because they are disabled, or people who have inherited wealth and choose to live off that wealth rather than work. In Canada, we don't count retirees as unemployed, either. (Some countries define the working-age population as sixteen to sixty-four, but Statistics Canada does not impose an upper age limit.)

If we want to refer to people of working age excluding retirees, stay-at-home parents, and so on, we instead talk about the *labour force.* The **labour force** consists of people in the working-age population who are either employed or unemployed. In other words, it is all the people who are currently working or who would like to work and are actively trying to find a job.

We now have the numbers we need to define the **unemployment rate**. This is the number of people who are unemployed divided by the labour force:

Equation 10-1

$$\text{Unemployment rate} \ = \ \frac{\text{number of unemployed}}{\text{labour force}} \times 100$$

$$= \ \frac{\text{unemployed}}{(\text{employed} + \text{unemployed})} \times 100$$

Table 10-1 shows the official unemployment and employment numbers for the Canadian economy for June 2008 and June 2009. The first date, June 2008, is just before the start of the economic downturn. The data for one year later show the recovering effects that a recession can have on a labour market. Over this one-year period there was a large increase in the number of unemployed people, from 1,079,100 to 1,585,700.

TABLE 10-1   CANADIAN EMPLOYMENT STATISTICS

Despite increases in working-age population and the number of people in the labour force, the overall number of people employed fell, and unemployment increased from 2008 to 2009.

Month	Working-age population (non-institutionalized)	Labour force	Employed	Unemployed
June 2008	26,808,500	18,079,800	17,000,700	1,079,100
June 2009	27,187,800	18,259,800	16,674,600	1,585,700

Source: Statistics Canada, CANSIM Table 282-0087, "Labour force survey estimates (LFS), by sex and age group, seasonally adjusted and unadjusted"

Dividing these figures by the labour force, also shown in Table 10-1, gives us the unemployment rate:

Unemployment rate, June 2008:

$$\frac{1,079,100}{18,079,800} \times 100 \ = \ 6.0\%$$

Unemployment rate, June 2009:

$$\frac{1,585,700}{18,259,800} \times 100 \ = \ 8.7\%$$

The June 2009 unemployment rate tells us that at the middle of 2009, nearly 8.7 percent of Canadians who wanted to work couldn't find work.

The unemployment rate describes what is going on in the national economy as a whole, but doesn't tell us much about *who* is affected. In general, the unemployment rate varies greatly by educational status, gender, age, and race. On average, younger people have higher unemployment rates than older people, and people with less education are more likely to be unemployed than people with more education.

We can also learn something interesting about the state of the economy by looking at the **labour-force participation rate**:

Equation 10-2

$$\text{Labour-force participation rate } = \frac{\text{labour force}}{\text{working-age population}} \times 100$$

This figure tells us what fraction of the population wants to be working, whether or not they actually have a job. During recessions we usually see the labour-force participation rate fall.

Some people who are unemployed eventually give up looking for work. Once these people stop actively looking for a job, they are no longer considered part of the labour force. Other people may drop out of the labour force in a recession because they choose to go back to school, or take early retirement, or become homemakers instead of looking for work.

Based on Table 10-1, we can compute the labour-force participation rate in June 2008:

$$\frac{18,\ 079,\ 800}{26,\ 808,\ 500} \times 100 \ = \ 67.4\%$$

This means that 67.4 percent of the total working-age population was in the labour force in June 2008. In June 2009 the labour-force participation rate was:

$$\frac{18,259,800}{27,187,800} \times 100 \ = \ 67.2\%$$

Over the one-year period, 0.2 percent of the working-age population stopped participating in the labour force. It is likely that at least some of these people would have been unemployed if they had stayed in the labour force, so the unemployment rate may understate the effect of the recession on employment.

Table 10-2 summarizes the two different measures of the Canadian labour market.

POTENTIALLY CONFUSING

When discussing unemployment, people often talk about *percentage point* changes—such as the unemployment rate increasing by 2.7 percentage *points,* from 6.0 percent to 8.7 percent. Sometimes people talk loosely about unemployment, referring to such a change as unemployment going up by "2.7 percent" rather than by "2.7 percentage points." There is a big difference, although people may guess what is meant.

If we want to, we could of course talk about changes in unemployment in terms of percent, rather than percentage points. For example, from 6.0 to 8.7 is an increase of 45 percent. That would be technically accurate, but you rarely hear economists talk this way.

Talking in percentage *points* makes a change easier to conceptualize. If you hear that the unemployment rate increased by "2.7 percentage points," for example, it means that 27 people out of every 1,000 in the labour force have lost their jobs. On the other hand, if you hear that an economy's unemployment rate increased by "45 percent," you have no way of knowing how bad the change really is. Maybe the increase was from 1 percent unemployment to 1.45 percent, which would be considered a small change. Or maybe unemployment went from 10 percent to 14.5 percent, which would be considered a huge change. This is why statisticians and economists report changes in percentage points, not percentages, when discussing unemployment.

TABLE 10-2   EMPLOYMENT IN CANADA, 2008 AND 2009

The recession increased the unemployment rate, while the percentage of the population participating in the labour force fell.

	Unemployment rate (%)	Labour-force participation rate (%)
June 2008	6.0	67.4
June 2009	8.7	67.2
Change	+2.7	−0.2

Source: Statistics Canada, CANSIM Table 282-0087, "Labour force survey estimates (LFS), by sex and age group, seasonally adjusted and unadjusted."

Beyond the Unemployment Rate

The unemployment rate is often used to summarize the state of the labour market, but it has significant limitations. Most obviously, it doesn't include people who gave up hope of finding a job, as the individual was deemed to have dropped out of the labour force and was no longer counted as unemployed.

This seems like a semantic trick. Why should we count individuals as unemployed when they're feeling optimistic and spend their days sending out resumés, but not when they turn pessimistic and give up the search? In fact, Statistics Canada has a term for theses individuals: **discouraged workers**. Discouraged workers are people who have looked for work in the past year but have given up looking because of the condition of the labour market.

Thinking about discouraged workers gives a broader view of who is affected by a recession. What about people who have part-time jobs but would like to work full time? Such people are defined as being **underemployed**. So are workers who are in jobs that are not suited to their skill level—for example, a law-school grad who can't get a job in law and reluctantly takes work as a barista at Starbucks. Statistics Canada collects data on the first kind of underemployment (people who are working fewer hours than they would like), but unfortunately not on the second kind (working in a job for which they are overqualified).

The other notable change that occurred during the recession was the increasing percentage of people who were unemployed for a long stretch of time. In 2007, people unemployed for more than fourteen weeks made up only 2.4 percent of the labour force. In 2009, this number rose to 4.2 percent of the labour force, or about half of all unemployed people. This change shows that unemployment during the recession wasn't just about short stints of joblessness between positions, but also about long-term inability to find work.

Discouraged workers are not counted as unemployed.

© Tony Biddle, Perfect World Design.

Where Does the Data Come From?

The main source of information on unemployment in Canada is a household survey that asks people if they are working and how much they are earning. This survey, performed by Statistics Canada, is called the Labour Force Survey. Every month, employees of Statistics Canada survey about 60,000 households. It's not exact—it would be prohibitively expensive to survey every single Canadian household every month—but the sample size is big enough to give a reliable estimate for the economy as a whole.

The survey is collected year-round, allowing Statistics Canada to analyze and adjust for changes in unemployment that are due to the season. If you're a trained ski instructor, for example, you'll more easily find work in February than in August. Farm workers and construction workers are also affected by seasonal changes. Statistics Canada publishes statistics that are *seasonally adjusted,* in order to help distinguish these expected seasonal patterns from deeper shifts in economic conditions. The data we show in the tables here are all seasonally adjusted.

✓ CONCEPT CHECK

☐ How is the labour-force participation rate calculated? [LO 10.1]
☐ Are discouraged workers counted as being unemployed? [LO 10.1]
☐ How is underemployment different from unemployment? [LO 10.1]

Equilibrium in the Labour Market

LO 10.2 Explain how wage rates above equilibrium cause unemployment.

The existence of *any* amount of unemployment is a bit of a puzzle. Labour is bought and sold in a market, just like other goods and services. There is demand for labour (from firms wanting to hire workers), a supply of labour (from individuals looking for jobs), and a price (called the wage). In most markets, we expect the price to adjust until the market reaches equilibrium, a point at which the quantity supplied equals the quantity demanded.

The existence of unemployment suggests that this simplest of models can't fully explain what goes on in the labour market. In this section we explore the predictions of the simple model. In the next section we'll add nuance to show that unemployment can arise when the wage is held above the equilibrium level or when real world frictions prevent labour supply or labour demand from adjusting perfectly to changes in the economy.

As in any other market, the labour market features a demand curve and a supply curve. Demand for labour comes from firms, which need labour to produce output. The **labour demand curve**, depicted in Figure 10-1, panel A, shows the relationship between the wage rate and the total quantity of labour demanded by all the firms in the economy. All things being equal, firms will want to hire more labour when wages are lower and less labour when wages are higher.

The supply of labour comes from people who are able to work and who choose to participate in the labour market. As we have seen, not everyone who could potentially work wants to work. Other things being equal, we expect that, across the economy as a whole, people will be willing to supply more labour at higher wage rates, and less labour at lower wage rates. The **labour supply curve**, pictured in Figure 10-1, panel B, shows the relationship between the total quantity of labour supplied in the economy and the wage rate.

Together, the labour demand and labour supply curves describe the national labour market, as shown in Figure 10-2. As in any other market, equilibrium occurs at the intersection of the supply and demand curves. At the equilibrium wage, quantity demanded equals quantity supplied, meaning that everyone who wants to work at prevailing wages, and has the required skills, is able to find a job.

FIGURE 10-1

Labour Demand and Labour Supply

(A) Firms and the labour market

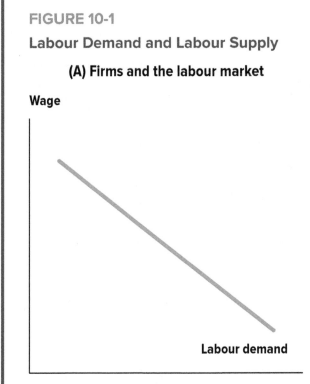

As the price of labour, or the wage, decreases, the amount of labour demanded by firms increases. This relationship is shown by the curve above.

(B) Workers and the labour market

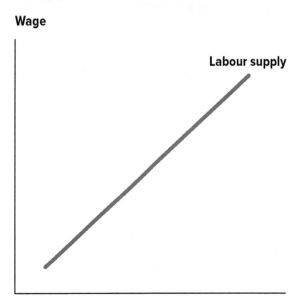

Conversely, as the wage rate increases, workers are increasingly willing to supply labour. This relationship is shown by the curve above.

Our definition of unemployment—people wanting to work, but being unable to find a job at the prevailing wage—is easy to rephrase in the language of supply and demand. The quantity of labour supplied at the prevailing wage (people wanting to work at that wage) is greater than the quantity of labour demanded (jobs offered by firms wanting to hire at that wage). In other words, there is a *surplus* of labour.

Surplus arises in a market when the prevailing price is higher than the equilibrium price. (Look back at Chapter 6, "Government Intervention," if you need to confirm this statement.)

Figure 10-3 shows how unemployment occurs when the wage rate is W_1—that is, higher than the equilibrium level of W^*. In this very simple model, unemployment is the gap between the number of people who want to work and the number of jobs offered at the prevailing wage. (However, we'll see in a minute that when a little nuance is added to the model, we can get unemployment even when the wage is not above the equilibrium level.)

FIGURE 10-2

The Labour Market in Equilibrium

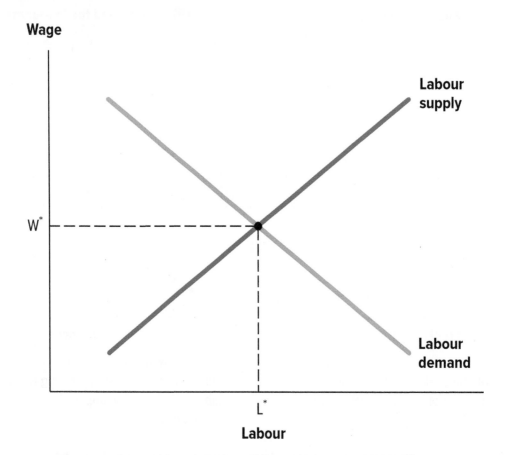

When the labour demand and labour supply curves are put together, they form a labour market of people willing to buy and sell labour. Like any other market, where the curves intersect the market is at equilibrium, with a stable wage (price) and amount of labour bought and sold.

Here's the puzzle: Why would wages remain above the equilibrium level? We know what *should* happen in a market when the price is too high: the price should fall until the market reaches equilibrium. So, why don't firms offer lower wages, or unemployed people offer to work for lower wages, until the equilibrium wage is reached? In the next section we'll look at several reasons this might not happen, as well as reasons unemployment can occur even at the equilibrium wage.

FIGURE 10-3

The Labour Market with Unemployment

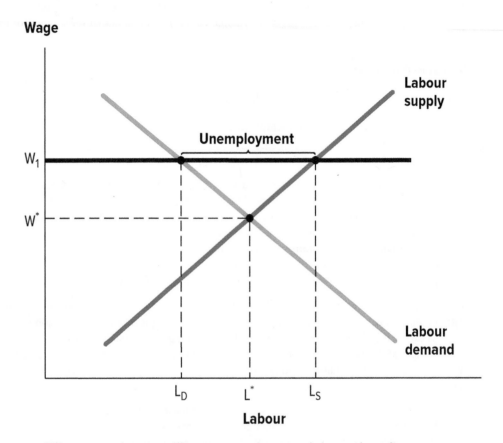

When people are willing to supply more labour than firms are willing to hire, the labour market has a surplus of workers, which is also known as unemployment.

✓ CONCEPT CHECK

☐ What is the equilibrium price of labour also called? [LO 10.2]
☐ What two curves intersect at the labour market equilibrium? [LO 10.2]

Categories of Unemployment

To start understanding the causes of unemployment, it's helpful to separate out two categories of unemployment. First is unemployment explained by the *natural* rate of unemployment. This is the normal level of unemployment that persists in an economy in the long run. Second is *cyclical* unemployment, which describes short-term fluctuations around this long-run norm. We'll see that some unemployment is an unavoidable part of a dynamic economy, but also that the amount of unemployment is affected by public policy.

Natural Rate of Unemployment

> **LO 10.3** Explain why there is a natural rate of unemployment in an economy.

The simplified model of the labour market described in Figure 10-3 suggests that we might reasonably expect to see *zero* unemployment when the market is in long-run equilibrium. The data in the first half of the chapter, however, showed that this is never the case (even when the economy is doing well). Instead, all economies experience some level of unemployment, regardless of how well or badly the economy is doing in the short term. We refer to this normal level of unemployment that persists in an economy in the long run as the **natural rate of unemployment**. The natural rate of unemployment is also sometimes called the *equilibrium rate of unemployment.*

Three contributors lead to the natural rate of unemployment. The first is **frictional unemployment**, which is unemployment caused by workers who are changing their location, job, or career. When people search for new jobs, it takes time to search for openings, submit applications, interview, move to a new city, and so on. How long it takes to make a job transition can depend on a lot of factors, including how well informed workers are about job openings, how picky they are about waiting to find the job that is the best possible match, and what resources they can draw on to support them while they search. Some amount of frictional unemployment is unavoidable—it's a natural and healthy part of life in a dynamic economy. Jobs in one company open up while others close, and ambitious workers leave their jobs to seek out better positions.

The second contributor to the natural rate of unemployment is **structural unemployment**. It is unemployment that results from a mismatch between the skills workers can offer and the skills that are in demand. Consumer preferences are constantly shifting and new technologies are being invented all the time. As a result, skills that are in demand today may not be in demand next year. If people could switch effortlessly from a job in a shrinking industry (like auto manufacturing) to one in a booming industry (like online services), then structural unemployment wouldn't exist. However, the reality is that people have educational qualifications, job experience, and family and community ties that are hard to change in the short run. These qualifications and ties make them better suited for jobs in some sectors and locations than others. A changing economy can lead to a mismatch between the types of jobs that firms are offering and the type of jobs for which people are qualified.

For example, consider the job of travel agent. If you want to book a flight, you probably just go online, right? A couple of decades ago, you would have gone to a travel agent who would have used a special database of routes and prices to propose an itinerary. The advent of websites such as Travelocity, Kayak, Priceline, and Expedia allow customers to do the travel agent's job for themselves easily and quickly. As a result, demand for the services of travel agents has plummeted; people who trained as travel agents lost their jobs and couldn't find new ones using the same knowledge and skills.

Some degree of structural unemployment is inevitable in an ever-changing economy, but governments can take steps to minimize it. One way is to provide information to unemployed people about which professions are experiencing rising demand for labour. Another way is to subsidize retraining programs for unemployed workers to learn new skills, improving their chances of finding work. These programs can help, but the changes can take years. If you were a middle-aged, unemployed auto worker, could you imagine moving to a different part of the country to start a new career from scratch?

The third contributor to the natural rate of unemployment is **real-wage or classical unemployment**. This idea captures the effect of wages remaining persistently above the market-clearing level. It's what we saw in Figure 10-3: anything that acts like a price floor in the labour market will create surplus labour, which we call unemployment. Examples include minimum wage laws, bargaining by unions, and strategic choices by employers to pay wages above the equilibrium rate. We'll explore each of these possible explanations later in the chapter.

The common thread in these different contributors to the natural rate of unemployment is that they reflect underlying features of the economy. As you'd guess, the features can change over time, which can raise or lower the natural rate. For instance, a new policy dramatically raising the minimum wage by $10 an hour would surely raise the natural rate of unemployment. An educational system that re-trains laid-off workers could lower the natural rate. The natural rate of unemployment, however, doesn't go up and down with every boom and bust in the economy. Those short-term fluctuations in unemployment need a different explanation, which we turn to next.

Cyclical Unemployment

LO 10.4 Explain why unemployment has a cyclical component.

The economy goes through ups and downs over time, and these fluctuations are reflected by changes in GDP growth. Economists call this pattern of ups and downs the *business cycle,* a topic we'll discuss further in Chapter 11, "Aggregate Demand and Aggregate Supply." The business cycle matters for unemployment because it affects the demand for labour. When the economy is going strong, demand for workers increases as firms expand their operations. When the economy slows down, demand for workers decreases as firms downsize. **Cyclical unemployment** is unemployment caused by these short-term economic fluctuations. Because GDP growth tends to go in *cycles,* speeding up and slowing down in an irregular pattern, we call the related unemployment cyclical, too.

Imagine the effect of an economic slowdown as a reduction in the total demand for labour at any wage. In other words, the labour demand curve shifts to the left. In the simple labour market model, this change would cause the equilibrium to move down along the supply curve, reaching a new equilibrium at a lower quantity of labour and a lower wage. Why don't wages simply fall during a cyclical slowdown, so that the market still clears and cyclical unemployment is zero? The typical explanation is that wages are *sticky* in the real world, meaning that they are slow to respond to shifts in the economy.

There are many possible reasons for wage stickiness. Some workers may be on contracts that are difficult to change, or employers may choose not to raise and lower wages all the time because it will upset workers and cause them to work less hard. The degree of wage stickiness in the real world is a controversial topic, even among economists. The result of wage stickiness is that actual wages are temporarily above the market-clearing level, which causes cyclical unemployment. When the economy swings back toward the boom part of the business cycle, labour demand will recover and cyclical unemployment will decrease.

In general, when growth goes down, unemployment tends to go up shortly after, and vice versa. The slight delay, or time lag, makes unemployment what we call a *lagging* or *trailing* indicator. It takes time for changes in the economy to translate into changes in employment. Employers wait to see how bad a recession looks before making the difficult decision to lay off workers, or how solid a recovery looks before taking on new employees. While playing wait and see, firms may first try to decrease or increase the hours of existing employees.

✓ CONCEPT CHECK

☐ What is the natural rate of unemployment? [LO 10.3]
☐ Contrast frictional and structural unemployment. [LO 10.3]
☐ With what measure does cyclical unemployment tend to move? [LO 10.4]

Public Policies and Other Influences on Unemployment

Addressing issues relating to unemployment can be tough. Unemployment is an important indicator of the overall health of the economy. It is also a very personal issue for those who experience it. As a result, discussions about the causes of unemployment—particularly those that have implications for public policy—can get heated.

In this section, we'll break down some of the policies and other factors in the economy that can influence the level of unemployment. Before we get into the details, though, consider one example of a controversial unemployment-related debate—do foreign workers cause unemployment by taking jobs? See the From Another Angle box, Canada's Temporary Foreign Worker Program (TFWP): Effects on the Labour Market, to see why economists generally disagree that this is the case.

FROM ANOTHER ANGLE

Canada's Temporary Foreign Worker Program (TFWP): Effects on the Labour Market

The temporary foreign worker program (TFWP) was created some forty years ago for employers in Canada who have trouble recruiting Canadian citizens or permanent residents for job openings. The original program was created to fill a short-term shortage of executives, academics, and other highly skilled individuals.

In 2002, the program was expanded to include occupations classified as *lower skilled* (these are occupations coded in the National Occupation Classifications at C or D skill levels). The program is jointly managed by Human Resources and Skill Development Canada (HRSDC), and Citizenship and Immigration Canada (CIC).

The number of temporary foreign workers has since increased drastically. Ontario, Quebec, and the Atlantic provinces saw the largest increase in temporary workers after the recession. (Incidentally, wages in some of these regions are also below the national average.) Thirty percent of new jobs created in non-agricultural sectors in 2011 were filled by temporary foreign workers, primarily in fast food restaurants, on construction sites, in nursing homes, and in nightclubs. In Alberta, they were also employed in extractive industries like mining, oil, and gas. Most of these workers had virtually no path to permanent residency, and employers could pay them up to 15 percent less than the prevailing wage.

But rising resentment and unemployment among domestic workers, along with public pressure regarding how foreign workers are treated, led the Harper government to make changes to the TFWP in May 2013. These changes included more stringent language requirements and shortening of the length of advertising periods for job openings that target foreign workers.

All of this suggests that Canada has a problem caused by foreign workers taking Canadian jobs. It looks like a straightforward case, right? Well, no. Applying some economic logic, we can add important details to the story.

For a start, foreign workers are living in Canada, so they are also spending money in Canada, increasing demand for the goods and services supplied by local businesses. Also, some of the money the companies save on wages will likely end up reflected in lower prices, saving consumers money. Some of the money consumers save will get spent elsewhere, in other businesses. This increased demand from consumers will lead local firms to hire more labour. That's good news for domestic workers who are looking for work.

There will, as always, be winners and losers, as foreign workers tend to compete for some kinds of jobs more than others. If there's an influx of new foreign workers who want to find jobs as construction labourers, this is bad news for Canadians looking for construction work: they'll face more competition for jobs, which will drive down wages. But it's good news if you're a Canadian who runs a construction company: you now have more candidates to choose from, some of whom might be willing to accept a lower wage. You might earn higher profits, which you will then spend in other parts of the economy, creating demand for labour elsewhere.

So we begin to see that it's an over-simplification to say that foreign workers are stealing jobs from domestic workers. Over time, these foreign workers can also expand the economy by increasing the size of the labour force, by contributing to economic growth by reducing the costs of production, and by increasing the demand for good and services. There's no doubt that importing foreign workers is a political hot potato. Rhetoric and emotion can get in the way of seeing the full picture, and the political debate more readily focuses on immediate job losses. And it's often hard to put numbers on society's longer-term gains.

But there are many reasons economists reject the simplistic assertion that foreign temporary workers necessarily cause unemployment. Economists see their role as trying to assess all of these trade-offs with as much balance as possible.

Source: Government of Canada, "Fact Sheet — Temporary Foreign Worker Program". http://www.cic.gc.ca/english/resources/publications/employers/temp-foreign-worker-program.asp.

Factors That May Stop Wage Rates from Falling

LO 10.5 Identify factors that may stop wages from falling to the equilibrium level.

In the previous section, we noted that unemployment can be influenced by forces that prevent wages from falling to the market-clearing level, either in the long run (through the natural rate of unemployment) or in response to short-term economic fluctuations (though cyclical unemployment). Why don't wages fall so that everyone with the skills and desire gets a job? In this section we will look at three possible explanations:

- The government might prevent it, through minimum wage legislation.
- Labour unions might prevent it, through bargaining backed by the threat to strike.
- Firms themselves might prevent it, by voluntarily choosing to pay higher wages than necessary.

Let's consider these three explanations in turn.

Minimum Wage

A *minimum wage* is the lowest wage that a firm is legally allowed to pay its workers. In Canada, the minimum wage ranges from $10.30 per hour in New Brunswick to $12.50 in the Northwest Territories. This wage is approximately the wage that entry-level workers at a fast-food restaurant earn. A worker who is earning the minimum wage and working forty hours a week earns just over $22,000 a year, before taxes.

Supporters of minimum wage legislation argue that workers deserve a basic standard of living. They say it would not be fair to allow firms to pay workers a wage that would leave them struggling to escape poverty. Opponents of minimum wage legislation point to graphs like the one we showed in Figure 10-3, which suggest that if the minimum wage is higher than the equilibrium wage, then we would expect unemployment to result. Of course, if the minimum wage is set at a level *below* the equilibrium wage, it will have no effect; this is called a *non-binding* minimum wage.

Does a minimum wage cause unemployment? The question can't be resolved by a theoretical analysis alone. We need to look at data. Economists have found evidence both for and against the idea that a minimum wage causes unemployment, and the debate rages on. Evidence from Newfoundland and Labrador indicates that raising the minimum wage did not cause firms to lay off employees. This implies that the real-world labour market does not work exactly like the model shown in Figure 10-3. In other cases, economists have found that minimum wages appear to cause a small amount of unemployment, or a change in *who* is employed, as firms substitute more skilled, older workers for unskilled, younger workers.

Another possibility some economists raise, given that the minimum wage applies only to people hired legally, is that it could drive jobs "under the table." That is, firms might respond to minimum wage legislation by employing undocumented migrants at below-minimum wages or pay workers in cash without telling the government.

Views on a minimum wage vary greatly. If the minimum wage does indeed cause unemployment, people who can't find jobs will lose out, while people lucky enough to be in jobs will benefit. If it *doesn't* cause unemployment, then all workers will benefit, while firms lose out by making lower profits.

Unions and Bargaining

In 2002, Alberta teachers went on strike. They picketed outside schools, refusing to work until the government accepted their demands for smaller classes and an increase in salary. The teachers' strike meant that schools had to shut down for 200,000 students, and the teachers gave up millions in lost wages. The strike was resolved after thirteen days (the government used an order-in-council to force an end), with the teachers gaining a substantial pay increase.

Strikes like this are made possible by the existence of labour unions. In this case the teachers were part of a union called the Alberta Teachers' Association. **Labour unions** are groups of employees who join together to bargain with their employer(s) over salaries and work conditions. In 2010, union membership had increased to 30 percent of wage and salary workers from less than 20 percent in the 1950s. But the opposite is true in the US. In the 1950s, one-third of US workers were in unions. The proportion is far lower today: about 12 percent of all wage and salary workers, or just under 15 million Americans, are in unions, and about half of these union members work for government entities.[3]

A unions benefits its members because it allows them to bargain as a group. If just a few disgruntled teachers had gone on strike, then other teachers could easily have been brought in to cover for them. But if workers strike together, they can bring the school system to a halt. This threat enables workers to drive a harder bargain with employers on wages and working conditions.

What does the existence of labour unions mean for the labour market and for unemployment? If labour unions drive a hard enough bargain, wage rates can rise above the equilibrium level. Then the effect of labour unions is the same as that of the minimum wage. To the extent that the labour market behaves like any other market, when unions manage to negotiate higher wages for their members, employers will, in theory, respond by employing fewer people. That means that being in a union is good for its own members, but can be harmful for the unemployed looking for work. There's some evidence, though, that the presence of unions pushes wages upward even for workers who are not in a union (if they work in a sector with a strong union presence). One reason is that employers with non-union workers want to keep their employees happy enough that they do not feel the need to form a union.

Beyond working to keep wages up, unions also try to ensure that working conditions are safe and that workers get benefits like health insurance, pension plans, and vacation time. Opinions about the role of unions on wages depend on whether you think that labour markets do a good job of determining fair wages and how much weight you put on the well-being of unemployed people versus people with jobs.

Efficiency Wages

What if paying wages above market-clearing levels is simply a smart decision by firms? Another reason wages may be above the market-clearing level is that some firms *want* to pay their workers more than the going wage. Why would they do this? There are two related reasons:

1. Paying a higher wage will make workers less likely to quit, saving the expense of advertising for, interviewing, and training new people.
2. Workers are more likely to fear losing their jobs and might work harder to keep the jobs they have.

Thus, it could be efficient for a firm to pay workers more than the going wage rate, especially in sectors where skills are scarce and worker motivation really matters. The idea is to give positive incentives to maximize productivity: job transitions, from one worker to another, harm productivity. Also, when workers exert more effort to keep their jobs, this improves productivity. The idea of deliberately setting wages above the market rate in order to increase productivity is captured by the term **efficiency wage**. Henry Ford is famous for instituting an efficiency wage at the Ford car factories in Detroit. He doubled his workers' wages in 1914 in order to reduce costly turnover and absenteeism, a move that turned out to be quite profitable.

How might efficiency wages prevent wages from falling in a recession? Imagine that you are running a firm with ten employees, and a recession causes the wage rate for labour to drop by 10 percent. Which would you rather do—force all your employees to take a 10 percent pay cut or fire one employee? You might calculate that the latter option is better. Sure, it would leave you with one fewer employee, but all nine remaining employees would be highly motivated to work hard and keep their jobs, knowing they are earning above the going rate. Among them, the nine employees may even end up producing more for the firm than ten employees (disgruntled because of their pay cut) would have produced.

In addition, the fact that efficiency wages can create unemployment can strengthen their impact. When employers fire workers (rather than cut pay), the rising level of unemployment worsens the consequences of losing a job. When workers fear an extended period of unemployment (rather than just having to work at a lower wage), they are likely to push themselves that much harder.

There is little clear evidence so far about how much of unemployment can be explained by efficiency wages. Some economists think that it's a key feature of labour markets; others argue that simply raising wages is unlikely to increase productivity. Recently economists have built on the efficiency wage idea that workers' effort is also determined by whether wages are seen as being "fair."[4] Needing to maintain "fair" wages might also limit employers' flexibility in cutting wages. The idea has support from laboratory-style economic experiments that explore made-up situations, and the idea awaits rigorous study in the real labour market.

Employment Insurance

> **LO 10.6** Describe the challenges policy makers face when designing employment insurance.

Frictional and structural unemployment are part of the normal working of the economy. Most economists, though, believe that some government policies can affect the level of these kinds of unemployment. One is employment insurance. **Employment insurance** is money that is paid by the government to people who are unemployed. There are usually certain conditions that determine eligibility—recipients must be actively looking for work and reporting work-related activities.

Employment insurance doesn't directly affect the wage rate, so it is not an explanation for why wages do not reach equilibrium. Rather, employment insurance can affect *how quickly* people find jobs. That factor will affect the natural rate of unemployment—that is, both frictional and structural unemployment. Employment insurance makes joblessness less painful by giving people income while they look for work.

The effect of employment insurance on unemployment is ambiguous. On one hand, if employment insurance is generous people might not look as hard for work. People may be more likely to take their time and wait for a better job, rather than accept the first job offered. This suggests that employment insurance could increase the equilibrium level of unemployment.

On the other hand, if people don't have to rush into taking the first job they're offered, they are more likely to find the right job for them. Having employers and employees better matched may mean that fewer people leave their jobs, which may reduce the level of frictional unemployment.

Which effect will be greater is up for debate. Another matter for discussion is the "right" level of employment insurance to offer if we want the two effects to balance out—giving people enough breathing space to find a suitable job, but not so much that they become unrealistic perfectionists.

The amount and duration of employment insurance varies widely between countries. In Canada, employment insurance is based on how much an individual earned over the previous year, up to a maximum level. The maximum duration of unemployment benefits is fifty-two weeks. However, this time period can be extended in times of unusually high unemployment. For example, during the recession of 2008–2009, the maximum limit was extended. What happens if you don't have a job when your employment insurance runs out? In Canada people can move onto other government welfare programs if they still cannot find employment after the insurance expires.

Not all countries offer employment insurance. For more on how such countries help those who are out of work, see the Real Life box, Unemployment and Developing Countries.

REAL LIFE

Unemployment and Developing Countries

Some developing countries have very high levels of unemployment. In South Africa, for example, more than 25 percent of the labour force is unemployed, even by the most narrowly defined measures. In developing countries, employment insurance is not the norm, and low-income countries must often devote government budgets to more pressing needs. Where does this leave the unemployed?

Governments in some low-income countries have implemented measures to help those without work. India, for example, has a program called the National Rural Employment Guarantee Act, which guarantees adults 100 days of work per year. The work usually is at the minimum wage on low-skilled projects such as building roads, but it's a job nonetheless. By 2012, the program had provided work for 38 million people.

Two survival options for those without a job are much more common in low-income countries than in Canada. One is the informal sector. The informal sector provides jobs without formal contracts and legal protections. These jobs include street-sellers, maids, taxi drivers, weavers, and small-scale factory workers.

Women in Informal Employment: Globalizing and Organizing (WIEGO) is an organization that has teamed up with the International Labour Organization to collect data about informal job activity. They estimate that, outside of agriculture, about one-half to three-quarters of workers in low-income economies are informally employed. If you include workers in agriculture (most of whom are farmers), the number can be as high as 90 percent, especially in South Asia and sub-Saharan Africa. The informal sector tends to offer lots of part-time, temporary jobs, and that makes it easier for people who lose one job to patch together income by taking other, short-term jobs.

The other option is to rely on extended family. Studies like *Portfolios of the Poor: How the World's Poor Live on $2 a Day* (co-written by one of the authors of this book) show that in Bangladesh and South Africa, where there is not much government support available, extended families use a complicated web of money transfers to help support each other in hard times.

In short, unemployment is a global problem—but like many problems, the solutions depend a lot on the resources available to address it within each country.

Sources: Government of India, Ministry of Rural Labour, Mahatma Gandhi National Rural Employment Guarantee Act, 2005: Report to the People, 2012, http://nrega.nic.in/circular/Report%20to%20the%20people_english%20web.pdf; Mari Megias, "Policy matters: The informal economy," Harvard Kennedy School, 2012, http://www.hks.harvard.edu/news-events/news/articles/policy-matters-the-informal-economy; and Daryl Collins, Jonathan Morduch, Stuart Rutherford, and Orlanda Ruthven, *Portfolios of the Poor: How the World's Poor Live on $2 a Day* (Princeton, NJ: Princeton University Press, 2009).

Other Factors: Taxes and Worker Rights

Employment insurance is just one policy we can expect to affect rates of unemployment. What are some others?

Taxes on wage income are important, as well. We would expect, all else equal, that lower taxes would reduce unemployment. The reasoning is that people have more incentive to find a job, knowing they will keep more of the income they earn from the job. The magnitude of the impact taxes have on job-search efforts, however, is inconclusive.

Another important factor is the ease with which employers can fire employees. In some countries, firing can be done on a whim, without explanation. In other countries, workers are legally protected and employers have to prove they have a good reason to let someone go. We would expect that policies to protect workers would lead to greater unemployment. Why? Because employers would be reluctant to hire people if they knew that it would be difficult to get rid of them. A particular aspect of this debate is explored in the What Do You Think? box, Youth Employees on Trial.

WHAT DO YOU THINK?

Youth Employees on Trial

When you start looking for your first professional job, you often hit a big challenge: without work experience, it can be tough to find a job. But how do you get work experience without having a job? This is one reason young people typically have a higher unemployment rate than older workers. If you look back at Figure 10-1, panel B, you'll see that youth unemployment peaked at close to 20 percent during the recent recession, compared with 10 percent for the whole population.

At the root of this issue lies a communication problem: young people looking for their first job lack ways to credibly demonstrate to employers that they will be good employees. Why should employers take a chance on a young person who has no job experience, when they could instead choose to employ someone with proven skills in the workplace? Of course, a particular young person with no job experience might turn out to be a great employee. But until you've employed the person, you have no way of knowing that. And once you've employed someone, it can be expensive, time-consuming, and even legally problematic to fire them.

This is the thinking that led New Zealand to implement a new policy allowing employers to fire new employees during their first ninety days at work, without the workers having any right to file legal action for unfair dismissal. Supporters of this policy say it helps young people to find jobs by removing some risk for the employer. The employer can test new employees for ninety days, and if it doesn't work out, can simply offload them.

Not everyone is happy with the idea. Some critics argue that the trial period is a way for firms to exploit young people, employing them without the same benefits and protections that other workers take for granted. Some worry that firms might never actually hire *any* permanent workers, instead relying on a constant turnover of employees under the trial period.

What do you think?

1. Is this policy a smart way to solve this information problem, or just a license to exploit young people?

2. What would keep employers from hiring and firing new workers every ninety days?

Source: New Zealand Institute of Economic Research, Inc. "90-day trial periods appear successful - NZIER Insight 25," http://nzier.org.nz/publications/90-day-trial-periods-appear-successful-nzier-insight-25 (accessed November 28, 2012).

✓ CONCEPT CHECK

☐ Why do some governments set a minimum wage? [LO 10.5]

☐ Why would an employer pay an efficiency wage? [LO 10.5]

☐ What are the trade-offs in the effect of employment insurance? [LO 10.6]

Conclusion

Most of our adult lives are spent working, and finding a great job can be a key to happiness. At the same time, not being able to find the right job—or not being able to find any job at all—can be one of the toughest life experiences.

We've discussed how the official unemployment rate is measured. Since the unemployment rate doesn't always give a full picture of labour-market conditions, economists and policy makers often pore over other measures, such as the labour-force participation rate.

We've described the main reasons for unemployment. Frictional and structural unemployment occur naturally; they will exist in any labour market regardless of policy. They are caused by people switching between jobs or shifting from one sector to another. Another type of unemployment, cyclical unemployment, mirrors the overall health of the economy and the business cycle. In boom times jobs are created and cyclical unemployment is small. But jobs are lost when the economy weakens and cyclical unemployment rises.

The labour market is in many ways like any other market. It's driven by the forces of supply and demand, and we can describe an equilibrium wage rate where the quantity of labour supplied equals the quantity of labour demanded. But there are differences too: minimum wages, bargaining by labour unions, and efficiency wages can all lead the wage rate to be above the market-clearing level for extended periods, which leads to unemployment.

Economists debate how much the rules of the labour market affect the overall rate of unemployment. We've seen that labour-market policies often come with important trade-offs. Policy makers have to decide how generous to make employment benefits, for example, and whether to make it hard for employers to fire workers. Providing more support for the unemployed may be desirable from a social perspective, but it sometimes increases unemployment rates. Similarly, raising minimum wages helps workers on the bottom rungs of the labour market, but raising minimum wages can also make it harder for unemployed workers to find jobs. The job for economists is to combine economic theory with careful empirical analysis.

Unemployment is not something that occurs in isolation from the rest of the economy. In the next chapter, the idea of unemployment will be combined with two other macroeconomic variables—price levels and national income—to create a simple model of the whole economy.

Key Terms

unemployment

labour force

unemployment rate

labour-force participation rate

discouraged workers

underemployed

labour demand curve

labour supply curve

natural rate of unemployment

frictional unemployment

structural unemployment

real-wage or classical unemployment

cyclical unemployment

labour unions

efficiency wage

employment insurance

Summary

LO 10.1 Explain how economists measure employment and unemployment.

To be considered unemployed a person needs to meet three conditions: (1) be part of the working-age, civilian population; (2) not have worked in the previous week; and (3) be actively looking for work. Economists measure unemployment with the *unemployment rate*. This is the number of people who are unemployed, divided by the labour force. The labour force participation rate is the fraction of the working age population that is working or looking for work. People who are not working but who are not actively looking for work—for example, students, homemakers, or discouraged workers—are not considered part of the labour force. Those, on the other hand, who are working jobs that don't fully use their skills or knowledge are considered to be underemployed.

LO 10.2 Explain how wage rates above equilibrium cause unemployment.

Like other markets, the labour market features a demand curve and a supply curve. The *total* demand for labour from all the firms in the economy is represented by the labour demand curve. On the whole, firms will want to hire more labour when wages are cheaper and less labour when wages are expensive, which means the labour demand curve slopes downward. The total labour supply is represented by the labour supply curve. We would expect that people will be willing to supply more labour at higher wage rates, and less labour at lower wage rates. This relationship gives the labour supply curve a positive slope. Equilibrium is reached at the wage (price of labour) where the labour demand and labour supply curves meet. Unemployment results when the market wage rate remains above the market equilibrium; it is effectively a surplus of labour at the inflated wage rate.

LO 10.3 Explain why there is a natural rate of unemployment in an economy.

We think of the economy having a long-run natural level of unemployment. This natural rate of unemployment is the amount of unemployment that is unavoidable in a dynamic economy. There are two reasons we expect the economy to have some unemployment when everything else is normal: Some unemployment is frictional, such as when people change jobs or locations. Some unemployment is structural, for example, when government policies affect the adjustment of the wage rate. Structural unemployment also includes people who are unemployed because of a mismatch between the skills demanded by firms and the skills the labour force has, perhaps as the result of developments in technology.

LO 10.4 Explain why unemployment has a cyclical component.

Some unemployment is related to changes in GDP. When GDP is higher than normal, unemployment is lower than the equilibrium rate. When GDP is lower than normal, unemployment is above the equilibrium rate. This type of unemployment is called cyclical unemployment.

LO 10.5 Identify factors that may stop wages from falling to the equilibrium level.

There are many factors that affect the level of the unemployment rate. Three reasons the wage rate may not fully adjust to the equilibrium wage rate in the labour market are: (1) a minimum wage that is above the equilibrium wage rate; (2) labour unions that negotiate a wage rate above the equilibrium wage rate; and (3) efficiency wages (wages paid by firms that are above the equilibrium wage rate).

LO 10.6 Describe the challenges policy makers face when designing employment insurance.

The design of the employment insurance programs is ultimately a balance of trade-offs. When benefits are not generous, losing a job can become a devastating financial hardship, but when benefits are *too* generous, incentives to actively search for a job are diminished. In Canada, unemployment benefits last only a short time and pay only a fraction of people's average working wages so as to minimize the incentive to shirk the job search. In European countries, unemployment benefits typically last longer and replace a greater percentage of average work income.

Review Questions

1. During the 1960s societal norms regarding working women were changing, and many women who had been housewives began working outside the home. How would you expect this new norm to change the labour-force participation rate? What about the unemployment rate? [LO 10.1]

2. List at least five categories of people who do not have paid jobs but would nevertheless *not* be considered unemployed. [LO 10.1]

3. Compare two countries, one that has unlimited employment insurance and one in which workers are eligible for twenty-six weeks of employment insurance. Explain one reason the country with more employment insurance may have a higher equilibrium unemployment rate. [LO 10.2]

4. Suppose the prime minister of a country comes to you to ask your advice. The country is currently at 8 percent unemployment, and the prime minister wishes to reduce unemployment in the country to 3 percent. As an economist, you determine that the country's natural rate of unemployment is 5 percent. What advice would you give the prime minister? [LO 10.3]

5. Innovation often requires *creative destruction*, in which a new product or technology makes previous products or technologies obsolete. For example, when the personal computer was invented, demand for typewriters plummeted; hence, the personal computer "destroyed" the typewriter. This process of creative destruction often results in structural unemployment because workers who knew how to build and maintain the old products have skills that are no longer in demand. Do you think the government has a role in either limiting how often new products are created or in helping those workers who are displaced because of the new product? [LO 10.3]

6. Suppose the government came out with a report suggesting that the economy will soon dip into recession. How do you think the levels of frictional, structural, and cyclical unemployment would change as the recession began? What would happen to the labour-force participation rate? [LO 10.4]

7. What happens to a country's levels of frictional, structural, and cyclical unemployment, as well as its labour-force participation rate, as a recession drags on for an extended period of time? [LO 10.4]

8. What happens to a country's levels of frictional, structural, and cyclical unemployment, as well as its labour-force participation rate, as a country begins to recover from a deep recession? [LO 10.4]

9. Give two reasons it may be rational for a firm to offer wages above the minimum wage. [LO 10.5]

10. In France, labour laws typically made it very difficult or even illegal for firms to fire workers during economic downturns. How would these laws affect cyclical unemployment as well as frictional and structural unemployment? (*Hint:* Think about how these laws affect firms' decisions to hire workers in the first place.) [LO 10.4], [LO 10.5]

11. Unemployment is often called a lagging or trailing indicator because unemployment tends to rise some time after the economy begins to slow down, and unemployment begins to fall again after the economy begins to rebound. In other words, unemployment trails GDP. Why do you think this might be the case? [LO 10.5]

12. The traditional goal of a government is to maximize its citizens' welfare. Given this goal, would you suggest getting rid of employment insurance? How would your answer change if the goal of the government is to maximize employment? [LO 10.6]

13. In Canada, during regular economic times, the maximum length of time a worker can collect employment insurance is forty-five weeks. During recessions, however, Parliament often increases the length of time for which workers can collect benefits. During the recent recession, workers could collect benefits for more than forty-five weeks in some regions. Comment on the advantages and disadvantages of this system. [LO 10.6]

Problems and Applications

1. For each of the following situations, is Rick Alexander counted as employed, unemployed, or not in the labour force by Statistics Canada? [LO 10.1]
   a. Alexander becomes self-employed in his job as a carpenter.
   b. Alexander moves from Alberta to Ontario and begins looking for work.
   c. Alexander feels discouraged looking for work and stops applying for jobs.
   d. Alexander starts looking for work again.
   e. Alexander starts work at a new job.

2. Using the data in Table 10P-1, calculate this economy's: [LO 10.1]
   a. Unemployment rate
   b. Labour-force participation rate

TABLE 10P-1

Working-age population	100,000
Labour force	60,000
Unemployed	10,000

Table 10P-2 uses data for the year 2014, adjusted to be comparable to each other. All population values are in thousands.

3. Refer to Table 10P-2, which uses data for the year 2014, adjusted so the numbers are comparable to each other. All population values are in thousands. [LO 10.1], [LO 10.4], [LO 10.5]
   a. Fill in the blanks in the table.
   b. You should have found that the unemployment rates of the three countries differ significantly from one another. Suggest three possible reasons to explain why the countries might have different unemployment rates.

4. Assume the equilibrium wage rate is $15. Draw a graph of the labour market to answer the following questions: [LO 10.2]
   a. When the government introduces a minimum wage of $12.00, does unemployment increase, decrease, or stay the same compared to no minimum wage?
   b. When the government introduces a minimum wage of $18.00, does unemployment increase, decrease, or stay the same compared to no minimum wage?

TABLE 10P-2

Country	Adult population	Labour force	Employed	Unemployed	Unemployment rate (%)	Labour-force participation rate (%)
Japan	77,550		62,886	2,416		
France		30,052		2,975		56.0
Germany	53,387	42,165			5.0	

5. Assume that the labour demand equation for a fictional country is $L_d = 30 - w$, where w is the wage per hour worked. Assume also that the labour supply equation for that country is $L_s = 0.5(w)$. [LO 10.2], [LO 10.5]
    a. Find the equilibrium wage and quantity of labour employed.
    b. At the equilibrium wage, how many people are unemployed?
    c. How would the number of unemployed change if the supply of workers increased? What if the demand for workers decreased?

6. Suppose a firm's labour demand equation is $L_d = 40 - 2(w)$, and the labour supply equation that it faces is $L_s = -20 + 3(w)$, where w is the wage per hour worked. [LO 10.2], [LO 10.5]
    a. Find the equilibrium wage and quantity of labour employed.
    b. The workers, thinking that their wages are too low, decide to strike. After tense negotiations, the firm decides to raise the wage by 50 percent. After the wage increase, how many people are unemployed?

7. Classify each of the following situations as either frictional, structural, or cyclical unemployment: [LO 10.3], [LO 10.4]
    a. Maria has started looking for work after taking time off to have a baby.
    b. Juan left high school without graduating and can't find any jobs he is qualified for.
    c. Rohit had a job working in the oil industry but lost his job during a fall in the oil price.
    d. Adam has just arrived in a new city and is looking for work.
    e. Max wants to work as an airline steward, but because the airline industry is heavily unionized there are very few jobs available.
    f. Jada has just lost her job in a web start-up that was affected by a downturn in the economy.

8. For each of the following situations, would the unemployment rate increase, decrease, or stay the same? [LO 10.5]
    a. A company begins paying efficiency wages above the equilibrium wage rate.
    b. The number of workers covered by union contracts falls.
    c. The government extends the duration of employment insurance.

9. Suppose a country has a twenty-six-week limit on the duration that an unemployed person receives unemployment benefits. You collect some data and notice that workers in their twenty-sixth week of employment benefits somehow manage to find jobs at a much higher rate than other unemployed workers. What would this statistic tell you about the incentives involved with employment insurance? [LO 10.6]

10. Understanding that unemployment benefits give workers the incentive to not look for work until their benefits run out, suppose an economist suggested that instead of giving workers up to fifty-two weeks of employment benefits that end once the person finds work, a person who loses his or her job would just get a single big check for fifty-two weeks of benefits, regardless of how long the worker is unemployed. What are the advantages and disadvantages of this idea? [LO 10.6]

PART FIVE

The Economy in the Short and Long Run

The two chapters in Part 5 will introduce you to ...

a basic model of the entire economy. The preceding four chapters presented the key economic concepts used to measure the health of the economy and how the economy changes over time. Now we'll put the pieces together.

Chapter 11 introduces a model to describe the state of the national economy as a whole. All of the transactions in the economy—from the snack you bought on the way to class to the purchase of new mobile devices—can be represented in a single demand curve, called *aggregate demand*. On the other side, everything that firms produce is represented by a single supply curve, called *aggregate supply*. Together, these two curves can be used to investigate changes in the entire economy, through booms and busts.

Using the aggregate demand/aggregate supply model, we can start to analyze how policy choices affect the national economy. Government decisions about taxes and spending make up *fiscal policy*, which is the focus of Chapter 12. The chapter compares the effects of taxes and government spending on the economy. It turns out that one dollar of government spending doesn't add just one dollar to overall GDP. Thanks to the effect of the *multiplier*, when the government spends money or changes taxes, the effect of this dollar is magnified throughout the economy. If you understand the role of the multiplier, you're a long way toward understanding what policy can and can't do.

Aggregate demand and aggregate supply are the main concepts used in macroeconomics to provide fundamental insights into changes in the broader economy.

CHAPTER 11

Aggregate Demand and Aggregate Supply

LEARNING OBJECTIVES

LO 11.1   List the components of aggregate demand and use these components to explain why the aggregate demand curve slopes downward.

LO 11.2   List some factors that could cause the aggregate demand curve to shift.

LO 11.3   Explain the difference between the short run and the long run in the economy.

LO 11.4   Demonstrate a shift in the short-run aggregate supply curve, and list some factors that cause it to shift.

LO 11.5   Demonstrate a shift in the long-run aggregate supply curve, and list some factors that cause it to shift.

LO 11.6   Explain the short- and long-run effects of a shift in aggregate demand.

LO 11.7   Explain the short- and long-run effects of a shift in aggregate supply.

LO 11.8   Describe the policy options the government can use to counteract supply and demand shocks.

Pop! Goes the Bubble

Between 2004 and 2008, oil market fundamentals changed. There was an unprecedented surge in global demand At the same time, non-OPEC supply underwent the first significant decrease since 1973. From Venezuela cutting off oil sales during a legal battle, to sabotage at oil fields in Iraq and Nigeria, to labour strife in Scotland, events propelled the price of oil from US$50 per barrel in early 2007 to US$140 per barrel in the summer of 2008 (before falling back to US$40 per barrel at the end of that year). The Alberta oil industry boomed as the increase in oil prices attracted newcomers from other provinces looking for a share of this wealth, and the cities of Calgary and Edmonton were transformed. At the peak of this boom, the city of Calgary issued $4- to $6-billion worth of construction permits annually (more than the city of New York). Vacancy for rental units approached zero as Ontarians and Maritimers arrived in flocks, searching for high-paying jobs. The housing market flourished; oil stocks rose.

Homeowners started feeling flush as they saw the value of their homes increase, and they started to spend on other things—a new car, a new kitchen, a holiday shopping splurge. In short order, the economy heated up. The provincial budget surplus was so large ($6.8 billion in 2005) that a prosperity bonus was announced in September 2005. It was a program that gave $400 back to every resident of Alberta (at a cost of $1.4 billion).

As unpredictably as it began, the Alberta oil boom turned out to be an example of what is called an *asset-price bubble*. Bubbles happen when people buy assets for no reason other than that they think the price will go up. During the oil boom, many people were willing to pay hefty prices simply because they believed prices would keep going up and they'd be able to sell for a profit.

But—inevitably—oil prices stopped rising. Excessive expansion in the industry and a world-wide economic recession hit the province hard. The price of oil, around US$100 between 2011 and early 2014, was in steep decline by mid-2014. During this period, the number of people coming to the province of Alberta started to slow down. Unemployment rose from 4.5 percent in July 2014 to 7 percent in November 2015 and the province lagged the nation in job creation and growth.

How can we describe what happened to the economy during this turbulent period? What is the connection between home prices, consumer spending, business investment, and the overall health of the economy? In this chapter, we will create a framework, called the *aggregate demand and aggregate supply model,* to understand how the economy operates as a whole. So far in this text we've looked at supply and demand

Larry MacDougal/The Canadian Press

in an individual market for a particular good or service. As macroeconomists, however, we need to think about *all* the goods and services in the economy. The aggregate demand and aggregate supply model is a way of adding up everything, leading to an *equilibrium* that describes the state of the national economy. We will use this model to understand how three important macroeconomic variables—output, prices, and employment—are determined and how they affect each other.

This bird's-eye view lets us see the economy from the perspective of policy makers and businesspeople, who need to consider macroeconomic shifts and frame strategies to respond to them. In the middle of 2014, the oil price crash plunged the economy deep into trouble. One of the first challenges government faced was figuring out how it should respond. In this chapter and the next, we'll see what policies are available to the government, and how they can affect the condition of the national economy.

Tying It All Together

Over the last three chapters, we've developed tools for measuring the major features of the macroeconomy: output (GDP), prices, and unemployment. But these aspects of the economy don't exist in isolation. Instead, they are different faces of one big, complex system. You probably have some intuitive sense of how they are tied together in determining the health of the economy. For instance, when we say the economy is "doing badly," most of us have a mental picture of both falling production *and* high unemployment. Similarly, you might associate crashing or skyrocketing prices of important goods, such as houses or gasoline, with economic troubles.

In this chapter, we're going to build an economic model on that intuition. The model shows how the condition of the economy—described in terms of GDP and overall price levels—is really an equilibrium outcome, equating the total demand for all goods and services with the total supply. In some superficial ways, this will look like a microeconomic model of demand and supply. In the macroeconomic model, *price* is the overall price level, calculated as a weighted average of the prices of all goods and services, usually represented by the GDP deflator; *quantity* is represented by real GDP, the measure of the value of all final goods and services produced by the economy. However, new forces come into play when we start to *aggregate* (add up) demand and supply across many different goods and services.

The model of aggregate demand and aggregate supply shows how output, prices, and employment are all tied together as part of a single economic equilibrium. This allows us to see what happens when an event like the collapse of resource prices or a natural disaster hits the economy, and why it is likely to affect all three measures. Using the same tools, we can see how a change in government policy—perhaps intended to counteract the effects of the bubble or disaster—will operate on the same system.

Aggregate Demand

This section will develop a picture of the demand side of the macroeconomy. The term *aggregate demand* describes the total demand for all goods and services in the economy. That means adding up demand across all of the individual markets for goods and services. It might seem strange to add up quantities of completely different items—literally, adding apples and oranges—but fortunately, we've already developed a tool for dealing with that problem. In Chapter 7, "Measuring the Wealth of Nations," we introduced the concept of GDP, which adds up all the goods and services in the economy by translating them into a common unit: market value. Thus, *aggregate demand* measures the total quantity of goods and services demanded in the economy in terms of their market value.

The Aggregate Demand Curve

> **LO 11.1** List the components of aggregate demand and use these components to explain why the aggregate demand curve slopes downward.

The **aggregate demand curve** shows the relationship between the overall price level and the level of total demand in the economy. When we graph aggregate demand, the price level is shown on the vertical axis and output (or GDP) is on the horizontal axis.

The aggregate demand curve slopes downward, just like the demand curves for televisions, haircuts, and any other individual good or service. But the reason for the similarity is not as obvious as it might seem. When we draw the downward-sloping demand curve for televisions, for example, we assume that the price of all other goods is held constant. Thus, the demand curve shows the change in the quantity of TVs that are demanded when *only* TV prices drop. With *aggregate* demand, though, we can't change the price of one good and hold the prices of all the other goods constant. By definition, aggregate demand represents *all* goods, so we're interested in what happens when the prices of *all* goods go up or down—as measured by the price index or inflation level.

So why does the aggregate demand curve slope downward? In Chapter 7 we saw that GDP consists of four components: consumption (C), investment (I), government spending (G), and net exports (NX):

$$GDP = \text{output} = \text{national expenditure} \quad = \quad C + I + G + NX$$

These four categories describe all the ways that people can spend in the economy. So the relationship between aggregate demand and price levels must reflect a deeper relationship based on one or more of these spending categories. Let's examine how each component reacts to changes in the overall price level of the economy.

- **Consumption:** In general, changes in the price level will change the real value of people's wealth and income. A rise in the overall price level means that a given number of dollars won't buy as much in terms of real goods and services. Thus, increases in the overall price level reduce people's wealth in terms of real purchasing power. When people are less wealthy, they reduce their consumption, creating a negative relationship between the overall price level and consumption spending. This relationship, called the *wealth effect,* gives us one way to explain the downward-sloping aggregate demand curve. As prices rise, people feel less wealthy and want to spend less, leading to a smaller quantity of goods and services demanded in the aggregate.

  There's one important caveat to note. If wages increase exactly as much as prices increase, the purchasing power of those wages will stay the same. Many employers have a standard practice of increasing wages along with inflation, and in that case the wealth effect won't come into play. But the same can't be said for wealth that you have stored as cash in your wallet, in non-interest-bearing chequing accounts, and in other dollar-denominated assets that won't necessarily increase along with inflation. Even when wages keep pace with increasing price levels, most people will probably still experience some reduction in real wealth, causing consumption to fall.

- **Investment:** When prices rise, the interest rate—roughly speaking, the price of borrowing—also tends to rise. Higher interest rates make it more expensive for firms to borrow, which means they invest less in new factories and working capital. (We'll come back to this idea in a later chapter.) The increased borrowing costs create an indirect negative relationship between the price level and investment spending.

- **Government spending:** Much of government spending is independent of the price level. Even when prices rise and fall, the government still needs to spend roughly the same amount on Social Insurance cheques and salaries for government employees. Thus, the government spending component does not contribute to the downward-sloping nature of the aggregate demand curve.

- **Net exports:** When prices in Canada increase, Canadian goods become relatively more expensive than goods from other countries, assuming that price levels stay the same in the other countries, so we would expect imports into Canada to increase and exports to decrease. This means that when the price level increases, net exports (exports minus imports) should decrease (because there is a negative relationship between the price level and net exports).

What have we learned? There is a negative relationship between price level and national expenditure for three of its four components (C, I, and NX), and no relationship between the price level and the fourth component (G). When we put this information together, we get a negative overall relationship between the price level and aggregate expenditures on GDP. In other words, we end up with a downward-sloping aggregate demand curve, as shown in Figure 11-1.

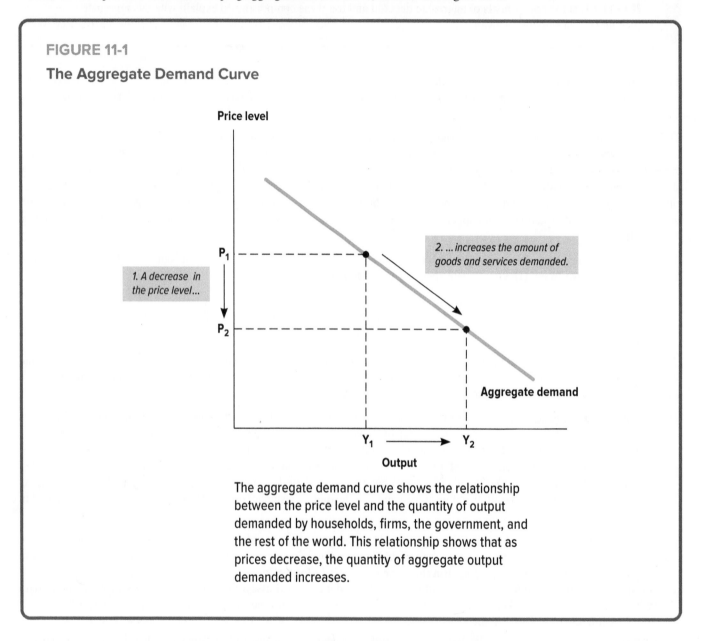

FIGURE 11-1

The Aggregate Demand Curve

1. A decrease in the price level...

2. ... increases the amount of goods and services demanded.

The aggregate demand curve shows the relationship between the price level and the quantity of output demanded by households, firms, the government, and the rest of the world. This relationship shows that as prices decrease, the quantity of aggregate output demanded increases.

Shifting the Aggregate Demand Curve

LO 11.2 List some factors that could cause the aggregate demand curve to shift.

Price changes generate movements *along* the aggregate demand curve. We saw that when the price level increases, for example, the wealth effect drives people to spend less and overall output falls. However, the entire aggregate demand curve can also *shift* in response to *non-price changes* in any of the four components of aggregate demand (consumption, investment, government spending, and net exports). These non-price changes move the entire curve to the left or right, making aggregate demand lower or higher at any given price level.

Big changes to the national economy can sometimes be described as shifts in the aggregate demand curve. Consider, for instance, the story of the oil price bubble in the 1970s. People felt confident when the increase in oil price led to higher housing prices. Homeowners could see the value of their houses increasing, which made them feel significantly wealthier and more optimistic. They started consuming more, which made all kinds of firms throughout the economy also feel good about their future prospects. They started investing more. The total effect of this boost in consumer and company confidence was to shift the aggregate demand curve to the right. Because confidence was high, people and businesses were willing to spend and invest more, increasing aggregate demand at any price level, as shown in panel A of Figure 11-2.

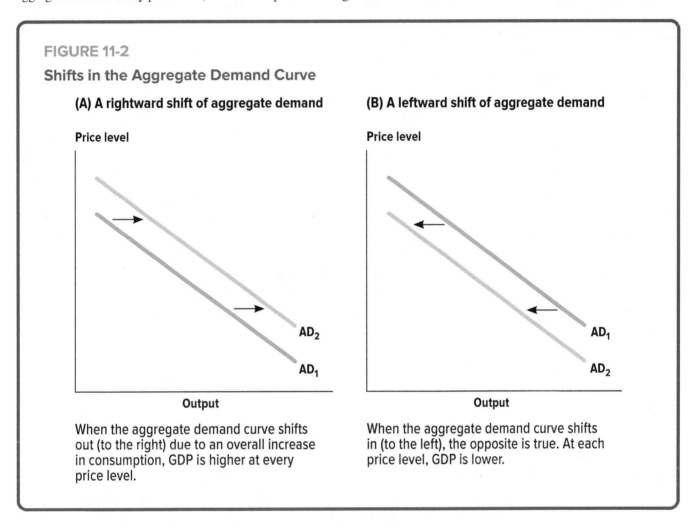

FIGURE 11-2

Shifts in the Aggregate Demand Curve

(A) A rightward shift of aggregate demand

Price level

AD₂

AD₁

Output

When the aggregate demand curve shifts out (to the right) due to an overall increase in consumption, GDP is higher at every price level.

(B) A leftward shift of aggregate demand

Price level

AD₁

AD₂

Output

When the aggregate demand curve shifts in (to the left), the opposite is true. At each price level, GDP is lower.

Unfortunately, that increase in housing prices turned out to be a bubble, which popped in the mid-1980s. House prices started to fall, and people became worried that they were not as wealthy as they thought they were. This concern reduced consumer confidence and people bought less. In turn, managers of companies became worried that they would not sell as many goods and services in the future, so they became less willing to invest. Together, this drop in confidence throughout the economy shifted aggregate demand to the left, as shown in panel B of Figure 11-2.

Confidence is a fuzzy concept, but as the example of the oil price bubble shows, it can be crucial to both consumption and investment. If people feel positive about their prospects for future income, they will be more likely to consume more. On the other hand, if people are worried about losing their jobs or paying higher prices in the future, they will probably start consuming less and saving more for a rainy day. Much the same reasoning applies to firms: if businesses are optimistic about the direction of the economy, they will want to invest more in new factories, warehouses, and machinery. But if prospects for the economy start to look bleak, managers will be less interested in expanding and increasing capacity, and will invest less. Increasing consumer and business confidence will therefore shift the aggregate demand curve to the right, while decreasing confidence shifts the curve to the left.

Some government policies, such as taxes and government spending, can also shift the aggregate demand curve. Cutting taxes paid by consumers is likely to increase consumption, because people keep more of the money they earn and so are in effect wealthier. Increased consumption spending shifts the aggregate demand curve to the right. By the same logic, raising taxes can dampen the desire to spend by leaving consumers with less money. Higher taxes shift the aggregate demand curve to the left.

The government can also affect aggregate demand through its own spending. Government spending increases aggregate demand directly, through the G in the demand equation. But as we'll see in detail in the next chapter, it can also have indirect effects on demand by encouraging more consumer spending. In the face of a recession, government can increase spending in order to shift the aggregate demand to the right. For example, this strategy could mean the construction of highways, more spending for the military, or added spending for schools. If, instead, the government sharply cuts its spending during a recession, it risks a decline in aggregate demand; in that case, the aggregate demand curve would shift to the left.

Table 11-1 shows examples of changes that can cause shifts in the aggregate demand curve. The middle column lists several factors that would increase aggregate demand, shifting the aggregate demand curve to the right. The right-hand column lists factors that would decrease aggregate demand, shifting the aggregate demand curve to the left.

TABLE 11-1   WHAT CAUSES THE AGGREGATE DEMAND CURVE TO SHIFT?

Category	Increase (shift right)	Decrease (shift left)
Consumption	• High expectations about future income increase consumer spending. • Tax cuts increase consumer spending.	• Low expectations about future income lead to greater saving and less spending. • Higher interest rates discourage borrowing.
Investment	• Confidence in the future of the economy leads firms to expand their businesses. • A tax credit for small businesses inspires firms to buy new company cars.	• Firms cut back on spending in order to weather a recession. • Taxes on capital increase, leaving less money for investment.
Government spending	• Increase in government spending spurs spending after a recession.	• Decrease in government spending in response to concerns about increasing debt leads to less spending.
Net exports	• A new free trade agreement with Europe reduces most tariffs and other restrictions on Canadian goods. • Economic growth abroad in the US increases demand for Canadian goods and services.	• Other countries increase their tariffs on Canadian goods, making the goods more expensive. • The dollar strengthens, making Canadian goods and services more expensive for international consumers, decreasing demand.

✓ CONCEPT CHECK

☐ What four components of spending make up aggregate demand? [LO 11.1]

☐ Is the relationship between price level and aggregate demand generally positive or negative? [LO 11.1]

☐ Would the construction of a new highway by the government shift aggregate demand to the left or right? [LO 11.2]

☐ Does a decrease in consumer spending after a tax increase shift aggregate demand to the left or right? [LO 11.2]

Aggregate Supply

Now that we've described the demand side of the economy, we'll turn to the other side. *Aggregate supply* is the sum total of the production of all the firms in the economy. Production occurs when factor inputs—technology, capital, and labour—are combined to produce output.

The **aggregate supply curve** shows the relationship between the overall price level in the economy and total production by firms (output). The aggregate supply curve is similar to a market supply curve, with two key differences:

1.   The aggregate supply curve represents production in the economy *as a whole* rather than just one good or service.
2.   At the macroeconomic level, there is a difference between how the economy operates in the short run and how the economy operates in the long run.

Because of the difference between the short run and the long run, there are actually *two* different aggregate supply curves: One describes aggregate supply in the long run; it is called the long-run aggregate supply curve (LRAS). The second describes how firms decide how much to produce in the short run; it is called the short-run aggregate supply curve (SRAS).

The Difference Between Short-Run and Long-Run Aggregate Supply

LO 11.3 Explain the difference between the short run and the long run in the economy.

In order to understand the two aggregate supply curves, we need to explore the difference between the short run and the long run in the economy.

Short-Run Aggregate Supply

The *short run* refers to the hourly, daily, or weekly decisions that firms have to make. If you're running a fast-food burger joint, short-run decisions include choices about how much beef and lettuce you want to order for the week, or how many hours you want each employee to work. In choosing these inputs, you are essentially deciding how much food you want to produce.

In the short run, the aggregate supply curve slopes upward, as Figure 11-3 shows. This means that as overall price levels increase, firms are willing to produce more. Why is this so? Because the prices of final goods and services—like burgers—tend to increase more quickly than the prices of inputs. So the burger joint is able to increase revenues faster than costs and wants to produce more.

The key idea is that when the price level increases, input prices don't all increase immediately. Instead, some prices are *sticky*, meaning that they adjust slowly in response to changes in the economy. Wages are a prime example. To understand why sticky wages cause the short-run aggregate supply curve to slope upward, think about a sudden increase in the price level. Firms are going to earn more revenue because the prices of their products are higher. However, wages don't adjust right away. In the short run, the burger stand can make higher profits because revenues have increased but labour costs haven't. Because of the sticky wages, firms will be prepared to hire new workers and produce more output.

But why are input prices sticky, when the prices of final goods can change instantaneously? Contracts and informal practices make wages and the prices of other inputs sticky. For instance, many firms re-evaluate wages only once a year; unionized firms typically have formal labour contracts that determine wage levels for several years at a time. If an employee wants higher wages, or an employer wants to implement a pay cut, they will have to wait until the next period in which wages are adjusted or when the present contract expires. Often, raw materials are supplied on the same basis. For example, a fast-food chain might have a contract with a beef supplier setting out how much it will pay for beef over the coming year.

Although contracts are common for input prices, the prices of final goods are rarely dictated by contract. It's not likely, for example, that a fast-food stand would ever get its customers to agree to a long-term contract that specifies how many burgers and fries they'll buy over a year. Instead, customers grab a burger whenever they're hungry, paying the price on the current menu. To change the price, the fast-food stand simply changes its menu. Although changing final prices isn't always easy, we generally assume that final prices can change far more easily than input prices.

FIGURE 11-3

The Short-Run Aggregate Supply Curve

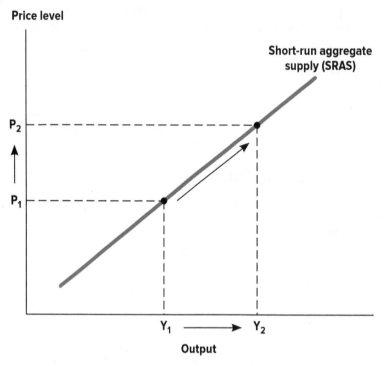

In the short run, the aggregate supply curve reacts to price changes. This means that firms are willing to change how much they supply based on price.

Long-Run Aggregate Supply

Now let's look at the long run. The first thing to know is that *the long run is not a set amount of time*, like one year, two years, or ten years. Instead, it is however long it takes for prices of inputs—such as wages, rent, and raw materials—to fully adjust to changes in economic conditions. In the long run, a burger stand can renegotiate the rent on its building, hire new employees, and negotiate new wages.

The adjustment process between the short and long run in macroeconomics differs from the adjustment process studied in microeconomics. In microeconomics, we focus on individual markets, and the key adjustment problem is one of quantities. Some costs are fixed because the quantity of an input cannot be adjusted in the short run; others are variable costs, because the quantity used can easily be adjusted in the short run. For example (back to the burger stand) basic equipment like deep fryers and heat lamps are fixed costs in the short run, but in the long run new equipment can be purchased and installed. In contrast, the amount of beef used is more likely to be a variable cost, increased or decreased as weekly burger sales dictate.

In macroeconomics, the focus is on how long it takes for *prices* to adjust through the whole economy, rather than the flexibility of *quantities* within an individual firm. What happens to the shape of the supply curve in the long run? Let's return to our example of the fast-food stand. In the short run, the burger stand's owners are making extra profits since revenues have risen but costs have not. That situation can't go on forever. Since goods are now more expensive, fry cooks and cashiers are going to ask for higher wages. Input prices, which have been under contract, will increase when the contracts are renegotiated.

Once these input prices adjust, the burger stand no longer makes higher profits. Its revenues may be higher, but costs are higher, as well; profits go back to where they were before the price increase. *This same process happens throughout the economy.* Once wages and input costs adjust to the new price level, the economy will go back to where it started.

In the long run, when input prices can adjust, our model says that changes in the prices of goods and services paid by consumers have no effect on aggregate supply. The long-run aggregate supply curve is a vertical line, showing that the same amount of output is supplied at any price level. Figure 11-4 shows an example of a long-run aggregate supply curve.

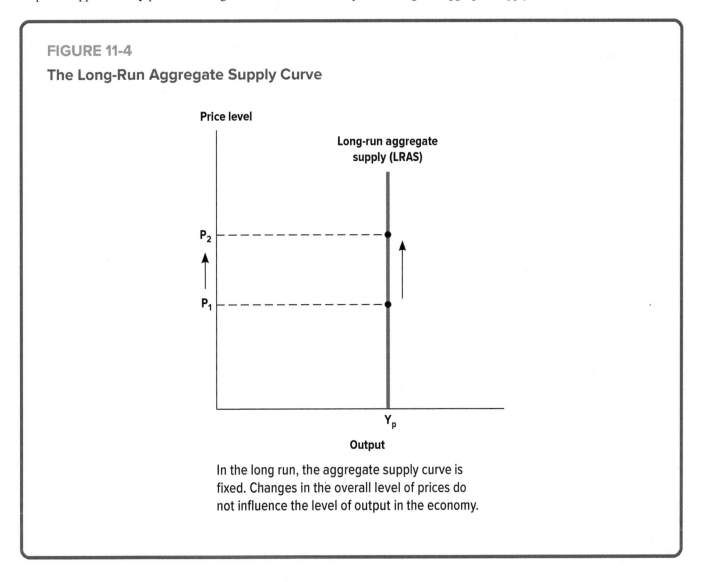

FIGURE 11-4

The Long-Run Aggregate Supply Curve

In the long run, the aggregate supply curve is fixed. Changes in the overall level of prices do not influence the level of output in the economy.

So, what determines the quantity of output supplied in the long run, if not prices? The long-run aggregate supply curve represents *potential output* in the economy—the level of output possible if the economy is operating at full capacity. It may help to think of the long-run aggregate supply curve as a production function. The production function shows how society's natural resources, labour, and capital can be combined to produce the greatest output. Changes in the long-run aggregate supply curve happen because something changes in the way that society's resources create output. Maybe there has been a new technological invention or the discovery of new resources, like a new oil reserve. The process of steadily pushing the long-run aggregate supply curve to the right—that is, increasing potential output—is the main driver of economic growth.

The economy does not always produce its potential output. Sometimes less output is produced, and sometimes more. We call these fluctuations around the level of potential output the **business cycle.** When output is higher than potential output, the economy is in a boom; when output is below potential, the economy is in a recession. Figure 11-5 shows the business cycle for Canada over the past fifty years.

FIGURE 11-5

The Business Cycle

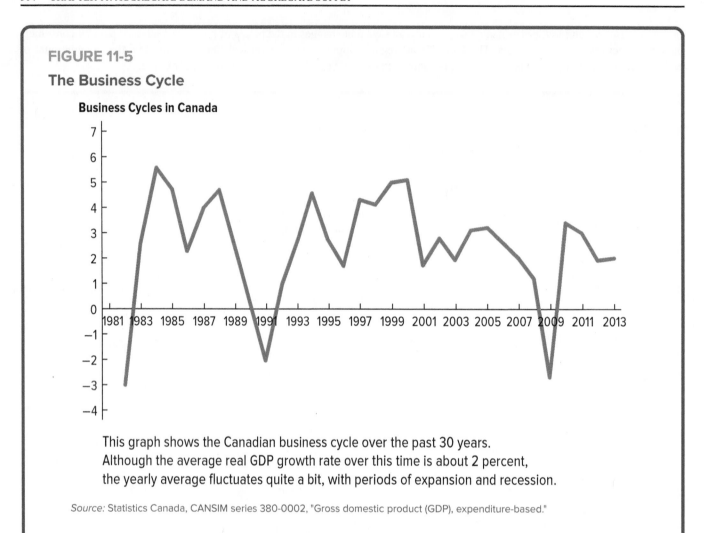

Business Cycles in Canada

This graph shows the Canadian business cycle over the past 30 years.
Although the average real GDP growth rate over this time is about 2 percent,
the yearly average fluctuates quite a bit, with periods of expansion and recession.

Source: Statistics Canada, CANSIM series 380-0002, "Gross domestic product (GDP), expenditure-based."

You might be wondering how we can ever have a boom. Put in terms of the model of aggregate demand and aggregate supply, how can short-run supply ever exceed the economy's level of potential output? It turns out that in the short run, production can be expanded beyond long-run potential by pressing all of the factors of production beyond their normal capacity. For instance, if firms ask workers to take on extra hours or run their factories around the clock, output can be temporarily pushed beyond the level of potential output.

To understand how this works, think about what happens at school during exam time. You may put in lots of extra hours to cram for a test. In doing so, you are operating beyond your long-run capacity for schoolwork. You may be able to study eighteen hours a day for a few weeks before mid-terms, but that schedule is probably not sustainable over an entire semester. Cramming for exams racks up costs that wouldn't occur with a normal schedule. These include the stress that comes from worrying about final grades or the health costs of eating too much junk food, not getting enough exercise, and not having enough leisure time. Once exams are over, these costs will push you to return to a normal workload in the beginning of the next semester. In other words, you will go back to your potential output.

In the same way that you incur costs by operating above capacity during exam time, firms incur costs by operating beyond potential output in the aggregate supply and demand model. When the economy is below capacity, ramping up production is easy. Firms can hire workers who were unemployed and rent warehouses that were sitting empty. This isn't the case when the economy is operating at full capacity. Since wages and input prices are fixed in the short run, firms often have to pay current employees overtime to work longer hours or hire workers who may not be fully qualified for the job.

Eventually, the intense demand for labour and capital when an economy is operating above capacity will drive prices upward. Hard-pressed workers will demand raises or leave to work for firms that are willing to pay them more money. As a result, input prices will increase, profits will shrink back to the original level, and supply will fall back to the long-run level. The end result of this short-term boost in output is higher prices in the long run.

Shifts in the Short-Run Aggregate Supply Curve

> **LO 11.4** Demonstrate a shift in the short-run aggregate supply curve, and list some factors that cause it to shift.

The short-run aggregate supply curve can shift—for example, if the costs of production change. Imagine that oil prices rise all of a sudden. Firms will feel the pinch. When oil prices rise, many firms will find that producing output is much more expensive. It's more costly for farmers to harvest and transport their crops, and transportation costs will make it more expensive to purchase the inputs that are needed for production. These changes shift the short-run aggregate supply (SRAS) curve to the left, as firms want to supply fewer goods at any given price level. Figure 11-6 shows this shift.

FIGURE 11-6

Shifts in the Short-Run Aggregate Supply Curve

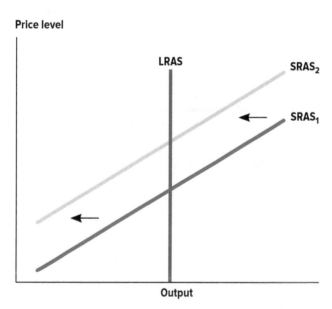

With an increase in the price of oil, prices increase for the same amount of production, so the aggregate supply curve shifts in (to the left).

POTENTIALLY CONFUSING

You may wonder at this point why a change in the world price of oil causes a shift of the SRAS instead of a movement along the curve. The reason has to do with the distinction between prices and costs. As oil prices rise, as we said, it's the increase in the *cost of inputs,* and therefore more costly production, that cause the SRAS to shift. An increase in the cost of production is different from an increase in the price level. An increase in the cost of production shifts the SRAS curve leftward, reducing the quantity of output produced at a given price level. In contrast, an increase in the price level itself—the weighted average of the prices of all goods and services we produce—would cause us to move from one point on the SRAS curve to another point on the same (unmoving) curve.

The short-run aggregate supply (SRAS) curve will also shift with other significant events that directly affect production—often called **supply shocks**. An example would be a major flood that disrupts the power grid and ruins crops. Expectations about future input prices will also shift the SRAS. If firms *anticipate* that the price of oil is likely to increase, for example, then suppliers will expect higher input costs in the future. This belief itself will reduce the quantity of goods supplied and shift the aggregate supply curve to the left.

Shifts in the Long-Run Aggregate Supply Curve

> LO 11.5 Demonstrate a shift in the long-run aggregate supply curve, and list some factors that cause it to shift.

In the long run, firms produce an amount dictated by available inputs, regardless of the overall price level. But that doesn't mean that the long-run aggregate supply curve never moves. Remember that the long-run aggregate supply (LRAS) curve is like a production function: a combination of land, technology, capital, and labour will produce a certain amount of output. Anything that affects the output that is possible using these factors will shift the LRAS curve. This includes new technologies, improved transportation systems, management innovations, and so on. The LRAS curve will shift to the right if the potential output of the economy expands. The LRAS curve will shift to the left if the economy loses productive capacity.

Consider the case of a new technology. When firms throughout the economy adopt a new technology, they can use same amount of resources to produce more output than before. Historical examples include the power loom during the nineteenth-century Industrial Revolution and the Internet in the past twenty years. These innovations shift the LRAS curve out to the right, as illustrated in Figure 11-7.

FIGURE 11-7

Shifts in the Long-Run Aggregate Supply Curve

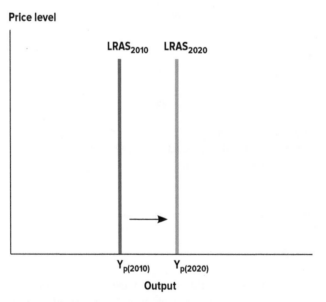

With an increase in technology, firms can produce more goods with the same amount of inputs. This shifts the long-run aggregate supply curve, the potential output of an economy, outward (to the right).

The long-run aggregate supply curve also shifts with changes in the factors of production in the economy. An increase in foreign investment will increase the capital stock of an economy, allowing production to increase and shifting the long-run aggregate supply curve to the right. In contrast, if levels of investment are low, and existing capital is not replaced as it wears out, we would see the opposite effect: potential output decreases, and the long-run aggregate supply curve shifts to the left. Table 11-2 gives some examples of changes that will shift the long-run aggregate supply curve.

TABLE 11.2   WHAT CAUSES THE LRAS CURVE TO SHIFT?

A variety of factors can shift the long-run aggregate supply curve by changing the potential output in an economy.

Factor	Increases LRAS	Decreases LRAS
Technology	Technological innovation allows for greater production using the same amount of inputs.	A new law stripping away intellectual property rights reduces the incentive to innovate.
Capital	Foreign investment in factories and machines increases available capital.	Depreciation and wear breaks down capital.
Labour	Immigration increases the available supply of labour.	Aging population takes workers out of the labour force.
Education	Universal primary education gives everyone a chance to go to school.	Reduction of federal university grants.
Natural resources	New energy sources allow factories to produce more with the same inputs.	Climate change permanently reduces the amount of land that can be farmed.

Do the LRAS and SRAS Always Shift Together?

Do the long-run and short-run aggregate supply curves always shift together? No. On the one hand, everything that shifts the LRAS curve will also shift the SRAS curve. The reason is that the available factors of production and technology that determine the position of the LRAS will also drive short-run supply. For instance, the spread of the Internet during the past twenty years shifted both the LRAS and the SRAS.

However, the opposite is not true. Not everything that shifts the SRAS curve will also shift the LRAS curve. Specifically, *changes in expectations* about future price levels affect only the SRAS curve. Before we discuss why this is so, it's a good idea to remind ourselves that although this situation involves the price level, it shifts the aggregate supply curve (a change in aggregate supply), rather than causing a movement along the curve (a change in aggregate quantity supplied). Why? Because we are focusing on *expected* changes in prices, not *actual* changes in prices. There must be an *actual* change in those prices to cause a movement along a curve, whether in the short run or long run.

Expectations about prices, on the other hand, are just guesses about the future. These expectations affect firms' production plans. Firms don't want to be caught unaware by changes in their costs. When they expect prices to rise at some future point, they also expect that workers will demand higher wages in order to keep up with the higher cost of living. As a result, firms reduce production at any given current price level, shifting the SRAS curve to the left.

Why don't changes in expected prices shift the LRAS curve? We can look at this in two ways. The first comes from our definition of the LRAS—as a representation of the production function, located at the economy's potential output. The only things that can shift the LRAS are those factors that affect how we produce, such as the amount of labour, capital, natural resources (land, for example), and technology. Expected prices aren't included in the production function, so they cannot cause the LRAS to shift. The second way to think about this is to consider our definition of the long run versus the short run. In the long run, expectations are fully incorporated into economic variables such as the price level. Since our expectations are fully accounted for, no shift occurs.

No matter how we look at it, while all other factors we mentioned shift the SRAS and LRAS curves in the same manner, changes in expected prices shift only the SRAS curve. In the short run, an expected increase in prices shifts the SRAS curve leftward; in the long run, these expectations are incorporated into the LRAS curve, and so we see no change at all. These changes will not affect the LRAS curve if they do not affect the number of workers, the amount of capital, or the amount of land and technology in the economy. In the long run, prices will fully adjust to take into account any changes in policies or expectations.

Economic Fluctuations

Now we have all the ingredients for a full model of the national economy: aggregate demand, short-run aggregate supply, and long-run aggregate supply. It's time to put them together.

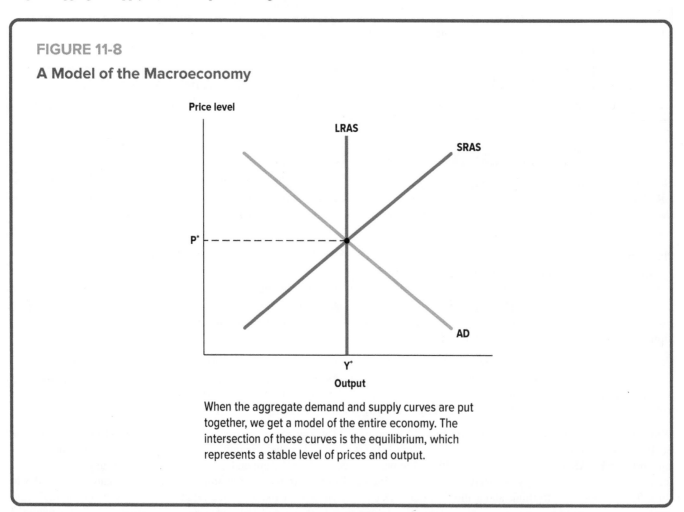

FIGURE 11-8

A Model of the Macroeconomy

When the aggregate demand and supply curves are put together, we get a model of the entire economy. The intersection of these curves is the equilibrium, which represents a stable level of prices and output.

Equilibrium in the national economy is the point at which aggregate demand equals aggregate supply. Short-run equilibrium is given by the intersection of the aggregate demand and short-run aggregate supply curves. In long-run equilibrium, however, the aggregate demand curve crosses the long-run aggregate supply and short-run aggregate supply curves *at the same point*. This means that prices are at expected levels and the short-run level of output is the same as long-run potential output. Figure 11-8 shows the macroeconomy in equilibrium: the intersection of the AD, LRAS, and SRAS curves gives the equilibrium price level and output.

A variety of shocks can push the economy out of long-run equilibrium. These shocks can shift ether the aggregate demand curve or the short-run aggregate supply curve, causing the economy to shift away from potential output in the short run. In the long run, prices will adjust and the economy will return to its long-run equilibrium. In reality, it's not always immediately clear whether a particular shock is shifting the aggregate demand or aggregate supply curve. In this section, we will show that supply-side shocks and demand-side shocks produce different implications for output and prices, which can help us to distinguish them.

Effects of a Shift in Aggregate Demand

LO 11.6 Explain the short- and long-run effects of a shift in aggregate demand.

Suppose there is a boom in the stock market and people who own stocks feel that their wealth is increasing, as well. Consumer confidence increases throughout the economy and consumption rises. We saw earlier in the chapter that increased consumption shifts the aggregate demand curve to the right. How will this affect the economy in the short run and the long run?

Panel A of Figure 11-9 shows how the increase in consumption during an economic expansion affects the economy in the short run. When the AD curve shifts to the right, the short-run equilibrium moves from point E_1 (the intersection of the AD, LRAS, and SRAS curves) to point E_2 (the intersection of the new AD curve and the AS curve). Point E_2 shows the effect of the housing boom: output was above the long-run potential level and prices increased.

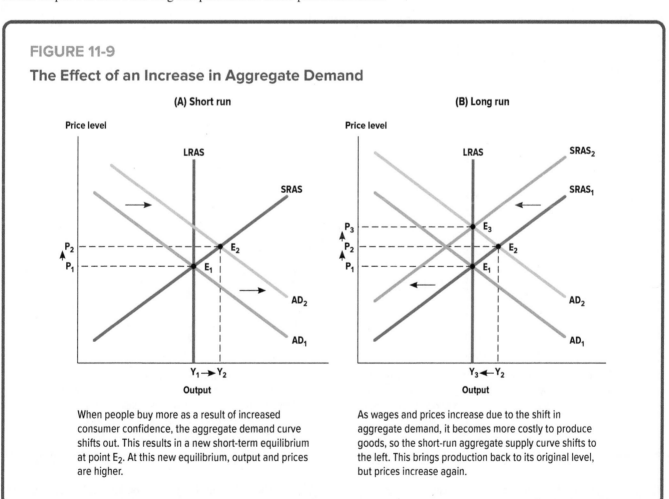

FIGURE 11-9

The Effect of an Increase in Aggregate Demand

(A) Short run

When people buy more as a result of increased consumer confidence, the aggregate demand curve shifts out. This results in a new short-term equilibrium at point E_2. At this new equilibrium, output and prices are higher.

(B) Long run

As wages and prices increase due to the shift in aggregate demand, it becomes more costly to produce goods, so the short-run aggregate supply curve shifts to the left. This brings production back to its original level, but prices increase again.

Point E_2 is an equilibrium point, but it is only a short-run equilibrium. How do we know this? The long-run equilibrium is determined by the *productive factors* in the economy, and this increase in consumption didn't change any of the land, labour, or capital that was available for production. Therefore we know that the LRAS curve hasn't moved.

How does the economy return to the long-run equilibrium? The SRAS curve has to shift again to restore the long-run equilibrium. As we'll see, this is where our model diverges from what actually happened during the stock market boom. If the economy had come down naturally, wages and other resource prices would have started to increase gradually because of inflation, causing an increase in input costs for firms and shifting aggregate supply. As contracts were negotiated and wages increased, the SRAS curve would have gradually shifted to the left until equilibrium was restored, as shown in panel B of Figure 11-9.

If you compare point E_1 to point E_3 in panel B of Figure 11-9—the movement from the initial long-run equilibrium to the new long-run equilibrium—you'll see that output didn't change, but the price level increased. Absent any other changes, the effect of a shift in the AD curve due to an increase in consumer confidence will be to increase both prices and output in the short run. In the long run, though, the gains to output retreat, and the only change that is left is higher prices.

The economy is in an opposite situation when a negative shock shifts aggregate demand to the left, as shown in Figure 11-10. For example, suppose the economy is humming along at equilibrium. Then, all of a sudden, stock prices collapse. Consumer confidence falls and consumption deceases, shifting the AD curve to the left. In the short run, shown in panel A, output will be below the potential level of output. However, this change exerts downward pressure on prices. As prices adjust and inputs get cheaper, firms will increase their output—shifting the SRAS curve to the right, as shown in panel B. The new long-run equilibrium will be at the original level of output, but with a lower price level (point E_3).

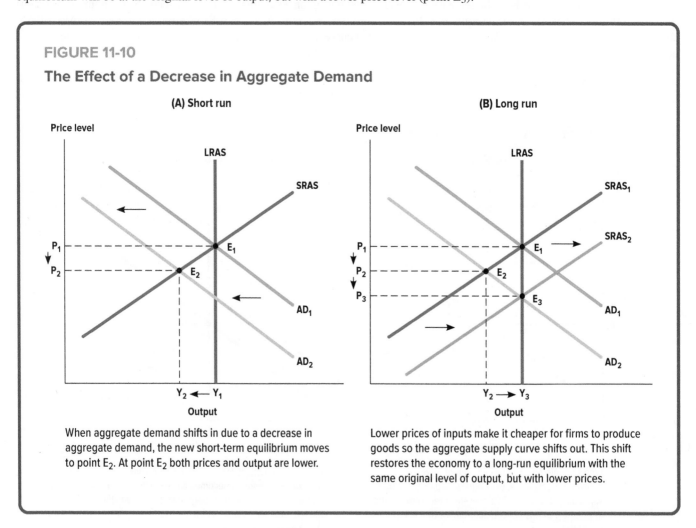

FIGURE 11-10

The Effect of a Decrease in Aggregate Demand

(A) Short run

When aggregate demand shifts in due to a decrease in aggregate demand, the new short-term equilibrium moves to point E_2. At point E_2 both prices and output are lower.

(B) Long run

Lower prices of inputs make it cheaper for firms to produce goods so the aggregate supply curve shifts out. This shift restores the economy to a long-run equilibrium with the same original level of output, but with lower prices.

Table 11-3 summarizes the effects of a change in aggregate demand in the short run and long run. The key is that demand-side shifts change only the price level in the long run, while output eventually returns to its long-run potential level.

TABLE 11.3   CHANGES IN AGGREGATE DEMAND IN THE SHORT RUN AND THE LONG RUN

The impacts of a shift in demand can be separated into two main paths. An increase in AD will increase both prices and output in the short run; in the long run, only prices will be higher as output slides back to the original equilibrium level. The opposite is true for a decrease in aggregate demand.

Shift	Example	Short run	Long run
Increase in AD	Increase in government spending: increases G	Output increases Price increases	Output unchanged Price increases
Decrease in AD	Reduction in consumer confidence: reduces C	Output decreases Price decreases	Output unchanged Price decreases

The bursting of the US housing bubble in 2007 had profound effects on the US economy. But the shock was also felt globally. One ripple effect was that people in the US cut back on the money they sent to relatives abroad, an idea explored in the Real Life box, Recessions and Remittances.

REAL LIFE

Recessions and Remittances

The next time you go to the hospital, look around at who is working there. You might see a nurse from the Philippines, or a doctor from Russia, or an X-ray technician from India. When people move to the United States to work, they often send money home to support their families. This flow of money, called remittances, is substantial. In the Philippines, for example, an amount equivalent to 10 percent of GDP comes from remittances. Families use these remittances to consume more goods and services, and to invest in starting new businesses.

Migrant workers are affected by the economy just as domestic workers are. When there is a downturn, they may lose their jobs and be unable to send money home. This decrease in remittances can cause a slump in consumption and investment in the migrants' home countries, which will then affect GDP in the home country through a leftward shift in the aggregate demand curve.

This is what happened during the recession of 2008–2009. There was a substantial increase in unemployment in both Europe and the United States—places that employ many migrant workers. Migrant workers were affected by the downturn, just as local workers were. In 2008, migrant workers from Latin America and the Caribbean sent home almost $69 billion. This amount fell to $64 billion in 2009—close to an 8 percent drop. In the Philippines, remittances decreased from more than 13 percent of GDP in 2006, to just over 11 percent of GDP for 2007 and 2008.

In today's interconnected global economy, a shock in one country can easily send shock waves rippling out all over the world.

Sources: http://blogs.worldbank.org/eastasiapacific/remittances-and-the-philippines-economy-the-elephant-in-the-room; www.oecd.org/dataoecd/48/8/42753222.pdf.

Effects of a Shift in Aggregate Supply

> LO 11.7 Explain the short- and long-run effects of a shift in aggregate supply.

The economy can also face shocks to the supply side. Supply-side shocks may be either temporary or permanent. When such changes are temporary, only the SRAS curve will shift. When the changes are permanent, both the LRAS and the SRAS curves will shift.

Let's first consider a temporary shock. Suppose there is a year-long drought in the prairies and a lot of wheat is damaged. This shock will shift the SRAS curve to the left, as shown in panel A of Figure 11-11. The economy will move from its long-run equilibrium at point E_1 to the new short-run equilibrium at point E_2. Prices will be higher and output will be lower. How does the economy adjust?

A situation in which output decreases while prices increase is often referred to as *stagflation*—economic stagnation coupled with high inflation. Adjustment from this short-run equilibrium is not easy. A drop in wages would help, but employees are usually reluctant to accept lower wages. We say that wages are generally *sticky downward*, meaning that it takes a long time for them to fall. Sticky input prices contribute to keeping the economy in this undesirable equilibrium.

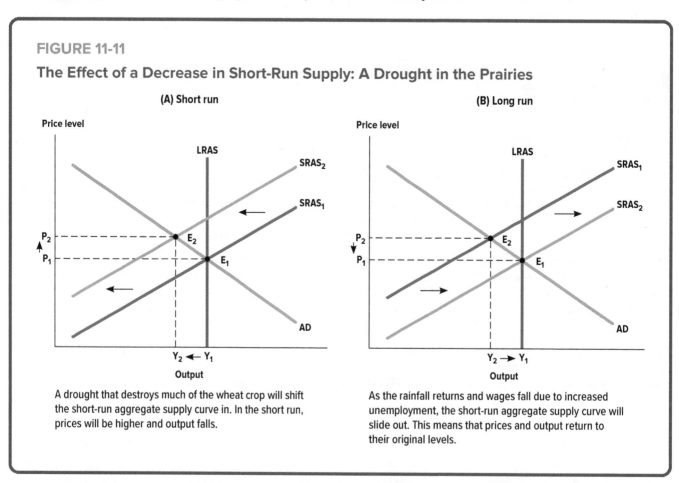

FIGURE 11-11

The Effect of a Decrease in Short-Run Supply: A Drought in the Prairies

(A) Short run

(B) Long run

A drought that destroys much of the wheat crop will shift the short-run aggregate supply curve in. In the short run, prices will be higher and output falls.

As the rainfall returns and wages fall due to increased unemployment, the short-run aggregate supply curve will slide out. This means that prices and output return to their original levels.

When the economy is producing at a level less than the potential output and wages are slow to fall, firms will lay off workers and unemployment will be higher than its natural rate. If the unemployment rate remains high, wages will eventually begin to fall. As labour becomes cheaper, the costs of production for firms will decrease. The short-run aggregate supply curve shifts back to the right, as shown in panel B. Eventually, costs will decrease to the point where the SRAS is back to its original level, and the economy will be back at its old long-run equilibrium (point E_1). In the long run, both prices and output return to their initial level.

Now let's think about a permanent supply shock. Instead of just a short-term drought, imagine that cataclysmic climate change makes it impossible to grow wheat or anything else with yields similar to those now possible in the prairies. Since the prairies are integral to Canadian food production, there simply isn't enough other land to make up the difference. With a loss of one of the factors of production (in this case, land), the LRAS curve will shift to the left, as in panel A of Figure 11-12.

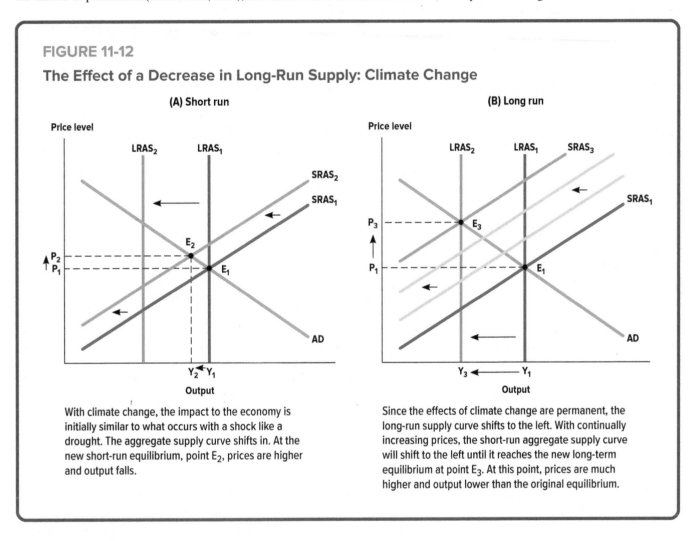

FIGURE 11-12

The Effect of a Decrease in Long-Run Supply: Climate Change

(A) Short run

With climate change, the impact to the economy is initially similar to what occurs with a shock like a drought. The aggregate supply curve shifts in. At the new short-run equilibrium, point E_2, prices are higher and output falls.

(B) Long run

Since the effects of climate change are permanent, the long-run supply curve shifts to the left. With continually increasing prices, the short-run aggregate supply curve will shift to the left until it reaches the new long-term equilibrium at point E_3. At this point, prices are much higher and output lower than the original equilibrium.

This change has effects in the short run, as well. Wheat grown in the prairies is important in the production of goods throughout the economy. Everything from the cereal you eat for breakfast to the food served in restaurants likely contains some wheat or product derived from wheat. The increase in food and other prices means that the costs of production will also rise, shifting the SRAS to the left.

The SRAS curve may not shift immediately to the new long-run equilibrium point; in the short run, the equilibrium may move only to point E_2. However, as long as prices are above the long-run equilibrium level, the SRAS will continue to shift to the left, as shown in panel B. This process continues until the economy reaches a new long-run equilibrium (at point E_3), with higher prices and a lower level of potential output.

Comparing Demand and Supply Shocks

The aggregate demand/aggregate supply (AD/AS) model is a powerful tool for understanding overall economic conditions and figuring out how to formulate policy response to shocks. However, successful economic policy hinges on being able to tell the difference between a demand shock and supply shock. If you apply a policy designed to fight the effects of one kind of shock and it turns out to be the other, you could potentially make things even worse.

This section describes the two main challenges that arise when using the AD/AS model to analyze events in the economy. First, if you see a specific shock, can you tell which side of the economy it is going to affect? Second, if you see a change in the economy, can you work backward to figure out what type of shock might have caused it?

First, think through who a shock will affect and what role they play in the economy. For example, higher oil prices are going to affect businesses that use oil to produce goods. This means that an oil-price change will be a shock to the supply side of the economy. Because the shock has to do with prices rather than real factors of production, it will affect only the short-run aggregate supply curve and not the long-run curve. In contrast, if you see a shock that affects consumers or government spending, it is likely to affect consumption and will therefore act on the demand side of the economy.

Table 11-4 shows some examples of demand and supply shocks. For each shock, think about which group of people the shock will affect, whether it is a demand-side or a supply-side shock, and then whether it is a long-run or a short-run shock.

TABLE 11-4   COMPARING DEMAND AND SUPPLY SHOCKS

The first task in determining how an event will affect the overall economy is to decide whether it is a demand or a supply shock. This means figuring out whom the shock most affects and what their role is in the economy.

Event	What kind of shock?
Temporary increase in the price of oil	Short-run supply shock
Technological innovation	Long-run supply shock
Drop in consumer confidence	Demand shock
Sudden increase in immigration	Long-run supply shock

When thinking in the other direction—from effect on the economy to figuring out the cause—there are clear predictions about how different types of shocks will affect prices and output; these can give clues about what the main shock must have been. For example, falling output, in the short-run, could be due to either a reduction in aggregate demand or a reduction in short-run aggregate supply. Go back and compare panel A of Figure 11-11, where we showed short-run aggregate supply decreasing, with panel A of Figure 11-10, where aggregate demand is decreasing. To distinguish between a demand shock or a supply shock, therefore, we need to see what happened to prices. The demand-side shock will reduce prices; the supply-side shock will increase the price level. So, an economy in which output has decreased and prices have decreased would seem to be undergoing a decrease in demand. On the other hand, an economy in which output has decreased and prices have increased appears to have been affected by a supply-side shock.

Sometimes, there can be a complex combination of overlapping shocks to untangle. For example, after 2008, growing pessimism about the economy made banks less willing to lend to businesses. For firms, borrowing became harder and more expensive. The increase in the cost of doing business was a short-run supply-side shock; it shifted the short-run aggregate supply curve to the left. That was on top of the demand shock that happened when consumers reduced their spending after the housing bubble popped. The demand shock led to a further decrease in the level of output in the economy.

Demand-side and supply-side shocks can also differ in the long run. Demand-side shocks will cause a change to the price level in the long run, since the short-run supply curve will shift in to restore the long-run equilibrium output. For a supply-side shock, there are no long-run changes to the price level. If the short-run supply curve initially shifts to the left, for example, prices will adjust to restore the long-run equilibrium.

We summarize the difference between supply-side and demand-side shocks in Table 11-5.

TABLE 11-5   DEMAND-SIDE VERSUS SUPPLY-SIDE SHOCKS

This table summarizes the impacts of a shock on the demand and supply sides of an economy. Each shock has a different effect on the economy in the long and short run.

Supply or demand?	Positive shock	Negative shock
Demand side	**Short run:** Output increases Price increases	**Short run:** Output decreases Price decreases
Demand side	**Long run:** No change in output Price increases	**Long run:** No change in output Price decreases
Temporary shock: Supply side	**Short run:** Output increases Price decreases	**Short run:** Output decreases Price increases
Temporary shock: Supply side	**Long run:** No change in output No change in price	**Long run:** No change in output No change in price
Permanent shock: Supply side	**Long run:** Output increases Price decreases	**Long run:** Output decreases Price increases

For an example of economic detective work to discover whether shifts in supply or demand were responsible for observed effects in an economy, see the Real Life box, The Kobe Earthquake and Aggregate Supply.

REAL LIFE

The Kobe Earthquake and Aggregate Supply

In January 1995, a large earthquake rocked the port city of Kobe, Japan. Many people lost their lives. Buildings and infrastructure were destroyed. The value of Japan's stock market dropped substantially. It was one of the most expensive natural disasters the world had ever seen, with a final damage bill equal to about 2.5 percent of Japan's GDP.

However, amazingly, only fifteen months after the disaster, Japanese manufacturing was back to 96 percent of pre-earthquake levels. How well can the aggregate supply and aggregate demand model explain the recovery of the Japanese economy?

George Horwich, an economist at Purdue, studied this question. The earthquake destroyed a large amount of capital, so we would expect the short-run aggregate supply curve to shift to the left. This shift would push the price level higher and would reduce output, increasing unemployment. However, when Horwich looked at the data, he saw a different picture. Surprisingly, the price level was relatively stable and employment was constant.

How can we match that data with the predictions of the AD/AS model? There are two possibilities in Kobe: either the aggregate supply curve shifted quickly back out again in the months after the earthquake, or the aggregate demand curve shifted out. We have a way to figure out what actually happened. If an increase in aggregate demand occurred, the price level would increase. But the data showed that the price level stayed constant or even decreased. This suggests that there wasn't an aggregate demand response.

Instead, Horwich argues, the aggregate supply curve shifted back out.

Although the damage in Kobe was significant, it seems that the Japanese economy was able to adjust to this very large shock in one part of the economy by rearranging how resources were used. In this process of adjustment, the aggregate supply curve shifted back out, returning the economy to its original position. The response to the Kobe earthquake tells us that the macroeconomy can sometimes adjust surprisingly quickly, even after large supply-side shocks.

Source: George Horwich, "Economic lessons of the Kobe earthquake," *Economic Development and Cultural Change* 48, no. 3 (April 2000), pp. 521–542.

✓ CONCEPT CHECK

☐ Will a positive demand shock lead to increased or decreased output in short-run equilibrium? What about in the long-run equilibrium? [LO 11.6]

☐ How do prices and output change with a leftward shift in aggregate supply? [LO 11.7]

The Role of Public Policy

LO 11.8 Describe the policy options the government can use to counteract supply and demand shocks.

It can take a long time for an economy to fully adjust to demand and supply shocks; waiting for adjustments often isn't very comfortable for people who experience changing prices and unemployment. When the economy hits a recession, voters often call upon politicians to do something. We will examine government's role in the economy in more detail when we look at fiscal policy and monetary policy in later chapters. For now, we will consider just one channel through which the government can try to boost the economy out of a recession: government spending.

Government Spending to Counter Negative Demand Shocks

Imagine that things are going badly in the economy: news outlets are full of stories about falling home prices, mass layoffs, and factory closings. With the steady beat of bad news, consumer confidence decreases and consumption falls. These changes cause the aggregate demand curve to shift to the left, shown in panel A of Figure 11-13. Output and the price level decrease.

Government can try to counter this negative demand shock by increasing spending. As we have seen, the effect of an increase in government spending is to shift the aggregate demand curve to the right. For policy makers, the goal is to counteract the negative shock to aggregate demand with a positive one and restore the curve to its original position.

This is not so easy to do. In practice, it can be hard to gauge the overall effect of government spending on aggregate demand. Even worse, it's rare to perfectly design government policy so that spending occurs at just the right amount to restore aggregate demand to its original level. Panel B of Figure 11-13 shows a case in which the policy is partly, but not entirely, successful: the increase in government spending shifts the AD curve only part of the way back to its previous position.

What about the long run? We know that for any demand-side shock, there can't be an effect on long-run output. According to our model, if the government did nothing, eventually prices would adjust downward until output rose to its previous level. This occurs through changes on the supply side, as lower prices reduce the costs of production, shifting the aggregate supply curve to the right.

When the government increases spending to stimulate the economy, the end result will be slightly different. Since, in this example, government policy was only partly successful, the economy still has to adjust before reaching long-run equilibrium. The process of adjustment is still the same as before, except that now SRAS doesn't have as far to go as it did when the government didn't act. In the end, the long-run effect of the government's increase in spending is that the previous level of output will be restored, but at a slightly higher price level than if the government hadn't acted, holding all else constant. The result is that with a given income or wealth, people can buy less. This trade-off between increasing the speed of adjustment and allowing higher prices is a genuine challenge the government faces in setting policies to fight downturns in the economy.

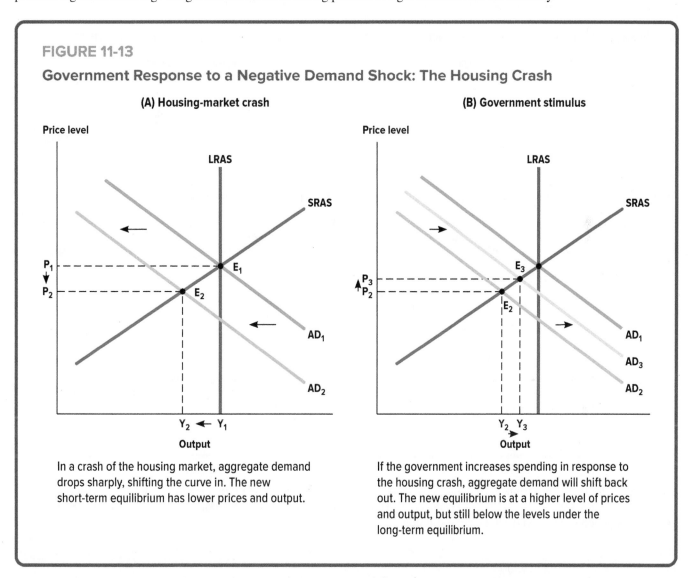

FIGURE 11-13

Government Response to a Negative Demand Shock: The Housing Crash

(A) Housing-market crash

In a crash of the housing market, aggregate demand drops sharply, shifting the curve in. The new short-term equilibrium has lower prices and output.

(B) Government stimulus

If the government increases spending in response to the housing crash, aggregate demand will shift back out. The new equilibrium is at a higher level of prices and output, but still below the levels under the long-term equilibrium.

Government Spending to Counter Negative Supply Shocks

Now imagine a short-run supply-side shock. A terrible drought has reduced the wheat harvest by 80 percent. The short-run aggregate supply curve has shifted to the left, as in panel A of Figure 11-14. The economy is now at point E_2: the level of output has fallen and prices have risen. In this case, policy makers are in a bind. If they choose to do nothing, the economy will be stuck in a period of higher prices and lower output (stagflation). We'll talk more about the challenges of stagflation in Chapter 15, "Inflation." For now, imagine a period in which prices increase, but with large amounts of unemployment and low output. It's a very hard situation to get out of. Remember that prices can be very sticky, especially when they have to adjust downward.

Instead of waiting for the aggregate supply curve to shift back out to the right, the government could choose to increase government spending in order to shift the aggregate demand curve. This action and effect are shown in panel B of Figure 11-14.

With the shift in aggregate demand, the economy moves to a new short-run equilibrium at point E$_3$. While this shift solves the problem of low output and unemployment, it actually drives prices even higher.

In both examples, the long-run result of government intervention is higher prices at the same level of output. So, why would the government ever choose to intervene? One reason concerns the speed of the recovery. Without the increase in government spending, adjustment might have been a long and painful process. In addition, lower prices are not always a good thing. As we will see in Chapter 15, falling prices, called *deflation,* carry another set of challenges for the economy.

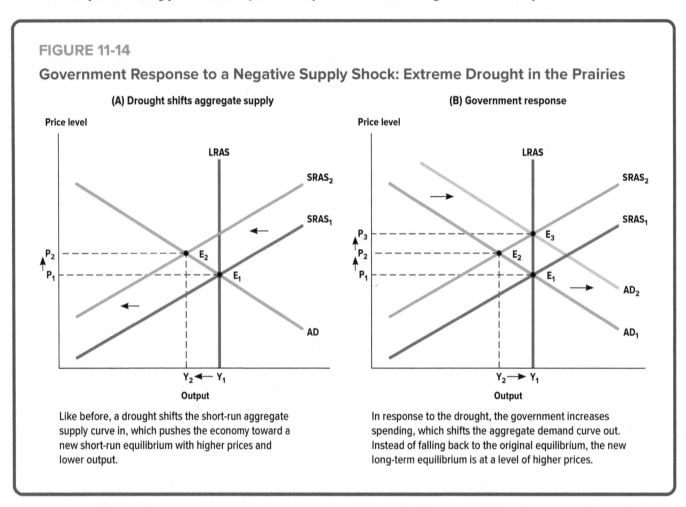

FIGURE 11-14

Government Response to a Negative Supply Shock: Extreme Drought in the Prairies

(A) Drought shifts aggregate supply

(B) Government response

Like before, a drought shifts the short-run aggregate supply curve in, which pushes the economy toward a new short-run equilibrium with higher prices and lower output.

In response to the drought, the government increases spending, which shifts the aggregate demand curve out. Instead of falling back to the original equilibrium, the new long-term equilibrium is at a level of higher prices.

The bottom line is that government spending is a short-term policy action that is often applied to address short-term demand shocks. Government spending is less effective in countering negative supply shocks, but political pressures can sometimes drive government action even when it's not a great solution.

✓ CONCEPT CHECK

☐   What is the long-term effect on prices and output when the government counters a negative demand shock with an increase in spending? **[LO 11.8]**

Conclusion

In this chapter, we created a model of the whole economy. This model is relatively simple, yet ambitious; it helps us to understand what drives key macroeconomics outcomes such as prices, unemployment, and GDP.

The aggregate demand/aggregate supply model breaks the economy down into two sides. The demand side is composed of all the components of expenditure in the economy: consumption, investment, government spending, and net exports. The aggregate demand curve identifies the relationship between overall price levels and aggregate demand in the economy. On the supply side of the economy, the aggregate supply curve identifies the relationship between overall price levels and total production in the economy.

In the long run, production is determined by the availability of inputs for production and the technology to convert inputs to outputs. In the long run there is no relationship between the price level and output. In the short run the economy responds to changes in the price level by increasing or decreasing output, so the short-run aggregate supply curve is upward-sloping. The long-run equilibrium occurs at the intersection of the aggregate demand and long-run aggregate supply curves.

We used the model of aggregate demand and aggregate supply to understand the 2008 recession that engulfed Canada, shifting the aggregate demand curve to the left. And we used it to understand the government's response, a stimulus package whose aim was to shift the aggregate demand curve back out, and stimulate output and employment. In the next chapter we'll talk about policy responses to economic shocks in more depth and explore the different effects of spending versus taxes.

Key Terms

aggregate demand curve

aggregate supply curve

business cycle

supply shock

Summary

LO 11.1 List the components of aggregate demand and use these components to explain why the aggregate demand curve slopes downward.

The aggregate demand and supply model captures the relationship between prices and output in the economy. It has two parts: the *aggregate demand* curve, which shows the relationship between the price level and total demand in the economy, and the *aggregate supply* curve, which shows the relationship between the price level and the total supply in the economy. The aggregate demand curve is downward-sloping because consumption, investment, and net exports all decline when the price level rises. The short-run aggregate supply curve is upward-sloping because it takes some time for input prices and/or wages to adjust.

LO 11.2 List some factors that could cause the aggregate demand curve to shift.

Since the aggregate demand curve is derived from the definition of GDP—$Y = C + I + G + NX$—anything that affects any of the components of GDP will shift the aggregate demand curve. For example, if government spending increases, the aggregate demand curve will shift out; if net exports decrease, the aggregate demand curve will shift in. When the aggregate demand curve shifts, there will be a short-run change in output, but no long-run shift in output. The price level will change in both the short run and the long run.

LO 11.3 Explain the difference between the short run and the long run in the economy.

The aggregate supply curve is actually two different curves: a *long-run aggregate supply* (LRAS) curve and a *short-run aggregate supply* (SRAS) curve. The long-run aggregate supply curve shows what the economy can produce if all the factors of production are being utilized. This doesn't depend on prices, so the LRAS is vertical. The SRAS is an upward-sloping curve between prices and output. There are factors that affect only the cost of production and do not change the amount of factors available for production. These changes will only shift the SRAS curve.

LO 11.4 Demonstrate a shift in the short-run aggregate supply curve, and list some of the factors that cause it to shift.

If the prices of *inputs* change, the entire aggregate supply curve will shift. Any change that makes production more expensive for firms will shift the supply curve in (to the left). Any change that makes production cheaper for producers will shift the aggregate supply curve out (to the right).

LO 11.5 Demonstrate a shift in the long-run aggregate supply curve, and list some factors that cause it to shift.

Anything that affects the output possible using these factors will shift the long-run aggregate supply curve. If the potential output of the economy expands, the long-run aggregate supply curve will shift out. If the production possibility frontier for the economy contracts, the long-run aggregate supply curve will shift in.

LO 11.6 Explain the short- and long-run effects of a shift in aggregate demand.

When there is a positive shock in aggregate demand, prices and output increase in the short run. Eventually, input prices and wages catch up to the increase in the price level. The SRAS curve slowly adjusts to the right. In the end, this adjustment further increases prices while decreasing output. The final result is that output falls back to its original level and prices are higher than originally. For a negative shock, the aggregate demand shifts to the left. Prices and output fall. The adjustment of the SRAS curve to the right brings output back to its original level, but prices fall even further.

LO 11.7 Explain the short- and long-run effects of a shift in aggregate supply.

The aggregate supply curve is a relationship between total supply in the economy and price level. Anything that affects the factors of production or the level of technology will affect both the long-run aggregate supply curve and the short-run aggregate supply curve; this shift is a permanent supply shock. Anything that affects the prices of inputs or the costs of doing business will affect the short-run aggregate supply curve, but not the long-run aggregate supply curve; this shift is a temporary supply shock. When there is a temporary supply shock, the price level and output changes in the short run but not in the long run. For a permanent supply shock, both the price level and output change in the long run.

LO 11.8 Describe the policy options the government can use to counteract supply and demand shocks.

Depending on the type of shock, the government can choose to increase or reduce government spending in response. The government often chooses to act because action is preferable to waiting for the economy to adjust after a shock. Shortfalls in aggregate demand can be corrected by increasing spending. The same is true of aggregate demand, although the government might want to be careful in this situation. Regardless of the shock, increases in government spending will produce higher prices in the long run.

Review Questions

1. Explain the aggregate demand and supply model for a closed economy where net exports are zero. What would aggregate demand consist of, and what would be the relationship between income and the price level? What would be the relationship between income and the price level in the short run and the long run? **[LO 11.1]**

2. The demand curves for individual goods are typically downward-sloping, due both to the substitution effect as well as to the income effect. Why does the income effect not affect the aggregate demand curve? **[LO 11.1]**

3. What effect does rising business optimism and confidence have on the aggregate demand curve? What effect does falling optimism and confidence in business prospects have on the aggregate demand curve? **[LO 11.2]**

4. List several events that could cause a *demand-side* recession (i.e., a recession caused by a fall in aggregate demand). [LO 11.2]

5. Which typically can change faster, the components of aggregate demand or the components of aggregate supply? Explain. [LO 11.3]

6. Explain the difference between sticky wages and sticky prices. How do these two ideas explain the sloped short-run aggregate supply curve? Why don't sticky wages or sticky prices affect the long-run aggregate supply curve? [LO 11.3]

7. List several events that could cause a *supply-side* recession (i.e., a recession caused by a fall in aggregate supply). [LO 11.4]

8. In the late 1990s, Canada experienced very high GDP growth, record low unemployment rates, and virtually non-existent inflation. Based on the conclusions of the AD/AS model, what could explain this combination of good economic results? [LO 11.4], [LO 11.5]

9. Why is long-run economic growth generally positive rather than negative? [LO 11.5]

10. Explain the mechanism through which the economy adjusts in the short run and the long run when consumer confidence falls. [LO 11.6]

11. Suppose a country is in the midst of an economic boom and is running large budget surpluses. The prime minister suggests that due to the good economic conditions, the time is ripe for a large tax cut. What are the arguments for and against this position? [LO 11.6], [LO 11.8]

12. Suppose a country is in the midst of a serious recession, with high unemployment and large government deficits. The prime minister suggests that in times like this the government has the obligation to "tighten its belt" and cut spending since so many families around the country have to do the same thing. Do you agree with the prime minister? Why or why not? [LO 11.6], [LO 11.8]

13. Using the aggregate demand and supply model, explain the difference between a one-year drought and permanent climate change. What happens to the price level and output in the short run and in the long-run for each type of shock? [LO 11.4], [LO 11.5], [LO 11.7]

14. Why does the government have a harder time counteracting shifts in AS than in AD? [LO 11.7], [LO 11.8]

15. Whenever AD or AS shifts, putting the economy out of long-run equilibrium, AS has a natural tendency to shift in such a way as to bring the economy back into long-run equilibrium. If the economy always eventually comes back to long-run equilibrium, why would the government ever try to implement policies to bring the economy into equilibrium through government means? [LO 11.8]

Problems and Applications

1. Is there a negative, positive, or no relationship between the price level and the following components of aggregate demand? [LO 11.1]
   a. Consumption
   b. Investment
   c. Government spending
   d. Net exports

2. If the government cuts taxes, what components of aggregate demand are affected? [LO 11.1]

3. For each of the following shocks, say whether it is a demand-side shock or a supply-side shock. [LO 11.2], [LO 11.4]
   a. Consumer confidence falls
   b. Government spending increases
   c. The price of foreign goods increases
   d. The price of oil increases
   e. A tornado destroys manufacturing plants

4. In the late 1990s, Canada experienced a technology boom. In part the boom was due to a revolution in communication technology that resulted in a massive expansion of the Internet; in part the boom was due to households and firms purchasing new computer equipment in anticipation of Y2K. What two curves of the model would be affected by these events? [LO 11.2], [LO 11.4]

5. Suppose that a statement by the governor of the Bank of Canada about the state of the economy causes a loss of consumer confidence. What will be the long-run impact on the economy if the government allows the economy to adjust without a policy response? [LO 11.3]
   a. Output will fall below its initial level in the long-run and the price level will decline.
   b. Output will return to its initial level in the long-run but the price level will be lower
   c. Output will return to its initial level in the long-run but the price level will be higher
   d. Output will rise above its initial level in the long-run and the price level will rise.

6. Say whether the following statements are true or false. [LO 11.3]
   a. In the long-run prices don't affect output.
   b. In the short-run prices may affect output.

7. *Fracking* is a new technology that allows drillers to extract significantly larger quantities of natural gas from existing deposits than was previously possible. How is this discovery likely to affect the economy? (*Hint:* Think about whether this will have a short-run or long-run effect.) [LO 11.4], [LO 11.5]

8. Throughout the nineteenth and twentieth centuries, the Canadian economy experienced frequent ups and downs, but over the past 140 years, the real GDP in Canada rose significantly. This growth represents a change in which curve? [LO 11.5]

9. For each of the following scenarios, say whether the shock was a demand-side shock, a supply-side shock, or a combination of both shocks. [LO 11.6], [LO 11.7]
   a. The price level and GDP both fell. GDP then increased, but the price level fell even further.
   b. In the long-run, the economy had the same level of output but a higher price level.
   c. In the short-run, the price level increased, but GDP fell.
   d. In the long-run, GDP increased, and the price level fell.
   e. In the long-run, GDP increased, and the price level was constant.

10. In 2009, during the height of recession, both real GDP and the Consumer Price Index fell. Was this recession likely caused by a shift in aggregate demand or aggregate supply? [LO 11.6], [LO 11.7]

11. In 1974, GDP fell but inflation increased. Was this recession likely caused by a shift in aggregate demand or aggregate supply? [LO 11.6], [LO 11.7]

12. For each of the following situations, use an AD/AS model to describe what happens to price levels and output in Canada in the short-run. In each case assume the economy starts in long- and short-run equilibrium, and show the appropriate shifts in the AS or AD curves. [LO 11.6], [LO 11.7]
    a. A stock market crash reduces people's wealth.
    b. The spread of democracy around the world increases consumer confidence in Canada.
    c. The European economy crashes.
    d. Canada enters into an arms race with the U.S., resulting in a significant increase in military spending.
    e. A revolution in Iran results in a significant reduction in the world's supply of oil.
    f. Terrorist activities temporarily halt the ability of Canadians to engage in certain productive activities such as transportation and finance.
    g. A computer chip manufacturer develops a new computer chip that is faster and cheaper than previous chips.
    h. A summer of perfect weather in the prairies leads to record harvests of wheat and barley.

Use an AD/AS model to answer the following questions. In each case assume the economy starts in long- and short-run equilibrium, and show the appropriate shifts in the AS or AD curves.

13. Suppose a stock market crash reduces people's wealth. [LO 11.6], [LO 11.7], [LO 11.8]
    a. Show what happens to price levels and output in Canada in the short-run.
    b. Suppose the government takes no action to help the economy. What happens to price levels and output in the long-run?

    c. Suppose, instead, the government decides to take action to help the economy. What action(s) would you recommend? Why?

    d. If the Canadian government makes the appropriate policy response, what happens to price levels and output in the long-run?

14. Suppose the spread of democracy around the world increases consumer confidence in Canada. [LO 11.6], [LO 11.7], [LO 11.8]

    a. Show what happens to price levels and output in Canada in the short-run.

    b. Suppose the government takes no action to help the economy. What happens to price levels and output in the long-run?

    c. Suppose, instead, the government decides to take action to help the economy. What action(s) would you recommend? Why?

    d. If the Canadian government makes the appropriate policy response, what happens to price levels and output in the long-run?

15. Suppose a revolution in Iran results in a significant reduction in the world's supply of oil. [LO 11.6], [LO 11.7], [LO 11.8]

    a. Show what happens to price levels and output in Canada in the short-run.

    b. Suppose the government takes no action to help the economy. What happens to price levels and output in the long-run?

    c. Suppose, instead, the government decides to take action to help the economy. What action(s) would you recommend? Why?

    d. If the Canadian government makes the appropriate policy response, what happens to price levels and output in the long-run?

16. Suppose a summer of perfect weather in the prairies leads to record harvests of wheat and barley. [LO 11.6], [LO 11.7], [LO 11.8]

    a. What happens to price levels and output in Canada in the short-run?

    b. Suppose the government takes no action to help the economy. Show what happens to price levels and output in the long-run.

    c. If the Canadian government reacts to the record harvests by increasing taxes or decreasing spending, what happens to price levels and output in the long-run?

    d. What is the problem associated with the government reacting to the record harvests by increasing taxes or decreasing spending?

CHAPTER 12

Fiscal Policy

LEARNING OBJECTIVES

LO 12.1   Explain the difference between contractionary fiscal policy and expansionary fiscal policy.

LO 12.2   Explain how fiscal policy can counteract short-run economic fluctuations.

LO 12.3   Discuss the main fiscal policy challenges faced by the government and how stabilizers can automatically adjust fiscal policy as the economy changes.

LO 12.4   Calculate the fiscal multiplier for spending and taxation, and explain why it differs for these two policies.

LO 12.5   Describe how revenue and spending determine a government budget.

LO 12.6   Explain the difference between the government deficit and public debt.

LO 12.7   Identify the benefits and costs of government debt.

From Prosperity to Recession

By late 2008, the warning signs were everywhere: Unemployment was increasing. Business confidence was down. The economy was at the start of a recession. What, if anything, could the Canadian government do to give the economy a boost?

The government (outlined in a November 2008 economic and fiscal statement titled Protecting Canada's Future) argued that since times were tough, the government should adhere to the basic fiscal approach of the 1990s and early 2000s, which emphasized healthy government finances as the foundation of long-term economic stability. The statement highlighted the government's past efforts in reducing the federal debt and its intention to balance the federal budget over the next five years. The document also announced several expenditure reduction policies (such as to reduce the cost of government, stabilize the wages of the federal public sector, and control costs associated with the equalization program).

Furthermore, the government believed that previously announced tax reductions (government estimated that its tax cut would amount to $31 billion in fiscal year 2009–2010) would be sufficient to stabilize the Canadian economy. They believed lower taxes would allow people to keep a larger share of their income, something the government hoped would encourage people to spend more, boosting demand.

The fiscal policy was short-lived. It was rejected by the opposition parties, who threatened to defeat the Conservative minority government and form a coalition government. The opposition parties argued that more aggressive increases in government spending would kick-start the economy. To that end, they advocated construction projects and other public investments, with the intention of creating badly needed jobs. This suggestion also conformed to the Washington Declaration made by the G20 (of which Canada is a member) in November 2008, in which countries agreed to use expansionary fiscal policy to stimulate domestic demand.

In the end, both sides got a little of what they wanted. One of the acts introduced in the House of Commons on February 6, 2009, was the *Budget Implementation Act of 2009*, more commonly known as the Economic Action Plan. That plan included both tax cuts ($20 billion in personal tax cuts) and a sizable increase in government spending ($40 billion). Its total cost was $60 billion (with nearly $47.2 billion financed by deficit)—about 4 percent of Canadian GDP.

By the end of 2014, five years after the plan was agreed upon, the economy had recovered. By that time, 431,000 people had lost their jobs and homes, and many businesses closed. The unemployment rate hit 8.6 percent at its peak in October, 2009, and had fallen below 7 percent by late 2014. The increased spending and decreased tax revenues put the Canadian government further into debt. By 2012, the dollar value of the debt had climbed past 80 percent of GDP.

Bayne Stanley/The Canadian Press

So, was the stimulus plan a success or failure? We can't judge this simply by looking at what happened before and after it was signed into law. Instead, we need to ask: What *would have* happened if the stimulus plan had *not* been enacted? What would have happened if the government had chosen an alternative balance of tax cuts and government spending? Would the level of unemployment and the health of the economy have been better, worse, or just the same?

To answer some of these questions, we'll create a framework for thinking about how taxation and government spending affect the national economy, based on the aggregate demand and supply model you saw in the previous chapter. By the end of this chapter you should be able to discuss the pros and cons of different policies, in terms of their effect on both short-run economic fluctuations and longer-run issues such as the national debt. These questions have crucial implications for the national economy, and have been hotly debated since 2009, as policy makers tried to steer the economy out of the recession.

Fiscal Policy

Each February, the finance minister and House of Commons begin the process of deciding how much to spend on all the varied functions of the federal government: how much to spend on building bridges, supporting the military, investing in medical research, and so on. At the same time, Parliament decides how much money should be collected in taxes to pay for all of these things. Government decisions about the level of taxation and public spending are called **fiscal policy**.

Expansionary or Contractionary?

> **LO 12.1** Explain the difference between contractionary fiscal policy and expansionary fiscal policy.

Fiscal policy is more than just simple budgeting. Choices about how much to spend, how to spend it, and how to raise the necessary funds can have dramatic effects on the economy. Recall from Chapter 7, "Measuring the Wealth of Nations," that government spending is one of the components of GDP. It is also part of the way we calculate the demand side of the economy in the aggregate demand and aggregate supply model from the previous chapter:

$$\text{Aggregate demand} = C + I + G + NX$$

Fiscal policy affects the economy by increasing or decreasing aggregate demand. As we saw in the previous chapter, shifts in the aggregate demand curve translate into higher or lower output and price levels throughout the economy.

Fiscal policy affects aggregate demand using two channels. The first is government spending, which directly affects the G in the aggregate demand equation. It can also have indirect effects on the C (consumption) and I (investment) components of aggregate demand. These effects come through mechanisms called the *multiplier effect* and *crowding out,* which we'll talk about later in the chapter. An increase in government spending will generally shift the aggregate demand curve out (to the right), and a decrease will shift it in (to the left).

The second channel through which fiscal policy drives aggregate demand is tax policy. This effect acts on aggregate demand directly through consumption, or the C part of the aggregate demand equation, although it can also indirectly affect the other components, such as investment. How much individuals consume is related to their incomes. But before anyone gets a paycheque, the government takes some money in taxes. Consumption therefore depends not on total income but rather on *disposable income*—what's left after taxes. If the tax rate increases, workers will take home less disposable income and we can expect them to reduce their consumption. As a result, the aggregate demand curve will shift in (to the left). If, on the other hand, the tax rate decreases, workers take home more money and will consume more. The decrease in the tax rate will shift the aggregate demand curve out (to the right).

Two broad terms differentiate types of fiscal policy:

- We use the term **expansionary fiscal policy** when the overall effect of decisions about taxation and spending is to increase aggregate demand. Increased government spending and lower taxes both have expansionary effects: they shift the aggregate demand curve to the right, as shown in panel A of Figure 12-1.

- In contrast, we use the term **contractionary fiscal policy** when the overall effect of decisions about taxation and spending is to reduce aggregate demand. Decreased government spending and higher taxes both have contractionary effects, shifting the aggregate demand curve in to the left, as shown in panel B.

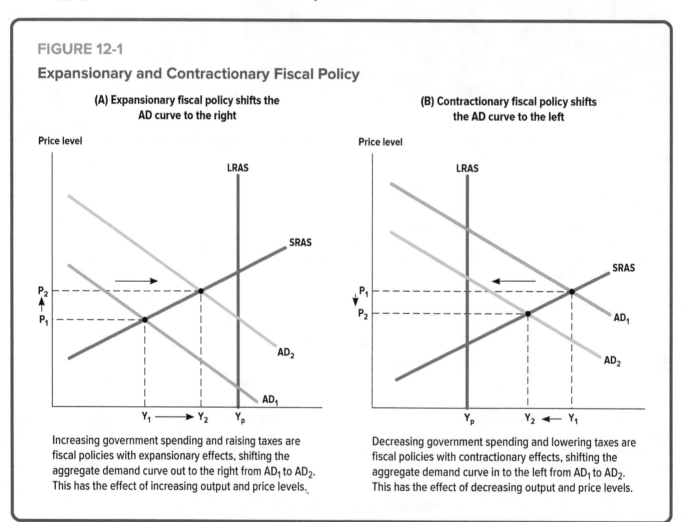

FIGURE 12-1

Expansionary and Contractionary Fiscal Policy

(A) Expansionary fiscal policy shifts the AD curve to the right

(B) Contractionary fiscal policy shifts the AD curve to the left

Increasing government spending and raising taxes are fiscal policies with expansionary effects, shifting the aggregate demand curve out to the right from AD_1 to AD_2. This has the effect of increasing output and price levels.

Decreasing government spending and lowering taxes are fiscal policies with contractionary effects, shifting the aggregate demand curve in to the left from AD_1 to AD_2. This has the effect of decreasing output and price levels.

Policy Response to Economic Fluctuations

LO 12.2 Explain how fiscal policy can counteract short-run economic fluctuations.

One of the most important ways that policy makers use fiscal policy is to smooth out fluctuations in the economy that might hurt consumers and businesses. In this section, we'll show how fiscal policy can be used to counteract the effects of economic shocks through the aggregate supply and aggregate demand model.

In the previous chapter, we saw how a shock like the financial crisis in late 2008 can affect the Canadian economy. The most immediate consequence of the steep decline in the Canadian stock market was that Canadian households felt poorer. This response shifted the aggregate demand curve to the left. Panel A of Figure 12-2 shows the leftward shift of the aggregate demand curve, from AD_1 to AD_2. The decrease in aggregate demand caused the economy to produce below its level of potential output. The result was lower GDP (output) and higher unemployment, seen in panel A as a reduction in output from Y_1 to Y_2.

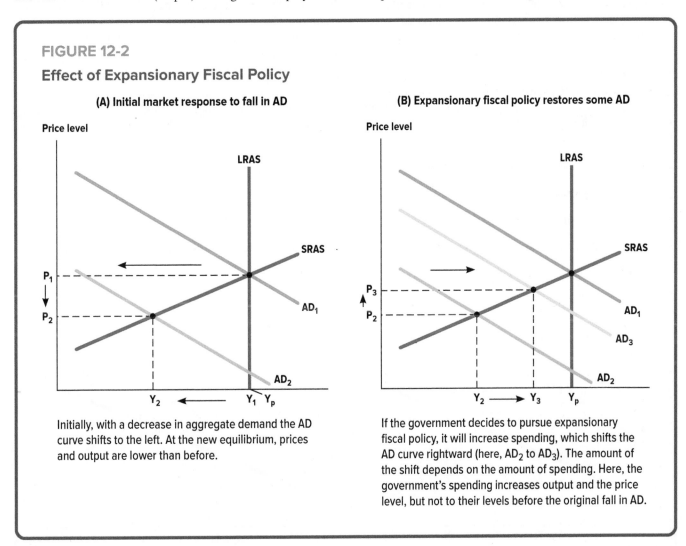

FIGURE 12-2

Effect of Expansionary Fiscal Policy

(A) Initial market response to fall in AD

Initially, with a decrease in aggregate demand the AD curve shifts to the left. At the new equilibrium, prices and output are lower than before.

(B) Expansionary fiscal policy restores some AD

If the government decides to pursue expansionary fiscal policy, it will increase spending, which shifts the AD curve rightward (here, AD_2 to AD_3). The amount of the shift depends on the amount of spending. Here, the government's spending increases output and the price level, but not to their levels before the original fall in AD.

According to the AD/AS model, if nothing else happened, the economy would eventually have automatically corrected itself. Wages would have fallen in response to unemployment, and lower production costs would bring other prices down. This response would cause the short-run aggregate supply curve to shift to the right until the economy returned to its original level of potential output level at Y_1. In the long-run, output would have recovered to its previous level, with lower overall prices in the economy.

Why didn't lawmakers simply wait for this to happen? It could have been a painful and very slow process. The wage rate would have had to fall along with other prices, and we saw in Chapter 10, "Unemployment and the Demand for Labour," that might not happen quickly or easily.[1] When businesses fail and people lose their jobs, they want their government to do something about it. They don't want just to hear that the economy will work the problems out if they wait long enough. As economist John Maynard Keynes once said, "In the long run, we are all dead."

We'll show in this chapter that fiscal policy can have real effects on the economy even in the short-run. Ideally, the government can counterbalance shocks, minimizing the damage to consumers and businesses without having to wait for the economy to correct itself in the long-run. However, we'll also see that the government may not always be able to improve matters—it might even make things worse, for reasons we describe in the next section. But if the government *is* going to act, for better or for worse, what should it do?

To counteract a decrease in aggregate demand, the government can try to boost demand by spending more or taxing less. This kind of expansionary policy is often called *Keynesian*, in recognition of John Maynard Keynes, who championed the strategy after the Great Depression of the 1930s.

The challenge is finding the dosage of fiscal policy that restores aggregate demand to its pre-recession level. As shown in panel B of Figure 12-2, a completely successful stimulus plan would shift the AD curve all the way back from AD_2 to its original position, AD_1. If the stimulus is only partly successful, then it would move the curve only part of the way back, from AD_2 to AD_3. Even a partially successful stimulus may be better than nothing. Full readjustment will take less time than in the absence of any stimulus, preventing the original shock from being as painful as it could have been.

What should the government do when the economy is suffering from the opposite problem—that is, when the economy is growing too quickly? People are often happy when the economy is booming, but government policy makers worry that big booms can get out of hand. Implementing contractionary fiscal policy to slow down the economy is a lot like shutting down a raging party because you are worried that the guests might regret their choices in the morning. It can be the smart thing to do, even though there will be plenty of grumbling.

FIGURE 12-3

Effect of Contractionary Fiscal Policy

(A) Economy overheats from too much AD

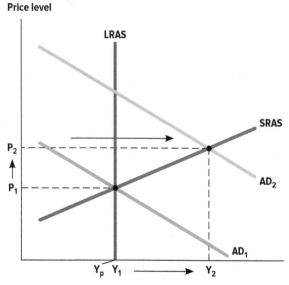

In an overheating economy, prices and output are above the long-run equilibrium in the economy.

(B) Contractionary fiscal policy lowers prices and output

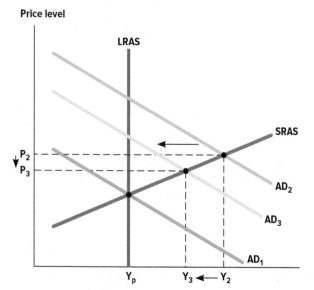

In order to slow down the economy, the government can cut spending or raise taxes, shifting the AD curve leftward. When this happens, prices and output fall, although the economy is still above long-run equilibrium.

A surge in aggregate demand, increases output and the price level, as shown in panel A of Figure 12-3. Contractionary fiscal policy slows down the economy by cutting government spending or increasing taxes, shifting the aggregate demand curve back in to the left, as shown in panel B of Figure 12-3.

Time Lags

> **LO 12.3** Discuss the main fiscal policy challenges faced by the government and how stabilizers can automatically adjust fiscal policy as the economy changes.

Fiscal policy can seem like a golden solution: Why should any government wait for the economy to correct itself in a slow and painful way when it can do the work much more quickly? Unfortunately, it's not so simple. Fiscal policy choices often amount to no more than educated guesses, made without the benefit of all the relevant information. Furthermore, time lags between when policies are chosen and when they are implemented mean that sometimes they are too late to do any good.

To see some of the difficulties of implementing fiscal policy, imagine that the economy is a bus. You're the driver and it's your job to prevent the bus from stalling if it comes to an uphill section of road, or from running out of control if it comes to a downhill section. You can step on the gas (in terms of the economy, use expansionary fiscal policy). Or you can step on the brakes (use contractionary fiscal policy). Sounds easy enough, right?

Now imagine that the windshield is blacked out so you can't see the road ahead, and that the speedometer indicates how fast you were going three blocks ago rather than how fast you're going now. Even worse, imagine that the bus is run as a democracy, so you also have to get the agreement of a majority of the passengers before you can hit the brakes or the gas, and they typically argue the matter for at least four blocks. Finally, once you actually hit the brakes or gas, it takes six to twelve blocks for that action to take effect.

This is how policy makers can feel when deciding about fiscal policy. Lags in the policy-making process come from three main sources:

1. Understanding the current economic situation. (You can't see out of the front of the bus, and the speedometer is three blocks delayed.)
2. Deciding on and passing legislation. (If the prime minister is the bus driver, lawmakers in Parliament are the arguing passengers.)
3. The time it takes for the policy to affect the economy. (Once you push the gas or the brakes, it still takes several blocks until the acceleration or braking engages.)

The first issue involves an *information lag*. It might seem pretty clear that the economy is in a recession or boom, just as it might seem pretty clear from looking out of the back window of a bus that you've started to go up or down a hill. But it can take a long time to collect data that tells policy makers about GDP, unemployment, and inflation. GDP figures, for example, are released every three months, and they report on economic activity that was happening three or four weeks before. These early numbers aren't always accurate, so it may be six months or more before the true figures are known.

Three to six months is a short time to register a trend in the overall economy. You certainly don't want to be the one who raises the alarm about a huge mountain up ahead of the bus, only to find that it was actually a tiny hill. It took several quarters' worth of data to trigger the announcement by Statistics Canada that the Canadian economy was slowing down. By then, the economy had lost thousands of jobs.

Just as it takes time to find out how bad things are, it also takes time to find out if the economy has reached the end of a recession. There will be news reports of companies hiring more workers, but it can take months to discover if this has translated into real gains for the economy. In both cases, policy makers have to make important decisions for the future, but they only know where the economy was a few months ago.

The second issue is *formulation lag*—the time it takes to decide on and pass legislation. First, a policy needs to be drafted and proposed in Parliament, where it becomes a bill. The bill is first debated in the House of Commons. If at least half of the MPs approve it, it then moves to the Senate. If a majority of the senators approve, the bill receives royal assent and becomes law. If the senators do not approve, the whole process has to start again. The 308 members of Parliament can take a while to make up their minds: it was clear in September 2008, with the collapse of the investment bank Lehman Brothers in the US, that the Canadian economy was in real trouble. But the stimulus act wasn't passed until February 2009.

The last hurdle for fiscal policy is *implementation lag.* Even after a policy has been proposed and passed, it may take time for it to take effect. It takes time for funds to be disbursed, employees hired, and materials purchased. Even tax cuts can take some time to kick in. When the government sent taxpayers a tax rebate, it took time to print and mail. Even after receiving the cheques, it took time for people to spend the money.

These three lags in the policy process—the information lag, the formulation lag, and the implementation lag—make conducting good fiscal policy a tough endeavour. In fact, the lags may be so large that by the time the policy takes effect, the economy might have corrected itself, making the policy unnecessary.[2] In the worst case, the economy might even have started to face the opposite problem, making the policy actively harmful—like slamming on the brake when it turns out the bus is just starting to go uphill, or stepping on the gas when it's now going downhill.

Policy Tools—Discretionary and Automatic

The 2009 stimulus bill is an example of targeted, or *discretionary,* fiscal policy. This is policy that the government actively *chooses* to adopt. Even if there had been no stimulus act at all, though, fiscal policy would still have had some effect on the economy due to already-existing taxes and spending policies. Called **automatic stabilizers**, these are taxes and government spending that affect fiscal policy without specific action from policy makers.

Taxes as Automatic Stabilizers

Taxes work as automatic stabilizers because the income tax system is designed so that people pay higher tax rates as their earnings rise. Income tax laws require you to pay a given percentage on each portion of your income that falls between certain ranges. For example, in 2014 single Canadians paid 15 percent in taxes on the portion of their income from $0 to $43,953, 22 percent from $43,954 to $87,907, 26 percent from $87,908 to $136,270, and so forth.[3] When the economy is booming, people earn more, so they pay taxes at higher tax rates automatically, without any new intervention from policy makers. When that happens, increased taxes serve to put a slight check on overall spending, just as they would if policy makers had intentionally implemented higher taxes as a contractionary fiscal policy. In the opposite case, when the economy is in a recession, people earn less and so automatically end up paying lower tax rates. The decrease in spending as a result of lower incomes decreases aggregate demand slightly, just as it would if the government had intentionally lowered taxes to implement an expansionary fiscal policy.

For the most part, *discretionary* fiscal policy via taxes (as opposed to fiscal policy using automatic stabilizers) requires policy makers to change *tax rates.* In other words, they have to decide to adjust the tax percentages owed on income. Changing the tax rates for discretionary policy allows active management of the economy, but information, formulation, and implementation lags can reduce the effect of such discretionary policy, or even make it counterproductive. Automatic stabilizers help when discretionary policy takes too long or is based on a misunderstanding of what's going on in the economy.

Using taxes as automatic stabilizers works by affecting *tax revenues*—the dollar amount the government collects in taxes. Since automatic stabilizers don't require specific policy action, lags are less serious. In addition, automatic stabilizers work to push the economy in the same direction that correctly timed and correctly formulated discretionary policy would. For example:

- When recession seems to be the major threat, discretionary policy through taxes would call for a government to encourage spending by lowering tax rates (expansionary fiscal policy). But because incomes are lower in a recession, people pay less in taxes, both in absolute dollars and also for some as a percentage of their income.
- When excessive inflation is of concern, discretionary policy through taxes would call for discouraging spending by increasing tax rates (contractionary fiscal policy). However, the increase in incomes during a boom means that more money is paid in taxes, increasing tax revenues and cooling down aggregate demand by taking away dollars that might have otherwise been spent.

It's true that changes in income during a recession or a boom affect the percentage of our overall income that goes to taxes as we move to different tax brackets (the ranges described above). However, as long as the government does not actively decide to change rates—in other words, as long as percentages changed only because income rose or fell due to economic conditions—automatic stabilizers are the primary factor at work. In general, it's a good idea to note the difference between tax rates and tax revenues, treating changes in tax rates as we discussed them as discretionary policy and changes in tax revenues as automatic stabilizers.

Government Spending as an Automatic Stabilizer

Some aspects of government spending also work as automatic stabilizers. Employment insurance benefits and welfare programs such as social assistance have set eligibility criteria based on income or unemployment status. When the economy is booming, fewer people are eligible for these programs, so government spending on them falls. This acts just like an intentional contractionary policy to lower government spending, reducing aggregated demand. In a recession, more people qualify for employment insurance and social assistance, so spending on those programs automatically rises. With higher government spending, the aggregate demand curve shifts to the right.

In sum, when the Canadian economy hits a recession, fiscal policy *automatically* becomes expansionary because average tax rates go down and spending on welfare programs goes up. In a booming economy, fiscal policy *automatically* becomes contractionary as tax revenues rise and welfare payments fall. The kind of *discretionary* stimulus bill approved in 2009 comes on top of these automatic effects.

Limits of Fiscal Policy: The Money Must Come from Somewhere

Politicians often cut taxes in response to recessions. The idea is that people will spend more money when they have more cash in their hands. That spending, in turn, will raise business profits, create jobs, and help the economy recover.

But it's not always so simple. Those tax cuts aren't free. The government will eventually have to find a way to make up for the lost tax revenue. That means either cutting an equivalent amount of government spending or, more frequently, raising taxes in the future. What happens if people see that today's tax cuts just mean higher taxes tomorrow? In that case, people won't want to spend as much from their tax cuts, and the stimulus strategy will be less effective.

This idea is known as *Ricardian equivalence.* This theory predicts that if governments cut taxes but not spending, people will *not* change their behaviour. Why not? Because people realize that the government will have to borrow money to cover the financial shortfall that's been created by cutting taxes. At some point in the future, taxes will have to go back up to repay the extra government debt. In other words, taxpayers realize that the money to maintain government spending must come from somewhere.

Taxpayers will get a nice-sized cheque from the tax cut today, but they will realize that they—or their children or grandchildren—will eventually have to pay it back through future tax increases. So the tax cut will feel more like a loan than a real windfall. According to classical economic theory, rational people should save what they receive rather than spending it today, in order to meet the financial obligation of increased taxes in the future. But if people save rather than spend, consumption does not increase and the tax cut will be unsuccessful in increasing aggregate demand.

Of course, in reality, people may not be so rational and forward looking. When they get a tax cut, they may go ahead and spend it. If so, Ricardian equivalence will fail to hold, and the fiscal policy will have the intended expansionary effect. Nonetheless, the theory of Ricardian equivalence is a good reminder that people often respond to changes in government policy by adapting their behaviour. Good policy has to take those responses and the unintended consequences that stem from them into account. In some cases, rational responses by individuals may be strong enough to make a well-intentioned policy fail. In practice, however, most people seem not to think about future tax increases when they open that envelope containing a tax refund.

✓ CONCEPT CHECK

- ☐ What are decisions about the level of government spending and taxation called? [LO 12.1]
- ☐ What type of fiscal policy increases aggregate demand? [LO 12.2]
- ☐ What are the three types of time lags involved in implementing fiscal policy? [LO 12.3]
- ☐ Are income taxes an example of discretionary or automatic fiscal policy? [LO 12.3]

The Multiplier Model

Imagine that you're the prime minister and you've just entered office in January 2009. With the economy in a recession, you are considering how to use economic policy to stimulate the economy and create jobs. Your economic advisors are divided over the best route to take. Some advise you to cut taxes. They figure that employees will take home more money and some of it will be spent, which will boost demand. Others advise you to increase government spending. Since thousands of people are out of work, the advisors argue, the government should create jobs by spending on infrastructure projects. The income paid to newly employed workers will then flow into the economy as these workers in turn spend their new income on food, clothes, energy, and other things. Both plans will stimulate the economy, but you want to ensure that you use government resources as efficiently as possible.

Which policy gives you the bigger bang for the government's buck? Economists answer that question using a measure called the *multiplier,* which measures the effect of government spending or tax cuts on national income.

Deriving the Multiplier

LO 12.4 Calculate the fiscal multiplier for spending and taxation, and explain why it differs for these two policies.

Consider what happens when you make a purchase. Let's say you hire a builder to construct a new deck for your backyard. The total bill is $5,000. This decision adds $5,000 to GDP, right? Yes, but that's not the end of the story. Let's say that the builder decides to take his family on a two-week vacation, which he couldn't have afforded before you employed him to build your deck. The money he spends on his vacation, including $3,000 on his family's hotel stay, also counts toward GDP. So your decision to build a deck has added $8,000 to GDP, not $5,000.

But that's still not the end of the story. Thanks to the builder's stay at the hotel, the owner feels able to buy a painting for the hotel lobby for $1,500. Your decision to build the deck has now added $9,500 to GDP. The artist celebrates selling her painting by spending $700 on a new digital camera, making your contribution to GDP $10,200, and so on. If you hadn't built the deck, none of this would have happened. Your decision has sent ripples through the economy, increasing GDP by considerably more than the $5,000 you paid your builder. Economists call this ripple of consumer spending the **multiplier effect**. The multiplier effect occurs when spending by one person causes others to spend more, too, increasing the impact of the initial spending on the economy.

The multiplier effect suggests that spending $1 increases GDP by more than $1. How much more? To be able to calculate this, we need to know what proportion of their incomes people spend. As a broad generalization, when income goes up, so does consumption. But the details of how much consumption goes up in response to an increase in income are important. First, consumption is based on the amount people have left after paying taxes. In other words, we need to look at after-tax income, rather than pre-tax income. Second, people usually consume part of their income and save the rest. When they get an additional dollar in income—for instance, because they receive a tax rebate—they will spend only a fraction of that dollar. The amount by which consumption increases when after-tax income increases by $1 is called the **marginal propensity to consume (MPC)**. The MPC is a number between zero and 1, indicating the fraction of an additional dollar that gets spent.[4] For example, an MPC of 0.8 means that people consume 80 percent of an additional dollar of income and save the other 20 percent.

Multiplier Effect of Government Spending

When the government tries to boost the economy through extra spending, it relies on the multiplier effect. Suppose, for example, that part of the stimulus plan is that government agencies buy new computers. The government pays $500 million to the computer manufacturer. Immediately, this expenditure increases GDP by $500 million, since government spending is one of the contributors to overall GDP. The computer company in turn uses the money to pay workers and make new capital investments, such as building a factory. The people employed to build the factory, in turn, spend money on goods and services elsewhere in the economy, and so on.

By how much will the $500 million computer purchase increase GDP? We can use the idea of marginal propensity to consume (MPC) to calculate the **government-spending multiplier**, which tells us the amount by which GDP increases when government spending increases by $1.

Let's say that, across the economy, people have an average MPC of 0.8. Therefore, every dollar that a person or business receives as a result of government spending will cause them to spend an additional 80 cents (80 cents = $1 × 0.8). That 80 cents is received by another person or business, which in turn spends an additional 64 cents (64 cents = 80 cents × 0.8 = $1 × 0.8 × 0.8), which in turn causes an additional 53.2 cents of spending (54.2 cents = 64 cents × 0.8 = $1 × 0.8 × 0.8 × 0.8), and so on. To find the total effect of the initial increase in government spending, we need to add up each separate addition to consumption: $1 + MPC + MPC^2 + MPC^3 + MPC^4 + \ldots$ all the way to infinity. After a lot of calculation, we would discover that the total increase in spending is $5. Fortunately, there is a much simpler way of getting to the same result, using an equation:

Equation 12-1

$$\text{Government-spending multiplier} = \frac{1}{(1 - \text{MPC})}$$

With a marginal propensity to consume of 0.8, we can calculate that the government-spending multiplier is 5:

$$\text{Government-spending multiplier} = \frac{1}{(1 - \text{MPC})} = \frac{1}{1 - 0.8} = \frac{1}{0.2} = 5$$

In other words, if the MPC is 0.8, then a $1 increase in government spending increases GDP by $5. In our example above, spending $500 million on new computers for government agencies will produce an additional $2.5 billion in GDP.

Of course, if the marginal propensity to consume is smaller, the government-spending multiplier will be smaller, too. If the MPC is just 0.6—that is, if people spend only 60 percent of an additional dollar of after-tax income—then increasing government spending by $1 will increase total income by 1/(1−0.6), or $2.50. In this case, the multiplier is 2.5, and the $500 million spent on new computers will increase GDP by $1.25 billion (1.25 × $500 million). The effect of government spending on GDP is still multiplied, but not by as much as with a higher MPC.

Multiplier Effect of Government Transfers and Taxes

Now imagine that, instead of spending that $500 million on new computers, the government decides to cut taxes by $500 million. The tax cut puts more money in people's pockets, which they can use for consumption. The multiplier effect comes into play under this policy, too.

To find out how much this tax cut will affect GDP, we can calculate the **taxation multiplier**. It tells us the amount GDP decreases when taxes increase by $1.

The taxation multiplier works in a similar way to the government-spending multiplier. A tax cut gives workers more after-tax income, which increases consumption. This consumption spending is received by other people, whose incomes go up; they consume more in response, and the loop continues.

The multiplier effect of tax cuts is smaller than the effect of government spending. To see why, remember that $500 million spent on computers counts directly toward GDP though the G in the GDP equation (Y = C + I + G + NX). On top of that, it has an indirect effect on C, when people increase their consumption in response to the increase in G. But $500 million in tax cuts does *not* count directly toward GDP. Instead, it boosts GDP only through the indirect effect on C, when people go out and spend the extra cash in their pockets. In other words, $500 million in government spending starts by adding $500 million directly to GDP, and follows with $400 million ($500 × 0.8) in consumption. But $500 million in tax cuts skips the direct effect and starts to affect the economy through the $400 million. As a result, the total effect of a tax cut on GDP ends up being smaller than the total effect of an equivalent amount of government spending:

Spending:

$$\$500m \times (1 + MPC + MPC^2 + \ldots) = \$500m + \$400m + \$320m + \ldots$$

Tax cuts:

$$\$500m + (0 + MPC + MPC^2 + \ldots) = \$400m + \$320m + \ldots$$

We can generalize this calculation to find the formula for the taxation multiplier. As the example above suggests, we need to subtract 1 from the spending multiplier, to account for the fact that the tax cut skips the direct effect on GDP. After a bit of algebra, this gives us:

Equation 12-2

$$\text{Taxation multiplier} = \frac{-MPC}{(1 - MPC)}$$

If the MPC is 0.8, then reducing taxes by $1 will increase income as follows:

$$\text{Taxation multiplier} = \frac{-0.8}{(1 - 0.8)} = \frac{-0.8}{0.2} = -4$$

The tax cut is actually a decrease in taxes, so we represent it mathematically as a negative number; in this case, −$500 million. When we apply the taxation multiplier to that tax cut, we find that:

$$-4 \times -\$500\,\text{million} = \$2\,\text{billion}$$

Thus, a tax cut of $500 million will provide a $2 billion boost to the economy, compared with the $2.5 billion boost the government spending provided.

If the MPC is 0.6 instead of 0.8, then the taxation multiplier is –1.5, meaning that a tax cut of $500 million will increase GDP by $750 million:

$$\frac{-0.6}{(1-0.6)} = \frac{-0.6}{0.4} = -1.5$$

and

$$-1.5 \times - \$ 500 \text{ million} = \$ 750 \text{ million}$$

This amount is less than the $1.25 billion boost to GDP we could expect from the government expenditure of the same amount. At any MPC, the taxation multiplier will be lower than the government spending multiplier.

Table 12-1 compares the amount of benefit provided by tax cuts and government spending under a variety of marginal propensities to consume.

TABLE 12-1   GOVERNMENT SPENDING AND TAXATION MULTIPLIERS

For the same marginal propensity to consume, the multiplier for government spending is higher than the multiplier for taxation. The difference is greater as the MPC decreases.

Marginal propensity to consume (MPC)	Government-spending multiplier 1/(1 — MPC)	A $500 million stimulus would increase GDP by:	Taxation multiplier–MPC/ (1 — MPC)	A $500 million tax cut would increase GDP by:
0.2	1.25	$625 million	—0.25	$125 million
0.4	1.67	$835 million	—0.67	$335 million
0.6	2.50	$1.25 billion	—1.50	$750 million
0.8	5.00	$2.50 billion	—4.00	$ 2 billion

Looking at the math alone, it appears as if there's a strong case for tackling a recession through government spending instead of tax cuts. However, we've made some big simplifying assumptions. In the real world, things are more complicated, and government spending can have side effects. For instance, we've assumed that government spending doesn't *crowd out* spending (through government borrowing) that would otherwise have occurred in the private sector.

The 2009 recession is one example of how complex it can be trying to figure out how the multiplier effect works in the real world. On one hand are those economists who suggested a huge increase in government spending, while on the other are economists who argued for tax cuts. The central focus of their debate was on the size of the multiplier for government spending. To see how this debate played out, read the Real Life box, The Great 2009 Multiplier Debate.

Fiscal policy can be a powerful tool, enabling the government to counteract short-run fluctuations in the economy by increasing spending or cutting taxes. However, there is catch: the government—and therefore, taxpayers—must pay for all the roads and bridges and tax rebates somehow. Where does the money come from? If spending increases without a comparable increase in taxes, or taxes are cut without a comparable decrease in spending, the government often goes into debt. This is the subject we turn to in the next section.

REAL LIFE

The Great 2009 Multiplier Debate

Ask different economists about the size of the multipliers for government spending and tax cuts and you'll get different answers. Differing views on the size of the multipliers lead to disagreements between experts on how to design the best fiscal policy. On the optimistic end, the Conservative government predicted that the government-spending multiplier on "shovel-ready" projects in the 2009 stimulus bill, like building roads or schools, would be 1.5. More pessimistically, Stanford University professor John Cogan and his colleagues argued that the government-spending multiplier was below 1. He thought that each dollar of government spending would add no more than 50 to 60 cents to GDP.

In the grand scheme of things, 1.5 may not sound that different from 0.6. But which figure you think is more accurate makes a huge difference to the economic impact you would expect from a policy to combat the recession. The difference in the expected impact of the 2009 stimulus under a multiplier of 1.5 versus 0.6 is about a billion more in GDP increases and thousands more jobs created.

Why is there such a large difference between different estimates of the multiplier? There are two significant reasons. One is that the multiplier is determined by overall economic conditions. Suppose the government employs a hundred workers to build a bridge, but the economy is doing pretty well and most of those hundred workers would have had little trouble finding other employment. In the worst case, the workers might actually get pulled into bridge building from another, potentially higher priority job. In that case, the impact of government spending on GDP would be much less than if those hundred workers had been sitting at home hoping for a job.

The second reason is that economists hotly debate whether government spending has a positive or negative impact on private-sector investment. Some argue that stimulus spending will inspire confidence in the economy and encourage firms to invest more. This would increase GDP. Others counter that government borrowing may drive up interest rates. As the government increases its demand for money in order to finance its spending, all else equal, the cost of borrowing—i.e., the interest rate—will increase, too. When faced with higher interest rates, firms may choose to invest less, decreasing GDP. This phenomenon is known as *crowding out*.

Taking these and other complicating factors into account, economists argue that different kinds of government spending and tax cuts will have different multipliers. Should the government invest in shovel-ready public works or put the money into widening the employment insurance program? Would it be better to cut payroll taxes or corporate taxes? The answers to these questions lie in which programs have the highest multiplier.

Sources: "Did Government Stimulus Fuel Economic Growth in Canada?" Fraser Institute. http://www.fraserinstitute.org/
publicationdisplay.aspx?id=15912&terms=do+government+stimulus+fuel+economic+growth

✓ CONCEPT CHECK

☐ Which multiplier is larger for the same marginal propensity to consume—the government-spending multiplier or the taxation multiplier? [LO 12.4]

The Government Budget

We've seen why the government may want to influence the economy by changing the amount it spends or taxes. In practice this can require borrowing money. If spending is higher than revenue, which is the current situation in Canada and in most other countries, then the government will go into debt. In the remainder of this chapter, we'll discuss the government budget and the effect that public debt can have on the economy.

Revenue and Spending

> **LO 12.5** Describe how revenue and spending determine a government budget.

A government budget is similar to a personal budget. Money comes in as tax revenues and goes out through government purchases and transfer payments. (**Transfer payments** refer to payments from government accounts to individuals for programs, like Social Insurance, that do not involve a purchase of goods or services. As such, these payments are not reflected in GDP.) Total government expenditure in 2013 was $760.26 billion. The government took in, through tax revenue, approximately $718.91billion. The gap between revenue and spending—the budget deficit—was $41.4 billion.

It may be hard to understand what an amount as large as $41.4 billion really means, so let's lop off a few zeros. Imagine that you spend $76,140 a year, but earn only $72,000 a year. To finance the gap, you have to borrow $4,140. Would you be happy about borrowing that $4,140? Or would you look for ways to make more money, or try to trim your expenses, or both? This is the same decision the Canadian government needs to make.

The Budget Deficit

This $41.4 billion shortfall in the Canadian government budget is called the **budget deficit**—the amount of money a government spends beyond the revenue it brings in. In other words, deficits occur when annual spending is more than annual revenue. Although it happens more rarely, it is also possible for the government to run a surplus. A **budget surplus** is the amount of revenue a government brings in beyond what it spends.

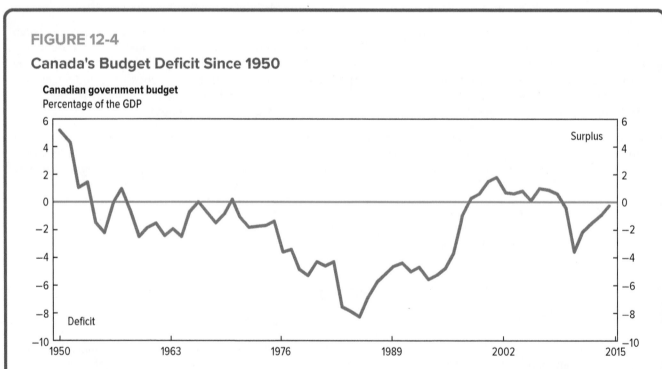

FIGURE 12-4

Canada's Budget Deficit Since 1950

Canadian government budget
Percentage of the GDP

The Canadian budget was relatively balanced until about 1970. For a few decades afterward, there was a persistent budget deficit. After a short surplus, the budget became more unbalanced as the government tried to spend the economy out of recession.

Source: Data from Government of Canada, Department of Finance; www.tradingeconomics.com/canada/government-budget.

Figure 12-4 shows the Canadian budget deficit/surplus for the last 60 years. Economists usually express the deficit as a percentage of GDP to emphasize the relationship between the deficit and the size of the economy. Every year between 1974 and 1997 there was a budget deficit. While there was a period of surpluses (1998–2008), the budget went into deficit again after the recession in 2009. Looking forward, the federal government expects to realize a surplus of $6.4 billion in 2015.

Spending increases can lead to larger deficits, but so can decreases in tax revenues. You may notice that the deficit was pretty high—on average 5 percent of GDP—during the 1980s, a time of economic growth and peace. This was due to changes on the expenditure side of the government budget, as employment insurance benefits were raised by Prime Minister Brian Mulroney and the government spent more money. Recessions also tend to increase deficits, as can be seen in the sharp spike from 2008 onward. During a recession, government spending often increases as part of an expansionary fiscal policy, while revenues tend to decrease because people are earning and spending less.

✓ CONCEPT CHECK

☐ What is the term for when the government collects more revenue than it spends? [LO 12.5]
☐ Name three reasons why the budget deficit might increase during a recession. [LO 12.5]

The Public Debt

Just a few blocks from the flashy billboards and dazzling displays of Times Square in New York City is a far more humble digital counter that keeps tabs on the debt incurred by the US federal government. Every time the government runs a deficit, the total debt increases. While Canada does not have a debt clock erected in public, the debt incurred by the Canadian federal government exceeded $614 billion in 2014 and is rising at a rate of $8 million per day. This $614 billion is the equivalent of over $17,300 of debt per citizen. If you add in the provincial debt, the national debt amounts to $1.2 trillion. Should we be bothered about the size of the debt?

Size of the Debt

LO 12.6 Explain the difference between the government deficit and public debt.

A country's **public debt** is the total amount of money that a government owes. The distinction between the *debt* and the *deficit* is an important one. The deficit tells us how much the government revenues fall short of spending *each year*. The debt is the *total* amount that the government owes. In other words, the debt is the cumulative sum of all deficits and surpluses.

To see why it's useful to think of the public debt as a share of GDP, consider it in terms of personal finances. Would you rather be making $20,000 a year and owe $10,000 in debt, or making $100,000 a year and owe $30,000 in debt? In the second case your debt is three times as large, but only 30 percent of your annual income. In the first case, your debt is smaller but amounts to 50 percent of your annual income. Even though you owe more in the second case, you'd be less worried about your ability to repay it. Similar logic explains why debt as a share of GDP actually shrank between 1950 and 1980, even though in dollar terms the debt was going up: the economy grew quickly in this time, much faster than the growth in the debt.

Almost every country in the world has debt, some much more than Canada as a percentage of GDP. (*Trivia:* Only the nation of Brunei is debt-free, according to the International Monetary Fund.) Figure 12-5 shows the amount of debt held by various countries. Three of them, Italy, Ireland, and Japan, owe more than 100 percent of GDP.

How exactly does government spending lead to debt? The process is more complicated than simply putting purchases on a charge card or getting a loan at a local bank. It involves selling Treasury securities, which are complex debt-financing arrangements that obligate the Canadian government to pay back the borrowed money over varying lengths of time and at varying rates of interest.

FIGURE 12-5

Debt in Various OECD Countries, 2014

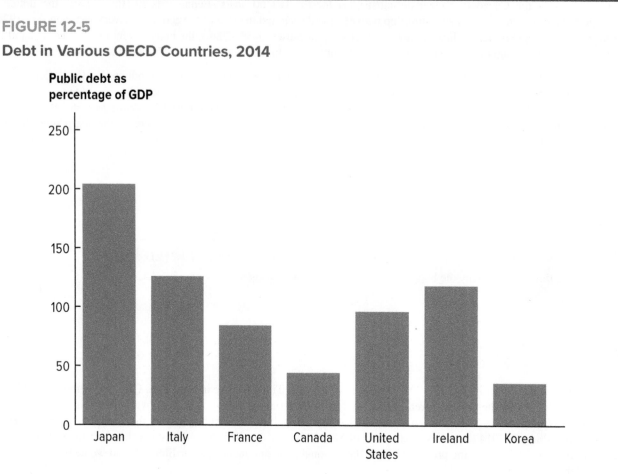

There is a wide discrepancy in the amount of debt owed among OECD countries. Japan has much more debt at more than 200 percent of its GDP. Most countries have a level of debt that ranges between 20 and 80 percent of their GDP.

Source: OECD StatExtracts, stats.oecd.org/index.aspx, accessed February 2015.

Is Government Debt Good or Bad?

LO 12.7 Identify the benefits and costs of government debt.

In the summer of 2011, more than 100,000 people marched in the streets of Athens. They were protesting austerity measures that would cut government spending in order to tame Greece's astronomical debt burden. At 1.5 times the size of GDP, debt had become a serious drag on Greece's economy. However, most economists believe that some debt is necessary to the smooth functioning of government. What are the costs and benefits?

Benefits of Government Debt

There are two main benefits of government debt. The first is that it allows the government to be flexible when something unexpected happens. Floods that devastated the city of Calgary in 2013 cost the governments more than $5 billion. (The Alberta government approved a preliminary $1 billion emergency fund, which represents almost 2.6 percent of Alberta government spending that year, and sought more than $3 billion in financial assistance from the federal government.) If the choice is between borrowing to cover the costs of responding to an emergency or not responding at all, many people would say it's better to borrow.

The second benefit of debt is that it can pay for investments that will lead to economic growth and prosperity (and presumably, higher tax revenues) in the long run. Just as you might decide to borrow to fund your university education because you expect it to lead to a better job and higher salary down the road, it can make sense for governments to borrow to invest in the education system or to construct roads and other infrastructure that will help the economy to grow more quickly.

Costs of Government Debt

There are both *direct* and *indirect* costs of government debt. The direct cost is the interest the government has to pay to the people it has borrowed from. Interest payments on the debt are substantial. Currently they amount to the second-largest budget expense, just behind spending on social services and ahead of "protection of persons and property" (the third-largest budget category).

The direct cost of debt depends on the interest rate. If interest rates increase, the government debt becomes more expensive to pay. Interest rates, in turn, depend on investors' confidence in the government's ability to pay back the debt. This can become a vicious cycle: if investors doubt that a government will be able to pay back its debts, they will demand higher interest rates before they are willing to lend to that government. Those higher interest rates increase the burden of debt, making it even more doubtful that the government can pay it back.

There are also indirect costs of government debt. In some circumstances, government debt can distort the credit market and slow economic growth. We have already noted the possibility that government borrowing can *crowd out* private borrowing. When the government borrows money, it increases the demand for credit and so increases the price of credit—the interest rate—in the wider economy. Higher interest rates increase the cost of borrowing for businesses that want to invest or consumers who want to buy new homes or cars.

Finally, there is the question of who bears the burden of government debt. People today benefit when the government borrows to spend more on services or cut taxes, but people tomorrow will have to repay the loans. The costs of services are being kicked down the road to our children and grandchildren.

✓ CONCEPT CHECK

☐ What is the difference between government debt and deficit? [LO 12.6]
☐ What is one possible effect of government debt on the amount of private investment? [LO 12.7]

Conclusion

We started this chapter by looking at why the government might want to change fiscal policy to counteract economic fluctuations. When the economy is in a recession, expansionary fiscal policy—cutting taxes, increasing spending, or both, as with the 2009 stimulus plan—can increase aggregate demand and speed up recovery. Unemployment remained high even after the stimulus, but ultimately there is no way of knowing for certain whether it would have been even higher without it.

We also looked at how the government can borrow, and how deficits lead to debt. Debt adds to government flexibility, but it can be costly and slow down economic growth. It also raises questions about the fairness of expecting future generations to bear the burden of paying off the debt.

Governments have an alternative to fiscal policy when they want to influence the economy: monetary policy. We will turn to this topic in the next chapter.

Key Terms

fiscal policy	government-spending multiplier
expansionary fiscal policy	taxation multiplier
contractionary fiscal policy	transfer payments
automatic stabilizers	budget deficit
multiplier effect	budget surplus
marginal propensity to consume (MPC)	public debt

Summary

LO 12.1 Explain the difference between contractionary fiscal policy and expansionary fiscal policy.

Together, the level of taxation and government spending is called fiscal policy. We say that fiscal policy is either expansionary or contractionary.

Expansionary fiscal policy involves changes to fiscal policy that cause the aggregate demand curve to increase (shift out to the right). It is expansionary because it expands demand. Expansionary fiscal policy occurs either because government spending increases or the level of taxation decreases and is a response to recessionary conditions.

On the other hand, contractionary fiscal policy involves changes to fiscal policy that contract aggregate demand, causing the aggregate demand curve to decrease (shift in to the left). Contractionary fiscal policy occurs when government spending decreases or when taxation increases, and is a response to an overheating economy with the accompanying threat of excessive inflation.

LO 12.2 Explain how fiscal policy can counteract short-run economic fluctuations.

The government can use fiscal policy to counteract business-cycle fluctuations. When the economy is sluggish, the government can conduct expansionary fiscal policy to stimulate demand. This will lead to a faster recovery than without the fiscal policy. On the other hand, if the economy is overheating, the government can undertake contractionary fiscal policy to reduce aggregate demand. This action also returns the economy closer to the long-run equilibrium level.

LO 12.3 Discuss the main fiscal policy challenges faced by the government and how stabilizers can automatically adjust fiscal policy as the economy changes.

The government faces two primary potential challenges when implementing fiscal policy: time lags and Ricardian equivalence. Time lags come in many forms. There are information lags (how long it takes to get the right information about the overall health of the economy), formulation lags (getting everyone to agree on the right policy), and implementation lags (how long it takes fiscal policy to have an effect on the economy). To get around these lags, some aspects of fiscal policy automatically stimulate or slow the economy. For example, income tax revenues will decrease when the economy is weaker, and increase as the economy is booming.

Ricardian equivalence is a theory that predicts that if governments cut taxes but not public spending, people will continue to save rather than spend, consumption will not increase, and the tax cut will be unsuccessful in changing aggregate demand. The government will have to borrow money to cover the financial shortfall that's been created, and at some point in the future, taxes will have to go back up to repay the extra government debt incurred through tax cuts.

LO 12.4 Calculate the fiscal multiplier for spending and taxation, and explain why it differs for these two policies.

The government-spending multiplier measures how much output increases when government spending increases by $1. The government-taxation multiplier measures how much output increases when taxation falls by $1. The multiplier effect from both spending and taxation occurs because there is a feedback effect between income and consumption: higher income (whether from increased government spending or lower taxes) increases consumption, which increases income, again increasing consumption, resulting in a feedback loop. The government-spending multiplier is larger than the taxation multiplier because government spending directly affects income, whereas taxation does so indirectly, through consumption.

LO 12.5 Describe how revenue and spending determine a government budget.

The government budget includes all of the revenue it collects in taxes and all of the money it spends on government programs. When the government spends more than it collects in revenue, it runs a deficit. When it collects more revenue than it spends, it has a surplus. In most years, the government spends more than it collects in revenue. In the effort to fight the latest recession, the gap between spending and revenue has increased drastically, making for a large budget deficit.

LO 12.6 Explain the difference between the government deficit and debt.

Deficits occur when annual spending is more than annual revenue. A surplus occurs when annual spending is less than annual revenue. The public debt is the total amount of money that the government has borrowed over time. The debt and the deficit are closely related: the budget deficit tells us how much the government borrows each year, and the debt tells us the total that the government has borrowed and not yet paid back over time. In other words, the debt is the cumulative sum of all deficits and surpluses.

LO 12.7 Identify the benefits and costs of government debt.

A deficit allows the government to spend more than its revenue. Allowing the government to run a deficit permits the government to respond to unexpected events and to undertake expansionary fiscal policy. However, there are also costs of running deficits. Interest needs to be paid on the debt, the government may not spend the money efficiently, and high government deficits may affect interest rates and reduce investment in the economy.

Review Questions

1. What is the best fiscal policy for a country suffering from high inflation? [LO 12.1]

2. If the government wants to slow down the economy by reducing GDP by $500 million via government spending, should it increase or decrease its spending? Must it increase or decrease spending by exactly $500 million, some amount more than $500 million, or some amount less than $500 million? Would this be expansionary or contractionary fiscal policy? [LO 12.1]

3. Alberta Premier Ralph Klein said the following in 1993 when announcing a 20 percent pay reduction for provincial public employees: "Never again will this government or the people of this province have to set aside another tax dollar on debt…" What do you think the intended effect of this policy would be, assuming the economy was in a recession at the time? Do you think it was the appropriate response? Why or why not? [LO 12.2]

4. If unemployment is high and spending is sluggish, what type of fiscal policy should be enacted? How would this be enacted via taxes? Via government spending? What is the intended effect of this policy on aggregate demand? [LO 12.2]

5. "The problem with democracy," your friend tells you as you debate politics, "is the time it takes to get approval for every action the government takes. If the prime minister didn't have to spend so much time arguing back and forth with Parliament, policy wouldn't take so long to affect the economy." Is your friend right or wrong? What would your response be? [LO 12.3]

6. Explain the difference between tax rates and tax revenues, and how each is related to recession and policy enacted to counteract it. Do you expect to see tax rates rise or fall during recession? What about tax revenues? Explain your answer. [LO 12.3]

7. Would it be more advisable to use government spending or tax cuts to stimulate an economy that is highly susceptible to the crowding-out effect? [LO 12.4]

8. Let's say that the government estimates that the average household spends 80 percent of each dollar of income and uses this estimate to determine the amount it needs to increase government spending to stimulate the economy by a given dollar amount. However, in reality, households actually spend 90 percent of each dollar of income. How will this affect expansionary fiscal policy via government spending? Will the amount of government spending calculated with the 80 percent figure be too much, too little, or just right? What will be the likely effect on output and employment in the short run? [LO 12.4]

9. Everything else equal, which will have a bigger effect on aggregate demand and GDP, a $100 million reduction in taxes or a $100 million increase in government spending? Is everything else equal in practice? Why or why not? [LO 12.4]

10. Why have budget deficits been so high in Canada since 2009? [LO 12.5]

11. You hear on the nightly news that the prime minister has vowed to decrease the nation's debt. "We'll have to buckle down and learn to do without, both the government and private citizens," he says. How can a nation lower its debt? How will the government and private citizens be affected? [LO 12.5]

12. A friend of yours looks at the state of the Canadian debt in 2011 and tells you, "Since the debt is so high, we must be running an incredibly large deficit every year." Is your friend's analysis valid? Why or why not? [LO 12.6]

13. Is it possible for a nation's government to run a budget deficit in some years but not have national debt? Explain your answer. [LO 12.6]

14. Taxpayers are clamouring for their government to be more responsible, and many strongly support a balanced-budget act (like the federal *Balanced Budget Act* of 2015). This would mean the country could no longer spend more than it takes in each year. Discuss the primary advantages and disadvantages of such legislation. [LO 12.7]

15. Is government debt good or bad for the economy and the nation as a whole? Give one argument for each side of the debate. [LO 12.7]

Problems and Applications

1. Is each of the following policies an example of expansionary or contractionary fiscal policy? Explain your answers in terms of the effect on aggregate demand. [LO 12.1]
   a. The government slashes funding for Natural Resources Canada, without changing any other spending.
   b. The government raises taxes on households making more than $250,000.
   c. The government decides to fill gaps in senior benefits by making it available to more people.

2. The economy is growing far too quickly, as high aggregate demand is causing inflation. What fiscal policy should be pursued in this instance—expansionary or contractionary? What will be the effect of the appropriate policy on aggregate demand? [LO 12.1]

3. Assuming that unemployment is high and spending is low, answer the following questions. [LO 12.2]
   a. Should the government pursue expansionary or contractionary fiscal policy?
   b. What will the appropriate policy do to the aggregate demand curve? Will the curve shift to the right or to the left?
   c. Through which component(s) of aggregate demand (C, I, G, or NX, or some combination of them) will the change occur?

4. The diagram in Figure 12P-1 shows aggregate demand for New Caprica last year (AD$_1$) and the aggregate demand for this year (AD$_2$). If you were to advise the president of New Caprica on economic policy, how would you answer the following? [LO 12.2]
   a. How large is current output? How large is potential output? What is the difference, if any, between the two?
   b. Is New Caprica in a recession or a boom?
   c. Given your findings, should the president enact expansionary fiscal policy, contractionary fiscal policy, or no policy at all?
   d. Which direction would the aggregate demand curve shift if the president used contractionary fiscal policy?

5. "Our fiscal policy was unsuccessful," an economic analyst says, "due to partisan bickering in Parliament that delayed the passing of the appropriate measures and our failure to realize we were headed into recession until it was too late." What type of lags is the analyst describing? [LO 12.3]

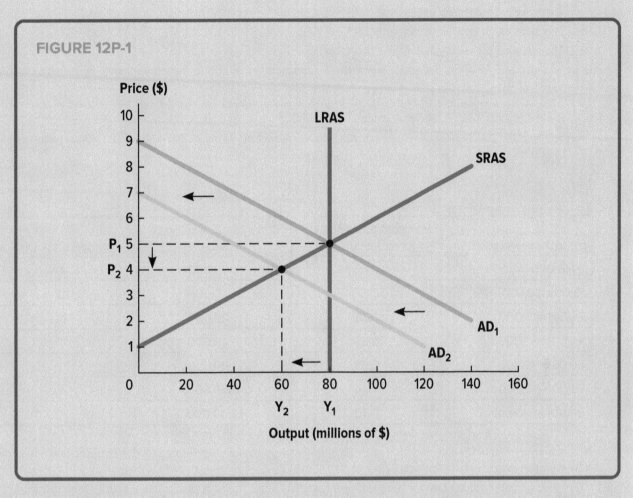

FIGURE 12P-1

6. Assume that the government in some nation intended to respond to low employment via fiscal policy, but that policy ended up having the opposite of its intended effect. Explain how this could happen in terms of formulation and implementation lags. [LO 12.3]

7. Calculate the government-spending multiplier in each of the following examples. [LO 12.4]
   a. The marginal propensity to consume (MPC) = 0.2.
   b. The marginal propensity to consume (MPC) = 0.5.
   c. The marginal propensity to consume (MPC) = 0.8.

8. Calculate the change in GDP for each of the following MPCs when the government increases its spending by $250 billion. For each, comment on the relationship between the MPC and the resulting change in GDP—as the MPC rises, does its effect on GDP increase or decrease? [LO 12.4]
   a. The marginal propensity to consume (MPC) = 0.2.
   b. The marginal propensity to consume (MPC) = 0.5.
   c. The marginal propensity to consume (MPC) = 0.8.

9. Calculate the government-taxation multiplier for each marginal propensity to consume given below. [LO 12.4]
   a. The marginal propensity to consume (MPC) = 0.2.
   b. The marginal propensity to consume (MPC) = 0.5.
   c. The marginal propensity to consume (MPC) = 0.8.
   d. What do your results imply about the relative strength of changes in government spending versus changes in taxation for fiscal policy, all else equal?

10. Calculate the resulting change in GDP for each of the following MPCs when the government decreases taxes by $250 billion (change in tax equals −$250 billion). [LO 12.4]

    a. The marginal propensity to consume (MPC) = 0.2.

    b. The marginal propensity to consume (MPC) = 0.5.

    c. The marginal propensity to consume (MPC) = 0.8.

11. In the country of Pythia, the marginal propensities to consume are related to income as shown by the chart in Table 12P-1. [LO 12.4]

    a. Assume the government of Pythia needs to pursue expansionary fiscal policy. If tax cuts are given to every income bracket, what is the value of the taxation multiplier in each bracket?

    b. Suppose the government increases spending on infrastructure. What is the value of the government-spending multiplier in each bracket?

TABLE 12P-1

Income range ($)	Marginal propensity to consume (MPC)	Total yearly income ($ in millions)	Income tax (%)
0–15,000	0.95	5,000	10
15,001–30,000	0.85	10,000	13
30,001–45,000	0.75	20,000	16
45,001–60,000	0.65	40,000	19
60,001–75,000	0.55	80,000	22
75,001–90,000	0.45	160,000	25
90,001 and above	0.40	1,000,000	30

12. If in some year a nation's budget deficit is $9.56 billion and government spending is $12.19 billion, how much must it have earned in tax revenue this year? [LO 12.5]

13. "The government shouldn't borrow so much," your uncle claims. "Look at that national debt! It's no different from someone borrowing on credit cards they can't pay." Is your uncle right? How is government debt spending like someone borrowing on a credit card? How is it not like someone borrowing on a credit card? [LO 12.5]

14. Econo Nation started 2008 with no national budget debt or surplus. By the end of 2008, it had a budget surplus of $304 million; in 2009, it had a budget deficit of $452 million; in 2010 it had a budget surplus of $109 million, and the amount of its budget deficit or surplus in 2011 is unknown. If at the end of 2011 Econo Nation's national debt totaled $50 million, did it run a deficit or surplus in 2011? Of how much? [LO 12.6]

15. "Though the national debt has increased, don't worry," the prime minister says in a televised speech. "We will not have to pay these funds back to bond buyers." How is this possible? How must the government have financed its debt in this case? [LO 12.6]

16. Which of the following are examples of the negative effects associated with government debt? [LO 12.7]

    a. Increased interest rates

    b. Increased taxes or lower spending in the future

    c. Increased investment in the economy

17. If the government could borrow as much as it liked with a zero-percent interest rate, would the government debt be cost-free? Explain your answer. [LO 12.7]

Chapter Sources

http://www.time.com/time/business/article/0,8599,1850269,00.html#ixzz1OtKQCoQM

http://www.brillig.com/debt_clock/

Jonathan Parker, "On measuring the effects of fiscal policies in recessions," *Journal of Economic Literature* 49, no. 3 (2011), pp. 703–718

PART SIX

The Financial System and Institutions
The four chapters in Part 6 will introduce you to ...

the financial and monetary systems, and the institutions that make them work. In Part 6, we'll discuss everything from the traders on Bay Street to the humble banknote in your wallet.

Chapter 13 runs through the basics of financial markets and describes the roles that individuals and institutions play in them—including everyone from a family buying their first house to the traders making million-dollar bets on Bay Street. Financial markets connect savers and borrowers, helping money flow to the parts of the economy where it is the most valuable at any given time, and allowing people to manage their money over time and minimize the risks they face.

Chapter 14 is all about money. Money helps the economy operate smoothly. As a *medium of exchange*, it enables you to buy a pack of gum, a car, or an entire commercial building. It is more than just bills and coins, though. In Canada, the Bank of Canada is the main institution responsible for creating and managing the overall money supply. This power gives it a unique ability to steer the economy through good times and bad.

Chapter 15 covers the delicate relationship between inflation and unemployment. Policy makers at central banks (like the Bank of Canada) have the task of controlling fluctuations in the value of money. They can also use the tools of monetary policy to influence the overall level of unemployment. With this power comes great responsibility: recent history is filled with examples of how countries have suffered from inflation and unemployment caused by poor monetary policy.

Although financial markets usually run smoothly, there are times when the system fails to efficiently manage risk and fund new ventures. Investigating how financial systems break down provides unique insights into how they actually work. In Chapter 16, we'll pick through the details of the worst financial crisis for generations and the problems that followed the 2007 crash in the US housing market, which plunged the US economy and others around the world into deep recession.

CHAPTER 13
The Basics of Finance

LEARNING OBJECTIVES

LO 13.1   Define a financial market, and list the three main functions it serves.

LO 13.2   Describe the market for loanable funds, and give examples of factors that affect the supply of and demand for loanable funds.

LO 13.3   Differentiate between debt and equity, and define the major types of assets in each category.

LO 13.4   Name the main institutions in financial markets, and describe the role that each plays.

LO 13.5   Explain the trade-off between risk and return in financial assets, and describe how risk can be analyzed.

LO 13.6   Give arguments for and against the assumption that markets are efficient.

LO 13.7   Explain why savings equals investment in a closed economy.

Safe Investment?

Prior to the summer of 2007, asset-backed commercial paper (ABCP) was considered a very attractive investment opportunity in Canada. This short-term instrument (usually matures between 1 and 270 days) is backed by residential mortgages and commercial loans that have a low risk of default. Financial institutions use this to protect important cash assets following profitable periods. However, as the mortgage situation deteriorated in the US during 2007, the Canadian market became unwilling to purchase ABCPs because of price drops in the backing assets as well as their similarity to mortgage-backed securities in the US. This caused a mismatch of funds for Canadian financial institutions, as they relied on the sales of short-term ABCPs to finance longer term investment. When no one is buying ABCPs, institutions are forced to liquidate their long-term investments at a substantial loss. This created a shock in a Canadian financial market that was already facing the impact of the financial crisis in the United States.

Aaron Harris/The Canadian Press

The story of the collapse of ABCPs, the financial-system implosion, and the recession that followed is one of the most fascinating economic tales of our time. To understand these events, we have to understand the financial system itself.

Why do we have a financial system? Traditional markets in goods and services are relatively straightforward—they help to match prospective buyers with those willing to sell. In comparison, financial markets can seem abstract and remote. What do they do? What exactly are Bay street firms selling, and on whose behalf are they selling it?

In fact, financial markets are very much like other markets—they match people who want to buy something (in this case borrowers who want money to spend) with those who have something to sell (people who want to save their money for later and are willing to lend it to borrowers in the meantime). In doing so, these markets also help people manage their money over time and protect themselves against risk. The *financial system* brings together savers and borrowers in a set of interconnected markets where people trade a variety of financial products.

The basic premise of a financial market is simple, but actual transactions can be quite complex. A wide variety of financial products are targeted at people with different investment or saving needs. Just as wholesalers and grocery stores mediate between farmers and hungry consumers, there are many different firms and institutions that mediate between savers and borrowers in financial markets.

Businesses, governments, non-governmental organizations, and individuals depend on the financial system to achieve their goals. It helps people get the money they need, in the right amount, at the right time, with as little uncertainty as possible. If you have a savings account, chequing account, credit card, student loan, home mortgage, or car loan, then you benefit from access to financial markets. It's easy to take these services for granted. The global disruptions in the credit market showed just how valuable a well-functioning financial system is.

In this chapter, we'll start by looking at the role of financial markets and the value they provide to savers and borrowers. We build a simple model of the market in which savers and borrowers participate. Then we look at the financial system from three angles: the functions it serves, the players involved in it, and the assets they trade. Finally, we'll look at some general features of financial products, like risk and return.

The Role of Financial Markets

LO 13.1 Define a financial market, and list the three main functions it serves.

The high-tech, elaborate dealings we associate with Bay Street are a relatively recent phenomenon, but basic financial markets existed at least as far back as ancient Greece. Moneylenders, based in temples, accepted deposits, changed money for travellers, and (as their name implies) made loans. A person's show of wealth went from precious metals, which were weighed, to coins stamped by the nation-state, which were counted. Stock markets as we would recognize them today first appeared in the seventeenth century. Why have financial markets been such a natural and useful institution in different societies throughout history? What do they do?

What Is a Financial Market?

In a **financial market**, people trade future claims on funds or goods. These claims can take many different forms. When you take out a loan, for instance, a bank gives you money now in return for an agreement that you will repay the bank, with interest, in the future. When you buy stock in a company, you have a right to a share of any profits earned in the future. When you buy an insurance policy, you make regular premium payments, and the insurance company agrees to pay out, if and when something bad happens to you in the future. We'll talk about the details of these and other types of financial assets later in the chapter. The important thing to notice, for now, is that they are all agreements that allow people to move funds around, from one time, place, or situation to another.

The key idea behind financial markets is that, at any given time, the people who have spare funds are not necessarily the same people who have the most productive ways to spend those funds. Financial markets allow funding to flow to the places where it is most highly valued at the moment. A well-functioning market makes everyone better off, by matching buyers and sellers who both have something to gain from a trade. In financial markets, buyers are people who want to spend money on something of value right now, but don't have cash on hand. Sellers are people who have cash on hand and are willing to let others use it, for a price. Among the buyers are families buying new houses, students paying university tuition, corporations building new factories, entrepreneurs starting new ventures, and often the government when it needs to finance public spending. Sellers are individuals, corporations, and government entities willing to forgo some spending right now in return for repayment down the road.

A Whirlwind History of Banks

These days, financial markets are extremely complicated—so complicated that when ABCPs fell apart in 2007 there were very few people who really had the full picture of what was going on. But the origins of financial markets are not so complicated. It starts with a bank, savers, and borrowers.

People face a problem: the times when they need to spend money almost never match up perfectly with the times when they earn money.

This problem crops up in a lot of different ways. Some mistiming is about the cycle of a person's whole life. For instance, you might want to earn more than you spend during your working years and then live on the savings during retirement. You might want to pay for a university degree or a house or a car early in life, before you've had a chance to do much earning. Other types of mistiming are shorter term: you might earn a paycheque once a month, but want to buy things in various places and times throughout the month. Or, if you run a business like a farm, your revenues might come in during one season (harvest) but most of your expenses come in another (planting).

A bank helps to solve these problems by taking in savings from people who are earning more than they're spending at the moment, and giving out loans to people who currently want to spend more than they earn. Why do we need banks for that? Why not just stuff cash under your pillow as you earn it, and lend to or borrow from family and neighbours as needed? In fact, that *is* the old-fashioned way of managing money. Even today, billions of people around the world don't have good access to modern banks, and they still rely on those simple methods.

But a bank serves a lot of useful functions. First, it acts as an *intermediary* between savers and borrowers. Without a bank, you'd have to make the rounds every time you need a loan, trying to cobble together bits and pieces of savings from the people you know. If they don't happen to have savings at the moment, you might just be out of luck. That sort of bad luck isn't terribly unlikely if the people you know are similar to you in some way. If they are about your age or work in similar jobs or farm the same crops, then they're likely to be short on cash at the same times that you are. A bank connects you to a much wider range of people who might have savings when you need to borrow. It also saves you (and them) the time and effort of managing dozens of small, person-to-person transactions. A bank is an easy, one-stop clearinghouse for everyone, whenever they need to save or to borrow.

Second, a bank makes it easier to have access to cash when and where you want it. In the old days, people had to literally have cash on hand to be able to buy something. They had to carry heavy gold or silver coins around and worry about them being lost or stolen. What's more, it was risky to let others borrow or invest your coins (even beyond the risk of not being repaid), because they wouldn't be available if you needed them back in a hurry. For instance, if you made a loan to your neighbour and then your child got sick, you might have trouble getting your coins back right away to pay the doctor. It was safer to keep some coins around, doing nothing, just in case they were needed.

A bank lets you enjoy the benefits of *liquidity*—having cash easily available when you want it—without these downsides. Some of these benefits are logistical. Banks and the tools they provide, like ATMs, chequebooks, and debit and credit cards, make it simple and inexpensive to have access to cash when you want it and not worry about it when you don't. But the real value is that you can deposit your savings at the bank without fear that you won't be able to withdraw the money if a need comes up. This works because there are many depositors at the bank, and it's very, very unlikely that all of them will need to withdraw their savings at once. So the bank can keep just a small amount of cash on hand, allowing most money to be loaned out and used in productive investments. Borrowers then pay the bank interest on the loans, and the bank can pay savers interest on their deposits, all without losing the benefits of liquidity for individual savers.

Finally, banks help savers and borrowers to *diversify risk*. Suppose that in the pre-bank system you made a big loan to your cousin, who wanted to open up a store. If the store did well, you'd get paid back, and everything would be fine. But if the store went bankrupt—as small businesses often do—you might be financially ruined. When you borrow and save on a person-to-person level, there's no getting around the risk involved in having a lot of your eggs in one basket, even if everyone is well-intentioned and trustworthy. A bank spreads your eggs around to many different baskets. Because the bank has a big pool of borrowers, the risk of everyone failing to pay back their loans at once is very small. A few borrowers will default on their loans, but most will repay, and no individual saver will have to bear the full burden of a failed investment.

In fact, it's not only banks that provide these benefits. The whole financial system—made up of many institutions, including banks, insurance companies, investors, stock exchanges, and government agencies—is designed to *intermediate* between savers and borrowers, *provide liquidity,* and *diversify risk.* We'll come back to these ideas over and over again throughout the chapter. In the next section, we take a look at how these buyers and sellers come together in a simplified type of financial market we call the *market for loanable funds.*

✓ CONCEPT CHECK

☐ What is traded in a financial market? [LO 13.1]
☐ What are the three main benefits that banks, and the financial system in general, provide to savers and borrowers? [LO 13.1]

The Market for Loanable Funds: A Simplified Financial Market

LO 13.2 Describe the market for loanable funds, and give examples of factors that affect the supply of and demand for loanable funds.

Consider a whole country of people earning and spending. At any given time, some of them want to borrow and others want to save. How much do they want to borrow, and how much are they willing to save? If the amount people want to borrow is higher than the amount saved, what determines which loans get approved? Financial markets mediate the forces of supply and demand by determining the price at which the quantity of funds saved will be equal to the quantity invested.

Real-world financial markets involve many products, with different prices, targeted at different types of buyers and sellers. You can get the flavour of this variety just by browsing the business section of a newspaper or looking at the types of accounts and loans offered by any bank. We'll dig into some of this nuance later in the chapter. For now, let's simplify all saving and borrowing into one market, which we'll call the market for loanable funds.

Loanable Funds: Savings and Investment

The **market for loanable funds** is a market in which savers, who have money to lend, supply funds to those who want to borrow for their investment spending needs. *Loanable funds* are the dollars that are on the table between them to be lent out and borrowed.

When talking about savings and investment, we have to be careful with terminology. When people purchase stocks or put money into a RRSP account for retirement, they often say they are "investing" the money. But to an economist, these are examples of *savings,* not investment. **Savings** is the portion of income that is not immediately spent on consumption of goods and services. Economists use the word **investment**, or more properly *investment spending,* to refer to spending on productive inputs, such as factories, machinery, and inventories.

Using these definitions, we can build a simple model of the market for loanable funds. The supply of loanable funds comes from savings; the demand for loanable funds comes from investment. Just as in any market, savings and investment are brought into equilibrium at the price at which the quantity supplied and the quantity demanded are equal.

The Price of Loanable Funds

Saving is like selling the right to use your money for a time, and borrowing is like buying the right to use someone else's money. The quantity of savings that people are willing to supply will depend on the price they receive, as will the quantity of investment funding that people demand.

The price of borrowing is known as the **interest rate**. The interest rate is the price charged by a lender to a borrower for the use of funds. It is typically expressed as percentage per dollar borrowed per unit of time until the loan is repaid. The interest rate determines the total amount that must be paid back on a loan in addition to paying back the original amount borrowed (called the principal). For instance, if you take out a one-year loan of $1,000 with a 10 percent annual interest rate, you'll have to repay the $1,000 principal plus $100 ($1,000 × 0.10) in interest.[1]

Just as in any market, the intersection of the downward-sloping demand curve and the upward-sloping supply curve determines the equilibrium interest rate and quantity of loanable funds. The market for loanable funds is shown in Figure 13-1.

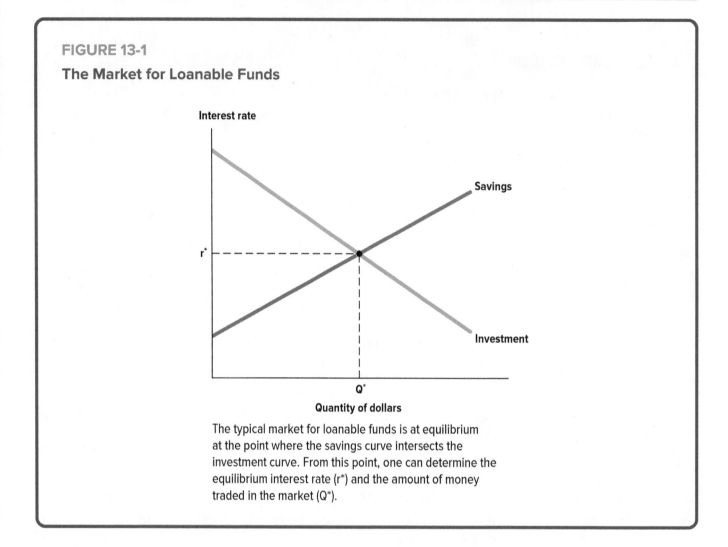

FIGURE 13-1

The Market for Loanable Funds

The typical market for loanable funds is at equilibrium at the point where the savings curve intersects the investment curve. From this point, one can determine the equilibrium interest rate (r*) and the amount of money traded in the market (Q*).

Why is the supply curve upward-sloping? This shape implies that the amount the population is willing to save increases as the interest rate increases. In markets for goods and services, the higher the price, the more people will find it profitable to supply the good. The relationship between price and quantity supplied in the market for loanable funds is essentially the same. The key is to realize that there is an opportunity cost of saving: saving money means that you can't consume as much right now.

People rationally calculate those trade-offs. If you save $100, you are trading off $100 worth of consumption now for the promise of getting some amount of money in the future. If the interest rate was zero, you would get just your $100 back. Some people will be willing to save even with zero interest—maybe they know they would rather consume $100 when they are retired than another $100 now. The higher the interest rate, however, the more people will find it worthwhile to delay their consumption in order to increase their future earnings. If you wouldn't save $100 in exchange for $101 a year from now, you might be willing to do it for $110. Even more people would set aside $100 if it was guaranteed that they would get $200 back in a year, and so on as the interest rate gets higher.

On the other side of the market for loanable funds, the demand curve is downward-sloping. This is because the cost of borrowing decreases as the interest rates decreases, making more and more investment opportunities worth the cost. When deciding whether to borrow, firms or households that are contemplating an investment—say, building a factory or buying a new home—must first try to estimate the rate of return on that investment.[2] The *rate of return* describes the expected profit that the project will generate per dollar invested.

If the rate of return (the benefit of borrowing) is lower than the cost of borrowing, then the investor will lose money on net after paying back the loan. In that case, the investment probably isn't worth making. If the rate of return is above the interest rate, the investment will yield a profit, and it makes sense to borrow the money. In the real world, a range of investment opportunities offer different rates of return. As the interest rate rises, fewer and fewer of these opportunities will have a rate of return higher than the costs involved in borrowing, and so the quantity of loanable funds demanded will decrease. The result is the familiar downward-sloping demand curve.

Changes in the Supply and Demand for Loanable Funds

The underlying factors that determine how much people want to save and invest can change over time, or differ from country to country. These factors shift the supply and demand curves in the market for loanable funds, changing the quantity of funds supplied or demanded at any given interest rate. As a result, the equilibrium interest rate and quantity will change. In this section, we'll discuss some of the important underlying determinants of savings and investment.

Determinants of Savings

Savings decisions reflect the *trade-off* people face between spending their income on consumption now and saving it for later. The upward-sloping supply curve reflects the fact that as the interest rate increases the value of saving relative to consuming increases, which causes people to supply more savings. However, factors other than the interest rate can also affect this choice. Typically, these factors are things that make people more or less interested in waiting to consume their income, such as expectations about how well the economy will be doing in the future and even how much value popular culture places on simplicity and frugality.

FIGURE 13-2

A Change in the Underlying Determinants of Saving Shifts the Supply Curve for Loanable Funds

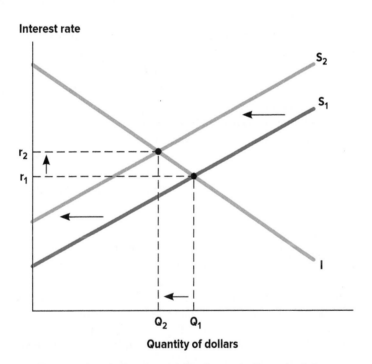

When the level of savings shifts dramatically to the left due to a change in one of the determinants of savings, the equilibrium interest rate is higher and the quantity of loanable funds in the market is lower.

A change in the underlying determinants of savings will shift the supply curve in the market for loanable funds. Imagine a change that makes people want to save less at any given interest rate—for instance, suppose people become more optimistic that the economy will do well over the next decade. Because they feel more confident that they will have jobs and earn plenty of money in the future, they become less concerned about saving now. This change in expectations will shift the supply curve to the left, as shown in Figure 13-2. The equilibrium in the market for loanable funds moves up along the demand curve, to a new point with a higher interest rate and a lower quantity of funds saved and invested. In contrast, a change that increased the quantity people want to save at any given interest rate would shift the supply curve to the right. The new equilibrium would have a lower interest rate and a higher equilibrium quantity of funds saved and invested.

What are these underlying factors that determine how much people want to save at a given interest rate? There are many, many issues that influence individuals' choices about savings. In this chapter, however, we are concerned with factors that affect the economy on a macro level—issues that will cause the population of the country as a whole to want to save more or less. These can change over time within a country, but they can also help to explain differences across countries. For instance, Canadian households have saved only a small percentage of their income in recent years, while Chinese households have saved upwards of 40 percent. Some of this difference is probably attributable to cultural factors and some to economic conditions.

The following are important factors that drive the supply of savings both over time and across countries:

- **Culture.** Different cultures and traditions place varying weights on being frugal, demonstrating wealth through material goods, leaving an inheritance for future generations, and so on. These cultural expectations are difficult to quantify, but almost certainly play a role in the differing savings rates across countries. For instance, Canada has a more consumer-oriented culture, while China's culture has traditionally been more frugal. Since average savings in China are higher at every interest rate, the supply curve for loanable funds in China is going to be far to the right of that of Canada's.

- **Social welfare policies.** Incentives to save at any given interest rate can be affected by public policies that determine what, if any, benefits people will receive if they lose their jobs, become sick or disabled, fall into poverty, or simply grow old. For instance, individuals in China may save more because they expect to bear more of the burden for their own health care and retirement costs in the future. In contrast, Canadian citizens expect to receive retirement benefits through Social Security and universal healthcare. (Of course, tax contributions to Social Security could be thought of as forced saving for retirement—but that type of "saving" isn't counted in the savings rate.)

- **Wealth.** Studies show that richer households tend to save more of their income than others. But the evidence regarding the relationship between wealth and saving is not fully consistent. There's also evidence, for example, that poorer households save more out of tax cuts than richer ones do. Both pieces of evidence, however, show that wealth matters.

- **Current economic conditions.** When we think about how people's savings decisions respond to economic conditions, it's important to distinguish between *current* economic conditions and how current conditions might change expectations about the *future*. If expectations about the future don't change at all, then an economic downturn will generally decrease savings at a given interest rate (i.e., shift the supply curve for loanable funds to the left). When times are bad and people lose jobs or have lower incomes, they will be less inclined to save and may even spend down past savings to pay for current expenses.

- **Expectations about future economic conditions.** People often take a recession as a bad sign about how the economy will be doing in the future, as well as how it is doing at the moment. This expectation about the future can affect the savings rate. When people expect their income to be lower in the future, they will be more inclined to save, all else equal, to make sure that they have enough down the road.

The relationship between current economic conditions and expectations about future economic conditions helps to explain why average Canadian household savings rates *fell* dramatically when the economy was doing well through most of the 1980s, 1990s, and early 2000s, as shown in Figure 13-3. By 2005, households on average were hardly saving at all—the average savings rate was not much more than 2 percent. Although we might think that good current conditions would make people willing to save more, it also made them optimistic about the future, which made them less inclined to save. When the economy hit a big bump, the savings rate moved back upward, starting in the depths of the recession around 2009. This suggests that people took the recession as a negative sign about the future, and in response they borrowed less and saved more.

FIGURE 13-3

Savings Rates in Canada Since 1981

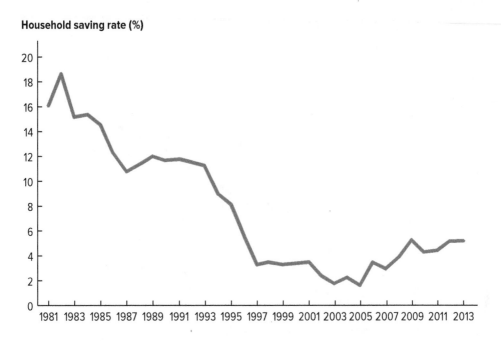

In the early 1980s, the savings rate in Canada was rather high, ranging from 11 to 18 percent. After this, the savings rate decreased steadily until it was about 2–3 percent in the mid-2000s. After the recession in 2009, the savings rate jumped to 5 percent.

Source: Statistics Canada, CANSIM Table 384-0040, "Current accounts - Households, provincial and territorial"

Determinants of Investment

Investment decisions are based on the *trade-off* between the potential profits that could be generated by an investment and the cost of borrowing money to finance that investment. The downward-sloping demand curve in the market for loanable funds reflects the fact that as the interest rate increases, there are fewer and fewer potential investments that will generate returns high enough to make the cost of paying back a loan worthwhile.

Just as on the supply side of the market, however, there are non-price factors that affect the demand for loanable funds. These factors are typically things that change the set of investment opportunities in the economy, increasing or decreasing the number of investments that are worth making at any given interest rate. A change that increases the value of potential investments throughout the economy will increase the quantity of loanable funds demanded at every interest rate, shifting the whole demand curve to the right, as shown in Figure 13-4. As a result, the equilibrium will move up along the supply curve to a new point with a higher interest rate and higher equilibrium quantity of funds saved and invested.

FIGURE 13-4

A Change in the Profitability of Investment Opportunities Shifts the Demand Curve for Loanable Funds

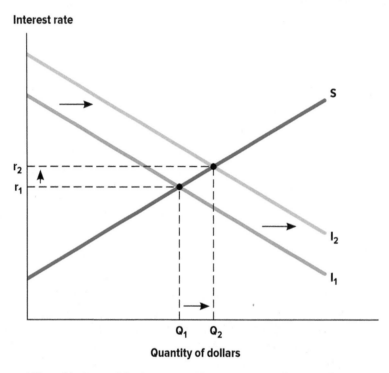

When the demand for investment increases, people are willing to invest more money at every interest rate. This takes the market for loanable funds to a new equilibrium, with higher rates and a greater quantity of loanable funds traded.

The essential non-price factor affecting the demand for loanable funds is expectations about the future profitability of investments made today. This view about future profitability usually goes hand in hand with overall expectations about future economic conditions. In 2006, the economy was booming and consumer demand was high, due in part to the thriving energy market. A booming economy can make investors eager to borrow money, because they expect ventures like new companies, products, shops, and real estate developments to earn large profits. This expectation shifts the demand curve to the right, as firms want to borrow more at any given interest rate.

The opposite was true once the economy soured in late 2008. Since consumer demand was weak throughout the economy, there was little incentive to take out a loan to expand production or start a new business. This lack of desire to borrow shifts the demand curve for loanable funds to the left as shown in Figure 13-5.

FIGURE 13-5

A Decrease in Borrowing Shifts the Demand Curve for Loanable Funds

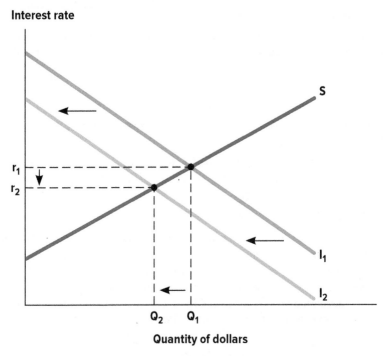

A weak economy decreases the demand for loanable funds. At every interest rate, people are less interested in making investments, fearing such investments will not work out. At this new equilibrium, the interest rate is lower, and the quantity of loanable funds traded is lower.

There's one final point to be made about the loanable funds market in a weak economy. Some have suggested that when the government borrows more, it can *crowd out* private investment. **Crowding out** is the reduction in private borrowing that is caused by an increase in government borrowing. Just as in Figure 13-2, the government's borrowing reduces the supply of loanable funds and can shift the supply curve to the left, forcing up interest rates. This shift in the supply curve, in turn, increases the cost of borrowing and so reduces private investment. This kind of crowding out of private investment is always a fear when the government intervenes in the market. Evidence from the recession suggests that crowding out was minimal then, but it is always a possibility that policy-makers need to take seriously.

A Price For Every Borrower: A More Realistic Look at Interest Rates

The simple model of the market for loanable funds illustrates the basic relationships between supply and demand in financial markets. In reality, however, there is no such thing as a single interest rate that is paid by all prospective borrowers. Instead, different borrowers pay different interest rates. For example, an individual may have to pay a higher interest rate to borrow money than an established company would, and almost everyone has to pay a higher rate than the Canadian government pays. The same borrower may also pay different rates on different kinds of transactions. For example, the interest rate will be less on a mortgage than on a credit card for a given individual. How is the interest rate for a particular loan determined?

Two basic factors drive differences in interest rates. The first is the length of time the borrower has to repay the loan. The reason for this is not immediately obvious. Isn't a lender already being compensated for lending over a longer period by earning interest over that longer period? Only partially. Think of it this way: lenders want to be compensated for the *opportunity cost* of being unable to get their money back quickly. When they lend money for twenty years at a fixed interest rate, they've tied up their money and must pass up any better investment opportunities and interest rates that could emerge in those twenty years. Since there's more uncertainty about potential future investment opportunities over a longer period of time, lenders generally want a higher interest rate to compensate them for the added opportunity cost when loans stretch over a longer period.

The second factor that drives differences in interest rates is the riskiness of the transaction. To understand why, ask yourself a simple question: To whom would you rather loan money—a stranger on the street or the local bank? Regardless of your answer, you probably had a simple criterion for deciding: Who is more likely to pay you back?

Lenders in the financial markets make this same calculation when they consider the likelihood that a borrower may default on a loan. A **default** happens when a borrower fails to pay back a loan according to the agreed-upon terms. If lenders think that a particular borrower might default, they will demand a higher interest rate to make it worth taking that risk.

Sometimes loans are secured against an asset, such as a house. If a borrower defaults on a mortgage loan, the lender takes ownership of the house as compensation for the loss. This explains why mortgages generally are made at a lower interest rate than credit card loans; if a mortgage borrower defaults, the lender can sell the house to get some money back (although usually not the full value of the loan). In contrast, credit cards aren't backed with valuable assets, so the lender's losses are higher if someone defaults.

The risk of a borrower defaulting on a loan is known as *credit risk*. It is measured against the **risk-free rate**—the interest rate at which one would lend if there were no risk of default. The risk-free rate is usually approximated by interest rates on Canadian government debt, because the Canadian government is considered extremely unlikely to default. All other borrowers must pay higher rates to compensate lenders for the higher possibility that they will default.

The difference between the risk-free rate and the interest rate a particular investor has to pay is called the *credit spread* or *risk premium.* The difference can be quite large, both among investors and over time. The recession, for example, caused credit spreads to rise dramatically, as borrowers of all kinds suddenly became more likely to default. Armed with data about the length of time of a loan and roughly how likely it is for the borrower to default, we can get an idea of the price a particular borrower might face for a particular transaction in the market for loanable funds. In general, the longer the term of a loan and the more likely the risk of default, the higher above the risk-free rate will be the interest rate on that loan.

✓ CONCEPT CHECK

☐ What is another name for the price of money in the market for loanable funds? **[LO 13.2]**

☐ What are factors that can cause the supply curve to shift right in the market for loanable funds? **[LO 13.2]**

The Modern Financial System

Now that we've covered the basic theory of financial markets, we'll turn our attention to some key realities of the modern financial system. We've already noted that the idea of a single market for loanable funds is an oversimplification. In reality, people and firms face different interest rates based on the length and riskiness of their loans. The institutions that make up the **financial system** bring together savers, borrowers, investors, and insurers in a set of interconnected markets where people trade financial products. This section takes a more nuanced look at the role the financial system plays in helping people manage their money and risk. It also defines some of the most important types of products that are traded in the financial system and identifies the people and institutions that trade them.

Functions of the Financial System

Financial markets help people save, borrow, invest, and insure by matching people who have funds with people who want funds. Why do we need institutions like banks, insurance companies, and stock exchanges to help us do those things? At the beginning of the chapter we saw how banks can help to fill three basic roles in the economy: offering *intermediation* between savers and borrowers, providing *liquidity,* and assisting in the *diversification of risk.* In this section, we expand on these ideas, and show how the financial system as a whole contributes to achieving them.

Matching Buyers and Sellers: Intermediation

Intermediation is the process of bringing together buyers and sellers in a market. Imagine you want to borrow to start a small business. How are you going to get enough money together? You could go to everyone you know and ask them to lend you as much as they can afford. This won't work very well unless you happen to know a lot of people with spare cash sitting around. But even if you managed to pull it off, the process of arranging and keeping track of all of those loans would be incredibly time consuming and complicated. The existence of banks lowers the *transaction costs* of this process. When banks exist, there is only one person you need to persuade to lend you the entire sum of money—the bank loan officer. This saves you—and the friends and family you'd otherwise be pestering for loans—time and money by replacing a lot of small, informal transactions with one big, professionalized one.

Various institutions act as **financial intermediaries**—channeling funds from people who have them to people who want them. A bank is one kind of intermediary. A different kind of intermediary is a mutual fund, which matches people with small amounts of money who want to buy a portfolio of various companies with institutions wanting to sell those shares. This intermediation reduces transaction costs by centralizing information about share prices and providing a marketplace for transactions.

Providing Liquidity

A second critical function of the financial system is providing liquidity. Earlier in the chapter, we talked informally about why people value liquidity. Formally, **liquidity** is a measure of how easily a particular asset can be converted quickly to cash without much loss of value. We say that an asset is *liquid* if it can be sold for cash quickly without much loss of value, and *illiquid* if it can't.

Consider two types of assets that many people own: cars and houses. If you needed cash quickly, which would you sell? A car is relatively easy to sell quickly. You can simply drive into a car dealership and ask the dealer to make you a cash offer. You won't get the best possible price, of course—but you'll get much of what the car is worth, in cash, right away. The house, on the other hand, is much harder to sell. You can't walk into most real estate agencies and expect a cash offer on the spot. The real estate agent will instead help you find a buyer, which can take time, and even then there are still mountains of paperwork and things that could go wrong.

In other words, the car is a more liquid asset than the house. Why is there such a difference in liquidity? Houses are more difficult to value and legally complex to purchase. Before you decide how much to pay for a house, you should do a thorough check of every part of it—make sure it doesn't have a leaky roof or that there aren't plans to build a waste-processing facility nearby. Cars are much easier to value. An experienced dealer can accurately size them up from a peek under the hood. That's why there are car dealers fulfilling the role of liquidity providers, but few equivalents in the real estate market. A liquidity provider is someone who helps make a market more liquid by being always ready to buy or sell an asset.

Financial intermediaries, such as stockbrokers, centralize information about prices and provide a marketplace for transactions.

© Alex Segre/Alamy Stock Photo

Various players in the financial system help ensure that markets are liquid. The very structure of financial assets such as stocks and bonds (as we'll define and discuss below) also serves to increase liquidity. If you want to sell a share of company stock or a government bond, there is almost always someone in the financial system willing to buy it from you. Often that someone is your bank or your broker, but it may also be a mutual fund or simply a large financial investor. We sometimes call these people *market makers* since they, in effect, make a market by being always ready to buy or sell, just like the car dealer.

Liquidity is important because it affects people's willingness to save. Savers generally want to know that their money will be there for them when they need it. If markets were not liquid, you couldn't count on being able to sell your assets quickly in order to get your money back, so you'd probably be extremely cautious about lending money out for investment in the first place. That would reduce the supply of loanable funds, which would drive up interest rates, reduce the amount of investment, and lead to slower growth in the economy.

Diversifying Risk

The third major role played by the financial system is that it spreads risk. Imagine that, as a saver, you could lend your money directly only to other individuals or companies. If the borrower defaulted, you would lose everything. If you lend your money to a bank, however, you know that the bank will pool your money with that of other savers and make thousands of loans to different borrowers. Some of those borrowers will default, but the bank won't lose everything at once and neither will its savers. The bank has *diversified* the risk. **Diversification** is the process by which risks are shared among many different assets or people, reducing the impact of a particular risk on any one individual.

Diversification is crucial for the functioning of the economy. People are more willing to save money, and entrepreneurs are more willing to start new ventures, if they don't have to worry too much about the risk of losing everything.

Major Financial Assets

> LO 13.3 Differentiate between debt and equity, and define the major types of assets in each category.

How does the financial system fulfill its roles of supplying intermediation, providing liquidity, and diversifying risk? It does so by creating financial assets that can be bought and sold within the financial markets. There are far more varieties of financial assets than we could possibly cover in this text, so we'll focus on just the major ones.

Equity

When you own part of a company and share in its profits, we say that you *have equity* in that company. Financial assets that represent this partial ownership are called *equities*. A *stock*—the financial asset you probably hear the most about—is the common name for an equity asset. The news media report figures from the stock market every evening, such as the Standard & Poor's (S&P) TSX 300 and the TSX Venture. There even are television networks dedicated to following every move of these indexes.

What exactly are stocks? A **stock** is a financial asset that represents partial ownership of a company. If a company has issued 100,000 shares of stock, then the owner of each share (called a *shareholder* or *stockholder*) owns 1/100,000 of the company.

Stockholders, as partial owners, are usually entitled to vote on certain aspects of how the company is run. They elect the board of directors, for example. Stockholders also are entitled to receive a portion of the company's profits, proportional to the size of their ownership stakes, in the form of dividends. A **dividend** is a payment made periodically, typically annually or quarterly, to all shareholders of a company.

Why do companies issue stock? For one thing, issuing stock allows a company to raise capital without borrowing. Imagine a store owner who wants to expand her business by opening a new store, but needs money to do so. She could borrow money from the bank, but she'd have to pay interest and pay back the loan even if the new store fails. Instead, the store owner may choose to sell some equity in her company. People who buy the shares of stock will become part owners of her company, taking on the risk of losing money if the new store fails, and expecting a percentage of the profits if it succeeds.

Stock is also a mechanism for turning an illiquid asset (ownership of a company) into a liquid one (a share that can be sold on the stock market). Ownership of an entire business is not easy to sell. Just like buying a house, there are many complicated things that a potential buyer will want to understand beforehand. On the other hand, stock can be easily bought and sold in small, standardized increments on the stock market. A privately held company is an illiquid asset, whereas stock in *public companies*—so called because anyone can buy a share—is a liquid asset.[3]

Debt

The main alternative to equity is debt. The most basic and familiar type of debt is a loan. A **loan** is an agreement in which a lender gives money to a borrower in exchange for a promise to repay the amount loaned plus an agreed-upon amount of interest. Banks make loans to individuals to make purchases like houses and cars, and they lend to businesses that want to make investments.

Making a loan is generally both less risky and less potentially rewarding than buying stock. A borrower might default on a loan. But people who have loaned money to a company that goes bankrupt have the first legal claim on that company's assets and will be paid as much as possible before stockholders earn anything. Buying stock in a company comes with a higher risk of losing everything, but buying stock also has a higher upside. If the company does very well and earns huge profits, stockholders are usually entitled to a share of those profits. With a loan, no matter how successful the company gets, the lender will never receive more than the amount specified in the original loan agreements.

Like any other financial asset, loans can be bought and sold. Imagine that a bank lends you money to buy a house. You sign a contract, and you have a legal obligation to pay the loan back at a specified interest rate by a specified date. The bank could then sell that obligation to somebody else. The buyer would pay the bank for the right to collect the money from you, according to the terms of the loan deal.

To make loans more liquid, they can be standardized into a more easily tradable asset, called a *bond*. A **bond** represents a promise by the bond issuer to repay the loan at a specified maturity date, and to pay periodic interest at a specific percentage rate. Because of the set interest rate, bonds are often referred to as *fixed-income securities*. The owner of the bond (bondholder) is legally entitled to receive scheduled interest payments (called *coupon* payments). These coupon payment are generally paid every three or six months.[4] The bond owner also receives a final payment of the original loan amount for the bond (the principal, sometimes called the *face value*, of the bond) at the maturity date.

Bonds are issued in varying maturities. Corporate bonds typically have maturities of ten to thirty years; government bonds (issued by the federal and provincial governments and municipalities) generally range from one to ten years. Governments and big companies often sell bonds as a way to borrow large sums of money, typically from a large number of lenders. Because bonds are standardized, it is easy for bondholders to sell them, making them a more liquid asset than regular loans.

Since a bond is essentially a loan, the basic risk–reward trade-off that applied to loans also applies to bonds: they are generally safer than stocks, but also less rewarding. Government bonds have historically averaged a real (inflation-adjusted) return of about 2 percent per year, while a broad index of stocks indicates a real return of nearly 7 percent per year over the same period. Why might savers be interested in buying government bonds, with so much lower returns, instead of stocks? Because stocks are more risky. They can easily go down in value, whereas the government is very unlikely to default on a bond.

Wouldn't it be useful if there were a way to take non-standard loans—say, loans to people to buy homes—and turn them into standardized, bond-like instruments that can be easily traded? It turns out there is such a process, called *securitization*. Securitization turns many loans into a single larger asset, thus reducing the risk to the lender of any individual borrower defaulting on the loan. Securitization became particularly prevalent in the early 2000s. Financial assets of all types, from student loans to mortgage loans, were securitized to create liquid assets that would be appealing to a wide array of lenders. In the "Financial Crisis" chapter we'll show how securitization played a starring role in the collapse of the ABCP market in Canada.

Despite its involvement in the recent recession, debt is not bad when done right. As we've mentioned, debt is behind many of the transactions we take for granted. When you're able to drive off the lot with a new car, or a firm is able to build a new factory, it's likely that debt helped make this possible.

Derivatives

Stocks, loans, and bonds are examples of financial contracts in which one person or firm agrees to pay another a certain amount, under certain circumstances. If you get creative, you can come up with much more complex arrangements based on the same fundamental idea. For instance, you can create a contract based on the future value of particular assets or goods, like mortgages, stocks, or the price of oil.

Financial contracts based on the value of some other asset represent a special category of financial assets, called **derivatives**. A derivative is an asset whose value is based on the value of another asset, such as a home loan, stock, bond, or barrel of oil.

The best example of this type of arrangement is a *futures contract*. The buyer of a futures contract agrees to pay the seller based on the future price of some asset. For example, through a futures contract you could sell all or part of your farm crops in advance at a set price. If the crops end up being worth more than the contract price, the person you sold the futures to will be able to sell them for a profit. If prices fall, the buyer of your crops will lose out, but you will still get the contract price. In effect, you have managed your risk by transferring both good and bad risks about the future price of wheat to your contract partner. In general, derivatives are meant to transfer risk to people who are more willing to bear it.

Major Players in the Financial System

LO 13.4 Name the main institutions in financial markets, and describe the role that each plays.

So far, we've seen the functions of the global financial system, and the major kinds of assets that get traded in financial markets. We'll now look at four key players without whom there couldn't be a well-functioning financial system: banks and other intermediaries, savers and their proxies, entrepreneurs and businesses, and speculators.

Banks and Other Financial Intermediaries

We've already mentioned that banks play a crucial intermediary role. Digging deeper, we can divide banks into two categories: *commercial banks* and *investment banks.*

Commercial banks are probably what you think of when someone says "bank." When you make a deposit at a bank or get a mortgage or student loan from a bank, you are interacting with a commercial bank. As well as acting as an intermediary between savers and borrowers, commercial banks help to create liquidity. The loans they make are relatively illiquid assets, typically taking years to be repaid.

Most savers, however, don't want their money to be tied up for years. How can banks *lend long* (make loans of long duration) while also *borrowing short* (using the money gained from deposits to make loans that allow them to be ready to give depositors their money back at short notice)? Banks assume that not all depositors will try to get their money back at once, so they keep on hand only a fraction of all deposits. If too many depositors want their cash back at once, the bank would run out of funds—a potentially disastrous situation known as a *bank run.*

Investment banks are part of what is commonly referred to as "Bay Street"—banks like TD Securities and BMO Capital Markets. These banks don't take deposits and they don't make loans in the traditional sense. Instead, they provide liquidity to financial markets themselves by acting as market makers. They help companies issue stocks and bonds by guaranteeing to buy any that remain unsold (a process known as *underwriting*).

Savers and Their Proxies

Most savers don't approach financial markets directly. Instead, they operate through a *proxy*—that is, they give their money to someone else to decide whom to lend it to. These proxies include banks, mutual funds, pension funds, and life insurance companies.

A **mutual fund** is a portfolio of stocks and other assets, managed by a professional who makes decisions on behalf of clients. Savers entrust their money to mutual funds to save themselves the hassle of researching the thousands of stocks and bonds they could buy; instead, they let a professional make the decisions.

There are many different types of mutual funds. One of the most popular types is an *index fund.* These funds buy all the stocks represented in a broad market like the Standard & Poor's (S&P) TSX 300, with the goal of mirroring the same return as the market on average. Managers of *specialized funds,* in contrast, try to beat the market by researching specific companies and picking stocks that they hope will earn higher returns than the market average. Mutual funds charge a fee for their services that can be as little as a tenth of a percent of assets (such as with a simple index fund) or as much as 3 or 4 percent (in the case of a fund that spends a lot on stock research).

Pension funds are also a major outlet for individual savings. Usually linked to an employer, a **pension fund** is a professionally managed portfolio of assets intended to provide income to company retirees. Two main categories of pension funds exist:

- *Defined-benefit* plans guarantee a fixed payout to employees who have met certain entry requirements, such as working a certain number of years with the company.
- *Defined-contribution* plans do not guarantee retirees a defined level of pension. Employees pay in a certain (defined) amount each year and their employers may match some portion of that contribution; the fund provides payouts that depend on how the stock market performs. Most defined-contribution plans allow contributions to grow tax-deferred until they are withdrawn.

In the past, defined-benefit plans were the rule, but today defined-contribution plans are much more common.

Life insurance policies are also a significant form of savings. The savings people put into these policies are called *premiums,* and as with mutual funds and pension funds, a professional decides how to use them in financial markets. Unlike mutual funds, where you can take money out at any time, and pension funds, which can be accessed when you retire, life insurance policies pay out to your dependents only when you die.

These three proxies are by no means the only ways in which individuals can entrust their savings to a third-party manager. Other options include hedge funds, private-equity firms, and venture-capital funds, to name just a few. Still, surprisingly enough, the simplest approach may be the best, as outlined in the Real Life box, The Incredible Index Fund.

REAL LIFE

The Incredible Index Fund

Entire TV networks dedicate their efforts to reporting the rise and fall of asset prices, from stocks to the price of gold. Bookstores are filled with advice on playing the stock market. If you're lucky enough to have money to put in the stock market, how can you make sense of this noisy deluge of information and find a way to outperform the market?

Maybe you shouldn't even try. Many savers have embraced index funds, now offered by a wide range of financial companies, attempt to replicate the exact movements of a given stock market index such as the S&P/TSX Composite, which is comprised of stocks in 300 leading companies that trade on the Toronto Stock Exchange.

Index funds have a big advantage over traditional, actively managed mutual funds: they cost much less to maintain. One reason for their lower costs is that index funds don't need to employ highly paid asset managers to research which stocks have the highest probability of beating the market. Instead, the goal is to simply mimic the market average. A second benefit of index funds is that, because the stocks that comprise an index like the S&P/TSX Composite don't change much, there is much less buying and selling of stocks. As a result, these funds minimize the capital gains taxes that are owed when stocks are bought or sold.

Professional fund managers point out that since index funds attempt to duplicate the exact movements of what is essentially the *average* performance of the market, they can miss out on large returns earned by specific subsets of the market. In the dot-com boom during the late 1990s, for example, the returns for some mutual funds that specialized in up-and-coming technological firms far outstripped the returns for index funds.

Who's right? According to the December 2014 Standard & Poor's SPIVA Canada Scorecard, just 26.47 percent of Canadian equity funds outperformed the S&P/TSX Composite.

Sources: John C. Bogle, "All about Index Funds: The easy way to get started," http://www.fool.com/mutualfunds/indexfunds/indexfunds01.htm; http://www.etfinsight.ca/blog/wp-content/uploads/2015/04/spiva-canada-scorecard-yearend-2014.pdf.

Entrepreneurs and Businesses

Entrepreneurs and businesses also are major players in financial markets, because they are often looking to borrow money to finance their latest ventures. Strictly speaking, these are the people who engage in economic investment, often with the advice of specialized investment banks that channel savers' money to them. Without these borrowers, much of the financial system would simply cease to exist.

Speculators

The last group of major players in the financial system is speculators, who play a unique and controversial role in the financial system. A *speculator* is anyone who buys and sells financial assets purely for financial gain. You may ask what's controversial about that—aren't the other three key players we've considered (intermediaries, savers, and entrepreneurs) also out for financial gain? Yes, but what sets speculators apart is that they are neither a "natural" buyer nor a seller, but are willing to play either role in an effort to make a profit.

There is fierce debate over whether speculators are good for the health of the financial markets, as summarized in the What Do You Think? box, Are Speculators a Good Influence on Markets?

WHAT DO YOU THINK?

Are Speculators a Good Influence on Markets?

From 2006 to 2008, prices of many staple commodities, such as wheat and corn, practically doubled. The sharp increase in food prices was caused in part by the combination of a fall in supply due to poor harvests and an increase in demand from people actually intending to eat the food. However, some say that this does not explain all of the increase. Instead, they say prices were pushed up by increased demand from speculators, who saw the opportunity to profit by buying food and then selling it again at a higher price. Pope Benedict XVI, former leader of the Catholic Church, concurred with a number of critics when he asked, "How can we be silent before the fact that food has become an object of speculation, or tied to happenings in a financial market that, lacking any certain rules and devoid of moral principles, appears to be still rooted to the sole object of profit?"

How might speculators defend themselves against such comments? The main argument in favor of speculators is their role in price discovery—that is, they help markets to find the "correct" price for an asset, reflecting all available information. What might the price of wheat be six months from now? Because speculators are trying to earn a profit, they will spend huge amounts of energy on understanding every nuance of this kind of question. Their goal is to figure out if they should be buying or selling wheat futures at the current price. Many believe that this is a valuable service, saving wheat farmers and bakeries and grocery stores from needing to do this research themselves. Instead, they can be confident that the market price already reflects the best information available.

Others believe, however, that speculation actually has the opposite effect. They say that it causes prices to swing wildly away from the "correct" levels, magnifying small fluctuations in the market and creating potentially destabilizing bubbles and busts. Consider the US housing boom of 2000–2007, which was driven in part by speculators buying houses in expectation that the price of real estate would continue going up. Critics argue that something similar happened with the prices of corn and wheat: speculators bid up the prices because they expected the price to continue to go up, creating a self-fulfilling prophecy.

This sounds like a puzzle. If speculators research the market thoroughly, wouldn't they realize that wheat was overpriced and want to sell, thereby returning wheat to its correct price? Some say that's what happens. Others believe that speculators might still want to buy overpriced wheat today, if they're confident that the wheat will be even more overpriced tomorrow, and that they'll be able to sell again for a profit before the inevitable crash comes. The "correct" price will be found in the end, but perhaps only after a period of hysteria and a lot of damage to consumers and savers.

What do you think?

1. What benefits can speculators provide through their participation in financial markets?

2. Do you think speculators' incentives to discover the "correct" price for a good are aligned with those of "natural" savers and borrowers like farmers and customers? Why might their incentives sometimes be different from those of other players in financial markets?

3. Do you agree with the Pope that there are moral issues that go beyond economics involved in speculation in food prices? Why or why not?

Source: http://www.nytimes.com/2008/04/10/opinion/10thu1.html.

✓ CONCEPT CHECK

☐ Which type of financial asset is included in the Dow Jones Industrial Average? [LO 13.3]

☐ Why would an investor wish to diversify his or her financial investments? [LO 13.3]

☐ What are the two different types of banks? [LO 13.4]

☐ What is a pension fund? [LO 13.4]

Valuing Assets

We've touched on a question a few times so far: How do buyers and sellers in the market for financial assets reach agreement on the correct price? We've already looked at how businesses balance the expected rate of return on an investment with the cost of borrowing. How do the suppliers of funds—that is, savers—decide whether to deposit money in a bank or to purchase stocks or bonds? (And if they choose to purchase stocks or bonds, how do they decide what to buy?) In this section, we'll explore some of the basic principles of *asset valuation,* which help savers make these decisions.

The Trade-Off Between Risk and Return

LO 13.5 Explain the trade-off between risk and return in financial assets, and describe how risk can be analyzed.

The basic trade-off in valuing any asset is between risk and return: if you face a high risk of losing your money, you're going to want the chance of a high return to make it worth taking that risk. Figure 13-6 shows the historical risk and return profile for various major financial assets. As you can see, cash and bond investments (both fixed income and inflation adjusted) are on the low-risk, low-return end of the spectrum. Stocks are on the high end of the spectrum, carrying both a hefty amount of risk but generally also providing larger returns. Different individuals have different appetites for risk: some savers may prefer to keep their money in low-risk bonds, while speculators enjoy chasing high rewards at the risk of losing everything.

FIGURE 13-6

Risk and Reward of Various Financial Assets

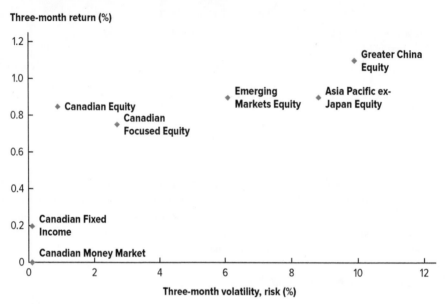

There is clearly a strong correlation between the expected risk and expected return in financial assets. Assets such as cash and fixed-income bonds carry very low risk and reward. At the upper end of the scale, financial assets in emerging countries carry a return that is high, but they also are quite risky.

Diversification, Market Risk, Idiosyncratic Risk

Another way to manage risk when purchasing financial assets is diversification. If you put all your money in one company's stock and that company goes bankrupt, you've lost everything. If you buy stock in many companies, especially those in different industries, they're unlikely all to go bankrupt at the same time. A *portfolio*—a collection or group of many different assets—will often have a higher return for a given level of risk than any individual asset could offer.

To better understand how diversification works, let's look at two different types of risk that exist with financial assets. First, **market risk**, or *systemic risk,* refers to any risk that is broadly shared by the entire market or economy. An example would be the risk of unexpected inflation. Of course, some businesses will be more affected than others by unexpected inflation, but all businesses will face the consequences of the rising prices.

For this reason, market risk is harder to eliminate via diversification. For the case of unexpected inflation, one strategy to eliminate some of the risk is to buy inflation-linked bonds issued by the government. The return to these bonds varies with inflation, so they hold their value even when prices rise without warning.

In contrast, **idiosyncratic risks** are unique to a particular company or asset—for example, the risk that a particular company will make a bad business decision, causing the value of its stock to fall. Idiosyncratic risks are the easiest to lower or even eliminate via diversification. If you buy stock in many different companies, it's unlikely that they're all going to fail at the same time.

A portfolio composed of many stocks succeeds in diversifying away idiosyncratic risks. As more stocks are added to the portfolio, idiosyncratic risk goes down without reducing the expected performance of the portfolio. Index funds are the natural extreme of diversifying to eliminate idiosyncratic risk: by investing in essentially all the stocks in the market, index funds achieve a very high level of diversification and face little to no idiosyncratic risk. A certain amount of market risk, just from having money in the financial market, remains in all portfolios and cannot be diversified away.

Measuring Risk

How is risk measured? The most commonly used measure of risk in financial markets is a simple tool borrowed from statistics: the standard deviation. The **standard deviation** is a measure of how spread out a set of numbers is.

In financial markets, the simplest way to measure risk is to look at the standard deviation of an asset's return over time. That means that we keep track of how much money it makes each day or month or year, and then measure how widely these numbers differ from period to period. For example, while the stock market has historically returned about 7 percent per year after inflation *on average,* the actual returns in a *particular* year have ranged anywhere from −80 percent to +120 percent. A 20–30 percent increase or decrease in any given year would not be particularly surprising. Government bonds, on the other hand, have historically gained about 2–3 percent per year after inflation on average; rarely have they experienced more than a 10 percent gain or loss. In other words, government bonds have a much smaller standard deviation—meaning they have much less risk than the stock market. Those historical figures don't necessarily give a good prediction of average levels of future stock prices, but they do show the bigger point that higher average returns usually come with substantially higher risk.

Predicting Returns: The Efficient-Market Hypothesis

LO 13.6 Give arguments for and against the assumption that markets are efficient.

Imagine you were asked to pick the stock most likely to go up in value over the next year. How would you do it? There are three basic approaches you could take.

The first approach would be to try to guess how much profit a company will make in the future and use that as a basis for calculating how much the company is worth now. We can use interest rates to translate between the *present value* and *future value* of money. If you estimate the future value of the profits the company will make, you can translate it into the company's **net present value** (often abbreviated as NPV). NPV is a measure of the current value of a stream of cash flows expected in the future. This tells you the "correct" price of shares in the company.

Of course, this presents a new problem: how to guess a company's future profits. Traditionally this is done through *fundamental analysis.* That is a fancy way of describing extensive research on an individual company: poring over financial statements, studying how the company is run, understanding the industry the company is in and who its competitors are, and so on. Specialized investment funds often employ hundreds of analysts to do this research.

The second approach is called *technical analysis.* It ignores any attempt to predict future profits or calculate NPV, or indeed to learn anything whatsoever about the stock in question. Instead it is used to analyze the *past* movements of a stock's price to try to predict future movements, looking for patterns in the data that could point to what's going to happen next. This method is usually done with the help of highly sophisticated computer software.

This is all pretty hard work. Is there an easier way? Well, yes. Here's the third approach: make a list of all the stocks, pin it to a wall, and throw a dart at it. Wherever it lands, that's your choice. This doesn't sound like a very good plan, does it? But if many academic researchers in the finance world are right, this approach is often just as good as either of the first two approaches, as well as being a whole lot cheaper, quicker, and simpler.

The idea underlying this third approach is called the **efficient-market hypothesis**. It holds that market prices always incorporate all available information and therefore represent true value as correctly as is possible. Both fundamental and technical analysis are ways of trying to outsmart the market; they work only if you find a stock whose current price is either higher or lower than the "correct" price. The efficient-market hypothesis (EMH) implies that finding incorrectly priced stocks is impossible. If prices already represent the best possible information about the true value of a stock, then all stocks are already correctly priced and there is no additional information you can use to predict which stocks will gain value.

The intuition behind this idea is pretty straightforward. Imagine that careful observers of the stock market have information that a particular company will announce high profits tomorrow. Such an announcement generally causes a stock's price to rise, so it makes sense to buy the stock today in the hope of selling at a profit tomorrow. The effect is to drive up the price of the stock today, until it reaches the price expected for tomorrow. The expectation of tomorrow's announcement is now *priced in.*

So what will happen to the stock's price tomorrow? According to the efficient-market hypothesis, the stock's expected movements might go in any direction—described as a *random walk*. Any attempt to predict the price of the stock tomorrow is foolish: if there were any credible information out there that suggested the stock would go up or down, then the stock would already have priced it in. This brings us back to our dart-throwing plan. If you can't possibly predict stock returns, you might as well just pin a list of stocks on the wall and throw darts at them.

Not surprisingly, the efficient-market hypothesis isn't very popular with the stock brokers and analysts who are paid handsomely for their attempts to pick winning stocks. They argue that some people simply have better information than others, or at least a better ability to put together all the complex pieces. However, the number of people who have consistently outsmarted the markets over a long period is extremely small.

One argument against the efficient-market hypothesis is that occasionally the same financial asset can be traded at different prices in different markets. That's evidence that the market isn't efficiently using all its information. If you can manage to simultaneously sell that asset in one place while buying it in another, you can make a risk-free profit. The process of taking advantage of market inefficiencies to earn profits is called **arbitrage**. Some fund managers specialize in scouring different markets in search of arbitrage opportunities. An example would be the recent surge in activities that try to find price differences in stock in the same company that is listed both in Hong Kong (H-share) and China (A-share). However, it takes a huge amount of effort to spot these opportunities, and if you get the timing even slightly wrong, you can end up losing a lot of money. Given what we know about risk and reward, though, if you get the timing right, you can reap big rewards.

Over the past couple of decades, some academic economists in a field called behavioural finance have also started questioning the validity of the efficient-market hypothesis, because they believe it might be possible to exploit the mistakes of stock analysts. See the Real Life box, Behavioural Finance and the Efficient-Market Hypothesis, for more.

REAL LIFE

Behavioural Finance and the Efficient-Market Hypothesis

The efficient-market hypothesis says that people have good information and make smart choices when buying and selling shares in the stock market. If that happens, it's difficult to systematically make money in the stock market. Other investors will have already snapped up bargains, and there will be no undiscovered gems overlooked by others.

But what if people *don't* use their information well and *don't* make good choices? Then it could be possible to systematically make money by taking into account how they actually make choices—and then creating strategies that exploit their mistakes. This is the thinking behind behavioural finance, a branch of behavioural economics.

✓ CONCEPT CHECK

- ☐ What is the general relationship between risk and return in financial markets? [LO 13.5]
- ☐ How does idiosyncratic risk differ from market risk? [LO 13.5]
- ☐ Is a stock that has a net present value lower than the current market price a good buy? [LO 13.5]
- ☐ What is the prediction of the efficient-market hypothesis? [LO 13.6]
- ☐ Does the possibility for arbitrage suggest that a market is efficient? [LO 13.6]

A National Accounts Approach to Finance

Earlier in the chapter, we showed that when the market for loanable funds is in equilibrium, savings (supply) must equal investment (demand). This applies the microeconomic logic of market equilibrium to the financial system, but we can also approach the analysis from a more purely macroeconomic angle. By looking at savings and investment through the lens of the national income accounting method introduced in Chapter 7, "Measuring the Wealth of Nations," we can track the quantity of funds on a national level and separate out different sources of savings.

The Savings–Investment Identity

LO 13.7 Describe why savings equals investment in a closed economy.

Start by imagining a simplified economy with no government and no international trade. All transactions happen within the borders of the country, between its residents. How could the residents of our simple economy use the money they earn? They have only two possible uses for their income: They can consume it (spend it now), or they can save it (keep it for later). In other words, income is equal to the sum of consumption and savings:

Equation 13-1

$$\text{Income} = \text{consumption} + \text{savings}$$

In this simple economy, with no government or international trade, all savings are **private savings**—the savings of individuals or corporations within a country.

Now let's think about how people in this simple economy earn their income. Since there are no governments or foreign countries to interact with, they earn income only when other people in the country purchase goods or services from them. All of these purchases can be categorized as spending on *consumption* (things like meals, clothes, and cars) or spending on *investment goods* (productive inputs like factories and machines). Income is equal to total spending, which in a closed economy is equal to consumption plus investment:

Equation 13-2

$$\text{Consumption} + \text{investment} = \text{income}$$

This result is related to the national accounts framework we developed in Chapter 7.

Next, to relate savings to investment, we can put together Equation 13-1 and Equation 13-2. Equation 13-1 says that consumption plus savings equals income. Equation 13-2 says that income also equals consumption plus investment. Putting the two together, we see that:

$$\text{Consumption} + \text{savings} = \text{income} = \text{consumption} + \text{investment}$$

Since consumption appears on both sides of this equation, we can cancel it out, and immediately see the *savings–investment identity:*

Equation 13-3

$$\text{Savings} = \text{investment}$$

which is commonly written:

$$S = I$$

The savings–investment identity tells us that savings always equals investment in an economy without governments or trade.

Private Savings, Public Savings, and Capital Flows

Our simple economy is missing a large reality: government. If government takes in more through taxes than it spends, it can run budget surpluses. These government surpluses are another form of saving: the government receives income in the form of taxes, and saves it by not spending it right away. On the other hand, if government runs a budget deficit (spending more than it takes in in taxes), it is *dissaving*. In that case, the government must borrow money from the rest of the economy in order to spend more than it collects in taxes.

If we look at how much the government takes in through tax revenue, and subtract what it spends, we get **public savings**:

Equation 13-4

$$\text{Public savings} = \text{taxes} - \text{goverment spending}$$

Adding public savings to private savings, we get **national savings**, which is the sum of the private savings of individuals and corporations plus the public savings of the government. When the government runs a deficit, national savings will be lower than private savings; the opposite is true when the government runs a surplus.

There are *three* things that citizens of our simple economy could do with the income they earn: they can consume, save privately, or pay taxes to the government. We can show this by adding taxes to Equation 13-1:

Equation 13-5

$$\text{Income} = \text{consumption} + \text{private savings} + \text{taxes}$$

There is also an additional way for citizens to earn income: they can sell goods and services to or receive benefits from the government. We can show this new income source as a variation on Equation 13-2.

Equation 13-6

$$\text{Consumption} + \text{investment} + \text{government spending} = \text{income}$$

Just as we did before, we can put together these two ways of arriving at "income" (from Equations 13-5 and 13-6):

$$\text{Income} = \text{consumption} + \text{private savings} + \text{taxes} = \text{consumption} + \text{investment} + \text{government spending}$$

Canceling consumption from both sides, this reduces to:

$$\text{Private savings} + \text{taxes} = \text{investment} + \text{government spending}$$

Now, let's rearrange that equation to isolate investment:

Equation 13-7

$$\text{Investment} = \text{private savings} + \text{taxes} - \text{government spending}$$

But we know (from Equation 13-4) that taxes minus government spending equals public savings. So, we can simplify further:

Equation 13-8

$$\text{Investment} = \text{private savings} + \text{public savings}$$

Therefore,

$$\text{Investment} = \text{national savings}$$

In other words, national savings are equal to the total investment in the economy.

Note that we are still assuming no international trade. The identity between national savings and investment holds only in a **closed economy**—an economy that does not interact with other countries' economies. The final piece of real-world complexity we need to add to our model is opening it up to international interactions. This is called an **open economy**.

When money is allowed to move freely across borders, two different types of international financial transactions can happen. A *capital outflow* occurs when the money saved *domestically* (within the home country) is invested in another country. Conversely, a *capital inflow* occurs when savings from another country finance domestic investment. The difference between capital inflows and capital outflows is **net capital flow**. A net capital inflow occurs in countries where investment is higher than national savings. In the opposite case, when national savings are higher than domestic investment, there is a net capital outflow.

For an *open* economy, national savings can be more or less than investment. But for the global economy as a whole savings must be equal to investment. This means that any excess savings in one country have to be soaked up as investment elsewhere. In the From Another Angle box, Is Saving More Always a Good Thing? we evaluate this possibility in practice.

FROM ANOTHER ANGLE

Is Saving More Always a Good Thing?

As children, we were often reminded of the virtue of saving. Many of us dutifully put our allowances in piggy banks, looking forward to blowing it all on a bigger and better toy down the road.

For the past decade, though, people in the United States haven't been saving much. The government has, for the most part, run large deficits. Households save only a small percentage of their income on average, with many actually spending more than they earn, financed by credit cards and loans. In addition, the country has long been running a sizable *current-account deficit,* meaning that it imports far more than it exports. All of these patterns suggest that people in the United States are spending way too much.

But could the problem be that other countries are *saving* way too much? This hypothesis, called the *global savings glut,* ties recent US economic ills to high savings rates in Asia and Latin America.

When economies are open to cross-border capital flows, savings no longer have to equal investment within a given country. It's possible for a nation to save more than its firms and individuals want to invest. When that happens, these excess funds end up searching for the best returns in other investments around the world. Most of these funds end up in the United States, largely because it is seen as a safe place to invest. In fact, economist Kenneth Rogoff estimated that in 2007 a full two-thirds of excess savings in the world ended up invested in the United States.

This represents a huge sum of money. In the years before the 2007 financial crisis, net capital inflows—the amount of money coming in, minus the amount the United States invested around the world—were around 6 percent of US GDP. Federal Reserve Chairman Ben Bernanke argued that this large inflow of money kept interest rates low, which translated to cheap borrowing for Americans. Cheap borrowing enabled the housing boom during the mid-2000s, when people borrowed heavily to buy houses they wouldn't have been able to afford at higher interest rates. Could the US housing bubble really have been caused in part by industrious savers in Asia and Latin America? It seems hard to believe, but it's possible that this played a role.

Sources: http://www.federalreserve.gov/newsevents/speech/bernanke20110218a.htm; Kenneth Rogoff, "Betting with the house's money," *The Guardian,* February 7, 2007, http://www.guardian.co.uk/commentisfree/2007/feb/07/bettingwiththehousesmoney.

✓ CONCEPT CHECK

- ☐ What are the components of national savings? [LO 13.7]
- ☐ What is it called when the amount of capital leaving a country is greater than the amount going in? [LO 13.7]

Conclusion

In this chapter we've explored the basic framework of the financial system: how buyers find sellers, how interest rates set the price of borrowing and the return on lending, and how the various players interact. We've also learned about a few of the major financial-asset classes and explored some of the ways that investors attempt to evaluate the risk and return potential of their investments.

You've seen that financial markets mostly operate like other markets. However, financial markets can sometimes behave in mysterious and opaque ways. We'll see more examples in the "Financial Crisis" chapter.

Now that we've covered the basics of how financial markets and the financial system works, it's time to look at the bigger picture by understanding more clearly how the financial system fits into the overall economy. In the next chapter, we'll look at the origins of money and how the modern financial system is responsible for both creating and destroying money. We'll also learn about the people who oversee much of the financial system, including influencing the money supply, and how their actions affect economic growth in ways both enormous and subtle.

Key Terms

financial market

market for loanable funds

savings

investment

interest rate

crowding out

default

risk-free rate

financial system

financial intermediaries

liquidity

diversification

stock

dividend

loan

bond

derivative

mutual fund

pension fund

market (systemic) risk

idiosyncratic risk

standard deviation

net present value (NPV)

efficient-market hypothesis

arbitrage

private savings

public savings

national savings

closed economy

open economy

net capital flow

Summary

LO 13.1 Define a financial market, and list the three main functions it serves.

A financial market is one in which people trade future claims on funds or goods. The financial market helps ensure that the world's wealth is constantly put to use, channeled to the individuals and organizations that can most effectively take advantage of it. A well–functioning financial market matches buyers and sellers as efficiently and effectively as possible. In financial markets, buyers are people who want to spend money on something of value right now, but don't have cash on hand. Sellers are people who have cash on hand and are willing to let others use it, for a price.

Financial markets act as intermediaries between savers and borrowers. They provide the benefits of liquidity—having cash easily available when you want it. And they help savers and borrowers to diversify risk by providing funds to a big pool of borrowers.

LO 13.2 Describe the market for loanable funds, and give examples of factors that affect the supply and demand for loanable funds.

You can think of the market for loanable funds as a hypothetical marketplace that brings together everyone looking to lend money (savers) and everyone looking to borrow money (anyone with investment-spending needs). The market for loanable funds clears at a price where supply and demand meet. This price is known as the interest rate. A key determinant of the supply curve for loanable funds is how much people decide to save. Many factors influence the demand curve for loanable funds, including the strength of capital flows within a country and the overall strength of an economy.

LO 13.3 Differentiate between debt and equity, and define the major types of assets in each category.

The major types of financial assets are debt and equity. Equity is ownership in a company, and the most common form of such ownership is stock. As partial owners, stockholders are entitled to receive a portion of a company's profits, in the form of dividends, in proportion to the size of their ownership.

The most basic type of debt is a loan. Loans are an agreement between a lender and a borrower in which the lender lends money to the borrower in exchange for a promise to repay the amount loaned (the principal of the loan) plus an agreed-upon amount of interest. A bond is a loan that has been standardized into a more easily tradeable and liquid asset. Bonds are a type of debt, issued by corporations or governments, as a way to borrow large sums of money. Stocks and bonds are liquid assets that are easily bought and sold in financial markets.

Financial contracts based on the value of some other asset represent a special category of financial assets, called derivatives. The best example of a derivative is a futures contract.

LO 13.4 Name the main institutions in financial markets, and describe the role that each plays.

There are many different players in the financial market. There are banks, which can be divided into two categories: commercial banks and investment banks. When you make a deposit at a bank, or get a mortgage or student loan from a bank, you are interacting with a commercial bank. Investment banks focus on providing liquidity to the financial markets themselves, by acting as market makers, helping companies to issue stocks and bonds (a process known as underwriting).

Individual actors in the financial market have to operate through a proxy—they give their money to someone else to invest for them. These proxies include mutual funds (professionally managed portfolios of stocks and other assets), pension funds (professionally administered portfolios of assets intended to provide income to retirees), and life insurance policies (in which people pay premiums that pay out to dependents upon the death of the insured). Entrepreneurs and businessmen are also major players in financial markets, as are speculators.

LO 13.5 Explain the trade-off between risk and return in financial assets, and describe how risk can be analyzed.

In general, there is a direct relationship between risk and reward in the financial market. The riskier the investment, the higher its potential return. Typically the investments with the lowest risk—and lowest return—are government bonds.

Stocks are a considerably more risky investment, but also offer the possibility of higher returns. Two different types of risk exist for financial assets—market risk (risk that is broadly shared by the entire market) and idiosyncratic risk (risk unique to a particular asset or company). A portfolio of assets can help diversify away idiosyncratic risk; a certain amount of market risk remains in all portfolios.

In financial markets, the most commonly used method of measuring this risk is a simple tool borrowed from statistics: the standard deviation. The standard deviation is a measure of how far apart a set of numbers is in a distribution.

LO 13.6 Give arguments for and against the assumption that markets are efficient.

The efficient-market hypothesis holds that markets are efficient—that market prices incorporate all available information, and as a result, accurately predicting stock returns is impossible.

Supporters of the efficient-market hypothesis describe the expected movements of a stock as a random walk, a term from statistics that describes any variable (like the price of a stock) that moves in a completely unpredictable (random) way from one moment to the next. Those who argue against market efficiency suggest that some people simply have better information than others or a better ability to put all the complex pieces together to predict stock price. Occasionally markets have certain information inefficiencies that savvy investors, through arbitrage, can exploit to profit from the differences between prices in different markets.

LO 13.7 Explain why savings equals investment in a closed economy.

In a closed economy, one with no international trade, citizens can consume or save. The amount of savings within an economy is necessarily the amount of investment that can occur. Thus, savings and investment spending (the supply and demand of the financial markets) are always equal, a relationship called the savings–investment identity.

Review Questions

1. In financial markets, who are the sellers? Who are the buyers? [LO 13.1]

2. Explain how a country with poorly developed financial markets might have a hard time sustaining economic growth. [LO 13.1]

3. Is it savings or investment when Collins Inc. uses the proceeds from issuing bonds to purchase equipment needed to start a new product line? If Daisy buys some of the Collins Inc. bonds, is her purchase savings or investment? [LO 13.2]

4. Why might a government want to encourage saving among its citizens? If the government enacts a successful policy aimed at encouraging saving, what would be the likely effect on the interest rate and the quantity of investment? [LO 13.2]

5. Explain the relationship between the quantity supplied of loanable funds and the real interest rate, and how this affects the slope of the supply curve in the loanable-funds model. [LO 13.2]

6. In a famous bet known as the Simon-Ehrlich wager, Paul Ehrlich bet that over the course of ten years, the prices of five commodities would be higher than they were at the start of the decade; Julian Simon believed the price of these goods would be lower. The loser had to pay the difference of the price from the starting point. What type of financial asset does this wager resemble? Why? [LO 13.3]

7. What is securitization? How did it contribute to the recent housing-market crisis? [LO 13.3]

8. How do economists generally define a bank? What kind of bank exemplifies this definition? Does an investment bank meet this definition? [LO 13.4]

9. What is an index fund, and why would a financial investor consider buying one? [LO 13.4]

10. Which is likely to have more risk, a government bond from a developing country or one from France? Which should have a higher return? [LO 13.5]

11. Define diversification and comment on how successful it is at managing market risk and idiosyncratic risk. [LO 13.5]

12. During the 1990s, securities related to technology and other dot-com firms experienced skyrocketing market prices, but around 2000 the market crashed. Was that crash an example that supports or offers evidence against the efficient-market hypothesis? [LO 13.6]

13. Describe the difference between fundamental analysis and technical analysis. Which, if either, does the efficient-market hypothesis suggest financial investors engage in? [LO 13.6]

14. Does the level of taxation in a closed economy have an impact on national savings? Explain. [LO 13.7]

15. Explain how a persistent government budget deficit can hurt a closed economy's ability to engage in economic investment. [LO 13.7]

Problems and Applications

1. The chapter discusses three main functions of a banking system. Classify each of the following by the function it best represents. [LO 13.1]
   a. Aaron can get cash out of the ATM at any time of day or night.
   b. Instead of lending all her savings out to one borrower, Barbara's bank makes the money in her savings account available to a variety of firms, with different characteristics and risk profiles, wishing to invest.
   c. When Charlie's car suddenly breaks down, he can quickly withdraw funds from his savings account to pay the mechanic and rent a car.
   d. Donna can get start-up funds for her new hair salon from a bank, instead of having to find people in her neighbourhood willing to lend their extra money.

2. After graduating, you take an unusual job: consulting with the queen of a small, newly populated island in the middle of the sea. You've provided advice to her on matters related to government and the economy, and while she has taken your advice most of the time, she has so far turned down your suggestion to have a banking system. She claims that banks will make the economy more complicated and do little to make the lives of her subjects easier.

   Over the past several months, though, the queen has discussed with you several issues that have arisen in the newly formed economy. For each of the three quotes from the queen below, refer to one of the three functions of banks discussed in this chapter to explain how a banking system could help with the issue described. [LO 13.1]
   a. "When my subjects have money left over after spending, they want to keep it somewhere safe and earn some interest on it. But that's hard for most of them because they have no way of finding out who wants to borrow and whether it would be a good idea to lend to them."
   b. "My subjects are lucky that we have very little crime, so they can safely keep their extra money inside their houses and take only what cash they need for a day's spending. However, many of them have complained that if an emergency occurs when they're all the way on the other side of the island, they can't access their funds."
   c. "Some of my subjects who are in the know about good borrowers have been making loans and earning interest. But lately there have been a couple of borrowers who defaulted on loans, and when they did, the lenders were totally out of luck. All that money just disappeared! And those bad experiences have made other potential lenders afraid, so that now borrowing and lending have dried up almost completely. If only there were some easy way for them to divide their savings among several different borrowers, they might feel safe enough to start lending again!"

3. Categorize each of the following as a type of savings or investment in the economic sense. [LO 13.2]
   a. You buy 100 shares of RBC stock.
   b. You place part of your income in a mutual fund.
   c. A delivery service buys 1,000 new trucks.
   d. You put $1,000 in a fixed term deposit, giving money to the bank in exchange for a set amount of return.

4. Use the following words to fill in the blanks in the statements below about the market for loanable funds. *Choose from: demanded/supplied, left/right, higher/lower.* [LO 13.2]
   a. A change that makes people want to save less will shift the quantity of loanable funds _____ to the _____. The resulting new equilibrium in the market for loanable funds would be a _____ interest rate and a _____ quantity of funds saved and invested.
   b. A change that makes people want to save more will shift the quantity of loanable funds _____ to the _____. The resulting new equilibrium in the market for loanable funds would be a _____ interest rate and a _____ quantity of funds saved and invested.

c. A change that makes people want to invest more will shift the quantity of loanable funds _____ to the _____. The resulting new equilibrium in the market for loanable funds would be a _____ interest rate and a _____ quantity of funds saved and invested.

d. A change that makes people want to invest less will shift the quantity of loanable funds _____ to the _____. The resulting new equilibrium in the market for loanable funds would be a _____ interest rate and a _____ quantity of funds saved and invested.

5. In each of following examples, name the financial product being described. [LO 13.3]
   a. A family borrows money to pay for a house.
   b. A new tech start-up offers investors the ability to purchase a small part of the company to raise needed capital.
   c. The Canadian government offers to pay investors a 3 percent return rate next year if they finance its debt today.

6. Evaluate each of the following statements and say whether it describes a loan, a bond, and/or a stock. [LO 13.3]
   a. It pays some form of interest, and principal is paid at maturity.
   b. It implies ownership in the issuing firm.
   c. Small businesses use these to raise funds for investment.
   d. This is also known as equity financing.
   e. We can think of this as a more liquid version of a loan.

7. In your spare time, you help out with a magazine for high schoolers that focuses on current events related to economics and politics. While the magazine aims to be readable and entertaining, it also wants to use terminology correctly. Knowing that you've taken an economics class, the editor turns to you to look over a paragraph in a story focusing on the roles of saving and investment after the recent crisis in the housing market. Go through the following paragraph and correct any errors in economic vocabulary, including an explanation for the editor about why the original was incorrect. [LO 13.2], [LO 13.3]

   > When Canadians invest by buying securities such as stocks and bonds or putting money in a bank, they provide funds for firms wishing to engage in diversification by buying assets used to produce goods and services. Households with extra money left over after buying things they want or need consume by purchasing securities or putting their funds in savings accounts, and banks help transfer those funds to firms. By matching and working with these borrowers and lenders, banks act as a source of liquidity.

8. Match each of the following players in the financial system with the financial product(s) it is most associated with. [LO 13.4]
   a. Commercial banks   i. Stocks
   b. Savers   ii. Bonds
   c. Investment banks   iii. Loans

9. Rank the following actors in financial markets by the level of liquidity they provide. [LO 13.4]
   a. Entrepreneurs offering equity in their businesses
   b. The Bank of Canada offering banks the chance to borrow short-term money
   c. Investment banks offering shares in mutual funds, which penalize you if you withdraw your money within thirty days
   d. A bank offering you a no-minimum reserve requirement chequing account

10. Which of the following is a way to describe the risk of a financial asset? [LO 13.5]
    a. Standard deviation
    b. Overnight rate
    c. Inflation rate
    d. Interest rate
    e. Beta

11. Rank the following assets based on their expected return. Then repeat the exercise, this time ranking the assets based on their expected risk. [LO 13.5]
    a. Real estate
    b. Commodities

    c. Canadian equities (stocks)

    d. Cash

    e. Canadian fixed-income bonds

12. Evaluate whether the following statements are true or false. [LO 13.5]

    a. Risk is measured by looking at the expected value (average) of an asset's returns over time.

    b. Market risk can be minimized with a well-diversified portfolio.

    c. Idiosyncratic risk is unique to a particular asset rather than applying to the market as a whole.

    d. A portfolio of well-diversified assets will often be less risky for the same level of return when compared to an individual asset.

13. "Listen," your buddy says. "Have you ever noticed that you can get the same type and size of tire for $30 cheaper in the next county over? I've got a way to make profits for years—we'll buy the tires where they're cheaper and bring them back here to sell." What is the term for the transaction your friend wants to make? Would the efficient-market hypothesis predict it will be as profitable as he says? Explain. [LO 13.6]

14. In each of the following examples say whether the market is behaving within the principles of the efficient-market hypothesis. [LO 13.6]

    a. The day after unrest in the Middle East, the source of supply for much of the world's oil, the price of oil falls.

    b. Investors find very few opportunities for arbitrage in the foreign exchange market.

    c. The Dow Jones Industrial Average, a major stock market index, changes in value by 5 percent for an entire week, even though very little economic news is released.

15. In 2010, US government spending was $3.8 trillion, tax revenue was $4.5 trillion, GDP was $14.12 trillion, and total consumer spending was $10.5 trillion. If the economy has no exports or imports, what was the national savings in 2010? How much was public savings? How much was private savings? [LO 13.7]

16. Consider the Canadian market for loanable funds in a closed-economy model. Answer the following questions about each scenario. [LO 13.2], [LO 13.7]

    a. The government starts offering a national savings bond to increase private savings, which pays a higher return than many other options available on the market. Which way will the supply-of-loanable-funds curve shift? Will the interest rate increase or decrease? Will there be more or less borrowing?

    b. Suppose the economy is now open. Due to rapid economic expansion in China, the Chinese government decides to invest in Canadian Treasury notes with some of its surplus. Which way will the supply curve shift?

    c. A new computer software program is introduced into the market, which offers businesses that purchase it promising returns on their investment. Which curve will shift? Which way will it shift?

    d. The government reduces the capital gains tax, which taxes earnings on assets in the stock market. Which curve will shift? Which way will it shift?

Chapter Source

Jeremy Siegel, *Stocks for the Long Run: The Definitive Guide to Financial Market Returns and Long-Term Investment Strategies,* 4th ed. (New York: McGraw-Hill, 2012).

CHAPTER 14

Money and the Monetary System

Cigarette Money

During World War II, millions of soldiers were captured and sent to prisoner-of-war (POW) camps. With no formal currency and little connection with the outside economy, the camps initially functioned with little more than an internal trading system: if a soldier had an extra bar of soap and really wanted a tin of salmon, he would have to find someone who had a spare tin of salmon and really wanted a bar of soap. Finding these kinds of trading possibilities sometimes worked, but it was time-consuming and inefficient.

Eventually a solution evolved. Prisoners began to use cigarettes as a common currency and a simple system of exchange with standardized prices developed: tins of food could be bought for a set quantity of cigarettes, soap for another quantity.

Why did the prisoners start using cigarettes as money? To start with, they were a lot easier to carry around than bars of soap or tins of salmon. Unlike food, cigarettes didn't spoil. And there was a fairly stable supply. Cigarettes came into the camps in shipments of food and other supplies from the Red Cross humanitarian agency and were distributed among the prisoners.

Hulton Archive/Getty Images

Sometimes, though, there would be a sudden influx of cigarettes—say, if the Red Cross managed to send an extra shipment one week. Soldiers, flush with cigarettes, would go on spending sprees, outbidding each other to get the things they wanted and sending prices skyrocketing. Soldiers would then need a lot more cigarettes to buy a bar of soap.

If the Red Cross missed a few shipments, though, there would be a steady decrease in the number of cigarettes in circulation, since prisoners smoked them, too. Prices plummeted and overall economic activity fell as trading slowed to a halt. Why would this happen? The reason is obvious if you think about it. With fewer and fewer cigarettes in circulation, and uncertainty about when the next shipment might arrive, cigarettes would become increasingly rare and valuable. This gave prisoners greater incentive to hoard rather than spend their cigarettes.

This unique system of money and trade was described by a British officer named R.A. Radford, who was captured by the Nazis and sent to a series of prisoner-of-war camps, where he remained until his rescue by Allied forces. After his return to Great Britain in 1945, Radford wrote a now-classic paper, "The Economic Organisation of a P.O.W. Camp." His paper showed that money—in whatever form it might take—is an intrinsic part of any economic system.

The challenges that made World War II prisoners adopt cigarettes as their currency are the same as those faced in any economy. What is money? What functions does it serve and what problems does it solve? What makes a particular item (such as cigarettes) a good or bad choice for use as money? How does the supply of money influence the broader economy, and who controls the supply?

In this chapter, we'll see how and why money works in the economy. And we'll show how the tools of economics are being used to make sure the dollar in your pocket keeps its value.

What Is Money?

We all have an intuitive grasp of what money is—we use it every day. But what is it that separates the cash we hold in our hands from any of the other items we own that have value? Economies used to work on a barter system in which one person could trade a few eggs from her chicken for some milk from a neighbour's cow. Why did civilization long ago abandon that system for one based on the exchange of small pieces of precious metal? And how did sheets of printed paper come to substitute for that shiny metal and then give way to records kept in a bank's computer? To answer these questions, we'll need a more formal understanding of the concept of money and the function it plays in society.

Functions of Money

LO 14.1 Describe the three main functions of money.

How much money do you have? When asked that question, you might answer by counting the cash in your wallet and maybe the balance of your bank account. You also might count the total value of any stocks, bonds, real estate, or any other assets you may be fortunate enough to own. By most definitions, money consists only of what you typically use to buy something—which includes the cash in your wallet and the balance in your bank account, but no stocks, bonds, real estate, or any other asset. More precisely, **money** is the set of all assets that are regularly used to directly purchase goods and services.

Money typically serves three major functions: it is a *store of value,* a *medium of exchange,* and a *unit of account.*

A Store of Value

We say that money is a **store of value** because it represents a certain amount of purchasing power that money retains over time. To have $100 or $1,000 or $1 million is to have the ability to acquire a certain quantity of goods. Money stores value in the sense that if you put a $100 bill in a safe, you can expect to be able to purchase roughly $100 worth of goods when you take the bill out, whenever that is. The value won't be absolutely the same, of course—we'll learn more shortly about how changes in prices create changes in the value of money—but holding money is nearly always the most convenient way to hold onto wealth over time. (If, by contrast, you stored all your wealth in apples, you would lose most of that wealth as the fruit spoiled.)

A Medium of Exchange

Of course, items other than money—such as stocks and land—also generally store value pretty well. So we need to add to our list of money's functions its role as a **medium of exchange**—you can use it to purchase goods and services. That is, you can make a transaction by exchanging your money for the goods or services you want to buy.

First, imagine a world without money, where the only way to acquire something you wanted would be to engage in **barter**—to directly offer a good or service (maybe your jacket or bike, or maybe the value of your labour) in exchange for some good or service you want. The reason barter is extremely inefficient is that you have to find someone who both has what you want and wants what you have.

Now add money to the world. Money makes life much easier because you need only find someone who wants what you have (say, your labour). You accept money in exchange for the labour because you are confident that, once you have money, the person who has what you want (say, groceries) will also, in turn, accept that money in exchange. There's no longer any need to find one person who fits both requirements.

Not surprisingly, an economy that uses money is dramatically more efficient than a society based on directly trading one good for another, since using money reduces transaction costs immeasurably. Without money people and firms would have to search constantly for mutually agreeable trades.

A Unit of Account

The final role of money is also important, though it is easily overlooked: Money provides a common **unit of account**—a standard unit of comparison. Imagine that you live in an economy without money and have to choose between two competing job offers: a farmer offers to pay you twelve big crates of eggs a week, and a shoemaker offers a pair of fine leather shoes as your weekly wage. Which is the better option? It's hard to tell. But if one offered you $300 a week and the other offered you $400 for the same amount of work, you could easily compare the offers. By giving us a standard unit of comparison, money allows us to make more informed decisions.

What Makes for Good Money?

> LO 14.2 Describe the characteristics that make something a good choice as money.

Now that we understand the functions played by money, we can ask a related question: What makes for good money? Economists differ on the exact answer, but two basic considerations offer a good starting point. Something makes for good money if it has *stability of value* and *convenience.*

Stability of Value

We saw the importance of stability in our chapter opening example, in which prisoners used cigarettes as a form of money. As long as shipments arrived predictably from the Red Cross, the value of a cigarette remained fairly stable. If there was either a sudden influx or a prolonged shortage of cigarettes, the functioning of the camp economy was disrupted.

Like cigarettes in the POW camp, the earliest forms of money were chosen primarily because they offered stability of value. These early versions of money generally took the form of a physical material that was durable and had *intrinsic value,* or value unrelated to its use as money. Goods that have intrinsic value will keep a more steady value; even if their value as money falls, the good is still useful to people for other reasons.

Gold is the traditional example of a good that has frequently been used as money due to its intrinsic value and stability of value. Its supply is relatively fixed. Of course, new supplies are dug out of the ground all the time, but usually in fairly small quantities relative to the total amount in existence. It is also durable. Gold coins made thousands of years ago are still being discovered intact today. In addition, gold has many uses outside of money. In early societies (and today) gold has intrinsic value because people like wearing it as shiny jewellery. The cigarettes in the chapter opener also had intrinsic value. After all, the reason the cigarettes were being shipped to the POW camp in the first place was that many soldiers smoked.

There is no reason, though, why money needs to have intrinsic value. A bank note has practically no intrinsic value. People don't typically eat it, or smoke it, or wear it as a necklace. We accept bank notes because we know that everyone else values them, too. Wide acceptance comes largely from the fact that dollars have stable value. This wasn't always the case. In the early days in Canada, there was no universal Canadian dollar; banks in each province produced their own currencies. It was not until 1867, under the *Dominion Notes Act*, that Dominion notes replaced the various provincial note issues. In 1935 Canada started phasing out the Dominion notes and replaced them with the new Bank of Canada notes for the entire country. This was a crucial decision in Canadian economic history.

Convenience

Why did we go from gold coins to bank notes? Paper money is more *convenient*. Compared to paper money, gold coins are heavy and hard to use for small purchases. A solid gold coin weighing just one ounce was worth over $1,200 at the time of this writing, making it hard to use to pay for a pack of gum or a bus fare.

Ultimately, as time goes on, technology allows for the development of more convenient forms of money. For an ingenious example of making money even more convenient in the developing world, read the Real Life box, Banking with a Cell Phone.

REAL LIFE

Banking with a Cell Phone

Imagine you grew up in a small village in rural Kenya and moved to the capital city to find work. You want to send money back to your village to support your family, but how do you do it? Your village does not have a bank branch—the nearest is hours away. You could take a wad of banknotes back to the village yourself, but that would involve a long day's travel on a crowded bus. Or you could entrust the money to someone else who is travelling back to your village, but what if no one's going soon?

A Kenyan mobile phone company called Safaricom came up with a solution to this problem. It's called M-Pesa—the M stands for mobile, while *pesa* is the local word for money. The system allows people to transfer money simply by sending a text message.

The process is amazingly simple. You go to an M-Pesa outlet (a small store usually located in the village marketplace) and deposit money into an account. This becomes your *e-float,* essentially an electronic representation of money. In this way, it's not all that different from the deposits at a traditional bank. You can then use a text message to transfer, say, $15 worth of your e-float to another M-Pesa user's account, which costs a small fee. The recipient then goes to the local M-Pesa outlet and withdraws the e-float as cash, paying another small fee.

With this ease of use, and the fact that M-Pesa outlets outnumber bank branches five to one, M-Pesa quickly became wildly popular. In its first five years of operation, M-Pesa reached 17 million subscribers—over 40 percent of Kenya's adult population. Annual transfers were equal to about 10 percent of Kenyan GDP. Three-quarters of M-Pesa members say they use their e-float accounts not just to transfer money but also to save money: it's safer than carrying cash around and much more accessible than a traditional bank account. Safaricom has now introduced a product called M-Schwari that includes interest-paying savings accounts and greatly expands access to banking services in rural areas.

The system hasn't eliminated the need for cash, since not everyone uses M-Pesa. Also, since there are small fees involved in sending money, sometimes it's better to use cash.

M-Pesa shows how new technologies can connect underserved areas and change the concept of money. Inspired by the success in Kenya, companies in over eighty countries—including the US—are developing similar mobile banking systems.

Sources: http://siteresources.worldbank.org/AFRICAEXT/Resources/258643-1271798012256/M-PESA_Kenya.pdf; http://www.bbc.co.uk/news/business-11793290; http://www.safaricom.co.ke/personal/m-pesa/m-shwari.

Commodity-Backed Money versus Fiat Money

The earliest forms of paper money could be converted at a bank into a specified amount of a named commodity.

Commodity-backed money is any form of money—usually paper money—that can be legally exchanged for a fixed amount of an underlying commodity, generally gold.

Canada had a long history in commodity-backed money. Since the early days of provincial notes (and eventually Dominion notes and Bank of Canada notes), our money was backed partially by gold (20 percent for the first $5 million to 25 percent for the next $3 million). By 1913, any issue that exceeded $30 million had to be fully backed by gold. Anyone who held Dominion notes could simply go to a bank and exchange them for a fixed amount of gold.

The gold standard was suspended at the beginning of the World War I with the expectation that, after the war, it would return. This return proved to be short-lived. The weakness of the Canadian dollar in the late 1920s and the export of gold set the stage for Canada to exit the gold standard in 1933 (the UK abandoned their gold standard in 1931).

If the Canadian dollar is no longer backed by the value of a commodity like gold, where does its value come from? What is it backed by? Well, it's backed by nothing—nothing tangible, at least. Instead, the Canadian dollar today is backed by "the full faith and credit of the Canadian government." In other words, the Canadian dollar has value only to the extent that people trust the Canadian government to keep using dollars and to keep their value roughly constant. The formal term for this type of money is **fiat money**. Fiat money is money created by rule, without any commodity to back it. (*Fiat* is a Latin term that roughly translates to "it shall be.")

When we say "to the extent that people trust the Canadian government," what exactly are the Canadians trusting it to do or not do? Essentially, they're trusting the government to maintain a reliable system of money—in short, to not create lots of new money. Creating lots of new money would reduce the value of existing money—just as, in our chapter opening example, an unexpectedly large shipment of cigarettes into the POW camp reduced the value of existing cigarettes.

Some people don't like the idea of trusting the government to manage the quantity of money responsibly. They advocate for a return to commodity-backed money, like we had under the gold standard. The What Do You Think? box, Back to the Gold Standard? addresses the arguments for and against.

WHAT DO YOU THINK?

Back to the Gold Standard?

From time to time, people call for Canada to return to the gold standard. For example, Eric Sprott, from Sprott Asset Management, is an advocate of a return to the gold standard. Many economists, however, think this is a bad idea. No major country in the world currently ties its currency to gold or any other commodity.

The arguments in favor of the gold standard boil down to a simple question: Would we rather place our trust in time-tested gold instead of governments composed of fallible politicians? Put that way, the issue seems simple—but there's more to consider.

✓ CONCEPT CHECK

☐ What kind of exchange happens when people trade goods without using money? [LO 14.1]
☐ How are cigarettes a good example of commodity-backed money? [LO 14.2]
☐ What kind of money is the Canadian dollar? What kind was it 100 years ago? [LO 14.2]

Banks and the Money-Creation Process

Earlier, we discussed how using actual gold coins in payment was eventually replaced by paper money that was backed by gold. We considered one obvious advantage of this: it's easier to carry around a piece of paper that says "ten gold coins" than it is to carry around ten gold coins. Here's another, less obvious, implication. Paper money made it possible for banks to *create money*, through a process called *fractional-reserve banking*. This is one of the most important, yet intuitively challenging, facts about our modern financial system. It's worth taking some time to make sure you understand it.

"Creating" Money

LO 14.3 Explain the concept of fractional-reserve banking and the money multiplier.

The easiest way to understand how banks create money is to picture an economy making the transition from gold coins to paper money. To start with, imagine that you live in ancient times and all transactions are carried out using actual gold coins. How much money exists in the economy? That's an easy question to answer—it's simply the amount of gold.

Next, imagine that banking is invented, and now you're offered the chance to store your gold coins so you don't have to carry them around. When you deposit a gold coin in the bank, the bank gives you a piece of paper (a banknote) saying "one gold coin." At any time, you could go to the bank, give the bank back this piece of paper, and get a gold coin. But you don't need to do this, because merchants are happy to accept the banknote instead of the gold coin. They know that the note is as good as the coin itself; at any point they could take the note to the bank to get a coin. And people find it so much more convenient to use notes than lug heavy gold coins around.

Now put yourself in the bank's shoes. As a banker, you observe that on any given day, out of the 1,000 coins that are in your bank vault, people come in and ask for only 100 of them. Since the other 900 are just sitting there doing nothing, why not lend them out, charge an interest rate on these loans, and make a profit? So, you decide to lend out the other 900 coins to people who want to use them to buy things—say, to pay construction workers to build a house. When the workers receive their coins as wages, the workers all decide to deposit them in the bank for safekeeping. For every coin they deposit, the bank gives them a piece of paper saying "one gold coin."

How much money is in the economy now? As Figure 14-1 shows, the bank again has 1,000 gold coins (the 10 percent on reserve plus the 900 more that were loaned out and then deposited by the borrowers). But it has now issued 1,900 banknotes saying "one gold coin." Because people are just as happy to trade banknotes as they are actual gold coins—and, thus, we can meaningfully consider the banknotes to be *money*—we can say that by making loans, the bank has *created money*. It has created 900 gold coins' worth of money, to be exact.

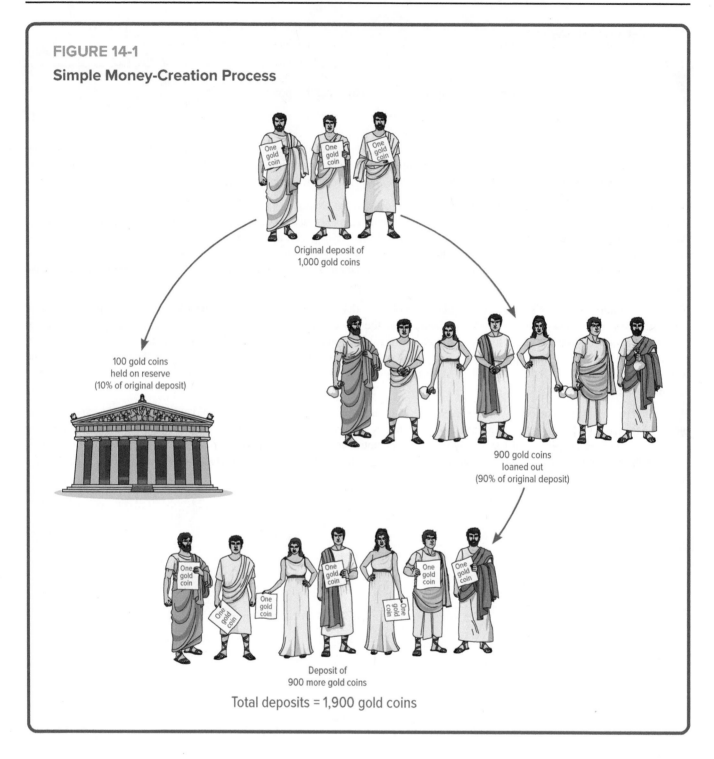

FIGURE 14-1

Simple Money-Creation Process

Original deposit of
1,000 gold coins

100 gold coins
held on reserve
(10% of original deposit)

900 gold coins
loaned out
(90% of original deposit)

Deposit of
900 more gold coins

Total deposits = 1,900 gold coins

How does the money-creation process work in today's economy? Let's work through another simple example with the aid of some basic accounting tools.

Money Creation in Today's Economy

Let's say that you walk into a bank with $1,000 in cash, and you make a deposit. The bank takes your cash, puts it in a vault, and adds $1,000 to your account balance.

Now the bank has $1,000 in cash. That $1,000 is an *asset* (a resource the bank possesses). But the bank also has a *liability* (an amount it owes): it owes you $1,000, and has promised that you can get your cash back any time you want. The fact that you can get your $1,000 back any time you demand it is why such deposits are called **demand deposits**—funds held in bank accounts that can be withdrawn (demanded) by depositors at any time without advance notice.

The primary way that banks earn money is through lending funds and collecting interest on those loans. So the bank wants to lend out as much of your $1,000 deposit as it (safely) can. As we saw in the example of the gold-coin bank, it's not necessary to keep on hand the total amount of the demand deposits. Instead, the bank decides to keep a certain amount on hand and to lend the rest.

We call the cash that a bank keeps in its vault its **reserves**. In practice, modern banks keep reserves either as cash or as deposits at the Bank of Canada, the central bank of Canada. As before, lending funds enables banks to "create" money. Currently, commercial banks are no longer required to hold a certain amount of reserves with the Bank of Canada. The ratio of the total amount of demand deposits at a bank to the amount kept as cash reserves is known as the **reserve ratio**. We'll assume throughout our discussion that the bank keeps a reserve ratio of 10 percent. The amount that the bank is desired to keep on hand is called the **desired reserves**. Any additional amount, beyond the desired reserves, the bank chooses to keep in reserve is called **excess reserves**. As with the earlier gold-coin example, banks "create" money by lending funds not kept as reserves.

The easiest way to visualize the bank's transactions is by means of a simple accounting tool called a *T-account*. We can use the T-account format to record how the bank's assets and liabilities change as a result of its transactions.[1] Panel A of Figure 14-2 shows, in T-account form, what happens to the bank's assets and liabilities when you make a $1,000 deposit. The left-hand side of the T-account for the bank shows the bank's assets—in this case, the $1,000 cash deposit. The right-hand side of the T-account shows the amounts owed—in this case, the demand deposits of $1,000.

Now let's see what happens when a new customer comes into the bank wanting to *borrow* $900—say, to purchase a new refrigerator. The banker takes $900 in cash out of the vault and hands the money over to the customer as a $900 loan. Panel B of Figure 14-2 shows the bank's new situation. Because the loan is an asset for the bank, the bank still has $1,000 in assets: $100 in desired cash reserves plus the loan of $900. The assets and liabilities both still total $1,000, though the composition of the assets has changed.

Here's where it gets interesting. The appliance store sells the refrigerator and gets paid $900 in cash. The store owner goes to the bank and deposits that amount in the store's account. Panel C of Figure 14-2 shows the bank's position now. It now has the following assets: a loan of $900, the new cash deposit of $900, and the $100 desired cash reserve, for a total of $1,900.

The bank has less actual cash on hand ($900 + $100) than the total of its deposits ($1,900). Is this reckless on the bank's part? Not if you remember the thinking of our ancient bank that stored gold coins. Observing that only a small number of customers wanted to convert banknotes into coins on any given day, it was happy to keep only 10 percent of its coins in its vault and lend out the rest. In the same way, modern banks count on the fact that not all of their customers will try to withdraw cash at the same time.

Let's say our modern bank keeps in its vault as desired cash reserves 10 percent of what its customers have deposited. Experience indicates that that amount will be enough to cover day-to-day requests from its depositors for cash withdrawals. With $1,900 in liabilities ($1,000 in the original deposit and the store owner's deposit of $900), the bank will now want to keep $190 desired cash reserves in the vault (10 percent of $1,900). That means it will be happy to lend money up to $1,710 (90 percent of $1,900).

The bank has already made loans of $900 and now lends another $810 to another customer, in order to have lent a total of $1,710. This new situation is shown in panel D of Figure 14-2.

FIGURE 14-2

How Banks Create Money

(A) Original deposit

Assets		Liabilities	
Cash:	$1,000	Deposit:	$1,000

(B) Bank makes its first loan

Assets		Liabilities	
Loan:	$900	Deposit:	$1,000
Desired reserves:	$100		

(C) The loan is deposited in the bank

Assets		Liabilities	
Loan:	$900	Deposit:	$1,900
New cash deposit:	$900		
Desired reserves:	$100		

(D) The bank loans out 90% of its new deposits

Assets		Liabilities	
Loans:	$1,710	Deposit:	$1,900
Desired reserves:	$190		

As the money comes in to the bank and then is lent out again, new money is created. In this example, by the time the money is lent out twice, the bank has created $1,900 from $1,000.

How far can this process continue? The bank will continue lending and taking deposits. Over time, the bank can end up creating as much as $9,000 in new loans. Why $9,000? Your original deposit was $1,000, and the bank has to hold 10 percent of that (= $100) as desired cash reserves. It then lends the rest and eventually gets the loans back as deposits.

Those deposits, in turn, create new reserve requirements. By the time the bank has lent a total of $9,000, it can expect $9,000 in deposits—which creates a need for 10 percent of those deposits to be held as cash reserves, too (= $900). The total sum of desired cash reserves is thus $100 + $900. Thanks to your original $1,000 cash deposit, the bank has enough cash to cover that. But that's all the bank has in cash, so it can't lend more. With $9,000 in loans and $1,000 in reserves, there is no money left for new loans. Still, your original $1,000 has had quite a run. The bank has used it to create $9,000 in new money, effectively turning $1,000 into $10,000.

From One Bank to an Entire Economy

So far, we have assumed that there's only one bank in the economy, so everyone has to use it to borrow and save. In practice, of course, there is more than one bank. Among the largest in Canada are CIBC, BMO, and the Royal Bank of Canada.

The logic of the example holds if we think of the bank in our example as representing the entire banking system. The first deposit might be made into CIBC, for example, and the next into BMO. The next might go to the Royal Bank. The key is that all money loaned out eventually gets put back into some bank within the banking system.

Let's round off our discussion with some formal terminology. We call the ratio of money created by the lending activities of the banking system to the money created by the government's central bank the **money multiplier**. In our example, the bank kept 10 percent of its deposits as reserves.

If the reserve ratio were 100 percent (a situation known as *full-reserve banking*), no lending would have happened in our example. Your entire original $1,000 deposit would just sit in the bank's vault. If banks aren't lending, it would be very hard to get the money needed to buy a house or car. The entire financial system would grind to a halt.

Rarely if ever do we observe full-reserve banking. Instead, we have **fractional-reserve banking**, a banking system in which banks keep on reserve less than 100 percent of their deposits. (That is, the reserve ratio is less than 100 percent.) Fractional-reserve banking allows the bank to lend out a portion of the money deposited in the bank. The size of the reserve determines the size of the money multiplier: As a simple approximation, we can calculate the money multiplier as 1/R, where R is the reserve ratio.

Equation 14-1

$$\text{Money multiplier} = \frac{1}{\text{reserve ratio}}$$

$$= \frac{1}{R}$$

Thus, a reserve ratio of 10 percent (or, equivalently, 0.10) means the money multiplier is 10:

$$\text{Money multiplier} = \frac{1}{0.10}$$

$$= 10$$

With $1,900 in liabilities ($1,000 in the original deposit and the store owner's deposit of $900), the bank will now want to keep $190 desired cash reserves in the vault (10 percent of $1,900). That means it will be happy to lend money up to the amount of $1,710 (90 percent of $1,900).

The bank has already made loans of $900 and now lends another $810 to another customer, in order to have lent a total of $1,710. You will notice the smaller the reserve ratio (R), the larger the money multiplier. Now, you may ask, what if a country like Canada (or the UK or Australia) has no reserve requirement (R approaches zero)? This will give a very large value of money multiplier, creating money without limit. The approximation in Equation 14-1 works as long as people don't hold any money as cash outside the bank, and banks lend out as much as they can beyond what's desired for them to hold as reserves.[2] If either assumption fails to hold, the multiplier will be smaller than the approximation. In addition, banks are also constrained by capital requirements, which are more functional than regulating reserve requirements.

Ultimately, the system of fractional reserve banking is what makes possible the existence of banks as we know them. However, you may be wondering if there are big risks involved. Is this a recipe for disaster? What if too many customers turn up at the bank asking for their dollar bills at the same time? A *bank run* occurs—the situation that arises from fear that the bank is in danger of running out of money. Read the Real Life box, Bank Runs and the Banking Holiday, for some real-life examples.

REAL LIFE

Bank Runs and the Banking Holiday

In 2007, hundreds of panicked customers lined up outside branches of the British bank Northern Rock in a desperate attempt to get money out of their accounts. Why did people suddenly lose faith in the bank that had been holding their money? The media had just reported that Northern Rock was heavily invested in nearly worthless loans and financial products that had been created during the US housing bubble. With heavy losses on these investments, the bank was near bankruptcy.

British banking regulations at the time offered some protection to savers: if Northern Rock went bust, customers would get most of their savings back from the government, up to a limit of £35,000 (about $55,000) each. But many customers decided they'd prefer to take their savings home in pound notes immediately rather than risk it. It was reported that about £2 billion in cash was withdrawn in just two days.

Bank runs are a problem because, under a fractional-reserve system, banks don't hold enough cash to pay out more than a small portion of their depositors' money. Ironically, a bank run can *create* the very thing customers are afraid of—the bank going bust—even if their fears are unfounded. If enough customers demand their deposits back all at once, a bank will inevitably go bankrupt, no matter its initial condition.

The most important response to a bank run, therefore, is to try to reassure savers and create time for their panic to subside. During the Great Depression, in March 1933, the governor of Michigan feared that one of the largest banks in the state, the Guardian Trust Company of Detroit, was on the edge of shutting down for good. In order to keep the bank from failing, the governor took the drastic measure of stopping transactions at all of the 800 banks in the state, leaving people to get by on only the cash they had in their pockets. Far from quelling the panic, though, this move sparked greater concern. Many reasoned that if the banks could be saved only by preventing all transactions, the entire system must be in danger of collapse.

Word of bank trouble spread throughout the country, and bank runs threatened to spiral out of control, destroying people's savings and crippling the economy. In response, Congress quickly passed what became known as the Bank Holiday, closing all banks in the country for four days (later stretched out to a week). Right before the banks were due to reopen, President Roosevelt talked to Americans through a radio broadcast (these were known as "fireside chats") and simply explained what was going on. Furthermore, the Federal Reserve pledged to supply unlimited currency to banks that reopened, so depositors essentially had 100 percent insurance on their deposits.

Amazingly, it worked. When the banks reopened, the panic had abated and Americans re-deposited two-thirds of the money they had drawn out in the bank runs. The outgrowth of this holiday was the creation of the Federal Deposit Insurance Commission (FDIC) through the *Glass-Steagall Act*, which reassured savers that if their bank failed the government would protect any deposit less than $100,000 (later changed to $250,000).

What happened to Northern Rock? After a second day of lines outside the bank's branches, the British government stepped in and announced that it would refund the entire value of customers' savings accounts if the bank went bust. The panic abated and Northern Rock lived to see another day. (However, it lost so much money in the US housing crash that the British government eventually had to take it over to keep it going.) These experiences remind us that bank runs—widely thought to have been consigned to the history books—can still happen in today's economy.

Sources: http://www.nber.org/papers/w12717; http://www.bos.frb.org/about/pubs/closed.pdf.

Measuring Money

> **LO 14.4** Describe M1 and M2.

Now that we know how money is created by the banking system, let's revisit our earlier question: How much money *is* there? If you are thinking to yourself, "That depends on what type of money you are asking about," you are exactly right. It is the job of the Bank of Canada to manage the **money supply**—the amount of money available in the economy—and it provides the most common definitions of the money supply. The Bank of Canada classifies different types of money by their *liquidity*—that is, by how easy an asset is to convert immediately to cash without losing value.

The narrowest definition of money includes the things that can be used in transactions *immediately*. It contains only two things: cash and bank reserves physically held at the Bank of Canada. (The Bank of Canada has complete control over these reserves and can ensure that they are instantly available as cash if necessary.) This definition of money is sometimes referred to as *monetary base.* In our discussion of the money multiplier, monetary base is what is being "multiplied" by the banking system, just as gold coins were in our initial example.

The Bank of Canada frequently uses two other broader definitions of money, known as M1 and M2:

- **M1** includes cash (*hard money*) plus chequing account balances (demand deposits, which are not exactly cash but are readily accessible for most people; this is also known as hard money).
- **M2** is broader still. M2 includes everything in M1 plus personal savings accounts and non-personal notice deposits where money is locked away for a specified period of time. Since these forms of savings can't be accessed quickly without penalty fees, they are slightly less liquid than other forms of money.

Both categories are legitimate measures of the money supply. Which one we use depends on our goals. If we want to look at spending (liquidity), we use M1. If we want to look at savings, we would use M2. You can think of M2 as a measure of the "multiplied" money. Comparing it to hard money can give you some sense of what the money multiplier actually is at a given point in time.

At this point, you might wonder who decides how much money is going to exist. Obviously, the banks play a large role in M1 and M2, but who decides how much hard money there is to multiply in the first place? And who sets the reserve ratios? We address these questions in the next section.

✓ CONCEPT CHECK

- ☐ What is a reserve requirement of 100 percent called? [LO 14.3]
- ☐ How does the money multiplier create money in the economy? [LO 14.3]
- ☐ What type(s) of money includes demand deposits (amounts in checking accounts)? [LO 14.4]

Managing the Money Supply: The Bank of Canada

Before the Great Depression of the 1930s, the federal government saw very little need for a central bank in Canada. Canada was mostly a rural economy and under British influence; the branch bank network worked relatively well to address the financial needs of the public and government.

After the Great Depression, Prime Minister R. B. Bennett directed a Royal Commission to study the arguments for and against the organization of a central banking institution. Shortly after the report was made public, the government adopted the recommendations and set up the Bank of Canada in 1935. Initially the Bank was set up as a privately held institution and it was not until 1938 that the federal government nationalized it. While the *Bank of Canada Act* has been amended many times since it was established, it has been the centralized institution responsible for coordinating the operations of the Canadian financial system.

The Role of the Central Bank

LO 14.5 Understand the role of the central bank.

Almost every major nation has a central bank. A **central bank** is the institution ultimately responsible for managing the nation's money supply and coordinating the banking system to ensure a sound economy. In Canada, the central bank is the Bank of Canada. Like any central bank, the Bank of Canada has four essential functions: being the sole issuer of Canada's bank notes, conducting monetary policy via managing the money supply, acting as the fiscal agent for the federal government, and acting as a lender of last resort.

Before we explain the four functions of a central bank, it may help to explain what a central bank is *not*. It is not a government department. In Canada, the financial operations of the government are conducted by the Department of Finance, while Revenue Canada is responsible for collecting taxes. In short, the Department of Finance executes *fiscal policy,* while the Bank of Canada conducts *monetary policy.* Formally, **monetary policy** consists of actions by the central bank to manage the money supply, in pursuit of certain macroeconomic goals.

So a central bank's most important function is to manage the money supply. A bit later, we'll learn more about the ways that the Bank of Canada does that. First, though, it's worth asking whether we, in fact, need a central bank to manage the money supply. Why not leave it to the private market to issue currency and control it? In principle, at least, there is no reason why a privately issued currency should not gain wide acceptance. For more about one attempt to create a new currency, see the From Another Angle box, Is Bitcoin the Currency of the Future?

FROM ANOTHER ANGLE

Is Bitcoin the Currency of the Future?

Some online communities have their own money: Farmville has "farm cash"; Second Life has "Linden dollars." Could virtual currencies ever take over from conventional currencies such as the dollar? In principle, it's a possibility. In practice, it's hard to imagine.

Think back to our discussion of what makes for good money. One of the most important features is stability of value. Why were people through the ages happy to store their wealth in gold? Because they thought it was unlikely that a huge new amount of gold would be discovered; such a discovery would slash the value of the gold they had. Why are people today happy to store their wealth in dollars? Because they are reasonably confident that the central bank will not suddenly decide to print trillions upon trillions of new dollar bills, thus rendering everyone's existing dollars nearly worthless.

Who has the power to "print" money in virtual worlds? Ultimately, it's the people who run those worlds. Would you really be happy to hold your life savings in a virtual currency, trusting that those in charge will never decide to create huge amounts of new money? Most of us wouldn't be so brave.

In 2009, a mysterious programmer using the fake name Satoshi Nakamoto created a new virtual currency—bitcoin—which proposed a solution to this problem: nobody is in charge of the bitcoin money supply. Instead, the supply of money increases at a rate predetermined by a mathematical algorithm.

In its early days, users of bitcoins were a small community of computer enthusiasts, and the value of a bitcoin was a tiny fraction of a cent. The first real-world purchase was made, for fun, by a Florida programmer named Laszlo Hanyecz, who paid 10,000 bitcoins to get two Papa John's pizzas delivered. (He transferred the bitcoins to another enthusiast, who paid in dollars.) But then bitcoins attracted the attention of the media, and speculators started to buy them. Their value took off, and by June 2011 the value of a bitcoin had soared to $27. The 10,000 bitcoins that Laszlo Hanyecz had paid for his pizza just a few months previously would have been worth over $270,000 at those prices. "I don't feel bad about it," he claims. "The pizza was really good."

With bitcoins worth so much, hackers started to look for ways to steal them out of users' accounts. In July 2011, an Internet site called Mt. Gox, which then handled 90 percent of all bitcoin transactions, was hacked. Other security scares followed, and one user reported that his $500,000 worth of bitcoins was stolen. The damage to the project's credibility saw the value of bitcoins fall to around $3 at one point. The currency has experienced big price fluctuations over time. Also, US regulators recently warned entities that exchange bitcoins to be aware of possible money-laundering activity using the currency.

Although the creator of bitcoin has disappeared without a trace, there are still plenty of enthusiasts for the bitcoin project working to bring the technology into the mainstream. Will the story of bitcoin eventually come to be seen as just the first chapter in how new currencies rendered central banks obsolete? Or will it be just another online idea that didn't live up to all the hype? The bitcoin saga shows that, even in the digital age, we still need to take seriously the very old problem of how to maintain stable, trustworthy currencies.

Sources: http://www.wired.com/magazine/2011/11/mf_bitcoin/all/1;
http://www.dailytech.com/Digital+Black+Friday+First+Bitcoin+Depression+Hits/article21877.htm;
http://www.economist.com/blogs/babbage/2011/06/virtual-currency.

Another role played by a central bank isn't strictly necessary, but it's certainly a very good idea: central banks can act as a *lender of last resort*. What does this mean? When nobody else is willing to lend to banks facing a bank run, the Bank of Canada can step in as the lender of last resort. The Bank becomes the last line of defense before an imminent financial collapse. These days, the Bank of Canada's job is to provide regulatory oversight of the clearing and settlement systems (one of the settlements is the large value transfer system).

Besides the above functions, the Bank of Canada is also responsible for issuing and distributing Canadian bank notes. Also, the Bank of Canada serves as a fiscal agent for the federal government. In other word, it acts as a government bank, managing the accounts for the Receiver General. It manages the government's foreign exchange reserves and the public debt via programs like Canada Savings Bonds.

How Does the Bank of Canada Work?

Now that we know what the role of a central bank is, let's look more closely at how the Bank of Canada—Canada's central bank—actually works. We will focus on two topics: the organizational structure of the Bank of Canada, and the key principles that guide the Bank in its policy-making.

How the Bank of Canada Is Organized

The Bank of Canada is managed by a board of directors. The board is composed of the governor, the senior deputy governor, and twelve independent directors, plus the deputy minister of finance (an ex officio non-voting member). At the time of writing, the governor is Stephen Poloz, who was appointed in 2013.

Since all the members of the board are appointed by the minister of finance, the Bank of Canada is controlled by the Canadian government. This structure is sometimes referred to as a subordinate central bank, as the government can issue directives to the governor with which he or she must comply.

In practice, however, you may notice that, for a governmental agency, the Bank of Canada has little connection with the rest of government. Though appointed by the government, the members of the board of directors enjoy the security of serving long terms (seven years for the governor and senior deputy governor, and three years for other directors), which helps them to be independent of politics. This is no accident. Politicians of all parties know the power of monetary policy. Giving the Bank of Canada a high degree of independence means that the members of the board will not be tempted by political pressure.

How the Bank of Canada Makes Policy

But what exactly does it mean to manage monetary policy for the benefit of the country? The objective of the Bank of Canada is "to preserve the value of money by keeping inflation low, stable and predictable."[3] In February 1991, the Bank and the federal government set out a path for inflation reduction (as measured by the CPI). The use of inflation targeting as a monetary policy framework provided a nominal anchor for monetary policy and helped to shape market expectations about future inflation. Currently the target is set at 2 percent. This is the midpoint of a 1 to 3 percent target range and is subject to review every five years. The target has been extended on five occasions to the end of 2016. The Bank sets an appropriate policy interest rate to guide the core inflation rate toward the target. The aim is to ensure a stable price environment over the medium term.

Tools of Monetary Policy

> LO 14.6 Explain the tools the Bank of Canada uses to conduct monetary policy.

To fulfill its inflation control target, the Bank of Canada manages the supply of money. In order to change the money supply, the Bank of Canada has a number of different options at its disposal. In this section, we'll walk through the three traditional ones to show how the Bank of Canada generally conducts business. These tools, from least to most commonly used are *reserve requirements, open-market operations,* and *changing the overnight rate.* Open-market operations and changing the overnight rate are the main tools of monetary policy; changing the reserve requirement is a backup tool, rarely used.

Reserve Requirement

The most powerful tool available to the central bank is its control of the **reserve requirement**—the regulation that sets the minimum fraction of deposits banks must hold in reserve. The tool can have far-reaching effects, so policy makers try to use it sparingly. You'll recall that the reserve ratio a bank maintains is one of several determinants of how much money is available in the economy and, by extension, how much lending occurs. If it wanted to, the central bank could even eliminate fractional-reserve banking altogether by mandating that banks hold 100 percent of their deposits in reserve, but that wouldn't be a very good idea.

Although changing the reserve requirement is a powerful tool, it is *too* powerful in most situations. Meaningfully controlling the money supply through reserve requirements would mean dramatically changing the amount of money banks are required to hold, an action almost certain to have significant and unpredictable consequences. Bank managers make their plans depending in part on a certain reserve requirement, so a rapid change in the requirement would make it harder for them to manage their money. Rapid change also would have ripple effects throughout the entire economy, affecting the availability of credit and confidence in the banking system. Despite this, some countries, most notably China, have used adjustments to the required reserve ratio as a primary tool of monetary policy (and have had mixed success). Canada abolished its reserve requirement in 1992. Think of changing the reserve requirement as a big shove; most of the time, monetary policy changes aim for more of a gentle push.

Open-Market Operations

Open-market operations are sales or purchases of government securities by the central bank to or from banks on the open (public) market. (The actual process is a bit more indirect than we'll present it here, but the ultimate end is the same: the central bank sells bonds to a bank or buys bonds from it.) These transactions directly result in an increase or decrease in the money supply.

When the central bank wants to increase the money supply, it can purchase a bond from one of the large banks it trades with (under the special purchase and resale agreement). The central bank pays for this purchase with reserves. Since the commercial bank now has more reserves, it can make more loans or buy more bonds, thereby creating money. On the other hand, if the central bank wants to decrease the money supply, it sells bonds, accepting reserves as payment. The central bank then effectively destroys the money it receives, which decreases the amount of money in existence.

Open-market operations have several advantages over other tools of monetary policy. First, the transactions—the buying and selling of bonds—take place on a daily basis. Since the central bank commonly wants to make small adjustments rather than sweeping changes in the economy, the frequency of these transactions adds to this tool's flexibility. The ability to act on a day-to-day basis helps maintain the central bank's reputation for steady, credible policy.

How exactly do open-market operations affect the larger economy? This tool works two ways. First, when the central bank sells bonds to a bank, the transaction is paid for with money that the bank keeps on deposit at the central bank. The sale thus reduces the bank's reserves. This in turn reduces the bank's ability to lend. Through the multiplier effect, the reduction in lending sets off a ripple effect with other banks' lending and slows down the growth rate of the money supply. This is an important way to conduct **contractionary monetary policy**—actions that reduce the money supply in order to decrease aggregate demand.

Or the central bank can buy government bonds to pursue **expansionary monetary policy**—actions that increase the money supply in order to increase aggregate demand. When the central bank buys bonds from a bank, it pays for those bonds by increasing the bank's deposit in the central bank, which increases the bank's reserves. The bank can then lend more and set off a ripple effect that increases other banks' lending. This is how the central bank can increase the growth rate of the money supply and pursue expansionary monetary policy.

The second way that open-market operations work is by affecting the overnight rate, the interest rate that banks charge when one bank makes a very short-term (usually overnight) loan of reserves to another bank. The Bank of Canada uses this rate as a target in open-market operations, pushing it upward by selling bonds and pushing it downward by buying bonds.

The Overnight Rate and Money Supply

The Bank of Canada rarely describes its policies in terms of changes in the money supply. Instead, it focuses on interest rates. Technically, the Bank of Canada announces a "target" for the **overnight rate** (eight times a year on fixed announcement dates)—the interest rate at which banks choose to lend reserves held at the Bank of Canada to one another, usually just overnight.

Banks choose to maintain a certain level of reserves. Thus, when a bank finds itself short at the end of the day, it may choose to make up the shortfall by borrowing from another bank that has excess reserves. Since both banks have an account with the Bank of Canada, it is easy and safe to borrow money this way.

How does the Bank of Canada affect the overnight rate? In contractionary policy, as we saw, the Bank of Canada sells bonds, taking reserves from banks as payment. This decrease in the supply of reserves pushes the overnight rate upward. Why? By reducing the supply of reserves, the price of borrowing reserves rises, just as in the standard analysis of supply and demand in a market for goods. Other interest rates move in the same direction as the overnight rate, so interest rates rise in general, discouraging spending on houses, cars, new machinery, and other things. Raising the overnight rate thus helps meet the goal of contractionary policy—which is to slow the economy down. A similar chain of logic applies to expansionary policy, in which the goal is to reduce interest rates to stimulate the economy.

These three tools comprise the traditional strategies of the Bank of Canada; we'll discuss examples of more unorthodox techniques used by other central banks in the "Financial Crisis" chapter. These innovations were used in the recent financial crisis to help shore up the entire financial system.

The Economic Effects of Monetary Policy

To understand why the Bank of Canada's control over the money supply is so powerful, we need a better understanding of the mechanism by which monetary policy affects the economy. Some economists, known as *monetarists,* argue that over the long run monetary policy is irrelevant because prices will adjust to a high or low supply of money without any change in overall economic output. (Consequently, monetarists say that "money is neutral.") However, most economists agree that in the short run, at least, the Bank of Canada's control over monetary policy allows it to combat recessions and cool an overheating economy. But how does this mechanism work?

Monetary policy primarily influences the economy through changes in the interest rate. Changes in the interest rate, in turn, affect the appeal of borrowing and lending, which can have significant effects on the economy. In this section, we'll walk through the connections in this process as well as some of the challenges of implementing monetary policy.

Interest Rates and Monetary Policy: The Liquidity-Preference Model

LO 14.7 Understand how monetary policy affects the prevailing interest rate and supply of money.

When the central bank increases or decreases the money supply, it changes the balance of money supplied versus money demanded. If the words *supply* and *demand* make you think about money in a market as depicted in the supply–demand graphs we've used so far, you're on the right track.

To understand how the relationships work, we first describe the nature of supply and demand using an idea, originally proposed by economist John Maynard Keynes in 1936, called the *liquidity-preference model.*

The Demand for Money

Economists use the term *liquid* to describe the ease of turning assets into cash. Cash is highly liquid by definition, and chequing accounts are nearly as liquid as cash. We need cash and easy-to-access bank accounts to be able to meet our daily spending needs. In other words, we have a preference for liquidity.

Government bonds, in contrast, are not very liquid. They have to be sold in order to generate cash for spending. Of course, government bonds have an important advantage over cash: they earn interest. The plus of interest is weighed against the minus of not being very liquid.

So, when the interest rate earned on government bonds is high, most people will try to hold more bonds and less cash. And when the interest rate on bonds falls, the advantage of bonds is reduced, making cash relatively more attractive. When you don't earn much interest on bonds, you may as well hold your money in cash and other liquid forms. This relationship is the central idea of the **liquidity-preference model**, which explains that the quantity of money people want to hold is a function of the interest rate. In this model, the money demand curve slopes downward, showing a negative relationship between the interest rate and how much money is demanded. Why? Think of *money* here as cash—specifically, cash as opposed to other assets, such as bonds that pay interest. (No matter how high interest rates are, though, you'll still have to hold onto some money to complete day-to-day transactions.)

On the whole, this means that people aren't going to demand much money when interest rates are high, but will demand more and more as interest rates decrease. A change in the quantity of money demanded in response to a change in the interest rate is represented by movement along the money demand curve. When the interest rate rises, we demand a lower quantity of money, moving leftward along the curve; when the interest rate falls we demand a high quantity, moving rightward.

Not all changes come about from movement along the demand curve. Some factors instead cause the demand curve itself to shift. The price level in the economy is one such factor. The demand for money in Canada is much higher today than it was fifty years ago, for the simple reason that almost everything is far more expensive today than it was then. Higher prices mean a greater need for money to meet the everyday needs of life, and that means more money demanded at every level of the interest rate. This increase in demand is represented by shifting the money demand curve to the right.

Increases in real GDP have a similar effect on money demand: more goods and services being sold means more money is needed to purchase them. Of course, decreases in real GDP would have the opposite effect. With less activity going on in the economy, less money will be needed. In addition to these economic factors, technological advancements can also play a role. Easier use of credit cards and greater availability of ATMs, for instance, reduce the demand for money. With these tools, people need to carry around far less cash in their wallets at any given time in order to make day-to-day purchases.

Money Supply

In the simple version of the liquidity-preference model, the supply of money is considered to be set only by the central bank: regardless of the interest rate, the central bank will ensure that there is a constant quantity of money supplied in the economy. As Figure 14-3 shows, this means that the money supply curve can be represented as a vertical line in the liquidity-preference model. It also means that the only way the supply of money can change is when the central bank changes it for policy reasons.

Figure 14-3 shows the basic relationship between money supply and money demand in the liquidity-preference model. The point where the supply of money meets the demand for money will determine the *nominal interest rate,* or stated price of money in the economy.

While this simple model assumes that the central bank has complete control over the supply curve, in reality an economy's money supply comes from a variety of sources. As the model currently stands, the central bank dictates the supply of cash and bank reserves it holds, and banks decide how much money is eventually created from deposits, through the money multiplier. As we'll see later, the central bank's ability to target the money supply and interest rates is not nearly as precise as this model suggests. Still, the assumption of a fixed money supply controlled by the central bank is useful for introducing the model.

Earlier, we discussed the ways that the central bank can adjust the money supply, which can be represented by shifts in the money supply curve. Any actions that increase the money supply will shift the money supply curve to the right. These actions include decreasing the reserve requirement, decreasing the overnight rate, or buying government bonds on the open market. In contrast, any actions that decrease the money supply will shift this curve left. As you can see in Figure 14-4, changes in the money supply increase or decrease interest rates.

FIGURE 14-3

The Liquidity-Preference Model

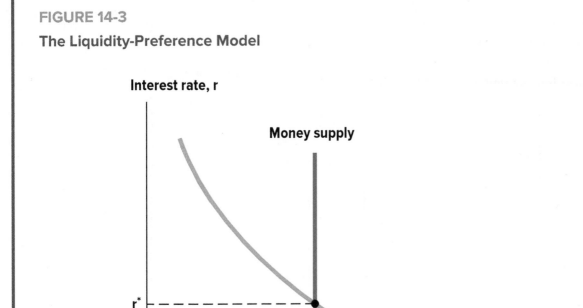

The liquidity-preference model shows the basic relationship between money supply and money demand. In this model we assume that the money supply is completely fixed by the Bank of Canada. The money demand curve slopes downward as a function of the interest rate. With high interest rates, people demand a small quantity of money, but as interest rates decrease, people demand more.

Knowing the slope of the money demand curve is important. The slope of the demand curve determines how a change in the money supply will change the interest rate. If the quantity of money demanded is really responsive to changes to the interest rate (a flat, elastic demand curve), changes to the money supply will have a smaller effect on interest rates than if demand is less responsive (steeper, more inelastic).

FIGURE 14-4

Shifts in the Money Supply Curve

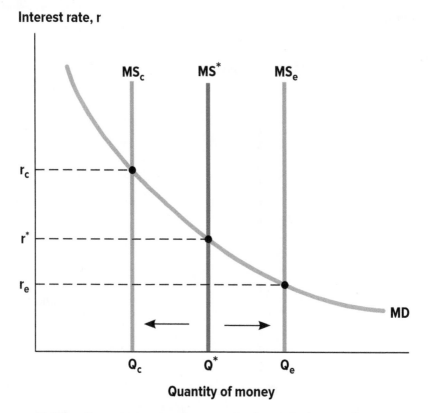

Shifting the money supply curve to the right (expanding the money supply) is called expansionary monetary policy (denoted with an e). The result is a greater amount of money in the economy, at lower interest rates. Shifting the curve to the left is called contractionary monetary policy (denoted with a c) and represents a decrease in the money supply. The result is less money in the economy, at higher interest rates.

Interest Rates and the Economy

LO 14.8 Explain how expansionary and contractionary monetary policy influence the broader economy.

The liquidity-preference model explains how the central bank's actions can change interest rates. The central bank can cause interest rates to fall by increasing the money supply, or it can cause interest rates to rise by decreasing the money supply. But why does the central bank care about the interest rate? The answer is that the interest rate has important effects in the economy. Many of the large purchases we make—buying a house, a car, or an expensive appliance—are made using money we've borrowed. Likewise, corporations borrowing to make investments must also pay the price dictated by the interest rate.

Expansionary Monetary Policy

Changes in interest rates affect aggregate demand and supply in an economy. Consumption increases when more people buy big-ticket items after a decrease in interest rates. Lower interest rates make it cheaper to borrow money and less rewarding to save money. People will spend instead, further increasing the consumption part of aggregate demand.

Monetary policy is thus an important way for policy makers to respond to changes in the health of the economy. For an example, let's say that the economy is in a recession. Aggregate demand is low and the economy is in a short-run equilibrium marked by sluggish output and lower prices. The central bank knows that lower interest rates would spur increased borrowing and spending—shifting the aggregate demand curve to the right. The Bank of Canada announces that it will lower the target for overnight rate. So the Bank of Canada conducts open-market operations to increase the supply of money in the economy. This action is called *expansionary monetary policy*. As you can see in panel A of Figure 14-5, lower interest rates are the result of this action.

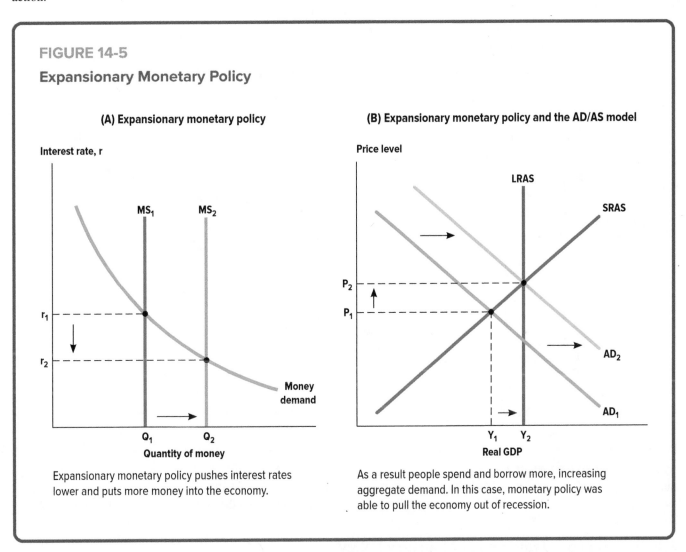

FIGURE 14-5

Expansionary Monetary Policy

(A) Expansionary monetary policy

Expansionary monetary policy pushes interest rates lower and puts more money into the economy.

(B) Expansionary monetary policy and the AD/AS model

As a result people spend and borrow more, increasing aggregate demand. In this case, monetary policy was able to pull the economy out of recession.

As described above, lower interest rates spur borrowing and spending, and discourage saving. With increases in consumption spending and investment, aggregate demand increases. The aggregate demand curve shifts to the right as shown in panel B of Figure 14-5. Ultimately the effect is the same as that of the expansionary fiscal policy we discussed in Chapter 13, "The Basics of Finance." Both prices and output increase, taking the bite out of the recession.

Contractionary Monetary Policy

Conversely, what should the Bank of Canada do when the economy is booming? Since the system was flush with cash, the aggregate demand curve was far to the right and price levels were high. Output was also high, which made the decision of what needed to be done in this situation slightly tougher.

On the one hand, strong economic activity is obviously a good thing. On the other hand, it is possible for an economy to be operating beyond its means. When short-run output moves above long-run equilibrium, the price level will inevitably increase. Such increases in the price level are contrary to the central bank's desire to maintain stable price levels. We'll go into this responsibility in more depth in the "Inflation" chapter, but for now, let's say that the Bank of Canada would be worried that these rising price levels might begin to adversely affect the economy.

When the Bank of Canada decides that the economy is a little too active—economists often call this *overheating*—it often moves to increase interest rates. This increase in interest rates shifts the aggregate demand curve leftward, leading to lower prices and equilibrium output in the short run. That result, shown in panel B of Figure 14-6, is the effect of a contractionary monetary policy, shown in panel A of the same figure.

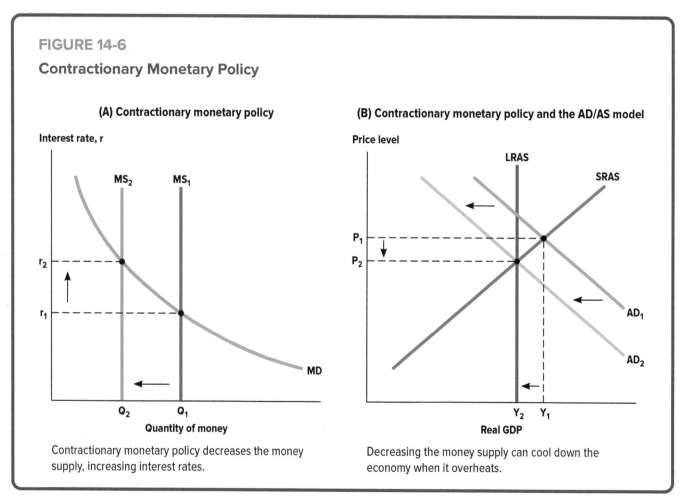

FIGURE 14-6

Contractionary Monetary Policy

(A) Contractionary monetary policy

Contractionary monetary policy decreases the money supply, increasing interest rates.

(B) Contractionary monetary policy and the AD/AS model

Decreasing the money supply can cool down the economy when it overheats.

You'll note that we left both of these examples in the short run. In the long run, the economy will adjust to changes in the money supply, leaving only changes in the overall price level. This fact leads to one of the challenges facing the Bank of Canada: how to maintain stable price levels while also ensuring full employment. As you'll see in the "Inflation" chapter, these two goals are often in fundamental conflict.

Challenges and Advantages of Monetary Policy

The above examples of the use of monetary policy show how policy can work in ideal cases, but it is rare for the world to work so cleanly. When we discussed fiscal policy, we noted that policy makers face practical challenges, such as time lags and imperfect information, when they try to make policy. The central bank faces the same problems as it seeks to steer the economy using monetary policy.

Although monetary policy usually does not take as long to implement as fiscal policy, a few months can pass before the central bank's actions start to have their desired impact. By that time the state of the economy might have changed. A boost in the money supply could push the economy past the level of long-run equilibrium output, for example, and cause the economy to overheat. Even worse, the central bank could inadvertently contract the money supply just as the economy starts sliding into a recession. This mistiming of policy would make the ensuing recession even worse.

Even so, monetary policy does have advantages compared to traditional fiscal policy. The central bank does not have to wait for squabbling politicians to come to a consensus about the best policy to help the economy. Instead, the board of directors and the governing council, if necessary, can change monetary policy immediately. In addition, the Bank of Canada is made up of prominent economic policy makers whose job is to make sure they fully understand the nuances of the overall economy in order to apply the right policy at the right time. Benefits like these make monetary policy a vitally important weapon against low employment and excessive inflation.

Coming Full Circle: Back to the Market for Loanable Funds

At this point you might be asking yourself, "What happened to the market for loanable funds?" (which we discussed in Chapter 13). If financial markets exist to match up borrowers and lenders, how is the extra borrowing spurred by lower interest rates financed when the central bank pursues an expansionary monetary policy? Wouldn't a lower interest rate create a shortage of loanable funds, as the demand from borrowers increased and the supply from savers decreased? It looks like we have two very separate models of the way the world works: In one, the central bank determines the interest rate by managing the supply and demand for money. In the other, the market as a whole determines the interest rate by the interaction of savers and borrowers.

Figure 14-7 shows how these two models are, in fact, connected by the dynamics of the economy. When the central bank acts to lower interest rates, it spurs borrowing and increases output in the economy. Some of this increase in output is saved, and this increase in savings is then multiplied by the banking system (through the money multiplier). As a result, the decrease in interest rates effectively shifts the supply curve for loanable funds to the right. That shift creates a new equilibrium at a lower interest rate and a higher level of borrowing.

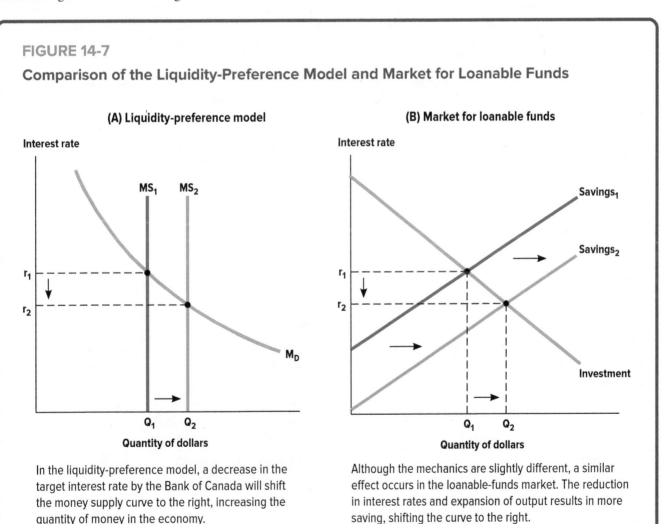

FIGURE 14-7

Comparison of the Liquidity-Preference Model and Market for Loanable Funds

(A) Liquidity-preference model

Interest rate

MS₁ MS₂

r₁

r₂

M_D

Q₁ Q₂

Quantity of dollars

(B) Market for loanable funds

Interest rate

Savings₁

Savings₂

r₁

r₂

Investment

Q₁ Q₂

Quantity of dollars

In the liquidity-preference model, a decrease in the target interest rate by the Bank of Canada will shift the money supply curve to the right, increasing the quantity of money in the economy.

Although the mechanics are slightly different, a similar effect occurs in the loanable-funds market. The reduction in interest rates and expansion of output results in more saving, shifting the curve to the right.

In fact, the shift to the right is exactly the amount required to bring the equilibrium interest rate in the market for loanable funds in line with the interest rate predicted by the liquidity-preference model. Taken together, these two ways of looking at the world simply show how developments in the financial system translate into effects on the broader economy.

✓ **CONCEPT CHECK**

☐ What is the overnight rate? [LO 14.7]
☐ What should the central bank do to fight low aggregate demand during a recession? [LO 14.8]

Conclusion

In this chapter, we've explored one of the most fundamental concepts in modern economics: money. We've looked at the roles money plays in the economy and explored some of the different forms of money that have existed in the past. We've also looked at how central banks and the private banking system interact to determine the size of the money supply. Finally, we've seen some of the tools the central bank has to manage the money supply and how those tools allow it to exert considerable influence over the broader economy.

This unique power gives the Bank of Canada and other central banks incredible responsibility for the economy. As you'll see in the next few chapters, this responsibility usually comes to ensure there is stability in the financial system in Canada.

Key Terms

money

store of value

medium of exchange

barter

unit of account

commodity-backed money

fiat money

demand deposits

reserves

reserve ratio

desired reserves

excess reserves

money multiplier

fractional-reserve banking

money supply

M1

M2

central bank

monetary policy

reserve requirement

open-market operations

contractionary monetary policy

expansionary monetary policy

overnight rate

liquidity-preference model

Summary

LO 14.1 Describe the three main functions of money.

The three main functions of money are as a store of value, a medium of exchange, and a unit of account. Money derives much of its true importance from its role as a medium of exchange—from the fact that you can use it to purchase the goods and services you desire. Money is also important as a way to register the value of transactions.

LO 14.2 Describe the characteristics that make something a good choice as money.

Money needs to have stability of value and be convenient. Items whose value varies from one day to the next will not be a good store of value and so are not suitable as money. Money also needs to be widely accepted in order to fulfill its function as a medium of exchange. Since 1933, Canadian money has been fiat money, created by rule rather than backed by a commodity such as gold.

LO 14.3 Explain the concept of fractional-reserve banking and the money multiplier.

Banks keep on hand a portion of the money deposited, in case depositors want to withdraw money. This money is known as the bank's reserves, and the ratio of the original deposit to the amount kept as reserves is the reserve ratio. If the reserve ratio were 100 percent (a situation known as full-reserve banking), no lending would take place; all deposits would sit in the banks' vaults, and the financial system would grind to a halt. Fractional-reserve banking allows a reserve ratio of less than 100 percent, enabling banks to lend a portion of the money that has been deposited. By means of that lending, banks "create" money. The ratio of money created by the lending activities of the banking system to the money created by the government's central bank is the money multiplier.

LO 14.4 Describe M1 and M2.

The Bank of Canada classifies different types of money by their liquidity—by how easy an asset is to convert immediately to cash without losing value. Cash and reserves physically held at the Bank of Canada are hard money, which can be used in transactions without delay. M1 includes hard money plus chequable deposits (which are not exactly cash but are fairly readily accessible for most people). M2 includes everything in M1 as well as things like savings accounts and term deposits that are generally harder to access immediately and so slightly less liquid than other forms of money.

LO 14.5 Understand the role of the central bank.

In any nation, the central bank's duties generally include maintaining the money supply and coordinating the banking system. In Canada, the central bank is known as the Bank of Canada. It has four essential functions: it is the sole issuer of Canada's bank notes, conducts monetary policy via managing the money supply, acts as the fiscal agent for the federal government, and acts as a lender of last resort.

LO 14.6 Explain the tools the Bank of Canada uses to conduct monetary policy.

The Bank of Canada has three tools to enact monetary policy. The first is changing the reserve requirement, or the regulation that sets the minimum fraction of deposits that banks must hold. It is usually seen as a rather blunt tool—powerful but inappropriate for most day-to-day economic maintenance. The second is the change in overnight rate, a lending facility run by the Bank of Canada that allows any bank to receive cash in exchange for certain non-cash assets like government bonds; the interest rate charged for these loans is the overnight rate. The change in overnight rate is one of the Bank of Canada's primary tools for providing liquidity to the markets and acting as a lender of last resort. The final and most used tool is open-market operations, in which the Bank of Canada sells or buys government bonds in the open market. Use of this tool alters bank reserves and influences overall interest rates.

LO 14.7 Understand how monetary policy affects the prevailing interest rate and supply of money.

The liquidity-preference model explains that the quantity of money people want to hold (the demand for money) is a function of the interest rate, which the Bank of Canada controls. As the quantity of money supplied changes, the price of that money, reflected in interest rates, will change as well. Increasing the money supply (such as by buying government bonds on the open market) decreases interest rates. Decreasing the money supply (such as by selling government bonds) will increase interest rates.

LO 14.8 Explain how expansionary and contractionary monetary policy influence the broader economy.

Depending on the circumstances, the Bank of Canada may want to engage in either expansionary or contractionary monetary policy. Expansionary monetary policy involves lowering interest rates; the lower rates increase aggregate demand, helping to expand the economy. This action is generally taken in response to recessionary forces. Contractionary monetary policy involves raising interest rates, which shrinks aggregate demand and slows the economy; it generally is taken in response to inflationary forces.

Review Questions

1. Describe how money contributes to economic activity and allows for a more complex society than barter does. [LO 14.1]

2. Explain how cigarettes fulfilled the three functions of money in POW camps during World War II. [LO 14.1]

3. Throughout time, metals such as gold have been popular choices for money in various societies. Explain why this might be, using our criteria for what makes good money. [LO 14.2]

4. On the Yap Islands in the middle of the Pacific Ocean, giant stone wheels, weighing as much as a small car, were used as currency. What were some of the likely problems with this currency? [LO 14.2]

5. Explain why keeping a reserve ratio of zero could be a very bad idea. [LO 14.3]

6. If banks keep 100 percent of deposits on hand as reserves, what would this imply about the reserve requirement and the multiplier? What would it imply about banks' ability to create new money? [LO 14.3]

7. Explain the role of base money and the money multiplier in the Bank of Canada's enactment of monetary policy. [LO 14.4]

8. Give an example where depositors changing the way they hold assets could increase the M1 measure of the money supply while leaving M2 unchanged. [LO 14.4]

9. What do we mean when we say that the Bank of Canada is politically independent, and how might this independence be a good thing for the Canadian economy? [LO 14.5]

10. Explain why using changes in reserve requirements to conduct monetary policy is generally not a good idea for Canada. [LO 14.6]

11. Which tool of monetary policy is used most frequently by the Bank of Canada? What makes this tool the best choice in most circumstances? [LO 14.6]

12. Are there any differences in the effects of fiscal policy versus monetary policy on aggregate demand in the short-run aggregate demand and supply model? [LO 14.7]

13. Describe the slope of the money supply curve in the liquidity-preference model. Are the assumptions behind the supply curve realistic? [LO 14.7]

14. Under the liquidity-preference model, how would the slope of the money demand curve affect the power of a central bank to conduct monetary policy? [LO 14.8]

15. Use the liquidity-preference model to explain how the Bank of Canada can react to the threat of exceedingly high inflation via monetary policy. Be sure to include the intended effect on the interest rate and quantity of money. [LO 14.8]

Problems and Applications

1. Determine whether each of the following would fulfill the three functions of money. If the item does not fulfill all three, name at least one function of money that it does not satisfy. [LO 14.1]
    a. Salt
    b. The barter system
    c. Baseball cards
    d. Canadian Tire money

2. Imagine you own a lawn-mowing business. Identify the main function of money exhibited in each situation below. [LO 14.1]

    a. You swipe your debit card to purchase gasoline for your lawn mower.

    b. You stuff your earnings from mowing lawns into a piggy bank.

    c. You pay your friend Cornelius $5 to help you mow lawns.

    d. You calculate your net earnings for the year on your tax return.

    e. You determine how much value your new lawn mower has added to your business.

3. From 2004 to 2009 the country of Zimbabwe underwent hyperinflation, in which prices rise rapidly. The government began printing bills as large as 100 billion Zimbabwe dollars. Explain how this situation would have affected at least one of the characteristics of good money discussed in this chapter. [LO 14.2]

4. Suppose you live in a country perfect for growing tulips and governed by King Balthazar, who proposes that you use the tulips for your currency. After all, says Balthazar, they are widely accepted in the community, they've been valuable for years, and are highly portable. If you were Balthazar's economic advisor, would you recommend using the tulips? If yes, list the traits of good money they satisfy. If no, list the trait(s) of good money they do not satisfy. [LO 14.2]

5. You decide to take $300 out of your piggy bank at home and place it in the bank. If the reserve requirement is 5 percent, how much can your $300 increase the amount of money in the economy? [LO 14.3]

6. Assume that $1 million is deposited in a bank with a reserve requirement of 15 percent. What is the money supply as a result? What would change if the government decides to raise the reserve requirement to 40 percent? [LO 14.3]

7. Say whether each of the following is a type of M1, M2, or both. [LO 14.4]

    a. Chequable deposits

    b. Dollar bills

    c. Money in your chequing account

    d. Money in your savings account

    e. Term deposit under $100,000

    f. Travellers cheques

8. Which of the following statements are true regarding the differences between M1 and M2? Check all that apply. [LO 14.4]

    a. M1 includes cash and reserves, whereas M2 does not.

    b. M2 represents a broader measure of the money supply than M1.

    c. Numerically, M1 is larger than M2.

    d. All items in M1 are more liquid than all items in M2.

    e. M2 includes savings deposits, whereas M1 does not.

    f. During the recent recession, M1 was a more stable measure of the money supply than M2.

9. Consider the POW camps described at the beginning of this chapter. Who played the role of the central bank? [LO 14.5]

10. Which tool of monetary policy is most likely being described by each of the following statements? [LO 14.6]

    a. It's the major way the Bank of Canada enacts monetary policy.

    b. This tool is good for emergency situations that require major, large-scale action.

    c. This tool goes through the Bank of Canada's role as lender of last resort.

    d. This tool is best for everyday monetary policy.

    e. A major disadvantage of this tool is that it requires that banks want to borrow from the Bank of Canada.

    f. Even if they aren't interested in buying, selling, or borrowing from the Bank of Canada, changes in this tool may inconvenience bank managers.

11. Name the monetary policy tool being used in each of the following examples. [LO 14.6]

    a. The central bank buys government securities from banks.

    b. The central bank raises the cost of borrowing money.

    c. The central bank changes the amount of depositors' money that banks must hold.

12. The economy is in recession and the Bank of Canada wants to increase the money supply. Should it increase or decrease the following? [LO 14.6], [LO 14.7]
    a. Reserve requirements
    b. The target for overnight rate
    c. Purchases of bonds in the open market

13. Using Figure 14P-1, answer the following questions. [LO 14.7]
    a. Is this economy in recession, just right, or overheating?
    b. What is the correct monetary policy in this situation—expansionary or contractionary?
    c. What is the effect on prices of that policy—will they increase or decrease?

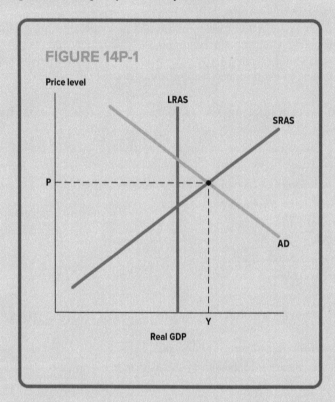

FIGURE 14P-1

14. What would happen to each of these components of the liquidity-preference model if the Bank of Canada decides to raise the reserve requirement? [LO 14.8]
    a. Money supply
    b. Interest rates
    c. Quantity of money in the economy
    d. Money demand curve

15. For each of the following situations, identify whether the Bank of Canada is likely to pursue an expansionary or a contractionary monetary policy. [LO 14.8]
    a. The unemployment rate is at 0.5 percent.
    b. The economy is experiencing record growth in GDP.
    c. The unemployment rate is at 15 percent.
    d. Inflation has reached 10 percent, a recent high.
    e. An earthquake recently demolished a major city, causing a major recession.

Chapter Source

Stephen G. Cecchetti, *Money, Banking, and Financial Markets,* 3rd ed. (New York: McGraw-Hill/Irwin, 2011).

CHAPTER 15

Inflation

LEARNING OBJECTIVES

LO 15.1   Explain the neutrality of money.

LO 15.2   Describe and illustrate the classical theory of inflation.

LO 15.3   Explain the quantity theory of money and relate it to inflation and deflation.

LO 15.4   Analyze the economic consequences of inflation.

LO 15.5   Analyze the economic consequences of deflation.

LO 15.6   Describe disinflation and hyperinflation, and explain the role of monetary policy in creating both situations.

LO 15.7   Explain the relationship between inflation, the output gap, and monetary policy.

LO 15.8   Analyze the relationship between inflation and unemployment, and explain how it is modelled by the Phillips curve and integrated into the non-accelerating rate of unemployment.

A Land of Opportunity . . . and Inflation

The story is a familiar one. In the closing years of the 1800s, millions of immigrants sought out the promised land—a country rich in natural resources and with the highest standard of living in the world. These immigrants sought a new life in one of the world's great cities—a modern, cosmopolitan city where the blending of cultures led to vibrancy nearly unrivaled in the world. At its peak, nearly 50 percent of the city's residents were immigrants.

They never set foot in the Maritimes or anywhere else in Canada. Instead, they headed for Buenos Aires—their promised land was Argentina. From the late 1800s to the early 1900s, more than 5 million immigrants from across Europe arrived in Argentina, a country with seemingly limitless opportunity. In 1910, Argentina's per capita GDP was relatively high, just slightly below that of Canada. In the century that followed, though, Argentina lagged behind economically, and its per capita GDP is now less than half of Canada's. What caused this divergence in fortunes? You could point to the political instability that led to a series of military coups and populist dictatorships. But dig a little deeper and you will find a common thread that came to define daily life in Argentina: out-of-control inflation.

More than almost any other country in the world, Argentina has struggled with rising prices. During the past seventy-five years Argentina has experienced three separate hyperinflations (*hyperinflation* refers to extremely long and painful inflationary periods). The worst of these, in the late 1980s and early 1990s, saw inflation peak at over 20,000 percent per year. (In other words, prices were doubling every month or two.) If this were to happen in Canada today, an iPod costing $100 at Christmas would cost $200 in February, $400 in March, and more than $20,000 by the following Christmas.

In between the periods of hyperinflation, Argentina has seen sustained high inflation unlike almost any other country in the world. In fact, the average annual inflation rate over the last seventy-five years has been greater than 200 percent—a tripling of prices every year! Argentina has brought inflation down to about 25 percent per year recently—which seems modest compared to historical levels, despite being one of the highest inflation rates in the world.

A century ago, Argentina seemed on the cusp of challenging Canada for supremacy in the Americas. Of course, this was not the only policy or geographic difference between Canada and Argentina, but it does help explain why that dream is gone. So what is so damaging about inflation for a nation's economy? And why do most economists believe that its opposite—deflation—is even worse?

In Chapter 14 we saw how money is created and how the supply of money can have an enormous impact on the overall economy, and in particular on interest rates. In this chapter we will look at the topic of inflation from various angles—theories about changing price levels, inflation in its various forms, and the effects of inflation on monetary policy.

© Simon Chavez/dpa/Corbis

Changing Price Levels

The price level, and especially changes in it, is one of the most important concepts in macroeconomics. An overall rise in prices in the economy is called **inflation**; an overall fall is called **deflation**.

As we saw in Chapter 8, "The Cost of Living," Statistics Canada measures overall prices in the economy by creating a consumption basket designed to resemble the purchases of the average household. This measure of overall prices is called the Consumer Price Index (CPI). Measuring inflation or deflation is done by calculating the percentage change in the ratio of the cost of the entire basket compared to the cost of that basket in a base year.

From that basket, Statistics Canada omits eight of the most volatile components—mainly expenditures for food and energy—when it calculate core inflation. **Core inflation** is a measure of inflation that excludes goods with historically volatile prices. It is one of Statistics Canada's official measures of changes in prices through the CPI. When the prices of food and energy are added to core inflation, we get *overall* inflation. That includes all of the goods that the average household buys.

Although they are essential purchases, food and energy are omitted when calculating *core* inflation because their prices tend to rise and fall more than most other prices. In March 2015, for example, the price of gasoline fell 19.2 percent, while core inflation rose by 2.4 percent.

Energy and food prices tend to be highly volatile from month to month, which means that changes in price levels caused by goods with volatile prices might simply be reflecting shocks to individual product markets rather than any sort of economy-wide inflation. Thus, when economists are interested in the underlying rate of inflation in the economy, they often differentiate between overall inflation and core inflation. Figure 15-1 clearly shows how much more stable core inflation (as represented by the core CPI) is than overall inflation (as represented by the CPI). Although overall inflation gives a more complete picture of how changing prices are affecting the average household, it's useful to subtract food and energy in order to get a better feel for underlying economic trends.

FIGURE 15-1

Running Annual Change in CPI and Core CPI, January 2001–March 2015

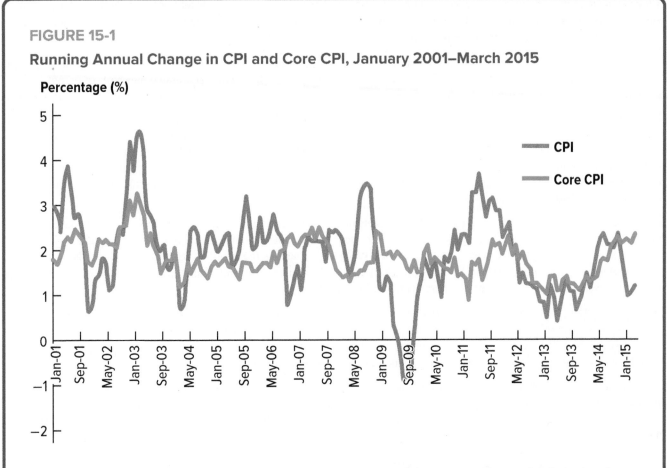

The figure shows actual annual inflation rates, as represented by CPI (representing overall inflation) and core CPI (representing core inflation). Core inflation is much more stable than overall inflation.

Source: Statistics Canada, CANSIM Series 326-0020, "Consumer Price Index", March 2015.

The Neutrality of Money

LO 15.1 Explain the neutrality of money.

When we say that the price level changes, what do we mean? To answer the question, it helps to think about what *output* really is. A country's GDP is simply an accounting of all of the purchases and sales that take place over a given period. In each transaction, somebody gives money to somebody else. All output, then, can be tied to the movement of money. But how do we measure that output?

It seems intuitive to measure output in terms of money, but this can become problematic. Imagine that the government were to simply add a few zeros to every piece of money (automatically turning $1 into $100, and $100 into $10,000). Prices would jump, and the measured "value of output" in the economy would increase tremendously. But we would know that the real output, the goods and services traded, didn't actually change. Yet that is what we want to measure—the output in terms of real, tangible goods and services: How many cans of soft drinks or tons of steel were created by the country?

As you may recall from earlier chapters, we call quantities measured this way *real values* because they represent an accounting of the actual amount of something that is produced, measured in terms of goods and services instead of in dollars. That accounting is independent of how many pieces of paper with a certain number of zeros on it you would need to purchase that output. In contrast, values measured in terms of how much money it would take to purchase something are called *nominal values*. We use changes in the *price level* to get from one to the other.

In Chapter 8, "The Cost of Living," we described the concept of a *deflator*—the idea of using a price index like the CPI or the GDP deflator to adjust between nominal and real prices. These indexes allow us to convert nominal measures of output into real measures of output. In other words, they let us measure how much real stuff we get for our money. The **aggregate price level** is a measure of the average price level for GDP and, in practical terms, is measured by either the CPI or the GDP price deflator.

Now, back to the hypothetical question: What if the government one day decided to add two zeros to the figure on every dollar bill? A bottle of water that was previously $1 would suddenly cost $100; that $20 haircut would now cost $2,000. Fortunately, as long as your job at the library now pays $900 an hour rather than $9 an hour, the change in the price of goods and services really wouldn't make much of a difference. (One important caveat: such rampant change in prices does wreak havoc; at a minimum it causes stores to constantly reprice items.)

This example helps show why, in the long run, the aggregate price level doesn't change real output. Since all prices have increased proportionately, what you could buy when you made $9 an hour is the same as what you can buy when you make $900 an hour. That's the basic intuition behind what is called the **neutrality of money** — the idea that aggregate price levels do not affect real outcomes in the economy. (However, as we'll see, the process of increasing prices, and the existence of *uncertainty* about increasing prices, matters a lot; money is more neutral in the long run than in the short run.)

In the above example, the change in the price level (prices and wages being 100 times higher than before) didn't dent your purchasing power. In other words, when the money supply increases by a given amount, prices eventually do, too, so that the *real* value of your money hasn't changed. Changes in the price level—that is, changes in the unit of measurement used to account for something—change only *nominal* values, not real values, given enough time.

The neutrality of money holds in many cases, but note that extreme situations, such as the story of Argentina that we discussed in the chapter opening, show that the neutrality of money did break down. Extreme and sustained inflation causes frictions in the economy, leading to slower growth. When prices change more rapidly, the cost of discovering (and updating) information about alternative prices rises.

The Classical Theory of Inflation

LO 15.2 Describe and illustrate the classical theory of inflation.

In Chapter 14, "Money and the Monetary System," we touched on the idea that the level of prices in an economy is affected by the quantity of money in an economy. It's time to explain formally how this process happens, using the *classical theory of inflation*. The classical theory of inflation illustrates the relationship between money supply, output (or GDP), and the overall level of prices.

Figure 15-2 illustrates the basic framework of the classical theory using the now-familiar aggregate supply and aggregate demand perspective. Suppose the economy is in long-run equilibrium at point E_1. Short-run aggregate demand matches short-run aggregate supply, which matches the long-run potential aggregate supply of the economy. What happens if the Bank of Canada increases the money supply, as in expansionary monetary policy? The increased money supply will result in lower interest rates and higher levels of borrowing; in turn, aggregate demand will increase. As Figure 15-2 shows, aggregate demand shifts right, creating a new temporary equilibrium where the new short-run aggregate demand curve intersects the short-run aggregate supply curve, and increasing output (real GDP). The economy is at point E_2.

We know from our discussion of the neutrality of money, however, that this situation can't survive for long. Eventually, prices will rise in proportion with the increase in the money supply. In practice, this can take a little bit of time, since prices are relatively *sticky* (slow-moving). For example, you don't get to renegotiate your wages immediately when prices go up; you have to wait until your contract is up for renewal or the time is right to renegotiate.

FIGURE 15-2

Increase in the Money Supply Under the Classical Theory of Inflation

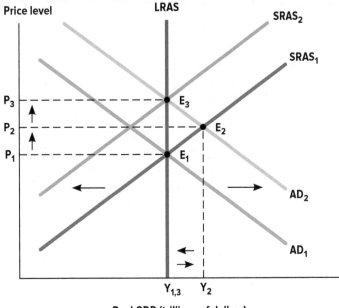

According to the classical theory of inflation, in the long run, increases in the money supply will lead to an increase in prices only; output will stay the same. In the short run, output and prices increase as aggregate demand shifts to the right. However, workers then begin to negotiate for a higher wage, which shifts the aggregate supply curve to the left. Output returns to the original level, while prices increase even more.

While it might take time for prices to rise, as long as money is neutral we know they will eventually tick upward. The increase in prices, especially in nominal wages, in turn leads to a leftward shift in the short-run aggregate supply curve. Why? Because the higher input prices of labour and other goods used in production make it more expensive to produce a given level of output. The economy eventually reaches a new equilibrium, indicated by point E_3 on the figure: aggregate supply and short-run aggregate demand once again meet at exactly the level of the long-run aggregate supply curve, and real GDP falls back to exactly the point at which it started. (This point is often called *potential output,* a concept we'll explore later in the chapter.) In fact, the only difference is that now *the price level is higher*—reflecting the lower value of money due to the increased money supply. In other words, it will now take a higher number of dollars to buy a given good or service. (Again, think back to the effect of more cigarettes in the POW camp in Chapter 14.)

It's important to emphasize that the classical theory of inflation is describing a long-run equilibrium. Some economists have used the eventual neutrality of money to argue that the Bank of Canada can't meaningfully guide the economy through the use of monetary policy. Others cite empirical evidence that suggests there is considerable scope for the Bank of Canada to affect the economy in the short run through expansionary or contractionary policy. This is one reason our analysis may yield different answers in the short run versus the long run.

The Quantity Theory of Money

LO 15.3 Explain the quantity theory of money and relate it to inflation and deflation.

The classical theory of inflation is strongly connected to a related theory: the **quantity theory of money**. The quantity theory of money states explicitly that the value of money (and thus the aggregate price level) is determined by the overall quantity of money in existence (i.e., the money supply). Further, changes in the price level (inflation or deflation) are primarily the result of changes in the quantity of money. An increase in the money supply leads to an increase in prices, as there are more dollar bills spent on the same number of goods and services. Likewise, a decrease in the money supply leads to a decrease in prices, as there are just as many goods and services but fewer dollars with which to purchase them.

The quantity theory of money depends on the velocity of money being relatively constant. The **velocity of money**, simply put, is the number of transactions in which a typical dollar is used during a given period. If you buy a hamburger, some of the money you spent to purchase it goes to the waitress, another part goes to the cook, and yet another part goes to the rancher who raised the cow; some goes to the dozens of other suppliers who provided everything from the bun to the booth you are sitting in. In other words, your consumption spending is someone else's income, and that person can (and usually does) go on to spend at least part of that income on something else. Intuitively, the velocity of money is a simple concept. If the average dollar is spent five times a year, then the velocity of money for that year would be five.

We can mathematically define the velocity of money (V) as equal to the price level (P) multiplied by real output (Y), divided by the money supply (M):

Equation 15-1

$$V = \frac{(P \times Y)}{M}$$

For example, if an economy produces 1,000 units of output (so that Y = 1,000) with a price level of $1 (P = $1) and the money supply (M) is $500, velocity is:

$$\frac{(\$1 \times 1,000)}{(\$500)} = 2$$

That means that over the course of the year, each dollar in the money supply was spent twice on average in order to generate $1,000 worth of output.

Rearranging Equation 15-1, we can see that the total amount of money in the economy (the money supply, M) multiplied by the number of times that money turns over during the year (the velocity of money, V) must equal the nominal value of output (Y). If we now adjust this formula to incorporate the concept of real output and aggregate price levels, we can see that total money supply multiplied by the velocity of money is equal to the price level times real output. This is the **quantity equation** that underlies the quantity theory of money:

Equation 15-2

$$(\text{Money supply}) \times (\text{velocity of money}) = (\text{price level}) \times (\text{real output})$$

$$M \times V = P \times Y$$

Until now, we've assumed that velocity is relatively constant, but is that true in practice? Figure 15-3 shows information about the velocity of money in Canada through history. As you can see, velocity has been relatively stable historically, though the Great Recession temporarily caused some significant changes. This means that real output (Y) will also not change in equilibrium (as long as the production process remains the same as well). Equation 15-2 implies that any increase in M (the money supply) has to eventually lead directly to an increase in P (the aggregate price level). Of course, a decrease in M would result in a decrease in P. In other words, increasing the money supply leads to inflation, and decreasing the money supply leads to deflation.

If the velocity of money were not relatively constant, then the quantity theory of money could not hold. With rapid increases or decreases in the amount of money changing hands in the economy, it would be possible for the money supply to double while people spend their money half as fast. Rather than increasing prices, as we would otherwise expect when the money supply doubles, the amount of money moving around in the economy would stay the same, and prices would stay roughly the same, as well. As an example of this, the Bank of Canada increased the size of the monetary base quite substantially in an attempt to stimulate the economy following the recession. If the velocity of money had not declined during this period (as shown in Figure 15-3), the result would have been far more inflation than was actually observed.

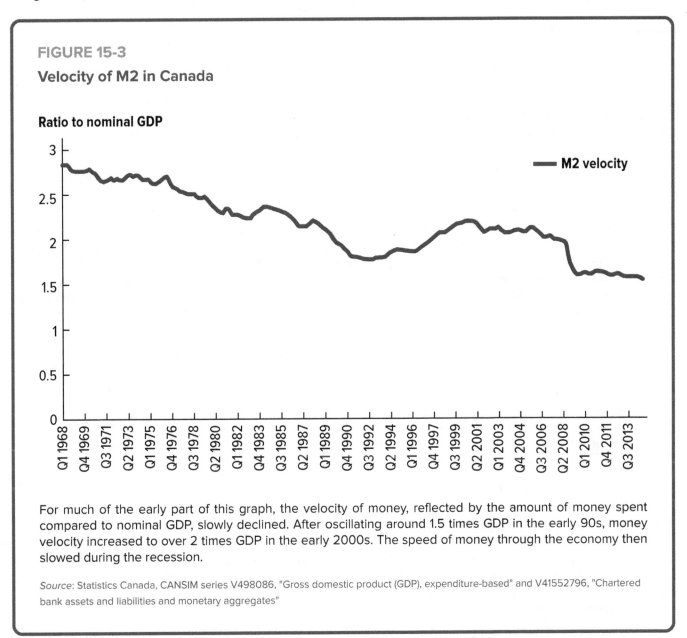

FIGURE 15-3

Velocity of M2 in Canada

Ratio to nominal GDP

For much of the early part of this graph, the velocity of money, reflected by the amount of money spent compared to nominal GDP, slowly declined. After oscillating around 1.5 times GDP in the early 90s, money velocity increased to over 2 times GDP in the early 2000s. The speed of money through the economy then slowed during the recession.

Source: Statistics Canada, CANSIM series V498086, "Gross domestic product (GDP), expenditure-based" and V41552796, "Chartered bank assets and liabilities and monetary aggregates"

One implication of this theory is that deflation occurs if the money supply remains constant but real output increases. Logically, the effect is the same as if real output stayed constant and the money supply declined. As we saw in Chapter 14, this relationship between output and the money supply is one of the main arguments against the gold standard. Barring a sudden discovery of gold, the supply of gold-backed money is relatively fixed. If M is constant, when the economy expands (that is, when Y increases), then one of two things must happen: either the velocity of money must go up, the price level must go down, or there must be some combination of the two. And if velocity is relatively constant, there is only one option: the price level must fall, a situation known as *deflation*. We will see in more detail later in this chapter why deflation can be extremely damaging to an economy.

The Where's George? website brings to life the idea of velocity. The site allows users to enter the serial number of a US dollar bill and see where it has been (assuming others have entered that bill, as well). See the Real Life box, Where's George? for more.

REAL LIFE

Where's George?

Have you ever looked at a crumpled dollar bill and wondered where that piece of paper had been before it got to you? If you were looking at a US dollar, you might have noticed a stamp on the bill leading you to the Where's George? website (www.wheresgeorge.com). Now that you know more about how money works you might find it interesting to see what happens there: users track the adventures of millions of bills as they travel through the economy. Tracking those travels captures what economists mean when they talk about velocity.

The website works like this. Users input the serial number found at the corner of any US bill. If the bill has already been entered on the site, you can see where the bill has been and how long it took for it to get around. If you are the first person to enter the serial number, the bill becomes part of the database that will record the story of that bill.

Statistics from the site can give a pretty interesting picture of who holds money in the United States. Overall, 140 million unique Georges have been added. The most bills are entered in California, Pennsylvania, and New York. This is not too surprising as these states are within the top five in total population. The individual stories can also tell a lot about how money moves through the economy. The site records such statistics as the distance the bills travelled after being recorded on the site, which is also converted into a miles-per-day figure. Most bills travel about five miles per day on average.

One of the more intrepid Georges visited fourteen cities in a 7,686 mile, four-year jaunt around the country that took it from the fast-food chain Whataburger in Tallahassee, Florida, to Aiken, South Carolina, via flashy Times Square and the hip streets of Portland, Oregon.

Most trips are far more mundane: 57 percent of the bills on the site travel only between 30 and 500 miles in the course of nine months. The website depends on users to add bills, and it has captured only a sliver of the 9.8 billion dollar bills in circulation. Still, the site reminds us that those crumpled dollars in your pocket might have had some interesting adventures.

Source: http://www.wheresgeorge.com/.

Other Causes of Changing Price Levels

We've looked at how the quantity theory of money explains changes in price levels: over the long term, any increase or decrease in the money supply—assuming that velocity and real output are held constant—will result in an increase or decrease in the price level. However, changes in the price level can also be created in a more temporary fashion by the actions of the business cycle or by sudden supply shocks to a key resource in production.

We've actually discussed the first type of inflation, also known as *demand–pull* inflation, many times before in our discussion of the business cycle in other chapters. Recall what happens when an economy goes through a boom. As companies look to expand rapidly to meet rising demand, competition for scarce resources heats up. It becomes harder to find workers, leading employers to bid against each other for the best talent, increasing wages. This demand pulls prices higher, as too much money is spent chasing too few goods. Of course, the opposite is also true. When economic activity is slow, fewer dollars are spent on the same amount of goods, pushing prices downward. These two effects combine to create a rise in price levels during the boom periods and, potentially, a fall in price levels during busts. We'll explore the relationship between inflation and the business cycle, and in particular unemployment, in more detail a bit later.

The other type of inflation, known as *cost–push* inflation, occurs when the price of a key input increases suddenly. A serious bout of cost–push inflation occurred in the mid-1970s in Canada when OPEC, the organization that controls most of the world's supply of oil, decided to cut the amount of oil they produced. Since oil in its many forms is absolutely essential, not only to the production of gasoline but also to many other goods, from wheat to plastics, increases in the price of oil increased the prices of goods throughout the economy.

✓ CONCEPT CHECK

- ☐ Do changes in the aggregate price level change overall real output? [LO 15.1]
- ☐ According to the classical theory of inflation, will inflation increase or decrease if the Bank of Canada pursues expansionary monetary policy? [LO 15.2]
- ☐ What is the velocity of money? [LO 15.3]

Why Do We Care About Changing Price Levels?

At this point you may find yourself wondering why changes in the price level matter. After all, we've seen from the theory of money neutrality that the economy should adjust itself to different levels of nominal prices, leaving no change in overall output. So why be concerned about them?

As we'll see in this section, while the price level itself is immaterial, *changes* in the price level can have a big effect on economic behaviour. We'll also see why many economists believe a modest and predictable level of inflation is a good thing, but that high or unpredictable levels of inflation—and any level of deflation—are economically damaging.

Inflation

LO 15.4 Analyze the economic consequences of inflation.

We've defined inflation as a rise in aggregate price levels. If the average price level rises 10 percent every year (that is, the prices of all the things in the economy go up by an average of 10 percent), we say that the economy is experiencing an inflation rate of 10 percent per year. Figure 15-4 shows inflation rates around the world in 1980, 1990, 2000, and 2010. Note that over the last four decades, the inflation rate has generally decreased.

FIGURE 15-4a

Inflation Around the World (1980)*

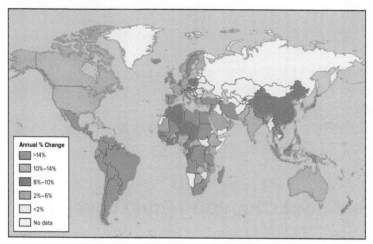

*National boundaries were slightly different in 1980, 1990, and 2000.

Source: World Bank World Development Indicators, 2012, http://data.worldbank.org/data-catalog/world-development-indicators.

FIGURE 15-4b

Inflation Around the World (1990)*

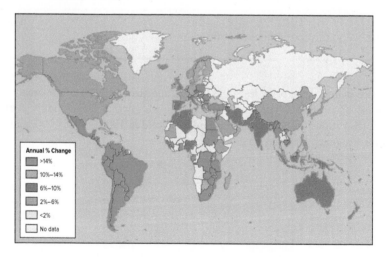

*National boundaries were slightly different in 1980, 1990, and 2000.

Source: World Bank World Development Indicators, 2012, http://data.worldbank.org/data-catalog/world-development-indicators.

FIGURE 15-4c

Inflation Around the World (2000)*

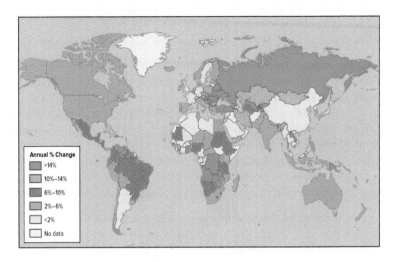

*National boundaries were slightly different in 1980, 1990, and 2000.

Source: World Bank World Development Indicators, 2012, http://data.worldbank.org/data-catalog/world-development-indicators.

FIGURE 15-4d

Inflation Around the World (2010)*

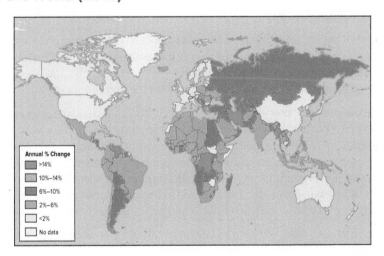

*National boundaries were slightly different in 1980, 1990, and 2000.

Source: World Bank World Development Indicators, 2012, http://data.worldbank.org/data-catalog/world-development-indicators.

Costs of Predictable Inflation

We've seen that money is neutral in the long run, so why is it bad if prices go up? Won't the rest of the economy adjust to any price change? As we'll see shortly, arguably the most damaging economic consequence of inflation is the uncertainty it can create, and that uncertainty is increased when the amount or timing of inflation is unpredictable. But even if inflation is predictable—say, if you are sure that prices will go up by about 20 percent every year—it still imposes costs. We will discuss three types of costs that even stable and predictable inflation imposes on the economy: menu costs, shoe-leather costs, and tax distortions.

The first, **menu costs**, refers to the cost (measured in money, time, and opportunity) of changing prices to keep pace with inflation. It comes from the simple idea that for restaurants, changing prices likely means reprinting menus. Consider a company that runs vending machines and has to send someone out to reprogram every machine when it wants to raise the price of a soft drink. Even if a company only has to update a website, it takes some time and effort.

The second type of cost that inflation imposes on the economy, **shoe-leather costs**, refers to the time, money, and effort people must spend managing cash in the face of inflation. Imagine you run a business that involves handling a lot of cash—a grocery store, say. If you know prices are fairly stable, you're going to be relaxed about keeping cash on your premises if it's more convenient (and safe) to do so. If prices aren't going up much, you aren't losing much buying power by holding the cash. But if you know prices are going up quickly, you're going to want to keep as much money as possible in an interest-bearing bank account. You'll earn at least a bit of interest to help offset the loss in buying power due to rising prices. In addition to other hassles, you'll likely waste a lot of time travelling back and forth to the bank to deposit and withdraw cash—wearing out your shoe leather, hence the name. (And even though with online banking your actual shoes may not wear so thin, the time you spend transferring assets from one form to another could be spent in more profitable—and enjoyable—ways.)

The third type of cost that inflation imposes on the economy is *tax distortion* (also sometimes called *bracket creep*). This one is a bit more subtle than menu costs and shoe-leather costs, but can be costly all the same. Tax distortions happen because tax laws take into consideration only nominal income—not what you can buy with it. Inflation reduces the purchasing power of your income, but when politicians don't respond by adjusting tax brackets and amounts, inflation can result in a situation in which you are essentially penalized via taxes for making more money in dollars, even though real purchasing power hasn't changed at all.

For example, let's assume that people pay one tax rate on their total pay and that those who make $60,000 a year are in a higher tax bracket; in other words, they pay more taxes than those who earn less. If inflation is 20 percent per year, then a family who earned $50,000 last year will enter the higher tax bracket and face higher taxes this year, even though they don't have any more real purchasing power than they did before. The tax system is treating them as if they've made more money, and it's true that they *have* accumulated more dollar bills, but those dollar bills are worth less than they used to be. The tax system is essentially penalizing the family for inflation. To minimize the impact on Canadian families, certain personal income tax and benefit amounts are indexed to inflation using the CPI data reported by Statistics Canada.

Problems of Unpredictable Inflation

We've just considered three costs that occur even when inflation is stable and predictable. It turns out that the problems that arise when inflation is *not* predictable are even worse. In many businesses, the profit margin (the difference between the cost of producing a product and the amount it can be sold for) is less than 10 percent. If the company can't be sure whether the prices of the inputs used to make its product will go up by 5 percent or 10 percent or 20 percent over the next year, planning becomes tough.

Uncertainty also lies behind a more complex "cost" of inflation that occurs because changing prices affect interest rates. Here, there can be a redistributive effect, effectively transferring money either from savers to borrowers or vice versa. To see how this happens, it might help to review the difference between *nominal* and *real* interest rates. The **nominal interest rate** is the everyday notion of the interest rate: it is the reported interest rate, not adjusted for the effects of inflation. For example, it is the percentage that the bank pays you for saving (or, if you're borrowing, the percentage that you pay the lender). Examples of the nominal interest rate can be found in the financial pages of a newspaper or on a loan contract. The **real interest rate**, on the other hand, is the interest rate adjusted for the effects of inflation. As we know, inflation means that each dollar becomes less valuable over time.

When you're deciding how much to save, then, you need to look at two things that work in opposite directions:

1. How interest will add to the value of your savings
2. How inflation will erode the purchasing power of each dollar in your savings account

To know which effect is dominant—that is, whether the real value of your money will increase or decrease over time—you have to calculate the real interest rate by subtracting the inflation rate from the nominal interest rate. Since both rates are typically stated as an annual percentage of the base level, the formula for calculating the real interest rate is simple:

Equation 15-3

$$\text{Real interest rate} = \text{nominal interest rate} - \text{inflation rate}$$

To see how important the difference between the nominal and real interest rates can be, look at Table 15-1. It shows an example of the same savings account with two different inflation rates. Suppose that in 2010 you had deposited $1,000 into an account with a nominal annual interest rate of 4 percent, keeping it there for five years. Here's what would happen with varying rates of inflation:

TABLE 15-1   REAL AND NOMINAL INTEREST RATES

Without inflation, the real and nominal interest rates are the same, so the interest rate you see is what you actually get. With inflation, the real interest you are earning is less than the nominal rate; if inflation is greater than the nominal interest rate, the investment actually becomes worth less in real value than the original investment.

Value in 2010 ($)	Nominal interest rate (%)	Inflation rate (%)	Real interest rate (%)	Nominal 2015 value ($)	Value in 2015 (2010 $)
1,000	4	0	4	1,217	1,217
1,000	4	3	1	1,217	1,051
1,000	4	5	−1	1,217	951

- If there is no inflation, then your real return is equal to the nominal interest rate—and you would end up with $1,217 in both 2015 dollars and 2010 dollars.
- If inflation runs at 3 percent per year over the five years, your real interest rate is only 1 percent (4 percent nominal interest rate minus 3 percent inflation rate). Then, in 2015, you will still have $1,217 in 2015 dollars, but they are worth only $1,051 in 2010 dollars.
- If inflation is 5 percent per year, then your money actually loses value. The real interest rate is −1 percent (4 percent nominal interest rate minus 5 percent inflation rate). You again end up with $1,217 at the end of the five-year period in 2015 dollars, but in this case it's worth only $951 in 2010 dollars.

Of course, the reverse situation applies to *borrowers*. Suppose you borrowed $1,000 in 2010 and agreed to pay it back at a rate of 4 percent interest. High inflation is now your friend: if inflation turns out to be 5 percent, then the real value of what you end up paying back is less than the amount you borrowed. That is good news for you!

In other words, when inflation is higher than nominal interest rates—when *real* interest rates are negative—the value of both savings and debts decreases. You do not want your savings to go down in value, but you do want the money you owe—your debts—to go down in value. Savers become worse off, as the value of what they have put in the bank becomes less valuable over time. Conversely, borrowers gain from inflation since inflation reduces the value of dollars; a loan made today will have a smaller value in real terms later. This debt will be easier to repay as its real value decreases. Effectively, we can say that high inflation redistributes wealth from those who save to those who borrow. (We should note, however, that borrowers may eventually suffer if savers/lenders stop making loans entirely because of these losses.)

If inflation is predictable, then this redistributive effect need not happen. Even if inflation is high—say, 20 percent—savers will not lose out as long as banks offer nominal interest rates above 20 percent. However, changes in the inflation rate often come as a surprise, and it can take time for nominal interest rates to adjust. (Storekeepers cannot immediately change all prices, nor can employers immediately change wages.). And, as we discussed earlier, there are other costs of inflation that apply even when its timing and amount are predictable.

These same ideas about the economic consequences of inflation apply to governments that have taken on debt and need to repay it. The only difference is that a government can control inflation, at least to some degree, through monetary policy. A government may thus be tempted to slowly "inflate away" the amount of debt it owes. The pros and cons of such a strategy are discussed in the Real Life box, Inflating Away the Debt.

REAL LIFE

Inflating Away the Debt

Picture this: you're the president of a country in an economic bind. Tax revenues are down. The prospect of economic growth is bleak. You face a growing government debt. What do you do? You could cut government spending or raise taxes, but both of these options are destined to make you unpopular. Fortunately, your chief economic advisor has an idea. "Just print money! That can solve your debt problems," he says. "Printing more money would increase prices, and this increase in inflation would reduce the real value of the debt that is carried by the government."

Zimbabwe used this scheme when it found itself owing more money to foreigners and government employees than it could easily afford. To get out of the bind, the regime headed by Robert Mugabe decided to start printing Zimbabwean dollars. In 2006, the government printed 21 trillion Zimbabwean dollars (roughly $210 million US) to pay off loans, and another 60 trillion (or $600 million US) to pay civil servants.

Did the strategy work? In a sense, yes. The government's debts, denominated in Zimbabwean dollars, soon became almost worthless as inflation predictably spiraled out of control. However, such high levels of inflation—it reached an incredible 11 million percent in 2008—caused utter chaos that crippled the Zimbabwean economy, leading to an unemployment rate of more than 80 percent.

Even when the economy stays strong, inflation is not an ideal solution. Debt represents a promise made to lenders, and they stand to lose money if the government decides to print its way out of debt. In the end, nobody is going to want to lend money to a government that has a track record of inflating away its debts. Economist Alan Auerbach calculates that with the way debt is designed, inflation could wipe out only $5.4 trillion of the roughly $53 trillion US budget shortfall projected over the next seventy-five years.

Still, it's easy to see the attraction of the idea. If you could simply print money to reduce the real value of your personal debts, wouldn't you be just a little bit tempted?

Sources: http://allafrica.com/stories/200602170023.html; http://economix.blogs.nytimes.com/2010/02/18/inflation-wont-solve-our-debt-problems/; http://sciie.ucsc.edu/workingpaper/2009/Using_Inflation_to_Erode_Debt_Nov27_09.pdf.

Deflation

> **LO 15.5** Analyze the economic consequences of deflation.

Inflation has a natural opposite: deflation. *Deflation* is a sustained fall in the aggregate price level—negative inflation, essentially. Periods of deflation occur far less often than inflation, and they generally occur in only the very worst economic circumstances. Deflation characterized the Great Depression of the 1930s, when aggregate prices in Canada fell by 25 percent in a few years. More recently, Japan experienced a so-called "lost decade" of deflation in the 1990s, which continues to pose challenges for its economy.

Why is deflation such a problem? For one thing, it increases the burden of debt. As we saw earlier, most loans are made in nominal terms. If you borrow $100 at an annual interest rate of 5 percent for one year, you will owe $105 at the end of the year. If the price level has gone down due to deflation, the real value of that $105 will be even higher. Since paying back loans eats up a greater part of what you can buy in real terms, consumption will decrease. Of course, the flip side is that your savings will be worth more in real terms.

Why don't savers spend more, given that deflation causes their savings to increase in value? Because if people *expect* deflation, they will likely want to spend less. It's easy to see why. Suppose you expect prices to be 10 percent lower in a few months than they are now. Will you buy that new car or wait for a few months? It's the expectation that prices will fall that explains at least in part why deflation can cripple an economy. In particular, companies that expect deflation to continue will be unwilling to borrow money to invest, because they expect the money they borrow will be worth more in real terms when they have to pay it back.

With consumption and investment both down, the net result of deflation is to reduce the level of aggregate demand in the economy. This, in turn, reduces prices, causing deflation to continue. This self-reinforcing cycle is referred to as a *deflationary spiral,* or *deflationary trap* and is particularly difficult to break.

Disinflation and Hyperinflation: Controlling Inflation . . . or Not

LO 15.6 Describe disinflation and hyperinflation, and explain the role of monetary policy in creating both situations.

Tsvangirayi Mukwazhi/AP Images

Imagine the complications of hyperinflation in daily life. This Zimbabwean man, at the height of the country's hyperinflation, is carrying enough money to buy some milk.

Controlling inflation is a crucial role of the Bank of Canada in managing the money supply. The Bank of Canada may want to reduce inflation from 7 percent to 2 percent, for example. The result is **disinflation**, the term for a period during which overall inflation rates, while still positive, are falling. (Be sure not to get this concept confused with *deflation,* in which inflation rates are negative.) In general, disinflation is usually discussed in the context of the central bank (the Bank of Canada in Canada) aggressively trying to contain inflation via contractionary monetary policy.

In Canada, the Bank of Canada famously applied disinflationary tactics to slow the increase in prices experienced as a result of the OPEC oil embargo in the 1970s, when inflation hit about 11 percent per year. Faced with the inflationary pressure, the federal government introduced wage and price controls in late 1975. On the other hand, the Bank of Canada tried to gradually reduce the pace of money growth by adopting a target for M1. Such efforts made little progress in reducing the ballooning inflation rate; the inflation rate remained elevated well into the 1980s.

To try to keep up with inflation, the Zimbabwean government kept printing bills in bigger denominations. Here is a 100-trillion-dollar note—not enough to buy a four-litre jug of milk.

Economists differ over how high inflation has to be before it becomes enough of a problem to merit such painful measures. Some countries have successfully coped with very high inflation (as much as 30 or 40 percent a year) for long periods of time without too much adverse effect on their economy. This is a high-risk situation, though: at such a high rate, inflation is extremely unstable, and it doesn't take much for an economy to slip further toward higher and higher inflation rates.

When inflation begins to spiral out of control, we say that a country is experiencing **hyperinflation**— extremely long-lasting and painful increases in the price level, usually enough to render the currency completely valueless or close to it. This happened pretty quickly in Zimbabwe after the Mugabe regime started printing money to inflate away their debts in 2006. The Zimbabwe dollar was no longer legal tender by the end of 2015 and transactions in Zimbabwe began to be conducted in other currencies, like the US dollar, the euro, and the South African rand. In December 2015, the Chinese yuan was added to Zimbabwe's basket of currencies.

© Finnbarr Webster/Alamy Stock Photo

In one of his first major involvements in public policy, John Maynard Keynes attended the meetings at Versailles that formally ended World War I. During these negotiations, Germany demanded, over the objection of Keynes, extensive reparation payments. Keynes left the Versailles meetings and returned to England to write *The Economic Consequences of the Peace* (1919). This popular work argued that the Versailles treaty demanded more in reparation payments from Germany than the German economy was capable of producing. Keynes predicted that it could lead to political and economic instability and the possibility of hyperinflation in Germany. Keynes's predictions materialized. While this was not the first or most severe hyperinflation experienced in Europe, it had far-reaching consequences. The resultant political and economic instability helped lead to the collapse of the Weimar Republic and the rise of Nazi Germany.

The worst hyperinflation ever recorded happened in Hungary in 1946. With the economy in ruins after World War II, and tax revenues covering only 15 percent of expenditures, the government began to print money to finance the gap. In January 1946 there were 16,500,000 *pengos* in circulation. By July 1946 there were 1,730,000,000,000,000,000. Prices were doubling approximately every fifteen hours. Clearly, this situation was not sustainable. In August 1946 the government abandoned the *pengo* and introduced a new currency, the *forint,* which is still in circulation today. By backing the new currency with gold, the government instilled confidence that it would not print huge amounts of forints.

Expectations can also perpetuate hyperinflation. In Brazil during the 1990s prices rose in part because everyone simply expected them to keep rising. The increase was slowed only by an unorthodox plan that included an entirely fake currency. The story can be found in the Real Life box, A *Real* Plan—with Fake Currency.

REAL LIFE

A *Real* Plan—with Fake Currency

In 1993, President Itamar Franco of Brazil appointed Fernando Henrique Cardoso to be the country's fourth finance minister in just seven months. As the rate of turnover suggests, it was not an enviable job. Price levels in Brazil had been steadily rising for seven years, and the inflation rate was approaching 2,000 percent per year. If he wanted to keep his job, Cardoso had to tackle the hyperinflation quickly. No one had high hopes for his success, though. Cardoso was a professor of sociology, with little training in economics. Furthermore, years of failed efforts had convinced Brazilians that the hyperinflation was impervious to government efforts.

Cardoso sought help from an academic economist named Edmar Bacha, who had been debating with colleagues about how to tame Brazil's stubbornly high inflation. Observing that the traditional tactics used to fight inflation—freezes on prices and wages—had been unsuccessful, they proposed an elegant, if slightly unorthodox solution: Brazil would create a system of fake money, called "units of real value," or URVs for short.

The plan, dubbed *Plano Real* (Real Plan) in Portuguese, worked as follows: Cardoso required everyone in the economy—grocery stores, the government, retail outlets, and all other businesses—to quote prices in both *cruzeiros* (the Brazilian currency at the time) and URVs. Even contracts with promises for future payment had to quote the payment in URVs as well as *cruzeiros*. People would pay in cruzeiros, but would always see the price in URVs as well. Changing conversion rates would ensure that the URV price remained stable: if prices doubled, the conversion rate between cruzeiros and URVs would halve, so that prices in URVs would remain the same. The price shown on a pint of milk might increase from 1,000 *cruzeiros* to 2,000 cruzeiros, but the price in URVs shown alongside would remain the same.

How could this simple accounting trick possibly help to get inflation under control? The genius of the idea is that it tackled what economists call the *psychological inertia* of hyperinflation. As inflation rises and rises, and all government efforts visibly fail to reduce it, people simply get used to the idea that things can only get worse. Businesses raise prices merely because they expect that prices will keep rising. When enough businesses do this, it becomes a self-fulfilling prophecy. A vicious cycle ensues.

The *Plano Real* broke this cycle. Since prices in URVs were stable, people began to trust that they would *stay* stable. Once trust in the stability of URVs developed, the government simply traded out the untrustworthy cruzeiros for a new currency called the *real*, which is still in use today. The government explained that one *real* was worth one URV. Convinced through experience that URV prices were stable, people expected *real* prices to be stable, as well. And because they expected prices to be stable, they were—relatively speaking, at least. In the first few years after the *real* was introduced, inflation fell to under 20 percent.

And what of Fernando Henrique Cardoso, whose job prospects as finance minister originally seemed so uncertain? A grateful nation promptly elected him president.

Sources: http://papers.ssrn.com/sol3/papers.cfm?abstract_id=518265; http://uk.reuters.com/article/uk-brazil-president-idUKTRE76119A20110702

Inflation as a Buffer Against Deflation

If deflation is bad and inflation is bad, then central banks must try to achieve perfect price stability with an inflation rate of zero, right? Wrong. In fact, for most central banks around the world, the preferred monetary policy is to promote modest positive inflation—something around 2 or 3 percent per year.

Why do most economists believe it's better to aim for modest inflation than completely stable prices? There are three main reasons for this belief. The first is that allowing for a little inflation reduces the risk of deflation. If the inflation rate tends to hover around zero percent, and the central bank miscalculates by making monetary policy too contractionary, the result would be deflation—which can have serious impacts on the economy. Keeping inflation at a modest positive level gives a central bank some leeway to make mistakes without running the risk of tipping the country into a deflationary spiral.

Second, keeping inflation at a modest positive level leaves more room for the central bank to engage in expansionary monetary policy. To understand why, we can work through a simple example. Suppose that inflation is at a healthy 3 percent per year. Investors are going to want an interest rate that is at or above the inflation rate to ensure that the real rate of return they earn on their money is positive. For monetary policy, this means that the overall nominal interest rate will likely end up somewhere at or above 3 percent. This gives the central bank some room to reduce interest rates before hitting zero (the lower bound). By contrast, if inflation was zero percent, nominal interest rates would be equal to the real interest rate (which is close to zero, as well). In the case of a recession, a central bank would have very little leeway to further reduce interest rates. (This situation is sometimes referred to as a *liquidity trap* and has been a major problem in Japan for more than a decade.)

In fact, during the latest recession, Olivier Blanchard, the chief economist of the International Monetary Fund (IMF), advised central banks to increase their inflation target from the traditional 2 percent to 4 percent. That extra room, he argued, could mean the difference between effectively fighting a deep recession and hitting the zero lower bound while the economy could still use some help from monetary policy.[1]

A third reason for having a positive inflation target is that the target makes it easier for firms to adjust real wages in the labour market in response to changing labour demand and supply conditions. Reductions in labour demand or labour supply result in reductions in the equilibrium real wage. If prices are stable, reducing the real wage requires employers to reduce the nominal wage; workers may respond to a 1 percent reduction in their nominal pay by reducing their work effort. But workers generally seem less bothered if they receive a 2 percent wage increase when there is 3 percent inflation.

The effect is the same—a 1 percent reduction in income—but the cause of the reduced income seems different. Furthermore, in cases in which there is a formal labour contract, nominal wages cannot be reduced during the life of the contract. With a low inflation rate, though, all that is required for firms to lower real wages is to increase nominal wages more slowly than the inflation rate. Thus, a low and stable inflation rate may help to "grease the wheels" of the labour market, allowing for more flexible real wages and more efficient labour markets.

✓ CONCEPT CHECK

- ☐ Why would people at the highest income level not worry about bracket creep? [LO 15.4]
- ☐ Why do people spend less in the present when deflation is expected in the future? [LO 15.5]
- ☐ What is a reduction in the overall rate of inflation known as? [LO 15.6]
- ☐ Why would lenders favour unexpected deflation, while borrowers favour unexpected inflation? [LO 15.6]

Inflation and Monetary Policy

Recall in Chapter 11, we asserted that when aggregate demand is high, it leads to higher output but a higher price level. On the other hand, when aggregate demand is low, both output and the price level tend to be low. Maintaining price stability, of course, is another way of saying that inflation rates should be consistently low. Ensuring full employment simply means that the economy experiences only frictional and structural unemployment and no cyclical unemployment.

The Competing Goals of Maintaining Price Stability and Full Employment

> **LO 15.7** Explain the relationship between inflation, the output gap, and monetary policy.

In practice, the goals of low inflation and unemployment are often incompatible. To understand why, it helps to think about how inflation rates change through a typical business cycle. During a recession, inflation is typically very low. Why is that? During a bust, the economy is operating well below its *potential*. Economists refer to an economy's **potential output** as the total amount of output the country could reasonably produce if all of its people and capital resources (i.e., machines and factories and the like) were fully engaged. In practice, this means that only frictional and structural unemployment—no cyclical unemployment—occur.

When an economy's actual output differs from its potential at some point in time, we say that it is experiencing an **output gap**. If output is below potential, then the output gap is negative. It is also possible for an economy to operate above capacity—if everyone was not only employed but working overtime hours as well. When an economy is working above capacity, we say that it has a positive output gap. Figure 15-5 shows the historical output gap for Canada.

What is going on when an economy has a negative output gap? For one thing, there are a lot of resources—either factories or workers—not being fully used. Workers are unemployed and factories are sitting idle, waiting for work. In other words, the economy is experiencing recessionary conditions. During recessionary periods, there is typically little threat of a rise in inflation (unless the economy is hit by an oil crisis or similar external shock). Low rates of inflation occur in part because there is so little demand for money in an economy experiencing recession. Borrowers, for example, are much less interested in taking out loans for big-ticket items during a recession, since they are less confident in their ability to pay back the loans. Firms have little incentive to borrow to expand their businesses when overall demand for goods and services is low. Why produce if you think there won't be buyers for the output you make? As long as the supply of money stays the same, decreased demand causes the overall price level to fall.

But what happens when the economy is experiencing a positive output gap? With nearly everyone employed (and working overtime), hiring new workers can be very expensive. Workers can eventually command higher salaries to switch jobs, since employers have to compete for them. Likewise, companies are competing to buy up machines, factories, or other inputs to meet soaring demand for their products, leading to a rise in those prices, as well. Rising prices across the economy, of course, mean inflation.

FIGURE 15-5

The Output Gap in Canada

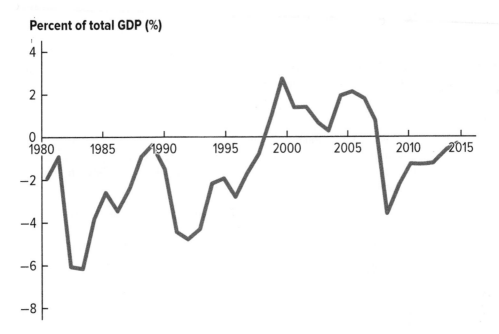

The output gap (measured as percentage of total GDP) registers the difference between actual GDP and potential GDP at full employment. Over this period, actual output has fluctuated around potential output.

Source: IMF, *World Economic Outlook* database, updated April 3, 2015, http://www.imf.org/external/pubs/ft/weo/2015/01/weodata/index.aspx

As you can see, there is typically a strong relationship between the output gap and inflation. But what does this have to do with monetary policy? To answer that question, we'll have to go back to what happens when the Bank of Canada conducts monetary policy.

We'll start with expansionary monetary policy. In a recession, an output gap implies that employment is low. A central bank knows that it can fix this problem by engaging in expansionary monetary policy. When it increases the money supply and lowers interest rates, borrowing may increase, which may help the economy rebound. An increase in economic activity puts more people back to work, which fulfills the mandate: prices have increased only a little bit and employment is high.

But, as you know, this is only a short-run equilibrium. The increased demand for goods and services will put upward pressure on prices. With an increase in the money supply, more money will be spent chasing the same amount of goods. In the long run, the economy will fall back to the long-run equilibrium. Employment will decrease, but prices will remain elevated. So what does a central bank do? It could continue to pump money into the economy in an effort to increase employment, but these gains will be short-lived, and inflation will worsen.

The opposite scenario occurs when inflation is above normal. When inflation is pulled high by demand, money in the economy is spent chasing a limited amount of goods. Firms want to buy machines and inputs in an effort to expand operations, while workers receive higher wages. In this case, employment is at full, or even beyond full, capacity. If a central bank decides that it needs to curb inflation it will pursue contractionary monetary policy—reducing the growth rate of the money supply to work toward a higher interest rate. As we described earlier, this slows the economy. The higher interest rate makes borrowing more expensive, and firms slow investment. Although inflation decreases, the slowing of the economy increases unemployment. Eventually, though, as the economy adjusts to lower prices and we move into the long run, employment will return to full-output levels, leaving just the decrease in overall prices.

So you can see that central banks, no matter how they conduct monetary policy, inevitably affect only price levels, with no lasting impact on employment, in the long run. Attempts to stimulate the economy through expansionary monetary policy will increase the inflation rate. Attempts to slow the economy through contractionary policy will lower the inflation rate and risk causing deflation. The Bank of Canada has to navigate this trade-off carefully.

Inflation and Unemployment

LO 15.8 Analyze the relationship between inflation and unemployment, and explain how it is modelled by the Phillips curve and integrated into the non-accelerating rate of unemployment.

We've seen that there is a trade-off between inflation and unemployment in the short run, which poses a challenge for the Bank of Canada. Ensuring full employment is really another way of saying "keeping actual output near potential output." Fulfilling this goal through expansionary monetary policy, however, risks violating the Bank of Canada's other goal, that of price stability. How can the Bank of Canada calculate the best way to make this trade-off?

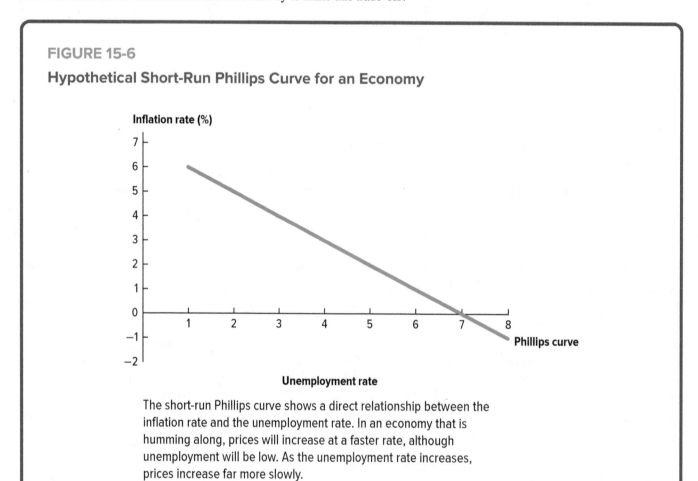

FIGURE 15-6

Hypothetical Short-Run Phillips Curve for an Economy

The short-run Phillips curve shows a direct relationship between the inflation rate and the unemployment rate. In an economy that is humming along, prices will increase at a faster rate, although unemployment will be low. As the unemployment rate increases, prices increase far more slowly.

The Phillips Curve

In 1958, an economist named A. W. Phillips plotted the change in prices against unemployment over a ninety-five-year period in Great Britain. A distinct pattern emerged. As inflation ran higher, unemployment was low; when inflation was low, unemployment was high. The line showing that relationship is now called the **Phillips curve**, and it forms the basis of a model that shows the connection between inflation and unemployment in the short run.

The most basic form of the Phillips curve is depicted in Figure 15-6. The hypothetical lines show that if the central bank of this economy wants zero inflation, then it will have to accept 7 percent unemployment. If it wants to target a modest positive rate of inflation of, for example, 3 percent, then it will have to accept 4 percent unemployment. If it wants to get unemployment down as low as 1 percent, it will have to accept a rate of inflation of 6 percent. And so on. This simple formulation fits our intuition about how the output gap—and by extension, unemployment—relates to inflation. In general, high amounts of unemployment in an economy will coincide with low inflation, and higher amounts of inflation come with lower unemployment.

We can now further investigate this relationship using the aggregate demand and aggregate supply model in the short run, as shown in panels A and B of Figure 15-7. If the economy is at short-run equilibrium with 4 percent unemployment and 3 percent inflation, an increase in aggregate demand above expectations is going to cause the economy to be at a point higher and to the left on the Phillips curve.

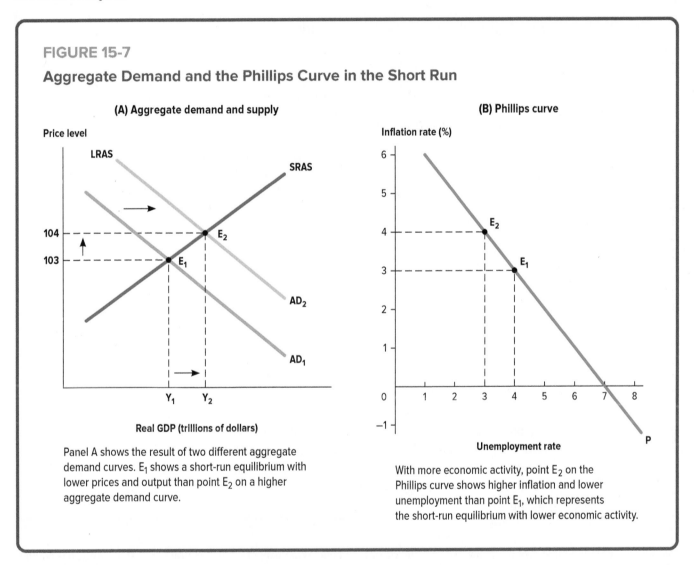

FIGURE 15-7

Aggregate Demand and the Phillips Curve in the Short Run

(A) Aggregate demand and supply

(B) Phillips curve

Panel A shows the result of two different aggregate demand curves. E_1 shows a short-run equilibrium with lower prices and output than point E_2 on a higher aggregate demand curve.

With more economic activity, point E_2 on the Phillips curve shows higher inflation and lower unemployment than point E_1, which represents the short-run equilibrium with lower economic activity.

However, this basic curve fails to consider an important factor: the role of *inflation expectations.* In any economy, people often come to expect whatever level of inflation has prevailed over the past few years. If inflation has been about 3 percent over the past few years, then the expectation of 3 percent inflation typically becomes "baked in" to prices. If prices are rising by 3 percent per year, employees will expect raises of at least 3 percent as a matter of course, and 3 percent inflation becomes a default for the economy.

Why does this matter? Let's assume that the economy represented in Figure 15-7 is humming along at a *long-run equilibrium* of 4 percent unemployment and 3 percent inflation. Now imagine that the central bank decides to try to reduce unemployment, accepting a slightly higher inflation rate as a result. When the money supply expands, unemployment falls to 1 percent and inflation increases to 6 percent.

So far, so good. However, we know that the economy was in long-run equilibrium at 4 percent unemployment. And we know from Figure 15-1, earlier in the chapter, what happens if a central bank pursues expansionary monetary policy when the economy is already at long-run equilibrium: it can increase output (and, hence, reduce unemployment), but *only in the short run*. In the long run, output returns to its earlier equilibrium and so do levels of employment.

Our hypothetical central bank finds that unemployment is now back at 4 percent, but inflation is now running at 6 percent. Effectively, by pursuing expansionary monetary policy when the economy was already at long-run equilibrium, it has shifted the Phillips curve upward, as shown in Figure 15-8.

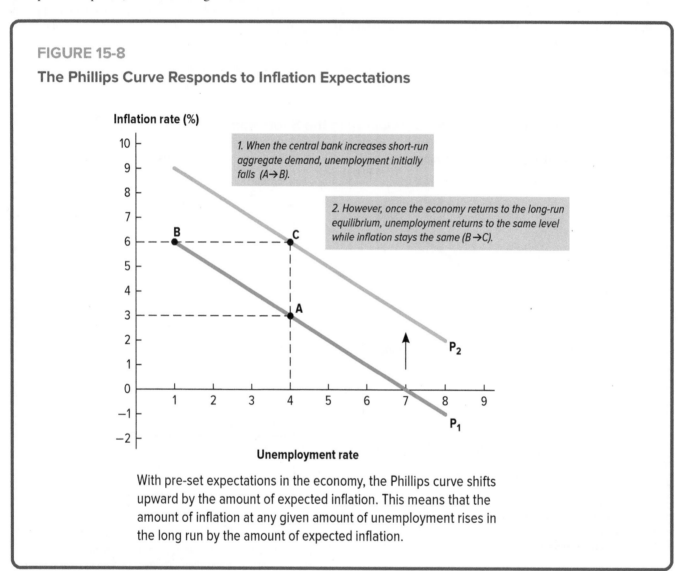

FIGURE 15-8

The Phillips Curve Responds to Inflation Expectations

1. When the central bank increases short-run aggregate demand, unemployment initially falls (A→B).

2. However, once the economy returns to the long-run equilibrium, unemployment returns to the same level while inflation stays the same (B→C).

With pre-set expectations in the economy, the Phillips curve shifts upward by the amount of expected inflation. This means that the amount of inflation at any given amount of unemployment rises in the long run by the amount of expected inflation.

People in our hypothetical economy now *expect* inflation of 6 percent. What happens if the central bank, stubbornly, has another go at reducing unemployment to 1 percent? It will succeed in the short run, but as we can see from the new Phillips curve, inflation will go up to 9 percent. And in the long run, we'll see unemployment rise again to 4 percent but inflation remain stubbornly at 9 percent because people will have adjusted their inflation expectations upward once again. Eventually, the central bank's efforts would simply spiral out of control, leading to more and more inflation and the unemployment rate never staying at the bank's goal in the long run.

Realizing this effect, economists proposed an improved version of the Phillips curve, showing also the long-run effect of changing inflation expectations. Figure 15-9 shows both the traditional Phillips curve, which we'll now call the short-run Phillips curve, and the long-run Phillips curve, for two different levels of inflation expectations. The two short-run Phillips curves in the figure tell us the trade-off facing monetary policy makers between inflation and unemployment at any given time. The vertical line in the figure is the long-run Phillips curve, which is at 4 percent. This line represents the idea that in the long run in our hypothetical economy, it is impossible to get the level of unemployment below 4 percent.

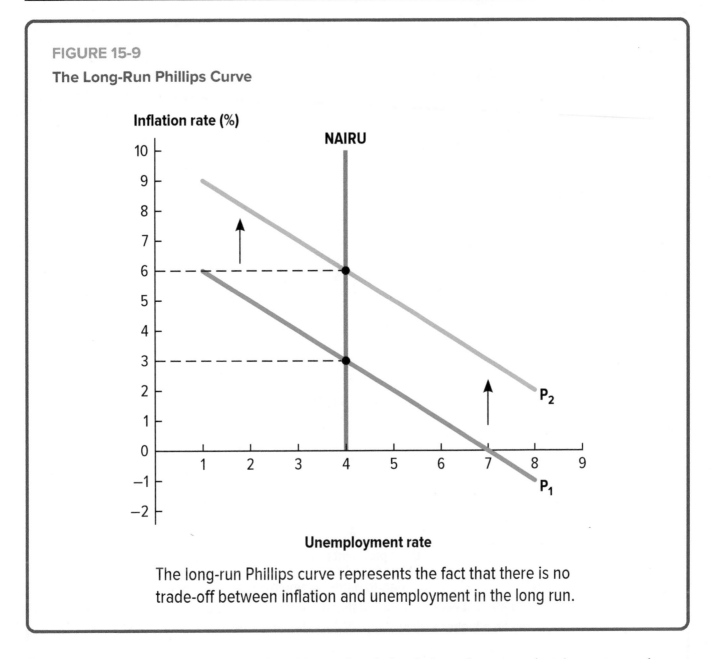

FIGURE 15-9

The Long-Run Phillips Curve

The long-run Phillips curve represents the fact that there is no trade-off between inflation and unemployment in the long run.

To see why, we'll run through a story that we've told many times before. Let's say the economy is at 4 percent unemployment and the economy expands. In order to expand, firms need more workers, but with such a low unemployment rate, few workers are just sitting around looking for work. As a result, trying to hire more workers is going to be expensive. Wages—the price of labour—are prices, after all, and are influential enough on the overall price level that with higher wages from the increase in demand for labour, prices throughout the economy will increase. In our diagram, the vertical line marks the minimum level of unemployment that can be sustained without creating runaway inflation.

Economists call this minimum level of unemployment the **non-accelerating inflation rate of unemployment (NAIRU)**. The NAIRU, sometimes also called the *natural rate of unemployment*, or simply *full employment* (even though it's not technically zero percent unemployment), is the lowest possible unemployment rate that will not cause the inflation rate to increase.

The NAIRU can change over time. Take, for example, the introduction of the Internet to job searches. This innovation reduced structural unemployment (and the NAIRU) on two fronts. One is from the increase of opportunities available to searchers. Before the availability of websites that allow you to search millions of job listings, job hunters had to scour local classifieds and attend job fairs. They essentially confined their searches to opportunities within a very narrow geographical range. With the Internet, that range has been greatly expanded. On the other side, the Internet has also been a boon to employers. Today, a job posting on the Internet will be seen by more job seekers and bring forward a wider pool of high-quality applicants.

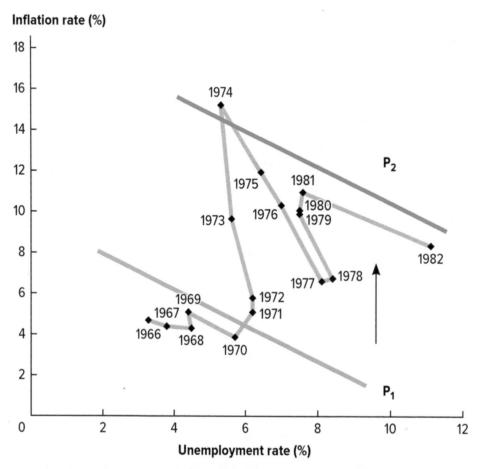

FIGURE 15-10

The Phillips Curve Shifts Upward

When the Bank of Canada tried to battle unemployment by allowing higher inflation, it eventually found that it had simply put the economy on a higher Phillips curve (P_2) as shown above.

Source: Statistics Canada, CANSIM Tables 380-0003, "Gross domestic product (GDP) indexes"; 384-0035, "Selected economic indicators," and 282-0087, "Labour force survey estimates (LFS), by sex and age group."

In practice, calculating the exact NAIRU is difficult. It differs among economies and over time due to variations in the structural components of unemployment, the regulatory and competitive environment, and a multitude of other factors. As a result, it can be difficult to know whether an economy is truly at full employment at any given time, a challenge for the Bank of Canada policy makers looking to fulfill their goals. Though we may not know the exact location of the NAIRU, we can fairly quickly determine if we are above or below it. If unemployment is below the NAIRU, inflation generally accelerates. If we observe involuntary unemployment rising, unemployment is above the NAIRU.

The Phillips Curve and NAIRU in Practice

To understand how the NAIRU and Phillips curve work in practice, we'll return to the story, from earlier in the chapter, of monetary policy after the OPEC oil embargo. When the oil embargo hit, the aggregate supply curve shifted sharply to the left. At that short-run equilibrium, prices were higher and output lower. Obviously, this combination is not desirable for policy makers;

it meant either permitting high rates of inflation, in order to keep unemployment in check, or slowing down the economy even further in order to rein in inflation.

During the 1970s, the Bank of Canada chose the first tack. The Bank of Canada thought that unemployment was a greater danger to the economy, and it even expanded the money supply to try to pick up the economy after the supply shock. As time wore on, inflation pushed higher and higher, but unemployment stayed relatively the same; the economy had shifted to a higher Phillips curve. Since inflation was expected in the economy, further attempts to boost the economy simply pushed the trade-off between inflation and unemployment even higher. By the end of the 1970s, inflation was running at double digits, while unemployment was high. Figure 15-10 shows this adjustment upward toward higher Phillips curves, from an inflation rate of about 3.9 percent in the early 1970s to the double-digit rate by 1980.

Gerald Bouey, governor at the Bank of Canada at the time, realized that shock therapy was needed to wean the economy off the expectation that inflation would continue to increase at relatively high rates. As a result, he employed the traditional tool used to fight inflation—he decreased the money supply through increases in interest rates. This blunt policy worked. Since people knew that the Bank of Canada was going to take a tough stand on inflation, expectations for price increases in the future evaporated. In just five years, the overall economy was in a position with a far more favourable trade-off between inflation and unemployment. In Figure 15-11 you can see the change in Phillips curves over this time period, resulting from a decrease in the inflation rate of about 10.1 percent in 1980 to a much tamer rate of about 3.3 percent in 1984.

Figure 15-11
The Phillips Curve Adjusts Downward

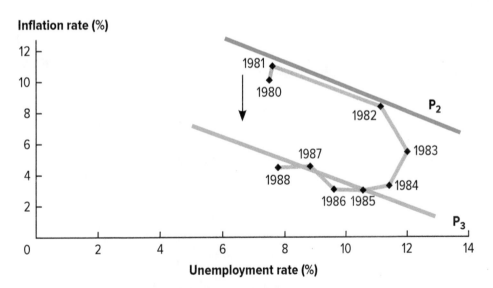

In the early 1980s, Gerald Bouey led an effort to raise interest rates, thereby decreasing the money supply and bringing down inflation. By 1985, the economy was on a lower Philips curve (P_3).

Source: Statistics Canada, CANSIM Table 380-0003, "Gross domestic product (GDP) indexes"; 384-0035, "Selected economic indicators," and 282-0087, "Labour force survey estimates (LFS), by sex and age group."

The Phillips curve remains an essential tool for understanding how the Bank of Canada works in practice. Effectively, setting the goal as full employment means ensuring that employment remains as close to the NAIRU as possible at all times. Pushing unemployment below that level all but guarantees that inflation will get out of control, failing to maintain price stability. On the other hand, allowing unemployment to remain at a higher level than NAIRU would mean failing to maintain full employment. The Bank of Canada's aim, then, is to keep unemployment levels near the NAIRU and inflation reasonably under control. As the story of the oil embargo shows, managing this trade-off is no easy task.

✓ CONCEPT CHECK

☐ What does it mean for the output gap to be positive? What will eventually happen if that occurs? [LO 15.7]

☐ What happens if unemployment is lower than the NAIRU? [LO 15.8]

Conclusion

In this chapter we've explored one of the most complex issues in economics: inflation. We've seen how mismanagement of the money supply can lead to runaway inflation, how even relatively modest inflation can have far-reaching consequences for healthy economies, and why deflation is a problem. We've also seen that expectations of inflation help determine whether savings will hold their value and whether it's a good time to borrow.

We've seen too that when people expect inflation to continue, those beliefs can, in themselves, perpetuate inflation. Thus inflation can be a self-fulfilling prophecy. Getting runaway inflation under control requires the right monetary policy as well as convincing people that inflation will indeed fall.

Key Terms

inflation

deflation

core inflation

aggregate price level

neutrality of money

quantity theory of money

velocity of money

menu costs

shoe-leather costs

nominal interest rate

real interest rate

disinflation

hyperinflation

potential output

output gap

Phillips curve

non-accelerating inflation rate of unemployment (NAIRU)

Summary

LO 15.1 Explain the neutrality of money.

Prices denote the nominal value of goods; the price level reflects prices when aggregated across the economy. The neutrality of money suggests that the money supply affects price levels throughout the economy, but in the long run has no effect on real variables in the economy, such as output. The neutrality of money implies that if the money supply suddenly doubled, nominal GDP would double as well, but real GDP would remain the same.

LO 15.2 Describe and illustrate the classical theory of inflation.

The classical theory of inflation describes the relationship between the money supply, output, and the price level. The theory argues that the money supply has no effect on output in the long run. However, it shows how adjusting the money supply can change output in the short run. If the central bank adopts expansionary policy, it could increase the money supply, shifting the aggregate demand curve to the right and causing output and prices to increase. The effect on the cost of production and anticipation that these high prices will continue causes the aggregate supply curve to shift leftward until it intersects the demand curve at the original level of output.

LO 15.3 Explain the quantity theory of money and relate it to inflation and deflation.

The quantity theory of money shows the relationship between the value of money in terms of the output we can buy and the quantity of it. Mathematically, the quantity theory of money indicates that the product of the velocity of money and the money supply (total spending) is identical to the product of the price level and real output (nominal GDP).

Changes in the quantity of money affect the price level. An increase in the money supply leads to inflation; a decrease in the money supply leads to deflation.

LO 15.4 Analyze the economic consequences of inflation.

Inflation is an increase in the price level in an economy. Over the long run, inflation is often caused by increases in the money supply. In the short run, it is more often a result of the business cycle. If inflation rates are unstable, they introduce uncertainty into the market, often causing a decline in output. Even a stable rate of inflation can impose costs on the economy, including menu costs and bracket creep.

LO 15.5 Analyze the economic consequences of deflation.

In contrast to inflation, deflation is a fall in the price level of an economy. Deflation is considered more dangerous than inflation. When prices are falling, borrowers have a more difficult time paying back their debts; deflation makes the debt more expensive over time, often causing borrowers to default. High default rates, in turn, lower prices, causing further defaults. A deflationary spiral often ensues, halting the economy.

LO 15.6 Describe disinflation and hyperinflation, and explain the role of monetary policy in creating both situations.

When central banks succeed at controlling inflation, disinflation often occurs. Disinflation happens when inflation rates are positive, but falling. A famous example of disinflation was Gerald Bouey's efforts to stem inflation in the 1980s. When central banks fail to control inflation, hyperinflation can occur. Hyperinflation is an extreme rise in price levels. It can cause economic crisis and drastically reduce the value of a country's currency.

LO 15.7 Explain the relationship between inflation, the output gap, and monetary policy.

The central bank uses monetary policy to control inflation. Central banks prefer to keep inflation low, but positive. When full employment occurs, the economy is said to be producing at its potential output, the total amount of output a country can produce if its resources are used efficiently. The output gap is the difference between potential and actual output. When the output gap is negative, inflation will decrease. Central banks will then pursue expansionary monetary policy by lowering interest rates, allowing inflation to rise and bringing back full employment. When the output gap is positive, inflation will increase.

LO 15.8 Analyze the relationship between inflation and unemployment, and explain how it is modelled by the Phillips curve and integrated into the non-accelerating rate of unemployment.

The relationship between employment and inflation in the short run is modelled by the Phillips curve. The curve shows that a decrease in unemployment will be accompanied by an increase in inflation in the short run. The relationship does not hold over the long run, in part because of inflation expectations. If central banks pursue aggressive expansionary policy to reduce unemployment, inflation may spiral out of control. The level of unemployment at which inflation will remain stable is called the non-accelerating inflation rate of unemployment (NAIRU), or full employment.

Review Questions

1. Your uncle comes to you with an investment idea. He tells you that the nominal GDP of Paradisia quadrupled over the past year and suggests that you invest there. Unemployment is at 20 percent and inflation over the last year was 500 percent. Do you think it's a good idea to invest? Draw on the neutrality theory of money to explain why or why not. **[LO 15.1]**

2. Why might we want to measure GDP in dollar terms? In output terms? How does the neutrality of money relate to your answer? **[LO 15.1]**

3. Suppose a country's currency is a gold coin. One day speculators find a large gold mine, which doubles the supply of gold coins in the economy. What will happen to output in the short run? What about price levels? What will happen to output in the long run? What about price levels? **[LO 15.2]**

4. Explain how some analysts might use the short-run and long-run effects on the aggregate demand–aggregate supply model to argue that monetary policy can't affect employment in the long run. **[LO 15.2]**

5. Why might the velocity of money increase around the holidays? If the central bank wants to avoid inflation in those times, what should it do? **[LO 15.3]**

6. Use the quantity theory of money to explain how expansionary monetary policy can be inflationary. **[LO 15.3]**

7. Imagine you own an ice cream store in Toronto. Write a brief note to your Member of Parliament explaining two ways in which unpredictable inflation hurts your business. **[LO 15.4]**

8. Is inflation harmful only when it's unexpected? If yes, why? If no, name two costs that occur with even predictable inflation. **[LO 15.4]**

9. Your MP now claims that lowering prices would be good for everyone—"Who doesn't like lower prices, after all?" He tells you he plans to lobby for deflation. Explain why falling prices could lead to a bad situation. **[LO 15.5]**

10. Is inflation always bad for an economy? Should we target a zero percent inflation rate? When does inflation become hyperinflation? **[LO 15.5]**

11. What could have happened to prices in the wake of the recent financial crisis, if the government and central bank had not intervened in the economy? How would this have affected the economy? **[LO 15.6]**

12. Are deflation and disinflation the same thing? Why or why not? **[LO 15.6]**

13. In the 1960s, policy based on the simple short-run Phillips curve worked better than similar attempts in the 1970s. How might better information availability have contributed to this result? **[LO 15.7]**

14. When we have a negative output gap, what is the proper monetary policy response in the short run? What are its intended effects on interest rates and employment? **[LO 15.7]**

15. Explain the effect contractionary monetary policy will have on the output gap, inflation, and unemployment if unemployment is currently at the non-accelerating inflation rate of unemployment. **[LO 15.8]**

16. Compare and contrast the effect of increased unemployment on inflation in the short and long run. **[LO 15.8]**

Problems and Applications

1. Which of the following can be affected by the money supply in the long run? **[LO 15.1]**
   a. Nominal GDP
   b. Real GDP
   c. Inflation
   d. Unemployment

2. Determine whether each of the following events is likely to cause deflation, disinflation, no change in the price level, or inflation. [LO 15.1]
   a. A bubble in the biomedical industry just burst.
   b. A new technology is introduced into the economy, sparking an economic boom.
   c. The Bank of Canada conducts contractionary monetary policy.
   d. The Bank of Canada is successful at meeting its goals of full employment and price stability.

3. To increase the self-esteem of dieters everywhere, powerful fashion designers lobby the government to redefine "five pounds" as "one pound." Under this system, what would have previously been five pounds of bananas will now be one pound of bananas and a 500-pound gorilla would now weigh only 100 pounds. [LO 15.2]
   a. How much would someone who originally weighed 180 pounds now weigh as a result of this redefinition?
   b. Has there been a nominal change in the person's weight? A real change?
   c. How is this story similar to contractionary monetary policy via a decrease in the money supply in the long run? (*Hint:* Parliament essentially shrank the "pounds supply" by redefining the word.)

4. "Monetary policy is incredible," your friend says. "Just a little manipulation of the money supply and interest rates, and we end up at just the right price level and amount of output." Is your friend overstating the central bank's control over price levels and output? Why or why not? [LO 15.2]

5. Your dormitory, Griffingate, has appointed you central banker of its economy, which deals in the currency of wizcoins. Assume that the velocity of wizcoins in Griffingate is constant at 10,000 transactions per year. Right now real GDP is 1,000 wizcoins, and there are 2,000 wizcoins in existence. [LO 15.3].
   a. What will be the value of each of the variables that make up the quantity equation—M, V, and P?
   b. Now indicate how the other variables will respond to each of the following scenarios, taking each case separately and assuming that velocity remains constant.
      (i)   *Real GDP:* You increase the money supply to 4,000, and prices increase twofold.
      (ii) *Price level:* Start with the initial values. Real GDP drops to 500 wizcoins, and the money supply remains constant.
      (ii) *Real GDP:* Start with the initial values. Prices increase threefold because of a sudden scarcity of soft drinks, and you decide to keep the supply of wizcoins constant.
      (iv) *Real GDP:* Start with the initial values. You increase the money supply to 5,000 wizcoins, and prices rise by 350 percent.

6. Express the following relationships using the equation for the quantity theory of money. [LO 15.3]
   a. The money supply is given by nominal GDP divided by the velocity of money.
   b. The relationship of the money supply to the price level is the same as the relationship between real GDP and velocity. (*Hint:* Start by dividing the money supply by the price level.)
   c. Real GDP is given by the flow of money divided by the price level.
   d. The price level of an economy can be found by dividing the product of the money supply and its velocity by real GDP.

7. Identify whether the following individuals will be affected by bracket creep next year, given the rates of taxation and levels of inflation found in Table 15P-1, [LO 15.4]
   a. Gabriela makes $9,500, and inflation is at 5 percent.
   b. Cooper makes $160,000, and inflation is at a record high of 20 percent.
   c. Shawna makes $140,000, and inflation is at 8 percent.
   d. Samuel makes $45,000, and inflation is at 6 percent.
   e. Marguerite makes $96,000, and inflation is at 6 percent.

TABLE 15P-1

Marginal tax rate (%)	Income level ($)
10	0 – 10,000
15	10,001 – 30,000

Marginal tax rate (%)	Income level ($)
18	30,001 – 50,000
20	50,001 – 100,000
23	100,001 – 150,000
25	150,001 and up

8. Cookie Monster has decided to channel his love of cookies into a new business, Me Want Cookies Inc., a new partnership he has formed with Miss Piggy. They are considering different countries in which to start their venture and would like to rank the countries based on the inflationary environment. They decide to give a country 10 "menu-cost" points for each percent of actual inflation in the last year, since inflation will cause their menu costs to increase. They also dislike unstable inflation, so they will give a country 20 "uncertainty" points for each percent difference in the actual inflation rate when compared to the projected inflation rate. Countries with the fewest total points will receive the highest rankings. Complete Table 15P-2 for Cookie Monster. [LO 15.4].

TABLE 15P-2

Country	Projected inflation (%)	Actual inflation (%)	Uncertainty points	Menu-cost points	Total points	Rank
Kermikopia	2	4				
Gonzoland	4	5				
Elmostan	7	8				
Oscaria	10	13				
Bertico	14	14				

9. Jack recently took out a loan from Diane at an interest rate of 5 percent. Diane expected this year's inflation rate to be 2 percent and the real interest rate to be 3 percent. The loan is due at the end of this year. Complete Table 15P-3, showing the real interest rate for each possible inflation rate. For each situation, determine whether the unexpected inflation level benefits Jack or Diane. [LO 15.5]

TABLE 15P-3

This year's actual inflation rate (%)	Actual real interest rate (%)	Who benefits?
1		
4		
0		
−2		

10. Assume the prices shown in Table 15P-4 are the prices of Big Macs in 2030, 2031, and 2032, and that changes in the price of Big Macs tend to closely keep up with inflation. For each of the four instances, determine the following. [LO 15.5], [LO 15.6]
    (i)   The percentage changes in price levels between each consecutive year.
    (ii) Whether the economy was experiencing inflation, deflation, disinflation, or hyperinflation over each period. (Assume that inflation above 100 percent constitutes hyperinflation.)

TABLE 15P-4

	Price in 2030 ($)	Price in 2031 ($)	Price in 2032 ($)
a.	1.00	1.02	1.03
b.	1.00	0.99	0.97
c.	0.01	0.05	1.00
d.	1.00	1.10	1.15

11. Assuming that inflation above 100 percent is hyperinflation, categorize each of the inflation rates in Table 15P-5 as deflation, disinflation, inflation, or hyperinflation as we move from one year to the next. [LO 15.5]

TABLE 15P-5

	Year	Inflation rate (%)	Description
a.	1900	90	
b.	1901	80	
c.	1902	120	
d.	1903	40	
e.	1904	−2	

12. Suppose you live in Frigidia, a country near the North Pole that is experiencing hyperinflation. You work for a Canadian company that pays you a monthly income of $100. Today, you can exchange those dollars for frigids, the currency of Frigidia, at a rate of 1,000 frigids/dollar. You pay a monthly heating bill that costs $10. Instead of paying the heating bill, you could simply burn Frigidia notes (which you can obtain in one-frigid denominations) at a rate of 1 million per month to supply heating. What would the exchange rate between frigids and Canadian dollars have to be for you to decide to burn bills instead of paying for heating? What level of inflation does this represent, assuming the real exchange rate remains the same? [LO 15.6]

13. "The problem wasn't having the wrong idea about interest rates," a sheepish central bank official says at a conference, "but rather not having the right idea about inflation rates." What does the official mean? How does the inflation rate affect the central bank's interest rate target, and how can a wrong prediction about inflation make monetary policy go awry? [LO 15.6]

14. Determine whether the Bank of Canada would pursue contractionary monetary policy, expansionary monetary policy, or no change in policy in each of the following situations. [LO 15.7]
    a. Inflation is 10 percent, above its average of 3 percent in the last several years.
    b. The output gap is positive.
    c. Unemployment is at a record high.

d. The economy is experiencing full employment.

e. The economy is on the brink of deflation.

f. A new technology causes output to surge.

15. Answer each of the following questions assuming the economy is experiencing a positive output gap. [LO 15.7]

a. Is inflation decreasing, increasing, or stable?

b. Is actual output greater than or less than potential output?

c. Is unemployment rising or falling?

d. Is the Bank of Canada more likely to pursue expansionary or contractionary monetary policy?

e. Is the economy likely experiencing an expansion or contraction?

16. Answer each of the following questions assuming the economy is experiencing a negative output gap. [LO 15.7]

a. Is inflation decreasing, increasing, or stable?

b. Is actual output greater than or less than potential output?

c. Is unemployment rising or falling?

d. Is the Bank of Canada more likely to pursue expansionary or contractionary monetary policy?

e. Is the economy likely experiencing an expansion or contraction?

17. Assume the Phillips curve is given by the simple equation $U = -I + 20$. The non-accelerating rate of unemployment is 10 percent. If inflation changes to 15 percent, what will be the unemployment rate in the short run? What will it be in the long run? [LO 15.8]

18. Using what you know about the Phillips curve, determine whether the following quantities will increase, decrease, or remain the same. [LO 15.8]

a. Unemployment in the short run after an increase in inflation

b. Unemployment in the long run after an increase in inflation

c. Inflation in the short run after a decrease in unemployment

d. Inflation in the long run after a decrease in unemployment

Chapter Sources

"Argentina's inflation problem: The price of cooking the books," *The Economist,* February 25, 2012, http://www.economist.com/node/21548229

Marco A. Espinosa and Steven Russel, "History and theory of the NAIRU: A critical review," Federal Reserve Bank of Atlanta, *Economic Review,* Second Quarter 1997, http://www.frbatlanta.org/filelegacydocs/acfc1.pdf.

Walking Away from a Mortgage

In 2015, Francis was in trouble. The value of his home had plummeted, and he owed more on his mortgage than the home was worth. Even if he sold his house, the proceeds still wouldn't be enough to pay it off. Like many Albertans who lived in Grande Cache, Francis's investment in his home was "under water."

In 2011, Francis bought a townhouse in the Grande Cache, Alberta, for $175,000 with a five percent downpayment (but still owes $150,000 on his mortgage). A realtor recently told Francis that the best price for his townhouse is $75,000. "At the time it seemed cheaper. I didn't want to spend money on rent. But now I think I can find something cheaper to rent," he said. Grande Cache, Alberta, is a mining town. When the price of mining products falls, so do the prices of houses.

With the mortgage "under water," if Francis walks away from his mortgage, CMHC (Canadian Mortgage and Housing Corporation) will need to cover the difference for his bank. And Francis will be sued by CMHC for any assets it can recover from him to offset the loss. Walking away from a mortgage is the defining act of any housing crisis that sends housing prices into deeper trouble. And it can happen in Alberta and Saskatchewan, as these two provinces have non-recourse mortgages[1] (subject to some caveats). In fact, during the economic downturn in 1983 and 1984, mortgage delinquency rates increased drastically in Alberta.

Paul Sakuma, File/AP Photo/The Canadian Press

In the years before the housing market slowdown, optimism was rampant. House prices continued to soar and risks appeared small. Then an incredible thing happened. Housing prices plummeted. The sustained fall in housing prices put many homeowners into default on their mortgages. The balances owed on the mortgages were more than what the houses were worth on the market. Many ended up defaulting. Financial investors who had thought they were parking their money in low-risk financial products were horrified to find themselves losing fortunes.

Markets are a powerful tool for the efficient allocation of scarce resources. Financial markets are, in many ways, the purest expression of the market mechanism. Relatively free from government intervention, financial markets are a global marketplace in which sophisticated investors make billion-dollar decisions nearly every second of the day.

So how can financial markets go so very wrong? And why do the failings of financial markets reverberate through the broader economy? Developing an understanding of the common causes of financial crises has become an urgently important task.

In this chapter, we'll introduce a few of the basic concepts of financial crises. We'll talk about why things sometimes go wrong in financial markets and how those problems might be corrected. In particular, we will take a close look at the crisis that began in December of 2007 in the United States after the collapse of the housing market.

Origins of Financial Crises

The first recorded example of a financial bubble was a "tulip mania" that afflicted investors in Holland in 1636–1637. At the time, a single tulip bulb was worth more than a handful of diamonds. Investors paid incredible sums for bulbs, hoping to profit by selling later at even higher prices. After a few years, however, the mania surrounding tulips died out and prices plummeted. Those who had invested in tulips lost fortunes.

This pattern has since been repeated many times. Prices go up and up and up, way higher than seems to make any rational sense, and then suddenly crash. Why does this happen? Two interconnected concepts lie at the heart of many financial crises: irrational expectations and leverage.

Irrational Expectations

> **LO 16.1** Describe the role of irrational expectations and leverage in the creation of financial crises.

In Chapter 13, "The Basics of Finance," we talked about how financial markets are supposed to allocate funds efficiently. Ideally, they allow money to flow to the places where it is most highly valued at any given time. What's more, the efficient-market hypothesis says that financial markets should incorporate all available information, so prices should represent the true value of an asset as correctly as possible. Where, in all of that, is there room for bubbles and crashes?

In reality, markets sometimes appear to be very irrational. The price of an asset can become inflated beyond the point where anyone can explain precisely why it should be so valuable. How does that happen? One hypothesis is that investors sometimes follow a herd instinct, investing in something simply because everyone else is doing it. Investors are just people—albeit often well-informed people with a financial interest in making good investments—and can get caught up in the moment and act emotionally, just like anyone else. A bubble starts to inflate when investors become irrationally optimistic that an asset's price will continue to rise. If the idea of herd instinct is true, it suggests that the efficient-market hypothesis doesn't always hold. An investor who sees through the irrational optimism and has a more realistic assessment of true value could earn a profit by betting against what everyone else is doing.

Where do irrational expectations come from? One possible explanation is a well-established cognitive bias called the *recency effect*. There is a basic human tendency to overvalue recent experience when trying to predict the future. When investors and speculators do this, it can lead to enormous miscalculations. For example, consider a company that enjoyed a spectacular few years of success: Research In Motion Limited (or RIM, now known as BlackBerry Limited for its most famous product). In 2005, RIM's total profits were just over US$213 million. Then it launched its new smartphones, followed by an upgrade to its server-related products and increased its global presence with new carrier launches around the world. In 2010, RIM reported profits of more than US$2.4 billion. That's a tenfold growth in profits over just five years.

With RIM's products still flying off the shelves, would an investor be justified in believing that RIM might continue its incredible run for another five or ten or fifteen years? That would mean that after another five years of tenfold growth, RIM would be earning more than US$24 billion a year. In ten years, the company would be earning more than US$240 billion. By 2025, RIM would be earning US$2.4 trillion annually—the current total GDP of Canada! When you look at it that way, it becomes clear that there would come a time for the company when future growth simply couldn't match past growth.

Although it's unlikely that anyone would project something quite that extreme, trends do influence our thinking. For example, in the housing markets, decades of rising house prices persuaded many Canadians that it was inconceivable that they could ever fall. However, not all investors in a bubble are necessarily caught up in irrational expectations. Some may be aware that assets are overpriced, but gamble on riding the rise in prices as close to the top as possible in the hope of selling at maximum profit just before the inevitable crash. This high-stakes game is described in the From Another Angle box, Do Investors Rationally Inflate Bubbles?

FROM ANOTHER ANGLE

Do Investors Rationally Inflate Bubbles?

On June 16, 2005, *The Economist* ran a story entitled "After the Fall." The magazine spelled out clearly why the fast-rising real estate prices around the world were a bubble that would burst, sooner or later. The only question was, when?

"Throughout history," the article notes, "financial bubbles—whether in houses, equities, or tulip bulbs—have continued to inflate for longer than rational folk believed possible...It is impossible to predict when [housing] prices will turn. Yet turn they will. Prices are already sliding in Australia and Britain. America's housing market may be a year or so behind."

As it happened, housing prices in the US stayed astronomically high for another two years after these words were written. Was this because house buyers had stubbornly plugged their ears to such warnings? Maybe. Or maybe many speculators were continuing to buy real estate knowing that a crash would come, but expecting that the bubble had a bit more inflating to do and hoping to maximize profits by selling at the peak price, *just before* the market came crashing down.

How do you make sure you get out before the market goes into free fall? If the timing is off, investors can get their fingers badly burned. Fund manager Stanley Druckenmiller lost a lot of money by not selling soon enough during the bubble in tech stocks in the 1990s. He explained his mistake, using a baseball analogy, "We thought it was the eighth inning, and it was the ninth."

The problem is that no one knows exactly when the bubble will end. A bubble pops when a critical mass of investors decides that the time is right to sell. This causes prices to dip, and everyone who was sitting tight will rush to sell off as well, turning the dip into a plummet. If you haven't managed to sell before this moment comes, then you'll struggle to find anyone who wants to buy.

The existence of speculators practising this sort of brinksmanship also complicates policy steps that could be taken to avert a crisis. If the bubble is being inflated by speculators who are poised to sell at the first sign of prices going into reverse, it might be impossible to prevent a gentle slowdown from turning into a crash landing.

Sources: http://www.princeton.edu/~markus/research/papers/bubbles_crashes.pdf; "After the fall: Soaring house prices have given a huge boost to the world economy. What happens when they drop?" © The Economist Newspaper Limited, London (June 16, 2005).

Leverage

Irrational expectations help explain how prices get so inflated during a bubble, but we have to go further to understand why the crash is so damaging after a bubble bursts. One culprit is the extensive use of leverage, which multiplies the effect of gains and losses in financial markets. In finance, **leverage** is the practice of using borrowed money to pay for investments.

The use of leverage means that a person or company can make an investment that is much larger in value than the amount they actually own. If the investment does well, you pay back the loan and get to keep the profits, which will be larger than you would have earned if you could invest only the cash you had on hand. If the investment does badly, you still have to pay back the loan, and that can require digging deep into your own resources. When financial markets are booming, leverage multiplies the gains; when they crash, leverage magnifies the losses.

On a personal level, people can leverage their funds through a *margin account*. A margin account allows you to use your existing investments as collateral to either buy more financial assets or withdraw cash. For instance, if you have $100 in an account that offers "2×" margin, you can effectively buy $200 worth of stocks even though you put in only $100. When stocks rise, you will earn twice as much profit, minus interest payments. But if the stock you bought goes down 10 percent, you are going to lose $20, which would bring your account value down to $80. If you did not buy on margin, your account value would go down to only $90. That doesn't sound so bad, but what if the stock goes down 50 percent? You would lose all your money, since 50 percent of $200 is your entire original $100. If the stock goes down more than 50 percent, you could actually end up owing money to your broker!

In practice, brokers exercise a *margin call* to ensure that they don't lose money. If it looks like you are in danger of running through your money, the broker will force you to sell your stock and use the money to pay back the loan. Since this probably means selling at the worst possible time—just as the market is collapsing—this situation is both bad for you and potentially destabilizing for the market as a whole. A rapidly falling stock price can trigger a flood of margin calls, leading to massive sales of the stock, which pushes the price down even more.

Companies and banks can also leverage their funds, which can lead to losses on a much larger scale than personal margin accounts. For instance, an investment bank or hedge fund might put down $5 million as collateral in order to buy a claim on $50 million worth of oil futures.[2] Gains or losses on that investment will be multiplied by the use of leverage, in exactly the same way that they are on a personal level. If the value of the investment goes down by a lot, the company can end up owing more than it is able to pay.

Leverage alone is not necessarily a dangerous thing—so long as it is limited and investors understand the risks well. Unfortunately, leverage combined with irrational expectations about a market can be a brutal combination. Imagine you believed that a company would keep growing at 60 percent a year for the next decade and borrowed heavily to leverage your investment. When the price of stock inevitably fell back to earth, you would take a huge loss.

The two-headed monster of leverage and irrational expectations is at the heart of most financial crises. In the next sections, we'll explore how these twin dangers have played out in two famous financial crises.

The South Seas Bubble

In the late seventeenth century, stock markets in England were in their infancy. One of the first issuances of stock, in 1688, was offered by the East India Company, which agreed to give investors a cut of the profits on a forthcoming voyage to India. By 1695, 140 companies were offering similar arrangements in London's Exchange Alley.

The South Seas Company took form in this new environment. The company was granted a government monopoly on trade between England and South America, and interest in its stock was intense. In just a single day, the price of South Seas Company stock rose from £130 to over £300. The company issued more stock, and the price jumped from £300 to £325 as investors used their existing stock as collateral to buy more. By June 1720, the bubble was in full swing, with a share of the South Seas Company trading at a price over £1,000.

It was never entirely clear how the South Seas Company was going to earn enough profit to justify this fantastic share price. After all, there wasn't much trade between England and South America, which at the time was made up of colonies that were mostly controlled by Spain. The company depended on an agreement with Spain to be able to run trading ships, and Spain allowed it to run only one ship a year. Still, wild rumours circulated of the fabulous profits that would one day flow from the South Seas, and investors were caught up in the frenzy.

Con artists saw the high prices that investors were willing to pay for shares in the South Seas Company and decided to cash in on the frenzy. They concocted their own companies, which promised investors riches through fanciful schemes. One claimed to be building a wheel of perpetual motion. Another company famously invited investors to buy stock in "a company for carrying out an undertaking of great advantage, but nobody to know what it is." Eventually, the English Parliament realized the dangers and moved to regulate companies that traded stock publicly, through a law known as the Bubble Act.

Inevitably, sanity returned, and the price of stock in the South Seas Company plunged. Many investors were ruined. Sir Isaac Newton, the great mathematician and one of the investors, lost 20,000 pounds—the equivalent of about 5 million dollars today. Kicking himself, Newton grumbled that he could "calculate the motion of heavenly bodies, but not the madness of people."

The Great Crash of 1929

While the South Seas bubble could be considered the first financial crisis of the modern stock market era, the worst was arguably the infamous stock market crash of October 1929 in the US. This event led to the Great Depression, which quickly reached Canada. It wreaked havoc throughout the 1930s. Production slowed and urban unemployment in Canada was 19 percent.

The Great Crash and resulting Great Depression had their roots in another bubble, a period of flashy exuberance known as the Roaring Twenties. In the early 1920s, the Canadian economy was growing at a high rate of 9 percent. There was some foundation for this increase in the economy: soldiers returning home from World War I had boosted production with additional manpower, while new technologies such as movies, radio, and mass-produced automobiles were causing widespread excitement. Many people began buying stocks on the margin. By 1928, however, the growth was stalled to zero percent. The reason behind this drop could traced to a disastrous wheat harvest, the plummeting in the stock market in the US and globally, prairie droughts, and rising trade protectionism around the world. In the next four years, output was cut almost in half—from $6 billion to just over $3.5 billion. It was not until 1933 that the Canadian economy started to gain traction as a result of higher foreign demand for our products. The economy grew 12 percent in 1933, 4 percent in 1934 and 8 percent in 1935. Exports increased from 20 percent in 1931 to 30 percent of our economy by 1936.

The 1970s and 1980s

The Canadian economy faced another challenge in the 1970s when it was hit with two global oil price shocks that led to stagflation in 1973 and 1974. Household and government spending were fluctuating with one or two quarters of contractions and growth. Unlike in the US, there was no prolonged contraction and the retrenchment of the different sections rarely happened at the same time. While

The Great Crash of 1929 wreaked havoc in Canada and around the world.

City of Toronto Archives, Fonds 1244, Item 1683.

unemployment rose from time to time, the growing concern was on inflation as consumer prices rose at a blistering pace of 10 percent a year over the decade.

Canada didn't experience another recession until the 1980s. Coupled with high inflation (and higher interest rate) and wage and price controls by the government, consumer spending started to fall. The higher cost of financing and falling demand means business investment did not expand. Governments were faced with fiscal stress and mounting deficits. The Canadian economy registered six consecutive quarters of decline in GDP (roughly a 4.8 percent drop from the peak). This made up the longest and deepest decline since the 1930s. The stock market crash in October 1987 did not bring a recession.

The Turn of the Century

Unlike previous contractions, the recession in the 1990s was triggered by public policy. After signing the Free Trade Agreement with the US in 1988, Canada's productive capacity underwent a continental restructuring. In addition, the Bank of Canada was using contractionary monetary policy (high interest rates) to fend off persistently high inflation. And part of the inflation was induced in 1991 by the introduction of the Goods and Services Tax (which replaced the Manufacturers Sales Tax). That meant part of the inflation fought by monetary policy was due to the shift in fiscal policy. While the US was facing its own recession, Canada's was far more severe. The contractionary monetary policy saw Canadian interest rates much higher than comparable US rates. The setting of higher interest rates by the Bank of Canada to fend off inflation resulted in Canadian interest rates higher than comparable US interest rates.This led to an overvalued Canadian dollar, which negatively affected our exports.

The recession was prolonged as governments tried to reduce deficits by cutting spending. Output fell 3.3 percent between 1990 and 1991. While the economy started to pick up in 1994, further spending cuts by governments in 1995 and 1996 put a lid on expansion. It was not until a year later that the Canadian economy finally started to recover, marked by low rates of inflation and a growth in household consumption. In addition, growing productive capacity in Asia and South East Asia led to higher demand for commodities. Since Canada is a leading supplier of commodities for the global supply chain, this growing demand fueled our economic growth further.

✓ CONCEPT CHECK

☐   Why does leverage exacerbate the effect of a financial crash? [LO 16.1]

☐   What is the name of the period of sluggish economic activity that followed the Great Crash of 1929? [LO 16.1]

The Financial and Economic Crisis in Canada: Case Study

Since the Great Depression, Canada has passed several laws intended to prevent similar crises in the future. It created the Canadian Deposit Insurance Corporation (CDIC) to insure bank deposits against possible bank failures, among other things. Each province also has its own securities regulator to administer its own securities act.

These reforms contributed to a long period of relative stability in financial markets. For decades, the Canadian economy chugged along without a major financial crisis or contraction in output. It seemed that the impact of the Great Depression might go down in history as the beginning of a new and more predictable era. Perhaps the global economy had moved on from the days of bubbles and panics. By the mid-2000s, this idea, sometimes dubbed the Great Moderation, had support in the academic and policy-making communities. Unfortunately, less than five years later, the global economy would again find itself in a major recession.

By 2008, the US was in the midst of the greatest global economic downturn since the Great Depression. Industrial and financial giants from General Motors to Merrill Lynch were under threat of collapse. Millions of people saw their life savings evaporate as housing prices collapsed and markets around the world plummeted.

In this section, we'll explore Canada's experience in the financial crisis and the extraordinary monetary and fiscal response from the world's governments, using the financial and macroeconomic concepts we've explored over the last few chapters. We will focus on Canada—in many ways close to the epicenter of the crisis—and how this US problem spread to the rest of the world. While countries from Spain to Greece to the UK faced enormous challenges of their own, Canada was one of the last industrial nations to be affected by this global crisis.

In order to really understand why Canada seemed to fare better in this downturn, we'll start by looking at some interrelated components of this financial crisis: subprime lending, the housing and mortgage market, and the broader world of consumer debt.

Subprime Lending

LO 16.2 Trace the role of mortgage-backed securities and tranching in the rise of subprime lending.

To understand the financial crisis that rocked the United States in 2008, we have to start with the housing market. From World War II to the onset of the financial crisis—a period of more than sixty years—housing prices never fell in the United States, staying steady, even when the rest of the economy went into recession. Buying a house was considered the safest investment anyone could make—a path to stability, wealth and the American Dream. Even the federal government joined the bandwagon in promoting home ownership, with policies ranging from tax deductions on home mortgage interest to government-created companies like Fannie Mae and Freddie Mac, which provided broader access to mortgage financing.

Some people still couldn't obtain a traditional mortgage loan—because of poor credit, low income, or job instability. But they gained a new path to home ownership through the growing availability of *subprime mortgages.* A subprime mortgage is a mortgage loan made to a borrower with a low credit score—that is, to someone who has a history of missing payments or otherwise struggling with debts. (The word *subprime* is in contrast to *prime* borrowers, who have better credit scores.) At first, these mortgages were seen as a triumph, allowing even more Americans to pursue the dream of home ownership for the first time.

Why were lenders willing to lend to subprime borrowers? These loans, after all, are especially risky, and banks had long been wary of lending to subprime-rated borrowers. But that all changed with the advent of securitization. **Securitization** is the practice of packaging individual debts, like mortgage loans or credit card debt, into a single uniform asset that can be easily bought and sold. In the late 1990s, investment banks began purchasing mortgages from the local banks that had created them. They then created *mortgage-backed securities,* which were tradeable assets made up of packages of individual mortgages whose value was tied to the revenues of those mortgages.

Securitization of mortgages allowed local banks to reduce their exposure to risk by effectively selling mortgage debt to investors. The investors got the revenues from mortgage payments in exchange for accepting the loss if borrowers defaulted. The security pooled all the idiosyncratic risks into one asset that had lower total risk. The reasoning is the same as that which leads a bank or insurance company to pool risks, as discussed in Chapter 13, "The Basics of Finance." If you make a single loan and the borrower defaults, you lose everything at once. If, however, you make 100 loans, it's very unlikely that everyone will default at once. A bank can take a thousand loans, estimate that *on average* 250 of them will default, and set prices so that it can still earn a profit on the total package.

Of course, an investor could go out and buy a thousand individual mortgages to accomplish the same goal. Doing that, though, takes time and involves scrutinizing each mortgage to guess how likely a particular homeowner is to default. The mortgage-backed security was supposed to be a single, uniform asset that pooled risk while still being easy to buy and sell quickly. It allowed local banks to pass the risk involved in holding mortgage debts on to an investor with a higher risk tolerance.

Some banks went one step further, dividing packages of debts into slices, each with different risk and return characteristics, a practice called *tranching*. Packages of reliable, low-risk mortgages could be sold to more risk-averse investors, while higher-risk subprime mortgages could be sold to risk-loving investors.

What was the point of this financial wizardry? It allowed local banks and mortgage companies to chase higher profits by making loans that they would have rejected as too risky in the past. Now they could sell those loans to investment banks, which in turn could chase profits by securitizing them and selling them on. Investors had such an appetite for mortgage-backed securities that local banks couldn't make loans fast enough. Real estate agents started pushing larger mortgages to customers who wouldn't traditionally have been able to afford them, and some mortgage brokers cut corners in paperwork to be able to pump out more loans. By 2006, a full 20 percent of the mortgage market consisted of subprime loans, a category that barely even existed a decade before. The sudden explosion of subprime mortgages in the US is shown in Figure 16-1.

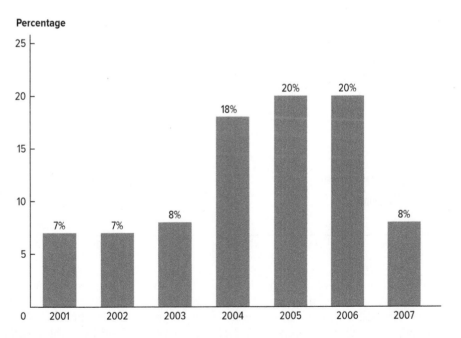

FIGURE 16-1

Growth of the Subprime Loan Market

This figure shows subprime mortgages as a percentage of all new mortgages from 2001 through 2007. Traditionally, new subprime mortgages comprised less than 10 percent of the total new mortgages in any given year. This changed in 2004, when the number of new subprime mortgages more than doubled as a share of new mortgages.

Source: The State of the Nation's Housing, Harvard University Joint Center for Housing Studies, 2008.

North of the border, our banking system and mortgage fundamentals are much more solid. A survey by the World Economic Forum has put Canada at the top of the soundest banking countries in the world. Subprime mortgages were a very small part of the Canadian market. Combined with low mortgage delinquency rate, this reduced the contagion problem seen in the US market.

The Housing Bubble

LO 16.3 Analyze the factors that led to the housing bubble and rising level of household debt in the US.

The sudden explosion of cheap and readily available mortgages in the US encouraged Americans to buy bigger and better homes. A mortgage is a form of leverage—you make a down payment that is only a fraction of the value of the asset (i.e., the house) that you are buying, and you borrow the rest. As down payment requirements got smaller and loans got cheaper, many homeowners became more and more leveraged. The frenzy of highly leveraged demand for houses was accompanied by a sharp run-up in housing prices. Figure 16-2 shows the rapid rise in US home prices during this period and the number of housing starts (a phrase that means new home construction—an indicator of increasing supply in the housing market) in the same period. At the height of the real estate bubble, American homeowners were seeing a very high ratio of home "value" to money actually paid.

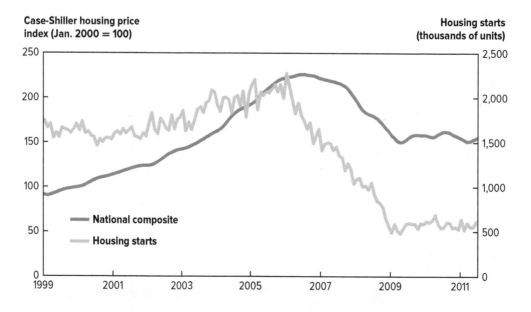

FIGURE 16-2

The US Housing Bubble Pops

The chart shows the rapid increase of housing prices from 1999 to 2006. As you can see, prices peaked in early 2007 and then quickly plummeted. The bubble was large nationally (as seen by the national composite index, represented by the blue line), as prices doubled on average in the span of seven years. The bursting of the bubble is shown by the sudden decrease in housing starts, followed by a sharp reduction in house prices.

Sources: Standard & Poor's; U.S. Department of Commerce, Census Bureau, accessed on the FRED, updated June 19, 2012.

The enormous run-up in housing prices was a classic bubble. People bought houses with the expectation that they would continue to go up in value. Banks began to offer special types of mortgages that allowed borrowers to defer payments for the first few years of the loan. Or they offered extremely low interest rates that would increase to much higher levels a few years down the road. As long as home prices kept going up, borrowers would simply refinance their homes when the bills came. That is, they would use the new, higher value of the home as collateral to take out a new mortgage with friendlier terms. When housing prices stopped rising, however, millions of homeowners found themselves with payments they couldn't possibly make on highly leveraged housing properties.

Why were these loans made? Economists continue to debate this question, but in many ways the housing bubble was no different from any other bubble. Banks and borrowers both got caught up in the moment and, convinced that housing prices would never go down, agreed to incredibly risky loans based on that assumption. Securitization encouraged the process by removing most of the risk from the lenders who created the original mortgage.

This removal of risk from the original lender may have also contributed to misaligned incentives when those lenders were assessing risk. Investment banks in the US relied on the local banks to evaluate each borrower. But local banks wanted to make as many loans as possible, since they earned fees for each loan. Investment bankers made money not by ensuring that local banks were making good loans but by buying as many loans as possible, packaging them into mortgage-backed securities, and selling them to investors. At some point up the chain, the people creating and buying complicated assets that were several steps removed from the original mortgage may not have fully understood what they were paying for.

Investors relied on the reassuringly high AAA scores given to many of these assets by credit-rating agencies. However, the rating agencies attracted business in part by keeping investment bankers happy. The ratings turned out to be much too optimistic.

Politicians in the US were driven by a vision of broader home ownership, but failed to pay enough attention to the economics. The same tools that were intended to allocate funds and spread risk more efficiently made it difficult for everyone to stay fully informed and diluted the incentive to do the research and refuse bad risks.

Although we are seeing a similar problem brewing in Canada's metropolitan areas (namely Vancouver and Toronto) today, housing prices in Canada did not increase at the same rate as those in the US in the early 2000s. This means the Canadian economy was not weighed down by the same degree of household debt as those in the United States. (That being said, today's Canadian household debt ratio of 163.7 percent of disposable income is at an all-time high—much higher than in the US during the crisis).

Buying on Credit

> **LO 16.4** Explain how the collapse of the housing bubble in the US created a credit crisis and subsequent contraction in output.

Flush with the feeling of wealth from their inflated home values, American consumers began saving less and spending more. Many used the value of their homes to secure loans and higher limits on their credit cards. In the context of the AD/AS models we used earlier in the book, this new spending represented a sharp increase in aggregate demand, with consumers taking on more and more debt to support their spending habits.

In fact, overall debt levels in the United States had been rising almost constantly since the Great Depression. As the housing market took off and consumers began borrowing more, however, the growth in household debt accelerated. Figure 16-3 shows the historical trajectory of debt in the United States, divided among household, corporate, financial, and government debt.

FIGURE 16-3

Historical Debt Trends in the United States

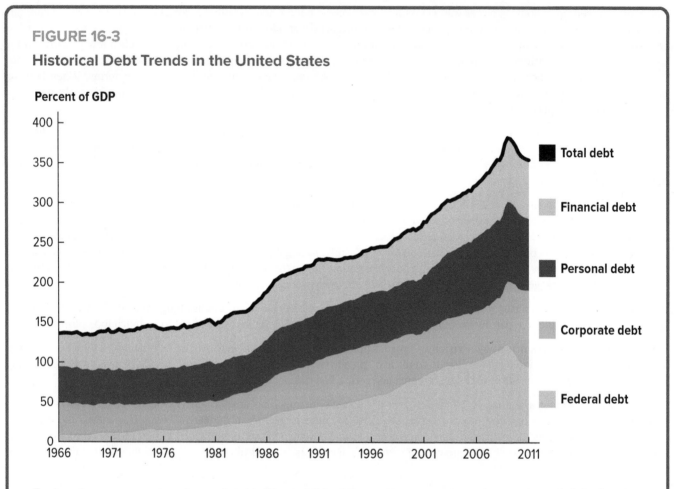

Each colour represents a type of debt. The height of the colour represents the amount of debt for that category, while the height of all the categories together, represented by the black line, shows the total debt. Since the 1960s, total debt in the United States has more than doubled its share of GDP, from just shy of 150 percent to over 350 percent of GDP today. Much of that drive has been from the government and financial sectors, the latter having grown from a single-digit share of GDP to about 100 percent of GDP.

Source: Board of Governors of the Federal Reserve System, accessed on the FRED, updated June 8, 2012.

Consumers could afford to pay for all this debt because interest rates were so low. During most of the 1990s and 2000s, the trend in interest rates was sharply downward. Declining interest rates made borrowing—and therefore going into debt—much cheaper. To understand consumer debt, economists look at a concept known as debt service. **Debt service** is the amount that consumers have to spend to pay their debts, often expressed as a percentage of disposable income.

Over the two decades leading up the 2008 crisis, falling interest rates meant that consumers could take on more debt without significantly increasing the amount of debt service they had to pay. Figure 16-4 shows the divergence between rising debt levels and relatively stable debt-service burdens. Unfortunately, that level of debt was sustainable only as long as interest rates remained low and home values remained high. Consumers would be facing serious trouble if anything unexpectedly went wrong.

FIGURE 16-4

Debt Payments and Total Debt

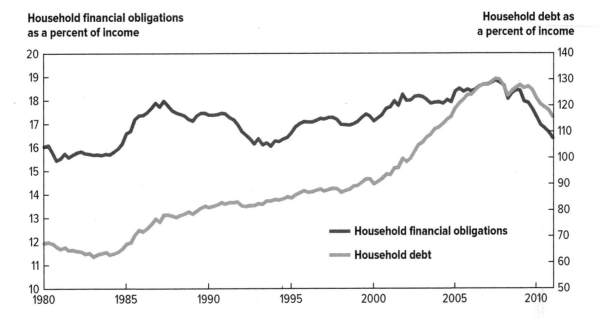

Household financial obligations as a percent of income

Household debt as a percent of income

Despite the fact that household debt has risen considerably, nearly doubling from about 70 percent of total disposable income to just below 120 percent of disposable income, household payments on this debt have not increased very much, as low interest rates have kept the price of debt low.

Source: Board of Governors of the Federal Reserve System, accessed on the FRED, updated June 8, 2012.

A Brief Timeline of the Crisis

The financial collapse in the US began in the subprime housing market. When housing prices were rising, consumers had become accustomed to *refinancing* their mortgages—paying off the existing mortgage and taking out a new mortgage based on the increased value of the home. Often the new mortgage was structured to result in lower payments (at least for a while), and often the appreciated value of the home enabled the homeowner to borrow some cash in the refinancing deal. But with housing prices no longer rising, and already falling in places like Nevada, Arizona, California, and Florida, consumers found themselves unable to refinance their loans.

Faced with impossibly high payments relative to their incomes, a massive wave of defaults occurred. Millions of people in the US found themselves in foreclosure, meaning that their homes became the property of the bank when they defaulted on a mortgage loan. Often the bank would then evict the homeowner and try to sell the house.

The wave of foreclosed properties hit the market, creating a big increase in the supply of housing. The increase in supply depressed housing prices even further, leading to another wave of defaults. Consumers who had used second and third mortgages, or borrowed in other ways to extract wealth from their homes, suddenly found themselves "under water," owing more in mortgage debt than their houses were worth. A vicious cycle of defaults and falling prices began that would ultimately cause home values to fall by more than 50 percent in the hardest-hit areas.

A number of large banks held massive quantities of mortgage-backed securities. When the crisis hit, riskier real estate investments became worthless, and even the supposedly safe, AAA-rated investments were badly affected. Banks lost trillions of dollars.

The opaque and complicated nature of mortgage-backed securities meant that it was difficult to tell which banks had been hit the hardest by the crash. As a result, the *entire* borrowing and lending engine of the economy ground to a halt. Nobody wanted to lend to anybody, in case they turned out to be a bad risk. Even the most venerable banks teetered on the edge of collapse.

Large institutions and companies that had deposited money with investment banks began withdrawing their funds, leading to a run on bank assets. Two of the largest and most respected banks—Bear Stearns and Lehman Brothers—collapsed, and the rest were perceived to be at risk as well. Figure 16-5 shows the dramatic collapse in stock prices of the largest banks.

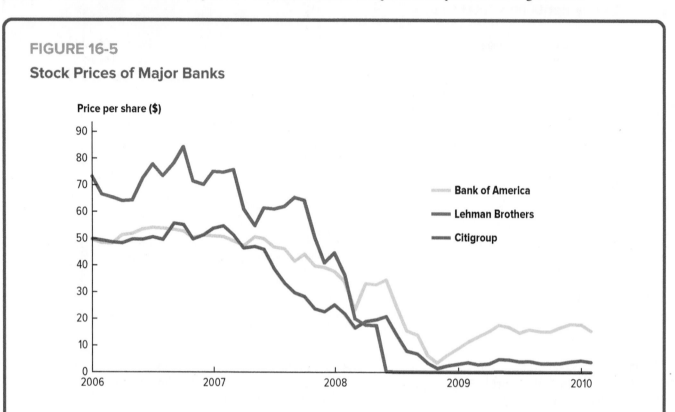

FIGURE 16-5

Stock Prices of Major Banks

Price per share ($)

Legend:
- Bank of America
- Lehman Brothers
- Citigroup

As a result of the housing boom, the financial sector performed well in the years leading up to the crisis. This ended when many of the banks announced that they held large amounts of toxic assets. Beginning in February 2007, prices began to fall. Come September 2008, prices of stocks throughout the financial sectors plummeted as the crisis hit.

Source: Yahoo! Finance, October 4, 2011.

As home prices fell, consumers were unable to refinance mortgages, and a cycle of defaults and falling prices followed, eventually engulfing the entire economy.

iStock Images

Because banks were unwilling to lend, many businesses were suddenly unable to access credit for their day-to-day needs. Even simple tasks like buying inventory or taking delivery of a container ship full of imported goods became nearly impossible for many companies. Effectively, the aggregate productive capacity of the entire world was reduced almost overnight. With no credit available for even the most routine of activities, the world economy was stumbling.

The combination of increasing interest rates and pessimism about future economic prospects decreased both consumption and investment spending. Businesses could no longer obtain credit to invest, and most would not have wanted to invest as the economy tanked. Households found themselves struggling to pay back debts, and some faced reduced income and poor job prospects. The fall in home prices meant they were no longer as wealthy as they thought they were, and people reduced their consumption accordingly. The reduction in consumption and investment spending shifted the aggregate demand curve to the left.

With demand flagging, businesses had to cut back further. Some employees were laid off, and others saw their wages or hours cut. Lower incomes led naturally to lower spending, a further reduction in aggregate demand and still more layoffs. Figure 16-6 shows the combined impact of these forces: as a result of the housing-market crash, both aggregate demand and aggregate supply shifted to the left. The combined shifts put the economy at a new equilibrium, with dramatically reduced output. Prices fell because the effect of the leftward shift in the aggregate demand curve was stronger than the effect of the leftward shift in aggregate supply. The combined effect left the economy reeling.

FIGURE 16-6

The Financial Crisis in Terms of AD and AS

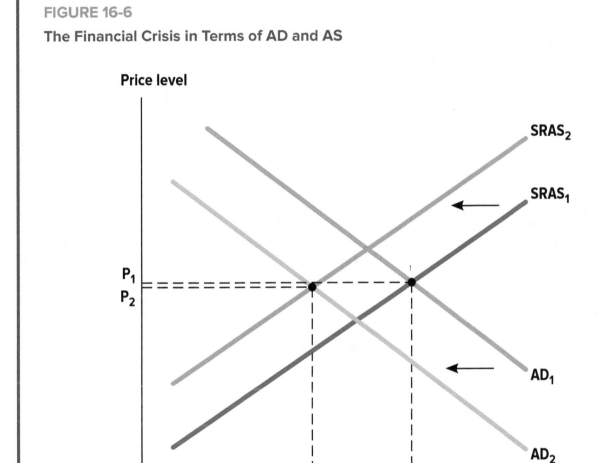

As a result of the housing-market crash, both aggregate demand and aggregate supply shifted to the left. This put the economy at a new equilibrium, with lower prices and dramatically reduced output.

It took barely two years for the bursting of a real estate bubble to tip the global economy into its worst downturn in over 75 years. Once housing prices collapsed and the bad loans in the financial system were revealed for what they were, it was only a matter of time before the convulsions in the financial market led to job losses and economic pain on the real economy.

While this seems far away from both in time and distance, higher and higher Canadian household debt ratios are making headlines across our country. Both the Bank of Canada and other international agencies have warned of the potential risk Canada might see in the future from the housing market and the high level of household debt.

The Immediate Response to the Crisis

LO 16.5 Describe the monetary and fiscal policy responses to the financial crisis of 2009.

With the private sector reeling from the impact of the shifts in both aggregate demand and aggregate supply, many looked to the government to provide stability and ensure that the situation did not become even worse. We've talked about how government can use monetary and fiscal policy to influence the economy. During the financial crisis, policy makers used these tools to try to avert a catastrophic economic collapse.

With more businesses failing, the goal of fiscal and monetary policy in 2009 was to "unstick" the frozen credit markets. Economists feared that any attempt to stimulate aggregate demand without first addressing the lack of supply would be ineffective at best and dangerous at worst. It could potentially have led to **stagflation**—that is, high inflation despite low economic growth and high unemployment.

The challenges facing the financial system stemmed from the two fundamental issues of liquidity and solvency. The most pressing was liquidity. Even though Canada has a strong banking sector, the uncertainty about which banks were facing losses meant banks were not willing to lend to each other. As a result of the lack of liquidity, there wasn't enough money moving through the system to keep transactions going. Concerns about the amount of the liquidity in the market were reflected in interest rates. In the depths of the financial crisis, interest rates on even the most secure loans soared.

Addressing the liquidity problem fell to the world's central banks, and primarily to the Bank of Canada in its role as lender of last resort. When a similar financial crisis shook the US in the early 1900s, one man—J. P. Morgan—stepped in to act as the lender of last resort, averting an US financial collapse. In 2009, the existence of the Bank of Canada meant that the situation played out very differently. In December 2008, the Bank lowered the bank rate to its lowest level since 1958. The European Central Bank and the Bank of England quickly followed suit, trying to help the financial system from seizing up completely.

At the same time, the US Treasury began the difficult task of dealing with banks that had a solvency problem. *Solvency problem* is a gentle way to refer to banks that had lost so much money that they would inevitably go bankrupt. While no banks in Canada required the kind of government bailouts that were required in the US, reports by the Canadian Centre for Policy Alternatives suspected the banking sector received secret bailouts from the federal government.[3]

After dealing with the banking sector, government also faced a request for help from the auto sector. With falling sales and the crunch in the financial market, the auto industry in mid-November of 2008 asked both the federal and provincial governments for loan guarantees. The auto sector was deemed **too big to fail**—that is, so large in terms of assets or workers, that the failure of one of these big automakers carried the risk of causing a domino effect in the highly integrated financial system, causing widespread loss in profits and employment.

Automotive companies considered too big to fail were eventually bailed out through fiscal policy—that is, through increased government spending. The bulk of this effort came through the bailout after the bankruptcy of General Motors and Chrysler. This represented the first wave of the federal government's fiscal policy response to the crisis, through which it invested billion of dollars in struggling automakers.

The Conservative government argued that these bailouts were absolutely necessary to save the economy, but debate raged. Chief among the concerns was the fear that blanket bailouts would create a class of sector that *knew* they were considered too big to fail and so would continue to take unnecessary risks.

This one-two punch of monetary and fiscal policy averted a systemic collapse and brought stability to the Canadian economy. By shoring up the capital of the heavily damaged auto sector and flooding the system with liquidity, the government and the Bank of Canada worked together to restore order within the economy.

The effect of these actions in the aggregate demand and aggregate supply model is shown in Figure 16-7, which builds from Figure 16-6. In response to the sharp reduction in the amount of credit available in the market, the Bank of Canada (by lowering interest rates) and the government (through rescuing General Motors and Chrysler) provided enough money in the market to restore aggregate supply to its original level. Once order was restored in the credit market, businesses were again able to finance their inventories and continue to grow their operations. This restoration pushed the SRAS curve back toward its original pre-crisis position. However, due to sluggish aggregate demand, output was still well below pre-crash levels (Y_1).

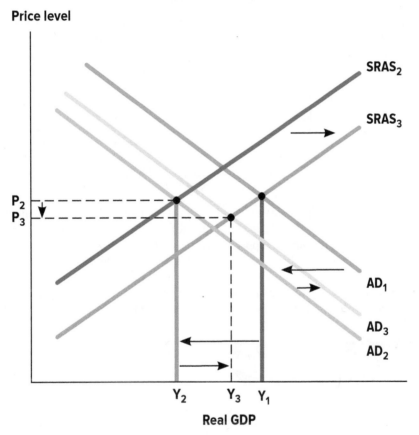

FIGURE 16-7

Bank of Canada and Government Intervention Restores Aggregate Supply

The Bank of Canada and the government both responded to the sharp reduction of credit available in the market. Their responses provided enough money in the market to spur aggregate supply and demand, although due to sluggish aggregate demand, output was still well below pre-crash levels (Y_1).

You might be wondering why all of that capital failed to stimulate aggregate demand. The short answer is that these programs did not have the same goal as traditional monetary policy conducted through the target overnight rate. Most of the offerings, instead, were used only by an auto sector that did not have the capital they needed to function normally—they were emergency programs for an extraordinary situation. So, even as the financial sector stabilized, Canada found itself with the classic problem of most economic downturns: depressed aggregate demand.

Stimulus at the Zero Lower Bound

LO 16.6 Describe the different tools that can be used to stimulate the economy when interest rates are at the zero lower bound.

The policy prescriptions for fixing low aggregate demand are relatively straightforward. The Bank of Canada can pursue expansionary monetary policy, lowering interest rates to encourage borrowing and investment spending, which pushes the aggregate demand curve to the right. Alternatively, the government can engage in stimulus through fiscal policy, increasing aggregate demand through tax cuts or increases in government spending.

In fact, both routes were pursued. The government of Canada passed fiscal stimulus legislation intended to support demand. The Bank of Canada slashed the target for the overnight rate from 4 percent before the crisis to 1 percent by January 2009. As demand stayed weak—even after stimulus spending—the Bank of Canada continued to cut the target overnight rate. By April 2009, the target overnight rate was at 0.25 percent, for all intents and purposes at the zero lower bound, and the economy was finally starting to recover. Since household debts were not very high at the time, the low interest rate created desire to borrow for investment in real estate—particularly when borrowing was essentially free. And with consumption rising, businesses were in the mood to invest in expanding their productive capacity as commodity prices continued to rise.

The situation in the US was different. The low interest rate after the housing bubble burst, together with households trying to pay down their debts (called de-leveraging) meant Americans were staying away from the real estate market. Businesses were also not investing in productive capacity due to the poor future prospects. And with interest rates already at zero in the US, what could the Federal Reserve do?

What came out of this impasse was a prescription for unorthodox monetary policy by the Fed: quantitative easing. **Quantitative easing** involves policies that are designed to directly increase the money supply by a certain amount, as opposed to the more common practice of indirectly adjusting the money supply through interest rates. The Fed accomplished quantitative easing by purchasing long-term government bonds. The aim was to get more money into the economy. In all, the Fed purchased more than $1 trillion worth of long-term bonds with newly created money, which meant that it added $1 trillion to the money supply. The Fed wanted to avoid what happened in Japan after a housing bubble inflated in the 1980s and then popped. For years, the Japanese economy was weak, and deflation was a recurring problem. The Real Life box, Japan's Lost Decade, tells the story.

REAL LIFE

Japan's Lost Decade

In the 1980s, Japan was one of the world's leading economies. In 1989, a real estate bubble threatened to destabilize the economy, and the Central Bank of Japan tried to gently rein in the price of housing by raising interest rates. The effect was dramatic: housing prices fell 87 percent from their peak. This shock reverberated throughout the economy and ravaged the stock market. With the combined crashes in housing and the stock market, Japan lost the equivalent of three years of GDP, one of the largest peacetime losses of wealth in human history.

In response, the government and central bank engaged many of the traditional tools used to fight financial crises and recessions. They bailed out banks that were in danger of collapse. Banks got enough capital to keep them afloat, but it wasn't enough for normal day-to-day lending. These banks became known as "zombie banks"—banks that were nominally alive thanks to continued government bailouts, but not able to play a useful role in the economy.

The government also embarked on an ambitious fiscal stimulus plan, mostly spending heavily on bridges and roads in rural areas. This stimulus also failed to improve the economy. Some argue the projects were ill-conceived, while others say the spigot of funding was turned off far too early to have a real impact.

In an especially drastic measure, the central bank dropped interest rates from 8 percent all the way down to zero. When that didn't work, the central bank said there was little else it could do—it had reached the *zero lower bound* on interest rates.

Japan's economy slipped into a downward spiral. Homeowners who had borrowed to purchase their houses when prices were high cut back on their spending so they could pay back debt. As a result, the economy became so weak that prices started to fall. The resulting deflation was incredibly damaging. Consumers held on to their money, knowing that they would be able to buy more in the future when its value increased, which drove prices even further downward.

With these headwinds, the Japanese economy stayed stuck in neutral for two decades. What was originally known as the Lost Decade eventually became the Lost 20 Years. However, one economist who closely studied Japan's experience suggested that much of this stagnation was avoidable. The government could have let some of the zombie banks fail, continued stimulus spending, and tried alternative monetary policy measures, such as quantitative easing, to stimulate the economy.

Who was the economist who proposed these measures? It was Ben Bernanke, who would be chairman of the Federal Reserve during the US crisis.

Sources: http://www.nytimes.com/2010/05/21/opinion/21krugman.html; http://www.time.com/time/magazine/article/0,9171,1884815,00.html.

After the Fed's first round of quantitative easing, the overall money supply remained nearly unchanged. When the economy continued to stagnate, however, the Fed engaged in a second round of quantitative easing. The second round dramatically increased the overall level of the money supply. By mid-2011, the money supply stood at nearly $3 trillion, more than triple its level going into the crisis.

This enormous increase in the money supply was unprecedented. Critics feared that it would cause very high inflation. With the economy stagnating, however, the increase in the money supply led to only a slight increase in borrowing. Why did this happen? The money multiplier collapsed as banks were unwilling to lend, and consumers and businesses were not very interested in, or capable of being approved for, borrowing. By 2014, the Fed halted the purchases when the economy showed signs of improvement as the program was successful in boosting demand. It appears that the Fed's efforts had at least prevented an outright fall in borrowing and lending, which would have further damaged an already weak economy.

Recurrence of the Financial Crisis

Given the severe downturn experienced in the US and Canada (and around the world), how likely is it that an event like this will reoccur? In order to answer this question, we need to look at the changes that have taken place after the crisis. As mentioned above, one of the key components of the crisis is the use of leverage (both by households and lenders). Basel III was developed to strengthen bank capital requirements by lowering bank leverage and improving liquidity. (Basel III is a global voluntary regulatory framework, set up by the Basel Committee on Banking Supervision after the financial crisis. Its purpose is to ensure that international banks maintain adequate capital in the event of another financial crisis.)

Although Canada is not a strong supporter of such a voluntary framework, the US Federal Reserve would implement a substantial number of the rules. In addition to the Basel III framework, the Financial Stability Board (FSB) was set up after the 2009 G20 summit. The purpose of the board is to "make recommendations for enhancing the resilience of financial markets and financial institutions."[4] Since 2011, the chairman of the board has been the former governor of the Bank of Canada (currently the governor of the Bank of England) Mark Carney. Together with the IMF, OECD, and central banks around the world, these improvements aim to reduce the recurrence of financial crisis.

✓ CONCEPT CHECK

☐ What is a subprime mortgage? [LO 16.2]

☐ Why did mortgage-backed securities lead to an increase in subprime lending? [LO 16.3]

☐ How did the 2007 financial crisis impact aggregate demand? [LO 16.4]

☐ What is the dilemma involved in deciding whether to bail out a sector that is considered "too big to fail"? [LO 16.5]

☐ Why would a central bank implement quantitative easing? [LO 16.6]

Conclusion

This chapter began with a simple question: Why do financial crises occur? Usually, financial crises arise from a combination of irrational expectations and leverage, which creates bubbles that burst with dire consequences for the real economy. Crises have been around since the very first financial markets, as the example of the South Seas Company in the 1700s shows.

These forces surfaced once again when innovations in the subprime lending market in the US led to a dramatic increase in home ownership and housing prices. When the real estate bubble burst in 2007 in the US, the result was a financial crisis, challenging economists' belief that economic crises had become a thing of the past.

Recent events show that we still have much to learn about the macroeconomy. Can we permanently moderate the business cycle? How will increasing global interdependency affect future crises? What can governments do to make financial markets work better? There are no quick and easy answers to these questions, but we are starting to better understand the complexity of the challenges. The unfortunate reality is that economies can collapse almost overnight, but they often take a lot longer to recover.

Key Terms

leverage

securitization

debt service

stagflation

too big to fail

quantitative easing

Summary

LO 16.1 Describe the role of irrational expectations and leverage in the creation of financial crises.

The existence of financial crises challenges the efficient-market hypothesis, showing that markets may not always accurately reflect all available information. Irrational expectations, often based on overly optimistic projections for the future, frequently lead to overvaluations. Combined with leverage, irrational expectations can create or fuel financial crises. The South Seas Bubble of the seventeenth century is one example: unrealistic expectations about access to trade with South America led to dramatic overvaluation and spawned fanciful investment schemes. Centuries later, in the Roaring Twenties, optimism and a rush to invest in the stock market gave way to the Crash of 1929 and a decade of economic decline during the Great Depression.

LO 16.2 Trace the role of mortgage-backed securities and tranching in the rise of subprime lending.

Securitization in the market for mortgage loans created a wave of subprime lending. Investment banks packaged these loans into larger mortgage-backed securities, which pooled the risk of subprime loans and enabled more loans to be made. Eventually, banks began tranching these securities, dividing them into segments with different risk and return characteristics. This process allowed the banks to tailor mortgage-backed securities to their clients' investment needs. It also contributed to asymmetric information problems, which later contributed to the crisis.

LO 16.3 Analyze the factors that led to the housing bubble and rising levels of household debt in the US.

Securitization of mortgage loans encouraged banks to offer more subprime mortgages, increasing demand for housing and pushing up prices. At the same time, homeowners found themselves with more wealth because the price of their homes had risen. Feeling wealthier, people increased their household debt, taking out more loans at attractive low interest rates, to pay for higher levels of consumption.

LO 16.4 Explain how the collapse of the housing bubble in the US created a credit crisis and subsequent contraction in global output.

Eventually, the housing bubble popped. Many subprime borrowers defaulted on their loans after teaser rates expired; home prices dropped, and banks found themselves with mortgage-backed securities worth a fraction of their original estimates. Many banks stopped lending and many failed. Credit markets dried up. Businesses were no longer able to finance economic investments. Households, facing a negative shock to wealth due to depressed housing prices, and began saving more and consuming less. The economy entered a recession.

LO 16.5 Describe the monetary and fiscal policy responses to the financial crisis of 2009.

In response to the crisis, the federal government acted quickly to stabilize the financial system. The Bank of Canada, in its role as the lender of last resort, offered short-term financing to banks that couldn't access credit otherwise. This provided liquidity to the market, a crucial step in raising aggregate supply. The government also tackled solvency issues by bailing out the auto sector. Once the crisis gave way to a contraction in output, the government used fiscal policy to increase aggregate demand by passing stimulus measures.

LO 16.6 Describe the different tools that can be used to stimulate the economy when interest rates are at the zero lower bound.

When the monetary policy hit the zero lower bound, the Fed undertook quantitative easing designed to increase the money supply by a certain amount. In three rounds of quantitative easing, it directly purchased a total of US$4.5 trillion in long-term government bonds, thus adding that amount to the money supply.

Review Questions

1. Your best friend comes to you for financial investment advice. She is wondering whether she should invest in (a) a sector of the economy that has been performing extremely well in the last five years relative to historical levels or (b) one that has been performing extremely poorly in the last five years relative to historical levels. What would you advise? How might irrational expectations affect your recommendations? [LO 16.1]

2. What is leverage, and how can it make an asset pricing bubble worse? [LO 16.1]

3. Explain why it's possible for tranching to make investing in a mortgage-backed security more risky than investing in a single subprime loan. [LO 16.2]

4. Explain how a mortgage-backed security can increase loan availability to those with little credit or bad credit. [LO 16.2]

5. Explain the role that leverage played in the recent US housing bubble. [LO 16.3]

6. How did government policies and asymmetric information problems make the recent US housing bubble worse? [LO 16.3]

7. In the US, many subprime borrowers entered into adjustable-rate mortgages with low teaser rates. These mortgages allowed borrowers to pay a low interest rate for the first two years on their mortgage before the rate jumped to market levels. But the loan documents sometimes made it difficult for borrowers to understand that the rate would increase. Explain why this practice could lead to a bubble in housing prices. [LO 16.4]

8. How did the recent US housing crisis affect the aggregate demand curve? [LO 16.4]

9. Imagine what would have happened if the Bank of Canada had not been in place to act as a lender of last resort during the financial crisis. Absent government involvement, what would have been the likely effect on aggregate supply? Why? What would have been the likely effect on aggregate demand? Why? [LO 16.5]

10. As the US Federal Reserve responded to the housing crisis in the US, how did this affect its balance sheet? Can you think of what caused the balance sheet's size to change so much? [LO 16.5]

11. What is the *zero lower bound* that must be considered in monetary policy, and how can it cause problems in enacting such policy? [LO 16.6]

12. What is quantitative easing, and when might it be used? [LO 16.6]

Problems and Applications

1. Determine whether or not each of the following is an example of irrational expectations. [LO 16.1]

   a. The price of BlackBerry's stock rises after tech blogs reveal that the company plans to release a new tablet, rumoured to be competitive with Apple's iPad.

   b. The CEO of a start-up producing applications for tablets is quoted as proclaiming a new era of media, in which thirst for content will rise indefinitely as information becomes more and more convenient for people to digest. An economics blog continues the discussion a year later, discussing returns to investment that have never before been contemplated. Stock prices for media companies are consistently outperforming historical levels by 50 percent and seem to be on a permanent rise.

   c. After an unusually cool summer, investors in Papa's Icepops decide to sell, believing demand for icepops will never reach historic levels again because of the weather.

   d. The Department of Justice reveals accusations against the CEO of a food and beverage company, alleging misconduct within the company. A trial could cost the company millions of dollars. The stock price falls by 5 percent by the day's end.

2. Ike, an investor, is considering opening a margin account and investing $1,000 in Mike's mutual fund. The terms of the account require that he pay back the amount he borrowed on the margin by the end of the year with 10 percent interest. Ike is trying to decide what level of margin he wants. For example, if he chooses an account at the level of 50 percent, the bank will let him borrow and invest an additional $500, or 50 percent of his original $1,000.

   Complete Table 16P-1 by filling in Ike's account value at the end of the year, given varying levels of the margin account and mutual fund performance. Assume that Mike's mutual fund will return 40 percent per year in a stellar market and 5 percent per year in a fair market, and that in a terrible market it will lose 30 percent. [LO 16.1]

TABLE 16P-1

Margin account level	Account value in a stellar market	Account value in a fair market	Account value in a terrible market
No margin			
60%			
100%			
150%			
200%			

3. Assume that a subprime mortgage involves a loan of $1,000 and is to be paid back in full with 30 percent interest after one year. [LO 16.2]

   a. Sometimes borrowers will not be able to pay off the entire mortgage or may default entirely. Calculate the final amount of money an investor earns under the payback rates shown in Table 16P-2. (Note that a rate of 130 percent means that the whole loan is paid off, plus the additional 30 percent of interest.)

TABLE 16P-2

Amount paid (%)	Final value	Probability
130		0.6
110		0.1
100		0.1
50		0.1
0		0.1

    b. Assume investors are unwilling to invest in these loans unless the expected rate of return is 10 percent. Calculate the expected rate of return for this loan by adding up all of the products of the final value and the probability that that value will occur. Will investors want to invest in this loan?

4. A single bank is considering two options: it can make a $200,000 mortgage loan for a customer with a 10 percent probability of default, or it can buy a $200,000 security representing a bundle of 100 mortgage loans, which can be broken down as shown in Table 16P-3.

TABLE 16P-3

Number of loans	Probability of default (%)	Weighted risk
40	3.0	40% × 3% = 1.2%
25	11.0	
15	1.5	
20	5.0	

You can calculate the weighted risk for each firm category by multiplying the percentage of loans represented (for example, the first tier includes 40 loans, which is 40/100 = 40% of the total) times the probability of default on loans of that category. Do so for each type of loan, then add together the weighted risks to come up with an overall expected default risk for this financial investment. If the bank is willing to take on only projects for which the default risk is 6 percent or less, which option(s) should it choose? [LO 16.2]

5. Table 16P-4 shows hypothetical levels of average household debt and debt service payments in two years, 2005 and 2008. At what annual interest rate would consumers have had to borrow for the debt-service payments in 2008 to equal the debt-service payments in 2005, despite the increase in household debt? Assume households are paying only interest on their debt and not part of the principal. [LO 16.3]

TABLE 16P-4

	2005	2008
Household debt	$20,000	$80,000
Annual debt-service payments	$800	?

6. Table 16P-5 gives information on income and debt for a small nation for the years 2008 through 2011. The nation had average household debt of $34,000 at the end of 2007. Use this information to fill in the blanks. [LO 16.3]

TABLE 16P-5

Year	Household income ($)	Financial obligations ($)	Financial obligations as % of income	Household debt ($)	Debt as % of income
2008	35,000	4,000			
2009	38,500	4,200			
2010	42,000	5,000			
2011	45,250	6,200			

7. Imagine that your personal finances are summarized by the account balances shown in Table 16P-6. Assume also that your decision to save is a function of your income and net worth. More specifically, assume that your savings each year will be equal to $0.2I - NW$, where "I" is your income and "NW" is your net worth. [LO 16.4]

TABLE 16P-6

Assets		Liabilities	
Home	$100,000	Mortgage	$90,000
Chequing account	15,000	Student loans	20,000
Car	10,000	Credit card	10,000
Total assets	$125,000	Total liabilities	$120,000

   a. If your income is $60,000, how much will you save this year?

   b. Assume the value of your house decreases by 20 percent. What is your net worth now? How much will you save?

8. If the rate currently payable on 10-year Treasury bonds is 4.8 percent and the risk spread is 2 percent, what is the average rate on other forms of commercial lending? [LO 16.4]

9. Which of the following policies were used in the US in response to the latest financial crisis? Of those used, which are examples of monetary policy? Of fiscal policy? [LO 16.5]

   a. Aggressive controlling of inflation by raising interest rates

   b. Providing short-term financing directly to small businesses to jump-start investment

   c. Bailing out banks having large amounts of risky mortgage-backed securities

   d. Purchasing long-term bonds to increase the money supply

   e. Raising the Social Security eligibility age by five years to encourage people to work

10. Table 16P-7 shows the balance sheet of a bank in millions of dollars. [LO 16.5]

TABLE 16P-7

Assets (in millions)		Liabilities (in millions)	
Cash	$ 800	CDs	$2,000
Commercial loans	2,000	Savings accounts	1,500
Consumer loans	600	Long-term debt	1,000
Prime mortgages	800		
Subprime mortgages	500		
Total assets	$4,700	Total liabilities	$4,500

    a. What is the bank's net worth?

    b. Assume housing prices decrease and defaults on subprime mortgages rise, causing the bank's assets in subprime mortgages to decrease from 500 to 350. What are total assets now? What is the bank's new net worth?

    c. How far would the value of subprime mortgages have to fall to cause the bank to be insolvent (that is, for liabilities to be greater than assets)?

11. Japan's economic situation throughout its Lost Decade and beyond can be explained in terms of problems with monetary policy via interest rates. Explain what happened. Identify what Japan's central bank should have done. [LO 16.6]

12. Consider an economy with $10 billion in base money and a multiplier of 4. The money supply is currently $10 billion × 4 = $40 billion. Now let's say that the amount of base money rises by 50 percent, to $15 billion. How must the multiplier change for the money supply to remain unaffected by this change in base money? [LO 16.6]

Chapter Sources

http://www.rhsmith.umd.edu/cfp/events/2011/GSE2011/papers/Explaining_the_Housing_Bubble.pdf

http://www.fsb.org

PART SEVEN

International Policy Issues
The two chapters in Part 7 will introduce you to ...

the international financial system and development policy. Chapter 17 covers the international financial system. If you've ever travelled abroad and traded your dollars for another currency, you've participated in one part of the international financial system. Yet it goes much further than that. Anything that was originally produced internationally and imported into Canada was made possible by the international trade of money. In this chapter, we'll introduce the markets that make this trade possible. Like the domestic financial system, the international financial system is vitally important to the smooth operation of the economy. We'll describe how it works and where it can get into trouble.

The final chapter, Chapter 18, turns to a large and pressing question: Why is the world filled with poverty amid so much wealth? This is one of the basic questions in development economics. We'll describe how the understanding of economic development has changed over time. We'll review the current state of research and introduce promising new methods to rigorously evaluate policies and innovations that aim to reduce poverty. Finally, we'll give some examples of solutions that draw on ideas developed in this book—solutions that are making a practical difference in people's lives.

Throughout the text we've seen how economics sheds light on many questions, decisions, and policy issues. Some (such as tax policy) are more obviously about "economics" and some less so. We hope that, in reading, you're learning how to apply the economic toolkit to help you solve everyday problems at home and investigate questions about the world around us.

CHAPTER 17

Open-Market Macroeconomics

LEARNING OBJECTIVES

LO 17.1   Define the balance of trade and describe the general trends of Canadian trade.

LO 17.2   Define portfolio investment and foreign direct investment.

LO 17.3   Explain the connection between the balance of trade and net capital outflow.

LO 17.4   Describe the determinants of international capital flows using the demand and supply for international loanable funds.

LO 17.5   Show how the international market for loanable funds can be used to explain events in the international financial system.

LO 17.6   Describe the exchange rate and its determinants, and explain how the exchange rate affects trade.

LO 17.7   Explain fixed and floating exchange rates and how monetary policy affects the value of currency in both.

LO 17.8   Describe the difference between the real and nominal exchange rates.

From Factory to Figures

Lululemon Athletica has been a runaway success. Since it was founded in 1998, Lululemon has sold millions of yoga pants around the world. You might think of Lululemon as an all-Canadian success story, given that Lululemon is a Canadian company. Technically, though, the yoga pants count as an import. That's because, like so many consumer goods, the yoga pants are put together in a factory in China before the finished product is shipped Canada.

The fact that the yoga pants are considered an import means that every pair of yoga pants bought in Canada contributes to the trade deficit Canada has with China. In 2014, Canadian consumers bought $35.7 billion worth of goods from China, while Canadian firms managed to sell only $20.6 billion worth of goods to consumers in China—an $15.1 billion trade gap between what Canada is buying from China and what it is selling there.

To see what this trade gap really means, imagine for a moment that China bought exactly as much from Canada as it sold to Canada. What would happen? Canadians would convert $35.7 billion Canadian into the Chinese currency, the yuan, and use it to buy Chinese goods. In turn, Chinese people would use that $35.7 billion to buy Canadian goods. Everything would balance out. In reality, the Chinese use only $20.6 billion to buy Canadian goods. So there must be $15.1 billion still sloshing around the Chinese economy. Presumably the Chinese don't just keep this money under their mattresses. Where does it end up?

Some dollars are spent or invested at home or abroad, searching for the best return. A lot of them end up being invested around the world, which means the money is used to make loans to governments around the world. The web of international financial connections is something to think about the next time you see Lululemon yoga clothing.

What explains trade flows? How and why does the rest of the world accrue debt to China? And why would China lend to the rest of the world? What determines the rate at which dollars can be converted into yuan? This chapter will answer those questions by exploring international economics. We examine the flow of goods and money around the world and then move on to discuss related shifts in the value of a country's currency.

Steve Rosset/Shutterstock

By showing how to understand the macroeconomy in an international context, this chapter sheds light on important policy debates about exchange rates, trade balances, and capital flows across countries.

International Flows of Goods and Capital

International trade is not a new thing. More than 3,000 years ago, China was exporting textiles along the famed Silk Road to the Mediterranean and Persian empires, and spices were travelling from India to the Roman Empire along the Spice Route. The voyage of Christopher Columbus was inspired by the desire to find a quicker route to the riches of India. But today, modern communications and ease of transportation have allowed international flows of goods and capital to reach unprecedented levels: consumers in Europe buy freshly cut flowers from Kenya, Americans dine on shrimp from Thailand, and Chinese utility companies import coal from Colombia.

In this section, we look at the different ways in which goods and capital flow around the global economy today.

Imports and Exports

LO 17.1 Define the balance of trade and describe the general trends of Canadian trade.

First, we'll describe some patterns of trade in Canada.

Figure 17-1 shows trade flows over the last fifty years. You can see that both exports and imports have increased dramatically over this period as the economy has grown. In 2014, exports of goods and services were $625 billion, or approximately 31.6 percent of GDP. Imports the same year were $643 billion, or approximately 32.5 percent of GDP.

It is interesting to look at the flows in and out, but the number that economists care the most about is the net value of these flows, called the balance of trade. The **balance of trade** is the value of exports minus the value of imports. For the last several years, Canada has imported more than it exported. Economists call this situation a negative balance of trade, or a **trade deficit**. In 2014, the trade balance was –$18.6 billion, or close to 0.9 percent of GDP. If a country exports more than it imports, the balance of trade is positive, or there is a **trade surplus**. Countries like Japan, China, and Germany run large trade surpluses For example, the trade surplus in Germany is worth around 5.6 percent of its GDP.

Figure 17-1 shows the total trade balance of Canada with all the other countries in the world. If you had to guess, which countries would you expect to be the main trading partners of Canada? Because trade requires transporting goods, which costs money, countries tend to trade with their neighbours. This holds true for Canada. Canada's biggest trading partner is the United States. Approximately 85 percent of Canadian exports go to the US and 75 percent of Canadian imports come from the US. Trade has also expanded as a result of the North American Free Trade Agreement (NAFTA) with the US and Mexico, a pact that eliminates barriers to trade and investment among these neighbours.

FIGURE 17-1

Imports, Exports, and the Balance of Canadian Trade ($ millions)

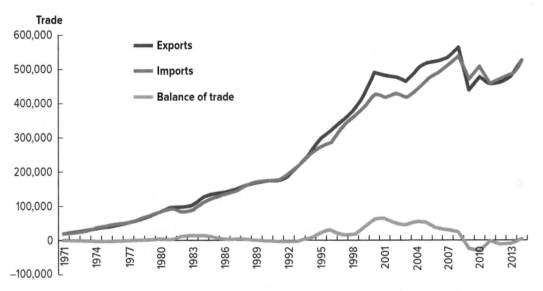

From 1970 until early 1990, trade by Canada was relatively balanced; imports were roughly equal to exports. Shortly thereafter, the amount of exports grew faster than the amount of imports, which led to a positive trade balance. Balance of trade turned negative in 2008, and by 2014 the trade deficit stood at $18.6 billion.

Source: Statistics Canada, CANSIM Table 228-0059, "Merchandise imports and exports, customs and balance of payments basis for all countries," May 2015.

Of course, as Figure 17-2 shows, not all trade partners are neighbours. In fact, with the exception of the US, Canada imports more goods from China than from any other country. As we noted, Canada imports much more from China than it exports to it. This difference generates a negative trade balance with China that is higher than with other trading partners. As we go through this chapter we'll examine explanations for the trade deficit with China. One factor is that Chinese products tend to be low in price. We'll also look at less-obvious factors such as the amount of savings in China and its exchange-rate policies.

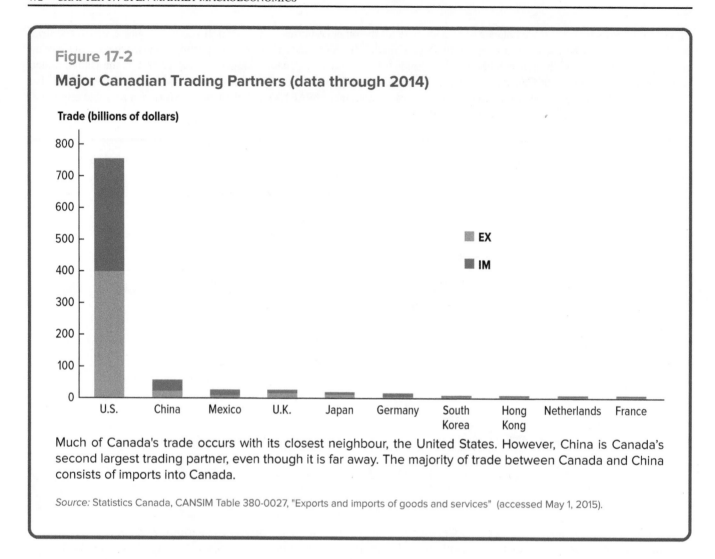

Figure 17-2

Major Canadian Trading Partners (data through 2014)

Trade (billions of dollars)

Much of Canada's trade occurs with its closest neighbour, the United States. However, China is Canada's second largest trading partner, even though it is far away. The majority of trade between Canada and China consists of imports into Canada.

Source: Statistics Canada, CANSIM Table 380-0027, "Exports and imports of goods and services" (accessed May 1, 2015).

We've seen how much Canada is trading and with whom—but *what* is it trading? As we described in Chapter 2, there are *gains from trade* when countries specialize in producing particular goods and then trade with others to meet their other needs. Looking at trade statistics shows exactly where the gains from trade in Canada come from. Figure 17-3 shows the main categories of goods that Canada exports and imports, and the contribution to the trade balance for each category.

The largest category of Canadian exports is energy products. Canada exported $128.7 billion in energy products in 2014. At the same time, it imported $43.6 billion worth of energy products, mostly natural gas and refined petroleum energy products. The balance of trade in energy products was $85.1 billion. Other than the category of energy products, Canada also has a positive balance of trade in fishery products, mineral products, forestry products, and transportation equipment.

Imports, however, are dominated by consumer goods—goods such as apparel, pharmaceuticals, and toys. The balance of trade in consumer goods was negative, −$47.4 billion, with imports of $106.2 billion and exports of $58.8 billion. In addition to consumer goods, Canada has a negative balance of trade in industrial chemicals, machinery and equipment, and motor vehicles.

FIGURE 17-3

What Does Canada Trade?

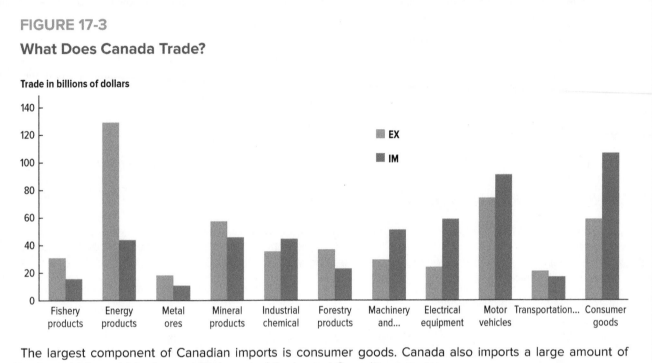

Trade in billions of dollars

The largest component of Canadian imports is consumer goods. Canada also imports a large amount of motor vehicles, which also constitute one of the largest Canadian exports.

Source: Statistics Canada, CANSIM Table 228-0065 "Merchandise imports and exports, customs and balance of payments basis for all countries" (accessed May 1, 2015).

Foreign Investment

LO 17.2 Define portfolio investment and foreign direct investment.

Imports and exports are the most visible and straightforward aspects of international economics. Countries interact in other ways, as well, including through investment. When a firm runs part of its operation abroad or invests in another company abroad this is called **foreign direct investment (FDI)**. Foreign direct investment often makes economic sense for businesses—it helps broaden markets and can cut wage costs, for example. Some people object that such investment can encourage "sweatshops" in other countries, where workers work for long hours under worse conditions than would be allowed in Canada. For a discussion of some of the issues surrounding foreign investment, see the What Do You Think? box, Are Sweatshops Good or Bad?

Of course, investment abroad isn't only in tangible assets such as factories. Often investors also want to buy foreign financial assets, such as stocks or government-issued securities. We call this type of investment *foreign portfolio investment*. **Foreign portfolio investment** is investment funded by foreign sources but operated domestically. Portfolio investment allows investors to hold financial assets that deliver greater profit and reduce overall risk relative to financial investments available at home.

One form of portfolio investments comes from Chinese purchases of Canadian government debt. Part of the reason for this is that Chinese investors have a reserve of Canadian dollars, so they want to buy assets that are Canadian dollar denominated. Why do they have a reserve of Canadian dollars? Because, as noted earlier, every time we buy Chinese goods, someone had to sell dollars in exchange for yuan to pay for these products. One option for all these dollars is to use them to buy Canadian Treasury bills.

When the total amount of direct investment and portfolio investment is tallied, we can find the net investment position of a country. The **net capital outflow** is the net flow of funds invested outside of a country. Countries that have a trade surplus have a positive net capital outflow. Countries that have a trade deficit have a net capital inflow.

Figure 17-4 shows net capital outflow for Canada over thirty years. You can see that the capital outflow is broken down into the two types of investment: direct investment and portfolio investment.

Portfolio investment can generally flow across borders quickly, since it mainly involves transfers between bank accounts. Foreign direct investment doesn't move as fast. You cannot just pick up a factory and move it across the border. For this reason, portfolio investment is sometimes called *hot money* since it can rapidly be withdrawn from a country. When a country is small, the rapid movement of money across borders can easily overwhelm the country's financial markets.

WHAT DO YOU THINK?

Are Sweatshops Good or Bad?

In 2001, an MIT graduate student named Jonah Peretti ordered a pair of sneakers from the NIKE iD service, which allows customers to personalize their shoes with a word of their choice. Peretti asked that his be emblazoned with the word "sweatshop." Nike refused, claiming that the word violated the NIKE iD terms and conditions because it was "inappropriate slang."

Peretti emailed back, with false innocence:

> After consulting Webster's Dictionary, I discovered that "sweatshop" is in fact part of standard English, and not slang. The word means: "a shop or factory in which workers are employed for long hours at low wages and under unhealthy conditions" and its origin dates from 1892... Your website advertises that the NIKE iD program is "about freedom to choose and freedom to express who you are." I share Nike's love of freedom and personal expression... I hope that you will value my freedom of statement and reconsider your decision to reject my order."

Nike again refused, doubtless not wanting the bad publicity of someone walking around in a pair of Nike Sweatshops. But Nike got bad publicity anyway when the email exchange with Peretti went viral, sparking media coverage around the globe. Peretti had a pointed goal—shaming Nike for the use of "sweatshop" labour to make its shoes. (Nike, for its part, has taken steps to improve labour standards and monitor conditions.) Yet here is the irony: although they are bad for publicity, it's not entirely clear that sweatshops are always such a bad thing.

Economists, including Jeffrey Sachs of Columbia University, argue that some kinds of sweatshops are good for an economy. After all, the fact that people choose to work in sweatshops indicates that these jobs are better for them than their other options. A lot of sweatshop workers are women, whose only alternative may be backbreaking agricultural work that pays even less than the low wages offered by sweatshops. By bringing people out of agriculture, sweatshops provide a source of relative financial security and contribute toward the growth of the economy.

Those who forwarded Peretti's email exchange with Nike presumably felt uneasy with Sachs's argument. Critics of sweatshops think it's wrong that workers can toil for as long as eighty hours per week for what most Americans would consider a tiny wage. Often, it is not just that wages are low by US standards; workers may be unknowingly exposed to hazardous chemicals and dangerous machinery. Such a problem could be a market failure due to information asymmetry if employees are not fully aware of the risks they are taking. Even where safety regulations exist, workers may be unable to report violations to local authorities without fear of retribution.

What do you think?

1. Why do rich countries tend to have stricter labour standards than poor counties, and how do you think these labour standards developed?

2. If consumers feel uneasy about buying goods made in overseas sweatshops, should they support efforts to enact minimum wage and worker safety legislation all over the world? Why or why not?

Source: "Making Nike Sweat," February 13, 2001, *Village Voice.* Used with permission of Voice Media Group, Inc.

The trade in goods, services, and capital comprises trillions of dollars around the world. Keeping track of the trade balance and capital inflow helps organize these transactions. In general, the accounting of trade in goods and capital is known as the *balance of payments.*

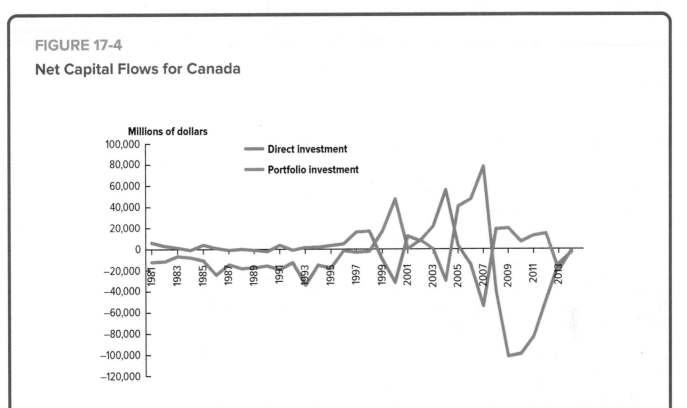

FIGURE 17-4

Net Capital Flows for Canada

For a long time, portfolio and direct investment flows in Canada were steady. Then, starting with the tech bubble, portfolio investment began to rise sharply. When the price of resources fell in 2004, so did the amount of portfolio investment. But with the global recession, the changes were more profound.

Source: Statistics Canada, CANSIM Table 376-0102 "Balance of international payments, financial account" (accessed June May 1, 2015).

Balance of Payments

LO 17.3 Explain the connection between the balance of trade and net capital outflow.

How are countries like Canada able to maintain a record of trade? It turns out that trade in tangible goods and different types of capital must balance each other out, balancing trade deficits with capital surpluses. This is shown through the **balance-of-payments identity**, an equation that shows that the value of net exports equals the net capital outflow.

Recall the income-expenditure identity from Chapter 7, "Measuring the Wealth of Nations." The identity for a closed economy—that is, one with no imports or exports—looks like this:

$$Y = C + I + G$$

Remember also that in a closed economy, savings (S) equals investment (I). We have two kinds of savings in the economy: *private savings,* which is the money left over that households and businesses don't spend, and *public savings,* which is the money left over that the government doesn't spend. Thus, rearranging the variables, we find:

1. $I = Y - C - G$

2. $S = S_{private} + S_{public} = Y - C - G$

3. $S = I$

What do things look like if we open up the economy and add in the variable of net exports? We get the typical equation for GDP, also known as the income-expenditure identity:

$$Y = C + I + G + NX$$

If we then rearrange the income-expenditure identity for an open economy, we get something that looks very similar to the equation above, except that savings equals investment plus net exports.

4. $I + NX = Y - C - G$

5. $S = S_{private} + S_{public} = Y - C - G$

6. $S = I + NX$

Finally, assume that people can choose where they want to invest. They can invest in the home country; those investments we'll call I, as before. Or they can invest in the rest of the world; those investments we'll call NCO, which stands for *net capital outflow*. The total amount of money that a country has to invest, its savings, must add up to I + NCO. Using this equation and (6) above, we find that net capital outflows to all other countries equal net exports to all other countries:

7. $S = I + NCO$

8. $S = I + NX$

9. $I + NCO = I + NX$

10. $NCO = NX$

The result—that net capital outflows equal net exports (NCO = NX)—is important and answers the question posed at the beginning of this section. A country that exports more goods than it imports, like China, will necessarily also send out more capital than it receives. That's because China's high net exports must be balanced by high net capital outflows. The capital outflows allow countries to sustain trade imbalances for long periods of times. This idea may seem tricky, so let's work through a simplified example.

Let's assume that China and Canada are both initially closed economies, so their savings equal domestic investment. Then, one day, a firm in Canada decides to buy a specialized battery made in China. The Chinese firm sends the battery to Canada, and the Canadian firm gives the Chinese firm a $100 bill.

What will the Chinese firm do with the $100 bill? It can do two things: It can keep the money in Canada (for instance, by depositing it in a bank account in Canada, or buying bonds or stocks or financial securities in Canada). Or it can buy something in Canada—say, a collection of economics books—and ship them back to China.

If the Chinese firm decides that it wants to keep the $100 in Canada, then it has made an investment in the Canadian economy. In other words, the *net capital outflow* from China to Canada is $100. The value of exports—the battery—from China to Canada is $100. Net exports are equal to net capital outflow.

What about from the Canadian perspective? Canada has $100 of its currency owned by China, so its net capital outflow is $100. (Or, in other words, Canada has a capital *inflow*.) Because the Canadian firm bought the battery from China, Canada has net exports of −$100. Net capital outflow equals net exports for Canada, as well.

What if, instead of investing the $100, the Chinese firm decides to use to it buy the books and import them back to China? Net exports for China are zero: the Chinese firm exported a $100 battery and imported $100 worth of books. Net capital outflow for China is also zero, because the money earned from the batteries was used to buy books, rather than being invested in Canada. Thus, none of its money remains in Canada. So, for China, NX = NCO.

Now let's look at the Canadian perspective. Initially, when Canada imported the battery, it had NX of −$100, but then it exported $100 worth of books, so NX became zero. No capital has been invested in or from China, so NCO is zero. For Canada, too, NX = NCO.

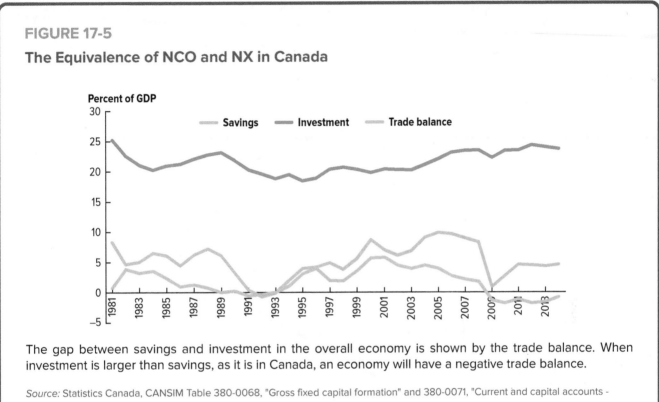

FIGURE 17-5

The Equivalence of NCO and NX in Canada

The gap between savings and investment in the overall economy is shown by the trade balance. When investment is larger than savings, as it is in Canada, an economy will have a negative trade balance.

Source: Statistics Canada, CANSIM Table 380-0068, "Gross fixed capital formation" and 380-0071, "Current and capital accounts - National" (accessed May 1, 2015).

The balance-of-payments identity tells us that the net capital outflow of a country equals the value of its net exports. Figure 17-5 shows savings, investment, and net exports in Canada in recent years. Notice that the gap between savings and investment is almost exactly the trade balance. (There may be small differences, which stem from the complexities of measurement.) In general, savings equals investment plus net exports, as we saw in the equations above.

✓ CONCEPT CHECK

☐ Which country is Canada's largest trading partner? [LO 17.1]

☐ What is portfolio investment? [LO 17.2]

☐ What is the relationship between net capital outflow and net exports in the balance-of-payments identity? [LO 17.3]

International Capital Flows

From time to time, seas of money have surged into the Canadian economy from abroad, in search of profitable investment opportunities. Why does capital flow into some economies and out of others? In this section, we'll develop a model to explain international capital flows.

Determinants of International Capital Flows

LO 17.4 Describe the determinants of international capital flows using the demand and supply for international loanable funds.

In Chapter 13, "The Basics of Finance," we developed a model of the market for loanable funds in a closed economy. In that model the equilibrium interest rate was determined by the intersection of the domestic investment curve and the domestic savings curve—the demand and supply of domestic loanable funds.

FIGURE 17-6

Expanded Market for Loanable Funds

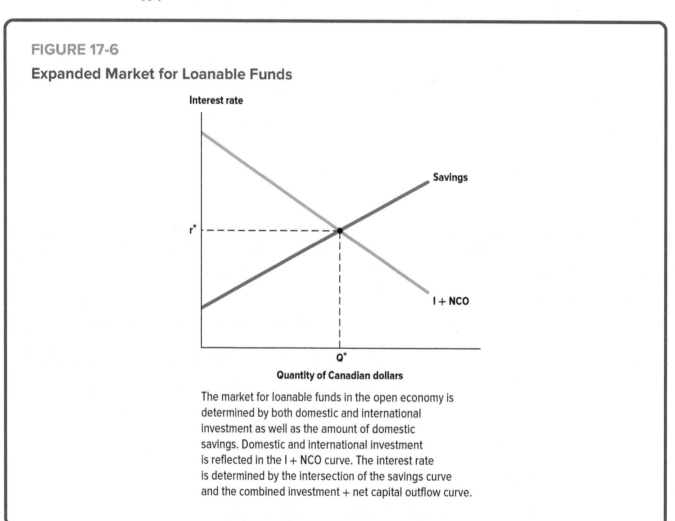

The market for loanable funds in the open economy is determined by both domestic and international investment as well as the amount of domestic savings. Domestic and international investment is reflected in the I + NCO curve. The interest rate is determined by the intersection of the savings curve and the combined investment + net capital outflow curve.

How does this model change in an open economy? The basic idea is the same: there still is a demand for and supply of loanable funds. Exactly as before, the supply of loanable funds is the sum of national savings. Savings has a positive relationship with the interest rate—as the interest rate increases, savers are going to supply a greater quantity of loanable funds to the market.

The demand for loanable funds (investment) comes from two sources: money that will be invested domestically, and money to invest internationally. *Domestic investment* is the same as it was in the domestic market for loanable funds, when we considered the economy to be closed. *International investment* comes in two forms: capital inflow (when money from abroad is invested domestically), and capital outflow (when domestic money is invested internationally). For the sake of this model, we will assume that all of these transactions occur through loanable funds. When we subtract capital inflows from capital outflows, we get *net capital outflows* (NCO). This NCO plus domestic investment forms the demand for loanable funds in the open economy. What does this demand curve look like?

We already know that domestic investment has a negative relationship with the interest rate (lower interest rates make it cheaper for firms to invest in equipment and factories). Let's use that knowledge to think about the intuition behind how capital inflows and outflows will be affected by Canadian interest rates. Suppose the domestic interest rate declines. People in Canada will start to look overseas for opportunities to earn more interest on their money. The result will be higher capital outflows. Meanwhile, people overseas will be less keen to invest in Canada because of the lower returns, so there will be lower capital inflows. Higher outflows and lower inflows both push *net* outflows in the same direction: higher.

Now suppose the interest rate goes up. In that case, the opposite happens: people in Canada will be more willing to keep their savings in the country; outflows will go down. At the same time, people overseas will send their financial investments to Canada in pursuit of better returns; inflows will go up. Lower outflows and higher inflows both push net outflows in the same direction: lower.

When we put this result together with domestic investment, as shown in Figure 17-6, we get the combined I + NCO curve—which is the demand for loanable funds in the open economy. In the open economy, the equilibrium interest rate is found at the intersection of national savings and the combined I + NCO curve.

For a real-life example of the power of domestic investment and capital inflows, see the Real Life box, Iceland and the Banking Crisis. In 2007, banks in Iceland held $90 billion in their accounts, far more than the entire country's GDP. When these banks ran into trouble, the whole country was thrown into crisis.

REAL LIFE

Iceland and the Banking Crisis

Iceland is a volcanic island in the North Atlantic Ocean, located between Greenland and the United Kingdom. The country is home to some 300,000 people, and until recently was best known as the home of the eccentric singer Björk. That changed in 2010 when a collapse of the banking sector in this quiet island nation nearly brought down the entire world economy.

Until the early 2000s, Icelandic banks were small and largely focused on catering to the basic financial needs of local citizens. Then Iceland deregulated its banking industry, and the country's banks expanded throughout Europe. This process was fueled by the Icelandic central bank's determination to control inflation by keeping interest rates high. We have seen that high interest rates lead to negative NCO (that is, a net *inflow* of capital).

Sure enough, money flowed into Iceland as savers from all over Europe rushed to deposit money in Icelandic banks. The banks grew bigger and bigger, eventually amassing foreign debt of more than $90 billion, six times larger than Iceland's entire GDP. (All the money people deposited with them constituted foreign debt.)

As the financial crisis and Great Recession of 2008 washed up on Iceland's shores, all three of its major banks collapsed. Savers saw their savings evaporate. Could the government of Iceland have decided to bail out the banks to keep the wider economy from derailing? In theory, yes, but unfortunately Iceland's banks had grown so big that even the state couldn't afford to bail them out.

The result was a mess. Iceland had to ask the International Monetary Fund, the global agency responsible for helping to maintain international financial stability, to step in with emergency funds of $6 billion to keep the country's financial system functioning. As the Icelandic economy shrank by more than 6 percent in 2009 alone, the British and Dutch governments undertook legal action to try to recover their citizens' billions in lost banking deposits. Not surprisingly, the people of Iceland reacted badly to the idea that their taxes should have to compensate British and Dutch savers. After all, ordinary Icelanders had had little to do with the risky behaviour of their nation's banks.

Icelanders vented their frustration on the politicians who had allowed this mess to happen by voting an absurdist comedian in as the new mayor of the capital city. His policy platform? "We should have this huge statue of Björk at the harbour like the Statue of Liberty." Sadly, the mayor did not find the money to enact this plan while in office.

Sources: http://www.nytimes.com/2010/06/26/world/europe/26iceland.html; debt statistics from the Central Bank of Iceland.

How Does Foreign Investment Work?

LO 17.5 Show how the international market for loanable funds can be used to explain events in the international financial system.

Using our model of international capital flows, we can begin to examine the impact of foreign investment—and understand why it's often economically beneficial. In short, foreign investment can:

- Increase the GDP of the host country by giving it access to additional resources
- Increase the GDP of the investing country by providing it with ways to earn higher returns on its capital
- Make the world a more efficient place by moving capital from places with low returns to places with high returns

To see how this works, imagine that people have a sudden increase in confidence in the economy of Canada and want to invest there. Figure 17-7 shows what happens. The shift in preferences toward investing in Canada means that the demand curve for loanable funds in the open economy will shift to the left. The shift indicates that net capital outflow has decreased. This results in a lower equilibrium interest rate in the economy. At the lower interest rate, the quantity of loanable funds demanded is less.

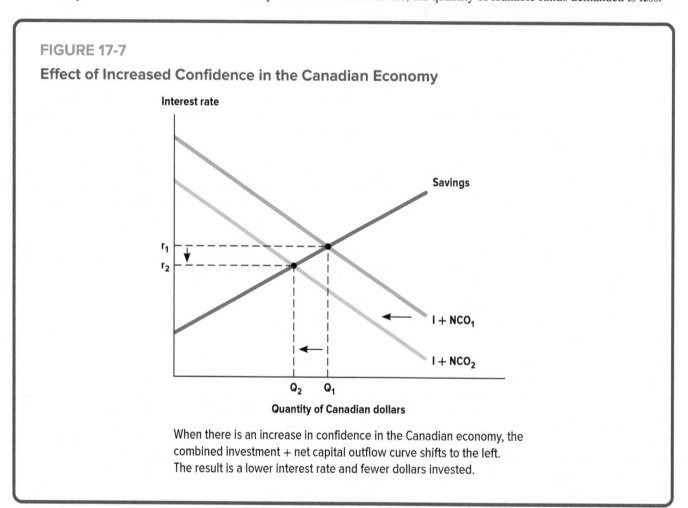

FIGURE 17-7

Effect of Increased Confidence in the Canadian Economy

When there is an increase in confidence in the Canadian economy, the combined investment + net capital outflow curve shifts to the left. The result is a lower interest rate and fewer dollars invested.

This might be confusing. In the domestic market for loanable funds, an increase in confidence in the local economy would shift the demand curve for loanable funds to the right. This still happens, but this effect is outweighed by the movements of capital in the open economy. In the open economy, the existence of better investment opportunities at home means that domestic investors are going to keep their money at home. Since the demand for loanable funds consists of I + NCO, the reduction in NCO directly reduces loanable funds demand. With a decrease in net capital outflow, this demand decreases.

Investment is a key component of GDP, so the Canadian economy benefits when foreign investment increases. Foreign investors also benefit from better investment opportunities in Canada, adding to the GDP of their countries.

We can also examine the relationship between foreign investment and public savings. Doing so will bring us closer to understanding the trade imbalance between Canada and China. Recall that the savings curve for the economy reflects the sum of private and public savings.

In order to see the connection, let's look at the case of a government budget deficit, which causes a decrease in public savings. When the government runs a deficit, the savings curve shifts to the left, as in Figure 17-8. When this happens, the new equilibrium interest rate is higher than before. With a higher interest rate there is more incentive to invest in Canada. Less capital flows out, and more capital flows in. Net capital outflow decreases and the quantity of loanable funds saved and invested in equilibrium drops.

Although net capital outflow is lower, the higher interest rate in the economy due to a decrease in savings means that there is a lower level of domestic investment. Foreign and domestic savings are used to finance the government budget, instead of being used to finance domestic investment. We say that the government deficit *crowds out* domestic investment because the higher interest rate reduces firms' investment in the economy.

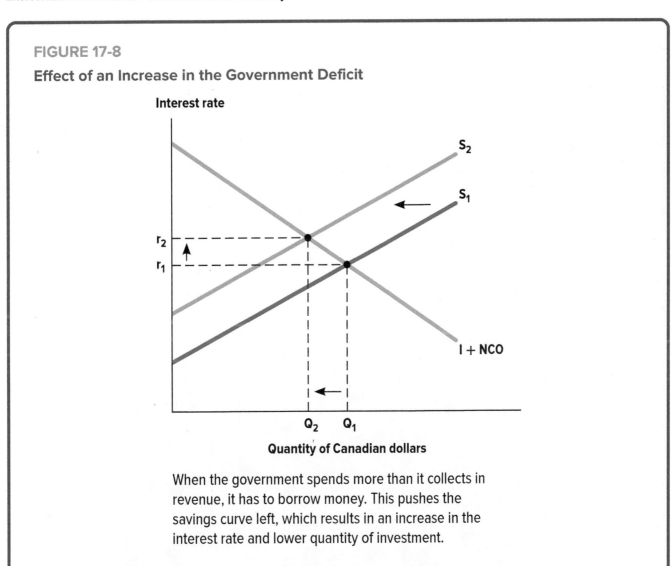

FIGURE 17-8

Effect of an Increase in the Government Deficit

When the government spends more than it collects in revenue, it has to borrow money. This pushes the savings curve left, which results in an increase in the interest rate and lower quantity of investment.

Can a Country Save Too Much?

Saying that it is possible to save too much is like claiming that it's possible to eat too much broccoli. It's true only at the most ridiculous extremes. But perhaps China is at that extreme. After all, it currently saves more than 50 percent of its GDP! In comparison, Canada saves only 3.6 percent of its total income. High domestic savings can keep demand for local products low as people consume less. There are empty malls and vacant housing projects in China, simply waiting for customers to open their wallets. Saving too much can also lead to trade imbalances.

We mentioned this idea in Chapter 13, "The Basics of Finance," but now we have the tools to evaluate the effects of a "global savings glut." A growing propensity to save shifts out the savings curve, decreasing the equilibrium interest rate. Low interest rates in China relative to other markets encourage capital to flow abroad, raising net capital outflow—which explains why China has so much invested around the world. The flip-side of that investment is the massive trade imbalance between China and the rest of the world.

If this explanation of the trade imbalance is right, how can it be corrected? One solution could be for China to reduce its saving levels and increase consumption. Imports should rise and exports should fall. Another solution is for each country to increase its own savings levels and spend a little less. If the rest of the world increases its total savings, either because households or the government saves more, then capital outflow will increase from the rest of the world, reducing the imbalance.

There's another story, however. Others, particularly politicians, suggest that the trade deficit between the rest of the world and China stems from China's fixed exchange rate, an idea we explore next.

✓ CONCEPT CHECK

☐ Which two curves make up the international market for loanable funds? [LO 17.4]

☐ What is the difference between the closed- and open-economy versions of the market for loanable funds? [LO 17.5]

☐ Which way does the savings curve shift when the government reduces its deficit? [LO 17.5]

Exchange Rates

If you arrive in a foreign country with a pocketful of Canadian dollars, chances are you won't be able to use them in most local shops and restaurants. They will require local currency, which you can get by exchanging your dollars at a bank or a specialized foreign currency dealer. The price at which the exchange happens is the *exchange rate.* Sometimes the exchange rate is at a level that gives you lots of local currency for your dollars. Other times, the exchange rate is at a level that requires you to give more of your dollars for the same amount of local currency. How does the market for currency work?

© Adiseshan Shankar/Alamy Stock Photo

The Foreign-Exchange Market

> **LO 17.6** Describe the exchange rate and its determinants, and explain how the exchange rate affects trade.

The market for buying and selling foreign currencies is often referred to as the *forex* market, short for *foreign exchange*. Every weekday people engage in trillions of dollars worth of transactions around the clock, trading dollars for euros or euros for Mexican pesos, for example. Like any other market, there is supply, demand, price, and quantity traded. And like any other market, the market for different currencies has a price, which is called the exchange rate.

Canadian dollars can be used all over the world, but need to be changed into local currency by currency exchangers. Sometimes this means a bank, and sometimes it is just a small shop, like the one in Manila pictured on the previous page.

The **exchange rate** is the value of one currency expressed in terms of another currency. For example, in May 2015, one Canadian dollar—abbreviated CAD—could be exchanged for 0.82 US dollars, 0.73 euros, 5.11 Chinese yuan, or 12.8 Mexican pesos.

Exchange rates can be expressed in two ways: either in terms of the domestic currency, or in terms of the foreign currency. When we examine the exchange rates between two nations' currencies, the exchange rates will be reciprocals of each other.

HINT

Recall that the *reciprocal* of a fraction or ratio is just that fraction or ratio turned upside down or flipped over, so that the numerator (portion above the fraction line) becomes the denominator (portion below the fraction line), and the denominator becomes the numerator. The reciprocal of 3/4 is 4/3, and the reciprocal of 2 (equivalent to 2/1) is therefore 1/2.

Furthermore, if one unit of domestic currency is worth six units of a foreign currency, then we can express this equivalently as the foreign currency being worth 1/6 of a unit of the domestic currency.

In the real world, foreign exchange rates are often expressed in decimal form rather than fraction form, but the same idea applies. If $1 is worth 0.73 euros, then 1 euro is worth $1.37 (since $1 divided by 0.73 is 1.37 $/euro). If $1 is worth 98 yen, then 1 yen is worth $0.01 (since $1 divided by 98 is 0.01 $/yen).

From this point forward, we will express exchange rates from the point of view of Canada, using the dollar as the domestic currency. That means that exchange rates will be expressed in terms of *units of foreign currency per dollar*. Of course, we could also look at things from the perspective of another nation—for example, from Japan's point of view. In that case, the yen would be considered the home currency, and exchange rates would be expressed in terms of the units of foreign currency—dollars, yuan, euros, and so forth—required to buy one yen. All concepts discussed in the chapter apply no matter which nation's point of view we assume.

You might wonder if discrepancies between the forex markets, located in so many places, might arise. For example, is it possible for a trader to convert dollars to pesos in a Mexican forex market, pesos to yuan in a Chinese forex market, yuan to euros in a European forex market, and euros back to dollars in a Canadian forex market, and end up with more dollars than she started with? This possibility is known as *arbitrage*, in this case, gaining financially by taking advantage of discrepancies in currency exchange rates. Since money can be made on these trades, forex traders have sophisticated software constantly scouring the world's different forex markets to see if any discrepancies exist. If they find them, they instantly trade the currencies until the discrepancy no longer exists. As a result, any opportunities for arbitrage are fleeting.

Another way in which speculators try to make money from forex is by betting on the direction that an exchange rate will move over time. When the value of a currency increases relative to the value of another currency, we say that a currency experiences **exchange-rate appreciation**. When the currency appreciates, it can buy more of another currency. For example, if the Canadian dollar appreciates against the euro, say from 0.73 to 0.83 euros, the result is that one dollar can buy 0.1 more euros than before.

Who benefits when the dollar appreciates against the euro? The Canadian dollar can buy more goods that are denominated in euros, so people who have Canadian dollars and want to buy goods from Europe will benefit. For instance, Canadian tourists in

Paris will find that things are cheaper as the dollar appreciates against the euro. For example, a French hotel room with a nightly rate of 73 euros would cost $100 at the exchange rate of 0.73 euros per dollar...

$$\left[73 \text{ euros} \times \left(\frac{\$1}{0.73} \text{ euros}\right) = \$100\right]$$

...but only $87.95 after the dollar appreciates to 0.83:

$$\left[73 \text{ euros} \times \left(\frac{\$1}{0.83} \text{ euros}\right) = \$87.95\right]$$

On the other hand, a Canadian company that sells DVDs in France will find that it has fewer customers: a $15 DVD that sells for 10.95 euros in Paris when the exchange rate is 0.73 euros per dollar...

$$\left[\$15 \times \left(\frac{0.73 \text{ euros}}{\$1}\right) = 10.95 \text{ euros}\right]$$

...would instead sell for 12.45 euros if the dollar appreciates to 0.83:

$$\left[\$15 \times \left(\frac{0.83 \text{ euros}}{\$1}\right) = 12.45 \text{ euros}\right]$$

When the value of a currency decreases relative to other currencies, we say that a currency experiences **exchange-rate depreciation**. In our example, when the dollar appreciates against the euro, logic tells us that the euro has *depreciated* against the dollar. Or, imagine the Canadian dollar goes from being worth 5.11 yuan to 5 yuan. We say the Canadian dollar has depreciated—it now buys fewer yuan than it did before. Who's going to be happy if this happens? Canadian consumers will have to pay more for Chinese goods, but Canadian exporters will have an easier time selling to Chinese consumers.

The Exchange Rate and Net Exports

Exchange rates affect nearly every dimension of international economics. The flow of goods is one example:

- When the Canadian dollar appreciates against a foreign currency, Canadian goods become more expensive to people abroad, and foreign goods become cheaper for Canadians. As a result, we would expect net exports to decrease.
- When the Canadian dollar depreciates against a foreign currency, foreign goods become more expensive for Canadians, and Canadian goods become cheaper for foreign consumers. We would expect net exports to increase.

Does this expectation hold empirically? Figure 17-9 shows Canadian net exports plotted against an exchange-rate index—the average value of the Canadian dollar against its main trading partners. Just as we expect, when the Canadian dollar goes up in value against other currencies, net exports tend to go down soon afterward. When net exports fall, the trade deficit rises. Similarly, when the Canadian dollar drops in value, exports tend to go up, which reduces the trade deficit. That's why we see that when the exchange rate rises, the trade deficit will usually rise, too. And when the exchange rate falls, so will the trade deficit.

FIGURE 17-9

Trade Deficit and the Exchange Rate in Canada

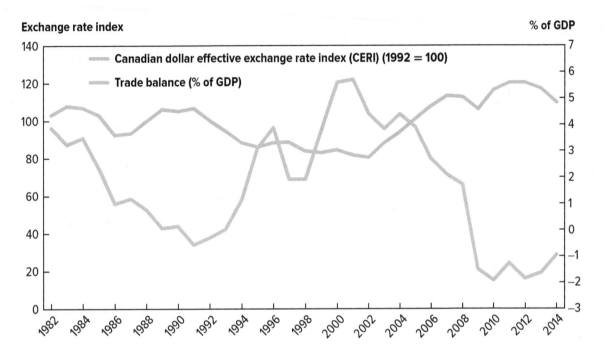

In Canada, there is a distinct relationship between the exchange rate (shown here relative to its 2005 level) and the trade deficit. When the exchange rate falls, the trade deficit decreases, although this effect operates on a lag, meaning that it takes time for trade to respond to changes in the exchange rate.

Source: Statistics Canada, CANSIM Table 176-0064, "Foreign exchange rates in Canadian dollars, Bank of Canada" (accessed May 1, 2015).

A Model of the Exchange-Rate Market

The foreign-exchange market is a market like any other: there is demand for a currency, a supply of that currency, and an equilibrium price and quantity, which is determined by the intersection of supply and demand. What determines demand and supply in the forex market?

We'll start with *demand*. Why would foreigners demand Canadian dollars? The demand comes from overseas consumers, businesses, and governments who want to use dollars to buy goods or services in Canada. For example, a British family might demand dollars to be able to vacation in Quebec. A Japanese shop might demand dollars to import Canadian-made DVDs for sale to Japanese consumers. The Chinese government might demand dollars to be able to purchase financial assets such as Canadian Treasury debt.

The demand for dollars also depends on interest rates, both in Canada and abroad. High interest rates in Canada relative to overseas will attract foreign capital. These assets need to be paid for in Canadian dollars, so demand for Canadian dollars will increase. On the other hand, if foreign interest rates are high relative to those in Canada, demand for dollars will decrease as investors sell their dollars to buy foreign currency for investment.

The last key variable in determining the demand for a country's currency is the perceived riskiness of investing in that country against the perceived riskiness of investing in other countries. If investors feel confident about putting money into emerging economies such as those of Russia or Brazil or South Africa, they will invest more there, all else equal. If investors decide it is risky to invest in such countries compared to Canada, then more people will want to invest more in Canada, increasing the demand for Canadian dollars.

To make an investment, one has to have the right currency. Anything that motivates investors to invest in a particular country will therefore increase demand for the currency of that country.

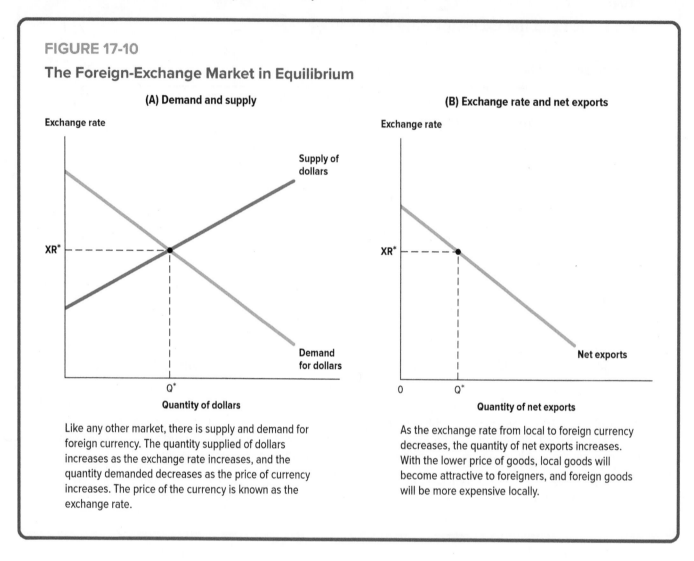

FIGURE 17-10

The Foreign-Exchange Market in Equilibrium

(A) Demand and supply

Exchange rate

Supply of dollars

XR*

Demand for dollars

Q*

Quantity of dollars

Like any other market, there is supply and demand for foreign currency. The quantity supplied of dollars increases as the exchange rate increases, and the quantity demanded decreases as the price of currency increases. The price of the currency is known as the exchange rate.

(B) Exchange rate and net exports

Exchange rate

XR*

Net exports

0   Q*

Quantity of net exports

As the exchange rate from local to foreign currency decreases, the quantity of net exports increases. With the lower price of goods, local goods will become attractive to foreigners, and foreign goods will be more expensive locally.

What about factors affecting the *supply* of foreign exchange? Interest rates and perceived risk matter here, too. If the Canadian interest rate is low relative to foreign interest rates, financial investors holding Canadian assets will want to sell them and purchase foreign assets. Similarly, if investors' confidence in foreign economies increases, the supply of Canadian dollars will increase as investors sell off Canadian assets. Finally, consumer preferences also play a role. If Canadian consumers prefer foreign goods, they will sell their dollars to obtain foreign currency, increasing the supply of Canadian dollars in the forex market.

Figure 17-10 shows how the supply of and demand for dollars determines the equilibrium exchange rate against any other given currency (panel A). It also shows how this equilibrium exchange rate in turn determines the level of net exports (panel B). When the price of dollars is high, foreigners will buy fewer goods from Canada and Canadians will buy more goods from overseas. As a result, net exports are low and may even be negative. When the price of dollars is low, the reverse happens: it's cheap for foreigners to buy Canadian goods and expensive for Canadians to buy foreign goods, so net exports will be high.

Let's look at an example of how this model works in practice. When the Toyota Prius was released to the Canadian market in 2003, many people wanted to get their hands on the first mass-produced hybrid gas/electric vehicle. Since the Prius was manufactured by Toyota in Japan, Canadian dealers had to exchange dollars for Japanese yen to be able to buy and import Priuses. This led the supply curve of Canadian dollars to shift to the right. The exchange rate from the Canadian dollar to the Japanese yen fell as a result. The new equilibrium is shown in panel A of Figure 17-11.

FIGURE 17-11

Increase in Demand for Prius cars

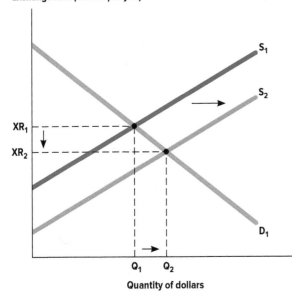

(A) Foreign-exchange market

When the demand for Priuses shifts to the right, the supply of dollars at equilibrium increases as more people are trying to sell dollars in order to purchase yen. This shift increases the quantity of dollars traded, but lowers the exchange rate.

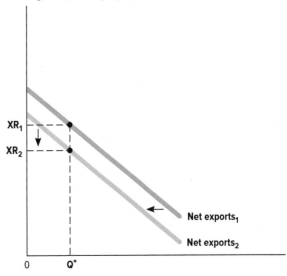

(B) Exchange rate and net exports

Since Canadians are now importing far more cars, the net exports curve shifts to the left. At the same time the exchange rate falls. Depending on the size of these two changes, the quantity of net exports could be higher or lower than it was before; in this instance the two cancel each other out.

What effect does this have on net exports for Canada? As we have seen, the net export curve is a demand curve. It shows the demand for net exports at different prices, or in this case, exchange rates. Just like a standard demand curve, shifts in preferences shift the net export curve. When Canadian consumers decide they want to buy Priuses rather than cars made in Canada, this shift in preferences moves the net export curve to the left (because more imports mean fewer net exports).

However, there is something else going on at the same time. Because the value of Canadian dollars depreciated, Canadian exports became cheaper, which increased the quantity of net exports. Panel B of Figure 17-11 shows the combined effects of a greater preference for Japanese cars are counterbalanced by the effects of the depreciation in the exchange rate. Depending on which effect is bigger, the quantity of net exports could end up being higher or lower than before the Prius was introduced. In this case, the graph depicts the effects as cancelling each other out exactly.

Now imagine another scenario: the Bank of Canada decides to tighten monetary policy by increasing the interest rate. This increase is going to affect both the demand for and the supply of Canadian dollars. Because the return on investment is higher in Canada, foreign investors want to buy Canadian assets, so the demand for Canadian dollars increases. At the same time, Canadian investors would rather invest in their own economy instead of buying financial assets abroad, reducing the supply of Canadian dollars. As shown in panel A of Figure 17-12, these shifts will cause the exchange rate to appreciate. Nothing in this story will shift the net exports curve, however, so panel B shows that the higher exchange rate translates directly into a reduction in net exports.

We can also look at the change in monetary policy in another way. We know that NX = NCO, so the higher exchange rate has also caused a reduction in NCO. (In other words, it has caused more capital *inflows*.) We know that there will be more capital flowing into Canada when interest rates go up, as foreign savers take advantage of the opportunity to get a better return.

FIGURE 17-12

Tighter Monetary Policy in Canada

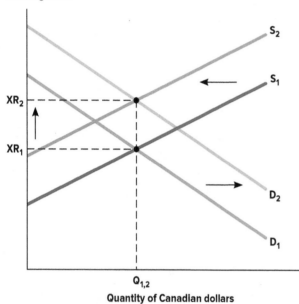

(A) Foreign-exchange market

When the Bank of Canada tightens the money supply, the price of the dollar initially rises and supply decreases. Demand shifts out as well, and the price of the dollar rises and the quantity of dollars traded returns to the initial amount.

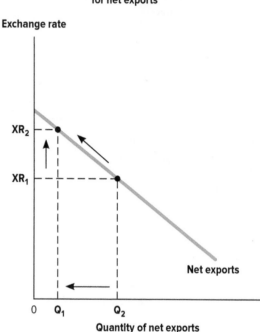

(B) Decrease in quantity demanded for net exports

With an increase in the exchange rate of the dollar, the quantity of net exports falls, as Canadian goods are now more expensive for foreigners.

Our model of the foreign-exchange market has shown us that monetary policy works on aggregate demand in two ways. Remember, by raising interest rates the Bank of Canada is trying to cool off the economy. One way it does this is by making it more expensive to borrow, reducing investment. We can now see that increasing the interest rate also causes the exchange rate to appreciate, which reduces net exports. Because net exports are also part of aggregate demand, this further reduces aggregate demand.

However, this result holds only in an open economy where the exchange rate is determined by the market. As we shall now see, some governments do not allow the market to determine the exchange rate for their currency.

Exchange-Rate Regimes

LO 17.7 Explain fixed and floating exchange rates and how monetary policy affects the value of currency in both.

The euro is used by nineteen countries of the European Union and a small number of other countries. Previously each had its own currency. Since many European countries are small, this made life difficult. A 150-mile trip from Dusseldorf, Germany, to Brussels, Belgium, with a stop in Maastricht in the Netherlands, would require the use of three separate currencies—the German mark, Dutch guilder, and Belgian franc. Now, tourists no longer have the hassle of exchanging money (and paying a commission to do so) every time they cross a border. Businesses that do a lot of trade with neighbouring countries no longer have to worry about exchange-rate fluctuations changing the prices they have to pay for their inputs or will receive for their products.

There are also disadvantages, however. In being so tightly joined to other economies, the members of the eurozone give up some of their ability to conduct independent macroeconomic policy. Let's say that Germany has low unemployment: wages are rising and so are concerns about inflation. We know that to tackle inflation, a central bank would usually tighten monetary policy—that is, increase interest rates. Let's say that at the same time Italy is experiencing *high* unemployment. There, a central bank would usually loosen monetary policy—that is, lower interest rates.

When Germany used the mark and Italy used the lira, these differing monetary policies would cause their currencies' exchange rates to change: in our example, the lira would depreciate and the mark would appreciate. The result? Italian products would become cheaper for other countries to buy, helping to boost aggregate demand in Italy and tackle unemployment. Meanwhile, just as we saw in the example presented in Figure 17-12, the appreciating German mark would help to reduce net exports in Germany, and hence aggregate demand, easing the upward pressure on prices. However, as soon as countries gave up their own currencies and began to use the euro, they could no longer pursue their own monetary policies to tackle their specific macroeconomic situations.

You may be wondering why this isn't a problem among Canadian provinces. What if Alberta is experiencing high demand for labour and rising prices and wages, whereas Newfoundland is experiencing high unemployment? The problem solves itself without any need for separate currencies and exchange rate changes. We would expect unemployed workers from Newfoundland to move to Alberta in search of higher wages, and Alberta-based businesses to relocate to Newfoundland in search of cheaper labour. The difference with the eurozone is that, unlike Newfoundland and Alberta, Germany and Italy speak different languages and have distinct cultures. In theory, Italian labourers can seek work in Germany and German businesses can relocate to Italy, but in practice it's not so easy—certainly not as easy as moving from one province to another in Canada.

Not all countries that share a currency are neighbours. In fact, Ecuador, a small country in South America, now uses US dollars exclusively. The barriers seem even greater than between Italy and Germany: Ecuador and the United States are much farther apart geographically, and unemployed Ecuadorans don't have the legal right to seek work in the US, as Italians do in Germany. Still, that hasn't stopped Ecuador from adopting the US dollar as its currency, as the Real Life box, Dollarization: When Not in the US... discusses.

REAL LIFE

Dollarization: When Not in the US . . .

In 1998 and 1999, Ecuador experienced a wrenching financial crisis that caused the value of the Ecuadoran currency, the sucre, to fall by 50 percent in just two months. Within two years, 70 percent of Ecuador's financial institutions went out of business, sending shockwaves throughout the rest of the economy. When the crisis was over, the country's GDP, at $10 billion, was half of what it had been two years earlier.

Rather than try to reboot the sucre, the government decided to "dollarize"—to replace all sucres with US dollars. This move immediately stabilized the Ecuadoran economy. In just three years, the annual inflation rate in Ecuador dropped from 20 percent to 2.7 percent.

However, dollarization has a drawback: it tied Ecuador's economy to that of the United States, for better or worse. In exchange for a stable currency and lower inflation, the government had to give up control of monetary policy. There is no way for Ecuador's government to print US dollars if the country's economy is in recession. Nor can it reduce the amount of US dollars in circulation if it wants to cool an overheating economy. Only the US Federal Reserve can do those things, and the Fed is not likely to take much account of Ecuador's macroeconomic needs when making decisions. If the US economy is doing well while Ecuador is struggling, a contraction in the money supply would further damage the Ecuadoran economy.

Ecuador is one of ten countries that have decided to dollarize, giving up their own national currency and throwing in their lot with the US in terms of monetary policy and exchange rates. Most of these countries are scattered throughout the Pacific (such as Palau and Micronesia) or Latin America (Panama and El Salvador, along with Ecuador). Although it is a rather dramatic step, for countries where inflation or financial instability is a persistent problem, the price of giving up control over monetary policy is one that's considered to be well worth paying.

Sources: www.imf.org/external/pubs/ft/issues/issues24/; http://www.utoronto.ca/plac/pdf/Conf_5_financial/-Delatorre-web.pdf

Fixed and Floating Rates

The dollar, euro, Mexican peso, and Japanese yen are all examples of currencies with a **floating exchange rate**. They can be freely traded and their value is determined by the market. The exchange rate is set by the intersection of the supply and demand curves for foreign exchange, shown in panel A of Figure 17-13.

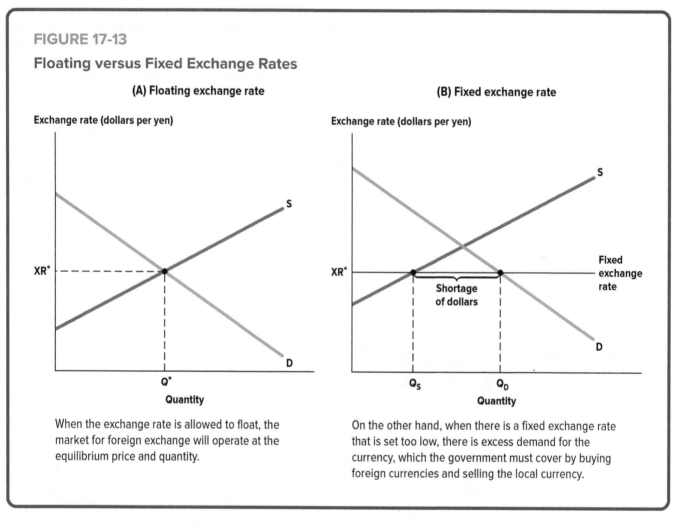

FIGURE 17-13

Floating versus Fixed Exchange Rates

(A) Floating exchange rate

Exchange rate (dollars per yen)

When the exchange rate is allowed to float, the market for foreign exchange will operate at the equilibrium price and quantity.

(B) Fixed exchange rate

Exchange rate (dollars per yen)

On the other hand, when there is a fixed exchange rate that is set too low, there is excess demand for the currency, which the government must cover by buying foreign currencies and selling the local currency.

Some currencies, however, have a **fixed exchange rate**—one that is set by the government, usually with reference to the US dollar or some composite index of major global currencies. A fixed exchange rate can be fixed at a price that is above the market equilibrium rate or below the market equilibrium rate, as shown in panel B of Figure 17-13.

Why might a government decide to fix its currency's exchange rate? The thinking is similar to Ecuador's decision to dollarize. The theory is that a fixed rate allows for more predictability and stability. More stability helps attract foreign investment and gives businesses that depend on overseas trade more confidence to invest. How is a fixed exchange rate kept above or below market rates?

To maintain a fixed exchange rate the government needs to be prepared to intervene in the foreign-exchange market, either buying or selling foreign currency. For example, let's say that suddenly consumers develop a greater appetite for imported goods. If the exchange rate were allowed to float, the increased supply of local currency would push the exchange rate downward. When the exchange rate is fixed, though, the exchange rate is not allowed to depreciate. The government then has to step into the foreign-exchange market and buy up local currency to balance out the increased supply. Governments generally try to increase demand for their currency by using their own reserves of foreign currencies to buy the domestic currency.

Economists use a slightly different vocabulary to describe changes in the exchange rate when the exchange rate is fixed. Instead of saying that a currency depreciates, we say that it is *devalued* if the government lowers the level at which the fixed exchange rate is set. Likewise, instead of saying that a currency appreciates, we say that the fixed exchange rate is *revalued* if the fixed exchange rate is set higher.

Maintaining a fixed exchange rate can be tough. This is especially true when investors begin to doubt the overall health of an economy. Then investors will start to sell their investments, increasing the supply of local currency. To counter that, the government will be forced to spend large amounts of foreign reserves to prop up demand for their currency.

Some investors, called *speculators,* look for these kinds of situations. The moment that they begin to doubt the ability or the resolve of a country to maintain its fixed exchange rate, they will sell that currency, converting it into a different currency, like dollars. If they dump a lot of the currency quickly, they may cause the government to run out of its stock of dollars and other foreign reserves. If that happens, the government has to give up its efforts to maintain the fixed exchange rate—and the result is that the value of the currency usually drops fast. At that point, the speculators come back in and buy the cheapened currency, pocketing a profit from having sold the currency at a high price and then buying it back at a low price. When this activity is happening, we say that a currency is experiencing a *speculative attack.*

In 1997, for example, the Thai baht came under intense speculative attack from investors. The Thai government had a fixed exchange-rate policy, so it needed to use foreign reserves to buy baht when the attack began. The government spent more than $33 billion (about 90 percent of the country's foreign reserves) trying to protect the currency. It also increased domestic interest rates to encourage investors to keep money in the country. However, the attacks continued, and the government eventually could not continue to defend the baht. The only choice was to untether the currency from the fixed exchange-rate system and let the baht float. Or, rather, sink: when the rate was allowed to float, the baht lost half its value. We show in Figure 17-14 how a speculative attack on the currency puts pressure on the exchange rate.

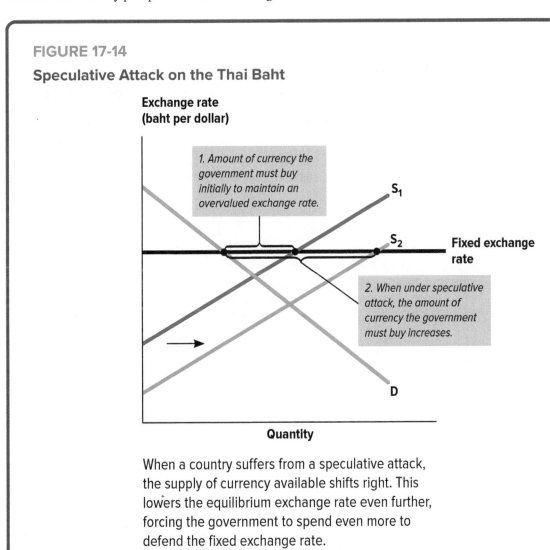

FIGURE 17-14

Speculative Attack on the Thai Baht

Exchange rate (baht per dollar)

1. Amount of currency the government must buy initially to maintain an overvalued exchange rate.

S_1

S_2 **Fixed exchange rate**

2. When under speculative attack, the amount of currency the government must buy increases.

D

Quantity

When a country suffers from a speculative attack, the supply of currency available shifts right. This lowers the equilibrium exchange rate even further, forcing the government to spend even more to defend the fixed exchange rate.

Even larger economies than Thailand's have suffered from speculative attacks when they tried to fix their exchange rates. In the United Kingdom in 1992, a single investor's speculative attack forced the government to devalue the British pound, as outlined in the Real Life box, The Man Who Broke the Bank of England.

REAL LIFE

The Man Who Broke the Bank of England

George Soros is one of the world's most well-known financiers. Known by some as "the man who broke the Bank of England," Soros made over $1 billion betting against the value of the British pound in 1992. At the time, the British pound was part of a managed system of exchange rates among countries. If the pound had been floating freely, it would have been able to depreciate, giving a boost to the UK economy. But Soros started to doubt the British government's resolve to keep to its fixed exchange rate in the face of recession. So he started selling pounds—lots and lots and lots of pounds.

For a newspaper report about this speculative attack on the British pound, go to http://www.telegraph.co.uk/finance/2773265/Billionaire-who-broke-the-Bank-of-England.htm.

Macroeconomic Policy and Exchange Rates

Now that we have outlined the difference between floating and fixed exchange rates, we'll look at monetary policy under the two exchange-rate regimes. Monetary policy is more effective under a flexible exchange rate than a fixed exchange rate because the flexible rate can affect two key variables: investment and net exports. If the exchange rate is fixed, then monetary policy can affect only investment.

Imagine there's a recession and the Bank of Canada wants to increase the money supply to stimulate aggregate demand. The lower interest rates that follow this action will make investing in Canada less attractive. Since the return on investment is lower, demand for Canadian dollars will fall. At the same time, the supply of Canadian dollars will increase as investors sell their Canadian financial assets and look to buy assets abroad. Under a floating exchange-rate system, the exchange rate depreciates and net exports increase.

Figure 17-15 shows what would happen if the exchange rate were fixed. Increasing the money supply would naturally cause the value of the dollar to fall. Since the government must maintain the exchange rate, however, it must buy its own currency in the foreign-exchange market. This purchase of dollars must be exactly the same as the increase of the money supply in order to maintain a fixed exchange rate. The end result is no change in the overall money supply, leading to a key point about fixed exchange rates: it is impossible to conduct monetary policy and maintain a fixed exchange rate.

FIGURE 17-15

Loosening Monetary Policy with Fixed Exchange Rates

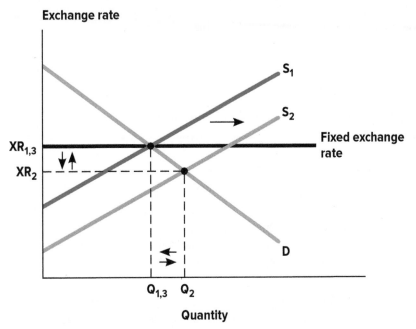

With a fixed exchange rate, monetary policy cannot be successful. When a country expands the money supply, the supply of currency increases and the exchange rate falls. Since this is unacceptable in a fixed exchange-rate regime, the government is forced to buy back the local currency on foreign markets, restoring the exchange rate.

Is the Chinese Currency Undervalued?

Our discussion of monetary policy and exchange rates leads us to the second explanation for the trade deficit between China and other countries, which we mentioned at the beginning of this chapter. During China's great economic expansion, China maintained a fixed exchange rate, keeping its currency pegged at 6.5 yuan per US dollar. This rate was *below* what the market would likely set. Why did it want to do that? Its goods would be cheap when measured in other currencies, so there would be lots of demand for Chinese exports.

The Chinese government keeps the yuan's value low by selling yuan in the foreign-exchange market, and it uses a portion of those dollars to buy US Treasury debt. The US argues that China's currency is intentionally undervalued, making China's exports more attractive to US consumers and making it harder for US companies to export to China. Chinese government officials, in turn, blame the trade deficit on US government budget deficits and lack of savings.

Would a floating exchange-rate regime eliminate the trade deficit between China and the US? If the Chinese yuan appreciated, Chinese exports would become more expensive and imports would become cheaper, so the Chinese trade balance would fall. The effect on the United States' overall trade balance is not so straightforward, however. The United States would import less from China, but it is possible that consumers in the United States would instead choose to import from other countries. Between 2005 and 2013, the Chinese yuan appreciated more than 20 percent and yet the US trade deficit was not reduced.

Suppose the US is right and China is undervaluing its currency to promote its exports. If having a low exchange rate is good for exports, we should ask, *Why isn't everyone already doing it?* Well, sometimes everyone does. This situation is known as *competitive devaluation,* or a currency war, and it occurs when multiple countries are trying to boost their economies by lowering their interest rates. Of course, because the value of a currency is measured relative to other currencies, it's logically impossible for all the world's currencies to devalue simultaneously.

There are reasons why a government might not want to have an undervalued currency, though. For one thing, it means that savers tend to send their money to be invested overseas rather than domestically, just as much of China's savings end up in the United States. This may not be the best way to develop the domestic economy. A second cost to China is that a low Chinese currency makes imported foreign goods relatively more expensive for Chinese consumers.

The Real Exchange Rate

LO 17.8 Describe the difference between the real and nominal exchange rates.

As we saw in Chapter 8, "The Cost of Living," currency exchange rates aren't the only thing that determine the relative price of goods in different countries. Even after converting exchange rates, the same Big Mac might be more expensive in Switzerland than in Canada, and more expensive in Canada than in China.

Up until now, we have been talking about the **nominal exchange rate**—the stated rate at which one country's currency can be traded for another country's currency. To really understand international trade, we also need to take into account the prices in two different countries by looking at the *real* exchange rate. The **real exchange rate** expresses the value of goods in one country in terms of the same goods in another country.

To take a simplified example, let's consider only one good—an apple. Say that you can buy an apple in Canada for $1, whereas in China an apple costs 3 yuan. If the nominal exchange rate is 6 yuan per dollar, then the *real* exchange rate is 2. We'll provide a standard formula for the real exchange rate in a few paragraphs, but for now, let's concentrate on the intuition behind this answer. Since $1 can be exchanged for 6 yuan, and 6 yuan can buy two apples (6 yuan/3 yuan per apple = 2 apples), the dollar that can buy only one apple in Canada can buy two apples in China. Note that our dollar "goes further" (buys more) in real terms in China than in Canada—our dollar can buy twice as many apples in China than it can buy in Canada.

Of course, people want to buy and sell more than apples. To calculate the real exchange rate properly, we need to look at all the prices in Canada and compare this total to all the prices in China. To do so, we need to look at the *price index* in both countries—the index that measures a typical basket of goods bought by a household. The real exchange rate uses the price level in each country to convert the exchange rate into a value that is in "real" terms. Just as we did with the apple example, to calculate the real exchange rate, divide the price level at home by the price level in the foreign country, and then multiply by the nominal exchange rate. Mathematically:

Equation 17-1

$$\text{Real exchange rate} = \text{nominal exchange rate} \times \left(\frac{\text{domestic price level}}{\text{foreign price level}} \right)$$

Note that the nominal exchange rate in this formula is expressed in terms of the foreign currency per dollar, as we've done throughout the chapter. So, for example, let's say that the price of a typical basket of goods in Canada is $100, and in China it is 300 yuan. Further, let's assume that the nominal exchange rate expressed in terms of yuan per dollar is 6; in other words, $1 can be traded for 6 yuan. With this information, we can calculate the real exchange rate to be 2:

Equation 17-1a

$$\text{Real exchange rate} = \text{nominal exchange rate} \times \left(\frac{\text{domestic price level}}{\text{foreign price level}} \right)$$

$$= 6 \text{ yuan/dollar} \times \left(\frac{\$100}{300 \text{ yuan}} \right) = 2$$

The *real* exchange rate is another way of saying "the exchange rate adjusted for *purchasing power parity,*" (PPP) an idea we discussed in Chapter 8, "The Cost of Living." If there were parity in purchasing power—that is, if an apple cost the same in China as in Canada, after adjusting for nominal exchange rates—then the real exchange rate would be 1.

The same factors that complicate calculations of PPP also complicate calculations of the real exchange rate. Consumers in China purchase different kinds of goods than do Canadian consumers—more rice, for example, and fewer burgers—so it's not easy to compare price levels using typical baskets of goods. Still, the real exchange rate is a useful way of comparing how far your money will go in another country.

✓ CONCEPT CHECK

☐ Does exchange-rate appreciation mean that the home currency gets stronger or weaker relative to other foreign currencies? [LO 17.6]

☐ When demand for a foreign good increases, what happens in the market for foreign exchange? [LO 17.6]

☐ What measurement gives the prices of the same goods in two different countries? [LO 17.7]

☐ What is another name for the real exchange rate? [LO 17.8]

Global Financial Crises

Although the international financial system works well most of the time, occasionally it falls out of order. In general, these crises can be labeled as one of two types: debt crises and exchange-rate crises. Throughout this section, you'll see how foreign direct investment (FDI) and international flows can be fickle, which can destabilize economies when things go wrong.

The Role of the IMF

Before working through some examples of disruptions in the financial system, we'll introduce the institution that is responsible for keeping the system together—the IMF, or International Monetary Fund. The IMF was created at the end of World War II. An international agency, like the United Nations and World Bank, the IMF headquarters is in Washington, DC.

Initially, when many countries had fixed exchange rates tied to gold, the IMF helped countries maintain their fixed rates. When countries ran into trouble maintaining their currencies, the IMF would step in and provide a loan to patch up a balance-of-payments deficit. Now that most exchange rates are flexible, the IMF's role has changed. Today, the IMF often steps in as a lender of last resort, making loans to countries when private investors flee. The loans can help to stabilize the economy and keep fears from building on themselves. As the recent financial turmoil in Greece and Iceland shows, international financial crises still occur, and the IMF is needed to help when things go wrong.

However, the IMF is not a magic solution for countries in need. Many IMF loans are made on the condition that the governments make certain policy changes. For example, a recipient country may be required to make efforts to reduce its budget deficit as a signal that it is committed to reform. In many cases, the IMF has been criticized for requiring economies to undertake contractionary fiscal policy and tighter monetary policy during the crisis itself. These policies usually depress the economy further and can exacerbate the crisis.

The role of the IMF and other global institutions is an area of ongoing debate. As globalization poses more risks of contagious collapse, how can the international system design institutions that will be able to prevent crisis?

Debt Crises

Although foreign capital often ends up invested in factories and international businesses, large shares of international capital end up purchasing government debt. When governments take on too much debt, though, investors begin to worry whether the government will be able to repay it, and investors move their money out of the country in a hurry. Why? If the government defaults, everyone who had invested in that debt stands to lose their money.

One such instance of investors losing confidence in the government's ability to repay debt occurred in Argentina in 2001. The debt crisis in Argentina started with heavy financing of a variety of industrial development projects during the 1960s and 1970s. The government then accumulated more debt in a war against the United Kingdom for control of the Falkland Islands.

As the country accumulated more debt, paying the interest on its debt formed a larger proportion of its budget. That wasn't the only problem in Argentina, though. The government had created a fixed exchange rate tied to the US dollar in an effort to curb inflation, but the currency became overvalued. Domestic industry and large amounts of trade went to Argentina's neighbours, where products were cheaper. Finally, the financial crisis in Russia in 1998 made investors far more skeptical of investing money in *emerging markets* like Argentina. The combination of overvalued currency and loss of confidence raised interest rates, making it harder and more expensive to borrow more.

To try to stop the flight of capital, the government promised several programs to reduce government spending, but as you might have guessed, these promises were not kept. What followed was a painful economic spiral. Increased capital outflows from the country led to higher and higher interest rates. The increasing rates made debt payments more expensive, which created further government deficits. By 2001, the problem had spun into a full-on crisis, with bank runs and public protests. Unemployment came close to 20 percent. The government finally defaulted on its debt, unable to meet the increasingly high debt payments.

We can analyze this scenario using the open economy loanable-funds market described earlier in the chapter. Figure 17-16 illustrates the stages of this debt crisis: when foreign investors started pulling their money out of the country, the net capital outflow curve shifted to the right. Interest rates then increased, which reduced investment. The higher interest rates also made the government's debt more expensive, and the government deficit increased. As the government deficit increased, this shifted the national savings curve to the left, increasing the interest rate again and reducing investment yet again.

FIGURE 17-16

The Argentine Debt Crisis

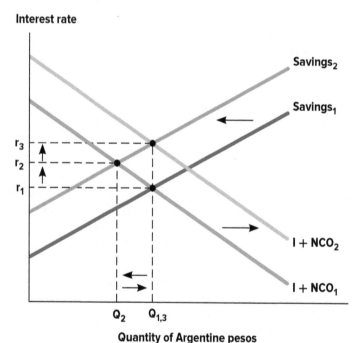

Once investors got word that the Argentine government was in danger, they pulled their investments out of the country, shifting the combined investments and net capital outflow curve to the right, increasing the interest rate. This higher interest rate made the government debt more expensive, which decreased savings. This led to a further increase in the interest rate, and a repetition of the cycle.

Exchange-Rate Crises

Loss of confidence in a government's ability to defend an exchange rate can also spook investors. If a government devalues an exchange rate, it essentially represents a loss for those holding investments in the country.

With this in mind, we turn to the story of the Asian financial crisis. In the early 1990s, emerging economies in Asia—Thailand, Indonesia, Malaysia, the Philippines—received a lot of capital from global investors. The influx of investment contributed to a remarkable spurt of growth.

With all that fresh capital, however, banks wanted to move money, and they started making loans to riskier entrepreneurs. Soon the signs of good fortune were fading. In Thailand, especially, most economic indicators started to create worries, and investors began pulling their money out of the country. But the crisis didn't end there. Because the world is so interconnected, crises can easily spread in a chain reaction called a *contagion*. The virus imagery is fitting. When Thailand got into trouble, investors immediately became nervous about other countries in the area, regardless of their condition. Soon, fearful investors were pulling their money out of the surrounding countries, as well, running them through the same financial crisis. In other words, the crisis was contagious.

After the financial fall of Thailand in 1997, speculative attacks spread to Indonesia, the Philippines, South Korea, and Malaysia. Like Thailand, each of these countries was unable to defend its fixed currency. Not surprisingly, their currencies rapidly depreciated once the fixed exchange-rate policies were abandoned and exchange rates were made flexible. GDP in these five countries fell about 10 percent between 1997 and 1998. The crisis lasted for about a year, and millions of people suffered. The overriding lesson of the Asian financial crisis was that the combination of fast-moving capital and fixed exchange rates can lead to devastating speculative attacks with the power to shake whole continents.

Following crises like these, it became important to determine how the destructive forces of contagion could be contained without losing the benefits offered by the free movement of capital. Among the many proposals to slow the flight of capital is the Tobin tax, which would apply a minuscule tax to all foreign-capital transactions, as described in the From Another Angle box, Cooling Down Hot Money.

FROM ANOTHER ANGLE

Cooling Down Hot Money

The largest financial market in the world is the market for foreign currency, with over $2 trillion exchanged daily. Incredibly, 90 percent of this trade is pure speculation, by traders making bets about the future price of currencies all over the world. Trades in currency happen incredibly quickly; short gaps in time can mean the difference between making money and losing it all. These flows can be incredibly destructive.

In response, two economists, one a Nobel Prize winner, have proposed measures to slow down lightning-fast currency transactions.

For more information, go to http://www.ft.com/intl/cms/s/0/6210e49c-9307-11de-b146-00144feabdc0.html; and http://www.wiwi.unifrankfurt.de/profs/spahn/pdf/publ/7-041.pdf.

Conclusion

In this chapter, we opened up the national economy to understand how countries trade and invest with one another. When we add net exports to our GDP equation, we get an interesting result: the difference between what a country buys and sells is also equal to the level of foreign investment. In effect, if a country is buying more than it is selling, it needs to borrow money from abroad to pay for its imports. This important equality is called the balance-of-payments identity, and the tight link between the trade balance and capital flows is the key to understanding trade deficit and some countries' debt with China.

We looked at two explanations for the trade deficit, which turn out to be different sides of the same coin. The first explanation is that countries are not saving nearly as much as China, so it is relying on investment from other countries. From the balance-of-payments identity, we know that if foreign investment is high, then there must also be a trade imbalance.

The second explanation is that exports from China are artificially cheap because the Chinese currency is set at a price below what it should be, i.e., below its market price. The cheap Chinese exports mean that the balance of trade is negative, and the rest of the world needs to borrow money to pay for its spending.

In extreme cases, we saw how international debt and fixed exchange rates can tip countries into economic crises. As the world continues to become more and more interlinked, economic policy in one part of the world will have global effects.

Macroeconomics may seem more abstract than microeconomics, with lots of moving parts, but trade policy, government fiscal policy, monetary policy, and decisions about how to set the exchange rate affect the daily lives of every citizen, usually in ways that are hard to see. In the concluding chapter, we will apply the lessons you've learned throughout the book to one of the most stubborn problems in economics—international poverty.

Key Terms

balance of trade	exchange rate
trade deficit	exchange-rate appreciation
trade surplus	exchange-rate depreciation
foreign direct investment (FDI)	floating exchange rate
foreign portfolio investment	fixed exchange rate
net capital outflow	nominal exchange rate
balance-of-payments identity	real exchange rate

Summary

LO 17.1 Define the balance of trade and describe the general trends of Canadian trade.

The balance of trade is the value of exports less the value of imports. It is also called net exports. Net exports respond to the value of the exchange rate: when the exchange rate is high, domestic goods are expensive and foreign goods are cheap, so net exports are low. When the exchange rate is low, net exports are high.

LO 17.2 Define portfolio investment and direct foreign investment.

There are two types of foreign investment. Direct investment is when a firm invests abroad with an active interest—for example, by building a factory and managing the factory. Portfolio investment is investment in financial securities, such as stocks or bonds, so that domestic residents still operate firms. Together, direct investment and portfolio investment give the net capital outflow of the country, a measure of the money a country invests outside its borders.

LO 17.3 Explain the connection between the balance of trade and net capital outflow.

The balance of trade and net capital outflow are related through the balance-of-payments identity which states that $NX = NCO$. This identity is an accounting identity: if a country has an imbalance of trade (positive net exports), it means that it has lent money to the rest of the world (positive capital outflow) to pay for these goods.

LO 17.4 Describe the determinants of international capital flows using the demand and supply of international loanable funds.

Net capital outflows are determined by the demand for and supply of net capital outflow. The supply of net capital outflows is national savings less domestic investment. The demand for net capital outflow is determined by the domestic interest rate and the foreign interest rate. When the domestic interest rate is high, net capital outflow is low, because foreign money flows into the country. When the foreign interest rate is high, net capital outflow is high, because money flows out of the country to take advantage of high returns.

LO 17.5 Show how the international market for loanable funds can be used to explain events in the international financial system.

Various events can influence the international supply and demand for loanable funds. An increase in confidence in an economy will cut net capital outflows, and lower the interest rate. A decrease in savings from an increase in the government deficit will shift the supply curve for loanable funds to the left, increasing the interest rate and decreasing net capital outflows.

LO 17.6 Describe the exchange rate and its determinants, and explain how the exchange rate affects trade.

The exchange rate is the value of one currency expressed in terms of another currency. Exchange rates can be expressed in two ways, either in terms of the domestic (home) currency, or in terms of the foreign currency. Exchange rates can appreciate or depreciate, as the currencies strengthen or weaken against each other.

The exchange rate is determined by demand and supply for domestic currency. Demand and supply are influenced by preferences for domestic and foreign goods and services, the domestic interest rate, the foreign interest rate, and the perceived riskiness of domestic and foreign investment.

LO 17.7 Explain fixed and floating exchange rates and how monetary policy affects the value of currency in both.

A fixed exchange rate is an exchange rate that is set by the government, not the market. Usually fixed exchange rates are set to be in relation to another stable currency. A floating exchange rate, on the other hand, is set by the market. In term of monetary policy, a fixed exchange rate necessarily means that monetary policy will not have any effect—any change to the money supply has to be counteracted by government actions on the foreign-exchange market. Monetary policy is possible under a flexible exchange rate.

LO 17.8 Describe the difference between the real and nominal exchange rates.

The real exchange rate is the nominal exchange rate corrected for the price levels in the domestic and foreign country. The real exchange rate is measured in terms of goods instead of currency. If the real exchange rate is 1, then a good can be exchanged in one country directly for a good in another country. If this is the case, we say there is purchasing power parity between the two countries.

Review Questions

1. What happens to the Canadian balance of trade as oil prices rise? [LO 17.1]
2. Suppose a candidate criticizes his opponent by saying his opponent's economic policies have made the dollar weaker and cost Canadian factory workers their jobs. What would be your response? [LO 17.1]
3. Why would a company want to make a direct investment in countries where the company's home currency has higher purchasing power? [LO 17.2]
4. Part of the North American Free Trade Agreement (NAFTA) opened the Mexican stock market to US and Canadian investors for the first time. How would this affect direct and portfolio foreign investment in Mexico? [LO 17.2]

5. If many factories that once made goods in Canada move to Mexico, what must also happen in order to correct the balance of payments in Canada? [LO 17.3]

6. Critics of the North American Free Trade Agreement argued that opening our borders to free trade with Mexico would result in Canadian firms moving all of their factories to Mexico and Canada running large trade deficits with Mexico. Comment on the concerns of these critics using your knowledge of international trade and net capital flows. [LO 17.3]

7. Rating agencies rate countries on the perceived riskiness of investing in their economies. Standard & Poor's, one of the main rating agencies, downgraded the credit rating for US Treasury bonds in 2011. According to this chapter, what impact should the downgrading have had on net capital outflows and interest rates? Why? [LO 17.4]

8. The interest rate on 10-year US Treasury bonds just before Standard & Poor's downgraded the US credit rating was 2.47 percent. One year later, the interest rate on these bonds had fallen to 1.60 percent. Explain this result, which seems to contradict the findings of this chapter. [LO 17.4]

9. List three policies that a government could engage in that would reduce interest rates. (*Hint:* Look back to Figure 17-6, Figure 17-7, and Figure 17-8.) [LO 17.5]

10. Why might a country's exporters want the country's government to have a balanced budget? [LO 17.6]

11. Some politicians argue for imposing trade restrictions in the hope that doing so will reduce the trade deficit of Canada. Assuming Canada has a floating exchange rate, give an economic argument against this proposed policy in terms of the supply and demand of money. [LO 17.6]

12. In response to a severe recession, a politician in a country with a fixed exchange rate proposes to allow the exchange rate to float. What impact would this move have on the economy? Do you think it would be a good response to the recession? [LO 17.7]

13. Suppose that in response to a severe recession, a country with an overvalued currency and a fixed exchange rate does, in fact, move to a floating exchange-rate system. Who are the winners and losers in this move? [LO 17.7]

14. Discuss what would happen to the real exchange rate between Canada and Australia if oil prices fell, which dramatically reduced the cost of transporting goods. [LO 17.8]

15. Is it ever possible for a country's nominal exchange rate to be depreciating while its real exchange rate is appreciating? Explain. [LO 17.8]

Problems and Applications

1. Suppose total Canadian exports in the month of June were $122.9 billion and total imports from foreign countries were $192.4 billion. What was the balance of trade? [LO 17.1]

2. Suppose a country's total GDP (Y) = $10 trillion, consumption = $7 trillion, government spending = $2 trillion, investment = $2 trillion, and taxes = $1.5 trillion. What is the level of net exports or balance of trade? What is the level of public savings? What is the level of private savings? What is the level of net capital outflow? [LO 17.1], [LO 17.3]

3. In 2010, Canadian investors purchased $50 billion in foreign assets, and foreigners purchased $100 billion in Canadian assets such as stocks and Treasury bills. In addition, Canadian businesses invested $150 billion in foreign factories and operations, while foreign companies invested $100 billion in Canadian factories and operations. What was the net capital outflow for the Canada? [LO 17.2]

4. Define each of the following as direct or portfolio foreign investment. [LO 17.2]
   a. Lululemon (a Canadian company) builds new factories in Cambodia.
   b. A Canadian hedge fund purchases 30 percent of the shares of a Brazilian paper manufacturer.
   c. Mercedes-Benz (a German company) builds a new manufacturing plant in Ontario.
   d. Hudson's Bay (a Canadian company) sets up a new call centre in India.
   e. A British chocolate maker buys a smaller Canadian rival.
   f. Fairmont Hotels (a Canadian company) builds a new resort in Nova Scotia.

5. Tom is stuck with his friends on an island that uses coconuts for currency, but they recently discovered Wilson's Island nearby. Tom's Island agrees to make only one transaction with Wilson's Island: it sells a fishing boat to Wilson's for 15 coconuts. Answer the following questions, assuming that yearly consumption on Tom's Island equals 500 coconuts, and domestic investments in huts and farm equipment equals 150 coconuts. [LO 17.3]

Help

a. What are net exports for Tom's Island?

b. What is the total national savings for Tom's Island?

c. Suppose Tom's Island imports a volleyball net from Wilson's Island for 5 coconuts. What is the total national savings now?

d. Now Tom purchases 1 coconut tree on Wilson Island at a cost of 10 coconuts. What is the balance of payments? (*Hint:* A coconut tree produces coconuts like a factory produces goods.)

6. Over the last five years, Portlandia's average income has risen and caused the supply curve of loanable funds to increase and shift right. [LO 17.4]

a. Would the domestic interest rate have increased or decreased?

b. Given the change in the interest rate, would a Canadian firm be more or less likely to open a plant in the country?

c. If Portlandia hits a recession and interest rates fall, which way must the demand curve for loanable funds have shifted?

7. Describe what happens to the supply and/or demand curves for Canadian dollars under the following scenarios. [LO 17.4]

a. A drought in Russia destroys the wheat crop, resulting in increased purchases of wheat from Canada.

b. Bollywood movies become extremely popular in Canada, increasing demand for foreign movies.

c. The Canadian government forces all government offices to purchase Canadian-made computer products, instead of importing them.

8. Suppose there is major unrest in the labour market in Canada, making European investors nervous about investing in Canada. [LO 17.5]

a. Draw the supply and demand curves for Canadian dollars, and show the appropriate shift(s) in supply and demand for Canadian dollars associated with the labour unrest.

b. Did the value of the Canadian dollar depreciate or appreciate?

9. For each case in problem 7, does the Canadian exchange rate appreciate or depreciate, and what happens to the Canadian balance of trade? [LO 17.6]

10. Suppose the new CEO for Lululemon Inc. decides to produce all the company's products in Canada instead of China. [LO 17.6]

a. Which way will the supply for Canadian dollars shift?

b. Which way will the demand for Canadian dollars shift?

c. Does the value of the Canadian dollars depreciate or appreciate?

11. Suppose that in Canada last season's hot holiday gift was the iPad (which is made primarily in China) while this season's big gift is media content for the iPad (which is made in Canada). Determine whether there will be an increase, decrease, or no change for each of the following variables compared to last year. [LO 17.4], [LO 17.6]

a. Supply and demand for dollars

b. Exchange rate between Canada and China

c. Net exports for Canada

d. Net capital outflows for Canada

12. In March 2009 the Canadian dollar was worth $0.78 US dollars. In April 2011 the Canadian dollar was worth $1.06 US dollars. What effect would this increase have on the trade balance between the United States and Canada? Why? [LO 17.6]

13. Suppose the Canadian economy slips into a recession. In response, the Bank of Canada cuts the interest rate in order to avoid unemployment. Consider what happens to the following under a floating exchange-rate regime. [LO 17.7]

a. Domestic investment

b. Capital inflow

c. Capital outflow

d. Exchange rate

e. Net exports

f. Aggregate demand

14. Reevaluate the previous problem assuming the Canadian economy follows a fixed exchange-rate regime. [LO 17.7]

15. Martha has $10,000 to invest in the foreign-exchange market. She's interested in trading Canadian dollars (CAD) for euros (EUR) and Japanese yen (JPY). Using Table 17P-1, determine the arbitrage profit/loss Martha will make in each of the following scenarios. (*Note:* Any value less than $10 should be considered zero.) [LO 17.8]

    a. CAD   EUR   JPY   CAD

    b. CAD   JPY   EUR   CAD

    c. Now look up the current exchange rates among any three currencies. Show that there are no arbitrage opportunities for the three currencies you chose.

TABLE 17P-1

Exchange rate	CAD	EUR	JPY
CAD	1.00000	0.78230	81.200
EUR	1.27830	1.00000	103.796
JPY	0.01232	0.00963	1.000

16. In Windsor, Ontario, a Big Mac from McDonald's costs $4.16 (Canadian dollars), and across the border in Detroit it costs $3.54 in US dollars. [LO 17.8]

    a. Suppose the nominal US exchange rate with Canada is US$0.80 per Canadian dollar. Does purchasing power parity hold between the two countries?

    b. What is the purchasing power parity exchange rate for the US?

17. Suppose the current Canada–UK exchange rate is 0.63 pounds (the pound is the UK currency) per dollar, and the aggregate price level is 170 for Canada and 140 for the UK. What is the real exchange rate? What does this real exchange rate mean in terms of the relative purchasing power of the dollar and the pound? [LO 17.8]

18. Imagine there are only two trading nations in the world. For each of the following scenarios, determine whether goods in one country will become more attractive relative to goods in the other country given their inflation rates and a shift in the nominal exchange rates. [LO 17.8]

    a. Inflation is 8 percent in the UK and 4 percent in Germany, but the UK pound–euro exchange rate remains the same.

    b. Inflation is 3 percent in Canada and 7 percent in Japan, but the exchange rate for Canadian dollars to Japanese yen increases from 70 to 80 Japanese yen.

    c. Inflation is 10 percent in Canada and 6 percent in Mexico, and the price of the Mexican peso rises from $0.08 to $0.15.

Chapter Sources

http://www.treasury.gov/resource-center/data-chartcenter/tic/Documents/shla2010r.pdf

http://fpc.state.gov/documents/organization/8040.pdf

http://www.fas.org/man/crs/crs-asia2.htm

CHAPTER 18

Development Economics

Poverty amid Plenty

In discussing macroeconomics, we've talked a lot about economic growth. But economic growth is not an end in itself. An economy can grow but still leave many people behind. Although the average level of real GDP per capita tripled in the second half of the twentieth century around the world, many people today don't have enough resources to escape from poverty.

About 1 billion of the 7 billion people on earth live on just US$1.25 per day, the World Bank's measure of extreme poverty, and billions more live on only slightly higher incomes. The depth and breadth of global poverty are not just a compelling humanitarian concern, but also an economic puzzle: How can such poverty persist amid such plenty?

Those with a pessimistic outlook believe that poverty will always be a part of life. They point to a decades-long legacy of failed bureaucracies and wasted foreign-aid budgets. Others who are more optimistic point to evidence of progress. Thanks to sustained efforts by governments, non-governmental organizations, and communities, many more children are attending school than a decade or two ago. Infant mortality has dropped by half since 1960: 9 million more kids lived to celebrate their first birthday in 2006 than would have if the mortality rate had stayed at the 1960 level.

Impressively, such improvements have occurred even in places where average incomes failed to grow. So although growth is good in general, the poorest can do better even if there is little growth. Nor does lots of growth necessarily mean higher incomes for the poorest. To use the language of economics, overall growth and income for the poorest are correlated, but not perfectly.

Courtesy of Robin Saidman

So, what can help the poorest lead better lives? One important step is improving access to markets and institutions that can expand opportunities and provide more choices. Think of how you rely on a basic bank account to pay bills and save money. About half of the adults in the world live their lives without access to a bank. By expanding access to banks, millions would be helped to save, invest, and provide for their families. The same goes for access to improved markets for transportation, health care, education, and other basic services, backed by responsive legal and political institutions to maintain fair practices.

These are the questions taken up in the field of development economics, the topic of this chapter. Development economists tackle a series of questions that span several core economic issues: What makes some people—and some countries—richer than others? What makes others poorer? How can markets be made more efficient and wide-reaching in developing countries? How should donors and investors choose among good options, given that resources are scarce?

In the first part of this chapter, we examine the relationship between economic growth and economic development. Then we look at the basics of economic development, taking a fresh perspective on some ideas we've encountered already in this book—human capital, good governance, investment, trade, and migration. In the final part of the chapter, we consider foreign aid—its history, the arguments for and against such aid, and how development economists are striving to understand what works.

Development and Capabilities

So far, we've talked a lot about economic *growth*. In this chapter, we talk about economic *development*. The concepts are intertwined, but distinct. Economic *growth* involves increases in GDP. However, GDP doesn't necessarily tell us much about what it's like to live in a country—its levels of inequality and poverty, what opportunities people have to better themselves if they're in the middle—or at the bottom—of the heap, how well basic institutions like courts and hospitals work, how many people can read and write, and so on. These are the kinds of things we're concerned about when we talk about economic *development*. Development economics looks beyond GDP growth to ask about the quality of life for all sectors of society. A helpful way to think about what matters comes from an idea called the *capabilities approach*.

The Capabilities Approach

> **LO 18.1** Explain how the capabilities approach relates to economic development.

The capabilities approach was developed by Amartya Sen, a Harvard professor who won the 1998 Nobel Prize in Economics. His idea provides a framework for economists to think about poverty, inequality, and human development. A **capability** is something a person is able to be or do. Examples of capabilities include being able to live a long and healthy life, have adequate food and shelter, get an education, speak one's mind, travel freely, live free of the fear of violence, be able to find secure and meaningful work, and be able to enjoy recreational and cultural activities.

In all, capabilities represent a vast spectrum of life—from basic survival and good health to self-expression and engagement in culture. Whereas economic growth focuses on expanding the economy, the capabilities approach to economic development instead looks to constantly improve what individuals can be and can do. Institutional and market failures restrict what people can do, and the restriction of capabilities often affects poorest citizens the most.

You might be wondering why we need a fancy new term like *capabilities* here. Aren't all of the things we've mentioned also simply things that increase utility? Why do we need to depart from the traditional economic framework of maximizing utility? Read the What Do You Think? box, Utility versus Capabilities, for more on that interesting question.

WHAT DO YOU THINK?

Utility versus Capabilities

We have seen throughout this text that the idea of *maximizing utility* is the foundation of individual decision making in economics. It captures the idea that people want to obtain more of what gives them satisfaction. Can't we, then, simply use the utility approach to think about development? Why do we need to introduce the capability approach to establish the value of things like education and health and free speech? After all, aren't they also going to increase people's utility?

While the utility approach serves us well when thinking about how *individuals* make decisions, it may not guide us toward the best decisions for *society*. The early founders of the utilitarian approach, philosophers Jeremy Bentham and John Stuart Mill, suggested that the best society is one that maximizes the collective utility of everyone in that society. Since then, other philosophers have argued that there are flaws in this idea. The capabilities approach addresses at least two of those flaws.

The first problem is that a simple utility-maximizing approach ignores the idea of fundamental rights. For example, what if slave owners received more utility from slave ownership than the utility slaves would get from being freed? Should society therefore allow slavery? Most people would say there are some rights, like not being enslaved, that are worth preserving even if it means accepting lower utility across society as a whole. As Sen says, "Happiness or desire fulfillment represents only one aspect of human existence. The capabilities approach attempts to fill the gap by looking at a much broader conception of life" (as quoted in Clark, 2011).

Second, simply trying to maximize utility ignores the *distribution* of that utility. Imagine that the president of an impoverished nation feels gnawing envy when he sees the presidents of richer countries flying around in private jets. His utility from owning a private jet is so great that it would outweigh the combined utility that citizens of a city would get from a new health clinic in their district. Should we, then, buy the president a private jet instead of improving health care? There seems to be something wrong with accepting this conclusion at face value.

On the other hand, by moving too far away from the utility approach, do we risk paternalistically giving the poor what we think they *ought* to want instead of what they really *do* want? In their book *Poor Economics,* Abhijit Banerjee and Esther Duflo tell of a man in a remote, dusty village in Morocco who, when asked by researchers what he would do if he had more money, said he would buy more nutritious food for his family. The researchers pointed out that he owned a television and a DVD player, and asked why he'd bought these things when his family didn't have enough to eat. "Oh," he replied, "television is more important than food."

What do you think?

1. Should the World Bank and local governments be building bridges, schools, and clinics in developing countries if citizens would rather have TVs?

2. Should development economists put more focus on capabilities or utility?

Sources: Abhijit Banerjee and Esther Duflo, *Poor Economics* (New York: Public Affairs, 2011); David A. Clark, "The capability approach: Its development, critiques and recent advancements," http://www.gprg.org/pubs/workingpapers/pdfs/gprg-wps-032.pdf (accessed November 7, 2011).

Economic Growth and Economic Development

> LO 18.2 Explain the relationship between economic growth and economic development.

We saw in an earlier chapter how growth in countries such as China has slashed poverty rates. The average person in China now earns about US$5,000 a year, compared with just US$250 three decades ago. Average levels of education and health have increased dramatically, too. That's not surprising. After all, when people have more money, you would expect them to spend more on improving their health and educating their children.

However, there is nothing inevitable about GDP growth improving health and education for everyone. For example, survey data show that in India the rate of children suffering from malnutrition essentially didn't change over the span of two health surveys conducted in 1998 and 2005.[1] Clearly, it is possible for a country to experience strong economic growth without comparably strong economic development. There needs to be additional attention paid to policy mechanisms that can help to translate higher average incomes into improved capabilities for the poorest citizens.

What about the other direction of the relationship? Does economic *development* lead to economic *growth?* There are plenty of reasons to think it does. As we saw in Chapter 9, "Economic Growth," economists hotly debate the fundamentals of economic growth. There is general agreement, though, that those fundamentals include such things as property rights and the rule of law as well as human capital. After all, an economy without healthy, educated workers is obviously going to have a hard time growing. We will turn now to considering in more depth some of the basic aspects of economic development.

✓ CONCEPT CHECK

☐ What are some examples of capabilities? [LO 18.1]

☐ Does economic growth always lead to economic development? [LO 18.2]

☐ Why may improving the education and health of the poorest help those who are more well off? [LO 18.2]

The Basics of Development Economics

Now that we've discussed the difference between economic growth and economic development, we can return with a fresh perspective on some ideas we've covered in earlier chapters. As we look at how countries can promote health, education, and good governance—all questions central to development economics—remember that we can think of these policies in two ways. We can see them as putting in place the conditions for economic growth. We also can see them as translating the fruits of economic growth into greater capabilities for people in society.

Human Capital

LO 18.3 Describe how improvements to education and health can develop human capital.

Countries all over the world have witnessed dramatic improvements in health and education. This is especially true in Asia, and even countries in Africa that once lagged in health and education progress are now coming close to having all kids in primary school. This is good news for both development and growth. Still, though, millions of kids die each year from diseases that could be prevented. These are improvements that could happen quickly and cheaply, but don't.

Health

Why do these improvements fail to happen? Part of the problem is that health care facilities don't exist in many parts of the world. In rural areas, especially, getting to a modern clinic may involve trekking on foot for miles. But another part of the problem is that even where clinics do exist, many people don't use them. Many choose instead to resort to home remedies and traditional village "doctors" who have little or no training in medicine but charge lower fees than modern hospitals do, and often are more attentive. Recognizing this, countries around the world, ranging from middle-income Thailand to poorer Ghana, have started national health insurance programs. For a nominal fee, usually a couple of dollars per year, families can visit any national clinic or hospital to receive basic services.

Still, often these national health care programs are not as effective as they could be. One study showed that in India, local health care workers were absent about 40 percent of the time. Even when the workers do show up, clinics sometimes run out of important drugs such as quinine (which fights malaria). One study of health care clinics in Delhi, by Jishnu Das of the World Bank and Jeffrey Hammer of Princeton, found that there were plenty of clinics available to poor households, but they provided much worse care than did private clinics in wealthier areas.

It's not because the doctors were badly trained. Rather, Das and Hammer found that doctors serving poor patients often operated below their "knowledge frontiers"—the doctors provided care below the standard of their medical training. One study, for example, showed doctors in public clinics failing to ask even the most basic diagnostic questions when patients appeared to be having heart attacks. Why? Partly because doctors in private clinics receive a fee for their services, while in public clinics, they receive a fixed salary. Doctors have a much higher incentive to get the treatment right when their income depends on customer satisfaction.[2]

One of the challenges for development economists working in health care is to figure out a way to give doctors the right incentives when their own intrinsic motivation isn't enough. On the other side of the equation, different incentives may also be needed for families to make better health care choices, such as immunizing their children. Read the Real Life box, Using Lentils to Fight Diphtheria, for one innovative example.

REAL LIFE

Using Lentils to Fight Diphtheria

Every year, 1 to 2 million children die from diseases that could easily have been prevented by the proper vaccines. Getting kids vaccinated also has positive externalities: the more kids are vaccinated against a disease, the less the disease will spread and affect unvaccinated kids. This is why many governments and non-profits work to provide immunizations at a very low cost—or even for free.

Unfortunately, though, even low-cost immunizations often aren't enough to raise immunization rates.

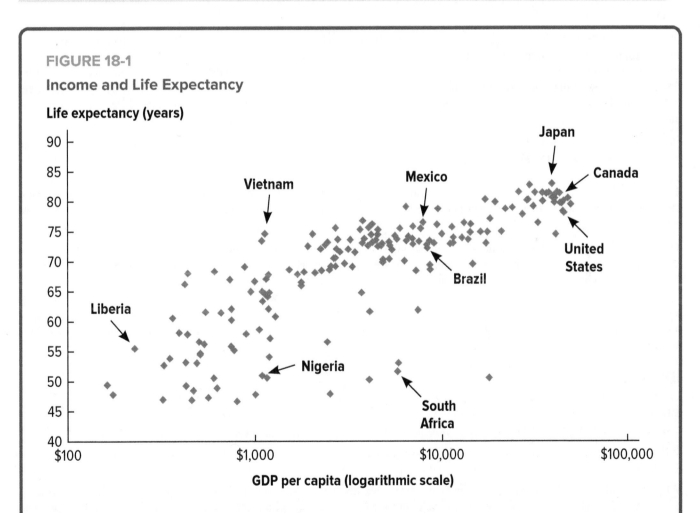

FIGURE 18-1

Income and Life Expectancy

Overall, the higher the income within a country, the higher the life expectancy of the citizens within the country. At lower levels of income, this relationship isn't perfect, however. Some countries have made strides in income with very little improvement in life expectancy, while others have high levels of life expectancy despite low incomes.

Source: The World Bank, *World Development Indicators 2011 Data Set*, data.worldbank.org.

Addressing these health care challenges can contribute greatly to economic growth as well as development. Well-nourished, healthy kids do better in school, making them more productive workers as adults. And epidemics that afflict young adults can have a profound impact on GDP. The AIDS epidemic alone has been found to lower economic growth rates by up to 1.5 percent per year throughout sub-Saharan Africa.

But is it necessary to achieve economic growth before it's possible to create better health care? Figure 18-1 shows the relationship between income measured in GDP per capita and life expectancy. As you would expect, people who live in countries with higher average incomes generally live longer lives.

Still, the correlation is not exact. Compare Vietnam and Nigeria, for example. They have about the same average income, but a baby born in Vietnam is expected to live about twenty-seven years longer on average than a baby born in Nigeria. Clearly, it must be possible to improve health outcomes dramatically even without achieving strong growth in average incomes.

Education

As with health, the reasons for investing in teachers, schools, and books are numerous. In terms of economic growth, educated workers are generally more productive: each additional year of schooling is worth about 10 percent more in overall earnings over the course of a lifetime. In terms of capabilities, education can be seen as worthwhile in itself, as well as contributing to other capabilities. For example, more-educated women tend to make better decisions about family planning. Considerable data also indicate that more education tends to make a society more democratic and reduce its levels of inequality.

In 1999, 106 million children around the world were not attending school; by 2011, that number had fallen by roughly half, with strong progress even in countries without strong economic growth. The abolishment of school fees is a major reason that more children are in school in a number of poorer countries. Even though the fees were usually small—about $30 a year—families living on just a few dollars per day simply could not afford them. Not surprisingly, when the fees were abolished, more kids went to school. In Kenya, for example, when school fees were eliminated in 2003, schools had to rush to find places for the 1 million more kids who enrolled around the country.

However, that posed a new problem—crowded classrooms and overburdened teachers. In some countries, there is only one teacher for 100 students. Development economists have recently started to pay more attention to the challenge of improving the *quality* of education. Even in middle-income countries such as Mexico, where all kids go to primary school, 91 percent of kids do not learn math well enough to be competitive on the international stage. The situation is worse for lower-income countries. One study in Ghana found that sixth graders on average performed at the same level on a basic literacy test as one could achieve simply by guessing.

There are many ideas for how to improve schools. Recent research by development economists has made great strides in assessing which approaches are effective and which are not. To work with children lagging behind on basic math and reading skills, Innovations for Poverty Action tested a remedial education program in India, Kenya, and Ghana, and found the program to be particularly successful. The approach included training women in the community to offer supplemental lessons to the students who were farthest behind in their learning. Other approaches, such as distributing textbooks, helped only the best students in the class. Providing parents with information about the quality of the children's schools had no effect at all.[3]

Institutions

> LO 18.4 Explain the importance of institutions and good governance in development economics.

When we studied the determinants of economic growth, we discussed the importance of *good governance*. Not surprisingly, good governance is also crucial to economic development. Many basic capabilities rely on having a competent, well-intentioned government and good *institutions*. Economist Douglass North of Washington University in St. Louis (and co-winner of the 1993 Nobel Prize for his contributions to economic history) defines **institutions** as the rules of the game in a society, or more formally, the humanly devised constraints that shape human interactions.[4] In addition to laws enforced by the government, this definition includes cultural norms, such as the unacceptability of shirking at work.

The term *institutions* is also commonly used to refer to government bodies (such as senates and ministries of education), development agencies (such as the World Bank), and international groups (such as the United Nations). According to North, to avoid confusion we should think of these as examples of *organizations* rather than institutions in development economics.

What exactly constitutes *good governance*? At first it seems like a highly normative question. Some think the best government is the smallest government, staying out of people's lives as much as possible. Others think that government should have its hand in many different sectors of the economy, all in the name of promoting stability, growth, and development. Most development economists agree that the most basic and important task of any government is to create a stable political system—one that ensures the important institutions of enforceable property rights and the rule of law.

Property Rights and the Rule of Law

Say you'd like to sell a bucketful of apples. This will probably work just fine without your having to prove you actually own the apples. You set up shop at a market, someone gives you the cash, and you give them the apples. What if you want to sell a house, though, or a field? Would you ever buy land if you didn't have clear proof that the person selling it is the owner? No, you would want to see the *title* to the land, a document that certifies ownership of property. In many countries, the system of *titling* (providing legal documents proving ownership of assets) is weak. Now imagine you own land and you want to use it as collateral for a loan—say, to buy a tractor so you can farm the land more effectively. Do you think the bank is going to lend you the money unless you can prove you own the land?

Hernando de Soto, a Peruvian economist and president of the Institute for Liberty and Democracy, says that that the weak titling system in Latin America results in "dead capital." Millions of people may have land or other assets, but without proper titles, they are effectively unable to tap the financial power of those assets. Titles would allow owners to take out billions of dollars in loans that could be used productively to invest in starting new businesses or improving their farms. If only they had titles, De Soto argues, their capital could be put to better use—it could become "alive." The evidence supporting his claim is mixed, suggesting that titling may be important only if other conditions are in place, too.

One of those conditions is the *rule of law.* There's no point in being able to prove you own something if the police and courts are corrupt or incompetent and won't help you if thieves take it away. The rule of law helps to create stability and provides a set of clear guides to govern transactions. Where crime is rampant and government unhelpful—or, worse, when a country falls into outright conflict—it's hard to sustain either economic growth or economic development.

Some countries have suffered for generations with problems related to property rights and the rule of law. If these problems are deeply entrenched in the culture, how do such countries begin the process of moving toward better governance? One radical idea was proposed by economist Paul Romer, as discussed in the From Another Angle box, Building Cities from Scratch.

FROM ANOTHER ANGLE

Building Cities from Scratch

The United Nations estimates that 3 billion people will move to cities in the next few decades. However, even now many cities have trouble providing the basics for their residents. From Lagos, Nigeria, to Port-au-Prince, Haiti, tens of millions of people around the world are packed into squalid slums. Rather than pour more and more people into these haphazardly expanding cities, what if we built new ones, from scratch, incorporating ideas learned about growth and development right from the start?

This idea, called *charter cities,* is championed by Paul Romer of New York University. The big advantage Romer sees for these cities is that they offer a chance to start again—that is, they allow for brand new institutions in countries that struggle with governance.

Is Democracy Necessary?

While studies indicate a link between economic growth and political stability, the correlation with democracy is less clear. Many of the stories of sustained growth in formerly poor countries occurred under governments that were far from democratic. Just think of China. The tiny, landlocked East African country of Rwanda is another illustration: over the last decade and a half, growth has averaged about 7 percent per year, and residents are provided with basic and almost universal health insurance. Despite this growth, journalists critical of the government are routinely jailed and political opponents are routinely harassed and barred from participating in elections. The current president, Paul Kagame, won the last election with 93 percent of the vote, achieved by keeping any serious opponents from getting on the ballot.

Rwanda shows that even a relatively autocratic government can promote economic development, as well as economic growth. Despite its democratic shortcomings, the government often makes good policy. Anti-corruption laws are some of the strongest in Africa. Also, women are encouraged to participate in the political process—so much so that the Rwandan parliament is the only one in the world in which women outnumber men.

So, if good policy and fair institutions do not require democratic elections, should we care about democracy? Amartya Sen's capabilities framework suggests that we should view democracy in its own right as an essential ingredient in improving lives and sustaining basic freedoms.[5]

Investment

> **LO 18.5** Evaluate the role of industrial policy and clusters in development.

We saw in Chapter 9, "Economic Growth," that investment is a key concern in promoting growth. Foreign direct investment is an important source of funds in many countries with low savings rates. Development economists debate which is the best way for developing countries to deal with these flows of capital from overseas, as well as the funds that come from domestic sources. *Industrial policy* has two traditional tactics: import substitution and export-led growth. It can also involve promoting a cluster of industries that share linkages through the economy so that they can develop in unison—an idea called *clustering*. Let's consider these ideas in turn.

Industrial Policy

South Korea's GDP per capita in 1960 was about twice the size of Brazil's; by 2009, it was more than four times the size. What accounts for these different rates of growth?

One important difference is that South Korea successfully pursued an industrial policy. **Industrial policy** is an effort by a government to favour some industries over others in the hope that coordinated investments in a chosen industry will help the overall economy to develop and will spur growth in the long run. The tools at a government's disposal in pursuing industrial policy include trade barriers, tax breaks, subsidies, incentives for foreign direct investment, and investment in research.

Traditionally, these tools have been used as part of two opposite philosophies of industrial policy. One is *import substitution,* which is the practice of using trade policy to protect domestic industries until they are efficient enough to compete on the world market. Imagine you want to nurture a successful electronics industry, but new electronics firms can't get off the ground because they have to compete with cheap imports from countries with more well-established electronics industries. Why not impose temporary trade barriers to stop the cheap imports, allowing time for the domestic *infant industry* in electronics to grow big and strong enough to compete?

Unfortunately, import substitution has failed to work well in the real world. One problem is that without the spur of foreign competition to drive down costs an infant industry might never grow up. For years, the Brazilian government protected domestic computer makers, but Brazilian-made machines still cost double the price of a foreign-made machine.

Another problem with import substitution is that decisions about which industries to protect are frequently driven by political rather than economic considerations. Naturally, companies would like to have their industry protected from foreign competition. That desire encourages large amounts of *rent-seeking* behaviour—that is, firms attempting to influence politicians in the name of profits. Many protective policies have persisted long after they were expected to lapse, at great cost to the taxpayer.

South Korea is achieving export-led growth by favouring companies, such as Hyundai, that are succeeding in the world market.

Realizing the problems with import substitution, some Asian countries have taken another tack: *export-led growth.* This involves investing heavily in an industry through tax breaks and export subsidies (government monetary support for exporters) with the aim of selling goods around the world. Rather than walling domestic markets off from international trade, export-led growth instead selects industries to push into the world market. Success depends on picking winners—something the South Korean government, for example, has managed to do, supporting companies such as Samsung and Hyundai. As a result, South Korea made the jump from poor to rich over the course of five decades. Japan, Singapore, and Taiwan used similar strategies to create the so-called "Asian miracle."

Bloomberg via Getty Images

Unfortunately, export-led growth doesn't always work. The unexpected and unprecedented success of these Asian countries led to many imitators, but not all succeeded. International markets are fickle and competition can be fierce. While the benefits of picking winners can be huge, so can the costs if you end up picking losers.

Clusters

As governments consider how to develop their industrial sectors, they often choose to focus on promoting not just one industry but *clusters.* **Clusters** are networks of interdependent firms, universities, and businesses that focus on the production of a specific type of good. Each part of the network is far less productive operating in isolation, so if governments can push each element of the cluster in unison, they should realize huge gains in productivity.

A successful example is Bangladesh's textile industry. Starting in the 1970s, the government made a concerted effort to develop a cluster around textiles, ensuring that complementary firms—such as those making fabrics and those sewing the fabric into clothes—were located in close proximity to minimize transportation costs, and providing incentives for these firms to work together. Ready-made garments are now a multi-billion-dollar industry in Bangladesh and in 2009–2010 accounted for 77 percent of the country's net export revenues.

Trade

In earlier chapters, we studied the benefits of international trade. When one country can produce a good more efficiently than another country, both can specialize in the industry in which they have comparative advantage and experience mutual gains. By opening up to foreign markets, countries gain access to a wide array of new products, save money through access to cheaper goods, and find new customers for their products. It's not surprising, then, that trade plays a major role in development economics.

In the last few decades, there has been great growth in free trade worldwide. Tariffs (taxes on imports) in developing countries have fallen by more than 20 percent. Part of this change has been due to the efforts of the **World Trade Organization (WTO)**, designed to monitor and enforce trade agreements, while also promoting free trade. But about two-thirds of the reduction in tariffs in the past twenty years comes from reforms by national governments changing their own policies, or making agreements with each other.

Wealthy countries increasingly feel that, in helping poorer countries develop, trade can be a more powerful lever than financial aid. In 2005, developed countries began to offer "aid for trade" programs to fund initiatives in developing countries that minimize barriers to trade and provide the infrastructure essential for imports and exports. Trade-related aid now accounts for over a quarter of official development assistance.

Migration

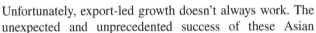

LO 18.6 Evaluate how migration and remittances promote development.

The prospect of a better life drives millions of people to move away from home to other cities, provinces, or countries thousands of miles away in search of opportunity. Research by economists Michael Clemens, Claudio Montenegro, and Lant Pritchett indicates that skilled workers in the United States earn about fifteen times more than workers with exactly the same skills in Nigeria.[6] It's hardly surprising, then, that according to the Gallup World Values Survey, 40 percent of those living in the poorest quartile of countries would like to emigrate (move out of their home country).

However, it's difficult to legally move to a high-income country. Every year, tens of thousands of people from developing countries apply to permanently immigrate to Canada. And the backlog for two federal programs, the Immigrant Investor Program and the Entrepreneur Program, was so large that it was terminated on June 19, 2014.

Some of those who are unsuccessful in legally immigrating to other countries are so desperate to find better-paying work that they set off on perilous journeys—taking rickety boats from Africa to Europe—to try to enter a high-income country illegally.

As we saw in the chapter on unemployment, in host countries such as Canada the influx of immigrants can be a highly controversial issue. But when we look at migration from the perspective of countries of origin, it presents a variety of opportunities to promote development. One important consequence of migration is remittances (money sent home by migrants). As shown in Figure 18-2, remittances are a major financial flow in some countries. The largest overall recipients of remittances are China and India, which each get more than $50 billion per year.

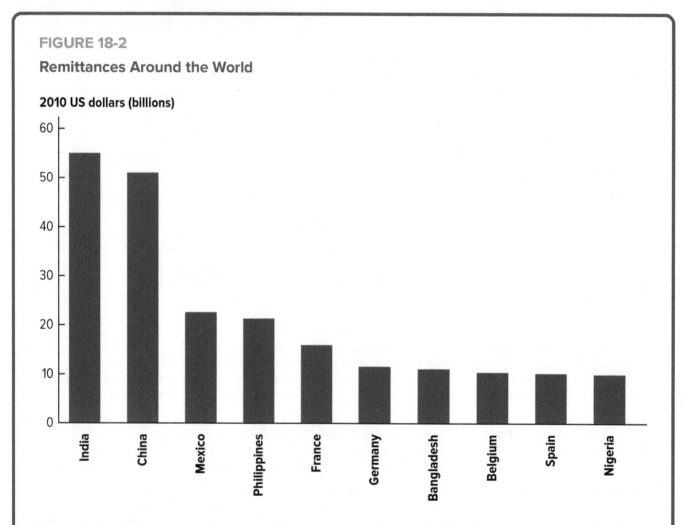

FIGURE 18-2

Remittances Around the World

2010 US dollars (billions)

The top ten countries in terms of remittances received are a diverse group. India and China are large countries, with many migrants abroad. Mexico and the Philippines are countries that have traditionally been associated with remittances. As the data for France, Germany, Belgium, and Spain show, remittances aren't strictly a flow from rich to poor countries.

Source: Dean Yang, "Migrant remittances," *Journal of Economic Perspectives* 25, no. 3 (Summer 2011), p. 134.

Overall, remittances have become a powerful force in the world economy, growing impressively even after accounting for inflation. In 1990, less than $50 billion in inflation-adjusted dollars was transferred. By 2010, this figure was over $300 billion, dwarfing the $120 billion spent by governments on foreign aid. As remittances increase, governments and aid agencies are increasingly wondering how to ensure that this money is used to its full potential, as described in the Real Life box, Sending Home the Riches.

REAL LIFE

Sending Home the Riches

In 1980, Emmet Comodas left his wife and eleven-year-old daughter in their tiny tin shack in a slum in the Philippines. He traveled 4,500 miles to Saudi Arabia to begin a job cleaning pools, a job that paid ten times his wage at home. In two-year stints, he managed to earn enough to send his kids to college and build a house on a farm far away from the crowded slum. Around the world there are 200 million people like Emmet Comodas, who as migrants abroad send money back to families in their home country.

By their very nature, remittances increase income, and thus have the potential to lift recipients out of poverty.

In addition to the benefits from remittances, migrants often return home after a few years working overseas, taking with them new ideas and skills that benefit their local economies. For Michael Clemens, an economist at the Center for Global Development, and Lant Pritchett, author of *Let Their People Come,* the world has much to gain by loosening migration restrictions so that workers can more freely seek jobs in other places.[7] See the From Another Angle box, Trillion-Dollar Bills on the Sidewalk? for more.

FROM ANOTHER ANGLE

Trillion-Dollar Bills on the Sidewalk?

In 2011, Alabama enacted HB56, a law punishing employers who hire illegal immigrants. After the law passed, tomato farmer Chad Smith found himself needing to hire Americans to pick his eighty-five acres of tomatoes. But picking tomatoes is hard, sweaty, poorly paid work, and most of his US workers quit after just a couple of days. Without immigrant labour, Smith argued, his farm couldn't operate competitively.

This story illustrates why studies find that the available evidence often doesn't back up common concerns that immigration takes away jobs and drives down wages among low-skilled workers: often, immigrants do jobs that natives don't want. On the flip side, in the countries that migrants move away from, evidence suggests the shrinking labour supply pushes wages up as the supply of labour falls. One study estimated the effect of emigration from Mexico to be worth about an 8 percent raise for low-income workers who stay in Mexico. On net, then, research finds that more migration boosts incomes across the global economy.

From an economic-development perspective, there is another worry about migration: brain drain. The workers who leave a country for better job opportunities naturally tend to be the most skilled. However, in a 2011 paper, John Gibson and David McKenzie concluded that lowering barriers to migration might actually *increase* the number of skilled workers in poorer countries. It makes sense, when you think about it: if workers in a low-income country know that it's possible to migrate, they may be more motivated to obtain crucial skills that would qualify them for jobs abroad. Not everyone in the end decides to move away—so the domestic economy ends up with more highly skilled workers as a result. This opens up the possibility of brain gain instead of brain drain.

Economist Michael Clemens has done the math and found that removing just 5 percent of barriers to the movement of workers between countries has the power to lift income around the world by trillions of dollars. Overall, this 5 percent reduction would have more of an effect than removing all existing tariffs, quotas, and barriers to capital movement around the world. The impact of making migration easier could dwarf anything foreign aid can hope to achieve.

Sources: Dean Yang, "Migrant remittances," *Journal of Economic Perspectives* 25, no. 3 (Summer 2011), pp. 129–152, http://pubs.aeaweb.org/doi/pdfplus/10.1257/jep.25.3.129; John Gibson and David McKenzie, "The Development Impact of a Best Practice Seasonal Worker Policy," Policy Research Working Paper, Impact Evaluation Series No. 48, http://www.wds.worldbank.org/external/default/WDSContentServer/IW3P/IB/2010/11/30/000158349_20101130131212/Rendered/PDF/WPS5488.pdf; Michael Clemens; "Economics and emigration: Trillion dollar bills on the sidewalk," Center for Global Development Working Paper no. 264.

✓ CONCEPT CHECK

☐ What do development economists mean by "institutions"? **[LO 18.4]**

☐ What are the three types of industrial policy named in this section? **[LO 18.5]**

☐ What are remittances and how do they promote development? **[LO 18.6]**

What Can Aid Do?

Foreign aid has long been seen as part of economic development, although a controversial part. Taxes in many countries go to provide aid to the poor around the world. Many citizens in these countries also give money to private charities such as Oxfam, CARE, Save the Children, and church-based organizations. In fact, private donations to some countries are sometimes larger than the entire budget for official foreign aid.

Why is foreign aid often the central focus of development efforts? It has direct intuitive appeal. If people are poor, then surely money would help make life a little easier. Are children not going to school? Why not give families money so that they don't have to choose between work and school? Are roads full of potholes, making it costly and difficult to get to markets and jobs? Why not help governments build and repair them?

These donations can be very important, whether in easing hunger in famine-ravaged areas or providing funding to would-be entrepreneurs. The problem is how to ensure these funds go to the best uses. After seeing many examples of misuse and waste, donating money seems like a very uncertain enterprise to many people. Later in the chapter, we'll discuss how development economists are helping to discover what works—so that these donations can provide the most bang for their buck.

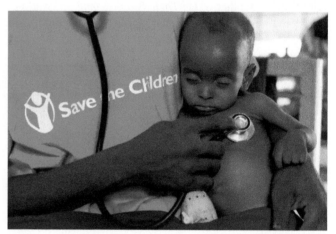

A child gets a medical checkup from Save the Children, an international relief and development non-profit organization.

Rachel Palmer/Save the Children

The History of Foreign Aid

Foreign aid got its start in the wake of World War II. In an unprecedented show of generosity, the United States distributed, as part of the Marshall Plan, $12 billion to help sixteen European countries rebuild after the devastation of the war. In today's money, the sum is the equivalent of over $100 billion. Of course, this aid wasn't entirely altruistic on the part of the US. There was a good deal of strategic self-interest involved, as it was seen as imperative to have strong European allies on the western borders of the Soviet Union.

Aid then shifted to the world's poorer regions, still retaining US political motivations. The 1947 Truman Doctrine pledged $650 million to help "free peoples who are resisting attempted subjugation by armed minorities or by outside pressures." In other words, the United States was willing to put forth money to spread development—and to try to halt the spread of communism. Russia, too, got involved in the aid business, trying to woo unaligned countries to join the communist bloc. During the Cold War, a period of competition between the US and Russia, many dams and bridges built in developing countries were the product of such altruism combined with political strategy.

Even though the Cold War has been over since 1991, foreign aid continues and is still largely dedicated to building public goods. Public goods tend to be under-provided, considering the positive externalities they provide to the economy. This is especially true in countries that already lack means for collecting taxes and making capital investment. The result is a **financing gap**—the difference between the savings rate within an economy and the amount of investment needed to achieve sustainable growth. To plug that gap, a large fraction of aid goes toward building schools, health care systems, and infrastructure networks. For much of the history of aid, the financing gap has been a driving force in decisions about how much to give.

In 2002, at the Monterrey Conference on Financing for Development, the leaders of the world's most industrialized countries reaffirmed a major pledge—to devote 0.7 percent of their gross national income (GNI, a combination of GDP plus net capital flow from abroad) to foreign aid, formally called Overseas Development Assistance (ODA). For Canada alone, this would mean around $5 billion per year. Hopes were high for what that money could accomplish. However, actual foreign aid budgets have fallen well below that goal. Of the twenty-two richest countries that made the pledge, so far only five have followed through to the extent promised. Canada devotes only about 0.2 percent of GNI to ODA, far below the 0.7 percent target and also below the average amount given by OECD countries. In 2014, Canada's net ODA fell 11.4 percent due to exceptional payments made in 2012 for climate change and debt relief, and to budget cuts affecting 2013. As you can see in Figure 18-3, this is part of an overall downward trend.

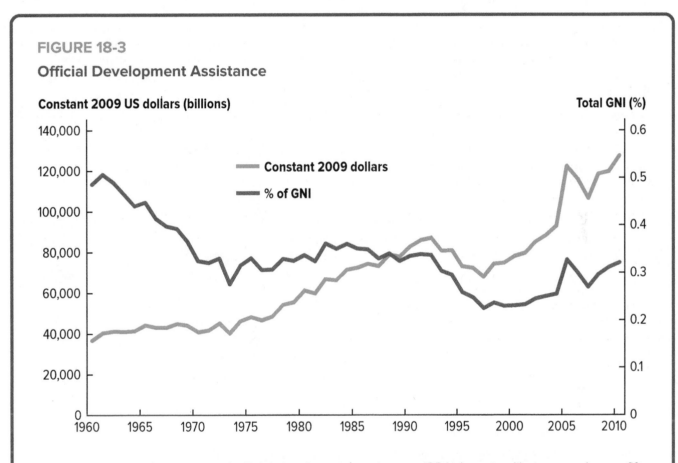

FIGURE 18-3

Official Development Assistance

In absolute terms, the amount of official development assistance (ODA) has steadily increased; over fifty years, the amount of money given by OECD countries in aid has tripled. Despite the 0.7 percent of gross national income (GNI) target set in the 1970s, however, the amount of ODA as a percent of the GNI has fallen and is not even half of this target.

Source: OECD, http://stats.oecd.org/index.aspx?datasetcode=ODA%5FDONOR.

Over the past fifty years, the amount given in aid has increased in dollar terms, but has steadily fallen in terms of aid as a share of GNI. Should Canada meet its pledge to give 0.7 percent? See the What Do You Think? box, Should Canada Give More in Foreign Aid? for more on this debate.

WHAT DO YOU THINK?

Should Canada Give More in Foreign Aid?

In the 2013–2014 fiscal year, the Canadian government spent $4.6 billion on official development assistance,[8] about 0.24 percent of the country's gross national income. This is well below the United Nations target of 0.7 percent of GNI, a goal that Secretary-General Ban Ki-moon urged all developed countries to meet when he shared a podium with Prime Minister Stephen Harper that year in Toronto.

Does that mean most Canadians would enthusiastically support the goal of spending more on foreign aid? Not necessarily. In 2011, the Harper government imposed a five year freeze on foreign aid, until 2015, in order to fight the deficit. According to a Gallup poll conducted in 2005, more than three-fourths of those Canadians polled would like to see foreign aid *reduced,* the largest share out of any of the other options presented. Maybe most Canadians feel at a gut level that however much Canada donates, it's too much.

If Canada is one of the richest countries, does it have an obligation to be generous to less-fortunate countries? Ten percent of the Canadian budget would represent an incredible sum of money, after all. A small increase in aid could potentially have large effects. Many development programs are funded with much smaller amounts of money. The World Food Program, which provides badly needed food aid to areas of famine around the world, costs about US$4 billion per year. A yearly investment of US$7 billion would be enough to reduce the global prevalence of AIDS from 38 million cases to 1 million by 2050.

The other side of the argument centers on the idea that Canada should focus on problems at home first. As Canada faces growing public debt, it has to make tough decisions about which taxes to raise or programs to cut. Money spent on foreign aid could just as easily go toward addressing domestic problems.

What do you think?

In a time when many Canadian government programs are facing cuts or elimination, does it make sense to help provide health insurance in Tanzania, roads in Afghanistan, hospitals in Iraq, or agricultural development in Mozambique?

Sources: UPI NewsTrack, July 1, 2005; http://www.wfp.org.

Poverty Traps and the Millennium Development Goals

Those who argue for ramping up foreign-aid budgets often assert that aid can help countries break out of poverty traps. A **poverty trap** is a self-reinforcing mechanism that causes the poor to stay poor. For instance, a poorly nourished and undereducated population is unlikely to have the energy or know-how to develop its economy. In the long run, it will never earn enough to feed itself and educate its children. Foreign aid, the theory goes, can break this negative self-reinforcing mechanism and create a virtuous cycle, in which improvements build on improvements.

Some theories of economic development hold that escaping from poverty traps requires there to be simultaneous investments in a wide variety of sectors, as well as improvement of institutions. One variant of this idea, championed by Columbia University economist Jeffrey Sachs in his book, *The End of Poverty,* is known as the "big push."[9] The idea that concerted efforts in different sectors are necessary underlie the United Nations' decision in 2000 to create eight Millennium Development Goals. These goals served as targets in all of the areas covered in Sachs's big push. The goals include establishing universal primary education and halving the number of people living on one dollar per day. They were supposed to be achieved by 2015. Some will be, and some will not. Of course, if a goal is not met, it doesn't mean the effort has been wasted. Even if universal primary education is not achieved by 2015, far more kids are going to school.

To showcase the big push idea, the United Nations and Columbia University's Earth Institute—headed by Jeffrey Sachs—together set up thirteen Millennium Villages scattered around sub-Saharan Africa. The villages are intended to show what can happen with sustained and targeted investment. For US$110 per person per year, new schools and clinics are built, sanitation improves, farmers receive improved varieties of seeds, and so on. However, not everyone is convinced that this is the right way for foreign aid to go. Critics argue that there is no guarantee the idea could work if rolled out globally, and it would be extremely expensive to try. They suggest other, cheaper ways to try to kick-start economic development, such as a focus on setting up better institutions or improving the quality of credit or insurance markets.

The Major Distributors of Aid

How do governments of wealthy countries give their foreign aid? Much of it is channeled through national development agencies or sectors of foreign-affairs ministries. The Canadian International Development Agency (CDIA) serves this purpose in Canada. About $4.6 billion is allocated by Canada toward official development assistance funds, which work to improve economic growth, trade, and agriculture, among other things.

Other resources are channeled through international institutions. About US$2.3 billion per year comes from the **World Bank**, a multinational organization dedicated to providing financial and technical assistance to developing countries. Formed in 1948 at the same Bretton Woods conference that spawned the International Monetary Fund, the World Bank is actually two development organizations: the International Bank for Reconstruction and Development (IBRD) and the International Development Association (IDA).

Much like a bank, the IBRD makes loans that are used by middle-income and creditworthy poor countries to finance a wide variety of investment projects. The IDA, on the other hand, more closely resembles what we think of as a traditional aid agency. In the past decade IDA has funded immunizations for 310 million children and clean water for 113 million. This work was accomplished on a budget that included US$15 billion worth of commitments in 2010.

Much development work is also conducted through a sprawling network of organizations under the **United Nations Development Program (UNDP)**. In all, the UNDP is on the ground in 166 countries, operating a diverse set of projects that provide information and resources in developing countries, including everything from halting the spread of HIV/AIDS to developing democratic institutions. Within the UNDP, specialized organizations fund more targeted types of aid. The World Food Program, for example, distributed 3.7 million tons of food aid to 90 million people in 73 countries in 2011. This largely went toward fighting hunger in famine-ravaged areas. Some government aid is also funneled through private, non-profit organizations such as Oxfam, CARE, and Save the Children.

Problems with Foreign Aid

LO 18.7 Identify the different arguments for and against foreign aid in development.

With such a large system of aid, it's not surprising that not everyone is on board with the idea of doling out billions of dollars to poor countries around the world. It's not hard to find these critics—including some notable economists—who believe that aid can be inefficient and even counterproductive. Jean-Claude Duvalier, president of Haiti from 1971 to 1986, lived a fantastically lavish lifestyle while ordinary Haitians lived in intense poverty. Duvalier would regularly showcase Haiti's poor to international donors and then divert much of the resulting aid (one estimate is 80 percent) into his personal bank account.

Foreign aid is now tracked more carefully than it was in Duvalier's day, and agencies and governments now require a greater degree of accountability. But problems still persist. An intriguing insight was provided in 2011 when WikiLeaks, an organization that works to make classified documents public, released 250,000 classified cables from US embassies. One of these cables revealed embezzlement and misplacement of funds from the UK Department for International Development (UK DfID) in projects around the world. In one example, almost US$2 million given by the UK Ministry of Defense to "support peacekeeping" in Sierra Leone was instead embezzled by top generals in the Sierra Leone Ministry of Defense to buy plasma televisions and hunting rifles. In Kenya, the Ministry of Education admitted to losing US$17.3 million worth of textbooks distributed through the Free Education program. In Uganda, officials managed to divert almost US$27 million from an education fund.

Disappearing money may be one reason why, despite the spending of half a trillion dollars in ODA from 1970 to 1994, productivity growth in developing countries was essentially zero and economic growth not much more. Another big problem is that organizations such as the World Bank are not held accountable for what happens to funds once dispersed. Abhijit Banerjee notes the example of a World Bank computer kiosk program implemented in India, which the Bank trumpeted as a rousing success in *Empowerment and Poverty Reduction: A Sourcebook*.[10] Many of these machines, however, were sitting uselessly in buildings that didn't have electricity or Internet connections. William Easterly, an economist at NYU who spent years working at the World Bank, argues that aid agencies typically have nebulous goals—such as promoting empowerment or economic growth or governmental reform—rather than being charged with completing a task that is specific and measurable. Without this, it's not surprising that organizations have little incentive to be sure that what they are doing actually works.

There are even stronger critics of aid than Easterly. Dambisa Moyo, in her book *Dead Aid,* argues that aid actually hurts the countries that receive it.[11] In many countries, aid is a substantial part of the budget. In Kenya, for example, aid averaged 10 percent of GDP from 1970 to 2010. Such large flows can have serious effects throughout the economy, notably crowding out domestic investment. When foreign aid flows in, it also has to be traded for local currency, bidding up the price of the local currency and hurting the competitiveness of the local export sector.

Aid can be particularly counterproductive when it involves trucking in goods for free or at highly discounted prices, a type of aid known as *goods-in-kind donations.* When aid agencies or governments distribute food, clothing, or other materials, they are giving goods in kind. To see the possible side-effects of well-intentioned donations, see the From Another Angle box, In Zambia, Did the Steelers Win Super Bowl XLV?

FROM ANOTHER ANGLE

In Zambia, Did the Steelers Win Super Bowl XLV?

Before the confetti from Super Bowl XLV was swept away, the victorious players for the Green Bay Packers donned T-shirts emblazoned with the words Super Bowl Champions. Of course, the Packers hadn't waited until after the game to get those T-shirts printed; instead they had thousands printed beforehand, just in case. So did the losing side, the Pittsburgh Steelers.

But as soon as the Steelers lost, their shirts became pretty much worthless. Who's going to buy a shirt that says the wrong team won? The NFL and a charity called World Vision came up with a solution: instead of letting the T-shirts sit around, getting mouldy in a warehouse, they could ship the T-shirts to Africa to give to the poor and needy.

Sounds great, right? Not if you're an African T-shirt maker. As it happens, T-shirts are not desperately needed in Africa. Africa has a solid homegrown and secondhand clothing market that supplies clothes at a fair price. Very few people go without T-shirts because they cannot afford them. An influx of Steelers T-shirts, instead of helping out, distorts the market, hurting everyone from secondhand clothes marketers to local clothing makers, who obviously can't compete with free T-shirts.

That's not the only problem with the idea of shipping all those Steelers T-shirts to Africa. Shipping costs money. One particularly glaring example of this is the One Million Shirts campaign, started by a young entrepreneur. In order to cover the shipping charges for the one million shirts he planned to send to Africa, the founder asked for a dollar along with each shirt. While this sounds noble, the plan comes with a considerable opportunity cost. Is shipping unneeded shirts to Africa really the best way to spend US$1 million, rather than, say, buying life-saving drugs or mosquito nets? In the end, the program was shut down after a firestorm of criticism.

The lesson is that it takes more than good intentions to solve the pressing issues of development. If good intentions were all it took, aid would have lifted everyone out of poverty long ago.

Sources: http://www.freakonomics.com/2011/02/15/what-happens-to-all-those-super-bowl-t-shirts-a-guest-post-by-dean-karlan/; http://www.nber.org/papers/w17456.pdf?new_window=1; http://www.time.com/time/world/article/0,8599,1987628,00.html.

Do these problems mean all aid should be stopped? Not necessarily. The lesson may be that more effort needs to go into improving the weak governments that embezzle aid or fail to use it productively. This idea was tested by economists Craig Burnside at Duke University and David Dollar, now at the US Treasury Department. They found that over the 1980s and 1990s, countries with sound fiscal, monetary, and trade policies, and strong rule of law combined with large amounts of aid grew at 1 percent, while countries with bad policy and high amounts of aid saw GDP shrink by 1 percent over the same time period.[12] In fact, for countries with bad policy, aid was actually a detriment to growth. The example of Duvalier's Haiti at the beginning of this section suggests why: with aid flowing in to embezzle, Duvalier had little incentive to work to improve Haiti's economy, since such improvements would reduce or eliminate aid.

Even though the research behind the Dollar and Burnside study has been questioned (it turns out that more recent data do not show the same patterns), their logic has spurred governments and aid organizations to think harder about links between aid and policy. In 2004, the United States created the Millennium Challenge Corporation to give cash to "worthy" governments, which have to meet seventeen requirements, including ruling justly, tamping down corruption, and maintaining a stable economy. So far, the Millennium Challenge Corporation has given out US$2.3 billion in arrangements called "compacts" to twenty-three countries.

Impact Investing

Most thinking about foreign aid has little to do with business. But businesses, after all, are extremely good at generating new products, producing at the right scale, marketing, and creating efficient supply chains. Those are the exact qualities needed to solve some of the toughest social and economic problems.

A group of private investors and institutions is supporting this new breed of socially minded business through an idea called *impact investing*. In some ways, it's an alternative to foreign aid, though in fact the two ideas can work together. **Impact investing** involves investing money in firms to generate both financial and social returns. These firms, called "social businesses," are involved in all kinds of endeavours from building cheap but effective private schools in the slums of Nairobi, to hospitals that serve the poor for free in South India.

The guiding idea behind impact investing is simple: markets can be powerful tools to promote human development, but not if investors are interested only in a quick financial return. Impact investors, who may be foundations, wealth managers, private managers, or non-profit organizations, are willing to be more patient, take greater risks, and sometimes accept lower financial returns as long as they're convinced that their money is being used to create social change.

One pioneering example of impact investing is the Acumen Fund, which describes itself as a non-profit global venture fund that invests only in businesses that aim for social impact. Since its start in 2001, it has invested more than US$50 million in health, housing, water, energy, and agriculture businesses across East Africa, India, and Pakistan. Among the firms supported by the Acumen Fund—to the tune of US$1.5 million—is d.light Design, which sells lanterns that produce light using solar energy. One out of four people in the world do not have electricity, and d.light's solar lanterns are a healthier solution than kerosene lanterns, which produce dangerous fumes.

Solar-powered lighting for a family in Tanzania makes things we take for granted in Canada, like studying at night, much easier to do.

© d.light design

Although the Acumen Fund's investments are a small fraction of the roughly US$1.1 trillion in foreign direct investment that flows around the world each year, impact investing is growing quickly, particularly in Europe. Large banks are getting involved, as are universities: Colorado State University, for example, offers a Global Social and Sustainable Enterprise (GSSE) Master's in Business Administration, while Stanford's Entrepreneurial Design for Extreme Affordability class teaches students to design products to serve consumers at the lowest income level (and was the group that incubated the solar lantern behind d.light Design).

How Do We Know What Works?

> **LO 18.8** Explain the need for impact evaluation, and analyze the role of randomized controlled trials in measuring impact.

There is no shortage of ideas for how to promote economic development. The Millennium Project, for one, offers 449 ways to reduce poverty, including hydrological monitoring systems, footpaths, road maintenance, electric power grids, women's empowerment initiatives, and industrial parks. As resources are limited, governments and aid agencies have to make some tough choices about which policies would be the most effective in reducing poverty. How do we know what works?

For most of the twentieth century, development efforts proceeded on a trial-and-error basis. Certain strategies were tried; if it seemed that they worked, they were kept, and if they were glaring failures, they were scrapped. The trouble is, many of the failures weren't glaring enough. Often, aid agencies simply couldn't be sure whether a particular strategy had helped or hurt.

In recent years, some development economists have started to argue against charging forward with ideas that might or might not work. Instead they promote a more informed approach by rigorously evaluating the impact of development programs and policies.

Evaluations

Impact evaluation entails answering one seemingly simple question: How did people's lives change after a program or policy was implemented, compared to how they would have changed without it? This would be easy if everything else were held constant except the program or policy, but that's not the case in the complexities of the real world.

Consider the challenge of enrolling kids in school and ensuring that they learn as much as possible while they are there. There are many options and promising programs. For example, since schools in developing countries often have to make do with old, battered learning materials, one strategy is to provide them with better textbooks. Another strategy may be providing kids with school uniforms—even when schooling itself is free, many schools require students to wear uniforms. When this is an expense that families cannot afford, their kids don't go to school.

At first glance, it seems as if it would be easy to evaluate efforts like these—just measure the test scores of kids in schools who receive the textbooks or the uniforms. If they're higher than before, great; if not, then back to the drawing board. Unfortunately, this is far from foolproof. Beyond the question of whether the tests measure learning in a meaningful way, how do we know that the better test scores are not the result of something else? What if there was an especially good harvest, and kids are learning better because they're no longer hungry while at school? Then we might be mistaken in thinking the textbooks are making the difference, and we'd keep pouring money into buying more textbooks when it could be put to better use elsewhere.

One way to avoid this problem is through the use of **randomized controlled trials (RCTs)**. Randomized controlled trials randomly assign people into groups in order to focus on the impact of a particular intervention. Some of the stories told in this book, such as the one about giving out mosquito nets to protect from malaria (see the Paying for Bednets box in Chapter 4), have been the result of such randomized controlled trials.

If we wanted to know the true impact of providing more textbooks on test scores, for example, we could select 100 similar schools and divide them into two groups of 50 at random. The first group doesn't get the textbooks, while the second does. If it's the textbooks making the difference, then schools in the treatment group will do better than those in the control group. The key to the process is assigning the schools randomly; the two groups will be similar on average before the study, so any factor other than the intervention should affect them equally. It doesn't completely control for other, confounding variables, but it's a start.

Evaluations using this method can unseat expectations. It turns out that if you want to boost school attendance, there's something you can buy and give out that's much more effective than either textbooks or uniforms—deworming pills.

Worms are tiny, parasitic organisms that cause chronic sickness that keeps kids out of school. Studies found that, overall, the deworming program led to a 7.5 percent gain in primary school participation.[13] Deworming pills are also far cheaper than textbooks or uniforms, costing just 50 cents per child per year. In comparison, the state-run *Progresa* safety-net program in Mexico, which links cash benefits for families to activities such as getting kids vaccinated and sending them to school, costs many times this amount. (Note that programs like Progresa also have other goals, not just increasing school attendance.)

Figure 18-4 shows the comparison between the two programs. The figure shows that there is one intervention that is even more cost-effective than deworming. When researchers crunched the numbers of the program costs versus how effective they were at increasing school enrollment, they found that a very simple program scored highest. That program involves simply informing parents—many of whom, in parts of the developing world, may never have attended school themselves—the potential benefits of giving their children an education.

Thanks to randomized controlled trials, policy makers and program managers can more confidently channel resources to approaches that work and are cost-effective. Two organizations are dedicated to this research: One is the Abdul Latif Jameel Poverty Action Lab (J-PAL), founded by economists at MIT and Harvard. The other is Innovations for Poverty Action (IPA), a non-profit organization started by Dean Karlan (one of the authors of this book). J-PAL and IPA conduct research in microfinance, education, health, agriculture, charitable giving, corruption, and social capital. They work with organizations to integrate this research into their operations to ensure continuous improvement and replication of successful ideas. Thanks to rigorous evaluations, the remedial education program we described earlier in this chapter, for example, is now being scaled up in Ghana, with the aim of reaching thousands of schools.

FIGURE 18-4

Impact of Programs Intended to Increase Years of Education

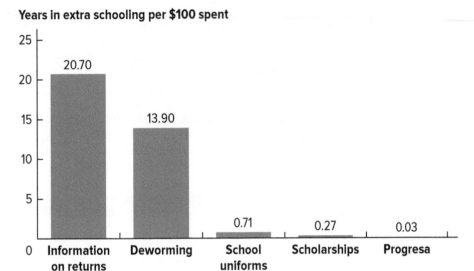

Evaluations allow researchers to compare the cost-effectiveness of various programs. Telling parents about the benefits of education (Information on returns) was by far the most effective intervention, and resulted in twenty extra child-years of education for every US$100 spent. Deworming is also very cost-effective. Although other programs were also effective at increasing schooling, they were not as cost-effective as these two.

Source: http://www.povertyactionlab.org/policy-lessons/education/student-participation.

This is not to say that these organizations have found the solution to global poverty. Like so many other tools, RCTs have challenges and limitations. Some questions, like the effect on economic development of changing monetary policy, simply can't be evaluated with an RCT. Even for those programs that can be evaluated, it's possible that the observed effects will change if the intervention is repeated on another continent or even in different areas of a country. And often it's hard to tell from an RCT exactly why the intervention worked or failed. Still, using economic theory to help design experiments, and replicating experiments at different times and in different places, can be crucial in moving knowledge forward. Along with other kinds of analysis, RCTs are helping to build knowledge, piece by piece, that is already pointing to some seemingly small interventions that can make large differences.

✓ CONCEPT CHECK

☐ How many countries pledged to participate in Overseas Development Assistance? How many of them actually gave the amount promised? [LO 18.7]

☐ What are the Millennium Development Goals? [LO 18.7]

☐ Why might goods-in-kind donations cause problems for local producers? [LO 18.7]

☐ What is a randomized controlled trial? [LO 18.8]

Conclusion

Although the work needed to put an end to global poverty may seem daunting, major strides have been made and continue to be made. Most obviously, decades of growth in the Chinese economy have lifted millions of people out of poverty. While what worked for China was a product of a time and place that can't simply be bottled and shipped to other regions, there are hopeful signs of improvements elsewhere, including Africa. Around the African continent, vigorously contested democratic elections are taking place, and some countries are posting impressive growth figures.

Progress is being made through different mixes of good governance, aid, strengthened institutions, investment, and careful testing of what works and what does not among aid programs. While there is a long way to go, progress like this can promote the expansion of capabilities and help expand markets that truly work for the world's poor.

Key Terms

capability

institutions

industrial policy

clusters

World Trade Organization (WTO)

financing gap

poverty trap

World Bank

United Nations Development Program (UNDP)

impact investing

randomized controlled trial (RCT)

Summary

LO 18.1 Explain how the capabilities approach relates to economic development.

Development is a field of economics that studies the causes and nature of international poverty. One way to think about development is known as the capabilities approach, developed by Amartya Sen. The goal of development is to increase human capabilities. There are many different types of capabilities, including very basic rights to health and education as well as other concepts like self-expression and reputation.

LO 18.2 Explain the relationship between economic growth and economic development.

The ideas of economic growth and development are similar but not identical. Economic growth can promote development. After all, when people have more money, you would expect them to spend more on improving their health and educating their children. There is general agreement, though, that the fundamentals of economic growth, including such things as property rights and the rule of law and human capital will spark development.

LO 18.3 Describe how improvements to education and health can develop human capital.

By providing access to more and better schools and clinics, countries can develop human capital. Many countries are now mandating universal primary education and providing health insurance on the cheap to make great strides in basic human capital development. These efforts must be of high quality to be effective, though. Human capital is an important part of economic development, as it allows for more productive workers and greater economic growth. Improvements in human capital can also promote capacities development as people are able to lead more complete (better educated and healthier) lives.

LO 18.4 Explain the importance of institutions and good governance in development economics.

Development often takes root in places where there are strong institutions. Institutions are human-devised constraints that shape human interactions. In contrast, organizations are groups of people that act according to those constraints. Several institutions are important for development, including a strong system of property rights, the rule of law, and a government capable of implementing good policy.

LO 18.5 Evaluate the role of industrial policy and clusters in development.

Governments have turned to industrial policy in an attempt to favour some industries over others. Two popular types of industrial policy include import substitution and export-led industrialization. An alternative industrial policy is clustering, which promotes networks of interdependent firms, universities, and customers focusing on a specific type of good.

LO 18.6 Evaluate how migration and remittances promote development.

Every year, millions of people leave their home countries and villages to migrate in search of better-paying jobs. The money they send home to their families, called remittances, represents a large and growing financial flow around the world. As a result, governments and aid agencies work to make sure that these remittances best help the families back home escape poverty.

LO 18.7 Identify the different arguments for and against foreign aid in development.

On the one hand, foreign aid can provide money needed to finance developments in infrastructure, clinic and school construction, and other important measures that simply would not happen without outside assistance. On the other, financial aid can be a destabilizing force that is wasted at best, and destructive at worse.

LO 18.8 Explain the need for impact evaluation, and analyze the role of randomized controlled trials in measuring impact.

Throughout history, ideas about how to spur development have mostly proceeded on a trial-and-error basis. Instead of wasting money on programs that may or may not work, economists have begun to evaluate the impact of various development programs. Impact evaluation tries to answer the question of how a particular program or policy changed people's lives.

A randomized controlled trial (RCT) is one way to answer that question; it compares a treatment group with a control group to show the effect of a program.

Review Questions

1. Are capabilities and utility the same thing? If so, why do economists use two different terms for the same concept? If not, explain the difference, both in terms of their definitions and when each is best used in economic analysis. [LO 18.1]

2. Determine whether each of the following is true or false. [LO 18.1]
   a. The chance to see a musical is an example of a capability.
   b. The freedom to practice religion is not a capability because it is not directly related to economic development.
   c. Economists will make the same conclusions and recommendations using the utility-maximization approach as they will using the capabilities approach.
   d. The capabilities approach works better for analyzing what's best for society, while the utility-maximization approach works better for analyzing what's best for an individual.

3. Are economic growth and economic development the same? Why or why not? [LO 18.2]

4. Does economic growth lead to development? Or does the causation run the other way, with economic development leading to growth? Explain. [LO 18.2]

5. How can health and education work together to spur economic development? What does this imply about the best way to spend aid funds with the goal of increasing educational attainment in a developing nation? [LO 18.3]

6. Explain how better health care in a developing nation, such as increasing the number of immunized children, can have economic effects beyond fewer sick kids. [LO 18.3]

7. "I'm thinking about writing a paper for a class on development economics," your friend tells you over lunch. "I'm going to focus on important institutions like government bodies and economic agencies." Is your friend using the term *institutions* correctly? Why or why not? [LO 18.4]

8. How can capital be considered "dead," and what do we mean by making this capital "alive"? [LO 18.4]

9. International trade is associated with economic growth and development—open economies tend to grow faster than closed economies, all else equal. Given this information, should a nation seeking to grow and develop faster use the method of import substitution or export-led growth? How would each of these two methods affect GDP through its net exports component? [LO 18.5]

10. Determine whether each of the following is an example of import substitution, export-led growth, or clustering. [LO 18.5]
    a. The government gives a $50 million grant to a leading university to work with car manufacturers and to research new ways to produce more fuel-efficient vehicles.
    b. The government gives $50 million to a domestic car company to subsidize its shipping costs to other countries.
    c. The government enacts a tariff on all cars imported from abroad.

11. How can emigration help the home economy in terms of income? Are the benefits of migration on income limited to those who actually migrate? Why or why not? [LO 18.6]

12. How does emigration affect wages and income in the migrant's country of origin? In the country they immigrate to? [LO 18.6]

13. Say that Canada is considering giving direct aid to a nation run by a dictator known for his lavish lifestyle while the nation's citizens suffer through a terrible famine. What might be a problem with giving aid to this nation? Name at least one way to fix the problem. [LO 18.7]

14. What are goods-in-kind donations, and how can they hurt the economies they're meant to help? [LO 18.7]

15. Explain briefly how you could set up an RCT to evaluate whether providing free breakfasts to elementary-school students helps them learn. [LO 18.8]

16. List three shortcomings of using an RCT to evaluate the success of a given economic program. [LO 18.8]

Problems and Applications

1. In a small town in Western Canada lives a drug dealer and manufacturer who supplies the illegal, addictive drug crystal meth. The drug dealer insists that making and selling the drug is what gives him the most satisfaction among any possible use of his time and resources. Using the utility-maximization approach, should he be allowed to continue supplying the drug? What about with the capabilities approach? Explain your answer. [LO 18.1]

2. Professor Bucks and Professor Liber are having a debate about the role of economic growth in contributing to economic development. Professor Bucks contends that economic growth is the only thing to consider in development, as people's utility is directly related to their income. Professor Liber agrees that income is directly related to development, but says that there are other things to consider. Given what we've learned in this chapter, pick the option that is most correct according to the capabilities approach. [LO 18.1]
    a. Professor Bucks is correct, because increases in income are the only way to measure economic development.
    b. Professor Bucks is correct, because capabilities always increase when income does.
    c. Professor Liber is correct, because income is unrelated to capabilities, which are the most important factor in development.
    d. Professor Liber is correct, because income is related to development, but it is not the only contributor to capabilities.

3. Table 18P-1 shows the levels and annual growth rates of economic indicators for two countries, Nationavia and Countrystan. Assume these growth rates will remain constant for the foreseeable future. Use these data to determine whether each of the following statements is true, false, or indeterminable. [LO 18.2]
    a. The theory of income convergence (that national incomes in poor countries will "catch up" to those in wealthier countries) holds for Nationavia and Countrystan.
    b. Countrystan has higher levels of human capital than Nationavia.

c. Inequality is greater in Nationavia.

d. In ten years, it's likely that Countrystan will have higher levels of human capital than Nationavia.

TABLE 18P-1

Indicator	Level	Growth rate (%)
GDP per capita—Nationavia	$50,000	3.1
GDP per capita—Countrystan	$30,000	3.0
Average years of education per capita—Nationavia	15 years	2.0
Average years of education per capita—Countrystan	5 years	8.0
Life expectancy—Nationavia	72 years	0.5
Life expectancy—Countrystan	56 years	1.8

4. In Nation A, GDP per capita is $21,000 and is growing annually at a rate of 1.4 percent. The average citizen in Nation A lives for 51 years, and this figure is growing at 6 percent per year. Additionally, the average person in Nation A has 9 years of education, growing annually at 5.1 percent, and 60 percent of Nation A's population is currently literate, growing at a rate of 2 percent.

In Nation B, GDP per capita is $40,000 and is growing annually at a rate of 0.8 percent. The average citizen in Nation B lives for 68 years, and this value is growing at 2 percent per year. The average person in Nation B has 10.5 years of education, increasing 2 percent annually, while 78 percent of its population is literate, a figure growing at 0.5 percent annually.

Which nation is experiencing more economic growth? Which is wealthier? Which currently has more capabilities for its citizens? And which is experiencing more economic development? [LO 18.2]

5. Imagine that you are the leader of a low-income nation. You have identified lack of access to health care as a major contributor to your nation's low income, and Canada has offered to help by providing funds to build more health clinics. Will this solve the problem? Why or why not? If it won't, what's one alternative to using these foreign aid dollars to build clinics? [LO 18.3]

6. While listening to the radio on the way to school, you hear a politician from a small, low-income nation say the following: "Over the last five years, there has been a 10 percent increase in the number of children attending school full time. We can expect to see these children grow up to be more productive workers, because their human capital has increased."

Is the politician's statement true, false, or somewhere in between? Explain your answer. [LO 18.3]

7. Classify each of the following as an institution or organization. [LO 18.4]
    a. The Canadian International Development Agency, a Canadian government agency that channels aid abroad
    b. The United Nations Development Program
    c. The UN Declaration of Human Rights, an agreement among members of the United Nations regarding the rights of individuals
    d. The United Nations
    e. The passing of a legislation which established rules for how publicly traded firms must report information in their financial documents

8. A given nation has a good titling system, but theft of productive equipment is rampant, with few consequences for those who steal. What is the term development economists use for what's lacking in this economy? What effect will this lack likely have on economic growth and economic development? Give one way to improve the situation. [LO 18.4]

9. The small, landlocked nation of Wheatleyton is just starting to develop an agricultural sector. Firms in this sector appeal to the government to temporarily limit imports of agricultural goods from other nations with more experience and larger economies of scale, because the prices of the imports are so low that domestic firms can't compete. What is this desired policy called? What problems are associated with it, and how can we reduce them? [LO 18.5]

10. The small nation of Movieheim wants to develop a film industry. It is considering two options for doing so:

    Option A: Reimburse relocation expenses for firms and give tax breaks to acting schools, film studios, digital artists, etc., to encourage them to work together and share ideas.

    Option B: Make the purchase and exhibition of foreign films illegal for the next ten years.

    What would development economists call each of these options? Which is more likely to encourage long-term economic development, and why? [LO 18.5]

11. Consider separately each of the following hypothetical scenarios about South Africa and answer the questions. Assume in each case that medical school has an 80 percent success rate—in other words, 80 percent of people who attend medical school graduate and become doctors. [LO 18.6]

    a. No doctors are allowed to emigrate, and the number of people going to medical school is given by $D = 100,000 \times I$, where I is an index relating the income of doctors to those in other professions. If $I = 4$, how many students will go to medical school? How many more doctors will there be in South Africa?

    b. Canada decides to offer visas to any doctors from South Africa. Additionally, I in the above equation changes from 4 to 10. Assume that 30 percent of doctors educated in South Africa immigrate to Canada. How many students will go to medical school? How many will become doctors? How many of those doctors will practise in South Africa, and how many will practise in Canada?

    c. Canada decides to limit the number of doctors from South Africa who can obtain visas to no more than 10 percent of those graduating from medical school. Assume that I remains at 10. How many students will go to medical school? How many will become doctors? How many of those doctors will practise in South Africa, and how many will practise in Canada?

12. Table 18P-2 shows the size of various flows to developing countries in 2009 and 2010 in billions of dollars. [LO 18.6]

    a. Rank each of the flows in 2010 as a percentage of ODA (official development assistance) in 2009, from highest to lowest.

    b. Rank each of the flows in terms of their growth rates from 2009 to 2010, from highest to lowest.

TABLE 18P-2

Financial flow	Amount in 2009 (billions of $)	Amount in 2010 (billions of $)
Official development assistance	128	119
Foreign direct investment	510	573
Remittances	307	324

13. The president of an organization specializing in foreign investment says the following at a shareholder meeting: "Our one-year program was a failure. We were hoping for a 6 percent return on our investment, but we got only 3 percent." Use the idea of impact investing to provide an alternative argument that the program was not a failure. [LO 18.7]

14. The following equation provides an alternative calculation to determine a developing country's financing gap:

$$FG = (A \times g) - I_D$$

In this equation, FG is the financing gap, A is a variable that captures the country's starting income together with its ability to turn investment into growth (expressed in dollars), g is the targeted growth rate, and I_D is the amount of domestic investment currently in the economy. Assume that A = \$50,000,000,000, g = 0.08, and I_D = \$500,000,000, and answer the questions that follow. **[LO 18.6]**, **[LO 18.7]**

a. What is the size of the financing gap?

b. Assume that the population of Canada is 35 million. How much would each Canadian citizen have to pay to fill the financing gap?

c. What percentage of GDP per capita in Canada does your answer from (b) represent if GDP per capita is currently \$45,000?

Now assume that Canada decides to donate the amount of the financing gap to the developing country as aid. Assume also that there are administrative and competitive costs associated with receiving aid. Specifically, 23 cents of every dollar spent on aid will go to administrative costs. Also, for every dollar received from abroad intended to be used for investment, 50 cents will be used for non-investment purposes.

d. Calculate the real increase in investment dollars the aid from Canada will provide in the recipient country.

e. Calculate the new financing gap by subtracting the above from the financing gap you calculated in part (a).

15. Table 18P-3 shows the results of a study on how to improve vaccination rates in a developing nation. The baseline numbers represent the rates of vaccination at the beginning of the study, while the endline numbers represent the rates of vaccination at the study's conclusion. Answer the following questions. **[LO 18.8]**

a. Which campaign(s) had a positive effect on vaccination rates in comparison with the control group?

b. Which campaign had the largest positive effect on vaccination rates in comparison to the control group?

c. Which campaign(s) had a negative effect on vaccination rates in comparison to the control group?

d. Which campaign(s) had no effect on vaccination rates in comparison to the control group?

TABLE 18P-3

Campaign	Vaccination rates (%)			
	Baseline—control	Baseline—treatment	Endline—control	Endline—treatment
Lectures	5	6	8	5
Free provision	5	4	8	8
Subsidy	5	5	8	10
Newspaper announcements	5	7	8	7

16. Table 18P-4 displays the results of a study on how to improve vaccination rates in a developing nation. The baseline numbers represent the rates of vaccination at the beginning of the study, and the endline numbers represent the rates of vaccination at the study's conclusion. Rank the campaigns in order, from most effective to least effective. Then refer to Table 18-P5, which shows the cost per person of each campaign. Combining information from the two tables, rank the campaigns that resulted in an increase in vaccinations from high to low in terms of cost effectiveness (based on treatment effect alone). **[LO 18.8]**

TABLE 18P-4

Campaign	Vaccination Rates (%)			
	Baseline—control	Baseline—treatment	Endline—control	Endline—treatment
Lectures	4	6	6	9
Free provision	4	7	6	8
Subsidy	4	5	6	9
Newspaper announcements	4	3	6	2

TABLE 18P-5

Campaign	Cost per person ($)
Lectures	10
Free provision	20
Subsidy	15
Newspaper announcements	5

Chapter Sources

Ursula Cassabone and Charles Kenny, "The best things in life are (nearly) free: Technology, knowledge and global health," http://www.cgdev.org/content/publications/detail/1425144

Alberto Chaia et al., "Half the world is unbanked," in Robert Cull, Asli Demirgüç-Kunt, and Jonathan Morduch, eds. *Banking the World* (Cambridge, MA: MIT Press, 2012).

Esther Duflo and Michael Kremer, "Use of randomization in testing development effectiveness," http://econ-www.mit.edu/files/765

Richard A. Easterlin, "The worldwide standard of living since 1800," *Journal of Economic Perspectives* 14, no. 1 (2000), pp. 7–26, Tables 3, 5, 8, http://pubs.aeaweb.org/doi/pdfplus/10.1257/jep.14.1.7

Jonathan Morduch, "Not so fast: The realities of impact investing," *America's Quarterly,* Fall 2011, www.acumenfund.org

http://econ.worldbank.org/WBSITE/EXTERNAL/EXTDEC/EXTRESEARCH/0,contentMDK:22263500~pagePK:64165401~piPK:64165026~theSitePK:469382,00.html

http://www.internationalpropertyrightsindex.org/userfiles/chapter%202%20property%20rights%20and%20economic%20development.pdf

http://www.unicef.org/publications/files/Children_and_the_MDGs.pdf

Glossary

absolute advantage: the ability to produce more of a good or service than others can with a given amount of resources

aggregate demand curve: a curve that shows the relationship between the overall price level in the economy and total demand

aggregate price level: a measure of the average price level; in practice, the CPI or GDP price deflator

aggregate supply curve: a curve that shows the relationship between the overall price level in the economy and total production by firms

arbitrage: the process of taking advantage of market inefficiencies to earn profits

automatic stabilizers: taxes and government spending that affect fiscal policy without specific action from policy makers

balance of trade: the value of exports minus the value of imports

balance-of-payments identity: an equation that shows that the value of net exports equals net capital outflow

barter: directly offering a good or service in exchange for some good or service you want

bond: a form of debt that represents a promise by the bond issuer to repay the face value of the loan, at a specified maturity date, and to pay periodic interest at a specific percentage rate

budget deficit: the amount of money a government spends beyond the revenue it brings in

budget surplus: the amount of revenue a government brings in beyond what it spends

business cycle: fluctuations of GDP either above or below the potential level of GDP in the economy

capability: a person's freedom to engage fully in life, including having economic and political freedoms

causation: a relationship between two events in which one brings about the other

central bank: the institution ultimately responsible for managing the nation's money supply and coordinating the actions of the banking system to ensure a sound economy

circular flow model: a simplified representation of how the economy's transactions work together

closed economy: an economy that does not interact with other countries' economies

clusters: networks of interdependent firms, universities, and businesses that focus on the production of a specific type of good

commodity-backed money: any form of money that can be legally exchanged into a fixed amount of an underlying commodity

comparative advantage: the ability to produce a good or service at a lower opportunity cost than others

competitive market: a market in which fully informed, price-taking buyers and sellers easily trade a standardized good or service

complements: goods that are consumed together, so that purchasing one will make consumers more likely to purchase the other

Consumer Price Index (CPI): a measure that tracks changes in the cost of a basket of goods and services purchased by a typical Canadian household as calculated by Statistics Canada

consumer surplus: the net benefit that a consumer receives from purchasing a good or service, measured by the difference between willingness to pay and the actual price

consumption: spending on goods and services by private individuals and households

contractionary fiscal policy: fiscal policy that decreases aggregate demand

contractionary monetary policy: actions that reduce the money supply in order to decrease aggregate demand

convergence theory: the theory that countries that start out poor will initially grow faster than rich ones, but will eventually converge to the same growth rate

core inflation: measure of inflation that excludes goods with historically volatile price changes

correlation: a consistently observed relationship between two events or variables

cross-price elasticity of demand: a measure of how the quantity demanded of one good changes when the price of a different good changes

crowding out: the reduction in private borrowing caused by an increase in government borrowing

cyclical unemployment: unemployment resulting from changes in GDP

deadweight loss: a loss of total surplus that occurs because the quantity of a good that is bought and sold is below the market equilibrium quantity

debt service: the amount that consumers have to spend to pay their debts, often expressed as a percentage of disposable income

default: the failure of a borrower to pay back a loan according to the agreed-upon terms

deflation: an overall fall in prices in the economy

demand curve: a graph that shows the quantities of a particular good or service that consumers will demand at various prices

demand deposits: funds held in bank accounts that can be withdrawn ("demanded") by depositors at any time without advance notice

demand schedule: a table that shows the quantities of a particular good or service that consumers will purchase (demand) at various prices

depression: a particularly severe or extended recession

derivative: an asset whose value is based on the value of another asset

desired reserves: in the absence of required reserves, the amount of reserves a bank wishes to hold

discouraged workers: workers who have looked for work in the past year but have given up looking because of the condition of the labour market

disinflation: a period in which inflation rates are falling, but still positive

diversification: the process by which risks are shared across many different assets or people, reducing the impact of any particular risk on any one individual

dividend: a payment made periodically, typically quarterly or annually, to all shareholders of a company

domestic savings: savings for capital investment that come from within a country; equals domestic income minus consumption spending

economics: the study of how people, individually and collectively, manage resources

efficiency wage: a wage that is deliberately set above the market rate to increase worker productivity

efficiency: use of resources in the most productive way possible to produce the goods and services that have the greatest total economic value to society

efficient market: an arrangement in which no exchange can make anyone better off without someone becoming worse off

efficient-market hypothesis: the idea that market prices always incorporate all available information, and therefore represent true value as correctly as is possible

efficient ~ ints: combinations of production possibilities that ___ the most output possible from all a~ ___ °s

___ hat has an absolute value of elasticity

___ ° how much consumers and producers ___ 'n market conditions

employment insurance: money paid by the government to people who are unemployed

equilibrium: the situation in a market when the quantity supplied equals the quantity demanded; graphically, this convergence happens where the demand curve intersects the supply curve

equilibrium price: the price at which the quantity supplied equals the quantity demanded

equilibrium quantity: the quantity that is supplied and demanded at the equilibrium price

excess reserves: any additional amount, beyond the required reserves, a bank chooses to keep in reserve

exchange rate: the value of one currency expressed in terms of another currency

exchange-rate appreciation: an increase in the value of a currency relative to the value of another currency

exchange-rate depreciation: a decrease in the value of a currency relative to other currencies

expansionary fiscal policy: fiscal policy that increases aggregate demand

expansionary monetary policy: actions that increase the money supply in order to increase aggregate demand

fiat money: money created by rule, without any commodity to back it

financial intermediaries: institutions that channel funds from people who have them to people who want them

financial market: a market in which people trade future claims on funds or goods

financial system: the group of institutions that bring together savers, borrowers, investors, and insurers in a set of interconnected markets where people trade financial products

financing gap: the difference between the savings rate within an economy and the amount of investment needed to achieve sustainable growth

fiscal policy: government decisions about the level of taxation and government spending

fixed exchange rate: an exchange rate that is set by the government, instead of determined by the market

floating exchange rate: an exchange rate whose value is determined by the market

foreign direct investment (FDI): investment when a firm runs part of its operation abroad or invests in another company abroad

foreign portfolio investment: investment funded by foreign sources but operated domestically

fractional-reserve banking: a banking system in which banks keep on reserve less than 100 percent of their deposits

frictional unemployment: unemployment caused by workers who are changing location, job, or career

gains from trade: the improvement in outcomes that occurs when producers specialize and exchange goods and services

GDP deflator: a measure of the overall increase in prices in an economy, using the ratio between real and nominal GDP

GDP per capita: a country's GDP divided by its population

government purchases: spending on goods and services by all levels of government

government-spending multiplier: the amount by which GDP increases when government spending increases by $1

green GDP: an alternative measure of GDP that subtracts the environmental costs of production from the positive outputs normally counted in GDP

gross domestic product (GDP): the sum of the market values of all final goods and services produced within a country in a given period of time

gross national product (GNP): the sum of the market values of all final goods and services produced plus capital owned by the residents of a country in a given period of time

human capital: the set of skills, knowledge, experience, and talent that determines the productivity of workers

hyperinflation: extremely long-lasting and painful increases in the price level

idiosyncratic risk: any risk that is unique to a particular company or asset

impact investing: investing money in firms to generate both financial and social returns

incentive: something that causes people to behave in a certain way by changing the trade-offs they face

income elasticity of demand: a measure of how much the quantity demanded changes in response to a change in consumers' incomes

indexing: the practice of automatically increasing payments as the cost of living increases

industrial policy: effort by a government to favour some industries over others

inelastic: demand that has an absolute value of elasticity less than 1

inferior goods: goods for which demand decreases as income increases

inflation: an overall rise in prices in the economy

inflation rate: the size of the change in the overall price level

institutions: the human-devised constraints that shape human interactions

interest rate: the price of borrowing money for a specified period of time, expressed as a percentage per dollar borrowed and per unit of time

inventory: the stock of goods that a company produces now but does not sell immediately

investment: spending on productive inputs, such as factories, machinery, and inventories

investment trade-off: a substitution of current consumption or investment in physical capital for future production

labour demand curve: a graph showing the relationship between the wage rate and the total labour demanded from all the firms in the economy

labour force: people who are in the working-age population and are either employed or unemployed—i.e., people who are currently working or who are actively trying to find a job

labour-force participation rate: the number of people in the labour force divided by the working-age population

labour supply curve: a graph showing the relationship between the total labour supplied in the economy and the wage rate

labour unions: groups of employees who join together to bargain with their employer(s) over salaries and work conditions

law of demand: a fundamental characteristic of demand: all else equal, quantity demanded rises as price falls

law of supply: a fundamental characteristic of supply: all else equal, quantity supplied rises as price rises

leverage: the practice of using borrowed money to pay for investments

liquidity: a measure of how easily a particular asset can be converted quickly to cash without much loss of value

liquidity-preference model: the idea that the quantity of money people want to hold is a function of the interest rate

loan: an agreement in which a lender gives money to a borrower in exchange for a promise to repay the amount loaned plus an agreed-upon amount of interest

M1: definition of money that includes cash plus chequing account balances

M2: definition of money that includes everything in M1 plus savings accounts and other financial instruments where money is locked away for a specified amount of time; less liquid than M1

macroeconomics: the study of the economy on a regional, national, or international scale

marginal decision making: comparison of additional benefits of a choice against the additional costs it would bring, without considering related benefits and costs of past choices

marginal propensity to consume (MPC): the amount that consumption increases when after-tax income increases by $1

market: buyers and sellers who trade a particular good or service

market basket: a list of specific goods and services in fixed quantities

market economy: an economy in which private individuals, rather than a centralized planning authority, make the decisions

market failures: situations in which the assumption of efficient, competitive markets fails to hold

market for loanable funds: a market in which savers supply funds to those who want to borrow

market (systemic) risk: any risk that is broadly shared by the entire market or economy

medium of exchange: the ability to use money to purchase goods and services

menu costs: the costs (measured in money, time, and opportunity) of changing prices to keep pace with inflation

microeconomics: the study of how individuals and firms manage resources

mid-point method: method that measures percentage change in demand (or supply) relative to a point midway between two points on a curve; used to estimate elasticity

model: a simplified representation of the important parts of a complicated situation

monetary policy: actions by the central bank to manage the money supply, in pursuit of certain macroeconomic goals

money: the set of all assets that are regularly used to directly purchase goods and services

money multiplier: the ratio of money created by the lending activities of the banking system to the money created by the central bank

money supply: the amount of money available in the economy

multiplier effect: the increase in consumer spending that occurs when spending by one person causes others to spend more, too, increasing the impact of the initial spending on the economy

mutual fund: a portfolio of stocks and other assets, managed by a professional who makes decisions on behalf of clients

national savings: the sum of the private savings of individuals and corporations plus the public savings of the government

natural rate of unemployment: the minimum level of unemployment that is unavoidable in a dynamic economy

net capital flow: the difference between capital inflows (investment financed by savings from another country) and capital outflows (domestic savings invested abroad)

net capital outflow: the net flow of funds invested outside of a country

net exports: exports minus imports; the value of goods and services produced domestically and consumed abroad minus the value of goods and services produced abroad and consumed domestically

net present value (NPV): a measure of the current value of a stream of cash flows expected in the future

neutrality of money: the idea that aggregate price levels do not affect real variables in the economy

nominal exchange rate: the stated rate at which one country's currency can be traded for another country's currency

nominal GDP: GDP calculation in which goods and services are valued at current prices

nominal interest rate: the reported interest rate, not adjusted for the effects of inflation

non-accelerating inflation rate of unemployment (NAIRU): the lowest possible unemployment rate that will not cause the inflation rate level to increase

normal goods: goods for which demand increases as income increases

normative statement: a claim about how the world should be

open economy: an economy that interacts with other countries' economies

open-market operations: sales or purchases of government bonds by the central bank, to or from commercial banks, on the open market

opportunity cost: the value of what you have to give up in order to get something; the value of your next-best alternative

output gap: the difference between actual and potential output in an economy

overnight rate: the interest rate at which banks choose to lend reserves held at the Bank of Canada to one another, usually just overnight

pension fund: a professionally managed portfolio of assets intended to provide an income to retirees

perfectly elastic demand: demand for which the demand curve is horizontal, such that demand could be any quantity at the given price, but drops to zero if the price increases

perfectly inelastic demand: demand for which the demand curve is vertical, in a way such that that the quantity demanded is always the same no matter what the price

Phillips curve: a model that shows the connection between inflation and unemployment in the short run

physical capital: the stock of equipment and structures that allow for production of goods and services

positive statement: a factual declaration about how the world actually works

potential output: the total amount of output a country could produce if all of its resources were fully engaged

poverty trap: self-reinforcing mechanism that causes the poor to stay poor

PPP-adjustment: recalculating economic statistics to account for differences in price levels across countries

price ceiling: a maximum legal price at which a good can be sold

price control: a regulation that sets a maximum or minimum legal price for a particular good

price elasticity of demand: the size of the change in the quantity demanded of a good or service when its price changes

price elasticity of supply: the size of the change in the quantity supplied of a good or service when its price changes

price floor: a minimum legal price at which a good can be sold

price index: a measure showing how much the cost of a market basket has risen or fallen relative to the cost in a base period or location

price taker: a buyer or seller who cannot affect the market price

private savings: the savings of individuals or corporations within a country

producer surplus: the net benefit that a producer receives from the sale of a good or service, measured by the difference between the producer's willingness to sell and the actual price

production possibilities frontier: a line or curve that shows all the possible combinations of two outputs that can be produced using all available resources

productivity: output produced per worker

public debt: the total amount of money that a government owes at a point in time

public savings: the difference between government tax revenue and government spending

purchasing power parity: the theory that price levels in different countries should be the same when stated in a common currency

quantitative easing: policies that are designed to directly increase the money supply by a certain amount

quantity demanded: the amount of a particular good that buyers will purchase at a given price during a specified period

quantity supplied: the amount of a particular good or service that producers will offer for sale at a given price during a specified period

quantity theory of money: theory that the value of money is determined by the overall quantity of money in existence (the money supply)

randomized controlled trial (RCT): a method that randomly assigns subjects into control and treatment groups in order to assess the causal link from an intervention to specific outcomes

rational behaviour: making choices to achieve goals in the most effective way possible

real exchange rate: the value of goods in one country expressed in terms of the same goods in another country

real GDP: GDP calculation in which goods and services are valued at constant prices

real interest rate: the interest rate adjusted for the effects of inflation

real-wage or classical unemployment: unemployment that results from wages being higher than the market-clearing level

recession: a period of significant economic decline

reserve ratio: the ratio of the total amount of demand deposits at a bank to the amount kept as cash reserves

reserve requirement: the regulation that sets the minimum fraction of deposits banks must hold in reserve

reserves: the money that a bank keeps on hand, either in cash or in deposits at the Federal Reserve

rise: vertical distance; calculated as the change in y

risk-free rate: the interest rate at which money would be loaned if there were no risk of default; usually approximated by interest rates on government debt

run: horizontal distance; calculated as the change in x

savings: the portion of income that is not immediately spent on consumption of goods and services

scarcity: the condition of wanting more than we can get with available resources

securitization: the practice of packaging individual debts into a single uniform asset

shoe-leather costs: the costs (measured in time, money, and effort) of managing cash in the face of inflation

shortage (excess quantity demanded): a situation in which the quantity of a good that is demanded is higher than the quantity supplied

slope: the ratio of vertical distance (change in y) to horizontal distance (change in x)

specialization: spending all of your time producing a particular good

stagflation: high inflation despite low economic growth and high unemployment

standard deviation: a measure of how spread out a set of numbers is

standardized good: a good for which any two units have the same features and are interchangeable

stock: a financial asset that represents partial ownership of a company

store of value: a certain amount of purchasing power that money retains over time

structural unemployment: unemployment due to a mismatch between the skills workers can offer and the skills in demand

subsidy: a requirement that the government pay an extra amount to producers or consumers of a good

substitutes: goods that serve a similar-enough purpose that a consumer might purchase one in place of the other

sunk cost: a cost that has already been incurred and cannot be recovered or refunded

supply curve: a graph that shows the quantities of a particular good or service that producers will supply at various prices

supply schedule: a table that shows the quantities of a particular good or service that producers will supply at various prices

supply shock: significant event that directly affects production and the aggregate-supply curve in the short run

surplus: a way of measuring who benefits from transactions, and by how much

surplus (excess quantity supplied): a situation in which the quantity of a good that is supplied is higher than the quantity demanded

tax incidence: the relative tax burden borne by buyers and sellers

taxation multiplier: the amount GDP decreases when government taxes increase by $1

tax wedge: the difference between the price paid by buyers and the price received by sellers in the presence of a tax

too big to fail: so large in terms of assets or customers, or so historically important, that banking regulators allow the bank or company to keep operating despite insolvency

total revenue: the amount that a firm receives from the sale of goods and services; calculated as the quantity sold multiplied by the price paid for each unit

total surplus: a measure of the combined benefits that everyone receives from participating in an exchange of goods or services

trade deficit: a negative balance of trade; a greater amount of imports than exports

trade surplus: a positive balance of trade; a greater amount of exports than imports

transaction costs: the costs incurred by buyer and seller in agreeing to and executing a sale of goods or services

transfer payments: payments from government accounts to individuals for programs, like Social Insurance, that do not involve a purchase of goods or services

underemployed: workers who are either working less than they would like to or are working in jobs below their skill level

unemployment: situation in which someone wants to work but cannot find a job

unemployment rate: the number of unemployed people divided by the number of people in the labour force

unit of account: a standard unit of comparison

unit-elastic: demand that has an absolute value of elasticity exactly equal to 1

United Nations Development Program (UNDP): a global United Nations network that provides knowledge and resources to developing countries

velocity of money: the number of times the entire money supply turns over in a given period

willingness to pay (reservation price): the maximum price that a buyer would be willing to pay for a good or service

willingness to sell: the minimum price that a seller is willing to accept in exchange for a good or service

World Bank: a multi-national organization dedicated to providing financial and technical assistance to developing countries

World Trade Organization (WTO): an international organization designed to monitor and enforce trade agreements, while also promoting free trade

zero-sum game: a situation in which whenever one person gains, another loses an equal amount, such that the net value of any transaction is zero

Endnotes

Chapter 1

1 "Grameen Bank at a glance," Grameen Bank, October 2011, http://www.grameen-info.org/index.php?option=com_content&task=view&id=453&Itemid=527

Chapter 3

1 http://qz.com/179897/more-people-around-the-world-have-cell-phones-than-ever-had-land-lines/

2 Ibid.

Chapter 4

1 http://www.canadaka.net/content/page/71-history-of-tim-hortons

2 http://www.huffingtonpost.ca/2016/01/07/canadian-national-parks-fees_n_8932042.html

Chapter 6

1 http://www.statcan.gc.ca/pub/11-010-x/00608/10626-eng.htm

2 http://www.time.com/time/magazine/article/0,9171,1727720,00.html; and http://www.nytimes.com/2008/06/22/nyregion/22food.html

3 "The new face of hunger," *The Economist*, April 17, 2008

Chapter 7

1 To find out more about the chain-weighted index, see this explanation from Statistics Canada: http://www.statcan.gc.ca/nea-cen/gloss/gloss_c-eng.htm#Chainindex

2 Below certain thresholds, some earnings from self-employment don't need to be reported, so failure to report isn't necessarily against the tax laws. In any case, if they're not reported, those activities are not captured in GDP calculations.

3 http://www.econ.jku.at/members/Schneider/files/publications/2011/IEJ_NewEstimates_ShadEc_World.pdf

4 Ibid.

Chapter 9

1 Reprinted from *Journal of Monetary Economics* 22, Robert E. Lucas, "On the mechanics of economic development," 3-42, July 1988, with permission from Elsevier.

2 Spending on research and development, 2014 (intentions); Statistics Canada, http://www.statcan.gc.ca/daily-quotidien/141017/dq141017c-eng.htm

Chapter 10

1 http://www.statcan.gc.ca (CANSIM table 282-0003) April 2009

2 http://www.statcan.gc.ca. Cansim Table 282-0004

3 Bureau of Labour Statistics, http://www.bls.gov/news.release/union2.nr0.htm, January 2012; http://www.statcan.gc.ca/daily-quotidien/131126/dq131126e-eng.htm

4 http://www.jstor.org/discover/10.2307/2646924?uid=3739576&uid=2&uid=4&uid=3739256&sid=21102140111277

Chapter 12

1 In Chapter 15, "Inflation," we will also see that there are other reasons to be concerned about *deflation,* or falling prices in an economy.

2 It turns out that many recessions last less than a year. The length of the 2008–2009 recession was ten months. Of course, it's impossible to know how long the recession would have lasted without the government's expansionary fiscal policy.

3 www.cra-arc.gc.ca

4 Although most of our discussion will be in terms of this marginal propensity to consume, there is another term related to the MPC, called the *marginal propensity to save.* An individual can either spend or save a given dollar, with no other options. Thus, the *marginal propensity to save* (MPS) is simply the opposite of the marginal propensity to consume (MPC). It is equal to 1 minus the marginal propensity to consume: MPS = 1 - MPC.

Chapter 13

1 For the moment, we are talking about the *real* interest rate. In the "Inflation" chapter, we'll talk about how the nominal interest rate can differ from the real interest rate when there is inflation; don't worry about that for now.

2 You may be wondering about how people measure the expected rate of return of a home purchase. That calculation involves estimating the resale value (price appreciation) of the home in the future as well as projecting the costs of borrowing, taxes, and other expenses (including the costs of renting versus buying). But people also think about non-monetary aspects of such borrowing—the non-quantifiable value and benefits they expect from home ownership.

3 Note that the word *public* in *public companies* indicates that ownership is open to the general public; it does not imply anything about government, as in the term public (i.e., government) spending.

4 In the past, bonds had actual coupons that bondholders would clip and return to the bond issuer in exchange for interest payments. Those coupons were quite different in purpose from the ones that people use to get price reductions on goods and services.

Chapter 14

1 The T-account format used here is a simplified representation of a balance sheet, which shows a company's assets, liabilities, and owners' equity. The underlying principle of the balance sheet is that assets must equal the total of liabilities plus owners' equity. We use that same basic principle in the T-account representations here (and assuming owners' equity of zero), showing that the bank's assets must equal its liabilities.

2 In reality, some dollars might get held as cash rather than being deposited, but usually we're safe to ignore those very small amounts relative to the total. That wasn't always true. In the past—and in some parts of the world today—few people kept their money in a bank, because either the closest bank was too far away or it wasn't worth the hassle.

3 http://www.bankofcanada.ca/core-functions/monetary-policy/

Chapter 15

1 Bob Davis, "IMF tells bankers to rethink inflation," *The Wall Street Journal,* February 12, 2010, http://online.wsj.com/article/SB10001424052748704337004575059542325748142.html

Chapter 16

1 A non-recourse mortgage is a mortgage secured by real property; if the borrower defaults, the lender can seize the collateral.

2 *Futures* are standardized financial contracts that obligate the buyer either to buy or sell a specified amount of some asset at a particular price at a specific future date. There are two main motivations for buying futures. One is *hedging*: companies and individuals use futures contracts to reduce uncertainty about prices in the future. The other is *speculating*: sometimes investors use futures contracts as a way to make bets on the direction of price changes—and, they hope, to make profits by betting correctly

3 https://www.policyalternatives.ca/publications/reports/big-banks-big-secret

4 http://www.bankofcanada.ca/core-functions/monetary-policy/

Chapter 18

1 http://blogs.ei.columbia.edu/2011/03/24/india-is-booming-so-why-are-nearly-half-of-its-children-malnourished-part-1/

2 Jishnu Das and Jeffrey Hammer, "Stained mercy: The quality of medical care in Delhi," World Bank Policy Research Working Paper Series No. 3228.

3 Unpublished data from Innovations for Poverty Action.

4 Douglass C. North, "Institutions," *Journal of Economic Perspectives* 5, issue 1 (Winter 1991), pp. 97–112.

5 For evidence on the link between democracy and economic growth, see http://as.nyu.edu/docs/IO/2591/Development.pdf

6 Michael Clemens, Claudio E. Montenegro, and Lant Pritchett, "The Place Premium: Wage differences for identical workers across the U.S. Border," Center for Global Development Working Paper no. 148, July 2008.

7 Michael Clemens, "Economics and emigration: Trillion dollar bills on the sidewalk," Center for Global Development Working Paper no. 264; and Lant Pritchett, *Let Their People Come* (Washington, DC: Center for Global Development, 2006).

8 http://www.international.gc.ca/development-developpement/dev-results-resultats/reports-rapports/d4r_1314-dar_1314.aspx?lang=eng

9 Jeffrey Sachs, *The End of Poverty* (New York: Penguin Press, 2006).

10 Abhijit Banerjee, *Making Aid Work* (Cambridge, MA: MIT Press, 2007).

11 Dambisa Moyo, *Dead Aid: Why Aid Is Not Working and How There Is a Better Way for Africa* (New York: Farrar, Straus and Giroux, 2009).

12 Craig Burnside and David Dollar, "Aid, policies and growth: Revisiting the evidence," WB Policy Research Paper no. O-2834 (Washington, DC: World Bank, 2004).

13 Edward Miguel and Michael Kremer, "Worms: Identifying impact on education and health in the presence of treatment externalities," *Econometrica* 72, no.1 (January 2004), pp. 159–217.

Index

Note: Boldface entries indicate key terms and the page numbers where they are defined.

and services, 213
Value creation, by voluntary exchange, 141–142
Valuing an economy
in macroeconomics, 204–205
in microeconomics, 204–205
by national income accounting, 204
Variables
dependent, 49
and direction of slope, 134
graphs of one, 46–48
graphs of two, 48–52
independent, 49
linear relationship, 94
nominal vs. real, 243, 245–246
omitted, 12, 13
and slope, 52–56, 134
Varian, Hal, 243
Velocity of money, 418
Canada 1968–2013, 418–419, 419*fig*
Venezuela, Big Mac index, 249*fig*
Versailles Peace Conference of 1919, 427
Virtual currencies, 398
Visa program for migrant workers, 512
Voluntary exchange, 141–142

W

Wage rates
effect of unions, 295–296
factors preventing fall in., 295–296
and labour supply, 288–290
and price level, 307, 427, 449
Wages
above equilibrium level, 289
above market-clearing level, 296
changes over time, 236, 237–238
controls, 427, 449
effect of unions on, 295–296
efficiency wages, 296
equilibrium, 289
and inflation, 247
minimum wage, 172, 236, 295
price controls, 427, 449
sticky downward, 293, 311, 322
undercutting, 294
Wage stickiness, 293, 311, 322

Wants, 4–5, 142
and gains from trade, 37
in production possibilities frontier, 28
and willingness to pay or sell, 142, 143
Washington Declaration, 334
Wealth, relation to savings, 362
Wealth effect, 307
Wealth of Nations (Smith), 39
Weimar Republic, 428
Welfare effects
of price ceilings, 174*fig*
of price floors, 178*fig*
Welfare programs, 340, 341
Well-being
vs. GDP, 223–225
Life Satisfaction Index, 224
measuring, 223–225
money and happiness, 224
national comparisons, 223–224*tab*
Where's George website, 420
White Paper on Employment and Income, 204
WikiLeaks, 517
Willingness to pay/buy, 66, **142**–144
and demand curve, 66, 143–144
factors affecting, 109
vs. haggling or bluffing, 146
and indifference points, 146
for Internet, 147
Willingness to sell, 72, **142**–144
vs. haggling or bluffing, 146
and supply curve, 72, 144–145
Women
as homemakers, value, 221
in Informal Employment, 297
participation in political process, 510
participation rate in workforce, 221, 269
value as homemakers, 221
Worker rights, 298
Workers
discouraged, 287
entry-level, 295
legally protected, 298

marginally attached, 287
Workforce, change in number of people in, 220
Working-age population
in Canada, 284, 285, 285*tab*, 286
percent of labour force, 284, 285, 286
World Bank, 495, **517**
absolute poverty measure, 251
on extreme poverty, 503
International Comparison Program index, 250
unaccountable for dispersed funds, 517
underestimating poverty, 251
World economic growth 1000 BC–AD 2010, 262–263
World Food Program, 516
World GDP per capita rates 1990–2010, 270, 271*fig*
World Trade Organization, 511
World Vision, 518
World War I, 427
World War II, cigarette money, 386–387, 388, 390

X

X-axis, 48–50
X-coordinates, 49
X-intercept, 98*fig*

Y

Yang, Dean, 512, 513
Y-axis, 48–50
Y-coordinates, 49
Y-intercept, 94, 95*fig*, 97*fig*, 98*fig*
Youth unemployment, 298
Yunus, Muhammad, 2–3, 4–5, 8, 9, 10

Z

Zambia, 518
Zero-sum game, 151
Zimbabwe, hyperinflation, 426, 427
Zombie banks, 460–461